D1601627

Whales

Whales

E. J. Slijper

Late Professor of General Zoology, University
of Amsterdam

Translated by A. J. Pomerans

Second edition
with a new foreword, concluding
chapter and bibliography by

Richard J. Harrison FRS

Professor of Anatomy, University of Cambridge

Cornell University Press
Ithaca, New York

First published, under the title *Walvissen*, by D.B. Centen's
Uitgeversmaatschappij, Amsterdam, 1958
Revised edition published in English 1962
Second English edition published by Cornell University Press 1979

Introduction, Chapter 14 © Hutchinson & Co. (Publishers) Ltd 1979
English translation © Hutchinson & Co. (Publishers) Ltd 1962

Printed in Great Britain

International Standard Book Number 0–8014–1161–0
Library of Congress Catalog Card Number 78–74217

Contents

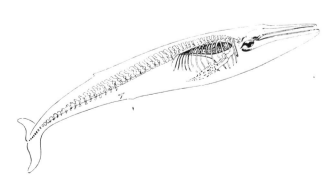

Foreword

by Richard J. Harrison FRS
Professor of Anatomy, University of Cambridge

ALL those interested in cetology should be pleased that it has been decided to reprint the late Professor E. J. Slijper's classic work on cetaceans. First published in 1958, in Dutch, and translated into English by A. J. Pomerans in 1962, his book *Walvissen* or *Whales* has probably done more than any other work to stimulate investigation of these remarkable animals. The publisher and I have decided to reprint the first thirteen chapters without any alterations even though knowledge of many aspects of cetology has increased considerably during the past twenty years. We made this decision for two reasons. First, a more complete revision would have been a monumental undertaking. Slijper had a background of comparative and veterinary anatomy that enabled him to analyse the structure of cetaceans in a way few could do today. He had acquired an immense amount of information and an unrivalled experience during the 1930s which led to *Die Cetaceen, vergleichend anatomisch und systematisch* in *Capita Zoologica*, vol. 7, pp. 1–590. He was fascinated by the problems posed in ascertaining the ancestry, evolution and relationships of living cetaceans as well as by their numerous adaptations. He had written papers on organ weights, asymmetry in the skull, variations in the vascular system, reproductive organs and reproduction as well as on the life-history of cetaceans. It was perhaps to be expected that Slijper would decide to write up all he knew in the form of a general text. What is remarkable is the way he did it, how he blended history, art and anecdote with scientific observations, results of museum studies and laboratory experiments, into a masterpiece. Second, the book, even unrevised, is still obligatory reading for beginners and, if my experience is anything to go by, a source for more advanced readers to consult repeatedly for information and ideas.

Slijper was also interested in the history of whaling and in the practical aspects of catching whales. He had become much concerned about conservation of cetaceans and the final chapter of his book was called 'The

Future of Whales and Whaling'. After some discussion it was decided to change its title slightly and to introduce new material without altering Slijper's intentions or his attitudes. This has been done with some reservations on my part in that I am not altogether convinced about certain arguments and statements. It is my fault if the chapter is not as blunt in its opinions as Slijper might well have made it had he been alive to revise it.

During the twenty years since *Walvissen* was published cetological investigations have burgeoned, as indeed have those on marine mammals generally. This has resulted not only because of concern about survival of the large whales but also due to other factors. The public became aware of the existence of small cetaceans after it had been found possible to catch dolphins and porpoises alive, transport them to specially designed pools on land and to maintain them for the education and entertainment of visitors. It became essential to discover more about these cetaceans in order to care for them and to provide veterinary treatment. Scientists had long been intrigued by cetaceans; now they had opportunities to study them in captivity and even to devise experiments. New techniques had become available to investigate structure and function, the needs of cetaceans and their life-style, their behaviour and their alleged 'intelligence'. Research during the past twenty years has demonstrated clearly that Slijper's enthusiasm for the future of cetology would be well vindicated, and also, as his book emphasized again and again, that it would be essential always to go and look first hand at any cetological matter before advancing hazardous guesses or making dogmatic statements. Almost every part of a cetacean differs in some way from that in a terrestrial mammal; some have considered cetaceans to be almost 'perfect' examples of biological adaptation, others find them the most 'aberrant' form of mammal.

It would be invidious to suggest which aspects of cetacean research have advanced most since 1958. Much has been done on the nervous system and behaviour but not sufficient to determine precise cortical activities and abilities.

A particular difficulty in studying true behaviour is that of observing cetaceans in the wild. Those held in captivity appear to develop activities related to their environment, to pleasing their trainers and to alleviating boredom. Certain types of behaviour can be considered aberrant in that they seem to result from 'apprehension', from restrictions of movement and from sources of aggravation. The propriety of keeping cetaceans captive for the enjoyment of man has been discussed as often as that of restricting any other fast-moving, wide-ranging wild mammal. A few have claimed an intelligence for cetaceans higher than for any other mammal except man. We cannot avoid some suspicion that this has arisen partly as a result of popular advertisement of a display of 'educated' porpoises and of inflated claims as to why grant money should be allocated. Owls are wise, elephants have long memories, cetaceans are intelligent, and long will it be so. P. J. Morgane and M. S. Jacobs have made considerable studies on cetacean brains. They have written: '. . . quantity of cortical material might lead one to place the dolphin extremely high in any hierarchical scale. The real question arises when one discusses the *quality* of cortex . . . this characteristic is under some great question in the case of the cetacean brain.'

The senses of hearing and sight have been much investigated as has the anatomy of sound emission. There is no doubt about the echo-locating skill of cetaceans but efforts to ascribe meaning to the whistles and related noises produced under water by many species of Odontocete have been unsuccessful. Many consider that it would be advisable to be certain where and how sounds are produced and received before attempting their analysis. The gross and microscopic structure of many tissues and viscera have been studied with increasing vigour as better-fixed material has become available. Numerous morphological and histological details have been revealed which seem to be associated with a marine existence, or which can be related to diet, to diving, to prolonged apnoea or some other cetacean characteristic. The use of telemetry, depth-time recorders and other methods of assessing dive profiles has provided more information about pinnipeds than about cetaceans but techniques applied to the latter will undoubtedly develop.

The need for knowledge on cetacean populations, migration, reproductive potential and life-histories has stimulated both field and theoretical studies. Conference after conference has been unable to reach universally acceptable conclusions, and for obvious reasons. Indeed, as commercial whaling declines, and unless special surveys are made, it could become increasingly difficult to assess what is happening to stocks of particular species. If there ever were a case to be made for sensible management of an animal stock by international cooperation, that for cetaceans is undeniable.

Serious efforts have been made to revise several cetacean genera on the basis of a variety of morphological and other criteria. The results are always interesting but have led to practical difficulties when a country lays claim to a species as its own or when a customs official asks why the living specimen of *Tursiops* in front of him at an airport really is *T. gilli* and not *T. truncatus*. The Classification of the Cetacea on pages 433–8 has been altered only slightly from that originally given by Slijper.

Slijper's Bibliography covered three centuries and was an interesting selection of references to numerous books, journals and publications of varying scientific standard. A similar selection today would demand an entire volume far larger in size than that, say, of Deborah Truitt (1974) *Dolphins and Porpoises* which was concerned in coverage only of a restricted number of delphinid genera. It was very tempting to retain most of the classical references: some can be consulted quite easily but others are difficult to obtain access to even at the best-stocked libraries. To make selection more difficult still, there have been many valuable works on Cetacea published since 1958 and not all could be included. Nevertheless, a selection had to be made and it is presented in the full awareness that it is incomplete. Slijper also included references to Abstracts and Proceedings of only a page or two: these have been omitted in favour of recent, more extensive works.

His bibliography has been thoroughly revised with the assistance of D. A. McBrearty MA. Duplication of entries has been eliminated: the reader should therefore look under more than one heading to find references to particular subjects. Much use has been made of the extensive *Bibliography of Cetacea* compiled by F. C. Fraser FRS, which is now in the Anatomy School, Cambridge University.

諸國名所百景

肥前
五嶌
鯨漁
の圖

Whaling off the coast of Japan (19th century woodcut)

Historical Introduction

THE PRIMITIVE man, clad in coarse wool, who began scratching the rocks on Røddøy (Northern Norway) in about 2200 B.C., could not have known that he was probably the first man in history to depict a Cetacean. All we know of him is that he lived in the Stone Age and that, metal being quite unheard of in his day, he must have scratched the rock with a sharp piece of flint. His drawing shows a man in a boat, close behind a seal and two porpoises (Fig. 1). On the right of the picture there appears an elk which obviously does not fit in with the rest. It is not clear whether the man was hunting the animals, but it seems likely, for coast dwellers have hunted seals and Cetaceans since the earliest times.

Other drawings discovered on Norwegian rocks portray various species of dolphin, probably animals that were washed ashore, and a drawing from Meling in Rogaland (Fig. 2) clearly depicts the encounter between a whale and four boats. From what is happening to the left of the animal's tail, we may reasonably infer that one of the boats was capsized by a stroke of the whale's tail and that the crew had been thrown overboard. Here, too, it is not clear whether the men were actually hunting the whale, but it is not unlikely if we bear in mind the primitive weapons with which people are still catching large whales to this day.

Another drawing of a whale, dating from about 1200 B.C., was discovered near Knossos, on the island of Crete, the site of the famous Palace of Minos. This drawing, however, is no longer pre-historic, since it dates from a time when Mediterranean people had known writing for more than 2,000 years.

Moreover, bones of whales found in the remnants of settlements of the original inhabitants of Alaska clearly show that the Eskimos caught whales as early as 1500 B.C.

The ancient Greeks (approximately 2000 B.C.) were well acquainted with Cetaceans, and many of their vases, coins and buildings were decorated with whale, and particularly with dolphin, motifs. These

Figure 1. The oldest drawing of Cetaceans. Neolithic rock-drawing from Røddøy.
(Petersen, 1930)

animals also played an important part in many Greek legends. We need
only recall what happened to Arion, the famous lyric poet and musician,
when he returned to Corinth from Italy where he had obtained immense
riches by his profession. When the sailors resolved to murder him for his
treasures, Arion begged to be allowed to play one last tune, and then
threw himself into the sea. His music had attracted a number of dolphins,
and one of them carried him safely ashore on its back.

This theme recurs in a great many Mediterranean fables. Pliny relates
the story of the little boy who was carried ashore on the back of a dolphin,
an event which, by the way, was commemorated by a special Dutch stamp
in 1929 (Fig. 5). Raphael immortalized this story in about A.D. 1500 with
a marble statue, now kept in the Hermitage Museum in Leningrad. His
dolphin has human teeth and eyes, its mouth is fish-like and its body is

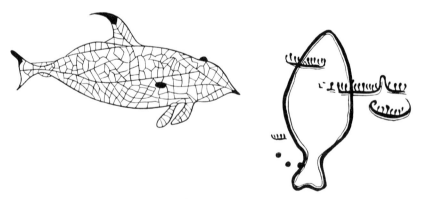

Figure 2. Norwegian rock-drawings. Left: a dolphin from Skogervejen. The original drawing
was 7 feet 6 inches long. Right: a whale and four rowing boats from Meling in Rogaland.
(Schäfer, 1956).

covered with scales – which is not at all surprising when we consider that
it was not until the eighteenth century that dolphins were first distinguished from fishes, and this despite the fact that Aristotle, the father of
biology and medicine, had pointed out as early as 400 B.C. that dolphins
have warm blood and lungs, that they are viviparous, and that they suckle
their young just as horses, dogs and human beings do. Aristotle also
mentioned the '*Mysticetus*', an animal which had 'pig's bristles' for
teeth. This was most probably his way of describing the hairy fringe at
the inner side of the baleen of the whalebone whales. He also knew the
Sperm Whale, which he called *Phalaena*, and he listed the most important
characteristics of porpoises and dolphins.

Though the Greeks were acquainted with Cetaceans, which are also
mentioned in various biblical passages, it seems that the ancients never
hunted the bigger species. While some Mediterranean people caught
dolphins, others thought it was a sin to kill or to hurt an animal that had
played so large a part in the sagas and myths of yore. Being the sailor's
constant companion on his long and distant journeys to every part of
the world, the dolphin was for long regarded as sacrosanct. Odysseus
proudly bore a crest with the dolphin device, and a dolphin always

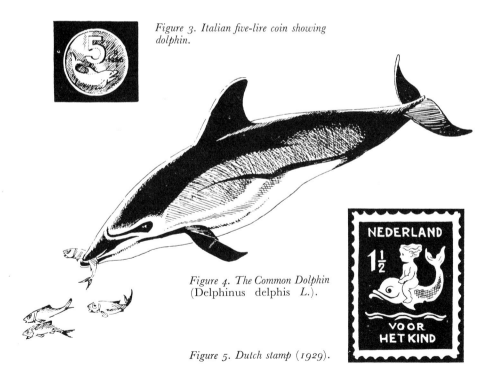

Figure 3. Italian five-lire coin showing dolphin.

Figure 4. The Common Dolphin (Delphinus delphis L.).

NEDERLAND
1½
VOOR
HET KIND

Figure 5. Dutch stamp (1929).

accompanied the god of the sea – the Roman Neptune, the Greek Poseidon and the Finnish Wellamo (Fig. 114). The dolphin gave its name to the heir to the French throne, and even in our own prosaic world, its image can be found on an Italian five-lire piece (Fig. 3).

We cannot leave the Greeks without mentioning a beautiful blown glass figure, 7 inches long, kept in the British Museum (Fig. 6). This figure, dating from the first century B.C., probably represents Cuvier's Beaked Whale or, as it is sometimes called, the Goose-Beaked Whale, a species which grows to a length of 26 feet and inhabits the Mediterranean to this day.

Roman authors such as Pliny and Galen added little to our knowledge of the Cetaceans. On the contrary, they did more harm than good by confusing them with fishes, and by allowing all sorts of fantasies to creep into their descriptions.

The Middle Ages turned their back on scientific observation and even Olaus Magnus, who published a book about the Arctic in 1555, contributed mostly fable and misinterpretation. A great number of imaginary animals are also described in Konrad Gesner's *Historia Animalium* (1551). To us, the most interesting of these is probably the unicorn (Fig. 8), a horse with cloven hooves, a lion's tail, and a horn in the middle of its forehead. The unicorn was first introduced into the English royal coat of arms by James I, and if we look carefully at it, we see that its horn resembles the greatly elongated spiral tusk of the male Narwhal, an Arctic dolphin some 13–16 feet in length (Fig. 7). Narwhal tusks, which were said to be endowed with miraculous properties, had undoubtedly found their way to Southern Europe, where they were ground into a powder with supposed medicinal qualities, since earliest times. Wormius (1655) was the first to identify them, and since his day their miraculous power seems to have waned. The tusks were relegated increasingly to museums and collectors' shelves, though in 1955 they once again attained prominence when nine Eskimos from Cape Dorset were commissioned to make a mace for the government of the N.W. Territories of Canada. The mace was to consist entirely of Canadian products, and when it was finished a Narwhal tusk served as its handle.

The fact that dolphins, porpoises and whales were known to Europeans long before the Middle Ages is also borne out by the derivation of the word 'whale'. The Norwegian *hval*, the Dutch and German *wal*, and the Anglo-Saxon *hwael* are thought to be related to the modern English *wheel*, and must have referred to the characteristic turning motions of whales when they come up to breathe.

Strandings of whales and large dolphins are reported in many medieval chronicles. They were generally looked upon as portents of important

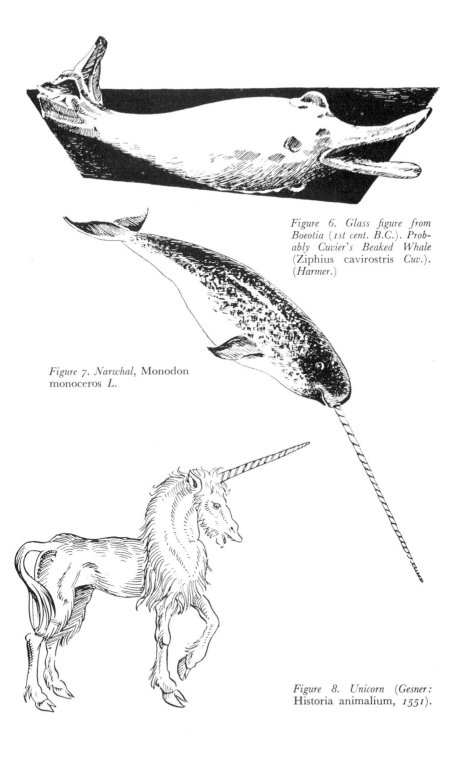

Figure 6. Glass figure from Boeotia (1st cent. B.C.). Probably Cuvier's Beaked Whale (Ziphius cavirostris Cuv.). (Harmer.)

Figure 7. Narwhal, Monodon monoceros *L.*

Figure 8. Unicorn (Gesner: Historia animalium, *1551).*

events – good or bad. Thus Crantzius thought that a young whale, captured near Lübeck in 1333, heralded the war between England and France which broke out soon afterwards, while the sudden Swedish invasion of Holstein (1643) was said to have been foretold by the stranding of two killer whales. Procopius, on the other hand, looked upon the capture of a large whale near Byzantium as an omen portending the end of the Gothic wars.

Greeks and Romans alike lived at peace with whales – at least with the large ones, but the early inhabitants of the coasts of Western and Northern Europe were quick to cast envious glances at the enormous wealth of flesh and oil stored within their colossal bodies. Probably it all began with a stranded animal, continued with 'forced landings', the animals being surrounded and chased ashore, and, as boats and weapons improved, ended by killing whales at sea.

Norway is a country rich in mountains, in trees and in ore, but with not very much arable or grazing land. It has, however, a long coastline with thousands of fjords, bays and small islands, a coastline that seems as if made by nature for supplying man with seafood. Throughout the ages, the population has relied on the sea for supplies, and we need not be surprised, therefore, that the oldest drawings of seals and porpoises come from Norway. And it is certainly no accident that the oldest whale hunters were Norwegians. No one knows when it all began, but as early as A.D. 890, one Ottar from Northern Norway reported his voyage through the Arctic Ocean to Alfred the Great of England, and mentioned that he had come across whalermen near Tromsö. He did not mention what kind of whales they had been hunting; they may have been walruses, or perhaps Biscayan (or North Atlantic) Right Whales, although the Norwegian *Kongespeiler* (which dates from about 1250) mentions that sailors were afraid of the *Slettibaka*, and *Sletbag* happens to be the modern Icelandic name for the North Atlantic Right Whale. The Icelanders probably learned whaling from the Norwegians.

The Biscayan Right Whale is called a Right Whale because in the early days of whaling it was the most profitable source of baleen and oil. In contradistinction to the Rorquals which are caught nowadays, Right Whales have no dorsal fin and no grooves on the underside. They have markedly arched upper jaws and long and narrow whalebone plates some 8 feet long. The Biscayan or North Atlantic Right Whale reaches a length of 46–60 feet and has characteristic white or yellow horny bumps round the chin and on the forward part of the upper jaw (Figs. 9, 136 and 139). Its 'head bump' has always been known as the 'bonnet' because it is so reminiscent of that article of female millinery. The Biscayan Right Whale, which has become a rare animal, may be found in the North Atlantic (either alone, in pairs, or in very small schools). Things were quite different once upon a time, when schools of over 100 of them were often found throughout the Northern Atlantic right down to the Azores, and particularly in the Bay of Biscay – whence the animal's name.

The Basques inhabiting the coasts of the Bay of Biscay, and particularly the inhabitants of Biarritz, Bayonne, St. Jean de Luz and St. Sebastian, began to hunt these animals in about the eleventh century. Although there is no direct evidence, it seems likely that they learnt this art from the Flemings and Normans who in turn picked up their knowledge from the Norsemen, who often raided their country. In any case, the Basques turned whaling into a large-scale industry, and extended it farther and farther across the Atlantic Ocean. As long as the whalers restricted their activities to the coast alone they could use the flesh of the animals, but as the hunt took them to distant parts their interest centred more and more exclusively on only two whale products: lamp oil and whalebone. At a time when steel and elastic were unknown, whalebone was the ideal material for whips, umbrellas, stays, crinolines, and countless other articles. With the increasing prosperity of Western Europe, whale oil and whalebone came into ever-greater demand. As houses required better lighting and women better clothes and as the local stock decreased, whaling spread from the Bay of Biscay to other parts of Western France, to the coasts of Spain, to Portugal and even to England, where the whale was proclaimed a royal fish, and the king was made an Honorary Harpooner, entitled to the head of all captured whales, while the baleen was given to the queen. Meanwhile whaling continued to spread farther afield still, so much so that by 1578 thirty Basque ships are known to have lain at anchor in Newfoundland.

The pursuit of Biscayan Right Whales continued well into the twentieth century (Hebridean 'fishery'), though Basques and Spaniards alike had ceased whaling almost completely by the end of the sixteenth century – not so much because whales had become too scarce, but rather because capital, ships, and crews could be far more profitably employed otherwise. It was the time of the great voyages of discovery and of colonial conquest. The expansion of Europe meant the doom of the Basque whaling industry.

Oddly enough, it was the desire for Oriental spices and other treasures that caused the development of Greenland whaling. Britain and Holland, anxious for their share of the good things of life, yet finding the southern trade route barred by the Spaniards and Portuguese, decided to pioneer a northern passage. As early as 1583 an Englishman, Jonas Poole, sailed to the Arctic, but failed to find the North-East passage he had sought. Three Dutchmen, Heemskerk, Barendsz and De Rijp, were equally unsuccessful and had to spend the winter of 1596 on Novaya Zemlya. However, those who survived this voyage returned with the news that the bays in Novaya Zemlya, Spitsbergen and Jan Mayen Island were teeming with whales. They had seen Biscayan Right Whales and also very similar animals which did not venture very far beyond the ice, and which had extraordinarily large heads with white or yellow spots on the chin and throat, but which lacked the usual bonnet. The Norwegians had met this animal much earlier, particularly off Iceland and the western coast of Greenland, and had called it the Grønlands-Hval (Fig. 9).

The Rorquals which are hunted nowadays, and which are distinguished from Right Whales by having small dorsal fins, also occurred in the Arctic Ocean, but they are so fast that they must have eluded primitive rowing boats. They can break surface as much as half a mile from the spot where they dive (or *sound*, as whalers call it) and do not float when dead, but sink to the depths of the ocean (Fig. 9).

Right Whales, on the other hand, are slow animals and usually do not come to the surface at such long distances from the spot where they dive. Moreover, their carcasses float on the surface and can be dragged to the beach or alongside a ship where they can be flensed and robbed of their precious yield. In addition, their whalebone is very long though of comparatively poor quality – that of the Greenland Whale can reach 13 feet while that of the Rorquals is very much shorter.

Reports about the abundance of whales in the Arctic caused a great deal of excitement in Western Europe, and shipbuilders found that a profitable new avenue was opening up to them. Since the Greenland Whale is found mainly in the Arctic sea ice, expeditions required years of careful preparation, and it took till 1611 for Thomas Edge to succeed in taking the first whaling ship to Spitsbergen. The first Dutch ship followed in 1612, and in 1614 the *Noordse Compagnie*, a kind of cartel as we might call it today, was founded in Holland.

The so-called 'Greenland whalers', who, by the way, went to Spitsbergen,[1] Novaya Zemlya and Jan Mayen Island rather than to Greenland itself, were ships of 250–400 tons, 100–120 feet long and 22–29 feet wide, and carried a crew of 30–50 men (some even double that number) and 4–7 sloops. It cost roughly £1,200 to equip such a ship – quite a lot of money for the time. But the profits, too, were considerable. A large Greenland Whale yielded about $1\frac{1}{2}$ tons of whalebone, and whalebone fetched as much as £2,250 a ton when the market was firm. Apart from that, each whale supplied some 25 tons of oil, so the capture of one whale

---

[1] Whalers refer to Spitsbergen as East Greenland.

Figure 9. A number of
Mysticetes shown side by
side with a man and a
Common Porpoise.
(Slijper, 1954.)

Greenland Whale

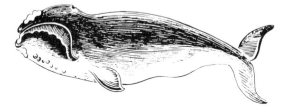

Biscayan Right Whale

Pigmy Right Whale

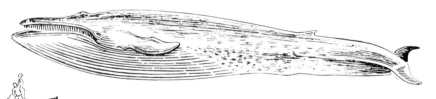

Blue Whale

Fin Whale

Sei Whale

would more than pay for the cost of the whole expedition. Of course, ships also came back empty-handed or damaged, and some never returned at all, but then other ships brought back the yield of as many as seventy-five animals in one season. No wonder that there was keen competition among sailors, and that such famous men as Admiral Michiel Adriaensz de Ruyter learned navigation on Arctic whalers in their youth (1633 and 1635).

Originally, whales were caught in the bays of Spitsbergen and of the other islands and then taken ashore for flensing (Fig. 11). As early as 1619 – the year in which they founded Batavia, the capital of their Far Eastern colonial empire – the Dutch also founded Smeerenburg, a settlement on Spitsbergen. In good summers, more than a thousand men were left behind here to look after the large boilers (try-works) and the repair dock. Later, when whales became scarcer in the bays, the men went out to sea, capturing the animals with hand harpoons and finishing them off with spears. The whales were then flensed alongside the boats. Since there were no boilers at sea, the blubber was cut up into small pieces and taken home in barrels. Holes were drilled into the bones to recover precious bone oil as well.

In the course of the seventeenth century, the pace of Arctic whaling increased by leaps and bounds. Whaling expeditions set out not only from Britain and Holland but also from Denmark, from the German ports of Hamburg, Bremen and Lübeck and finally from France, the latter manned with Basque harpooners who had seen better days. In 1680 Holland had 260 whalers with a total crew of 14,000, and in 1697, 182 ships of various nationalities caught 1,888 whales off Spitsbergen alone. Every country had its own settlement in the Arctic, and the new industry also brought prosperity to many a home port. In the eighteenth century America, too, joined the hunt for Greenland Whales, not only in the Davis Straits and Baffin Bay but also – albeit somewhat later and not in very great numbers until the nineteenth century – in the Bering Straits and in the Sea of Okhotsk. The Greenland Whale is found over the entire Arctic, and until the end of the nineteenth century whalebone remained a valuable commodity. In 1897 one pound of whalebone fetched four dollars on the San Francisco market and, together with the oil, the profit from a single Greenland Whale could be as much as £8,000. During the 1849 season whalebone to the tune of 2 million dollars was sold in Honolulu alone.

In 1720 European whalers, too, shifted their activities towards the Davis Straits and Baffin Bay, to look for new hunting grounds.

Even so, by the eighteenth century the Greenland Whale was still far from extinct, and the decline of, for instance, the Dutch whaling industry

 Little Piked Whale

 Humpback

Grey Whale

 Sperm Whale

Figure 10. Three Mysticetes and a Sperm Whale (on the same scale as Figure 9).
(Slijper, 1954.)

*Figure 11. Try-works on Jan Mayen Island. After a painting by C. W. de Man, 1639.
(Rijksmuseum, Amsterdam.)*

at the beginning of that century must be attributed to quite different causes: wars, occupation, keener British competition, and new political and economic factors. But by the nineteenth century it was too late, for when sporadic Dutch expeditions set out for the Arctic they had little success. The last Dutch ship to catch a Greenland Whale was the *Dirkje Adema* in 1860. From 1870–1872 Captain C. J. Bottemanne hunted Rorquals off Iceland, with equally poor results.

But it was not the Dutch who were responsible for so decimating the Greenland and Biscayan Whales that nowadays they have become a rare and highly protected species. This dubious honour is due to Britain, which unlike all other countries continued to hunt the animals during the entire nineteenth century with better and better equipment, penetrating the ice more and more deeply for longer and longer periods and causing whole-sale slaughter even among very young animals. At the beginning of the twentieth century this game, too, was no longer worth the candle. In 1910 ten ships from Dundee still managed to catch eighteen whales, but by 1912 the one ship to leave Dundee returned empty-handed. At the moment the number of Greenland Whales is growing again. They are still absent or at least very rare in European waters but put in a regular appearance in Hudson Bay, Eclipse Sound and Lancaster Sound, as well as in the Bering Sea. Now and then, Eskimos and the inhabitants of eastern Siberia manage to capture an odd specimen; they are allowed to do so since the local population is exempt from international restrictions. Siberian sledge-runners continue to be made of whalebone to this day, though clock-springs are now increasingly being manufactured of other materials.

The reader might well think that, since whales have been caught in their thousands from the fourteenth century on, their structure and habits must have been described in detail by whalers and biologists of the time, but if he does, he will be disappointed. True, the books on fish by Belon (1553) and Rondelet (1554) rejected medieval fable and fantasy and, for the first time in more than fifteen hundred years, gave a useful and accurate description of Cetaceans, but Greenland whaling which, after all, was so important to England, Holland, and Germany, was carried on for almost a century before the first book on the subject appeared in 1675. It was called *Spitzbergische Reisebeschreibung* and was written by a Hamburg barber and surgeon, Friedrich Martens. Clearly, scientists attached little importance to the Arctic, and since ship's surgeons were barbers rather than physicians they were quite indifferent to animal biology. Martens was the first to describe the characteristics of the Greenland and Biscayan Whales accurately, but his work was very quickly outstripped by Sibbald's *Phalaenologia nova* (London 1692).

The sixteenth and seventeenth centuries were of the greatest importance to the study of human anatomy. It was the age of Vesalius, of Ruysch and of Nicolaas Tulp, the Dutch anatomist, whose fame was immortalized in Rembrandt's *Anatomy Lesson*. It was the age in which dissections of human bodies had become a kind of ritual, and it is therefore not surprising that the work was extended to animals as well, and particularly to porpoises, which were caught and sold all over Europe, so that there was no lack of illustrative material. The first known dissection was carried out in 1654, when Bartholinus dissected a porpoise in the presence of King Frederick III of Denmark. Thereafter our knowledge of the structure of the animal was greatly amplified by the writings of Ray (1671), Major (1672) and Tyson (1860). In the eighteenth century Frisch and De la Motte (1740) both gave descriptions of the porpoise. Little, however, was written about the great whales. True, Zorgdrager (1728) and Fabricius (1780), in their detailed accounts of Greenland whaling, mention quite a few salient facts, but they were far more concerned with the industry than with the structure and habits of its victims. Anthony van Leeuwenhoek investigated the structure of a whale eye brought to him pickled in brandy by a whaling captain. Field work must indeed have been very difficult, if we reflect that one young ship's surgeon whom the great John Hunter instructed to collect and preserve specimens returned with no more than a piece of whale skin covered with parasites. It all seems very strange, for the whalers themselves brought back all kinds of trophies: jaws, vertebrae, scapulae and parts of the ear. The jaws were frequently used as gate posts or as rubbing posts for cattle (Fig. 162). In fact, complete young whales were sometimes brought back to Europe. Thus, it was no novelty when, in 1952, two Fin Whales, pickled in formalin, travelled through western Europe – the one, Jonas, by ship, and the other, Miss Haroy, in a 65-foot railway car specially constructed to carry her weight of more than fifty tons. Similar sights could have been seen in 1892 and in 1903, and even during the eighteenth century. According to J. Bicker Raye's reliable account of daily life in Amsterdam, 'Mr Waterman's Greenland whaler brought back an eighteen-foot-long whale on the 30th September 1736, the whale being displayed full length in pickle'. Judging by its size, the animal must have been a very young Greenland Whale, for this is their length at birth.

It seems odd that the great English anatomist John Hunter (1787) complained of difficulties in obtaining whale material, when there are so many excellent etchings of whaling conditions at that time. Hunter, by the way, was the first to give good and accurate descriptions of the big whales and particularly of their internal structure. Though the British had almost completely eradicated the Greenland Whale by the nineteenth century, they had at least made sure of providing posterity with an excellent description of this important animal. Supplementing the work of Hunter, William Scoresby published his *Account of the Arctic Region* (1820) in Edinburgh. Scoresby, the son of a whaling captain, made his first journey to the Arctic in his father's company when he was only ten years old. He then went back to school, and later studied biology and anatomy at Edinburgh University. In 1810, when he took command of his father's *Resolution*, he was the first academic whaling expert to sail a ship, and I believe that this feat has not often been repeated since. I might add that his schooling did no harm to his commercial success, for in 1820, the year in which his book appeared, he brought back to Liverpool the biggest of all Greenland catches. Yet another scientist to whom we owe much of our knowledge of the Greenland Whale is the Danish biologist, Eschricht, who published his accounts in about the middle of last century.

So far we have discussed whaling in Europe and the neighbouring seas, but elsewhere, too, the whale was given little peace. The Greenland Eskimos and the Indians of the American West Coast probably began whale-hunting early in the sixteenth century. It seems likely that they originally picked up the trade from the Basques, but they very quickly developed a method of their own. This method was either an adaptation of Basque techniques to the special conditions prevailing off the American East Coast, or else the original contribution of the Indians of Cape Flattery (which is now in the state of Washington). Twenty to thirty small hand harpoons or spears are thrust simultaneously into the whale's body. Each harpoon is attached to a block of wood or an inflated sealskin which floats above the water and thus keeps the animal buoyant. Moreover, the animal's movements are so impeded that it can be finished off fairly easily (Fig. 12). This method is still being used in a few places for catching sharks, but in the case of very large animals petrol drums, which have a much greater buoyancy, have replaced the wooden blocks.

The Indians on the East Coast probably caught Biscayan Right Whales, while those on the West Coast (Cape Flattery and later Vancouver Island across the Juan de Fuca Strait) hunted mainly Californian Grey Whales (Fig. 10). Nowadays Grey Whales are found only in the Northern Pacific, though it is possible that they may have once occurred in the North Atlantic as well. The animal reaches a maximum length of 45 feet, and is dark grey in colour flecked with white spots. Its general structure can be regarded as intermediate between Right Whales and Rorquals, though like the Right Whales it has no dorsal fin, and is a very slow swimmer (average speed $3\frac{1}{2}$ knots; maximum speed 7 knots, as compared with the Rorquals' 18 knots and more). This fact must have helped small Indian boats a good deal.

The Grey Whale spends the summer in the Arctic, and particularly in the Bering Sea. In autumn, it migrates south along the coast to winter in the bays and lagoons of California. It is here that the females give birth to their calves and can therefore be caught fairly easily. Oddly enough, it took the white man until 1846 before he began to hunt Grey Whales intensively in these waters. From then on they were captured in such great numbers that the Grey Whale has become very scarce and, like the Right Whale, is protected. Only the local population is allowed to catch Grey Whales for their own needs. In this way, about fifty animals are caught every year in Kamchatka, and Russian as well as American biologists think that the whales are once again gradually increasing in number.

Europeans started whaling much earlier off the American *East* Coast, and it is believed that the seventeenth-century British settlements in New England were established because whaling off Cape Cod had proved so profitable. In the eighteenth century, coastal fishing extended as far as Maine in the north and South Carolina in the south. At first the catch consisted predominantly of Biscayans, but as these became scarcer, whalers were increasingly forced to switch to Humpbacks. The Humpback Whale (Fig. 10) with its normal length of up to 50 feet is the smallest of the big Rorquals. It has two properties which make it the Rorqual *par excellence* for primitive coastal whaling. Firstly, it is a very slow swimmer – its cruising speed never exceeds $3\frac{1}{2}$ to 5 knots – and secondly, like the Grey Whale, its yearly migrations take place close to the shore. Moreover its blubber is proportionately much thicker than that of other Rorquals. One serious disadvantage to whalers is the fact that dead Humpbacks

sink to the bottom and only rise to the surface when decomposition gases
have formed. Humpbacks have been pursued since ancient times by the
local population, although on a small scale.

During the seventeenth and eighteenth centuries whaling was also
practised in other parts of the world but, with the exception of Japan,
where it was an important industry, only locally and on a modest scale.
In many respects Japan is very similar to Norway. A large part of the
country is mountainous and in the coastal plain every inch of fertile
ground must be utilized for the cultivation of staple crops – in the case
of Japan, rice. Unlike Norway, however, Japan is a very highly populated
country whose own paddy fields are inadequate to meet the population's
requirements of carbohydrates, let alone of proteins. Stockbreeding is
largely restricted to Hokkaido, the northernmost island, and milk and
other dairy products are regarded as luxuries in Japan. Japan therefore
has to look to the sea for her proteins, and there is probably no other
country on earth (with the possible exception of Norway) where fish plays
so important a part in the daily diet.

The Japanese have probably been whale-hunters since time immemorial,
though the oldest records go back to no earlier than 1606, when the
beaten army of the Kamakura Shogunate dug in at Taiji (Central Japan)
and took to whaling seriously. The industry quickly spread across the entire
coastal belt. At first the animals were killed with simple spears and hand
harpoons, but in 1674 nets were introduced in Kishu, a method of whale
catching ideally suited to Japanese conditions. The Japanese coast is
studded with thousands of small islands from which spotters can alert
the land stations by means of smoke signals, and rowing boats, manned
by scores of oarsmen and carrying one or even two harpooners each, can
quickly set out in pursuit of their prey. The crews of these boats used to
stand upright facing the bows as they surrounded the whale and drove
it into the nets. Once enmeshed, the animals could be attacked with
spears and harpoons. When the whale was clearly exhausted, one of the
sailors climbed on to it, drove his spear straight into its heart and tied a
rope through the blow hole. The carcass was then pulled ashore. The
Japanese generally hunted Biscayan Whales (which also occur in the
North Pacific), Grey Whales and Humpback Whales. Occasionally they
would also capture a Fin Whale.

The Japanese recorded their experiences in a number of books and on
some exquisite prints. The oldest books date from 1774, and this is very
old indeed, for Japan is a country with few relics older than 1700. The
earliest books are rice-paper scrolls kept in beautiful wooden chests. Text
and plates illustrate all the different species of whales frequenting Japanese
waters to this day. Single prints, which are generally no more than a

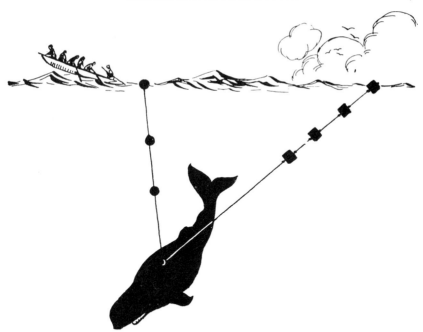

Figure 12. Sperm Whale being caught with floats made of sealskin (left) and of wood (right).
(Crisp, 1954.)

hundred years old, also depict whaling in all its aspects. These prints are often veritable little jewels of Japanese art, full of warmth and beautifully designed. In 1954, I was lucky enough to acquire one of these prints in an antique shop in Tokyo (see frontispiece).

Whaling off the Japanese coasts is still carried out intensively now, of course, by up-to-date methods. In 1891 the Russians first established land stations in Korea, hunting mainly Grey and Sei Whales, but these stations are no longer in use. At the turn of the century whales were still caught with nets on a few land stations in Kamchatka and New Zealand, a method that had been practised for centuries off the coast of Norway near Bergen. Once the animals' retreat from a fjord was cut off they were bombarded with darts, previously dipped into dead whales. The bacteria caused the poor beasts to die of gangrene within a few days.

We have so far restricted our discussion to the hunting of Biscayan, Greenland, Grey and Humpback Whales, and we must now conclude our historical survey with a few words about the Sperm Whale. The Sperm Whale has teeth instead of whalebone and is therefore an Odontocete (Toothed Whale) unlike the Right Whales and Rorquals which are Mysticetes (Baleen or Whalebone Whales).

Since Sperm Whale meat is thought unpalatable the world over, it is not surprising that the animal was left in peace until relatively recently, despite the fact that it is slow-swimming and easily caught by even the most primitive boats. Moreover, their curiosity often brings Sperm Whales into close proximity with the ships, and they like to 'doze' on the surface of the water. A Sperm Whale will generally break surface close to the spot at which it last sounded. All these characteristics are very helpful to whalers. What is less advantageous is the fact that, since the Sperm Whale feeds on cuttlefish, it generally keeps to deep waters, and only where the coast is steep can it be found close to the mainland. The Sperm Whale is furthermore a predominantly tropical animal which prefers to keep to waters between 40°N and 40°S. While small schools of mature bulls, who fail to become the leaders of a herd of cows and calves, migrate to the Arctic or Antarctic in the summer, the vast majority keep to tropical and sub-tropical waters – regions which are far away from the main centres of the early whaling industry.

During the eighteenth century, when there was an increasing demand for lamp oil and candles, for which Sperm Whale oil is so ideally suited, New England whalers turned their attention increasingly to this animal. American whalers from New Bedford and Nantucket were the first to extend Sperm Whale hunting from coastal waters to the high sea. It all started in 1712, and by 1770, 125 ships participated in pelagic (i.e. open sea) whaling. Frenchmen, Englishmen and Portuguese soon joined in, and at the end of the eighteenth century hundreds of ships were combing the Atlantic for likely prey. Sperm Whales are, however, found in every ocean, and so, in 1789, the *Amelia* left London as the first Sperm Whale hunter to round Cape Horn in order to try her luck in the Pacific. The expedition proved so successful that others soon followed. In 1802 the first Sperm-whalers reached New Zealand, and during most of the nineteenth century such ships were regular callers there, in Australia, in the Indian Archipelago and on hundreds of small South Pacific islands.

Hawaii, in particular, became a very important whaling centre and its economic rise must indubitably be attributed to Sperm Whale hunting. In 1846 Honolulu harboured more than 600 ships, and by then many oil merchants and ship's chandlers had set up in business there. A large number of adventurous sailors decided to turn their backs on the hum-drum existence in their cold native countries for good, and deserted their ships to dally in the shade of the palm trees and in the arms of some beautiful Polynesian girl. Thus the racial composition of the population of many South Sea islands owes much to Sperm Whale hunting.

Catching Sperm Whales under a clear Southern sky was more attractive than Greenland whaling. The animals were caught from boats carrying six oarsmen and one harpooner; they were towed to the mother ship to be flensed alongside, and the blubber and head were boiled on board. Still, even this relatively pleasant occupation made great demands on the crew. The ships were very small (generally less than 300 tons) and a journey could last up to four years. The men had to make do with poor food, they often lacked drinking water, and they were tossed about by storms, particularly off Cape Horn. Even Sperm Whale hunting demanded tough sailors who knew how to take the rough with the smooth. Nor are things so very different nowadays. Take the story of 36-year-old Roa Hansen, captain of a Norwegian whaler, who fell overboard in the Atlantic in 1955. When he was found seven hours later swimming on his back, he refused to take the line that was thrown to him and climbed up the man-rope unaided. Formerly, tales of heroism and legends about Sperm-whalers were the order of the day. It was the time of Moby Dick, the formidable white Sperm Whale which inspired Herman Melville's great book of that name.

Moby Dick was by no means the only Sperm Whale to have achieved notoriety. There were also Timor Tim, Don Miguel (Chile), Morguan (Japan), New Zealand Jack and Newfoundland Tom, all of whom have become legendary because of the havoc they caused amongst sailors, boats and even big ships. Generally, though, Sperm Whale hunting is a relatively safe occupation. It has repeatedly been noticed that cows and young bulls allow themselves to be slaughtered almost impassively. The only danger comes from some of the older bulls who put up a fierce resistance, and often jump full-length out of the water to lash out with their tails or to ram the boats with their dangerous blunt heads. Anyone unlucky enough to be caught between a Sperm Whale's jaws is unlikely to get away with his life. Even the most modern catchers have to be on their guard. Thus in December 1955, when the Dutch *Johannes W. Vinke* (714 tons) was rammed by a Sperm Whale in the Antarctic, her propeller was put out of action and she had to be towed to Melbourne for repairs.

The years 1820–1850 saw the heyday of Sperm Whaling. In 1842, 594 American and 230 ships from other countries provided work for 70,000 men and caught about 10,000 Sperm Whales a year. This is more or less the annual total still caught throughout the world. Apart from killing Sperm Whales, the men also wreaked what can only be described as carnage amongst the Southern Right Whales, which belong to the same species as the Biscayan Right Whale and whose geographical distribution in the south is roughly the counterpart to that of the Biscayan in the North. During the first twenty years of the nineteenth century an annual average of just under 14,000 of these animals was caught, chiefly off New Zealand,

Australia and Kerguelen Island, and their number became greatly reduced.

From 1846 onwards Sperm whaling went into a steep decline, again not so much because Sperm Whales had become too scarce – their present number is probably no smaller than it was in those days – but for a host of economic reasons. The rapid development of the American cotton industry was attracting capital and manpower, and then, in 1849, sailors in San Francisco deserted in their hundreds to join the great gold rush. Also, a great number of ships were lost during the American Civil War. Finally, in 1859, mineral oil was discovered in Pennsylvania and began slowly but steadily to oust whale oil and spermaceti candles from the fuel market. The real old salts stuck it out as long as they could, but by 1925, when the *John R. Manta* and the *Margarett* returned to New Bedford for the last time, the romantic epoch of Sperm Whale hunting, which to all intents and purposes had come to an end in 1860, was definitely over. That epoch, so rich in profits and adventure, had yet been rather disappointing from the scientific point of view.

Even today we lack a really accurate description of the muscles and internal organs of an animal of which specimens have been captured in their hundreds of thousand over the centuries. The Sperm Whale still holds a number of secrets that other animals have yielded up long ago. The most valuable scientific heritage from that period consists of the many old log-books now kept in the New Bedford Public Library and other New England institutions. In 1935 Townsend made a thorough study of some of the available material, from which at least some facts about the geographic distribution of the species and about its migratory habits emerged.

As transport and our knowledge of human and animal anatomy improved, biologists the world over paid increasing attention to stranded whales. Occasionally a whale or a dolphin would be washed ashore dead or alive, particularly when it entered shallow waters and was caught by sandbanks or cliffs. Van Deinse in his 1931 thesis and in later papers gave a detailed account of all such strandings off the Dutch coast. During the second half of the eighteenth century the great anatomist Petrus Camper also did a great deal of work on stranded whales, van Breda supervised the dissection of a Bottlenose Whale stranded off Zandvoort on the 24th July, 1846, and Vrolik, the founder of the anatomical collection of the University of Amsterdam, investigated a great many Cetacean organs. In Belgium, van Beneden was responsible for the splendid collection of skeletons, which form so important a part of the Brussels Museum of Natural History; in France, Gervais and Delage; in Scotland, Struthers and Turner; in England, Murie; in Sweden, Malm; in Germany, Kükenthal and his many pupils – all did a great deal to increase our knowledge of the Cetaceans.

But to return to whaling itself. Since the Sperm Whale was pursued all over the world, and since whalers had to break their long voyages now and then, it is not surprising that they imparted their skills to some of the native population. Thus the foundations of the Mozambique, the Australian and the New Zealand whaling industries were laid. From 1792 to 1930 New Zealand Maoris used open boats to hunt Sperm Whales, Southern Right Whales and Humpbacks with hand harpoons, as the Americans had first taught them to do, and on the Friendly Islands the hunters continue to operate in this primitive way even now. Here the catch consists almost exclusively of cows, often accompanied by calves. The villagers of Lamakera on Solor, and Lamararap on Lomblen, small islands in the Timor Sea, still capture Sperm Whales, dolphins and an occasional Rorqual with harpoons attached to a bamboo shaft. They use small boats with a special platform in the prow for the harpooner. But not all natives were brave enough to tackle these large animals, and once, when a Sperm Whale appeared off the coast of Manokwari, the Papuans gave the sea a wide berth for quite some time. The most important reminder of the great past, however, is found on the Azores. Here the coast is very steep, and Sperm Whales can therefore approach very close. They are still caught from rowing boats with hand harpoons, and to this day some of the blubber is boiled down on land in old-fashioned iron pots. The only innovation in an industry which today operates from about fifteen land stations is a motor launch for towing the boats out and the dead whales in. The launches keep up radio-telephone contact with look-out posts on land.

Probably not since 1600 have whales known a more peaceful era than the second half of the nineteenth century. Greenland voyages were over, and Sperm Whale and Southern Right Whale hunting was declining from year to year. Local activities in, for instance, Japan, Norway, and California excepted, the whale was relatively safe. Unfortunately the Golden Age was soon over. The Norwegians, seeing that the Biscayan and Greenland Whales were rapidly disappearing from under their eyes, turned their attention to the faster Rorquals. With the advent of steamships, the problem of speed was in the process of being solved, and all that remained was to discover a way of killing the animals from a distance of, say, 40 yards. From 1732 British whalers in the Arctic, in particular, had begun to experiment with all sorts of harpoon guns and even with bomb-lances, though with no noticeable success. In 1868 it fell to the Norwegian Svend Foyn from Tönsberg to perfect a practicable harpoon gun and to improve it further by introducing the shell harpoon. The shell of this harpoon was connected to a time fuse, and exploded inside the whale a few moments after it was fired. The explosion caused so much damage to the whale that it was killed very quickly.

Fast catcher-ships, harpoon guns and shell harpoons thus made it possible to pursue Rorquals, animals which had previously eluded the whalers. As we have seen, Rorquals have slim bodies (Fig. 9), a small dorsal fin, longitudinal grooves on their throats and chests, flat heads and shorter whalebone plates than Right Whales, from which they are furthermore distinguished by their speed and by the fact that their carcasses do not float. To keep them afloat in the water, air must be pumped into them. The biggest Rorqual is the Blue Whale, a gigantic animal that can attain a length of 100 feet and a weight of 130 tons (Fig. 135). Its average length, however, is just under 79 feet. The somewhat smaller Fin Whale has an average length of 68 feet and a maximum length of 82 feet. Both species behave in much the same way as the Humpback Whale, which we have discussed earlier; in the summer they keep to the colder waters of the Arctic and Antarctic and they winter in tropical or subtropical oceans, covering vast distances during their yearly migrations. The Sei Whale is yet another Rorqual – smaller and slimmer than the Fin Whale, and generally found in warmer waters. Finally, there is Bryde's Whale which differs little from the Sei Whale but which is found exclusively in warm waters, i.e. off the coast of Southern Africa, in the Bay of Bengal, in the Malacca Straits, in the Caribbean and in the Northern Pacific. (There are some indications, however, that it also occurs off Australia.) The Little Piked Whale, too, is a Rorqual, but it is a dwarf, less than 30 feet long, and we shall discuss it separately because it is of no interest to what is called the big whaling industry.

Svend Foyn's discoveries quickly led to a vast expansion of land stations all along the Norwegian coast and it was not long before similar stations were set up in Iceland, Ireland, the Faroes and the Shetland Islands. As early as 1885, 20 Norwegian companies with 34 stations caught 1,287 whales off the Finmark coast (Norway), and other countries soon followed suit. As land stations in Newfoundland, Labrador, Murmansk, British Columbia, California, Japan, Korea, Australia and New Zealand were brought up to date, the peace of Rorquals was shattered all over the world. In 1908 South Africa established her first land station, soon to be followed by Chile, Brazil and Peru.

The great discoveries of Koch and Pasteur had caused such changes in antiseptic techniques, particularly in North America and Western Europe, that the population of these areas increased by leaps and bounds. Simultaneously there occurred a general increase in the standard of living caused by a variety of factors. Both sets of circumstances led to an increasing demand for fats. Whalebone had by then fallen out of favour because other elastic substances had taken its place; America supplied beef in abundance; and paraffin, gas and electricity provided all the illumination that was needed. But with greater emphasis on bodily hygiene there arose an ever-increasing demand for soap, and with a larger population a greater demand for edible fats. Now, butter has forever been in short supply and hence a luxury, and margarine, which is not a dairy product, had to serve as substitute for the poorer classes. Ground-nuts and coconuts had long been the only source of this fat, as whale oil, because of its smell and taste, was thought unfit for human consumption. But disaster struck the whales in 1901, when Sabatier and Sendérens discovered a new process which Bedford, Norman, and others applied to the hardening of fat some years later. By hardening is meant the saturation of unsaturated fatty acids (see page 326), and during this process the taste and smell of the oil are so improved that it can be mixed with vegetable fats. In 1929 chemists working for the Margarine Union (later merged into Unilever) managed to improve this process to such an extent that whale-oil could be used entirely by itself.

Still, Norwegian whalers did not immediately derive all the benefits they would have liked from the new situation. While increasing demand caused a steep rise in prices, there was a shortage of Rorquals within reach of the land stations. However, the Norwegians soon remembered that the Northern Arctic, where the Greenland Whale had by then become almost extinct, had an annual influx of Rorquals, which came there in search of food. It was decided to return to the old trade, but now in modern guise. The first modern factory ship, the 450-ton *Telegraph*, was sent to Spitsbergen waters by Christian Christensen in 1903. In 1904 the *Admiralen* followed, and by 1905 seven 'floating factories' were operating in the Arctic.

A brief glance at a map will show that the Arctic is a fairly small area, particularly when we compare it with the Antarctic. It soon became apparent that the lucrative trade would have to be extended to southern waters with their far greater number of whales. Now, the Antarctic was very far away from Europe, but after all, Jacques le Maire, who had rounded Cape Horn in 1616 in his small ships *Eendracht* and *Hoorn*, had pointed out that he had come across so many whales 'that he had his time cut out keeping them at bay'. Moreover, Cook, Ross, Weddell, and other subsequent explorers had also stated time and again how many great whales they had encountered in the Antarctic. Since then, however, the Southern Right Whale had become so reduced in numbers that a Dundee expedition which set out in 1892 returned almost empty-handed, and the same fate befell the three ships which were sent out in 1894 by a number of Hamburg shippers. But Captain C. A. Larsen, who took part in the

Hamburg expedition, and who led the Swedish South Pole expedition in 1901, was struck by the great number of Rorquals off South Georgia and the small islands in the neighbourhood of the southern tip of South America.

European financiers were slow to realize the vast potentialities of Antarctic whaling, but Larsen managed to find the necessary capital in Argentina. In 1904 he established the land station of Grytviken on South Georgia, and in 1905 he sent the *Admiralen* to the Antarctic. By 1910 six land stations and fourteen factory ships were in operation, and 10,230 animals were caught by forty-eight catcher boats. The factory ships were all kept at anchor in the sheltered bays and inlets of South Georgia, the South Shetlands, the South Sandwich Islands and the South Orkneys. Now, all these islands happened to be British territory, and the British government demanded a great deal of money for the anchorages. Moreover, the number of whales in these regions was far from inexhaustible, and this led to the idea that modern factory ships might just as well operate like the old Sperm Whale hunters – on the open sea.

A start was made in the winter of 1923. At first, flensing alongside the mother-ship proved very awkward, but in 1925 the *Lancing* first employed the slipway and the whole process was revolutionized. The slipway is a stern-ramp over which the whales can be hauled to the cutting-up deck (Fig. 13). The intestines are thrown overboard, while the blubber and also the bones (which are first cut up by steam saws) are fed into the boilers below, where the oil is drawn off.

In the beginning of the thirties came the modern 'claw' which engaged the tail of the whale and ingeniously lifted the dead giant as it was moved astern of the ship. Other modern improvements included radio-telephones to the catcher boats, together with radar and asdic. After the Second World War attempts were made to locate whales first from seaplanes, and later from helicopters, but these have not been very successful so far.

Equally unsuccessful were attempts to kill the animals by electrocution, a method particularly dear to the UFAW (Universities Federation for Animal Welfare), a British society who consider this much more humane than shell harpooning. Technically this method, which at first caused more shocks to the whalers than to the whales, has now been mastered, but it can still happen that instead of being killed, the whale is merely stunned. It then regains consciousness with all the unpleasant consequences that can be expected. Some investigators are, moreover, of the opinion that the electrocution of whales has much the same effect as curare, an American Indian arrow poison which has also been tried out for catching whales. In both cases it is thought that the motor nerves become blocked with the consequent paralysis of an otherwise conscious animal. Only when the heart itself is paralysed does the animal die, so that it is quite possible that this method is by no means as humane as UFAW originally thought. Even so, Hector Whaling Ltd, a British company, continued tests with an advanced type of electric harpoon during 1956–7, and other companies have carried out (so far unsuccessful) tests, using a harpoon grenade containing compressed carbon dioxide, whereby the animals are meant to be killed quickly, while being inflated simultaneously.[1]

However, it is very difficult to adapt complicated modern instruments to whaling needs. Thus the bones are still cut up by somewhat primitive steam saws before they disappear into the boilers, a method which has proved the safest of all, and safety is a prerequisite for an industry where every interruption may lead to disastrous losses.

Southern whaling is no longer restricted to South Georgia, but takes place right round the Antarctic Ocean. For a long time, the waters south of the Pacific were prohibited territory, but in 1955 the prohibition was lifted to afford some measure of relief to other hunting grounds. Although the area in question is not very large and though it is far removed from suitable harbours, ships moved in right away, amongst them Holland's *Willem Barendsz II*, then on her maiden voyage. In some sectors, at least, they came across a good number of whales, and the South Pacific has therefore been revisited by many whalers since (1956–9).

During the first half of the twentieth century whaling was a very lucrative trade indeed, and fleets became bigger and bigger, particularly in the thirties. The Norwegians were the first to build up the industry, but Britain, South Africa, Japan, Panama, Germany, the United States and Chile also played an important part. Whaling in the last three countries fell off during the Second World War. Since 1945 the Soviet Union and Holland have also joined in, and of the twenty-two factory ships which sailed to the Antarctic in the season 1960–1, nine were Norwegian, two were British, seven were Japanese, one was Dutch and three were Russian. After the war, Japan increased her Antarctic whaling fleet from two to seven ships, and the second and third Russian mother-ships made their maiden voyage in the winter of 1959–60 and 1960–1. It is believed that Russia is increasing the number of whaling expeditions as well.

Since the overall annual catch of all whaling fleets is limited by international agreement, Antarctic competition has become extremely keen. Every country tries to get the lion's share of the total quota, with the consequent construction of ever-greater ships accompanied by the greatest

[1]In 1959 a special international committee set up by the International Whaling Commission discussed at length the different methods of humane killing of whales. Some progress with regard to electrocution was made by exchange of information and W. H. Dawbin reported successful electrocution by New Zealand's Humpback whalers.

number of catcher boats. Clearly, a ration of a certain number of animals per ship is called for, and would effect considerable economies, but this measure has so far been opposed because it is felt that it would curb free competition on the open seas. Still, a national quota has once again become an important subject of discussion. Meanwhile, Holland, which started whaling in 1946 with a rebuilt Swedish tanker, is using the new *Willem Barendsz II*, built in 1955, a 26,830 tonner which, with its contingent of 506 men is a really big factory-ship. The Russian ship *Sovietskaya Ukraina* (36,000 tons) is the biggest of all.

The crew of a modern whaler is kept hard at work during the entire season. Once the first harpoon has been fired and a successful catch has been made, the winches on deck rattle away day and night, the boilers keep bubbling ceaselessly and the catchers are out for 24 hours a day. To keep the mother-ship well stocked, the crew have to work in two shifts with only short breaks for meals. Life is extremely hard and very tiring, and for three long months it revolves round two questions only: how many tons of oil have we got today, and how big will our bonus be? Everyone from the captain to the lowest deck hand shares in the proceeds and returns home with jingling pockets. Whaling is a lucrative but also a very fatiguing and often an icy cold job. Still, it is not nearly as dangerous or arduous as it used to be. All mother-ships and catcher boats are adequately heated, the berths are comfortable, washing facilities are good, and there are many pleasant distractions. The ship's doctor watches over the crew's health and has the most up-to-date medical equipment; the diet is both pleasant and balanced. Vitamin and other nutritional deficiencies are things of the past.

The most important whaling product nowadays is oil, but before we deal with this product more fully, we must first remove a persistent error: the constant confusion of whale-oil with fish-liver oil. The whale supplies no fish-liver oil whatsoever; fish-liver oil is the product of the livers particularly of halibut and cod, fish which abound in northern waters. The remedial effects of cod- and halibut-liver oil are based on the presence of vitamins A and D, both of which are essential to human health. Thus, if children lack vitamin D, they may get rickets. Whale oil, too, contains some vitamin A, and the livers particularly of Blue Whales and Sperm Whales are so rich in it that they are an excellent source of the substance. But no part of the whale contains any vitamin D whatsoever, so that real cod-liver oil is quite a different product.

Whale-oil is primarily a fatty oil used in the manufacture of soap and margarine, and to a lesser extent as a drying oil as used in the paint industry. Inferior grades are used for tanning, and particularly in the manufacture of chamois leather. Sperm oil (a mixture of Sperm Whale

Figure 13. Working up a whale aboard the Willem Barendsz II. *Photograph:
A. F. M. Drieman, Amsterdam.*

oil and spermaceti) falls into a category of its own. Scientifically speaking, it is a waxy substance and not an edible fat at all. It was used to a great extent in the manufacture of candles, so much so that the first unit of light to be introduced, the standard candle, was defined as 'a candle of spermaceti, of which six weigh a pound, burning at a rate of 120 grains per hour'. Nowadays Sperm Whale oil is primarily used for the manufacture of cosmetics (lipsticks, skin-creams, etc.), while spermaceti, the oil found in the cavities of the animal's head, is used by chemists for making a number of ointments. It so happens that sperm oil is readily absorbed by the skin; it is an excellent lubricant, particularly for aeroplane and submarine engines, and can also be used in the manufacture of certain detergents. The Japanese even use it to make boot polish.

The price of whale-oil fluctuates a great deal, and reflects the prices ruling in the world market of fats and oils on which whale-oil itself has only a minute effect. Immediately after the Second World War, prices were high and most whaling companies did well. Since then prices have dropped again and there is great concern about how to make ends meet. Antarctic expeditions are very expensive and the costs keep rising from year to year.

The Japanese are less affected, for they kill whales primarily for their meat. We have already seen that Japan is short of protein foods, and it is therefore understandable that whale- and dolphin-meat has been consumed there for centuries. When Japan first sent out her Antarctic whalers in the 1930's, they used refrigerator ships kept at a temperature of $-25°$ C., in which the meat was transported back to cold storage installations at home. Whale-meat is sold in Japan with a great deal of high-pressure advertising (Fig. 14), and the Japanese have learned how to turn it into all sorts of dishes. They cut it into thin strips and eat it raw with condiments, but then they do the same with chicken and fish.

Europeans, too, have eaten whale-meat for centuries. As early as A.D. 1000, traders from Rouen brought it to London, and we know that whale-meat was sold in Utrecht in 1024, in Nieuport in 1163, in Damme in 1252 and in Calais in 1300. Ludovic van Male, Duke of Flanders, had it sent regularly to his daughter Margaret, the wife of Philip the Bold (1342—1404), as a special delicacy. In modern Europe, whale-meat is used predominantly in Norway. In fact, the Norwegian land stations have proved profitable precisely for that reason, though their annual catch is relatively small. The captured whales are cut up with a special 'spade' while they are still in the sea so that the carcasses can cool and the meat be brought fresh ashore. Here it is inspected scrupulously and then kept in refrigerators, so that it can be consumed with perfect safety all over Norway. Inferior grades of meat are sent to fox-breeding farms. Norway, the Faroe Islands and Iceland export a proportion of their catch to

Figure 14. Japanese poster advertising whale-meat.

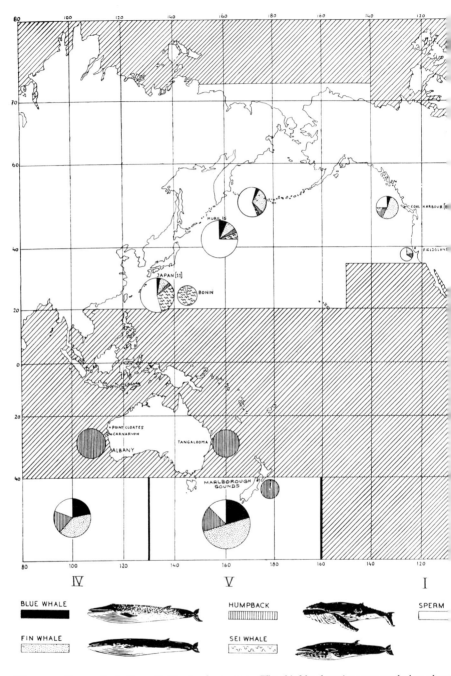

Figure 15. Survey of whaling activities in about 1950. The chief land stations are marked on the m
but Area I (S. Pacific) was opened in 1955. The dimensions of the circles reflect the size of th
averages.) Some land stations have since ceased operating, while others (e.g. Saldanha Bay and
three catchers) at Dairen, and she is at present building another station on

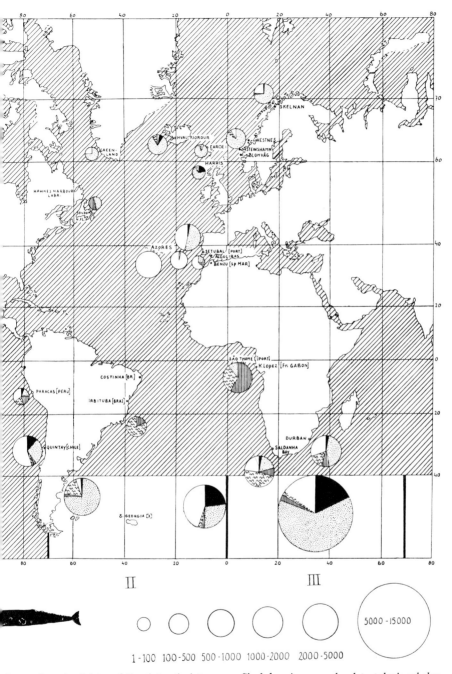

II   III

1-100   100-500   500-1000   1000-2000   2000-5000

5000-15000

figures show the division of the Antarctic into areas. Shaded regions are closed to pelagic whalers,
ch; the shading reflects the proportion of the various species in it. (Both are calculated from 5-year
bour) have resumed activities after a prior interruption. In 1958, China opened a land station (with
land. Sperm Whales have been caught also at Cape Lopez and Saõ Thomé.

Germany and to Britain where it is used to some extent for human consumption and more generally for dog meat. Britain also imports some
whale-meat from the Antarctic. The *Balaena* (Hector Whaling Ltd)
particularly, processed a great deal of whale-meat which was sent home
in special refrigerator ships. At the Low Temperature Station (Cambridge)
scientists have done much work on the correct way of preserving the
meat.

Other European countries use little, if any, whale-meat, which is
rather a pity since in this way a great deal of meat, eminently suitable for
human consumption, is wasted in the Antarctic. A single Antarctic Fin
Whale can provide up to 5 tons of excellent meat, but unfortunately the
long-distance transport in refrigerator ships turns out to be so expensive
that, for instance, frozen Argentine beef can be bought for the same price.
Moreover, most Europeans have an unfortunate prejudice against whale-
meat, believing that it is inferior and that it tastes of fish or oil. This is a
fallacy, for if the lean meat of the young animals is prepared and kept
properly, it is almost indistinguishable from good beef. I myself am sent
frozen whale-meat every year, and my friends and acquaintances always
tuck in with relish – provided they are not told beforehand what they are
eating. If I tell them afterwards, they rarely believe me. At a meeting of
the Dutch Zoological Association held on 8th December, 1956, more than
fifty guests ate whale beefsteaks with obvious enjoyment.

But even when whalers have no use for whale-meat itself, there is no
reason at all why they should throw it overboard. First, they can turn it
into meat extract for the manufacture of stock and soup cubes, and
secondly it can be turned into excellent cattle meal by mixing it with
other foods. One difficulty is that the meal must be stored in bags and must
be dried very carefully. If more than 8–10 per cent moisture is present,
a great deal of heat is generated with consequent risk of fire. Ingenious
attempts have also been made to render the meal colourless, odourless
and tasteless so that this protein-rich substance may become fit for human
consumption. Russian scientists seem to have succeeded, for the members
of the Whaling Conference in Moscow were served with a delicacy,
somewhat reminiscent of marsh-mallow, consisting of refined whale meal.

Another edible whale product is the blubber itself, though only a few
countries hold it in esteem. In Japan, it is served either raw or salted and
often with a spicy sauce. I myself do not like it; it seems to be an acquired
taste. In Iceland they use the belly, in particular, for preparing a dish
called *rengi* which is made by pickling the fat in acid. According to
experts, *rengi* tastes of cucumbers, and it, too, is an acquired taste; at least
foreigners rarely like it.

The bones and some skeletal tissues can be used for preparing glue and

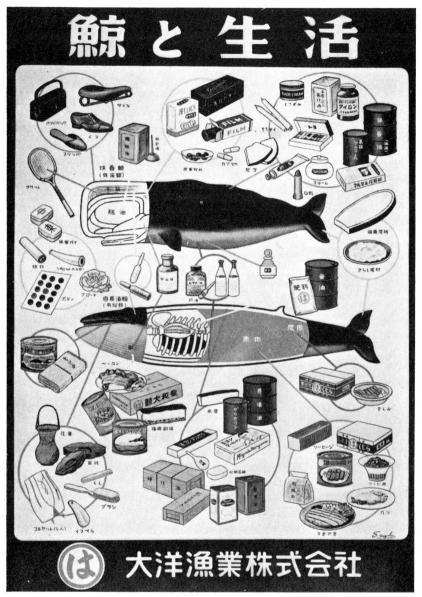

Figure 16. Japanese poster showing the various products derived from a Sperm Whale and a Rorqual.

also gelatine, not only for photographic films and other technical purposes, but also for jellies and similar sweets (Fig. 16).

Apart from foodstuffs, a host of other articles can be made from whales. Incompletely boiled bones make an excellent fertilizer; the tendons can be used as strings for tennis raquets, and for surgical stitches. Whalebone is still used in a number of countries, such as Japan, for all sorts of articles, corsets included. In Europe, whalebone can still be found in riding crops, in some types of top boot, and as a support for the busbies of British and Danish Guardsmen. Moreover whalebone is occasionally used in the manufacture of brushes, though the industry is none too keen on this practically indestructible substance, and prefers to sell articles that require regular replacement. Sperm Whale teeth can be turned into chess men, mah-yong counters, buttons and all sorts of 'ivory' articles which are often very beautifully carved. Such carving, called scrimshaw work, is a very old skill indeed. Whalers, particularly during the eighteenth and nineteenth centuries, were masters of it, and practised it during the long spells of fog and lulls at sea. The teeth were often decorated with Indian ink, and by far the greatest proportion of these drawings represent women, ships and Sperm Whales. Even modern whalers, during the long voyages out and home, still have plenty of time to carry on this ancient craft. Their acquaintance with the Antarctic has given them a liking for the penguin, and the curved teeth of the Sperm Whale are admirably suited to reproducing its form. The Japanese and Norwegians even have small handicraft centres for scrimshaw work, and their products are sold in the gift shop attached to the United Nations headquarters in New York.

The skin of the whale is not suitable for leather products, though the Japanese use certain parts of Sperm Whale skin for that purpose. The liver supplies vitamin A, and the endocrine glands all sorts of valuable hormones used in medicine and veterinary surgery. In a later chapter we shall return to these hormones and also to ambergris, an intestinal product which is often washed ashore or else found in the gut of the Sperm Whale. Ambergris used to play a very important role in the perfume industry. It must be stressed that in spite of the similarity of their names, there is no resemblance at all between amber and ambergris, as has so often been thought.

It will have become clear by now, that, although oil is still the most important whale product, whales have much more to offer mankind. In fact, apart from the intestines which can adversely affect the colour of the oil, no part of the whale needs to be discarded.

The number of whales killed annually is surprisingly large. Until recently the overall catch of factory ships operating in the Antarctic was restricted to 15,000 Blue Whale Units[1] (one B.W.U. being equal to 1 Blue Whale, 2 Fin Whales or 2·5 Humpbacks), and since nowadays by far the greatest number of whales killed is made up of Fin Whales, the figure is equivalent to just under 30,000 animals. Apart from this quota, however, whales are also caught by land stations in South Georgia, Norway, Iceland, Greenland, the Faroes, Morocco, Spain, Portugal, Madeira, the Azores, Gabon and Saô Thomé, South Africa, Brazil, Peru, Chile, British Columbia, Labrador, Newfoundland, Australia, New Zealand, Japan, China, the Bonin Islands and the Kuril Islands. In addition, a few Japanese and Russian mother ships still operate in the North Pacific (Fig. 15). Some of the land stations may close down when prices are low or catches bad, but the moment the industry picks up they resume their activities. Thus during the 1952–1953 season, 18 factory ships, 50 land stations and 375 catcher boats caught 43,669 whales all over the world, of which 4,208 were Blue Whales, 25,553 Fin Whales, 2,172 Sei Whales, 3,322 Humpback Whales, 8,317 Sperm Whales, and 97 belonged to other species. They supplied a total of 420,000 tons of oil and 47,000 tons of sperm oil, but this is less than 2 per cent of the annual world production of fats and oils, and only 4–5 per cent of the world production of animal fats.

If we realize how many whales lose their lives each year, we may feel pangs of conscience, and become perturbed that if things are allowed to continue in this way whales may become extinct or be reduced to such numbers that the whole industry may fold up. Are we perhaps killing the goose that lays the golden egg?

And when all is said and done, it is the golden egg which tips the balance. In 1924 and in 1927 the League of Nations made sustained efforts to produce some international agreement, but all attempts proved fruitless. On 21st June, 1929, Norway passed a law regulating the national catch, and on 18th January, 1936, the so-called Geneva Convention was accepted by many whaling countries. The Convention was superseded on 8th June, 1937, by the London Conference, and on 2nd December, 1946, delegates of the member states met in Washington and founded the International Whaling Commission, with a secretariat in London. The Commission has meanwhile met twelve times: seven times in London, and once each in Oslo, Cape Town, Tokyo, Moscow and The Hague. The eighteen affiliated countries are: Argentina, Australia, Brazil, Britain, Canada, Denmark, France, Holland, Iceland, Japan, Mexico, New Zealand, Norway, Panama, South Africa, Sweden, the U.S.A. and the U.S.S.R.[2] Jointly, they make up by far the largest proportion of whaling

[1] Owing to some serious objections this overall limit was abandoned in 1959.
[2] While the English edition of this book was being prepared, Norway and Holland withdrew from the Commission. Later on Norway cancelled its withdrawal.

countries. Spain, Portugal and Gabon have so far refused to join the Commission, while on 11th August, 1952, Chile, Ecuador and Peru concluded a separate agreement in Santiago. They found some of the international conditions unacceptable and, moreover, insisted on a 200-mile territorial limit. Needless to say, not even the members of the International Whaling Commission are in full agreement on every point. If we bear in mind that, of the 17,387 men employed in Antarctic whaling during 1958–9, 40 per cent were Norwegian and 46 per cent Japanese, and if we remember that quite apart from her land stations, Norway has nine factory ships for a population of 3·5 million, while Holland, for instance, has only one ship for 11 million inhabitants, we see at once how much greater and more important a part whaling plays in the economy of Norway than it does in that of most other countries. While Norway, in particular, is forced to take a long term view of the problem, other countries, and particularly the newcomers, are often more concerned with the immediate results. Australia and New Zealand, by virtue of the geographical location of their land stations, are primarily interested in Humpbacks and in limiting the annual Antarctic catch of that species, so that a maximum share is left for their own whalers. Countries such as Denmark and Iceland, which are mainly interested in the North Atlantic catch, and countries such as Russia and Japan which are concerned with the North Pacific, are clearly more opposed to whaling limits in their respective domains than, say, Holland or South Africa. Thus the divergent interests of eighteen countries must be balanced, while the whale population in general and every species in particular must be preserved.

Despite many conflicts, however, we are on safe ground when we say that compared with all kinds of other international bodies, the atmosphere in the Whaling Commission is fairly good. Members have some idea of one another's needs, and are usually ready to strive for a common solution. This good atmosphere is in no small part due to the offices of the first four Presidents: Professor B. Bergersen (Norway), Dr R. Kellogg (U.S.A.), Ir. G. J. Lienesch (Holland), each of whom held office for three years, and Mr R. G. R. Wall (Britain), who was elected in 1958. International understanding was also greatly fostered by A. T. A. Dobson (Britain), the first Secretary of the Commission, who served until 1959. The Commission has drawn up a number of regulations laid down in the 'International Convention for the Regulation of Whaling' (Washington, 1946). By the Washington Convention member states have to agree to observe an overall catch limit, to refrain from capturing individuals belonging to species that are endangered, to observe the closed season and areas, to spare animals below a fixed size and particularly cows accompanied by a calf, to process whale carcasses quickly and correctly, etc. Still, the most controversial issue is the overall limit of the annual Antarctic catch from factory ships. In 1946 this limit was fixed at 16,000 B.W.U., but this figure was subsequently reduced to 14,500 B.W.U. and raised again to 15,000 in 1959. During the 1955–6 season, the quota was caught by 19 factory ships operating with 257 catcher boats, and in 1957 by 20 factory ships with 237 catchers. In future this yield will have to be shared with the U.S.S.R. which is extending her whaling fleet considerably. The International Bureau for Whaling Statistics (Sandefjord, Norway) receives weekly reports about how many units have been caught by every ship, and on the basis of these the Bureau decides when the season is to be declared closed. During recent years, this happened on about the 18th March, but during 1955–6 the quota was exhausted by 4th March. That season was the shortest ever recorded.

The general season usually opens on 7th January, but Blue Whales, which need special protection, may not be hunted before 1st February. Humpbacks may be hunted for no more than four days every year.

Thus the season lasts for two and a half months, and the fixing of the opening date is a point of the utmost importance. It might be argued that the later that date the better the results, since whales grow fatter during the season. However, the weather in the Antarctic deteriorates and storms, fogs, snow and hailstorms can hold up the work for days, so that it is essential to get the catch in before the bad weather sets in.

The reader might wonder why there is a sanction against killing females accompanied by their calves and no protection for cows in calf or even for cows in general, when the females of, for example, some types of deer, are completely protected. As things are, when a cow in calf is killed a future whale and all the oil it could yield are completely lost.

Unfortunately, it is impossible to tell what sex a whale is before it is taken out of the water, let alone whether a female is in calf or not. The only exception is the Sperm Whale, for here the males have an average length of over 50 feet, while the females are always less than 40 feet long. Hence the size limit below which it is prohibited to kill Sperm Whales has been fixed at 38 and 35 feet for pelagic catchers and land stations respectively. In practice, this means that nearly all cows are spared, and that the species is kept up to strength. The South American Convention has fixed this limit at 30 feet, since Chile uses Sperm Whale meat for animal consumption, and can therefore not afford to be very fussy.

The reader might also wonder how the size limit is assessed. After all, it is impossible to take a tape measure to a whale before it is killed. In fact, this question is settled by the harpoon-gunners, who have generally served on whaling ships since their earliest youth and for whom whaling is a family tradition. Their experience is such that they can estimate the length of a whale within a few feet from the appearance of any part of its body. How well they know their jobs is best seen from the fact that the number of reported mistakes is very small indeed. Thus during the 1954 season only 1·2 per cent of all the whales killed in the Antarctic were found to be below the limit.

Are these figures reliable? Is there any reason why the crews should not simply conceal their mistakes? In fact, there is, for the sizes are checked not by the whalers themselves but by government inspectors. Every factory ship carries two such government officials who supervise the measurements and whose task it is to see that international agreements are fully observed. It would appear that they do their job very conscientiously and that, while some governments may be laxer than others in reporting mistakes to the international body, no serious lapses are suspected anywhere.

What happens when an error is discovered? There are no international sanctions, but each country deals with the problem separately. All member states make it a rule to withhold payment and bonuses in respect of illegally killed whales. This rule and the excellent tradition among whalers have so far helped a great deal. Of course, international inspection would lead to even better results, and there has been talk lately of neutral observers from non-whaling countries.

Clearly, if protective legislation is to be effective, it must be based on accurate knowledge of the biology and habits of whales, in particular of the distribution, the growth, and the method of reproduction. All this requires much biological study, and twentieth-century whaling, therefore, gave rise to a new discipline: applied whale biology. Actually, this discipline was not altogether new, for as early as 1796 the Dutch Academy of Science at Haarlem held a competition for 'the best biological description and natural history of whales, such as would help to discover their habitat and the best methods of killing or catching them'. J. A. Bennet, a Leyden Doctor of Philosophy and Medicine, was awarded the gold medal for his paper on capturing whales, his description of a new kind of harpoon, and his anatomical account of a whale foetus.

Modern biologists are primarily concerned with statistical data on the number, the sex, the length and other characteristics of captured animals. It may be said that the spade-work was done by Major G. E. H. Barrett-Hamilton who went to the land station at Leith Harbour (South Georgia) in 1913 to make anatomical investigations of the carcasses of whales. Unfortunately, he died at his post a year later and it was not until 1925 that his data were published by Hinton. Norwegian whaling companies are all members of *Norges Hvalfangstforbund* (formerly *Hvalfangerforening*), and when S. Risting became its secretary in 1919, he immediately started to organize a statistical survey based on data collected by all ships. The first paper was published in 1927, and on 16th August, 1929, the Norwegian government, at the suggestion of the International Council for the Exploration of the Sea, founded the Committee for Whaling Statistics. The headquarters of the committee are the offices of the *Hvalfangstforbund* in Sandefjord. Its first Secretary was S. Risting, the second H. B. Poulsen, and it is now under the capable directorship of E. Vangstein. The Committee now receives data from practically every ship and land station the world over. The data are entered on punch cards, and the results are published annually in the International Whaling Statistics. We can safely state that there is no other form of hunting or fishing on which there exists comparably comprehensive information.

Meanwhile the British, too, who after all were in control of South Georgia and the Falkland Islands and who, moreover, were generally concerned with the Antarctic, had begun their own investigations. The Discovery Committee was founded in 1920; and it dispatched the Royal research ship *Discovery* to make investigations in the vicinity of the Falkland Islands. The *Discovery* was a sailing ship, and has since been replaced by the *Discovery II*, a steel-built steamer which is a veritable floating laboratory. She has cruised throughout the length and breadth of the Antarctic, gathering material wherever she went. At first the investigations were concerned with a study of oceanography and the Arctic fauna and flora, but from 1925–7 the present deputy director of the National Institute of Oceanography, Dr N. A. Mackintosh, turned his attention to an inquiry into whaling resources. Together with J. F. G. Wheeler he examined no less than 1,683 whales in South Georgia and South Africa, primarily with a view to throwing greater light on their method of reproduction. The results were published in *Discovery Reports* Vol. I, and *Discovery Reports* have to this day remained one of the chief sources of whaling information. In 1949 the Discovery Committee was reorganized as part of the National Institute of Oceanography, which is continuing the good work, though on a somewhat smaller scale.

The Norwegians did not stop at purely statistical work, and as early as 1924 the *Hvalfangerforening* requested Professor J. Hjort to join the Michael Sars expedition to the Davis Strait. On 4th May, 1930, the *Hvalrådt*, the supreme Norwegian whaling authority, founded the State Institute for Whale Research (*Statens Institutt for Hvalforskning*) as a special department of the Institute for Marine Biology of the University of Oslo. Its director, and the leading Norwegian authority on whaling research, was and is Professor J. T. Ruud. The Institute published its papers both in the *Hvalrådets Skrifter* and also in the official journal of the *Hvalfangstforbund*, the *Norsk Hvalfangst-Tidende* whose editor is E. Vangstein.

In 1936 Germany set up the *Reichsstelle für Walforschung* (Government Office for Whaling Research) with headquarters in Hamburg, and Japan followed suit in 1946 by setting up a whale research institute in Tokyo under the directorship of Dr H. Omura. In Paris, Professor Dr P. Budker directs whaling research at the *Musée National d'Histoire Naturelle*; in Australia the C.S.I.R.O. finances the work of Dr Chittleborough; in British Columbia the work is directed by G. C. Pike; and in Russia the V.N.I.R.O., with its numerous sub-committees in different parts of the country, directs the work from Moscow. Amongst Russian scientists, Dr M. M. Sleptsov, Dr B. A. Zenkovich, Dr S. V. Dorofeev and Dr S. E. Kleinenberg have made important contributions to the study of Cetaceans.

Holland, too, has appreciated the importance of biological investigations ever since she first entered the field in 1946. Shortly after the maiden voyage of the *Willem Barendsz* (on 3rd October, 1947) the Dutch organization T.N.O. founded a Research Group which is at present directed by W. L. van Utrecht from the Zoological Laboratory of the University of Amsterdam. It relies for its data primarily on information gathered by biologists on board the *Willem Barendsz*, and also by inspectors, particularly Mr W. H. E. van Dijk.

Apart from research for commercial motives, the twentieth century has witnessed a great deal of purely scientific work on Cetaceans. It would take up far too much space to list all those scientists and other who have made important contributions in this field, though many of their names will crop up in subsequent chapters. I must, however, make an exception in the case of Sir Sidney F. Harmer and his successor, Dr F. C. Fraser, of the British Museum (Natural History), who did such remarkable work on living Cetaceans, and also in the case of Dr R. Kellogg, the Director of the U.S. National Museum in Washington who, apart from his work as an administrator, made a very thorough study of extinct whales and dolphins.

In our discussion so far we have ignored the smaller Cetaceans, though man, not content with his big booty, has for centuries been killing the smaller species as well. In fact, it seems to be pretty certain that he first began by hunting porpoises and dolphins, and that it was only subsequently that he was bold enough to tackle the larger whales.

Porpoises (Fig. 18) have been caught through the ages wherever they have approached close to the shore. Sometimes they were caught sporadically, and at other times regularly and in such numbers that we are justified in speaking of an industry in the true sense of the word. This happened off Normandy in the eleventh century, to such an extent that by 1098 legal limitations had to be imposed on the catch. The oil was used

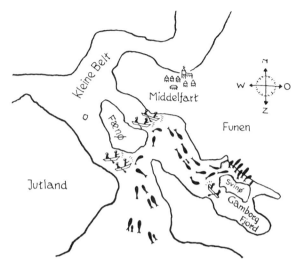

Figure 17. Porpoise hunt in Middelfart (Denmark). (Møhl Hansen, 1954.)

for burning and the meat for human consumption. Porpoise meat was in fact considered a great delicacy at the time, and a chronicle from the year 1426 reports that Henry VI of England was very fond of it. We also know that during the Coronation Dinner of his successor, Henry VII, it was served up in various guises – both as a main course and also in pies. Bound to tradition though they are, the English have now relinquished this delicacy, although we know for certain that the Court continued to enjoy it until late in the seventeenth century.

Porpoises and Bottlenose Dolphins have also provided food for the inhabitants of Middelfart, a small Danish town on Fyn, ever since the beginning of the sixteenth century. Porpoises are caught mainly from November to February, when they migrate from the Baltic to the North Sea (Fig. 17). The animals' path is blocked, and the water is beaten with sticks, until the porpoises are driven into a small fjord which is quickly sealed off. They are then chased ashore and killed with long knives. During good years in the past, the villagers have often caught more than 3,000 animals annually in this way. When the oil market dropped, regular catches ceased, and in 1892 the whole business on Fyn folded up altogether, though since then it has been revived on occasion and particularly during the lean years of the First and Second World Wars. Still, the villagers never forgot their old tradition, for a Dutch expedition which visited the region from December 1957 to January 1958 with the aim of capturing live porpoises returned with excellent results. While the people of Middelfart were primarily interested in the oil, other people, particularly on the Mediterranean and the Black Sea, hunted porpoises and

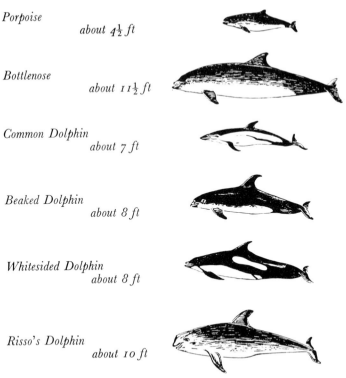

Porpoise

about $4\frac{1}{2}$ ft

Bottlenose

about $11\frac{1}{2}$ ft

Common Dolphin

about 7 ft

Beaked Dolphin

about 8 ft

Whitesided Dolphin

about 8 ft

Risso's Dolphin

about 10 ft

Figure 18. Some North Atlantic Dolphins. (Slijper, 1954.)

dolphins for their meat also. Off the Black Sea, porpoises are caught mainly with nets, and at the beginning of this century Odessa had a full-fledged oil factory. In Holland, porpoises are not usually considered fit for human consumption, though many people ate and even liked them during the war years. In Belgium and France, porpoise meat is still sold regularly, and in previous centuries the same thing happened in Holland, for the *Great Ordinance for the Amsterdam Fish Market* of 1569 lays down a fee of one penny for the killing of a porpoise, a seal, or a tunny. On some South Pacific islands the natives hunt and eat the Finless Black Porpoise (Fig. 187). Here, the witchdoctor withdraws to his sanctuary for half a day and uses magic to lure the animals close to the coast. The men then put to sea, surround the animals, which have meanwhile responded to the spell, and drive them ashore by clapping their hands and making other noises.

Dolphins are caught in a similar, if less magical way, in other parts of the world also. Thus Russians, Rumanians, Bulgarians, and Turks have so far caught about 120,000 dolphins off the Black Sea coast partly with nets (Russia) and partly with guns (Turkey and Bulgaria).

The natives of many tropical islands, as well, go in for dolphin hunting on a big scale. On the south coast of New Guinea, for instance, the Papuans capture Malayan Dolphins (*Prodelphinus malayanus*) which visit the area in schools of up to one thousand, and whose meat is considered a great delicacy. Fresh-water dolphins (the *Platanistidae*) are caught in rivers. The Susu, or Gangetic Dolphin (Fig. 117), which is blind, is confined to the Rivers Ganges, Indus and Bramaputra; the Amazonian Dolphin or Boutu occurs in the Upper Amazon and its tributaries, 1,500 miles from the open sea; the La Plata Dolphin occurs in the estuary of the River Plate; and the Chinese River Dolphin (Fig. 188) is never seen except in Tung Ting Lake (roughly 600 miles up the Yangtze Kiang). The Gangetic Dolphin, in particular, is caught with nets. Its flesh is eaten and its oil used for lighting and as a cure against rheumatism. The Boutu, on the other hand, which is a prodigious hunter and even gobbles up the voracious *Piraya*, is never killed deliberately by the natives, who think that blindness strikes anyone who uses Boutu oil in his lamp. This belief is probably due to the fact that the animal has a very small eye aperture. The natives, moreover, believe that the Boutu comes ashore during certain festivities, to join in the celebrations. Many a local child is said to have been fathered by a Boutu on such occasions, particularly when the merry-making was at its height.

Some dolphins occur in large schools, and if they happen to get into shallow waters they may panic and dash against the beach or rocks with great speed. Wherever the natives value the meat and know how to process it, they look upon such an event as a godsend, but where they do not, the stench of the rotting carcasses soon becomes obnoxious, particularly in the tropics. Often the local population 'helps' this kind of panic by chasing schools ashore as soon as their arrival is signalled by watchers. On 10th March, 1952, for instance, 52 White-Sided Dolphins (Fig. 18) were caught in this way near Kalvåg (Norway). The yield from this catch was 1·3 tons of blubber, 1·8 tons of bone, and 3 tons of meat which was sent to the fox-breeding farms.

In some parts of the world dolphin-hunting is carried on regularly and on a large scale, in particular off the coasts of Japan where various dolphins congregate in big schools. During May and June 1949, one whaling company alone harpooned 1,163 dolphins of three different species near Onahoma. Since the products are in great demand and since, moreover, there are no limitations as to the overall catch, this industry is expanding rapidly. At the time the ruling market price was 2,000–3,000 yen, i.e. £6–£9 per animal. Another spot where dolphins, and Bottlenose

Pilot Whale
about 20 ft

Killer
about 26 ft

Bottlenose Whale
about 33 ft

Figure 19. Three large North Atlantic Dolphins. (Slijper, 1954.)

Dolphins (Fig. 18) in particular, have been caught for more than two centuries, mainly for the sake of their oil, is Cape Hatteras in North Carolina, about 350 miles south of New York; here the fishermen usually drive the animals ashore with nets.

An animal that has proved very profitable for centuries, particularly to North Atlantic fishermen, is the Pilot Whale (Fig. 19), an almost entirely black dolphin which attains a length of up to 28 feet. The Pilot Whale has a nearly spherical forehead, very long flippers and a rather low and elongated dorsal fin. It always moves about in schools, which often number hundreds and sometimes thousands of individuals. These gregarious animals are known to frequent bays and even to strand in great numbers. The local fishermen take advantage of this fact, and for instance on 20th October, 1954, in Vejle Fjord on Jutland (Denmark) they killed sixty-three animals at one fell swoop. Their sale provided the captors with the rather disappointing sum of about £250, but they did not seem to mind, since reminiscences of their windfall still help to while away their long winter evenings. However, there are beaches where the

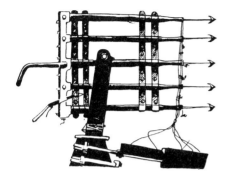

Figure 20. Japanese harpoon gun firing five harpoons simultaneously, and used for hunting Pilot Whales. (Ōmura, 1953.)

Pilot Whale appears so frequently and in such great numbers that Pilot-whaling is an important trade. This is the case, above all, on the Shetland Islands, the Orkneys, and particularly the Faroes, where Pilot whaling has a history that can be traced back to 1584. Between that year and 1883, i.e. in a space of 300 years, about 117,000 Pilot Whales were caught here, and their capture continues to represent a good source of revenue for the local population to this day. During July 1947 alone over a thousand animals were caught, and a special winch was used for hauling the carcasses out of the water. Similar sights can be seen in Dildo (Trinity Bay, Newfoundland), where 3,000–4,000 Pilot Whales may be caught annually. Mink breeders here depend a great deal on the catch. In Japan, the animals are pursued with small boats, and are killed with a harpoon gun that fires five harpoons simultaneously (Fig. 20).

In the Arctic, and seldom far from the icy northern polar seas, we find the Narwhal (Fig. 7), a spotted dolphin some 13–18 feet long. The males have the peculiar 'unicorn tusk' which we have discussed earlier. Though Narwhals have occasionally stranded in North Sea countries, they do not as a rule occur farther south than 70° N., roughly the latitude of North Cape. But even so far north the Narwhal is far from safe, for the Eskimos go out in their kayaks and catch every Narwhal they can lay their hands on. They are not so much interested in the meat, most of which they feed to their sledge dogs, or in the oil, as in the animal's skin which contains a great deal of vitamin C, just like the skin of the Greenland Whale which is valued for the same reason by the inhabitants of Eastern Siberia. Vitamin C is essential to human health, and since man is one of the few mammals which cannot manufacture it internally, he must find it elsewhere. In Western Europe, the chief sources of this vitamin are potatoes, vegetables like cauliflower and Brussels sprouts, and fresh fruit such as strawberries, oranges and melons. Clearly, the Eskimos have no means of cultivating these plants and so must get their vitamin from animals, which are generally poor sources. Vitamin C occurs in small quantities in the livers of seals, wild ducks and musk oxen, and since man requires about fifty milligrammes of Vitamin C per day, the Narwhal, which contains 31·8 mg. per 100 g. of skin, is a welcome provider of this essential substance. The figures compare favourably with those of potatoes, raspberries and melon, and are only slightly less than those of lemons, Brussels sprouts and oranges. The skin is generally eaten raw, which is probably the best way of obtaining most of the vitamin. After all, we are always being told to eat raw greens and raw fruit for the same reason. Whether the raw skin is a tasty dish is, of course, quite another question, but we have already seen that the tastes of different peoples vary.

Another Arctic dolphin is the White Whale, more commonly known by its Russian name – the Beluga. Like the Narwhal it has a rounded head and lacks a dorsal fin, but the whiteness of the adult is quite unique. The very young Beluga is dark grey; it later becomes mottled and then yellow before assuming its final colour. The Beluga is a coastal species, often moving far up river in large schools. It can be found much farther south than the Narwhal. The Hudson Bay Company started Beluga whaling as early as 8th February, 1688, and has continued this activity to this day, with periodic interruptions. Belugas are also caught either in nets or with harpoons in the Gulf of St. Lawrence, in Alaska, in the Okhotsk Sea where they enter the mouths of rivers, and off Greenland, Northern Russia and Siberia. During the second half of the nineteenth century, Norwegians from Tromsö started Beluga-whaling off Spits-bergen. At first, they caught roughly 2,000 animals per year, but since 1900 the number has become greatly reduced. The Beluga is valued primarily for its oil, which is excellent for lighting and tanning and par-ticularly for the manufacture of chamois leather. The meat is usually fed to dogs or foxes, and the skin is tanned locally into a kind of leather known as 'porpoise hide'.

We have already seen that the second half of the nineteenth century was a very difficult period for Norwegian whalers. The North Atlantic Right Whale and the Greenland Right Whale had practically disappeared, and even the invention of the harpoon gun and the consequent capture of other Arctic species did little to cover the mounting costs. No wonder, then, that whalers turned their attention to the smaller Cetaceans. We have just spoken of the Beluga, but in addition to it, the Arctic and the Northern Atlantic abound with Bottlenose Whales, which are another rich source of oil. The Bottlenose Whale grows to a length of between 24 and 30 feet and is almost entirely black on the dorsal surface. The mature males in particular have a very prominent forehead (Fig. 19), containing a substance very similar to the spermaceti of the Sperm Whale. In the autumn the animals migrate from the Arctic to sub-tropical and even to tropical waters. They generally move in fairly large schools. The Scots began to hunt the Bottlenose in 1877, and the Norwegians followed in 1882. However, the Norwegians set to with a will, and in 1895 seventy Norwegian ships caught 3,000 of the animals in Arctic waters. Nowadays, the Arctic catch of Bottlenoses is insignificant, but a few Bottlenoses are still caught by Norwegian land stations.

The 'great' whaling industry had always been uninterested in such 'dwarfs' as the Little Piked Whale or Lesser Rorqual, since the yield from this 30-foot animal was too small to bother about. Externally, the Piked Whale resembles the Fin Whale (Fig. 10), of which it seems to be a dwarf replica, except for the fact that it has a white band on the outer surface of the flipper. In whaling circles, it is referred to as the Minke Whale, supposedly because one of Svend Foyn's men, Meincke by name, mistook a school of Piked Whales for Blue Whales. His error so amused whalers the world over that his name became a household word amongst them. It was during the Second World War (1940) that Norway first turned her attention to these whales also. The meat of the Piked Whale is very tasty and the carcass small enough to be flensed aboard the catcher boats themselves. The meat and blubber are taken ashore, which involves carrying enough ice for a trip of two to three weeks. In 1949, the best year, approximately 4,000 Piked Whales were caught, and the Norwegian government was forced to take protective measures. Piked Whales are also caught in other parts of the world, particularly off Japan and New-foundland, for they occur in most seas.

We have at last told the story of men and whales, the story of man's age-long hunt for food and other valuable products, a story that is unfolded all the way from the coasts of Greenland to the South Sea Islands, over all the seas from the Arctic seas of the barren north right across the warm waters of the tropics to the bleak Antarctic. The story began in the Stone Age and may end — if we ever let it come to that — when the last whale has been killed and the last dolphin harpooned. Let us hope that this will never be, and that man will show himself a more capable administrator of his earthly trusteeship. Let us hope there will be whales in the sea, and whale-meat in our larders, as long as man con-tinues on earth. If that is to happen we need much more knowledge of the structure and behaviour of animals that have always excited the interest of all serious naturalists, who are particularly anxious to know what happens when a mammal becomes adapted to an unusual environment – water. The study of whales is at one and the same time the study of life on earth, and it is my earnest hope that this book may contribute its small share towards it.

2

Evolution and External Appearance

ONE NIGHT aboard the *Willem Barendsz*, I was woken in my bunk by two of the ship's officers, who asked me to settle a heated argument. 'Doctor, Doctor, please wake up and tell us something!' 'If I can,' I replied, still groping blindly. 'What is it you want to know?' 'Can you tell us how many legs a whale has?' they pressed me. 'Five,' I told them, 'four normal ones and an extra one for hitting you over the head if you worry them at night.' My answer seemed to satisfy them, for they left me to catch up on my sleep. But was it really correct, or only my means of getting rid of them?

To find out, we had best dress in warm clothes, put on an overall, and get up on deck. Ear muffs well down, lined waders pulled right up (make sure they have hobnails, or you will break your neck), we emerge from our cabins. The great winches amidships have just dug their claws into one of the giants, and have pulled it up the slipway on a steel cable. The whistle has gone for a half-hour break, the work has stopped, and we can count the whale's legs at our leisure.

A superficial inspection of its enormous bulk will convince us that it has no real legs at all. True, it has two small pectoral fins (flippers) in front, but it has nothing at all resembling legs – just a powerful tail, its tip flattened into flukes which stick out quite a bit on either side of the body. Actually, we cannot see much of the flukes here on deck, for the whalers have hacked part of them off to make their work easier. But where are the hind legs? To find them, we must make a fairly deep incision in the body. If we can locate the correct place, just a little anterior to the anal vent, we shall find a slender bone some 12 inches long, hidden amidst masses of muscle tissue on either side of the body. Occasionally there is a fairly pronounced process in the middle of the bone (Fig. 21). If we remove and clean the bone, we find that another small bone may be attached to it, at least in the Blue, Fin, Sperm and some Humpback Whales (Fig. 22). The second bone is absent in Sei Whales and Little Piked Whales.

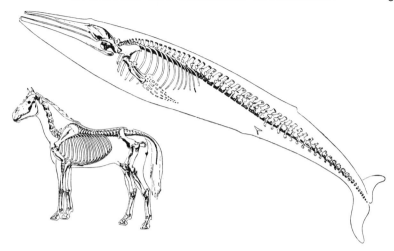

Figure 21. Comparison of the body shape and skeleton of a Blue Whale and a horse. Note the difference in the development of limbs, neck, and tail, and the presence of chevron bones on the lower side of the Blue Whale's caudal vertebrae.

The longer bone makes up the entire Cetacean pelvis, but unlike the pelvis of normal mammals it is not attached to the vertebral column, though, in the males, the penis has remained anchored to the bone. The smaller bone which is generally just over an inch in length and which is sometimes fused with the larger, may be thought of as a vestigial femur (Fig. 227). In some Right Whales, e.g. the Greenland and the Biscayan, another small bone, representing the tibia, is attached to the femur. Occasionally a tibia is also found in Sperm Whales. Thus, at Ayukawa Whaling Station (Japan), a Sperm Whale was brought in in 1956, with a 5-inch tibia projecting into a $5\frac{1}{2}$-inch external 'bump', and a Russian factory ship in the Bering Sea had a similar experience in 1959. All other Odontocetes have only single pelvic bones. Moreover, in some species,

Figure 22. Left view of left pelvic bone of a male Sperm Whale with vestigial femur fused to it. The animal was found stranded in Holland (Texel) on 9th July 1950. (Van Deinse, 1954.)

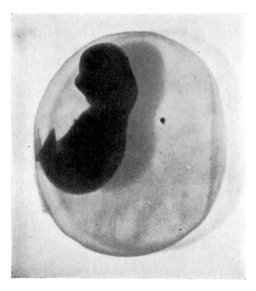

Figures 23 and 24. The beginnings of a giant. Photograph of a very young Blue Whale embryo surrounded by embryonic membranes. Note the complete absence of flukes. – 24. Drawing of an 8 mm. Porpoise embryo showing rudimentary limbs. In the centre, the severed umbilical cord. (Müller, 1920.)

e.g. the Pigmy Sperm Whale and Sowerby's Whale, only the males have even this vestige, to which their penis is anchored.

But while adult whales show no external traces of hind limbs, things are different with embryos. If we examine a very young embryo (20 mm. long) of a whale or a dolphin, we shall in fact discover the presence of rudimentary hind limbs. They appear as round and spatular extremities, and very much resemble the hind limbs of other mammals at this stage of their development. But while such extremities develop into proper limbs in normal mammals, they generally disappear in Cetaceans by the time the embryo has grown to about $1\frac{1}{5}$ inches. Of course, there are exceptions, and the Russian biologist Sleptsov once came across an adult dolphin with tiny pelvic fins. Such vestiges of former limbs can also be distinguished on an etching by Hendrik Goltzius of a Pilot Whale stranded at Zandvoort on 21st November, 1594.

In any case, the whale's typical flukes can in no way be identified with the pelvic limb. Formerly it was believed that the flukes had arisen from a fusion of the hind limbs, but a single glance at Fig. 24 is sufficient to show that this belief was false and that the flukes are an outgrowth of the skin and connective tissue of the tail.

The fore-limb, though flat and fin-shaped, has survived to a far greater extent (Fig. 21), and all the bones which are present in, say, our own arms, can also be found in the flipper of the whale or the dolphin. True, the humerus is short, and the forearm bones (radius and ulna) are short and flattened, but the flippers of all Cetaceans (with the exception of Rorquals which lack a thumb) have five digits. The digits – although separately distinguishable internally, are enclosed in a common integument, thus giving the flipper its characteristic flat shape. The fin as a whole is a stiff but elastic paddle with the shoulder joint as its only true movable part.

In normal mammals, man included, every finger has three phalanges, except the thumb, which has two. In Cetaceans, however, the central digits have a larger number of phalangeal elements. Hyperphalangy is most pronounced in the long flippers of the Pilot Whale, whose second and third digits have 14 and 11 phalanges respectively (Fig. 25).

But like the pelvic limb, the flipper of the very young embryo started as a normal limb, just like our own arm, which began as a flat, leaf-shaped outgrowth of the trunk. Subsequently, it becomes a kind of stalk, flattened at the end. In man, the wrist develops from the notch just below the thickened end which gives rise to the five fingers, but in whales the notch disappears again and the 'arm' assumes its characteristic fin shape (Fig. 26).

From the fact that whales have vestiges of pelvic limbs which arose in the same way as those of normal mammals, we may infer that whales did not originally have their present form but that, in the dim and distant

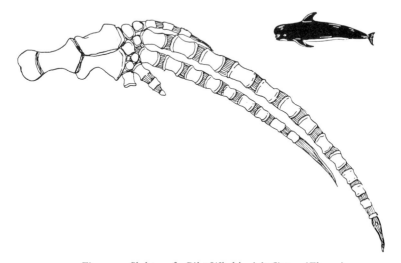

Figure 25. Skeleton of a Pilot Whale's right flipper. (Flower.)

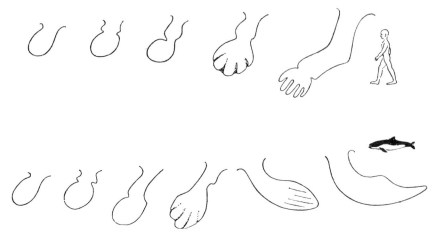

Figure 26. Comparison between the embryonic development of a Cetacean flipper and a human arm.

past, they probably had fully developed limbs. In other words, whales must have descended from terrestrial mammals. To discover what these animals were like, we must first find out what position the Cetaceans occupy in the Animal Kingdom, i.e. how they are classified.

Aristotle (about 400 B.C.), as we have already seen, lumped whales and fish together, not because he was unaware that whales breathe through lungs, that they have hair, that they are viviparous and suckle their young, and that they have horizontal flukes instead of a vertical tail fin, but because his criteria for classifying the animal kingdom were different from ours. To Aristotle, aquatic life was, in itself, a crucial criterion, and not only Pliny, but Belon (1553), Rondelet (1554), and even Linnaeus at first followed in his footsteps. Ray (1693) and Linnaeus, however, subsequently took the decisive step of classifying the Cetaceans as mammals, and since that time their classification has never been challenged. All that remains is to investigate the place of the Cetaceans among their mammalian relatives.

Now, if we examine all the characteristics of the Cetaceans, and if we compare them with other mammals, it becomes clear that their nearest relatives belong to two orders: the Carnivores and the Ungulates. It would take us too far afield to muster all the arguments for this assertion; suffice it to say that their close relationship, particularly to Even-toed Ungulates (Artiodactyls), e.g. cattle, sheep and camels, has become quite clear from similarities in their protein structures. Protein comparisons tell us, *inter alia*, whether two animals can be interbred to produce fertile offspring or not. The method itself falls outside the scope of this book, but its results are pertinent to our investigation, since Boyden and Gemeroy used it in 1950 to discover that 11 per cent of all Cetacean and Artiodactyle proteins were identical, while only about 2 per cent of the proteins of either group agreed with those of other mammals. Moreover, study of fossils has shown that a group of small, primitive mammals appeared in the Cretaceous period (which began about 125 million years ago). These animals which probably lived on land, and partly in trees, had characteristics strongly reminiscent of primitive Carnivores and of primitive Insectivores. As yet, little is known about these small animals, the fossils of which were discovered in the interior of Mongolia, but it is thought that the mammalian line can be so constructed that both the Carnivores and the Ungulates can be traced back to this group of primitive Creodonts-cum-insectivores. Even modern insectivores, bats and apes are said to be descended from these ancestors, and so are the Cetaceans whose line of descent is close to that of the Carnivores and Ungulates, but especially to the latter and quite particularly to the Even-toed Ungulates (Fig. 27).

A glance at Fig. 27, will reveal a preponderance of stippled lines. These indicate the absence of fossils, so that the picture may have to be modified once new evidence comes to light. Meanwhile, it represents the best interpretation of all the available data. From it, we can see clearly that the first-known fossils of fully-fledged Cetaceans date back to the Eocene epoch which began roughly 45 million years ago. Cetacean fossils from that epoch were first discovered in Louisiana in 1832, when a column of twenty-eight vertebrae was unearthed. They were classified as *Basilosaurus*, i.e. King of the Reptiles. As early as 1839 Owen realized that *Basilosaurus* was a mammal and not a reptile, and he renamed it *Zeuglodon*, the Greek for the yoke-shaped teeth of a skull that had meanwhile been discovered.

In 1845 Albert Koch, a German collector, discovered a part of a skull and a great number of vertebrae. He joined up the vertebrae of two animals and obtained a specimen 112 feet long which – ignorant of the work of Owen – he called *Hydrargos* (Water Chief) and which he exhibited as the 'Sea Snake', first in the Apollo Rooms on Broadway, New York, and afterwards in a number of European cities. Later, it emerged that the actual skeleton of the animal he was exhibiting could only have had a length of 50 feet and that the skeleton belonged to a Cetacean (see Fig. 28). Further Cetacean skeletons from the Eocene, more or less complete, have since been discovered in North America, Europe, Nigeria, New Zealand, the Antarctic, and near Cairo in particular.

All these skeletons belonged to a group of primitive Cetaceans, the Archaeocetes, which were, however, not the direct ancestors of the two extant sub-orders, and must be looked upon as a branch that died out

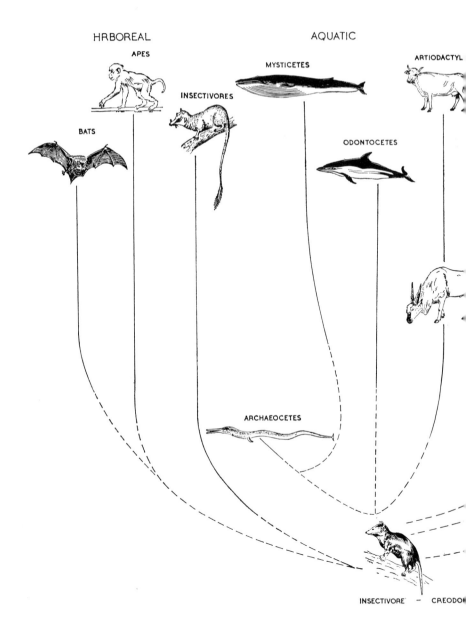

HRBOREAL

AQUATIC

APES

MYSTICETES

ARTIODACTYL

INSECTIVORES

BATS

ODONTOCETES

ARCHAEOCETES

INSECTIVORE — CREODO

Figure 27. Possible family tree of mammals related to Cetaceans. Right: Geological perio

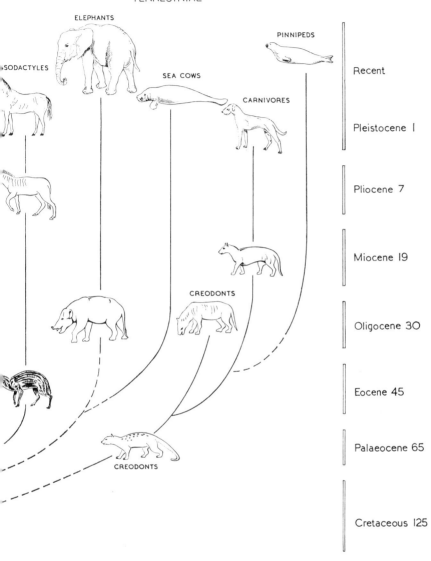

TERRESTRIAL

ELEPHANTS

PINNIPEDS

SODACTYLES

SEA COWS

CARNIVORES

CREODONTS

CREODONTS

Recent

Pleistocene 1

Pliocene 7

Miocene 19

Oligocene 30

Eocene 45

Palaeocene 65

Cretaceous 125

illions of years. Dotted lines indicate the absence of fossils from the period in question.

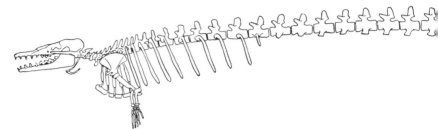

Figure 28. Reconstructed skeleton of snake-shaped Basilosaurus cetoides *(Owen) which lived some 35 million years ago, in what is now Alabama, and was then the sea. The skeleton is in the U.S. National Museum in Washington. (Kellogg, 1936.)*

some 25 million years ago. Some of its members were snake-shaped, while others had the torpedo shape so characteristic of modern whales (Fig. 29). From the different characteristics of their skeletons, it would appear that all of them had horizontal flukes which, however, were less pronounced than those of the more recent species. Their necks were fairly short even then, but they still consisted of seven independent vertebrae. The fore-limbs were short and fin-shaped, though they were probably still movable at the elbow, whereas the ulna and radius of the modern Cetaceans are rigidly attached to the humerus.

As we might have expected, Archaeocetes had a more pronounced pelvic girdle than the extant species, even though it was no longer attached to the vertebral column (Fig. 30). The pelvic bones were much broader and the three components which make up the *ossa innominata* of the pelvis of terrestrial mammals: ilium, ischium, and pubis, were clearly distinct, and so was the innominate foramen. The most striking fact, however, was the presence of a distinct ball and socket joint whereby the femur articulated with the pelvis. The femur was well developed, and though no traces of a tibia were discovered, it is quite possible that vestiges of it existed in the living animal. In any case, all the bones were so small that we may safely assume that the animals showed few, if any, signs of an external fin – at most a small bump.

All these characteristics make it clear that the Archaeocetes, which became extinct some 25 million years ago, were structurally much more like terrestrial mammals than are modern Cetaceans. We may take this fact as additional proof that the original ancestors of our whales lived on land and that they were built just like all other terrestrial mammals.

This assumption is borne out further by another characteristic of the Archaeocetes, viz. the position of their nostrils. In the horse, the dog, and all other terrestrial mammals, the nostrils are at the tip of the snout. However, if we examine a whale on the deck of our factory ship, or a dead porpoise on the beach, we shall find that the nostrils, i.e. the blowholes,

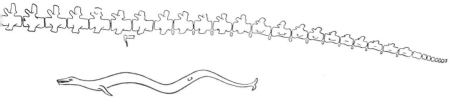

have migrated to the top of the head. In very young embryos (4–5 mm. long), the nostrils are still in the normal mammalian place, but by the time the foetus is 22 mm long, they have taken up their final position.

Why the nostrils are found where they are is not yet entirely clear, but the explanation must probably be sought in the distribution of body weight, and the consequent position of the animal at the water surface. The specific gravity of the normal mammal, once its lungs are filled with air, is such that its body floats in the water. In man and probably in the anthropoid apes also, the nostrils are submerged when the body is floating, but all other mammals naturally assume a position in which the nostrils lie above the surface, and the animal has no difficulty in breathing. This position is the result of two forces: the force of gravity which pulls the body down, and the upthrust of the displaced water, which pushes the body up. The centre of gravity of ordinary terrestrial mammals always lies behind the point of application of the upward thrust (centre of buoyancy), and the two forces therefore form a couple, with the result that the animal is tilted upwards until its centre of gravity comes to lie perpendicularly below the point of application of the upward force. When that happens, the animal will float obliquely, a position that greatly helps to raise the nostrils out of the water.

Since whales and dolphins have such an unusual shape, their case differs from that of all other mammals. First, they have no hind legs, and while the tail is thin and light, the head is exceptionally large and heavy. Moreover, the lungs (which are very light, particularly when they are filled with air) stretch far back into the thorax (Fig. 79). For these reasons, the centre of gravity may be assumed to lie more at the front than it does

Figure 29. Skeleton of a dolphin-like Archaeocete, Dorudon osiris (Dames), reconstructed from bones in museums in Stuttgart and Munich, and found in 35-million-year-old deposits in Fayum (Egypt). (Slijper, 1936.)

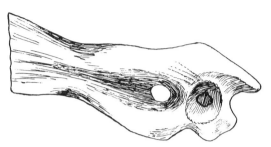

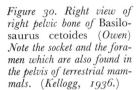

Figure 30. Right view of right pelvic bone of Basilosaurus cetoides *(Owen) Note the socket and the foramen which are also found in the pelvis of terrestrial mammals. (Kellogg, 1936.)*

in ordinary mammals, and therefore to coincide with the point of application of the upward force. Hence the whale will float almost horizontally.

And that is in fact what we observe. Whenever whales come up slowly to breathe, they emerge almost parallel to the water surface (Figs. 32 and 51), in a way strongly reminiscent of submarines. While the top of the head and the back as far as the dorsal fin can be seen clearly, the tip of the snout itself always remains submerged. This is also the attitude in which whales and dolphins often doze at the surface. In the great Marineland Seaquarium in Florida, which we shall discuss later at some length, McBride and Hebb observed female Bottlenose Dolphins dozing so that only the blowhole appeared above the surface. Oddly enough, the males, which also doze almost horizontally, do so some 12 inches below the surface and come up now and then to breathe in the same way as the larger whales.

Further experimental data on this subject are still needed, but if we take into account all the available evidence, it seems clear that, from hydrostatic considerations alone, the whale's nostrils ought to lie right on top of the head and behind the tip of the snout – and that is precisely where they are found in all living Cetaceans, with the exception of the Sperm Whale where they lie a little to the left and near the tip of the head (Fig. 33). This is probably due to the fact that the Sperm Whale's gigantic head holds the spermaceti case, an almost rectangular cavity in its upper surface. This enormous 'case' is made up of connective tissue, with enormous quantities of fat cells containing spermaceti. Spermaceti is not a true oil, but a glistening wax-like substance which separates out on cooling. Its low specific gravity probably causes the anterior part of the head to break surface first.

If we make a longitudinal section through the head of a Sperm Whale, we shall find many unsuspected phenomena. That part of the nasal passage which lies inside the skull, and which is therefore enclosed in bone, has the same location as in all other Cetaceans, viz. posterior to the snout. From the skull, however, two long canals run through the spermaceti

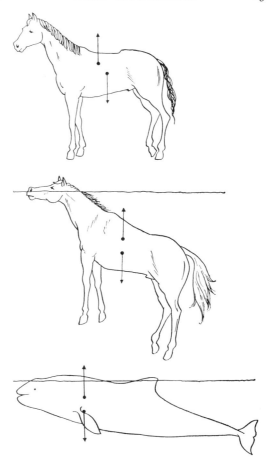

Figure 31. Relative position at the surface of the water due to gravity and upthrust of (a) a horse and (b) a dolphin.

case to the tip of the head where together they constitute the blowhole (see Fig. 33). This is probably best explained by the fact that, the more Cetaceans became adapted to their aquatic mode of life, the more essential it became for the nostrils to migrate to their present posterior and superior position in the head. This must have happened to the ancestors of the Sperm Whale as well, but as the large spermaceti case developed and filled with light material, the nostrils were obviously in the wrong place. Now there is a biological law, Dollo's 'law of irreversible evolution', which states that evolution never retraces its steps. Hence, once the nasal passage of the Sperm Whale had migrated to its present position, it could not return to its original situation, and a new solution had to be found: the elongated passage through the spermaceti case. Further evidence for this assumption is found in the position of the nasal passage in the Pigmy Sperm Whale, a black or nearly black species with a maximum length of 13 feet, which occurs in all temperate waters, and whose head is much smaller than that of the Sperm Whale ($\frac{1}{6}$ as compared with $\frac{1}{3}$ of the total length). The Pigmy Sperm Whale, therefore, has a much smaller spermaceti case, and its head is, moreover, more spherical, so that the case has a much smaller effect on the animal's centre of gravity. The nostrils therefore lie right on top of the head, just as they do in other whales and dolphins (Fig. 33).

Our remarks about the position of the blowhole in the more recent Cetaceans have interrupted our discussion of the Archaeocetes. In most of their representatives the nostrils were neither in front of the snout, as

Figure 32. A Fin Whale surfacing while swimming slowly, when the tip of the snout always remains submerged. (Gunther, 1949.)

they are in terrestrial mammals, nor as far behind the snout as in modern whales, but half-way between the two – another pointer that these animals were not as well adapted to aquatic life as the more recent species, and that they were still much closer to their terrestrial ancestors.

While we are discussing the migration of the whale's nostrils in the course of its evolution, we might also look at what has happened to the bones of the skull during this process. For side by side with the retrogression of the nostril there occurred a strong development of the jaws, making it possible for them to hold the long row of uniform, sharp teeth of the Odontocetes, or the great number of baleen plates of the Mysticetes. As a consequence, not only has the nasal bone migrated far to the rear; the maxilla and pre-maxilla have been extended to overspread the braincase. In Odontocetes, these two bones were pushed right over the frontals, while the parietals became depressed laterally (Fig. 34). In Mysticetes, the pre-maxilla and also the tip of the maxilla were pushed across the frontals, while the bottom of the maxilla was pushed beneath them. The whole process is known as the *telescoping* of the Cetacean skull.

The Archaeocetes showed no signs of this telescoping, with the exception of one of the latest representatives, the fairly short *Patriocetus*, a skull of which was discovered in the upper Oligocene (roughly 20 million years ago) deposits at Linz on the Danube. The structure of its skull strongly resembled that of the Mysticetes, although *Patriocetus* could not have been a direct ancestor since, according to fossil evidence, Mysticetes had already existed some seven million years earlier. The fact that *Patriocetus*

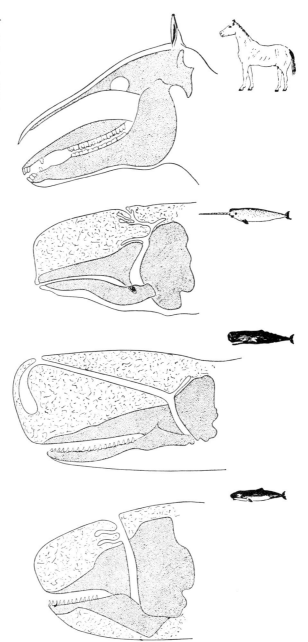

Figure 33. Position of nostrils in a horse, a Narwhal, a Sperm Whale and a Pigmy Sperm Whale. Note the size of the connective tissue cushion (spermaceti case of Sperm Whale) in the three Cetaceans.

had teeth, albeit very simple ones, is not in itself sufficient evidence for excluding the animal from the list of possible ancestors, for we have clear indications that the distant forefathers of the Mysticetes were in fact toothed animals. We do not know with any certainty how long ago these animals lived, though it must have been well over 27 million years ago, since their oldest-known Middle Oligocene representatives had lost all traces of teeth – at least the known fossils of adults had. This qualification is important, for even modern Mysticetes cannot be said to be entirely devoid of teeth, which still occur in their foetuses.

This has been known for the last 150 years, for foetal teeth were first discovered in the lower jaw of a Greenland Whale by Geoffroy St. Hilaire in 1807. Such tooth buds can also be found on the deck of every modern factory ship whenever the foetus of a cow in calf is removed. If an incision is made into the soft mucous membrane of the upper or lower jaw of a Fin Whale foetus aged 4–8 months (ca. 4 feet 3 inches – ca. 10 feet long) a row of conical tooth buds will appear (Fig. 35). In the upper jaw, these tooth buds lie slightly sunken within a white, smooth and glistening ridge from which the young baleen will later develop. The beginnings of the baleen, a row of small cornified transverse ridges, first appears in foetuses when they exceed a length of 10 feet; at this stage the rudimentary teeth of both the lower and upper jaw disappear without a trace. However, their presence during the early stages of foetal development is clear evidence that the Mysticetes are descended from a line of ancestors with teeth in both jaws.

We have already seen that Archaeocetes could not have been the direct ancestors of the Mysticetes, and it appears that no primitive Odontocetes could have been their ancestors either, for the two differ too radically in structure and in many other respects. For instance, their oil has a different chemical composition – the oil of Odontocetes being a wax rather than a fat – and secondly, their blood proteins are different, too. Moreover, Dr Kendrew of Cambridge and his colleagues recently showed that there exist differences also in the crystalline form of their myoglobin – the iron-holding pigment in the red muscle. For all these reasons, it is generally assumed that the three great groups of Cetaceans developed quite separately from their terrestrial ancestors, but that the Mysticetes are closer to the Archaeocetes than are the Odontocetes.

It is even thought that we can form some picture of the ancestors of the different groups, in the sense that both Mysticetes and Archaeocetes can be said to be descended from terrestrial animals with short, and the Odontocetes from animals with long tails. This is inferred from a careful study of very young embryos, those of Mysticetes having the shortest and those of Odontocetes the longest tail in proportion to total body length.

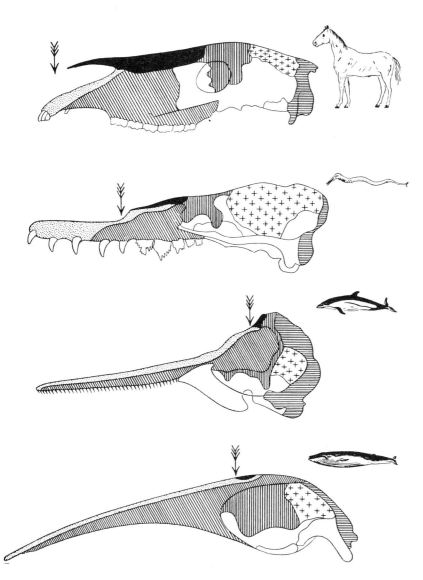

Figure 34. Skulls of a horse, an Archaeocete (Basilosaurus), *an Odontocete* (Common Dolphin) *and a Mysticete* (Fin Whale), *illustrating the migration of the nostrils and the telescoping of the cranial bones. Dots – premaxilla; black – nasal; vertical lines – frontal; diagonal lines – maxilla; crosses – parietal; horizontal lines – occipital.*

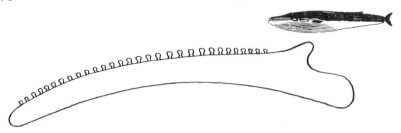

Figure 35. Right lower jaw with tooth buds of a 4 foot Fin Whale foetus.

During subsequent embryonic development the tail of the former increases in relative size, while that of the latter decreases. This may well be connected with a characteristic distinction between Mysticetes and Archaeocetes on the one hand, and Odontocetes on the other: the course the spinal arteries take along the various vertebrae. Beneath the vertebral column lies the aorta, which continues as the caudal artery in the tail (Fig. 95). From the aorta, small spinal arteries connected with the blood-vessels in the vertebral canal branch off at every vertebra. Now the skeleton shows clear traces of these spinal arteries, since they penetrate the vertebrae to leave a slight groove. In the Odontocetes, these grooves run behind the transverse spinal processes of the lumbar and anterior caudal regions, and in the posterior caudal region they penetrate the processes from the rear (Fig. 37). In Archaeocetes and Mysticetes, the arteries also run behind the transverse processes in most of the lumbar area, but in the posterior lumbar region they change course so that, in the anterior caudal region, they run in front of the transverse processes and penetrate them from the front (Fig. 38). The difference can be explained by assuming that during embryonic development the aorta and the caudal artery on the one hand, and the vertebral column on the other, grow at different rates. Since in Mysticetes the tail grows faster than the trunk, and in Odontocetes the trunk grows faster than the tail, we may take it that these differences give rise to the differences in the arterial grooves.

We have already seen that the beginnings of the Mysticetes go as far back as the middle Oligocene, about 27 million years ago. From the Oligocene and Miocene, i.e. roughly 27–7 million years ago, fossil remains of a primitive group of Mysticetes, the *Cetotheriidae*, have been discovered in various parts of the world. The arrangement of their skulls and other characteristics is such that they are considered to be the original ancestors of the recent Mysticetes. They were, however, strikingly smaller (9–33 feet).

From the Pliocene (7–1 million years ago), a number of species are known which can be fitted into the modern sub-orders. These were discovered mainly in the second half of the nineteenth century during excavations near Antwerp, and also in some eastern parts of Holland. Only recently, thirty pupils at a technical school in Hengelo, led by their teacher, dug up an almost complete vertebral column of a fossil whale from a pit at Neede. The Brussels Museum of Natural History has a particularly fine collection of such fossils. Pliocene Right Whales were 16–50 feet long and, even in this respect, strongly resembled some modern whales, for the Pigmy Right Whale has a maximum length of 20 feet. But the Rorquals were still very much smaller than their modern representatives (10–50 feet as against 30–100 feet). During the last few million years of the earth's history, these whales increased their size, so much so that in ancient times it would hardly have been worth the trouble to go whale-hunting on a large scale. In any case, because he appeared only half a million years ago, man could never have met live species of these animals.

The oldest known representatives of the Odontocetes come from the Upper Oligocene, and cannot, therefore, be more than 30 million years old. They belonged to the *Squalodontidae*, so-called because their jagged teeth strongly resemble those of the shark (Figs. 39, 148). In the older representatives of this group, the nostrils still lay much further to the front than they do in modern Odontocetes, but the more recent members were practically indistinguishable from our own kind. The size of their brain was smaller than that of modern Odontocetes, but considerably larger than that of *Patriocetus* (see page 70).

Their skulls were built symmetrically or almost symmetrically, and while the same can be said of the skulls of most mammals, Odontocetes form a rather strange exception to this rule. Externally, these animals are in fact built symmetrically, and their other organs, too, show the bi-lateral symmetry characteristic of normal mammals, man included. However, the blowholes of a number of species are found, not in the centre of the head, but a little to the left. The lack of symmetry in the skull is not equally pronounced in all Odontocetes, but is very striking in, for instance, the Narwhal (Fig. 40) and the Bottlenose Whale, in which the nasal septum is frequently tilted.

The explanation of this phenomenon has caused experts a great many headaches, but no satisfactory solution has yet been found. We know that this assymmetry was absent or insignificant in the geologically older Odontocetes, and that even during the embryonic development of more recent skulls it occurs fairly late. Clearly, Odontocetes are derived from ancestors with symmetrical skulls, and the change must have occurred during the Miocene, i.e. about 20 million years ago. Apart from the

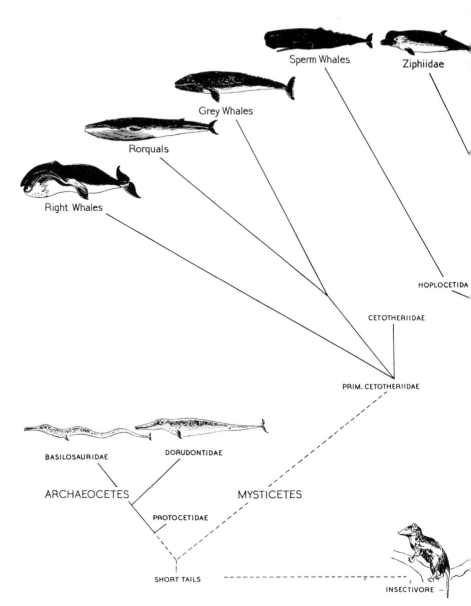

Sperm Whales

Ziphiidae

Grey Whales

Rorquals

Right Whales

HOPLOCETIDA

CETOTHERIIDAE

PRIM. CETOTHERIIDAE

BASILOSAURIDAE

DORUDONTIDAE

ARCHAEOCETES

MYSTICETES

PROTOCETIDAE

SHORT TAILS

INSECTIVORE —

Figure 36. Probable pedigrees of the various Cetaceans (see also Fig. 27). Geological ages are marked on the right (in millions of years). Broken lines mean that no fossils are known from the period in question. (After data by Slijper, 1936.)

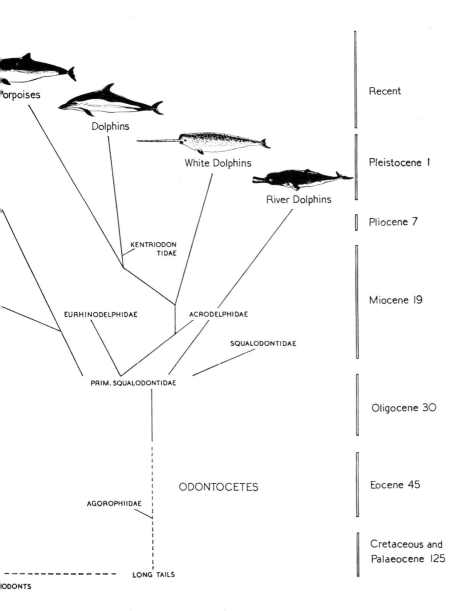

Porpoises

Dolphins

White Dolphins

River Dolphins

KENTRIODON
TIDAE

EURHINODELPHIDAE   ACRODELPHIDAE

SQUALODONTIDAE

PRIM. SQUALODONTIDAE

ODONTOCETES

AGOROPHIIDAE

- - - - - - - - - - - - - - - -   LONG TAILS

ODONTS

Recent

Pleistocene I

Pliocene 7

Miocene 19

Oligocene 30

Eocene 45

Cretaceous and
Palaeocene 125

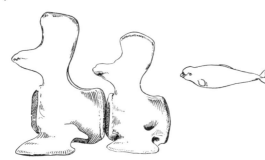

Figure 37. Left view of first and second caudal vertebrae of a Beluga. In this Odontocete the arterial grooves run behind the transverse processes and enter them from the rear. (Slijper, 1936.)

Squalodontidae, which are extinct, Miocene specimens of all extant Odonto-cetes are known, some with fairly symmetrical and others (e.g. the ancestors of the Sperm Whale) with asymmetrical skulls.

Now we have dealt not only with the question of whale's limbs, but with his ancestry also. But we are still on deck of our factory ship right next to a freshly-killed whale, and we must take the opportunity of examining the rest of the carcass before the men hack it into a thousand pieces and throw it into the boilers.

Let us take a closer look at the animal's shape. If we stand close by, its bulk is too great for an overall view, and so we must climb up to a vantage point on the afterdeck from which we can appreciate its beautifully streamlined contours, so reminiscent of a torpedo. We know that this shape offers minimum resistance to the water and thus guarantees maximum speed.

The shape is not the same in all Cetaceans (Fig. 41). The Right Whales are a little more rotund, although they are certainly more streamlined in their natural habitat than the formless mass we sometimes find at land stations. The Rorquals, too, which look so squat when they lie on deck, are in fact very slim – much slimmer even than some dolphins and porpoises, whose maximum girth lies much farther back and whose tails are not so slender.

The heads, too, of the different Cetaceans show very marked differ-ences, that of the Rorqual being fairly pointed, while those of porpoises and dolphins are much blunter, since despite their long and pointed snouts, their foreheads are bulbous (Figs. 19 and 99). This is due to the presence of a thick, hard cushion above the snout, sometimes caused by a thickening of the blubber, but sometimes due to the presence of much harder and tougher connective tissue containing fat cells (cf. the Sperm Whale's spermaceti case). A great deal of study is still needed before scientists have a clear idea of the relationship between shape and water

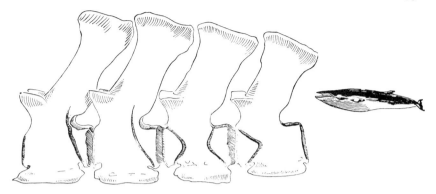

Figure 38. Left view of 11th–13th lumbar and first caudal vertebrae of a Little Piked Whale, from a skeleton in the Natural History Museum in Leyden. In this Mysticete, the arterial grooves run behind the transverse processes of the lumbar, and in front of those of the caudal vertebrae. (Slijper, 1936.)

cleavage. Perhaps it will then become clear why in Odontocetes the upper jaw protrudes over the lower jaw, and vice versa in Mysticetes.

The pectoral fins, the dorsal fin and the flukes of Cetaceans are almost as streamlined as the wings of an aircraft. While the dorsal fin is well-developed in some species, it is poorly developed in others such as the Humpback and the Sperm Whale. In yet others (Grey Whale, Narwhal, Beluga, Finless Black Porpoise) it is entirely lacking.

Clearly the dorsal fin cannot play as important a part as it does in fish. Now, fish have an air bladder situated well below the backbone. Its position is such that the fish has a tendency to capsize and to float upside down. Aquarium owners are quite familiar with this phenomenon – dead fishes always float belly upwards. Cetacean lungs, on the other hand, lie high up inside the body and there is little danger of capsizing, and hence less need for a stabilizing fin.

One of the prerequisites of good streamlining is smoothness of contours. It has been shown that even the smallest projection has a measurable adverse effect on motion. For this reason, the door-handles of modern cars and trains are generally built in, i.e. they fit into the general contours. In whales, Nature has seen to it that all those parts that are external in other mammals are also 'built in'. Thus the penis lies within an abdominal fold, and so do the mammae whose nipples are concealed in two slits on either side of the female genital opening. There is no external ear, but then aquatic animals do not need pinnae, which serve for collecting and reflecting *aerial* vibrations. In their stead, the whale has small ear holes flush with the surface of the body, halfway between the eye and the base of the pectoral fin. In order to examine this aperture more closely, we

Figure 39. Four teeth (molars with two roots) of a Squalodon from the Miocene deposits of Belluno, Italy (about 15 million years old). (De Zigno, 1876.)

descend again from the afterdeck, and we can use the opportunity to inspect a few other peculiarities also. The umbilicus is generally fairly distinct, and a little anterior to the small slit hiding the retractile penis. The female genitalia open much nearer to the anal vent, i.e. much further tailwards (Fig. 42).

As we examine our whale, we are immediately struck also by a series of parallel grooves running longitudinally on the lower surface of the throat and chest region, from the jaw to the umbilicus. The grooves are about 2 inches deep, and are separated by ridges $2\frac{1}{4}$–$3\frac{1}{4}$ inches wide (cf. Fig. 135). In the case of the Grey Whale, we find no more than a few grooves under the throat, and Right Whales have no grooves at all. Rorquals, on the other hand, have 40–100 of them.

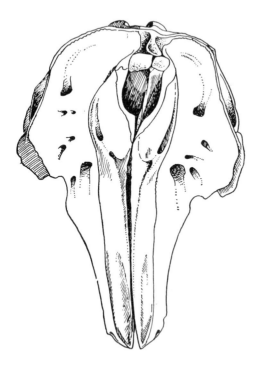

Figure 40. Top view of the skull of a female Narwhal, showing its asymmetrical construction. (Van Beneden and Gervais, 1880.)

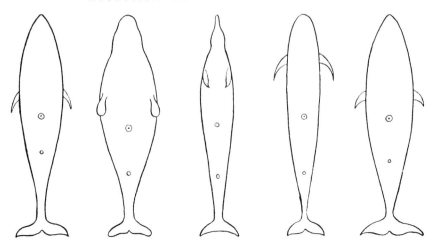

Figure 41. The shape of different Cetacea, seen from below. Umbilicus and anal aperture have been ringed. From left to right: Sei Whale, Sperm Whale, Beaked Whale, Pilot Whale, Porpoise. Note the differences in shape of head and tail, and in pectoral fin attachment. Note also that maximum girth need not coincide with maximum breadth, since girth is largely determined by height.

For almost a hundred years, scientists have vainly tried to discover the significance of the grooves. Lillie, one of the greatest experts on Cetaceans, who lived in the nineteenth century, showed that the grooves made possible local expansion of the skin. This is quite apparent in recently killed whales. Whenever air is pumped into them, or when putrefaction has set in, the carcasses become so distended that the folds disappear completely and the skin beneath the snout and chest looks like a gigantic blown-up balloon. Lillie thought that this elasticity enabled Rorquals to increase the capacity of their mouths and to swallow the enormous quantities of *krill* (see page 255) on which they feed. This might explain why Right Whales have no grooves – their strongly arched jaws provide adequate space as it is, and their feeding habits differ radically from those of Rorquals (cf. Chapter 10). However, none of these explanations really tells us why the grooves run so far back. Possibly, long grooves obviate undesirable skin tensions or else they have some part to play in breathing. We shall see later that Rorquals have a very large diaphragm and that abdominal breathing plays an important part in their respiration. The grooves might very well help the expansion of the otherwise rigid skin.

Other biologists believe they have found a connexion between the grooves and the animals' speed. Smooth whales are always slow swimmers, while most Rorquals can develop great speeds. The grooves might well serve to remove hydrodynamic friction, and thus provide better water

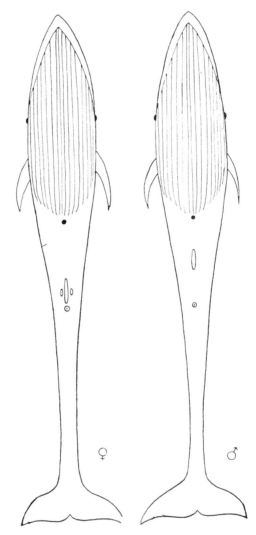

Figure 42. Ventral view of female and male Fin Whales, illustrating differences in external form.

cleavage. The Admiralty Experimental Station at Haslar, in England, has carried out experiments with models on this subject, but the results has so far been inconclusive.

Hydrodynamic friction, however, is indubitably reduced by the fact that Cetaceans are hairless. When we say that someone is as 'bald as a coot', we might equally well say that he is as 'bald as a whale'. Cetacean skin is as smooth as glass, and we know that the smoother, for instance, the hull of a boat, the greater its speed, and that barnacles can greatly impede its progress. In fact, Cetaceans have no need of hair, since hair (or clothing) by surrounding the body with a layer of still air, acts as a thermal insulator which prevents rapid cooling or heating. Now, if water enters the hair (or the clothing) the thermal effect is lost at once. True, aquatic animals which regularly come ashore, such as seals, and sea lions, have a short-haired fur, but to Cetaceans, who always remain in the sea, fur would merely be an impediment. It might be argued that apart from being a thermal insulator, hair also offers protection against injury from sharp objects with which terrestrial animals may often collide. But then such sharp objects rarely exist in the ocean (as distinct from the ocean bed).

Connected with this lack of hair, there is also a lack of sebaceous glands. These small glands which secrete a fatty substance, are usually attached to the hair follicles, and protect the skin from flaking or the hair from splitting. Now a dry skin is something a whale need not bother about in its normal habitat, but when living specimens of dolphins or porpoises are transported overland to an aquarium, great care must be taken to keep them wet all over, for otherwise they will most certainly perish through injury to their skin. (We might just mention here that Cetaceans also lack sweat glands, but we shall return to this subject at greater length in Chapter 11.) When we say that whales are completely hairless, we are not, strictly speaking, correct. In fact, the Greenland Whale has about 250 bristles on its chin and the tip of its upper jaw. Rorquals have a total of 50–60 hairs: one row along the edge of the upper jaw, and another on either side of the axis of this jaw – from the tip of the snout to just behind the blow-hole (Fig. 43). Dolphins generally have no more than 2–8 hairs, usually close to the tip of the snout. In some species, e.g. the Sperm Whale, hair is only found during foetal development, while the Narwhal and the Beluga have no hair at any stage. In any case, what few hairs Cetaceans have are not really 'hairs' so much as 'vibrissae' – just like a cat's whiskers. They are tactile organs, rather than fur (cf. Chapter 9), and therefore have a special structure. Not only are they stiffer, but the follicles are surrounded with greatly distended veins, the so-called blood sinuses, and with a great number of nerve endings whose structure is identical to that of tactile corpuscles. No less than four hundred nerve fibres run to every hair. Now we can understand why the Cetaceans have bristles over their jaws, for this is precisely where vibrissae are normally found in terrestrial animals also. We do not know what it is that Cetaceans feel with their hair, but it is unlikely to be very important or else the hair would be longer.

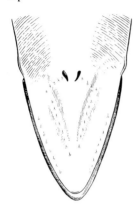

Figure 43. Dorsal view of the head of a 3 feet 9 inch Fin Whale foetus, showing position of tactile hairs in relation to eyes and blowhole.

Since we are on the subject of the external appearance of whales, we must not forget to mention their colour. A number of species – Right Whales, Sperm Whales, Pigmy Sperm Whales, Bottlenose Whales, False Killers, Pilot Whales, Gangetic Dolphins, and Indian Porpoises – are practically black, though in most of them the black shades off into dark grey on the ventral side. The Beluga is creamy white, and the Narwhal is yellowish with dark grey or blackish spots on the back, the colour becoming markedly lighter on the ventral side. The same is true of the Grey Whale, of Risso's Dolphin, and of the Blue Whale. All other Rorquals and most other Odontocetes, i.e. most Dolphins, are black on the dorsal and white on the ventral side. In some cases, e.g. the Common Dolphin, the black is relieved by brown or violet shades, and there may be light spots on the black, or dark spots on the white surface, but, on the whole, black and white are the predominant colours and the transition from one to the other is gradual.

Now the same distribution of colour – dark on top and light beneath – can also be found in most fishes, in seals, penguins, and in a great number of terrestrial animals. It has a clear biological significance, for it serves as an excellent means of camouflage – countershading. This is best illustrated by means of a model. If light is allowed to fall perpendicularly on a grey cylinder held horizontally in front of a grey screen, the cylinder will not merge with the screen but be clearly visible, since the light will illuminate its upper surface, while the cylinder's own shadow will darken its lower part. Now, if we colour the cylinder dark on top and whiten it beneath, the two colours will merge imperceptibly, for less light will be reflected from the top and more from the bottom. The cylinder will fuse into the background. Countershading enables animals to hide both from their pursuers and their prey. Amongst the Cetaceans there is, however, an exception to the general rule of countershading, viz. Cuvier's Beaked

Whale, an animal some 17–26 feet long, found in all warm and temperate seas. Though some individuals are, in fact, countershaded, the front of the body at least of the majority of these dolphins is white on top and dark at the bottom. The Pilot Whale, which is entirely black, may well owe this peculiarity to its being a nocturnal animal (cf. Chapter 6). Albinos, i.e. completely white or creamy-white specimens, are also found in Cetaceans, just as they are in other mammals. I myself came across an albino Bottlenose Dolphin near Harlingen, and on 19th April, 1957, a white Sperm Whale was killed off Japan – a reincarnation of the famous Moby Dick.

While the two sexes in Cetaceans do not differ in colour, they often differ in length. It seems that in Mysticetes, the average female is 3–6 feet longer than the male, while the female Odontocete is shorter than her mate. As a rule, however, the difference is smaller than in Mysticetes, and in porpoises, for instance, there seems to be no difference at all. In young porpoises, the male is probably longer, but in mature animals the reverse is the case. In other species, e.g. in Sperm Whales, Bottlenose Whales, Killer Whales and False Killer Whales the difference between males and females is about 19, 13, 8, and 3 feet respectively. Ziphiids of the genera Berardius and Ziphius form the exception, for the males are shorter. In some species, there is moreover a clear difference in *shape* between the sexes. Thus male Bottlenose Whales have a more protruding forehead than females, male Killers have a much larger dorsal fin, the two sexes of the Bottlenose Dolphins have differently shaped dorsal fins, and the tooth of the male Narwhal has already been mentioned.

A careful look at the skin of many dolphins will reveal the presence of a number of long parallel stripes (Fig. 100). The distance between the stripes agrees exactly with the distance between the animal's teeth, and we may therefore infer that they have resulted from fights with members of the same species. Such stripes are also found on Sperm Whales, where the distance between them is 4–8 inches, i.e. the exact distance between their teeth. But Baleen Whales, too, have scratches on their skin, which cannot possibly be due to wounds inflicted by members of the same species, which, as we know, have no teeth. In fact, these scratches do not run parallel, but fan out in all directions. They are possibly due to abrasions caused by ice-floes. Impressions inflicted by the suckers of squids are commonly found on Sperm Whales and those dolphins which feed on squids, e.g. the Pilot Whale and Risso's Dolphin.

Our attention is frequently arrested by peculiar scars, often with a radiating pattern, found particularly on the skin of Blue Whales, Fin Whales and Sei Whales. These round, oval or crescent-shaped skin

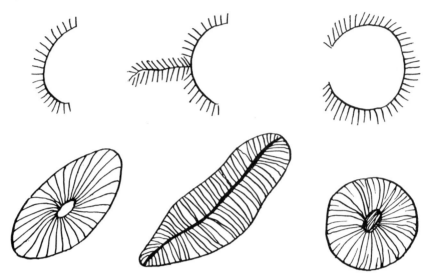

Figure 44. Scars found on the skins of Rorquals

lacerations (Fig. 44) are well known to all whalers. They are generally
2 to 6 inches long, and are found mainly on the posterior part of the body.
Against black skin, they appear to consist of a dark centre, from which
fairly fine white stripes fan out in all directions, but against white skin,
on which, by the way, they are far less frequent, they form a completely
black pattern. Although these scars are found predominantly on the
species listed above, they occasionally occur on the skin of the Grey
Whale, the Humpback Whale, and the Sperm Whale also. The scars are
found on whales in both hemispheres, and the reason why they are rarer
in Humpback Whales and Sperm Whales must probably be sought in
the fact that their skin and, even more, their blubber, is so much harder
and tougher than that of their larger relatives.

Nor are the scars restricted to these species. Mr W. L. van Utrecht, who
made a thorough investigation of them, reports that similar scars are
found in three species of Beaked Whales belonging to the genera *Mesoplodon* and *Berardius*; in Bottlenose Whales, in White-sided Dolphins, in
Finless Black Porpoises, and also in the Common Porpoise. In the latter,
though the species has been known for centuries, they were first described
by van Utrecht in a specimen caught on 31st January, 1955 (see Fig. 45).
Subsequently, it transpired that such scars on Common Porpoises are
quite frequent.

How did these marks come about? The answer is rather difficult, for the
simple reason that no dolphin or whale has ever been caught with any

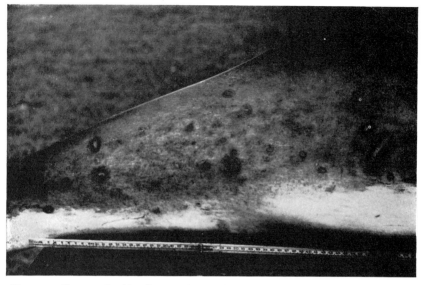

Figure 45. Scars on the skin of a porpoise caught at the entrance to the Channel on 31st January 1955. Photograph: W. L. van Utrecht, Amsterdam.

direct evidence of the identity of its perpetrator on its skin. The biologist has had to turn detective, trying to sift what clues he can from the available circumstantial evidence.

In this process, what strikes him is the fact that no skin-wounds ever occur in species which keep exclusively to cold seas, e.g. Right Whales, Belugas or Narwhals. The cause must therefore be sought in warmer waters, and this is, moreover, borne out by the fact that in migratory whales caught in cold water the scars are always healed – open wounds are only found in the tropics and the sub-tropics, and particularly between approximately 45 degrees north and 15 degrees south. Between the polar seas and these regions, the wounds are partially healed.

The peculiar radiating pattern of the scars is associated with the direction of the papillary layer between the epidermis and the dermis (cf. Chapter 11 and Fig. 171). Hence it appears most clearly in scars whose axis is nearly perpendicular to the direction of the papillary layer of the corium.

Now, what inhabitant of the warm seas can possibly inflict these wounds? The credit for having found an acceptable solution must go primarily to G. C. Pike, a biologist who spent many years on a lonely post in the Pacific – the land station of Nanaimo on Vancouver Island (British Columbia) – and did outstanding research on whales. Pike discovered

Figure 46. Left: mouth of lamprey, showing teeth. (East, 1949.) Right: fish with lamprey attached to its skin.

that many of the round scars coincided precisely with the shape of the mouths of a species of lamprey common in the North Pacific (*Entosphenus tridentatus*). Moreover, Pike managed to see the actual impression of lamprey teeth on more than one occasion. His findings were confirmed by Nemoto, and later also by van Utrecht. Lampreys are very strange eel-shaped creatures which fasten to other aquatic animals with their round mouths. In fact, the same sort of scar has been found on many fishes also. It would appear that round or oval scars occur whenever the lamprey attaches itself to the whale with its entire mouth, crescent-shaped scars whenever it uses part of its mouth only, and longitudinal scars whenever it shifts from its original position. Moreover, contractions of the whale's skin may very well cause the wounds to open out into longitudinal slits, as happens with human scars also, which are often fan-shaped.

Still, this is by no means positive proof of the lamprey being the real culprit. A judge would dismiss the evidence as uncorroborated, and call for eye-witnesses. Fortunately, we can comply, for, as early as 1913, the Norwegian biologist, Olsen, reported that whalers attached to a West African land station had found eel-shaped animals dangling from a freshly-killed whale. Their description leaves no doubt that these animals must have been lampreys. Pike, too, reported similar eye-witness accounts from the North Pacific. Apparently, the lampreys let go of their host soon after he is killed, or whenever he moves to colder waters, even though lampreys themselves are not restricted to temperate or tropical seas. Possibly they dislike the faster speed which whales develop on their migratory journeys, but this will have to be investigated further. In any case, lampreys do not necessarily have to bear the entire blame, and it is possible that other 'guests' are responsible also.

Apart from lampreys, the skin of whales and dolphins is often studded with other animals which, for convenience, we shall lump together under the general heading of 'parasites', although many of them do not batten

Figure 47. Acorn Barnacles and Stalked Barnacles on the skin of a Humpback.
Photograph: A. F. M. Drieman, Amsterdam.

on their hosts, but merely attach themselves to their skins without doing any damage. Now the smooth skin of fast swimming animals does not really provide safe anchorage for parasites, and for that reason by far the overwhelming majority of these guests entrench themselves firmly in the epidermis and even in the blubber beneath. With the exception of one encapsuled representative of the unicellular Ciliate, *Haematophagus* by name (cf. Chapter 10), and of a Nematod (*Odontobius*), which both live on the whalebone, all these guests are Crustaceans, first appearances notwithstanding. Unlike the external parasites of terrestrial animals (e.g. fleas and lice) all of which are air-breathing insects (with the exception of mites and ticks which are classified with spiders), aquatic parasites naturally breathe in water and must therefore be equipped with gills or similar organs.

The most striking of these guests are the Acorn Barnacles, sessile crustaceans with a hard shell of calcium, which most of us have seen

washed up on the beach or attached to the bottom of ships. The Norwegians call them 'Knøllus' since they occur in great number on Humpback Whales (Knølhval), especially on the head and the pectoral fins
(Fig. 47). In Sperm Whales they can be found between the teeth as well.
A common type looks like a six-pointed star, and against the black background of its host strongly reminds us of a decoration worn on a dress
suit. It was probably for this reason that Darwin named it *Coronula reginae*
(Queen's Coronet). In other, generally larger, members of *Coronula*, the
resemblance to a coronet is more striking still (see Fig. 48).

Another sessile crustacean often found on Cetaceans is called *Penella*.
It looks like a long wire, and its anterior appendages burrow deep into
the skin. Its abdomen is feather-shaped and trails a number of filiform
egg strings (Fig. 48). *Penella*, and also the Acorn Barnacles, occur less
frequently on Rorquals in the Antarctic than in the tropics, and old
animals are generally more strongly infested than young ones. In addition
to the parasites listed, whales also harbour the cirripeds known as Stalked
Barnacles (Figs. 47 and 48). These barnacles seem to prefer a firmer
support than skin provides, and hence they generally cling to Acorn
Barnacles, to *Penella*, to the baleen, and to the teeth of Sperm Whales.
The only non-sessile parasites are small crustaceans (maximum length
$\frac{1}{2}$ inch) known as whale lice. Like *Penella*, these are true parasites, which
feed on the whale's skin, to which they cling with sharp little claws. They
generally keep to grooves and slits – the lips, the corners of the mouth, the
ear slit or the genital folds – where they are more protected against water

*Figure 48. Some common parasites found on
whales.*
A = Penella balaenopterae; *B* =
whale louse, Cyamus spec.; *C* = *Stalked
Barnacle*, Conchoderma auritum *attached
to* D = *Acorn Barnacle*, Coronula
diadema; *E* = *Acorn Barnacle*, Coronula
reginae.
    Approx. $\frac{5}{9}$ *their natural sizes.* (*Peters,
1938.*)

Figure 49. Whale lice in a groove on the skin (old scar) of a Rorqual. Prep: W. H. E. van Dijk; Photograph: W. L. van Utrecht, Amsterdam.

friction (Fig. 49). They are found abundantly in these slits on dead whales.

When we examine dead whales, we are struck by the fact that some are more infested with lice and other parasites than others. Parasites are most common in Right Whales – a Greenland Whale may have hundreds of thousands of whale lice. Humpbacks and Sperm Whales also play hosts to a multitude of unwelcome visitors, and Zenkovich mentions the case of a Humpback carrying over 1,000 lb. of Acorn Barnacles and Stalked Barnacles. Quite likely, the guests prefer these whales because they swim more slowly than other Mysticetes. Among Odontocetes, not only Sperm Whales, but also Bottlenose Whales, Pilot Whales, Killer Whales, Narwhals, Belugas and even Common Dolphins, are known to be infested, while Common Porpoises and Bottlenose and many other dolphins seem to be free of parasites. Of course, a more thorough investigation may reveal external parasites on these species as well, but only in exceptional cases. Even among infested whales, there are marked individual differences, so that we can distinguish between 'clean' and 'dirty' animals, though the causes of this distinction are not yet understood. In terrestrial animals, particularly of the domestic kind, such differences are often the result of the animal's condition. Lice are not the causes of disease, they simply multiply far more readily in sick than in healthy specimens. In whales, a contributory factor may well prove to be their seasonal habitat. This is certainly true for another group of external parasites: diatoms (Fig. 133). These microscopic plants often form a yellowish film over the sides and bellies of some whales and dolphins, and particularly of Antarctic Blue and Fin Whales. When such animals are hauled up on to the deck of a factory ship, they often look like an entirely different species, whence the name 'sulphur bottom' for some Blue Whales. Once this filmy layer is scraped off, however, the normal colour reappears. 'Sulphur bottoms' are most prevalent in the Antarctic, simply because diatoms are most wide-spread in this region (cf. Chapter 12).

Our long discourse on the whale's external appearance has led us from our giant's early beginnings to the lice which infest its gigantic bulk. We have seen that the external features of this strange animal still keep a great number of secrets from us, and when we come to discuss its internal organs and its behaviour in subsequent chapters, we shall see that these secrets are by no means its only ones.

3

Locomotion and Locomotory Organs

'DOLPHINS AHEAD!'... What passenger on an ocean liner has not been enticed to the deck by this cry, to hang eagerly over the rails as he watches the animals' graceful play? Generally, what he sees is a small school of five to ten Common Dolphins, though in tropical waters he might see other species as well. The dolphins usually swim ahead of the ship, or sometimes alongside, but never in the ship's wake. Unlike sharks, which follow ocean liners for their refuse, dolphins merely come up to play, sometimes jumping right out of the water, darting across the bow waves and even diving under the ship. They are not covetous and never beg. On the contrary, they are the envoys of Neptune, the God of the Sea, and as such they accompany the ship and see it safe to harbour.

Not only dolphins, but large whales, too, are sometimes inquisitive enough to come close to a ship so that they can investigate the interloper from all sides and even from underneath. When they do (Fig. 72), passengers and crew are given a wonderful opportunity of observing their aquatic skills and particularly their method of surfacing, which is rather important to whalers, for from the small part of the body protruding above the water, and even from the way it surfaces, they must be able to tell to what species it belongs. The method of surfacing may, however, alter with the animal's speed. Thus, when a Fin Whale is swimming slowly, it generally surfaces almost horizontally (Figs. 32 and 51). The blowhole comes up first, then a small section of the back, followed by the dorsal fin, and then our whale is gone again, almost in the same way it came up. But whenever a Fin Whale is swimming quickly, it surfaces at an angle, snout breaking water first (Fig. 73), curves its body to display a great deal of the back and tail (Fig. 53), and then dives down again at an angle (Fig. 54). Gunners much prefer the whale to come up this way, for if it does, it offers a much larger target area than when it surfaces horizontally.

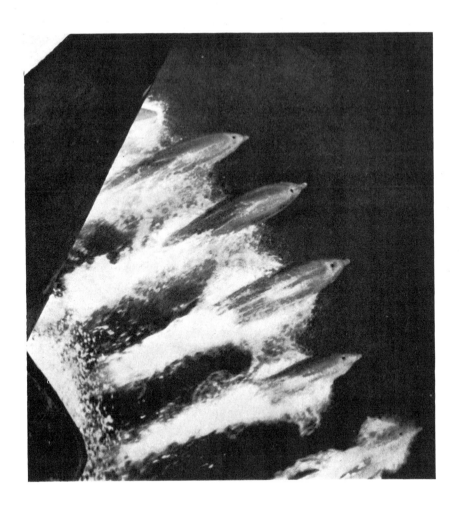

Figure 50. Dolphins in the bow waves of S.S. Rondo (*N. V. Stoomvaartmaatschappij Nederland*). *Note the wide-open blowholes. Photograph: W. L. Wolff, Membang Muda.*

Figure 51. Rorquals surfacing slowly. (From Discovery Committee Report, 1937.)

Before the Second World War, catcher boats rarely made more than 14–15 knots, and therefore had to 'stalk' the much faster whales. The Norwegians called this method of whaling *Luse-jag*, but since 1945 *Luse-jag* has generally given way to another method called *Prøyser-jag*, in which fast vessels not only force the whale to swim faster and thus to surface at an angle and to present a larger target area (see Fig. 55), but also to come up for air at more frequent intervals. For the faster a whale swims, the more, of course, it 'pants'. The spot where a whale sounds is usually betrayed by a smooth and 'oily' patch, called the blow-wake and this was once believed to be the result of a special secretion. It would, however, appear that the blow-wake is, in fact, caused by a current churned up by the diving flukes. Some whales stay submerged for large distances, but the Sperm Whale, for instance, usually sounds vertically, to reappear some thirty minutes later at almost the same spot.

Fig. 54 shows clearly that when Fin Whales surface, their flukes normally remain submerged. The same is true also of Blue, Sei, and Little Piked Whales, but Right Whales, Humpbacks, and Sperm Whales generally display their flukes, particularly before deep dives (Figs. 56 and 70). The Greenland Right Whale is even known to shake its flukes to and fro in the air, and it is generally believed that the animal does so because its thick blubber so reduces its specific gravity that it has difficulty in diving normally. The Grey Whale, too, displays its flukes just before diving, but not when swimming near the surface. All these characteristics, together with the shape of the head, the profile of the back, the shape and size of the dorsal fin, and particularly the shape of the 'blow' – the cloud of vapour which the whale exhales – often enable whalers to identify the species. Even so, Blue, Fin, and Sei Whales are not easily distinguished except by very experienced whalers.

The surfacing of many dolphins, and particularly of porpoises, is very similar to that of Fin Whales (Fig. 54). The animals come up at an angle of 30°, and depending on their speed, either the tip of the snout or the blowhole emerge first out of the water. When they swim slowly, some dolphins, such as the Boutu, can surface almost horizontally.

What we have said so far applies to normal swimming only, but just as we sometimes skip and dance rather than walk, whales too, often behave extraordinarily. Thus it is said that Fin Whales occasionally swim on their side when they are feeding. It is believed that these large animals cannot turn very easily, and have to 'roll' instead. Many dolphins are real high-jumpers; they sometimes shoot out of the water in a wide arc, and some-times jump right up into the air, with their bodies almost perpendicular to the water (Fig. 57). Sometimes they dive back into the water snout first; at other times chest or belly first. The large whales, despite their

Figure 52. Sperm Whale surfacing slowly. Note blowhole (left) and dorsal 'bump' (right).
Photograph: R. Stephan aboard M.S. Pool, *New Guinea.*

Figure 53. A Humpback surfacing. Photograph: W. H. Dawbin, Sidney.

enormous weight, are no less agile, particularly the Humpback, a real acrobat, which can jump right out of the water and then flop back with a resounding smack (Fig. 58). This animal also likes to roll on the surface, slapping the water with its flukes and wing-shaped pectoral fins as he does so. The slaps can often be heard many miles away. Moreover, Humpbacks like to swim on their backs for a while and to display their white bellies. They often turn whole series of somersaults both above and also under the water. On 21st October, 1955, W. Bannan and T. J. Hermans, two officers aboard the *Sibajak* (Royal Rotterdam Lloyd) came across this kind of play off the Australian East Coast, and made a little sketch of it (Fig. 59). The Humpback's antics are, moreover, commemorated on a postage stamp, one of quite a few, by the way, on which various Cetaceans appear. This is the Falkland Island sixpenny stamp (1833 to 1933).

Other Rorquals, though less proficient, can also jump right out of the water. J. B. Colam watched a Blue Whale doing so off Durban in 1950, and Captain Mörzer Bruins stated that, on 28th January, 1956, during a trip on the *Piet Hein*, he saw a Sei Whale jump full length out of the water, south of Waiglo (New Guinea). Sperm Whales (and to a lesser extent, Little Piked Whales) are past-masters at jumping, too, but often half their body remains submerged.

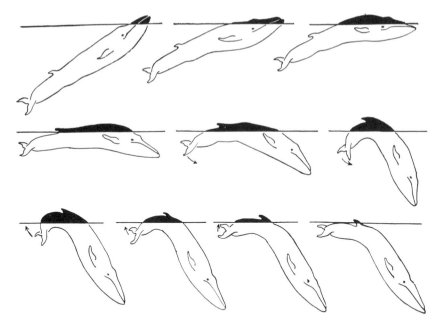

Figure 54. The surfacing of a fast-swimming Fin Whale. The snout comes up first. Cf. Figure 32. (Gunther, 1949.)

Figure 55. Characteristic view of a Humpback. Photograph: Dr W. Vervoort, Leyden.

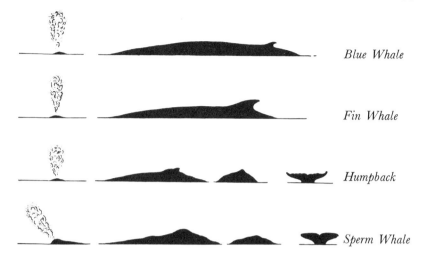

Figure 56. The most important clues for identifying various whales from the way in which they surface. (Modified after Peters, 1938.)

How do whales and dolphins manage to swim so fast and to manoeuvre so skilfully? We know that, by and large, they swim like fish. In fish, too, the pectoral fins are too small to affect forward motion, their function being to help the animal to balance and steer, particularly when they are fully extended. Propulsion of the body is brought about either by flexions of the whole body, as is the case with shark and trout, or else by flexions of the tail alone, as with many other fish. Now the whale's flukes are in a horizontal plane, while those of fish are vertically placed, and hence the whale's propulsion is clearly based on up and down motions of the tail and not on lateral flexions, though Scoresby (1820) thought he had detected horizontal motions also, during which the tail acted very much like a ship's screw. On the whole, however, whales move their flukes very much as frogmen move their flippers, though they do not, of course, beat alternatively with right and left.

Everyone who has watched a swimming whale or dolphin knows how difficult it is to follow its movements accurately. Dolphins do not seem to move their bodies at all, or at best show a small quiver, while big whales so churn up the water surface that they become practically invisible. Townsend, during observations of Bottlenose Dolphins in New York Aquarium (1907) saw nothing apart from vertical tail motions, and True fared no better with a captive Beluga. Russian investigators, e.g. Shuleikin (1935) and Stass (1939), however, hold that not only are there undulations of the whole body but that the tail acts like a screw, i.e. it moves horizontally, as well as vertically. Shuleikin based his opinion on a film of a dolphin suspended in air, a method singularly unsuited to the study of the animal's motion in its natural habitat. Stass greatly improved matters by attaching a special vibrograph to the back of a dolphin which swam while attached to the ship by a long rope (100 yards) (Fig. 60). The research was directed by a scientific institute on the Black Sea, and it appeared that the vertical beat of the tail was one and a half times as great as the lateral beat. Still, even these investigations are not altogether convincing, and Parry (1949) pointed out that certain defects in the apparatus might easily have produced the lateral effect.

The most reliable work about the swimming of dolphins is unquestionably that based on underwater films of swimming Bottlenose and other dolphins, and of a Pigmy Sperm Whale in Marineland Aquarium (Florida). These films, of which parts have been incorporated into Rachel Carson's film 'The Sea Around Us', show very clearly that the animal's bodily movements are confined to the tail, which consists of the peduncle of the tail and the flukes. The same conclusion can be drawn from Williamson's film on underwater life, and also from the beautiful colour film of the underwater movements of Sperm Whales and dolphins, taken

Figure 57. A dolphin jumping thirteen feet out of the water.

Figure 58. A Humpback jumping clear of the surface. (Glassell, 1953.)

aboard the French research-ship *Calypso*. All the films show that the tail beats absolutely vertically about a point near the vent, i.e. roughly the base of the tail (Fig. 62; cf. also Figs. 101–105). This is in perfect accordance with the motility of the animal's body, for if we examine a dead porpoise (Fig. 61) we find that these apparently so flexible animals have an extraordinarily rigid trunk. The head is movable to some extent, but the base of the tail forms a very distinct pivotal point.

Fig. 61 illustrates that, in addition to this fulcrum, another one is found at the base of the flukes. This agrees with the evidence of the films analysed by Parry (1949), which show clearly that, as the peduncle of the tail moves up and down, the flukes carry out related movements of their own. In fact, without these movements, the whale would be perfectly motionless, no matter how vigorously it beats the water with its tail. Similarly, if we were to sit in a boat and simply beat the water with a pair of oars, our boat could hardly be expected to move forward. Now, the fact that the flukes keep beating behind the peduncle of the tail, causes them to 'scull' at an angle to the peduncle in all positions of the tail, and

Figure 59. A Humpback's somersaults after a sketch by Bannan and Hermans of an observation made off East Australia in 1955.

hence to exert a continual thrust in a forward direction (Fig. 63). The effects of the tail's vertical motions naturally cancel out, so that this forward thrust determines the propulsion. (The same principle operates in fish, though here the tail is waved in a horizontal plane.) The peduncle of the tail may even be said to have a braking effect, but the latter is negligible since the tail is not only streamlined but so laterally compressed, that it cuts through the water very much like a knife. The reader might wonder how so relatively small a part of the whale as the flukes can manage to propel the animal's gigantic bulk, but he need only think of a large ship's small screw to realize that mere size is unimportant. Woodcock (1948) observed that dolphins accompanying a ship at 20 knots beat their tails at a rate of two beats per second, while Gunther (1949) measured 1–2 beats per second in the case of a Fin Whale making 10–12 knots.

Even though the whale is thus propelled as a result of its tail's vertical beat, the tail can also bend horizontally. However, here there is no special 'fulcrum' at the base of the flukes. The lateral motion is undoubtedly needed for steering and particularly for quick turns, in short for most of the animal's aquatic feats. The flippers contribute a small share to the steering effect and particularly help to balance the animal on its course, and the dorsal fin also plays a part as a stabilizer, though stability, as we have seen, is primarily assured by the high-up position of the lungs.

We have also seen that the trunk in Cetaceans is fairly rigid, and the typical curved appearance of the back when the animal is surfacing is mainly due to the fact that head and tail are bent down. Oddly enough, while Cetaceans have a very short and rigid neck, the head of some species, e.g. Bottlenose Dolphins and Boutus, can make an angle of 45° up or down with the trunk, and somewhat smaller angles in a lateral direction. However, the head is not equally movable in all species, and that of the Pilot Whale is particularly immobile. This may well be due to the fact that its food consists exclusively of cuttlefish which, on the whole, are not as mobile as fishes. Since the neck is fairly rigid in most species, the head is moved by the joint between the atlas (the first cervical vertebra) and the occipital bones at the rear of the skull. This joint which

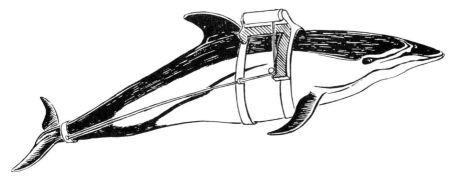

Figure 60. Stass's experiment for recording the motions of the flukes in a swimming dolphin.
(Stass, 1936.)

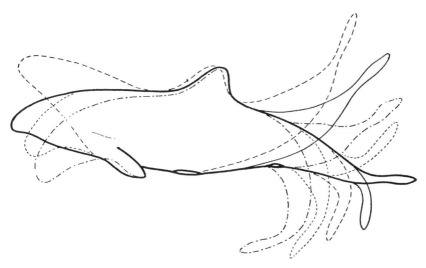

Figure 61. Experiments with a 3 feet 6 inch porpoise to determine the vertical mobility of
various parts of the body. (Slijper, 1936.)

consists of two rounded prominences, enables the whale to 'nod' but not
to shake its head, i.e. to turn the head about its own axis. Even so, the
head can be inclined sideways, for the joint acts as a kind of neck, though
not sufficiently to enable the whale to look back.

The reason why whales and dolphins cannot shake their heads is the
absence of a joint between the atlas and the axis (the second cervical
vertebra), and the great compression of the other cervical vertebrae.
The extent of the compression (and the consequent short neck) is best

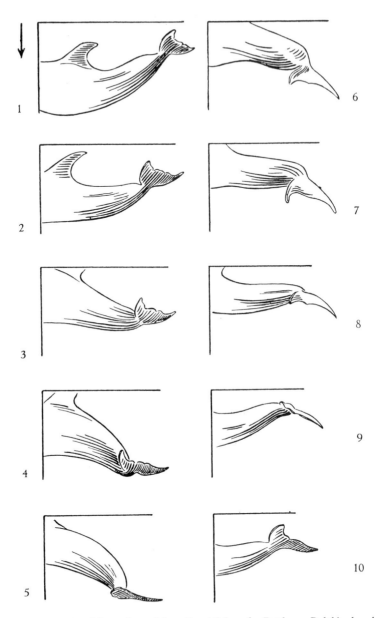

Figure 62. Analysis of the motions of the tail and flukes of a Bottlenose Dolphin, based on a film made in the Marineland Aquarium, Florida. 1–5: downstroke; 6–10: upstroke. (Modified after Parry, 1949.)

appreciated by comparing the skeleton of a whale with that of a terrestrial mammal (Fig. 21). Cetaceans have a full complement of seven cervical vertebrae as found in most mammals irrespective of whether their neck is as long as the giraffe's or as short as the dolphin's, but while Rorquals, River-dolphins, Belugas and Narwhals still have independent cervical vertebrae, Right Whales, Dolphins and Porpoises have all the seven vertebrae fused into one osseous unit (Fig. 64). The resulting short and rigid neck not only adds to the streamlining effect of the rest of the body, but also aids propulsion in other ways for, since the motive force lies in the tail, a less rigid head would flop in all directions and impede the animal's progress through the water.

The rest of the vertebral column also shows characteristic modifications to aquatic life. Even a superficial examination of Fig. 21 will reveal the extraordinary extension of the lumbar part of the vertebral column. This may be partly associated with the formation of a streamlined body, but it is also connected with the fact that it is to the lumbar vertebrae that the tail muscles are attached. A long tail which is expected to develop a great deal of power must naturally lead to an increase of the surface to which its muscles are attached. In some species, e.g. the snake-shaped *Basilosaurus* (Fig. 28) and also – though to a lesser extent – in *Ziphiidae* (e.g. the Bottlenose Whale), increase in body length goes hand in hand with longer vetebrae. At the same time these animals have a shortened thorax. In most other Cetaceans, however, the lumbar region has become extended through increases in the number of individual lumbar vertebrae.

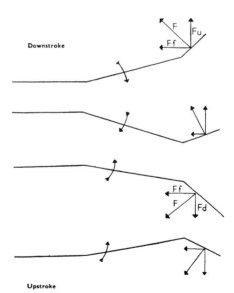

Figure 63. Forces operating during vertical motions of a Cetacean tail. The force F resulting from the resistance of the water can be resolved into a forward (Ff), and into an alternatively up (Fu) and downward (Fd) component.

Downstroke

Upstroke

This can be seen clearly in Rorquals, and particularly in Dolphins, some of which not only have an increased number of lumbar but also of caudal vertebrae (Fig. 67). Generally, each of these vertebrae is so flattened antero-posteriorly that their bodies resemble draughts counters. Such vertebral bodies, with or without their spinous and transverse processes, are often washed up. The greatest number of vertebrae is found in White-sided Dolphins (93); the Common Dolphin has 75, the Porpoise has 66 and the Blue Whale has 63, as compared with the dog's 50. If we examine the history of Cetaceans, we shall find that the geologically oldest types always have the smallest, and the more recent types the greatest number of vertebrae. The advantage of this sequence of adjoining short discs is probably not so much the possibility of increasing their number within a given space as the consequent increase in the number of cartilaginous pads between the vertebrae. As a result, the vertebral column has proportionally more cartilage and less bone, and hence much greater suppleness and elasticity. Bone which is primarily a means of supporting the body is not so important in aquatic animals, most of whose weight is borne by the water.

The fact that Cetaceans lack a sacrum is obvious from the fact that the pelvis has been reduced to a slender bone which, moreover, is quite unattached to the vertebral column. However, because of the nerve roots which emerge from the spinal cord behind certain vertebrae, we can still say that these – otherwise quite ordinary – lumbar vertebrae correspond to the sacral vertebrae of terrestrial mammals. If we regard them in this way, it appears that the tail does not start directly behind these 'sacral' vertebrae, but that a number of so-called post-sacral vertebrae are interposed. The Porpoise, for instance, has six of these.

Although it is difficult to tell superficially just where the lumbar region ends and the tail begins, since, externally, the body has smoothly flowing lines, the distinction is quite easy to make on skeletons, for here every caudal vertebra is provided with chevron bones (Figs. 21 and 226). The first vertebra to have these bones at its anterior side can therefore be distinguished as the first caudal vertebra. Chevron bones, which occur in all caudal vertebrae with the exception of those in the flukes, are so called because they strongly resemble the chevrons worn by N.C.O.s. Chevron bones also occur in other mammals, but in the more anterior caudal vertebrae only, where they are so small that they can be located only with the greatest difficulty. The reason why they are so well developed in Cetaceans is quite obvious: the muscles which raise the tail are provided with adequate levers by the spinous processes on top of the caudal vertebrae. However, no such levers are normally found on the lower side of vertebrae, and the chevrons found here consequently help to

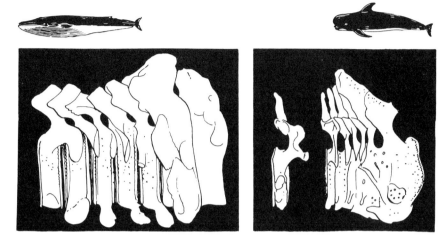

Figure 64. Right view of the seven cervical vertebrae of a Blue and a Pilot Whale. In the Blue Whale, the vertebrae are fairly short and independent; in the Pilot Whale only the 7th cervical vertebra is free (it is shown separately in the figure). (Van Beneden and Gervais, 1880.)

depress the tail. Large blood vessels, to which we shall return in Chapter 5, are found in the chevron canal, surrounded by chevron bones. The vertebrae of the flukes have neither chevrons nor other processes. In conformity with the overall shape of the flukes, they are small bones flattened vertically as well as laterally.

We have seen that the neck, thorax, and abdomen of most Cetaceans are fairly rigid. All this, too, must naturally be reflected in the structure of the vertebral column, and moreover, in such a way that the mutual mobility of any two successive vertebrae is restricted. And, in fact, intervertebral joints and articulating processes (zygapophyses) are lacking in the greater part of the vertebral column of many Cetaceans. In most Baleen whales, in Sperm Whales and in Ziphiids they are only present in the second to fourth thoracic vertebrae, and in Common Dolphins and Porpoises they extend no farther back than the fifth to tenth vertebra. The mutual mobility of the vertebrae, already greatly reduced by flattening the ends of the vertebral bodies, is restricted further by the fact that the metapophyses of the posterior thoracic, and of all, or certainly the anterior, lumbar vertebrae, are so long that they embrace the spinous process of the preceding vertebra (see Fig. 65). Moreover, beneath the centre runs a strongly developed ligament, the longitudinal ventral ligament, whose main function it is to prevent the vertebral column from sagging. In the caudal vertebrae, however, these restrictions are absent, and hence they can be moved far more freely.

We have already seen that the Cetacean skeleton, unlike that of terrestrial mammals, does not so much have to carry the entire weight of the body, as to anchor the musculature. This function is very important, for the muscles of a Blue Whale weigh roughly 40 tons, i.e. 40 per cent of the animal's total weight, while the skeleton accounts for only 17 per cent. In Fin and Sei Whales these proportions are respectively 45 per cent and 16 per cent, and 54 per cent and 13 per cent. Dolphins and porpoises, too, have proportions of about this order, and it seems clear that muscles play a predominant part in these animals. Sperm Whales, whose muscles make up 10 per cent of the body weight, are the only exceptions; their special position in the list is probably due to their large heads.

The great mass of muscle which moves the tail and the flukes is thus situated in the lumbar region. For here a whole system of long and powerful tendons gradually fans out to become attached to each of the various caudal vertebrae, which can therefore be moved separately. Moreover, whole sections, such as the flukes, can be moved with respect to the other sections, so that the fact that, during motion, the flukes make an angle with the rest of the tail (see above) is not due to their passive reaction to the pressure of the water as it is in the fish, but to an active muscular exertion. Though the tendons are attached to the vertebrae of the flukes, they are also joined to the complicated system of tough fibres and lamellae of which the peculiar white connective tissue of the flukes is built up. As early as 1883 the great German anatomist Roux made a study of Cetacean flukes, and showed how complicated and how ingenious the structure of these organs really is. It appears that whenever the tendons exert a pull on the vertebrae of the flukes, the entire tissue system is tensed, giving the flukes their characteristic shape and rigidity.

A close examination of Figs. 66 and 67 will show that there are great differences between Cetaceans, particularly in respect of the form of their lumbar and anterior caudal vertebrae. In some species, e.g. Sperm Whales and Ziphiids, the transverse processes of these vertebrae are short, the spinous processes are long, and the metapophyses placed low. In dolphins

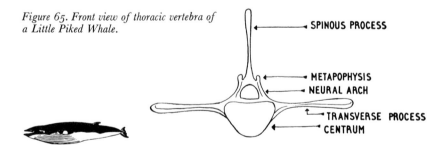

Figure 65. Front view of thoracic vertebra of a Little Piked Whale.

SPINOUS PROCESS

METAPOPHYSIS
NEURAL ARCH

TRANSVERSE PROCESS
CENTRUM

and porpoises, the transverse processes are long and the metapophyses placed high, particularly in the posterior lumbar and the anterior caudal regions. In these regions, the spinous processes incline forward, while those of the first group incline backwards just like all their other spinous processes. The big whales share the last two characteristics with the first group, and the long transverse processes with the second group. It is very difficult to enter into a detailed explanation of this phenomenon, because to do so would involve giving a full account of the structure of the muscles (see Slijper, 1946). Moreover, it is far from clear in what way the differences are connected with the animals' respective methods of propulsion. In any case the shifting upward of the mammillary processes of the posterior lumbar and anterior caudal region in porpoises and dolphins gives a longer lever arm to the muscles attached to these processes. Consequently, in porpoises and dolphins these muscles can work with a higher degree of efficiency than in the other Cetaceans (Slijper, 1960).

As we stand on the deck of the factory ship and watch the heavy bone-saws chewing through vertebrae, jaws and other bone, we cannot help being astonished by the lightness of the material. Now, a whale's bones consist of only a very thin shell of compact bone, the rest being made up of thin bony bars with large spaces between them. This gives the bone a spongy structure. Spongy bone is found also in all terrestrial mammals, but there it is surrounded by a much thicker shell of compact bone. Consequently the bones are very much heavier. Now the bones of terrestrial animals have to bear their owners' entire weight, while aquatic animals are supported by the water – hence the difference.

All bones have the cavities in their spongy part filled with bone marrow. The skeletons of young animals contain red bone marrow, a vascular soft tissue in which the red and white blood corpuscles are formed. In the course of development, however, most of the red marrow is replaced by yellow marrow. In the vertebral column this process starts simultaneously from the cervical and the caudal vertebrae, until red marrow is restricted to the thoracic vertebrae only and, here and there, to the ribs. Yellow bone marrow consists entirely of fatty tissue, and fatty tissue is also found in red bone marrow, though to a much smaller extent. For this reason, oil is obtained not only from the blubber of a whale but from its bones as well. The fat content of the skeleton is 51 per cent – 84 per cent in the head, a maximum of 24 per cent in vertebrae containing red bone marrow, and 32–68 per cent in vertebrae containing yellow marrow, and in other parts of the skeleton. The bones therefore contribute a third of a whale's total oil yield.

Because of this large proportion of fat in the skeleton and also because of the presence of large quantities of blubber, the specific gravity of

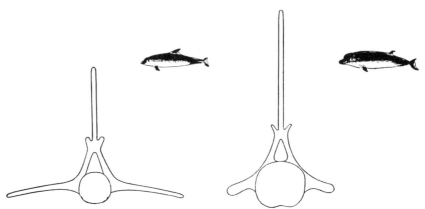

*Figure 66. Front view of lumbar vertebrae of a Bottlenose Dolphin and a Bottlenose Whale,
showing differences in length of spinous and transverse processes.*

Cetaceans is approximately one. In other words, most dolphins and whales neither sink nor rise but float in the water. However, this is merely a generalization, for we have already seen that there are whales, such as the Sperm Whale and the Right Whale, whose carcasses rise to the surface, while Rorquals generally sink to the bottom. Some dolphins are known to rise while others are known to sink, after they are killed or dead. Dead terrestrial mammals generally sink, and the same is true of hippopotami, which are so heavy that they can walk along the bottom of a river.

In whales, individual differences in this respect are probably due mainly to differences in the thickness of the blubber. Flensed carcasses always sink. Right Whales and Sperm Whales, particularly, have a relatively thick layer of blubber, and so has the Humpback Whale which, though air is always pumped into its carcass for safety, generally floats after it has been killed. The carcasses of Blue and Fin Whales often float towards the end of the whaling season, by which time their blubber has become much thicker. Floating also depends on the extent to which the lungs are filled with air. Thus animals which sink after death, e.g. Rorquals and dolphins, can, thanks to the air in their lungs, float at the surface when alive, with their blowholes just above the water. Two American scientists (Woodcock and McBride) managed to demonstrate a clear difference in the specific gravity of a dead and a living Rough-toothed Dolphin.

The reader may have wondered what speeds these powerful swimmers can develop. Sailors and whalers the world over have told us a great deal on this subject, but before we discuss their figures, a few cautionary remarks are needed. A point to be borne in mind in arriving at the correct

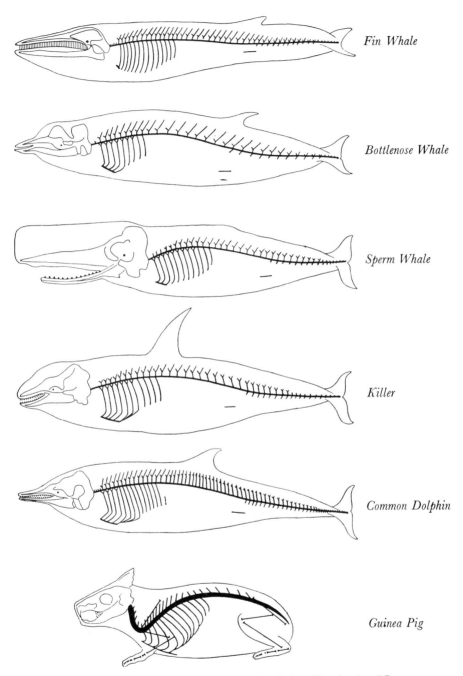

Fin Whale

Bottlenose Whale

Sperm Whale

Killer

Common Dolphin

Guinea Pig

Figure 67. The skeletons of a number of Cetaceans and a Guinea Pig, showing differences in length of the various parts of the vertebral column and in the direction of the spinous processes. (Slijper, 1946.)

picture is the duration of the observation, i.e. the time during which the whale or dolphin keeps up the observed speed. Now we know perfectly well that the speed of a sprinter is far greater than that of a long distance runner, and the same applies to whales also. Moreover, dolphins in particular like to ride the bow waves, and that is how they are usually observed from ships. In so doing, they are said to 'surf-ride' almost passively, or to be propelled by the water of the bow-wave welling up (Scholander, 1959), but these claims may be based on errors of observation, and special caution is needed in accepting them (see Fejer and Backus, 1960). Woodcock thinks that dolphins allow themselves to be carried by the ship's waves, and that they subsequently surface by changing their specific gravity.

The Right Whales are very slow swimmers and rarely exceed 5 knots, their average speed being 2 knots. Similar figures hold for the Grey Whales, for which Wyrick obtained a maximum speed of 6·5 knots off the Californian coast. The Humpback, too, is a slow swimmer. Chittleborough, who observed these animals near Point Cloates (Australia) from a helicopter, established that they made just over 4 knots. Females accompanied by calves swam more slowly still (3 knots), and the average speed during migrations is between 1·3 and 3·6 knots. The second mate of S.S. *Murena* (Shell Tankers) noted a speed of 5 knots for Humpbacks, and this agrees pretty well with Chittleborough's figures. When chased, however, they may show bursts of 9–10 knots (Dawbin). Sperm Whales are much faster. On S.S. *Utrecht* (Royal Rotterdam Lloyd), the third mate measured a speed of 10 knots, while other observers measured 8, 12, 16 and even 20 knots. The faster speeds were probably those of short spurts, and 10 knots would be a fair estimate of the Sperm Whale's average speed. It must be remembered that Sperm Whales like to preserve their energies, and that, as a rule, they prefer swimming slowly. Blue and Fin Whales are said to be capable of keeping up a spurt of 18 to 20 knots for 10–15 minutes, though their normal speed rarely exceeds 14 knots, 10–12 knots being the average. Observations with the Asdic apparatus have shown that even Fin Whales can achieve a sprint of about 30 m.p.h. under water for a very short time. These differences are not surprising when we consider that among athletes sprinters have roughly twice or three times the speed of stayers. On S.S. *Tamo*, speeds of 14 to 18 knots were recorded for a Little Piked Whale. The champion swimmer is probably the Sei Whale which is reported to reach a speed of 35 knots at the surface of the water, though Andrews states that the animal cannot keep this up for long. The Sei Whale is therefore the aquatic sprinter *par excellence*, just as the cheetah with its maximum speed of 65 m.p.h. is the leading sprinter among terrestrial mammals.

Two different observers recorded that Common Dolphins, swimming at some distance from their ship and hence unlikely to have benefited from the bow waves, kept up 20 knots for a considerable period of time. Speeds of 30–32 knots were measured in dolphins swimming in the bow waves of a destroyer. Captain Mörzer Bruins reported that dolphins had no difficulty in keeping up with the *Tarakan* whose speed was 14·5 knots. Dolphins of the genera *Steno* and *Prodelphinus*, however, fell behind the *Tarakan*, though they could keep up with the slower *Enggano* which was making 11·5 knots. River dolphins swim much more slowly, and Layne measured a normal speed of 2 and a maximum speed of 10 knots in the Boutu. Six knots appears to be the top speed of *Sotalia plumbea*, a marine species of Dolphin from the Malabar coast of India, and Vladykov measured a maximum speed of 10 and a normal speed of 6 knots in the Beluga. In the case of False Killers, Captain Mörzer Bruins measured 14·5 knots, and he also established that a Bottlenose Dolphin from the Red Sea (*Tursiops aduncus*) could swim faster than a ship making 17 knots. This is in agreement with the figures for the ordinary Bottlenose Dolphin (*Tursiops truncatus*) which is said to elude all boats making less than 22 knots. Comparing these speeds with those of ships, we find that the faster whales and many dolphins can keep up with modern liners. Still, the comparison is a little unfair, since ships are not submerged and have to overcome much less resistance. A submarine would, therefore, provide a much better analogy, and using it we find that many Cetaceans are far superior, for submarines only make 6 knots when submerged and 15 knots on the surface.

On the whole, it is true to say that the larger a ship the faster it is. In fish speed appears also to be directly proportional to size. Now this does not hold for Cetaceans, since an 8-foot dolphin can easily keep up with a 70-foot Fin Whale which weighs almost 1,000 times as much. True, speed boats of less than 100 tons can also keep up with 1,500-ton destroyers, but, once again, there is really no comparison, for the destroyer has to cut through the water, while the speedboat skims the surface. The fact, then, that two similarly built animals of such tremendous difference in size can yet reach the same speed, is unique, so much so that not only biologists but all sorts of marine engineers are very interested in this phenomenon. It is therefore not surprising that the Admiralty Experimental Station in Haslar (England) feels that scientists have much to learn from Cetaceans, and that the British Association for the Advancement of Science, during their annual meeting in Newcastle in 1949, devoted an entire joint session of the zoological and technical sections to the study of this problem, with Prof. Burrill presenting the technical, and Dr Richardson and Prof. Gray the biological aspects. Though their deliberations did not lead to an entirely satisfactory conclusion, it has nevertheless by now become clear what the crux of the problem is, and where its solution must be sought.

The speed of a body in water depends on its kinetic energy on the one hand, and on the resistance of the medium on the other. The resistance depends not only on the density and viscosity of the medium (in syrup, for instance, it is greater than in water), on the body's velocity (to be precise, on the square of the velocity) and on the surface area presented to the medium, all of which are known for Cetaceans in water, but also on the nature of the flow past the body. When a fluid flows past a streamlined body, as happens during the body's motion through the water, the particles of the fluid in the immediate vicinity of the body are held on to it and retarded in their original motion. The fluid layers lying farther and farther away from the body are retarded less and less until we reach the region of steady flow. If the drag on the particles nearest the body is small, the outer layers execute a gliding motion over one another, and we speak of *laminar flow*. However, if the drag becomes too great, the innermost particles are so slowed down that they no longer glide within the outer layers. Their velocity is then called the critical velocity, at which laminar flow changes into *turbulent flow*, and eddies are formed. Now turbulent flow of the medium greatly impedes the motion of the body placed within it. The nearer to the front of the body the source of the turbulence, the greater the adverse effect.

So much for resistance. We cannot solve the question of how much power a whale must develop to overcome this resistance until we have learned that the amount of work a single muscle fibre of given length and thickness can do is by and large the same for all healthy animals. Thus if we know the power of one animal, we can calculate the power of another from its total muscle fibre, though other factors must also be taken into consideration. Luckily, the effect of these factors can be determined from a formula, and so, once we know the work a man can do – and man has, after all, been studied more extensively than any other animal – it is easy to determine what work a whale or dolphin can do, also.

Now, scientists, and particularly Prof. Gray and A. V. Hill, have calculated that a dolphin making 15 knots must develop 0·235 h.p. to overcome the resistance of the water. This is the same amount a man of equal weight must develop in order to climb a mountain at the rate of 5 m.p.h. Most men would boggle at this task, though it is by no means beyond the realms of human endeavour – a trained athlete can develop as much as 0·35 h.p. Thus the dolphin is by no means an unusual animal in that respect provided – and this is an extremely important stipulation – we have been right in assuming that the flow along the entire body is laminar. If the flow is turbulent, 1·7 h.p. would be needed, i.e. roughly seven times as much. To equal this, man would have to climb the mountain at a rate of well over 30 m.p.h., and the dolphin would have to have about seven times the amount of muscle fibre it does in fact possess. Hence it follows that the flow past its body must be laminar.

If we make similar calculations for, say, the Blue Whale, we find that, in order to make 15 knots, the animal must develop 10 h.p. in laminar and 168 h.p. in turbulent flow. From the weight of its muscles it appears that it can probably develop up to 62 h.p., which enables the animal –as reliable sources tell us – to pull a catcher boat behind it at a rate of 4–7 knots, even though the boat itself is pulling in the opposite direction.

Sixty-two h.p. would in fact be required of the animal if we assume, for instance, that the flow is laminar along the first two-thirds, and turbulent along the last third of the body.

The reader might wonder with what right we assume that the flow is laminar in the case of dolphins and only partly laminar in the case of Blue Whales. Now, in the same way that the flow past a ship can be determined by experiments with laboratory models, experiments have in fact also been carried out with models of Cetaceans and fishes. It appeared that the resistance of the water was so great that the only explanation seemed to be turbulent flow along the entire body. Our theoretical picture would have had to be discarded completely, were it not for the fact that there are tremendous differences between rigid models and flexible living animals. It is by no means impossible that it is precisely the powerful flexions of the abdomen and tail which cause the flow to become laminar. So far no methods have been found to determine the nature of the flow along living fish or dolphins, but Prof. Gray of Cambridge has constructed a model of a dolphin using very flexible material, and though he could not establish that the flow was laminar, he showed, in any case, that it differed radically from the flow past a rigid model.

Another possible explanation is that the laminar flow may be connected with the way in which the epidermis of the Cetaceans is attached to the underlying layer of blubber (see also Chapter 11). Technicians in the U.S.A. have constructed some models with the aid of a silica-gel, but definite results are not yet available.

G. A. Steven, a biologist attached to the Marine Biological Station in Plymouth, who served in the Royal Navy during the Second World War, one evening saw a number of seals and dolphins swimming about in the phosphorescent sea. Countless phosphorescent unicellular organisms gave him a clear picture of the flow, just as aluminium powder sprinkled on water gives experimenters a clear picture of currents in the laboratory. Steven saw that the dolphins produced two straight glowing lines as they swam through the sea, while the seals caused a great deal of turbulence – just one more bit of circumstantial evidence in favour of our assumption.

The difference between whales and dolphins is primarily due to their difference in length – the longer the body the greater the turbulence, and the farther back the maximum girth the smaller the disturbance. We have already seen in Fig. 41 that dolphins have their maximum dimensions much farther back than Rorquals. Apart from the other explanations, the difference between whales and dolphins may also be ascribed, at least partly, to the fact that the structure of the spinal musculature in dolphins shows a higher degree of efficiency than in whales (see page 109). Though this, too, is circumstantial evidence, we see that scientists have begun to approach the solution to the mystery of the speed of whales and particularly of dolphins. As investigations continue, more and more evidence will no doubt come to light, and this evidence will probably be applied to improving the construction and speed of ships, and especially of submarines. May I express the hope that by the time such improvements are made, there will no longer be any need for military measures, and also that faster and better ships will not mean a more extensive persecution of whales and dolphins. It would be very tragic, indeed, if these animals were made to suffer for the knowledge they have imparted to us.

4

Respiration

THOSE OF US who have been fortunate enough to go on an ocean cruise may have come across the impressive sight of a blowing whale. On the monotonous stretches between Las Palmas and Cape Town or between Aden and Colombo, this spectacle is a particularly welcome distraction, and passengers will drop their pastimes and climb up to the highest deck for a good look at the jets of vapour which the whale emits at regular intervals (Fig. 68). These jets are highly reminiscent of geysers, with which most of us are familiar from films or our school geography books. The vapour hovers in the air for a few seconds before it disperses, and then the spectators wait for a repeat performance. Watches are consulted, and it emerges that it takes about one minute before the next jet shoots up.

Up on the bridge, they have, of course, spotted the whale long before, and probably altered course to give the passengers a better view of this spectacle. Moreover, if the liner belongs to one of the big whaling nations, the officers themselves probably have an interest in reporting their observations to the competent authorities. Thus some British ships send their reports to the National Institute of Oceanography in Wormley, Dutch ships to the Netherlands Whale Research Group in Amsterdam, etc., and we shall see later why these reports are important. Meanwhile we shall merely point out that the type, shape and direction of the jet – the blow or *blåst* as it is called in whaling circles – are important means of identifying the species.

In this, the height of the blow is probably the least reliable pointer, not only because a great deal of experience is needed to judge it accurately, but also because it depends largely on the size of the individual whale. Adult Greenland and Biscayan Whales have blows from 10–13 feet high, and the figures for other whales are: Grey, 10 feet; Blue, 20 feet; Fin, 13–20 feet; Sei, 6–8 feet; Humpback, 6 feet; Little Piked Whale, 3 feet; Sperm Whale, 16–25 feet; Bottlenose Whale and Beluga, 3 feet.

Figure 68. The blow of the Sei Whale. (Andrews, 1916.)

Figure 69. Various surface views of the Southern Right Whale. (Matthews, 1938.)

The remaining Odontocetes emit vague blows which only last for a moment.

Whereas the contours of the blows of Bottlenose and Little Piked whales are also somewhat vague, the shape of other blows during calm spells is an excellent indication of the species (Fig. 56). Right Whales have a double V-shaped blow and can therefore be easily distinguished from Rorquals which have a single blow (Fig. 69). Californian Grey Whales, which are an intermediate species in respect of many characteristics, sometimes have a double and sometimes a single blow. The blow of all Rorquals is single and vertical, and the individual species cannot easily be distinguished by it (Fig. 56). However, the Blue Whale has a high and often pear-shaped blow that gets progressively broader towards the top while the blow of Fin and Sei whales is shorter and less conical. The blow of the Humpback is shorter still and more pronouncedly pear-shaped. Even so, none of these differences are very clear-cut, and even experienced gunners often confuse the blows of Rorquals, particularly on windy days. Identification is easier in the case of Sperm Whales whose pear-shaped blows emerge at an angle of about 45° from the left side of the tip of the head, instead of from the top (Fig. 70). On fairly calm days, therefore, identification is very easy, but on stormy days even the Sperm Whale may be confused with a Rorqual whose blow may appear oblique in the wind (Fig. 71). The Sperm Whale's blow is, by the way, much longer than it looks, because its oblique direction has a misleading optical effect.

If the ship sails up close enough, we may even see the blowhole of our whale, as it is likely to be quite unafraid of the ship, diving playfully beneath it. When it surfaces to exhale in a shrill vibrato, we catch our first glimpse of the blowhole opening (Figs. 72 and 73). We may also hear

a much gentler inhalation before it closes the blowhole and dives down
once more. The huge back with its small dorsal fin comes up for a
moment (Figs. 3 and 55), the impressive flukes, gleaming white beneath
and black on top, wave through the air, and then the whale is gone, almost
straight down. The flukes tell us that we have just seen a Humpback
Whale, for other Rorquals rarely bring their flukes up out of the water.

We might have gathered this from the shrill vibrato of its blow alone,
for other Rorquals produce a deep lowing noise, while dolphins and
porpoises emit 'sighs'. On a still summer evening these sighs can often be
heard from many North Sea piers, and holiday-makers rarely forget this
weird sound. But to return to our Humpback. From the fact that its flukes
came up, we can tell that its dive will be long and deep, and that the
animal will be submerged for the next 10–15 minutes. Our ship resumes
its original course, and the passengers return to their interrupted pastimes,
unless some of them are interested enough to wonder what really happens
when a whale blows. Clearly, it is a form of respiration since, being
mammals, whales must replenish the air in their lungs above the surface.
This is rather unfortunate for them, for if they had gills instead of lungs
they would be almost safe from human pursuit.

Though it was formerly thought that whales blew water, our own eyes
have shown us that this is not so. We have seen that the nostrils – the blowhole – do not open until they break surface and we know that what
emerged from them was condensed vapour, just like our own breath on a
cold winter's day. Vapour appears whenever breath is cooled suddenly,
and hence the whale's blow is particularly distinct in polar seas, though,
as we have seen, it appears in the tropics also, and Layne reports that even
in the heat of the Upper Amazon, the Boutu's blow can be seen to a height
of 6 feet.

The explanation is therefore not so much the climate, as the fact that

Figure 70. J. Stel's drawings of two Sperm Whales seen from S.S. Breda *off S. America
on 31st May and 2nd July, 1955.*

Figure 71. Blow of the Sei Whale bent forward by the wind. (Andrews, 1936.)

Figure 72. Humpback surfacing and blowing. Photograph by W. H. Dawbin, Sydney.

Figure 73. Humpback inhaling. Note that the blowhole is wide open.
Photograph: W. H. Dawbin, Sydney.

whenever a gas escapes under pressure, it becomes cooled. We all remember from our elementary science lessons that when a gas expands it loses heat, and from the way the whale whistled when it blew, we could tell that the air was being forced through a narrow opening under great pressure, subsequently to undergo great expansion outside. It is here that the moisture (which is present in all exhalations) condenses by cooling and turns into the small visible drops that constitute the blow. This explanation is confirmed by an observation of Gilmore (1960): when California Grey Whales exhale very slowly, the blow is hardly visible.

Recently, F. C. Fraser and P. E. Purves, both of the Natural History Museum in London, offered a new explanation of the blow. In the trachea of all Cetaceans there is a foamy substance, which is also present in the bronchi of rabbits. Moreover, the wall of the auditory air sacs (see Chapter 7) produces foam in its large glands. The authors claim that the foam has a strong affinity for nitrogen. We shall return to this question later, and meanwhile note that Fraser and Purves believe that during every blow large quantities of this substance are exhaled and that it is droplets of foamy mucus which we see as the blow. However, as long as we do not know whether in fact such large quantities of mucus are produced, and until the foam has actually been isolated in the blow itself, it would be safer to work on the orthodox explanation, though it is quite possible that even very small quantities of mucus may act as condensation nuclei, in much the same way that impurities in the air cause London fog.

So much for the blow. What of the dive? We might have wondered how deep the animals go down, and why they 'sound' in the first place. William Scoresby studied this problem during the nineteenth century, and by running out a harpoon line he concluded that the whale could dive to a depth of more than 50 fathoms, and modern whalers would agree with him. The harpoon lines, of which every catcher boat carries two, are as a rule 1 km (3,280 feet) long, to allow for the fact that trapped whales never dive down vertically but try to get as far away from the boat as possible. Moreover, the line must be paid out carefully if it is not to break.

For more precise information we must turn to P. F. Scholander, a Norwegian physiologist. In 1940, working from Steinshamn, a Norwegian whaling station, he attached manometers to harpoons used for shooting Fin Whales, and from their maximum pressure determined the maximum depth. Discarding data of whales which came up dead, he found figures of 46, 57, 74, 126 and 194 fathoms. (The record for a skin diver is about 60 fathoms.) Experts, however, think that uninjured whales do not usually descend to more than about 25–50 fathoms, though, if need be, they can dive down 200–250 fathoms without any adverse effects, for some of Scholander's Whales continued to behave quite normally and had to be finished off with a second harpoon. Actually most animals are capable of exceptional spurts of effort when they are under stress. Thus a normally placid Zebu cow is capable of clearing a 6-foot hedge from a standing start, and captive animals have often astonished spectators in zoological gardens by their unsuspected athletic prowess.

Even so, it seems odd that Rorquals should want to go down to a depth of 50 fathoms, when *krill*, their main food, is predominantly found in the first 5 fathoms of the sea. This was established by the very comprehensive investigations carried out by J. W. S. Marr (National Institute of Oceanography, Wormley) who showed that, though krill can be found as deep as 500 fathoms, it is most highly concentrated near the top. However, Rorquals, like humans, may grow tired of their monotonous diet, and since it is known that their food is not exclusively restricted to krill, this may well be the explanation for their deep dive.

Much more is known about the feeding habits of Sperm and Bottlenose Whales. These animals feed principally on cuttlefish, different species of which occur at certain fixed depths. From undigested parts of such cuttlefish in the stomachs of dead Sperm and Bottlenose Whales, we can state with certainty that these animals regularly dive down to 250 fathoms, and probably much deeper also. Thus, in 1932, the crew of the cable-ship *All America*, which was plying between Balboa and Esmeralda (Ecuador) discovered that almost 200 feet of submarine telephone cable was twisted round the skeleton of a Sperm Whale, which had probably been trapped. The first mate stated that part of the cable had caught in the jaw, and the rest had twisted round the tail. Now, since the cable was 500 fathoms below the surface, it seems clear that the whale must have dived to that depth. Altogether, thirteen similar cases have been reported – eight off the American Pacific coast between 13° N and 13° S; one off Nova Scotia; one in the Persian Gulf; one off Cape Frio (Brazil); and two elsewhere off the coasts of South America. In six of these cases, the cable was 450 fathoms deep, and in the rest 50–175 fathoms. Some of the cables had snapped and, during repairs, recently killed Sperm Whales had to be disentangled. A similar fate also befell a Humpback Whale off Alaska, but at a depth of only 60 fathoms.

Little is known about the depths to which other Odontocetes can descend, though it is thought that they do not make very deep dives. Scholander measured the dive of a porpoise by attaching a harness to it, and found that the animal did not go lower than 10 fathoms, slightly less than pearl and sponge divers who usually keep to within 15 fathoms. Otoliths of fishes found in the stomachs of Bottlenose Dolphins off the West African coast (Dakar) show that these animals dive to depths of at least 11 fathoms (Cadenat, 1959). Sea otters usually stay within 10 fathoms of the surface, while different species of seal are said to descend to 40, 50, and 140 fathoms and thus to rival the performance of some of the big whales.

What is involved in deep diving, you might wonder? First of all, of course, the ability to hold the breath while submerged, and secondly immunity to great pressures. With every 5 fathoms from the surface, the pressure of the water increases by about one atmosphere, and a descent to 250 fathoms therefore means that the body has to withstand a pressure of 50 atmospheres. Our Sperm Whale at 500 fathoms must therefore have wrestled for its life under a pressure of 100 atmospheres.

But this is by no means as astonishing a feat as we might be inclined to think, since living matter is largely made up of water, and water is practically incompressible in our bodies. The only thing that is easily compressed is, in fact, the air in the lungs, whose pressure consequently increases until it equals that of the water outside. Now if the external pressure becomes too great and exceeds the contractibility of the thorax, there is great danger of breaking a few ribs. In Cetaceans this critical depth is estimated to be about 50 fathoms, based on the fact that the volume of air in their lungs can be compressed to about $\frac{1}{10}$ (cf. Fig. 75). Hence it was formerly thought that at greater depths their ribs would in fact crack. As evidence for this mishap, Buchanan (1910) cited the case of a Fin Whale skeleton in the Monaco Museum, whose ribs showed clear evidence of having been broken. Actually, a fight with another Fin Whale is a far better explanation, for, as we now know, whales have emerged quite sound from much greater depths. Obviously, the ribs can withstand fairly high pressure differences. We know that the air bladders of fish are provided with special glands for increasing the quantity of gas in them, and fish can therefore maintain the bladders at a pressure equal to that of the water outside. Whales, however, are not fish and have no glands for producing air in their lungs, and so the only thing they can do is take in as little air as possible before they dive to great depths. The less air there is in the lungs, the less danger from the consequences of its compression.

But does not a diver gulp in as much air as he can before he dives, so as to remain submerged for as long as possible? We have already seen that whales can stay under water for a very long time, and we would therefore expect them to take down with them large quantities of air, which as we know would prove fatal. How has nature resolved this problem?

Before we can answer this question, we must first find out for how long the animals do in fact remain submerged, and how often they have to come up for air after deep diving. Unfortunately, not enough is known about their respiratory rhythm. Accounts of observations are scarce and, particularly in dolphins, most of the evidence is contradictory – the direct result of the conditions under which the observations were made. When a whale is being hunted and makes great efforts to elude its pursuers, it begins to 'pant' in the same way that, say, a hunted stag breathes twice as quickly as a walking stag. The rate of respiration of a cow increases by 50 per cent even when it is merely ruminating. No wonder then, that Caldwell noted that Spotted Dolphins in the Gulf of Mexico came up for air 6–12 times a minute when they swam fast as against 0·5–1 times a minute when they swam slowly.

It is, moreover, obvious that the respiratory rhythm after deep diving must be different from that during slow swimming or dozing at the surface. Sperm Whales are known to be capable of staying underwater for more than an hour, subsequently to come up looking quite exhausted. They regain their breath by staying just beneath the surface of the water for some time and by coming up for air roughly six times per minute. Normally swimming Sperm Whales do not pant, and the officer commanding the watch on the *Piet Hein* (Royal Dutch Navy) recorded

Figure 74. *Respiratory frequency in different Cetacea. The crests represent respiratory movements at the surface, the troughs represent dives. The horizontal axis represents time. 1. Sperm Whale diving deeply; 2. Sperm Whale swimming quietly at the surface; 3. Fin Whale diving from 10-15 minutes; 4. Dolphin, diving occasionally.*

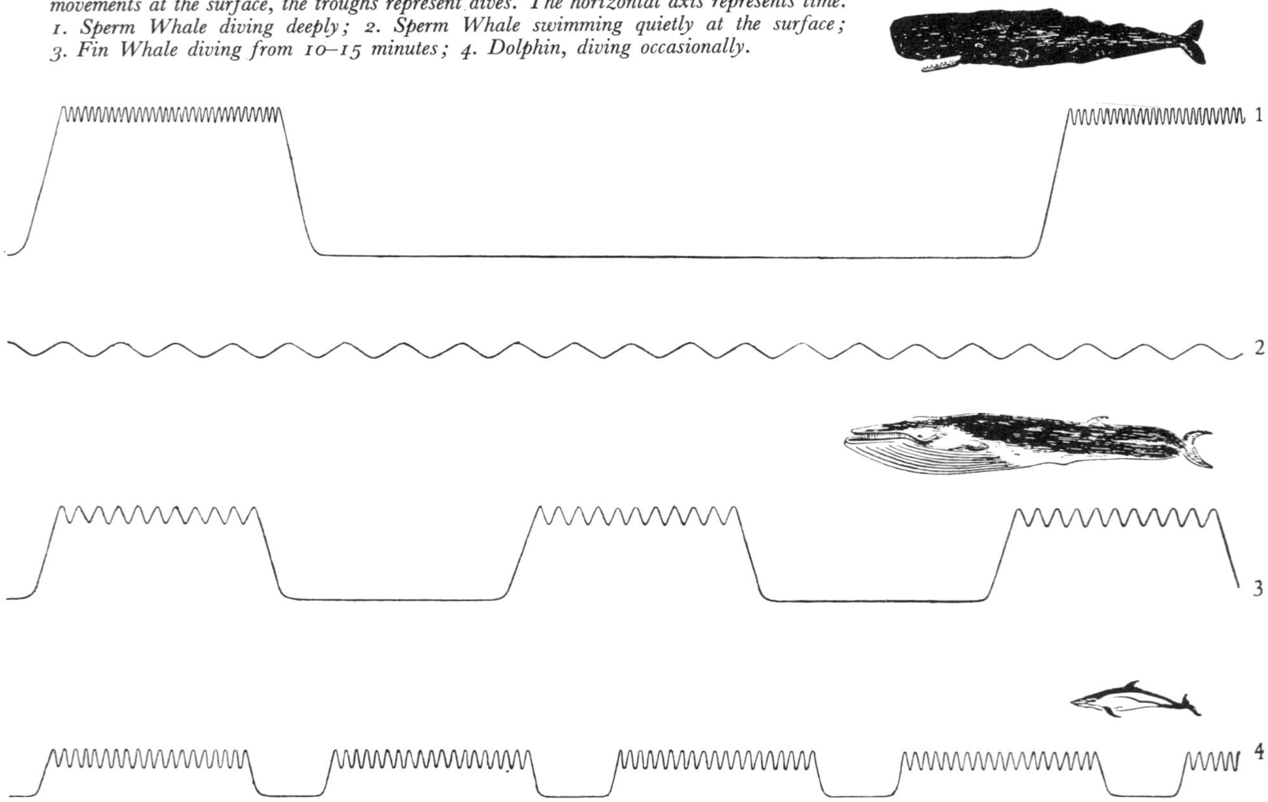

that on crossing the equator on 7th July, 1955, at 130° E, he observed a Sperm Whale peacefully swimming at the surface and blowing every two or three minutes. Clearly, after a deep dive, breathing may increase to up to fifteen times the normal rate.

Basing our case on what few data we have, we may say that, by and large, three types of respiration can be distinguished in Cetaceans, based on the length of their respective dives. The first group includes such deep-sea divers as Sperm Whales and Bottlenose Whales, which have been reliably reported to be capable of staying under for as much as 90 and 120 minutes respectively. But then, these are record performances. Normally, the animals dive for 50 minutes, and then stay at the surface roughly 10 minutes to take about six breaths per minute before they dive down again (Fig. 74). It is quite possible that Cuvier's Dolphin, which is very closely related to the Bottlenose Whale, belongs to this same group, but what data we have on it require further checking.

Right Whales and Rorquals represent the second type of respiration. The Greenland Whale is reported to stay submerged for up to 60 minutes, and Rorquals for up to about 40 minutes. Clark cites the case of a Fin Whale that became enmeshed in a drag-net cable off Cape Cod on 8th April, 1958. The animal struggled furiously to get out but died after 30 minutes. Had it not been fighting for its life, it would probably have been able to stay submerged for at least another 10 minutes. Animals in this second group usually remain underwater for 10–15 minutes, coming up for 5–10 minutes at a time. At the surface they take about 5–20 breaths, with an average of one breath per minute. Frequently, however, they dive for only 4–7 minutes, the difference in time depending on their agility or possibly on their method of feeding. Chittleborough (1956) noted that Southern Right Whales dive for 2–3 minutes and then come up for 8–9 minutes, blowing 6–9 times during that period. If Fin Whales are chased by a catcher, they may come up every 70 seconds. This may be called panting (van Utrecht).

The third group is made up of dolphins and porpoises which do not descend to very great depths. They usually dive for up to about 5 minutes, and surface to blow up to six times per minute. However, when they swim near the surface, they can manage with only two breaths per minute. Kleinenberg (1956) noted that Common Dolphins in the Black Sea dive for $1\frac{1}{2}$–3 minutes,[1] porpoises from 4–6 minutes and Bottlenose Dolphins (which find their food in lower regions of the sea) for 13–15 minutes. A 15–minute dive by Belugas was noted by Vladykov.

If we compare these figures with those for other mammals, we discover

[1] According to Tomilin (1948), these animals die when their breathing is impeded for more than 5 minutes.

that Cetaceans are by far the best divers. A dog dies if it is kept underwater for more than 4 minutes, cats and rabbits die after 3 minutes, and
normal human beings do not last for more than one minute, though
experienced sponge and pearl divers can stay submerged for up to $2\frac{1}{2}$
minutes. Aquatic mammals are, of course, far better adapted to underwater life. Thus, the hippopotamus can remain underwater for up to
15 minutes; the beaver for up to 20; the muskrat for up to 12; the platypus
for up to 10; and the sea-cow for up to 16, while the figures for sea-otters
and polar bears are only 5 and $1\frac{1}{2}$ minutes respectively. Seals and sea-
lions can dive for 5–15 minutes, i.e. considerably longer than porpoises
or Common Dolphins. Even so, we may say of Cetaceans in general that
they excel over terrestrial mammals in their ability to hold their breath.

What of this respiratory frequency? Here comparisons are not so straightforward, since this is largely determined by body size. The number of
breaths per minute is roughly 100 in mice and rats, 70 in squirrels, 58 in
rabbits, 35 in cats, 20 in dogs, 16 in men, 10 in lions, 7 in bisons, and 6
in elephants. On closer investigation it would appear that the number of
breaths per minute is a function of the ratio of surface area to lung
capacity. This is quite logical since oxygen needs depend on the rate of
combustion. Now, since combustion serves, *inter alia*, for compensating
heat losses, and since animals lose heat primarily through their skin, the
greater the surface area, the greater the demand for oxygen. Now, with
diminishing body size, the surface area decreases proportionally to the
square, while the capacity of the lungs (which have to provide the
oxygen) decreases proportionally to the cube, of the decrease in total size.

Do Cetaceans fit into this picture? In other words, is their respiratory
frequency regulated by their size to the extent that it is in other mammals?
In considering this question, we must, of course, ignore 'panting' and
consider normal breathing alone. Thus the Sperm Whale's rate of six
breaths per minute between deep dives is exceptional, and we must
consider instead its *total* respiration, diving and surfacing included. If
we do so, we shall find that the animal takes only one breath per minute.
Now these figures are precisely what we would expect judging from the
animal's size, and so are the figures for Rorquals and Right Whales.

Things are, however, different with dolphins, whose overall respiratory
frequency is about 1–6 breaths per minute, and 3–8 breaths per minute
between dives. Comparing these figures with those for terrestrial mammals
of corresponding weight (150–400 lb.), e.g. bears, stags, pigs, antelopes,
sheep, and men who breathe 14–16 times per minute, we find that
dolphins have an exceptionally low respiratory frequency, the more so
since the figures for terrestrial mammals refer to normal breathing, while
those for dolphins refer to animals in motion and sometimes in very quick

motion. Admittedly, the relatively small surface area of dolphins is part of the explanation, but it is by no means the whole story, which can only be told after we have taken a closer look at the Cetacean lung.

A mere comparison of its weight with that of the lungs of other mammals would tell us very little; far more relevant is a comparison of the respective lung-to-body weight ratios. Unfortunately, the measurements involved are hard to come by. The lungs of a Blue Whale can weigh up to a ton, and the animal itself more than 100 tons. For accurate measurements, the whole animal must first be cut up carefully, and this involves much time and labour. Since whalers have little time to spare for such tasks, most measurements have been carried out at land stations, where the men are not in quite so great a hurry. Even so, it is astonishing that enough time has been found to weigh as many as forty-six big whales to date. The record is held by a Blue Whale, weighed by Winston in 1950. The animal tipped the scales at 134·25 tons. Captain Sørlle measured the runner-up in 1926 at South Georgia: a Blue Whale weighing 122 tons. The Japanese have done a great deal of work in this field, in order to be able to establish an average weight. In 1950, Omura weighed 16 Sei Whales and 10 Sperm Whales, and in 1956, Fujino weighed another 15 Sei Whales in another area. Much of our knowledge is also due to the work of G. Crile, an investigator who devoted a good deal of time to weighing the organs of many wild animals. The figures he obtained are much more valuable for our purpose than the available wealth of data on captive animals. It is thanks to Crile that we have what little information there is on the weight of the dolphin's organs, though the Dutch whaling-research group of the TNO organization has recently begun to do field work in this sphere.

From the available data, it would appear that the lungs of terrestrial mammals represent 1–2 per cent of the total body weight, while the figures for Rorquals, Sperm Whales, Pigmy Sperm Whales and Bottlenose Whales are only 0·6–0·9 per cent. In dolphins and porpoises, however, the figures are 1–6 per cent, the average being 3·5 per cent. The great differences between various dolphins are associated with the respective duration of their dives. Thus the Bottlenose Dolphin which dives for longer periods than the Common Dolphin also has bigger lungs. Porpoises, according to Kleinenberg, fall half-way between the two, while the figures for beavers, muskrats and seals would seem to resemble those for terrestrial mammals.

Now, while the relative weight of the lungs is an important indication, what is even more important is relative lung-capacity, i.e. the amount of air that can be stored up in the lungs, and also the amount of tidal air, i.e. the air inhaled and exhaled with every normal breath. However, it is by no means the easiest of experimental tasks to establish these figures. Nevertheless, as early as 1873, Jolyet carried out such experiments with a Bottlenose Dolphin kept at the Biological Research Institute at Arcachon (France). The animal was so tame that it did not object to swimming about with a bag over its blowhole. The bag was connected by a tube to a spirometer, an instrument for determining both the volume and composition of exhaled air. Other investigators have tried to solve the problem in their own ways, but pride of place must be given to the Norwegian physiologist P. F. Scholander, who based his investigations on the work of L. Irving of Swarthmore College (Pennsylvania). Irving had previously investigated the respiration of ducks, beavers and muskrats, and Scholander decided to apply the same methods to porpoises and seals. Unfortunately, his experimental subjects proved less tractable than Jolyet's dolphin, and he was forced to tie them up in a tub, and to simulate diving by alternatively raising and lowering the water level. Despite this handicap, Scholander's investigations proved so fruitful that, in 1938, he was awarded a Rockefeller grant to work under Irving in Swarthmore. Their collaboration has produced many important results, particularly on the respiration of Bottlenose Dolphins and sea-cows.

It appeared that the estimates of lung capacity calculated from the animals' lung-to-body weight ratio was substantially correct. The lungs of a 70-foot Fin Whale were found to have a maximum capacity of 2,000 litres of air, and those of an 18-foot Bottlenose Whale and a young porpoise of 40 and 1·4 litres respectively. By comparison, the lung of man has a maximum capacity of 5, and the lung of a horse a maximum capacity of 42 litres. If we refer these figures to body weight, it appears that the lung capacity of Bottlenose Dolphins and porpoises is roughly one-and-a-half times that of terrestrial mammals, while that of Rorquals, Sperm Whales and Bottlenose Whales is only about half that of their relatives on land. Seals and sea-cows were found to have approximately the same lung capacity as terrestrial mammals.

We have learned why deep divers must take down a minimum of air, while those which stay submerged for long periods but remain close to the surface can take down a large volume of air. In this connexion we might well ask whether, irrespective of their lung *capacity*, the animals completely fill their lungs before diving. Now, while Grey Seals and sea-elephants are known to make a point of exhaling before they dive, Cetaceans do the reverse and Scholander gained the clear impression that they fill their lungs to capacity.

That being the case, we might wonder why Rorquals and Sperm Whales with their relatively small lungs do not breathe more frequently than terrestrial mammals and why the respiratory rate of dolphins is so much lower still. The answer is that the respiration of terrestrial mammals is generally very shallow. Take our own lungs, for example. Their maximum capacity is 5 litres of air, but they generally contain no more than 2·5 litres, i.e. they are only half-filled. Nor do we inhale and exhale even that smaller amount for, with normal exhalation, 2 litres of air are left in the lungs, and only if we breathe out as hard as we can is the residue reduced to one litre. Our thorax, which protects the lungs, is so constructed that only if we drill a hole into it can we get rid of more air still. Even if the lungs are completely collapsed about 300 c.c. of residual air are left in them. We shall have to return to this subject, and meanwhile note the fact that man inhales and exhales no more than half a litre of air with every breath, while his lungs are capable of taking in 4 litres at a time.

Cetaceans, on the other hand, particularly when they dive regularly, fill their lungs to capacity and, moreover, change 80–90 per cent of their supply with every breath, unlike terrestrial mammals for which the corresponding figures are 10–15 per cent (Fig. 75). The difference is due not only to the fact that Cetaceans expand and contract their thorax to the maximum, but also because that maximum happens to be 10 per cent greater than it is in terrestrial mammals – so much so that their relative volume of residual air is only half that of the latter. This was discovered when, by drilling a hole into the thorax of a dead Bottlenose Dolphin, it appeared that far less air escaped, i.e. that the lungs were less collapsible than those of, say, dogs or horses, for the very good reason that most of the air had been expelled during exhalation. Even so, some residual air there certainly is, as is proved conclusively by the fact that the lungs float when they are thrown into the water.

Possibly, whales and dolphins swimming quickly near the surface do not breathe as deeply as they do during diving, but divers certainly make up for their small lung capacity or their small respiratory frequency by inhaling and exhaling as much air as they can. As a result, they may be said to have no means of taking in special quantities of air when special emergencies arise. Man, if need be, can breathe more deeply than he normally does, but these animals, whose lungs as we have seen are already filled to capacity, can get more air only by increasing the frequency of respiration. In other words, they must surface more frequently, and this fact is used by modern whalers who no longer trail the whales, but chase them with very fast corvettes. The speed of the hunt is such that the poor beasts are forced up to the surface much more often than usual, thus presenting the gunners with excellent targets.

We must now ask ourselves whether deep breathing really has the same effect as shallow breathing with greater lung capacity or a faster respiratory rate. Obviously, Cetaceans take down adequate supplies of oxygen, for

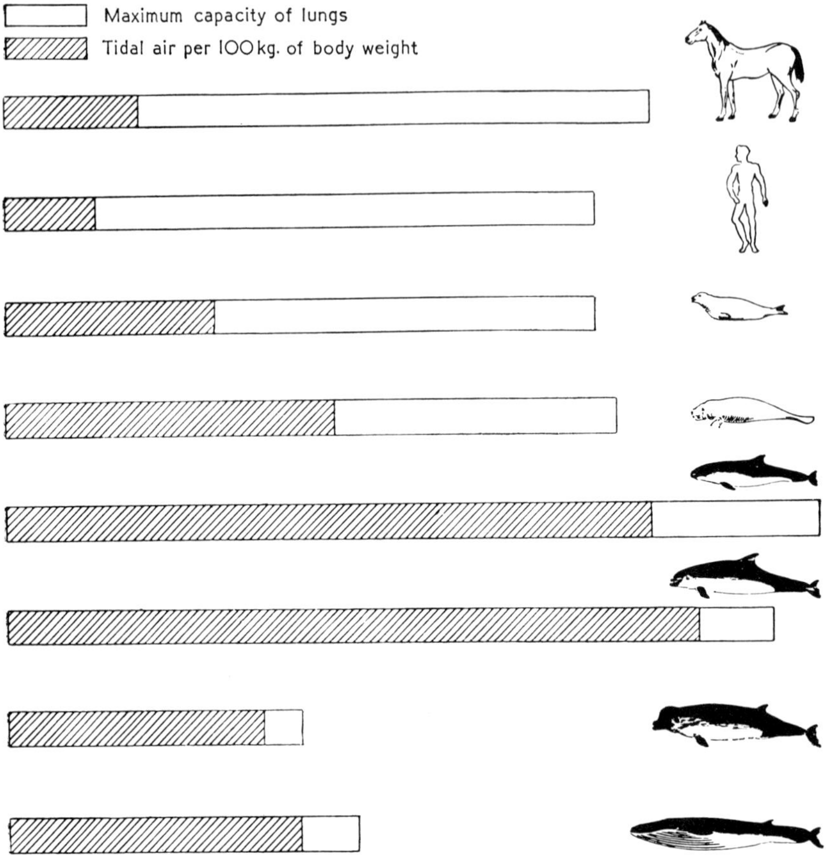

Figure 75. Maximum capacity of lungs and tidal air per 100 kilograms of body weight in a horse, a man, a seal, a sea-cow, a porpoise, a Bottlenose Dolphin, a Bottlenose Whale, and a Rorqual. After data by Scholander and Irving.

otherwise they would perish, and the only question is how they get it. It would appear that their method of respiration alone cannot supply the required amount, for calculations have shown that, weight for weight, about half as much air is contained in the lungs of Cetaceans as in those of terrestrial mammals, while other calculations have shown that the amount of oxygen Cetaceans use up in equal time is roughly the same. Hence Cetaceans must have some special means of utilizing twice as much oxygen from a given volume of air, and the only way in which they can do so is by having blood that is adapted to this situation. In fact, the total surface of their red blood corpuscles is very large, and it is here that we must seek the key to our mystery. In Chapter 5 we shall return to this subject in greater detail.

However, we have still not answered the question of how these animals, using half the amount of air that we do, bulk for bulk, can yet stay submerged 5–15 times longer than most terrestrial mammals, even allowing for the fact that they can derive twice as much oxygen from the air. The answer is simply that the lungs are not the only parts of the body in which oxygen reserves can be stored. If we take a few deep breaths before diving, some of the oxygen combines with the haemoglobin in our blood and some with the myoglobin in our muscles, while further small quantities are stored in other tissues. Of the total quantity of oxygen which a human diver takes down with him 34 per cent is found in the lungs, 41 per cent in the blood, 13 per cent in the muscle and 12 per cent in other tissues. In diving whales, these proportions are quite different: their smaller lungs contain only 9 per cent, their blood 41 per cent and their tissues 9 per cent, while 41 per cent of the oxygen is found in the muscles. In other words their smaller lung capacity is compensated for by the enormous oxygen-storing properties of their myoglobin (muscle haemoglobin). Moreover, the proportion of myoglobin in their muscles is far greater than that of terrestrial mammals. Tawara (1951) found that Sei Whales had twice as much and Sperm Whales eight to nine times the amount of myoglobin found in terrestrial mammals. It is, in fact, apparent at first glance that the meat of freshly killed Cetaceans is much darker in colour than beef, and that it is almost black in Sperm Whales and Bottlenose Whales. Since myoglobin is a dark red pigment, this is only to be expected.

A calculation will show that the amount of oxygen which Fin Whales take down with them is roughly 3,350 litres. You might think that is a good deal, but calculations show that, if we assume that their metabolism, i.e. their rate of combustion, is of the same order as that of terrestrial mammals, it is a quantity of air which would enable them to dive for only half their normal time. Hence, not even the large quantities of myoglobin they have provide an adequate explanation for their long stay under water. We have almost run out of explanations – only one remains: a metabolism that differs radically from that of all terrestrial mammals. In Chapter 11 we shall see that while such differences have not been established for the metabolism as a whole, it is quite possible that temporary metabolic changes occur during the process of diving.

Some authors believe that whales require a minimum of energy while submerged, not only because underwater swimming is easier than swimming at the surface, but also because breathing itself takes up energy. However, we now know that only 1–4 per cent of the total metabolism of terrestrial animals is devoted to this purpose, and Irving and Scholander therefore think that, during diving, basic changes in the metabolism must occur particularly in the muscles.

Normally, the chemical processes which supply the necessary energy for muscle contractions, can be divided into two phases. In the first (anaerobic) phase the combustible material (glycogen) is broken down in the muscles into lactic acid without the intervention of oxygen, and in the second (aerobic) phase part of this lactic acid is oxidized, while another part is re-synthesized into glycogen. This, at least, is what happens in theory. Now, Irving and Scholander believe that in a number of animals the anaerobic phase predominates during diving with a consequent saving of oxygen resources. The aerobic phase, however, predominates during surface swimming, when the animals have to take up oxygen with increased intensity. This hypothesis was corroborated by experiments with ducks, rats and seals which showed that during diving the proportion of lactic acid increases considerably in the muscles, but accumulates in the blood shortly after surfacing. From these and other facts which we shall examine more closely in Chapter 5, it has been concluded that during diving the muscles require very little oxygen, and that the blood circulation is switched to the heart and brain instead. Unfortunately, it has not yet been possible to prolong the experimental submersion of Cetaceans sufficiently for a significant amount of lactic acid to accumulate in the blood. Though direct proof is, therefore, still lacking, it seems probable that the secret of the whales' record diving time rests not only in the oxygen reserve in their muscles, but also in the extremely economical use which they make of their oxygen reserves during diving.

In other organs, such as the brain, they are probably unable to effect similar economies, and here oxidization is complete, with the consequent formation of carbon dioxide, and increase of the carbonic acid content of the blood. Now we know that in all mammals, man included, such an increase stimulates the medullary respiratory centres. In the case of man, it means that he cannot hold his breath, which, in skin-divers, would be disastrous, and we are therefore not surprised to learn that the Russian biologist, E. Kreps (1941), came to the conclusion that the central nervous system of diving animals is singularly unresponsive to carbonic acid.

During public discussions of the problem of diving and respiration in whales and dolphins, somebody invariably gets up to ask whether these animals show no signs of caisson sickness – the 'bends'. Whenever men working in diving suits or caissons at great depths are brought to the surface suddenly, they run the risk of paralysis and consequent death. Autopsies will then reveal the presence of bubbles in the heart and in the blood vessels, and particularly in the blood vessels of the lungs. Since these fatal bubbles are generally filled with nitrogen, it is believed that they are due to the fact that air is continuously being pumped into the caisson at the same high pressure as the water outside. At that pressure considerable quantities of the nitrogen in the air of the lungs leak into the blood, from which the gas is liberated in the form of bubbles when the pressure is suddenly decreased as the caisson is pulled up. (Cf. the carbon dioxide bubbles in soda-water bottles when the stopper is taken off.) However, if the caisson is hauled up very slowly, the dissolved nitrogen in the blood has a chance of re-entering the lungs, and there are no adverse effects.

Now, though whales surface very quickly from great depths, no cases of caisson sickness have been reported, and scientists have wondered why. A number of improbable hypotheses were put forward before the simple and obvious solution became generally accepted. Thus, in 1934, *Nature*, the British journal devoted to the natural sciences, gave much space to the discussion of this problem. One author thought that Cetacean lungs became filled with water at great depths, another that all the air was expelled, and a third that the blood circulation to the lungs was cut off. In 1933, Laurie, investigating the blood of whales aboard a whaler, discovered the presence of bacteria which, he thought, could absorb nitrogen, and which he called micro-organisms X. Only two years later, however, he changed his mind and admitted that 'organisms X' were nothing but putrifying agents which do not occur in living whales. Speculation would have remained rife, had not L. Hill (1935) shown that there is a basic difference between diving inside a caisson and diving straight into the water. In a caisson, there is a continuous supply of fresh air and thus also of fresh nitrogen with which the blood can become saturated, while the normal diver takes down a fixed quantity of air so that, despite the high pressure of the water, only a small quantity of nitrogen is available for solution in the blood. The experimental proof of this simple hypothesis was given by Scholander, using frogs (Fig. 76). Two frogs were placed into a vessel of water under a pressure of three atmospheres. While one frog was supplied with air, the other was not. When the pressure was suddenly decreased, the first frog showed clear signs of caisson sickness, and the other behaved quite normally.

While we are on the subject of respiration, we would do well to take a closer look at the lungs

Figure 76. Two frogs in a vessel under high pressure. The frog at the bottom does not suffer caisson effects, while the frog on top does, when pressure is released.

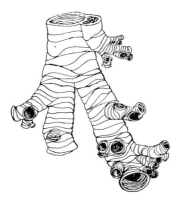

*Figure 77. Dorsal view of the
end of the trachea and bronchi of
a False Killer. Note the
eparterial bronchus.*

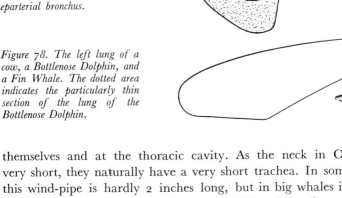

*Figure 78. The left lung of a
cow, a Bottlenose Dolphin, and
a Fin Whale. The dotted area
indicates the particularly thin
section of the lung of the
Bottlenose Dolphin.*

themselves and at the thoracic cavity. As the neck in Cetaceans is
very short, they naturally have a very short trachea. In some dolphins
this wind-pipe is hardly 2 inches long, but in big whales its diameter
can be more than a foot, so that a small child could easily crawl through
it. Still, in view of the whale's size, this is by no means surprising.
It might be thought that a short trachea is a great advantage, since
the more air there is in the trachea, the greater is the dead space in
the pump system. Now, in porpoises the trachea does in fact represent no
more than 4 per cent of the lung capacity, but in Rorquals, with their
small lungs, the dead space represents 8 per cent, just as it does in
terrestrial mammals.

In Cetaceans, the cartilage rings which support the trachea either
surround it completely or else have breaks here and there. Moreover, the
rings are sometimes fused with one another, so that the whole structure
looks more like a pitted cylinder than an annular cartilage system. At the
entrance of the thoracic cavity, the trachea branches into two bronchi,
supplying the left and the right lungs respectively – just as in all other
mammals. In Cetaceans, however, the trachea also divides into a third,

smaller, bronchus (Fig. 77) which supplies the apical part of the right lung. A similar extra bronchus is also to be found in all Artiodactyles (with the exception of the camel and the llama); thus cattle, sheep, deer, and so on, are once again shown to be close relatives of the Cetaceans (see Chapter 2).

In most mammals, the lungs, viewed laterally, look like a triangle with the apex at the under side. Dolphins have retained this triangular shape to some extent, though the ventrally placed apex looks extraordinarily thin and contains a minimum of lung tissue. Most of that tissue is found on the dorsal side of the thoracic cavity, and this phenomenon is even more marked in Bottlenose Whales, Sperm Whales and Rorquals (Fig. 78), whose lungs are long, fairly flat and even more dorsally placed (Fig. 79). Similar lung characteristics are also found in sea-cows, and, although to a lesser extent, in seals and sea-lions, and must clearly be considered adaptations to aquatic stability. We have seen in Chapter 2 that the higher the light, air-filled lungs are placed, and the lower the heavy heart and liver, the greater the animal's stability in the water.

As a consequence, the thorax, too, shows characteristic differences from that of terrestrial mammals. A great many authors, not only of elementary but also of advanced textbooks, have made contradictory statements on this subject, and while I do not wish to take issue with them in detail,

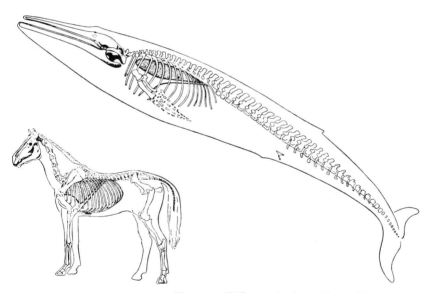

Figure 79. Differences in the position and form of the lungs and the angle of the diaphragm between (a) a Fin Whale and (b) a horse.

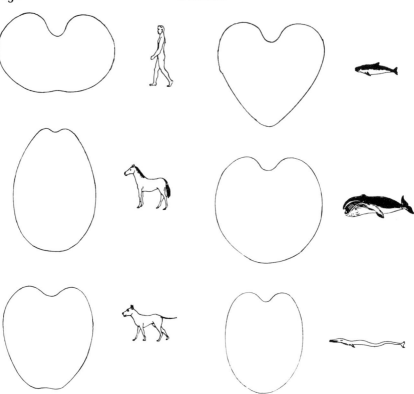

Figure 80. Cross-section of the thorax of three terrestrial mammals (man, horse and dog) contrasted with that of three Cetacea (Porpoise, Greenland Whale and Archaeocete). The figure shows, inter alia, *that the shape of the thorax of Archaeocetes was closest to that of quadrupedal terrestrial mammals. (Slijper, 1936.)*

I should like to draw attention to the fact that the differences between Cetaceans and terrestrial mammals rest mainly on three factors: the peculiar barrel-shape of the Cetacean thorax, the dorsal position of the lungs, and the peculiar angle of the diaphragm. The barrel-shaped thorax (which in terrestrial animals is much narrower in front) is connected with the general stream-lined form of the body in which neck and body have become fused, and with the fact that the fore-limbs, not having to support the body, can be placed more laterally. The dorsal position of the lungs, and also the fact that they thin out towards the ventral side, is, as we have just seen, associated with stability. As a result, the dorsal part of the thorax is wider than the ventral part. (The reverse is true of terrestrial mammals.) In cross-section, the thorax of Odontocetes therefore looks heart-shaped, while that of Mysticetes and Archeocetes is fairly circular. The peculiar slope of the diaphragm (Fig. 79) is a direct consequence of the dorsal position of the lungs. Particularly in Mysticetes, the diaphragm is far more horizontally placed than in terrestrial mammals, and the same is also true of sea-cows. All these factors cause the surface of the lung facing the diaphragm to be much larger than it is in terrestrial mammals, and the diaphragm to play a more important part in breathing than the ribs. This is also borne out by the fact that the diaphragm is relatively large and consists almost exclusively of muscle fibre, a central tendon being absent or rare.

The exceptional development of the diaphragm, its predominant role in breathing, and the dorsal position of the lungs have undoubtedly had an important effect on the structure of the ribs. In Cetaceans, the number of true ribs and false ribs, i.e. those attached to the sternum, is small, while the number of floating ribs is comparatively large. In dolphins, the number of true ribs is 8 to 11 out of a total of 11 to 15, and the last or the last two ribs are frequently not even attached to the vertebrae. Moreover, in dolphins, as in Archaeocetes, the costal cartilages are ossified, but in Sperm Whales and Ziphiids they are cartilaginous and are, moreover, very short, amounting to between 3 and 5 only. In Mysticetes, they are completely absent, all ribs being floating ribs, with the exception of the first which is attached by ligaments to a much-reduced sternum (Fig. 21). In terrestrial mammals, the ribs usually articulate with the vertebrae by capitular and tubercular attachments (heads), and while 10 of the 13 ribs of the oldest Archaeocetes were two-headed, only 7 are so in their youngest representatives. The oldest fossil Mysticetes still had 8 two-headed ribs, but extant species have no more than 3, and the Little

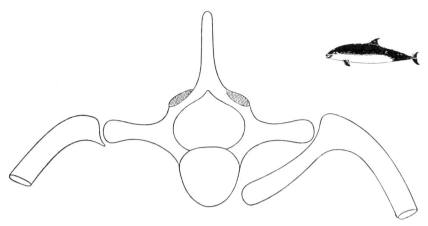

Figure 81. Thoracic vertebra of a Bottlenose Dolphin with (left) a one-headed and (right) a two-headed rib.

Piked Whale has just one. In Odontocetes the number fluctuates between 4 and 8 (Fig. 81).

How all these phenomena have arisen from the fact that, in Cetaceans, the thoracic cavity is expanded primarily from the diaphragm and the dorsal side, still needs to be investigated more closely. What is clear, however, is that the mobility of the thoracic wall has been greatly enhanced by the increase in floating and one-headed ribs. This increase may thus be a form of adaptation to the strong fluctuations in pressure which occur during diving and surfacing and possibly during respiration.

Let us now take another look at Fig. 78, which may already have impressed upon us the great difference between the lungs of Cetaceans and other mammals. The left lungs of most terrestrial mammals have two fairly deep clefts which divide the organ into three lobes, while the right lung is often divided into four. The actual figures vary from mammal to mammal, the greatest number of lobes being found in porcupines which have 10–12 lobes in each lung. While it is not absolutely clear why there are these differences, it is believed that they are connected with the changes of form which the lungs undergo during inflation and collapse, i.e. during respiration. The greater the changes, the greater the number of lobes, and the smoother the action. Now from the very fact that the lungs of Cetaceans have no such clefts, we may deduce that they expand and contract far more evenly and change shape less than those of terrestrial species. (The same kind of undivided lung is also found in sea-cows and seals.)

While the dorsal position and shape of the lungs are thus not so much connected with respiratory processes during diving, they are clearly associated with achieving stability in the water.

Most of us remember from our elementary biology lessons that the lungs not only supply the blood with oxygen, but also remove carbon dioxide from it. To effect this type of gaseous exchange quickly and efficiently, the blood must be brought into close contact with the air, i.e. blood and air must be separated by only the thinnest of membranes. In essence, our lungs are nothing but an enormous ramification of the trachea and the bronchi. Within the lungs each bronchus divides repeatedly into successively thinner tubes, the thinnest of which are no longer supported by cartilage and lack internal ciliated epithelium. Ultimately, the finest tubes pouch out into alveolar sacs with pulmonary alveoli resembling so many bunches of grapes (Fig. 82).

The alveoli are so squashed up against one another that the dividing wall (septum) between any two consists of only two rows of flattened epithelial cells between which there is room for only one thin layer of capillaries (Fig. 84). Hence every capillary obtains its oxygen from two

Figure 82. Highly simplified diagram of the structure of the lung of terrestrial animals. The bronchiole surrounded by cartilage (top) branches into ever finer bronchioles devoid of cartilaginous support, finally to pouch out into the alveolar sacs. The septa between the alveoli are shaded in, and are much thinner than they are shown on the diagram.

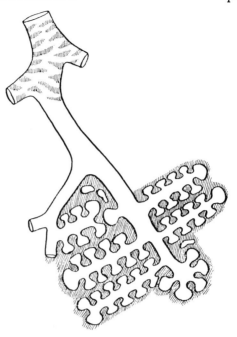

neighbouring alveoli. The capillary wall, just like the wall of the alveoli, is only one layer thick. Moreover, while the cells between capillaries are normal cells whose nuclei can be seen under an ordinary microscope, they are connected to each other by flimsy platelets covering the capillary wall. These platelets can only be seen with an electron microscope. Clearly, the thinnest possible wall divides the air in the alveoli from the blood in the capillaries.

The septa generally widen towards the top, where we find elastic fibres and smooth muscle. Since the smooth muscle is so arranged that it surrounds the opening of the alveolus, it can close this opening by contracting. In the tissue of the septa and also in the alveoli themselves there are large numbers of special cells whose function it is to collect what particles of foreign bodies may have reached them from the outside. In many town-dwellers and in all coal-workers these 'dust cells' are black.

Though scientists first turned their attention to the microscopic structure of Cetacean lungs during the nineteenth century, the first important results were not published until 1914, by Barbosa. In 1916 the German scientist Fiebiger published a further paper, and then came contributions from Neuville, Lacoste and Baudrimont (France), Laurie (Britain), Wislocki and Engel (U.S.A.), Belanger (Canada) and Murata (Japan). It is largely to them that we owe our knowledge of the fine structure of the lungs of twelve different species of Cetaceans and, to some extent at least, of how that structure is adapted to an aquatic form of existence.

One of the first characteristics, little connected with breathing or diving, which struck the investigators, was purely negative, though of positive value to the animals: the complete absence of mucous (goblet) cells in the epithelium of the trachea and the bronchi, and their almost complete absence in the glands terminating in the air passages. Moreover, the bronchioles and other parts of the lung are somewhat deficient in lymphoid tissue, and the trachea is said to be lacking in cilia. Since cilia have, however, been found in the bronchi, their alleged absence in the trachea may have been due to the fact that the histological material examined was poor. Bearing in mind that all the above characteristics are associated with the removal of dust and bacteria from the air passages, and that dust cells have never been discovered in whales or dolphins, it becomes clear that in the clean and moist environment in which these animals live, they can dispense with structures that are essential to animals living in a dry, dusty and germ-ridden atmosphere. Not surprisingly, W. Ross Cockrill, a veterinary surgeon who inspected many thousands of whales in the Antarctic, never once diagnosed an infection of their air passages. (In 1959, pneumonia was first diagnosed in a Fin Whale.) And we, who use up considerable quantities of handkerchiefs, who are plagued by colds and bronchitis, have every reason to be jealous of animals which, according to the Russian biologist Tomilin (1955), are quite unable even to cough. He found that in dolphins the so-called coughing reflex is completely absent, and that water which accidentally finds its way into the air passages is removed during ordinary exhalation. We have, however, seen that the blow of a whale is so intense that it may almost be called a cough.

Another characteristic, on the other hand, is directly associated with diving: the structure of the bronchi. We have already seen that in terrestrial mammals these ramifications of the trachea have cartilage supports at the beginning, but not at their terminal branches. Now in Cetaceans the cartilage, in the form of spirals, rings or irregular pieces, reaches right down to the alveolar sacs. There is only one known exception to this rule, viz. a species of *Berardius*, found off Japan, a relative of the Bottlenose Whale, in which the cartilage support stops higher up.

As a result of this extra support, all the air pipes are provided with a rigid wall which is constantly kept open and hence is far less sensitive to pressure changes than the rest of the lungs. This, as we shall see, is a great advantage, particularly during the strong fluctuations in pressure which occur in the course of vertical dives.

It is also of considerable importance during fluctuations in pressure which take place on respiration at the surface. Man takes about four seconds to breathe in and out normally, during which roughly half a litre of air is displaced. But big Rorquals displace some 1,500 litres of air in 1·5–2 seconds, two-fifths of the time being used for exhalation and three-fifths for inhalation. We have seen under what great pressure the air escapes, and clearly a system of fairly rigid tubes is a great advantage to the pumping action of the thorax. On the other hand, some elasticity is clearly needed, if only for emergencies, and hence, as we have seen, the cartilage support is not uniformly annular and allows for a certain amount of expansion (Fig. 77). Also, the walls of the bronchi are provided with a double system of predominantly longitudinal, elastic fibres, which add extra resilience.

Great quantities of such elastic fibres are also found in the lining (pleura) of the lungs. This is immediately apparent when we look at this organ aboard a whaler, for the lungs have a yellow and crinkly appearance, the colour being due to the fibres, and the crinkles to their contractions. In addition to being found on the walls of the bronchi and the pleura, elastic fibres occur throughout the tissue of the lung, where they are very much more profuse than in terrestrial mammals. By increasing the flexibility of the lungs, great pressure changes can be more easily effected.

The presence in Cetacean tracheas and bronchi of an extensive network of small veins distended with blood is not yet clearly understood, though, apart from warming the air, they may also act as shock absorbers during the violent respiratory movements of Cetaceans. The position of this moist cushion itself seems to make such an assumption probable.

Another phenomenon particularly associated with diving is the presence of a peculiar system of sphincters (valves) in the respiratory bronchioles. Such systems have been found in all dolphins so far investigated, including *Berardius*. The mucous membrane of the bronchi involved is here provided with a succession of annular folds which serve to restrict the diameter of the bronchioles (Fig. 83). Each fold is provided with a layer of smooth muscle, also annular in shape, which is joined by strands of elastic fibre running radially to the cartilage support. It follows that, when the muscles are relaxed, the air passage is kept wide open, and when they contract, the passage narrows. The number of such successive valves varies from 8–12 in the porpoise, and from 25–40 in the Common Dolphin and the Bottlenose Dolphin.

What part do these valves play during diving? As the water pressure mounts, the air in the highly compressible alveoli would normally be squeezed into the incompressible part of the bronchial system. Since it is

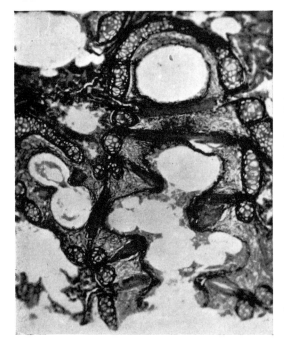

Figure 83. Top: Photograph of a microscopic preparation of the lung of a Bottlenose Dolphin, showing longitudinal-section of bronchiole with cartilage and annular muscles. Photograph: W. L. van Utrecht of a preparation made by Miss J. R. Goudappel, Amsterdam.

Bottom: Longitudinal and cross-section of a bronchiole of a dolphin showing system of annular muscles in the walls. Annular muscle fibres = Af; circular and radial elastic fibres = Ef; cartilage = C, surrounded by longitudinal elastic fibres (Ef).

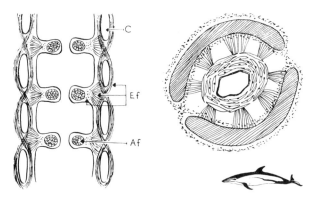

in the alveoli, however, that the air is most needed, as essential gaseous exchanges take place in them, the alveoli must be shut off from the rest of the respiratory system by a kind of tap, or else the animal could not make full use of the air it has taken down.

But why is there a system of successive taps instead of a single one? The best person to answer this question is your plumber, who will tell you straight away that it is unsafe to regulate great water pressures by means of a single stop-cock, as the water would gush out far too forcefully. Only if there is a series of regulating taps can the pressure be adjusted safely and smoothly.

If the animals remain at a given depth, no further great fluctuations in pressure will occur. However, in diving and surfacing there may still be differences in pressure between the soft and hard parts of the lung, and between the soft part of the lung and thorax, with adverse effects on the delicate walls of the alveoli and the capillaries surrounding them. In this case, too, the valves act as essential safeguards.

We have dealt with dolphins and porpoises, and the reader may wonder whether whales which dive so much deeper have a similar mechanism. Oddly enough they have not, or at least not to a significant extent. However, they have a regulating mechanism of their own in the alveolar ducts, i.e. the air pipes going to the alveoli themselves. These fairly wide ducts, which are unsupported by cartilage, can be shut off by powerful annular muscles, and so can each alveolus separately. Now, smooth muscle fibres are also found in the alveolar ducts of all other mammals, in which, however, they are not nearly as strongly developed. The overall effect in whales is probably similar to that of the dolphins' valves, though it must be remembered that deep divers take down far less air than animals which stay closer to the surface.

Until recently little was known about the fine structure of the lungs of Bottlenose Whales. In 1957, however, microscopic investigations carried out by Miss J. R. Goudappel, a student at Amsterdam University,

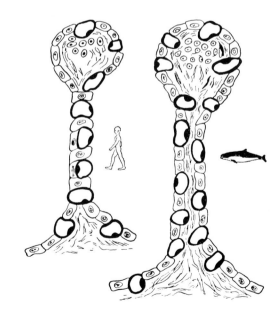

Figure 84. Septum between alveoli in (a) man and (b) a porpoise. Note that the former contains one and the latter two layers of capillaries. At the top of the septum: smooth muscle and elastic fibres.

revealed that these whales also lacked a bronchial valve system. The fact that Bottlenose Whales, Sperm Whales and Rorquals, all of them deep divers, share this characteristic deficiency may well indicate that this particular lung structure has certain advantages during diving.

Another striking characteristic of all Cetaceans is the presence of a thick septum between adjoining alveoli, instead of the thin septum of terrestrial mammals (Fig. 84). In this way the resilience of the lungs and the resistance to external pressure fluctuations of the thin alveolar walls are greatly increased. Moreover, every septum can now hold two layers of capillaries, instead of the one found in terrestrial mammals. While the capillaries seem to be embedded in the epithelium cells in much the usual way, the double layer does, of course, provide for more rapid gaseous exchanges with the alveoli, and this is a great advantage, particularly during inhalation at the surface. The thick septum leads to the optical illusion that Cetacean alveoli are extraordinarily small, but closer microscopic observation reveals that they are comparable in size to those of other mammals. Experimental work on the total number of alveoli and the surface area of the epithelium is still too incomplete for any further conclusions to be drawn.

Another interesting topic, about which too little is still known, is the structure of the blood vessels in Cetacean lungs. In fact, only two French investigators, Lacoste and Baudrimont, have really gone into this question. They discovered, *inter alia*, that the smaller arteries suddenly branch out into a network of still finer arteries, which twist and turn on their course. Similar phenomena occur also in other organs whose form can change radically, e.g. the spleen. Thus it may be taken that the phenomenon is an adaptation to the marked changes in volume which the lungs undergo during respiration, changes which, as we have seen, are far more intense than in terrestrial mammals. Another adaptation is the presence of an annular valve system in the blood vessels, very reminiscent of that in the bronchioles. The two French investigators thought at first that these 'valves' occurred in the arteries, but on closer examination Baudrimont (1955) discovered that, in fact, they occurred in the veins. In any case, they, too, are undoubtedly an adaptive mechanism to quick changes in pressure. Additional evidence for this assumption is the fact that each blood vessel is surrounded by a sheath of lymph vessels, which probably acts as a shock-absorber during sudden changes of volume in or round the vessel.

So far we have only dealt with the structure of the trachea, the lungs and the thorax. Now we must briefly examine the remaining parts of the respiratory system: the larynx, the pharynx, and the nose. The larynx, as we know, is situated at the beginning of the trachea, and its walls are supported by special laryngeal cartilages; the pharynx (throat) is the intersection of the trachea and the oesophagus; and the function of the nose requires no special discussion. In mammals, nasal and buccal cavities are separated by a bony plate called the hard palate and its continuation, the soft palate, consisting of mucous membrane and muscle. In most mammals, the soft palate is rather long and extends back to the region of the glottis. In this way the connexion between the naso-pharynx and the larynx is kept open, and air from the nose can reach the respiratory tracts while the animal is eating. During swallowing the soft palate is pulled up, and food has the right of way. In men and apes, the soft palate lies above the epiglottis enabling them to breathe through their mouths with the utmost facility.

Mysticetes show no great differences from terrestrial mammals in the structure of their pharynx and larynx, except for the fact that the epiglottis is relatively longer. The only real distinction is an opening on the lower side of the thyroid cartilage through which the mucous membrane of the larynx swells out like a large bag at the lower side of the trachea. Although this phenomenon was discovered by Hunter as long ago as 1787, its exact significance is still not known. It is, however, thought to be some sort of pressure-regulating structure.

The larynx of an Odontocete, however, differs greatly in structure from that of terrestrial mammals, so much so, in fact, that even the first whale anatomist was struck by it. For this is what Bartholinus had to say about the larynx of the porpoise in his *Historarium anatomicarum rariorum* (1654): *Larynx singularis figurae, anserinum caput refert* – the strange larynx resembles the head of a goose. In fact, in all Odontocetes two of the laryngeal cartilages are greatly elongated and beak-shaped: the epiglottis, and the arytenoid cartilage above it. Often the elongated epiglottis looks like an open gutter covered by the arytenoid cartilage, the two together forming a fairly narrow pipe which, however, can be distended by muscles (Fig. 85). In practically all Odontocetes, there is a swelling at the tip of the epiglottis which looks something like a collar stud. The only exception is the Pilot Whale whose epiglottis is shorter and in which it is the arytenoid cartilage which holds the 'stud'. However, the function of the two structures is identical.

If we now look at the throat itself, we find that the elongated 'beak' of the epiglottis protrudes into the inferior part of the sloping nasal duct, the soft palate being extended towards the rear and being considerably thickened at its posterior edge. The thickening is continued along the lateral walls of the pharynx, and also just over the entrance to the oesophagus. Hence the nasal passage is greatly narrowed down at its

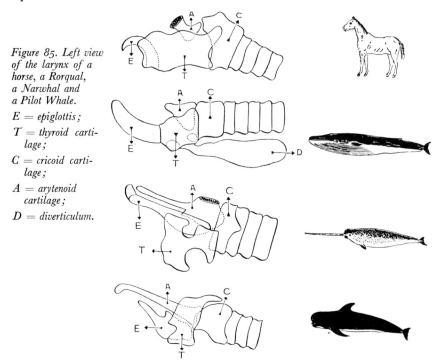

Figure 85. Left view of the larynx of a horse, a Rorqual, a Narwhal and a Pilot Whale.

E = epiglottis;

T = thyroid carti-lage;

C = cricoid carti-lage;

A = arytenoid cartilage;

D = diverticulum.

point of entry into the throat, i.e. where the beak-shaped cartilage protrudes into it (Fig. 86). As a consequence, there exists a much more direct connexion between the nose and the trachea than is found in terrestrial mammals and Mysticetes and, moreover, air is prevented from entering the mouth during exhalation, and water from entering the trachea during inhalation. The system works particularly efficiently since the specially thickened walls of the throat are provided with annular muscles which act as a tight ring round the 'beak'. This ring is not easily dislodged by movements of the throat or the epiglottis, mainly because the beak, as we have seen, is equipped with a stud at its tip. In Sperm Whales and Pigmy Sperm Whales the beak does not lie in the centre but a little to the left, so that the left passage to the oesophagus becomes narrower and the right passage wider. It was formerly believed that this was due to the fact that Sperm Whales swallow their food in large gulps, but considering that Killer Whales swallow seals whole and yet have a central 'beak', this explanation must be discarded. The phenomenon is probably associated with the asymmetrical blowhole position of Sperm Whales and related species.

While the peculiar beak and the associated structures provide a complete separation between the air and food passages, the question remains why such a strict separation was needed in the first place. The great eighteenth-century Dutch anatomist, Petrus Camper, who devoted a great deal of attention to the structure of Cetaceans, pointed out that it enabled the animals to breathe and swallow simultaneously. His explanation has ever since been repeated by a host of authors and would sound feasible, were it not that Boenninghaus (1903) and other authors have pointed out that there is really no need for such a mechanism in animals which breathe exclusively above the surface and swallow their food exclusively below. An alternative explanation might be that by sealing off the trachea while food is ingested, air is prevented from escaping through the mouth, or from going down the oesophagus. But this explanation, too, will have to be rejected, for we know that man can swallow fluids and solids underwater without any adverse effects. And aquatic mammals (Mysticetes with their 'normal' throat and larynx included)

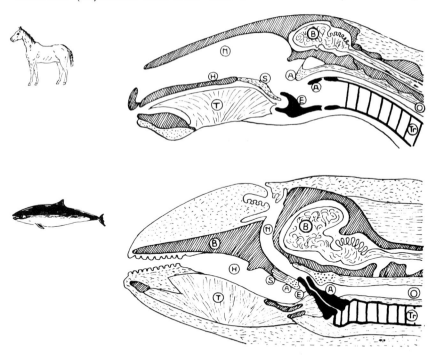

Figure 86. Longitudinal section through the head of (a) a horse and (b) a porpoise, to show the position of the larynx and the structure of the throat and nasal passage. N = nasal passage; H = hard palate; S = soft palate; A = annular muscle, which surrounds the beak of the epiglottis of the porpoise; T = tongue; E = epiglottis; A = arytenoid cartilage; Tr = trachea; O = oesophagus; B = brain (and also – in the porpoise – upper jaw). (Partly after Rawitz, 1900.)

always swallow their food under water, though it is known that young seals must first be taught to do so. When they start feeding on fish, they bring their prey up to the surface where they swallow it, but after about two weeks they join their parents in swallowing their food below.

A better explanation might be connected with another characteristic distinction between Odontocetes and Mysticetes: the presence or absence of diverging diverticula or membraneous folds in the upper nasal passage. We shall return to these diverticula later, but here we should like to point out that they can be filled with air during diving, the beak mechanism preventing this air from escaping through the mouth. Moreover, as we shall see, it seems likely that during strong pressure fluctuations these animals expel some air from the trachea. To do so gradually, they need a successive tap system of the kind found in the bronchioles (see above). This is clearly provided by the beak as the first tap, and the air plug formed by the diverticula in the nostril as the second.

In most terrestrial mammals the nasal passage, though long, does not have the capacity we might think it has. From the lateral wall of each nasal cavity spring three twisted laminae of cartilage (conchae), dividing each side of the nose into a number of narrow passages (meatuses). The meatuses are lined with ciliated epithelium which serves as a dust filter, and they contain small glands for keeping the air moist. They are also provided with a network of veins which help to keep the air warm. The posterior part of the uppermost compartment of the nose is provided with olfactory receptors embedded in the mucous membrane lining the numerous lamellae of the ethmoid bone.

We have seen that in all Cetaceans, with the exception of the Sperm Whale, the blowhole, i.e. the nostril, is found on top, rather than at the front of the head, so that the nasal passage rises up almost vertically from the throat. The passage is not only relatively short but also relatively wide when open, since conchae are absent in Cetaceans. All this obviously makes for quicker air displacement, and we know that Cetaceans breathe far more violently than we do. In Cetaceans there is no ciliary epithelium, which they do not need, since the air they breathe is free of impurities, and there is also a complete absence of small moisture-producing glands – the air being moist enough as it is. However, the absence of veins in this large nostril is a disadvantage, and is probably compensated for by the presence of a highly developed network of veins in the wall of the trachea and the bronchi which have probably taken over the function of warming the air.

In Odontocetes, the olfactory receptors (and the olfactory nerve) are entirely absent or present in rudimentary form only. Mysticetes, however, are said to have retained a slight sense of smell (see Chapter 9), for close

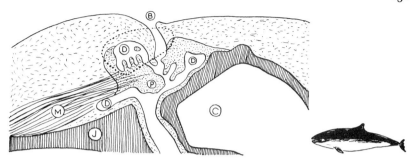

Figure 87. Longitundinal section through the blowhole and diverticula of a porpoise. The dotted line shows the area of the lateral diverticulum. Note the hard connective tissue along the diverticula, the 'plug' (P), and the muscle (M) running from the plug to the top of the skull bones. B = blowhole; D = diverticula; J = upper jaw bone; N = nasal passage; C = brain cavity.

under the blowhole they have three cartilaginous nasal conchae which are in fact lined with olfactory epithelium.

In the Mysticetes, the nostrils are in the form of two slits, and the septum is so high up that we are justified in speaking of two nostrils. The slits run in a sagittal direction converging to form a V with the angle pointing forward (Figs. 43 and 73). In Right Whales this division is so pronounced that two separate blows emerge, but in Rorquals both nostrils combine to produce a single blow. The openings of the blowhole are surrounded with thick 'lips'. If we climb up a dead whale and try to push our arm into the blowhole, we shall find that a great deal of strength is needed to do so. This is due to the fact that the 'lips' consist of highly elastic tissue which normally keeps the blowhole closed by tension even when the whale is at the surface. To open it during breathing, the whale has numerous muscles which run from the 'lips' to the skull below. Obviously, this method of closing the blowhole is much more effective than the method found in seals, sea-lions and hippopotami whose nostrils are normally open and must be closed underwater by an active contraction of annular muscles. Some whales do have annular muscles as well, but they are of minor importance.

In Sperm Whales, the blowhole is more or less S-shaped, but in other Odontocetes it is a single transverse slit situated right on top of the head (Fig. 50). Since the front of the skull slopes so steeply, all Odontocetes carry some form of adipose cushion on their foreheads (see Chapter 2 and Figs. 33 and 86), but Mysticetes, whose integument is much closer to the bone, do not possess such a cushion. Where the nasal passage of Odontocetes traverses the bones of the skull, it is divided into two by a nasal septum, but no such septum is found in the part of the passage which lies in the adipose cushion, or in the blowhole. Just where the nasal passage emerges from the skull, the adipose cushion sticks out over it like some sort of plug and forms a narrow passage which may be completely closed during respiratory intervals (Fig. 87). The plug can be pulled forward by means of a powerful muscle attached to the bones of the snout, and the passage is thus widened. Above this plug are found the peculiar diverticulae (or air pockets) mentioned earlier, which extend to the top, to the back and to the side of the adipose cushion. While the diverticulae themselves may be fairly wide, their openings into the nasal passage are generally very narrow. Their shape and position differs from species to species but the principle is the same in all Odontocetes, with the exception of the Sperm Whale, which has a single diverticulum between the spermaceti cushion and the skull, and another anterior to the cushion. This is shown clearly in Fig. 33. The diverticula of the Odontocetes are not equipped with special muscles, but are partly surrounded by a very characteristic layer of particularly tough and non-elastic connective tissue. According to Kükenthal (1893), some sections of the diverticulae still show traces of an olfactory mucous membrane. It is his contention that the species in which these traces occur also have olfactory nerves at an early stage of their embryonic development. A number of other zoologists have tried to solve the problem of the function of the diverticula, including Cuvier himself, who thought that they served to remove water which had accidentally entered the nostrils. Since, however, no special muscles are attached to the diverticula, this explanation sounds improbable, and the same can also be said of many other theories which have been put forward during the past 150 years. From the recent and very thorough research work of Lawrence and Schevill (1956) it is clear that at least one of the diverticula, i.e. the lateral, does in fact act as a plug for the blowhole. These two scientists not only made a profound study of the structure of diverticula in Common Dolphins, but also in the Bottlenose Dolphins of the famous Marineland aquarium in Florida. Their project was financed by the American Office of Naval Research, evidently in the hope that their research might have useful applications in the naval field. It emerged that the animals could seal off their blowholes most effectively by blowing air into the lateral diverticula. Moreover, Lawrence and Schevill discovered that this plugging effect was by no means their only function, and it seems feasible that the diverticula form a part of the valve system of Odontocetes, a hypothesis first put forward by Raven and Gregory in 1933. The simultaneous occurrence of diverticula and epiglottal 'beaks' in Odontocetes and the absence of both in Mysticetes points clearly to the conclusion that these two structures must be interrelated in some way. If this is so, it is possible that during fluctuations in pressure the air from

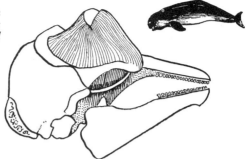

the larynx is first expelled into the diverticula, and then released through the blowhole. The exceptionally tough connective tissue surrounding the diverticula and keeping the air pockets open is additional evidence in favour of this hypothesis. This extra 'safety valve' is very useful indeed, since, as we have seen, it regulates the escape of air under pressure, and since whales are, in fact, known to release air while diving, possibly in order to produce sounds (see Chapter 8).

For the sake of completeness we must add that diverticulae apart, the blowholes of Odontocetes and Mysticetes are opened and shut in identical ways. True, Bottlenose Dolphins and Pigmy Sperm Whales are known to have special muscles for closing the aperture, but nevertheless, the tensed lips remain the main factor in shutting even their blowholes, which are dilated in all Cetaceans by rays of muscle running down and attached to the skull beneath (Fig. 88). Russian scientists have shown that in dolphins the blowhole is opened by a reflex that is set off whenever the animals surface, and that it is permanently shut underwater unless the dolphin needs to open it for a special reason. This reflex may also be linked with certain movements of the flukes which force up the blowhole so that it is clear of the water. On the other hand, it must be stated that when the blowhole of a porpoise is forcibly held above water, it opens automatically at regular intervals, and the same phenomenon has been observed in stranded whales and dolphins.

5

Heart, Circulation and Blood

I N 1955, when President Eisenhower had a heart attack, Doctor Paul
Dudley White of Boston was immediately summoned to the President's
bedside. No wonder, for there are few men who know as much about
hearts as Dr White. Not content with probing the secrets of our own, he
took his complicated instruments to the giants of the animal kingdom as
well: first to elephants and then, finding their hearts a little on the small
side, to whales and dolphins.

He began with Belugas, mere 14-footers found in the Arctic, schools of
which visit bays and estuaries where they are caught fairly easily. White
started operating from Clarks Point (Bristol Bay, Alaska) where he could
count on the help of experienced gunners. Now gunners do not normally
take a whale's pulse, but in this case they helped to do so. The electro-
cardiograph, an instrument for recording small electric changes during
contraction of the muscles of the heart, has two electrodes which are
attached to the subject's body. Attaching such plates to a living whale is
no easy matter, and that is where the gunners came in – they used
harpoons as electrodes. At first it was thought that one harpoon would
do the trick, and that the current would return through the water to a
special copper plate attached to the boat. However, it soon appeared that
this method was inadequate and that two electrode harpoons were needed.

Luckily, White had been given a grant to cover most of the expenses,
and, for the rest, he drew liberally on his private income. Flying a small
aeroplane, he spotted a school of Belugas on 6th August, 1952, and sent
out a motorboat with the necessary instruments in pursuit of the animals.
After a number of unsucccessful attempts, he finally managed to get an
adult Beluga to trail the wires for half an hour and thus obtained a number
of electrocardiograms. Encouraged by his success, White felt he could
now tackle the slow-swimming Californian Grey Whale also, but despite
assistance from the U.S. Navy and biologists from the Scripps Ocean
Institute (University of California) his attempts proved abortive. The

animals reacted so violently that some of the investigators nearly lost their lives. In 1957, when President Eisenhower had recovered, White made a fresh attempt, this time using a helicopter and a gun that fired two electrode harpoons simultaneously. But once again he failed to register the heartbeat of the Grey Whale, one reason being that the animals were frightened away by the currents of air which the helicopter churned up. However, it has been announced that further attempts will be made shortly.

In any case, White did manage to take the Beluga's pulse. Now, the pulse of an animal swimming about with three harpoons in its body might be expected to be exceptionally high and irregular, as would our own in similar circumstances, but White measured a regular 16 to 17 beats a minute – remarkably little, we might think, for an animal weighing some 22 cwt, particularly if we bear in mind that elephants were found to have an average rate of 30 beats a minute. Actually, the bigger an animal the slower is its pulse. Thus, horses have 40 heartbeats a minute, pigs and humans 70, cats 150, hedgehogs 300, and mice 650. From these figures, we should expect the Beluga to have a pulse of roughly 35. Now, all White's electrocardiograms were taken while the Beluga was swimming under-water, and we know that the pulse rate of all animals drops when they dive. Thus our own pulse rate falls from 70 to 35, and in aquatic mammals the decrease is far greater still. Irving and his colleagues established experimentally that, while diving, the pulse of a beaver drops from 140 to 10, that of a penguin from 240 to 20, and that of a seal from 120 to 10. In applying their work to Cetaceans, they had an easier task than White, since they experimented with tame Bottlenose dolphins in the Marineland Seaquarium (Florida). They managed without much trouble to apply electrodes to these animals and also to some others in the bay, and found that their pulse rate was 110 beats a minute at the surface and 50 beats a minute below; it began to increase just before the animal surfaced.

Irving and his colleagues think that the drop in the pulse rate during a dive is due to the fact that part of the blood circulation is shut off. In the last chapter, we saw that, in a dive, very little oxidization may occur in the muscles, and that more oxygen is consequently made available for the organs which cannot do without it: the heart and the brain. How sensitive these organs are to oxygen deficiencies can best be seen from the fact that, in man, while the blood supply to all the muscles can be cut off for some 15 minutes, and that to the arms and legs for a few hours, without appreciable damage, the heart would suffer serious injury after a much shorter time, and the brain after only 3 to 5 minutes. Fifty per cent of human beings would die after the blood-flow to the brain had been stopped for 2–3 minutes.

The decrease of blood-flow to the muscles of aquatic mammals and the consequent increase to the other organs would naturally lead to a great distension of the blood vessels in the latter, and a contraction in the former. That this is in fact the case was discovered by Irving and his collaborators, who found that the blood pressure in the large arteries supplying the muscles was increased, while it was greatly decreased in the smaller arteries. Somewhere between the large and small arteries, a contraction of the vessels must therefore take place. In fact, hardly any blood can be drawn from the muscles or the intestines of a diving animal.

The Norwegian physiologist P. F. Scholander, whose work we have discussed in the last chapter, took an electrocardiogram of a porpoise swimming at the *surface*, from which it appeared that the animal had a pulse rate of about 130 beats per minute. These figures agree with the available data on Bottlenose Dolphins and also with a nineteenth-century count made by Eschricht (150 beats a minute). Accordingly, the Beluga would have a pulse rate of about 30 at the surface, and the bigger whales a correspondingly lower rate – which was calculated by Pütter (1924) to be no more than 5 beats a minute. On 5th December, 1959, a 45-foot Fin Whale was stranded alive at Cape Cod. The animal lived for 24 hours and during that time its electrocardiogram was taken by J. Kanwisher (Woods Hole). It showed a heartbeat of 25 a minute. Because the respiratory rate of the stranded animal was three times as fast as in a normal swimming whale, we may assume that the pulse rate of a normal Fin Whale is about 8, which agrees quite well with Pütter's calculations.

Although the available data are still far too few for a final conclusion to be drawn, we may say provisionally that, judging by body weight, the heartbeat of the smaller dolphins, at least, is abnormally accelerated at the surface. We can therefore say that the pulse rate is normal in diving, and increased in surfacing. This is not so peculiar when we consider that Cetaceans are permanent aquatic animals which, after all, have to replenish the oxygen in their blood very quickly during the short time they are at the surface. Belugas, and perhaps the bigger whales also, would then be the exceptions to the rule, for their pulse rate seems normal at the surface, and abnormally low below.

By and large, therefore, the pulse rate itself gives no indication that there is anything special about the output of the Cetacean heart, particularly since little is known about the blood pressure, for though Pütter thought it must be very low in big whales, his data require further confirmation. Only one anatomical facet of the problem has been more fully investigated, viz. the extension of the elastic part of the arterial system.

From our pulse and from spurts of blood from a severed artery it is clear that the blood in our arteries does not flow evenly, but intermittently.

This is due to the fact that the heart contracts roughly once every second, forcing large quantities of blood into the aorta and the pulmonary artery as it does so. In order to temper the effects of these sudden spurts and to avoid excessive pressure changes in the smaller blood vessels, the main arteries leaving the heart have thick, strong walls containing a large proportion of elastic tissue which make them look yellow. In the medium-sized and smallest arterial branches, smooth muscle is more abundant, the elastic tissue being correspondingly reduced. As we grow older, the general elasticity of the arteries decreases, and more force is needed to push the blood through them. As the blood pressure rises, a greater strain is put on the heart which now has to force the blood through a more and more rigid pipe. Elasticity is, therefore, a *sine qua non* of sound circulation.

The more blood is squeezed out with every heartbeat, and the greater the force of the contraction, the longer the elastic region of the arteries needs to be. Now from my own comparative study of the arteries of a horse and a Bottlenose Dolphin (see Fig. 89), it appeared that in both animals the elastic region had the same length, and that consequently, in this respect, too, Cetaceans do not differ greatly from other mammals.

'*Le coeur est énorme,*' the well-known French physiologist, Paul Portier, wrote in 1938, in his excellent little book on aquatic animals. How right he was emerges clearly when we realize that, while the hearts of the rhinoceros and the elephant can be handled on a dissection table, the heart of the whale has to be dragged over the slippery deck of a whaling ship by seven strong men – and then with some difficulty. The poor biologist who wishes to cut up this huge mass, almost 6 feet wide and 10–11 cwt in weight, may well shy from such an Augean labour. Still, with the occasional help of a derrick or steam winch, he has managed to solve this problem remarkably well.

Since mere weight tells us very little about the comparative size of the heart, biologists are much more concerned with the weight of the organ expressed as a percentage of the total body weight. Now, while earlier workers, e.g. Zenkovich (1937), found the heart of the Sperm Whale and some larger Rorquals to represent 2·6–3·9 per cent of the animal's total weight, more detailed Japanese investigations made since the Second World War have revealed that the average percentages are 0·5 per cent in Blue Whales, Fin Whales and Humpback Whales and 0·4 per cent in Sei Whales. I myself measured averages of 0·5 per cent in Little Piked Whales, 0·85 per cent in porpoises, 0·93 per cent in Bottlenose Dolphins, and 0·6 per cent in all dolphins taken together, the Beluga included. Figures of 0·34 per cent and 0·7–0·8 per cent are reported for Sperm Whales and Biscayan Right Whales respectively.

We have already seen that in mammals there exists a close correlation

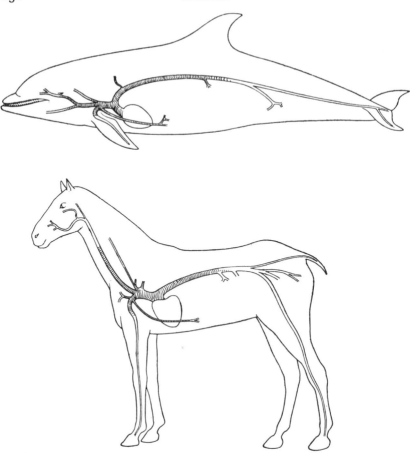

Figure 89. The main arteries of (a) a Bottlenose Dolphin and (b) a horse. Shaded areas consist mainly of elastic tissue.

between total size on the one hand and lung weight or pulse rate on the other. Thus, we might expect a similar correlation to exist also in respect of the size of their hearts. Now, if we look at Crile's very accurate tables, we find that the ratio of heart to body weight in hippopotami and sea-cows is 0·3 per cent, in elephants, giraffes, rats, beavers and seals 0·4 per cent, in rabbits, cats, guinea-pigs, chimpanzees and cattle 0·5 per cent, in mice and bisons 0·7 per cent, in horses 0·8 per cent, and in zebras and bats 1·1 per cent. It would therefore appear that the size of the heart is not as closely related to the size of the body as we might have expected. Experts believe that the size of the heart is also connected with other factors, such as the speed and power the animal develops, and while the whole problem is still far from being solved, we may safely state that, in this respect too, the Cetacean heart is not radically different from that of other mammals.

Everyone who has seen the flensing of a whale, particularly of a Sperm Whale, is struck by the quantities of blood that keep pouring from the carcass. However, calculations have shown that the ratio of blood to body weight is only 6·5 per cent in Blue Whales and 5·5 per cent in Belugas, the corresponding figures being 4–8 per cent in rabbits, 5 per cent in rats, 6·6 per cent in horses and 8·1 per cent in sheep. Clearly, this is another respect in which Cetaceans are very much like other mammals.

Some hint about the strength of an animal's heart can be gleaned from its shape. In porpoises, the heart is a little longer than it is broad, in most other toothed whales length and breadth are approximately equal, while in Mysticetes and Sperm Whales the breadth exceeds the length. The Biscayan Right Whale has the broadest heart of all. All these peculiar shapes, which are characteristically different from the more elongated shapes of the hearts of most mammals (Fig. 90), are undoubtedly the result of the peculiar shape of the Cetacean thorax. In the last chapter, we saw that because of the dorsal position of the lungs, the peculiar angle of the diaphragm and the barrel-shape of the thorax itself, the available space for the organs in the ventral part of the thorax has become broader and

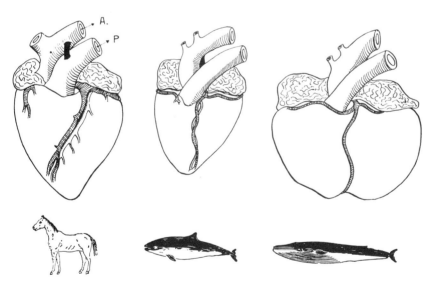

Figure 90. Left views of the heart of (a) a horse, (b) a porpoise and (c) a Fin Whale to show differences in shape. A = aorta; P = pulmonary artery. Note the ductus arteriosus between the two arteries in (a) and (b), where it has become fused into a ligament. The hearts are not drawn to scale.

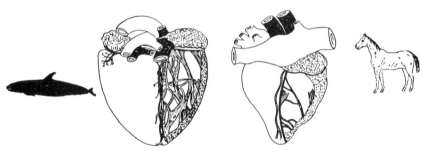

Figure 91. Right views of the heart of (a) a False Killer and (b) a horse. The right chamber is shown in section to reveal the trabeculae. (Slijper, 1939.)

shorter. Undoubtedly, similar factors have also affected the shape of the hearts of elephants and sea-cows. Zimmermann's investigations (1930) have moreover shown that there is a certain correlation between the shape of the heart and its strength, so that a racing horse has a more elongated and narrower heart than a carthorse, a wild rabbit a narrower heart than its tame relatives, and so on. The shape of the Cetacean heart would, in that case, indicate that the animal is not equipped with a specially strong organ. Moreover, the ventricles are intersected by a considerable number of muscle bundles or *trabeculae* (Fig. 91), and according to one of the leading experts on the structure of the mammalian heart, the German anatomist Benninghoff, hearts with highly developed trabeculae generally have a smaller output than others. In this connexion we might also mention that the wall of the right chamber is 2–3 times as thick as that of the left – just as it is in men and other mammals.

From the entire preceding discussion, we can therefore conclude that no single characteristic of the Cetacean heart makes it more efficient or powerful than that of a terrestrial mammal – if anything, the reverse seems to be the case in the larger species. The reader might wonder why so much time has been spent on showing that there is nothing remarkable about the Cetacean heart. The answer is that this fact is not generally appreciated and, moreover, that without looking at the heart, we would have been unable to go on to a discussion of the rest of the vascular system, and here we shall in fact find the most astonishing peculiarities.

One of the strangest Cetacean characteristics is undoubtedly the presence of numerous and widespread vascular networks (the so-called *retia mirabilia*) in the blood system. We may remember from our school days that the arteries, i.e. the vessels that carry blood from the heart to the rest of the body, branch out into ever-finer vessels till finally they become a capillary network. Here, the blood surrenders its oxygen to the tissues and takes up carbon dioxide, then goes on to join up with a system

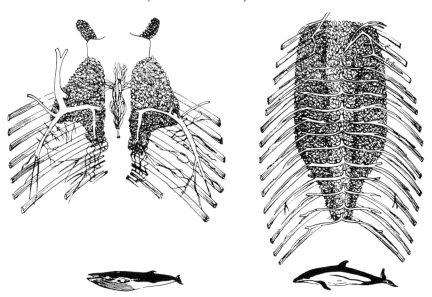

Figure 92. View into the thorax of a Little Piked Whale and a Common Dolphin to show the position of the vascular networks, the ribs, and some afferent vessels. (Bouvier, 1889.)

of ever-bigger veins which carry the deoxygenated blood back to the heart. This, at least, is the normal situation, but sometimes arteries and veins branch out into a network of small vessels which have neither the very thin walls nor the other characteristics of capillaries. There are very small arteries or veins, with arterial networks interposed between two arteries and venous networks between two veins. Although such networks occur in various terrestrial mammals as well (including cows) they were once thought so unusual that they were given their present name of *retia mirabilia*, meaning 'wonder-networks'.

If we can get hold of a very recently killed porpoise and remove its heart and lungs, we shall lay bare a thick, spongy, vascular mass on either side of the vertebral column and between the ribs. We can trace this mass going right up into the cervical and down into the lumbar region, though it clearly thins out in the posterior part of the body (Fig. 92). Even so it continues right into the chevron canals of the caudal vertebrae and ends just in front of the flukes. On closer examination the networks can be seen to consist of twisted blood vessels, and this becomes quite obvious at their intercostal termini, where the convolutions can be seen with the naked eye. Though Tyson (1680) and Monro (1787) were greatly struck by these networks while dissecting porpoises, the first accurate and detailed description was given by the French anatomist Breschet, who published

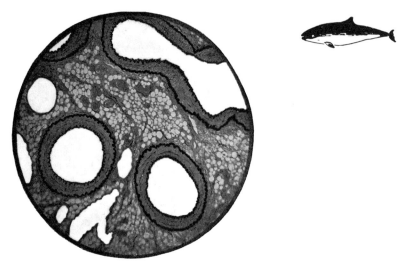

Figure 93. Histological section through the thoracic rete of a porpoise. The elastic tissue is stained dark, showing that the walls of the arterioles have only a very thin inner and outer elastic layer, and that the wall consists mainly of smooth muscle. Between the arterioles lie thin-walled venules and fat cells.

a beautifully illustrated book on the subject in 1836. His copperplates convey a very clear picture of the retia and even of their fine structure, and this despite the fact that microscopy was still in its infancy in his day.

The blood is carried to the vascular networks principally by the inter-vertebral and intercostal arteries as well as by the costocervical and supreme intercostal arteries which divide into innumerable branches in a serpentine course. All the branches are of equal diameter, and the terminal branches are, moreover, imperceptibly interwoven and are anastomosed so as to form a complete network. From the functional point of view, it is important to note that while the afferent vessels are pre-dominantly of the elastic type, the vessels of the network itself are strongly muscular, i.e. their wall consists mainly of a thick layer of smooth muscle at the expense of elastic fibres (Fig. 93).

A microscopic examination will show that, in addition to being built up of arteries, the retia are also built up of veins, although to a much lesser extent. In contrast to the arteries, these small veins have very thin walls without muscle tissue. Moreover, they lack valves so that the blood in them can flow in two directions. In a very few places, the arterial retia are joined to the venous retia by capillaries. Erikson is quoted by Scholan-der (1940) as stating that in these mixed networks, the arterial parts are directly connected to the venous parts by arterio-venous anastomoses, but no such anastomoses have ever been seen under the microscope. The *retia*

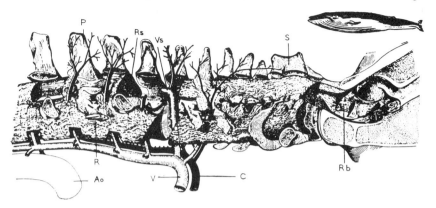

Figure 94. The vascular networks with their afferent and efferent blood vessels in the anterior thorax, the neck, and cranium of a Fin Whale foetus. Ao = aorta; C = costo-cervical artery carrying blood from the aorta to the retia; V = costo-cervical vein returning blood from the retia and the spinal veins to the anterior vena cava; R = thoracic and cervical retia; Rb = basi-cranial rete; Rs = spinal rete; Vs = spinal vein; P = spinous process of a thoracic vertebra; S = spinous process of a cervical vertebra. (Walmsley, 1938.)

mirabilia lie embedded in adipose tissue consisting of a large mass of fat cells separated by connective tissue septa.

This type of tissue can be found in other animals as well, particularly when the fat has a mechanical function as, for instance, in the pads of a dog's foot. Here the fat is not so much a food reserve as a shock-absorber. The very structure of the tissue, which resembles a quilt, would seem to bear out this contention. Thus the structure, the serpentine course of the small vessels, the many branches, the anastomoses, and the thick muscular wall of the small arteries, all strongly point to the conclusion that the retia are subjected to very great and quick changes of volume. By quick distensions and contractions of their muscular wall, the small arteries enable the retia to absorb and expel large quantities of blood very quickly, and some form of shock-absorber is obviously essential if they are to function smoothly. Moreover, it is quite possible that the venous retia also act as shock-absorbers for the arterial retia.

We have discussed the retia mirabilia of a porpoise because it has the most highly developed system of vascular networks of all Cetaceans. Common Dolphins, too, have considerable thoracic retia, but in other Cetaceans they are neither so thick nor do they extend so far or so wide. In Ziphiids, including the Bottlenose Whale, they are found only in the cervical region and half-way down the thorax, while in Sperm Whales they extend down to the lumbar region. Rorquals show vascular networks in the cervical region, and in the thoracic region down to the sixth rib. I

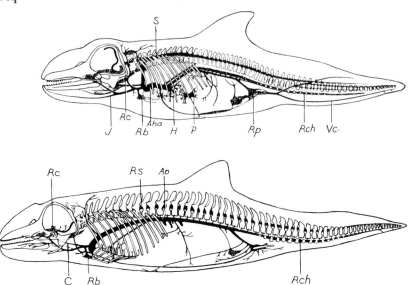

Figure 95. Top: The main veins and their retia in a porpoise. (The cervical and thoracic
retia are not shown.) J = jugular vein; Rb = brachial rete; Rc = basi-cranial rete;
Aha = anterior vena cava; H = hepatic vein; P = portal vein; S = spinal vein; Rp =
pelvic rete; Rch = chevron-canal rete; Vc = superficial caudal vein. (Slijper, 1936.)
Bottom: The main arteries and some retia in a porpoise. (The cervical and thoracic retia are
not shown.) Rc = cranial rete; C = partially closed internal carotid artery; Rb = brachial
rete; Rs = spinal rete crossed by two arteries carrying blood to the brain cavity; Ao = aorta;
Rch = chevron canal rete. (Slijper, 1936.)

myself found that in Little Piked Whales the networks, at least in the
anterior thorax, spread out fairly wide in a lateral direction.

Mixed networks containing arteries and veins are, moreover, found in
other parts of the Cetacean body as well (Fig. 95). We have already
mentioned their presence in the chevron canal, where, by the way, they
are only found in Odontocetes and in Little Piked Whales. In big Rorquals,
which have only one large artery and one large vein in the chevron canal,
the retia are particularly well developed in the neural canal, i.e. the space
in the neural arch in which the spinal cord is also situated. The neural
retia are joined to the thoracic retia, and continue into the cranium where,
in all Cetaceans, they join a particularly well-developed basi-cranial
network in the vicinity of the hypophysis. From here the retia continue
along the optic nerve, and together with the arteries which, in Odontocetes, lie embedded in it, they supply most of the brain's blood requirements, since, in Cetaceans, the internal carotid artery has a very narrow
lumen. These retia act as a shock-absorber against the effects of the intermittent spurts of blood to the brain. All Cetaceans also have a particularly

well developed vascular network towards the outer side of the brain case, especially near the joint of the jaws, the bulla tympani, and the foramen magnum. Smaller networks occur particularly in the pelvic region and in the sexual organs, but by far the largest mass of retia is found in the head, the neck, and the thorax. Another remarkable network at the base of the pectoral fin will be discussed later, since it probably has quite a different function from the other retia.

Similar networks are also common in sea-cows, but are not found in sea-lions, seals, or other Pinniped Carnivores.

Before we discuss the function of the retia in greater detail, we must look at some other characteristics of the vascular system, and particularly at those retia which consist entirely of veins. Unlike the mixed arterial-cum-venous retia we have discussed, they are found almost exclusively in the abdominal cavity.

These retia, too, are generally most highly developed in porpoises and less so in other Odontocetes. In Rorquals, they are restricted to the pelvic region and the sexual organs, but in porpoises, tremendous networks which, during dissection, are shown to be greatly distended with blood, stretch right round the dorsal and lateral sides of the abdominal and pelvic cavities. They obtain their blood mainly from a large vein running close under the skin on the side of the tail and carrying venous blood from tail and flukes. The retia give up their blood chiefly to the inferior vena cava which runs close to the aorta on the dorsal side of the abdominal cavity and which returns the blood to the heart. Hence it looks as if all the blood from the abdomen and tail returning to the heart by way of the inferior vena cava must pass through these retia on its way (Fig. 95). However, in all mammals, man included, the blood returning from the stomach, the intestines and the spleen must first go to the liver by the portal vein, usually to return by the hepatic veins to the inferior vena cava, after first passing through the capillaries of the liver. In Cetaceans, this blood therefore by-passes the abdominal retia. In addition, the portal system itself has certain peculiarities, at least in all Odontocetes investigated so far, i.e. porpoises and different species of dolphins.

At the turn of this century, French scientists, in particular, were responsible for showing that the two main hepatic veins and also that part of the inferior vena cava into which they run are very much distended in these animals (Fig. 96). Moreover, the hepatic veins are sometimes, and the inferior vena cava in the region of the diaphragm is always, equipped with a muscular sphincter by which their diameter can be decreased or by which they may be closed. I found that such distensions and annular muscles were very pronounced in a $6\frac{1}{2}$-foot female Bottlenose Dolphin. While other Odontocetes still need to be investigated I have personally

Figure 96. Highly diagrammatic rear view of the liver of Risso's Dolphin, showing position of distended hepatic veins and their connexion with the posterior vena cava. (Richards and Neuville, 1896.)

confirmed that Rorquals show no traces of such special hepatic distensions or annular muscles, though it is known that they are present in sea-lions, seals, walruses, and probably also in beavers, so that they are clearly connected with diving habits. (Such annular muscles occur in some terrestrial mammals as well, although in a more rudimentary form.) In Common Dolphins, the branches of the portal vein are, moreover, provided with a special valve system similar to that found in their bronchioles and pulmonary veins (see Chapter 4). However, nothing is known about this phenomenon in other Cetaceans.

As the factory ship's powerful bone saws rip their way through the vertebral column, we often get an excellent view of it in cross-section. Below the strikingly small section of the spinal cord and the predominantly arterial vascular network there appear two wide veins which, in Blue Whales, can have a diameter of up to 4 inches. Such spinal veins are found in all Cetaceans, where they are the principal vessels for returning the blood from the brain, the jugular vein being very narrow. Moreover, the spinal veins receive blood from all the thoracic intercostal veins, and are connected at each lumbar vertebra with the posterior vena cava by special vessels. Only in the caudal region do they thin out, for the caudal blood returns either through the lateral veins found close under the skin of the tail, or through the vein in the chevron canal. Two wide vessels, which lie behind the second and third ribs (in Odontocetes on the right side only) join the spinal veins (which also communicate with each other) to the anterior vena cava, through which the blood is returned to the heart.

The spinal veins are by and large of uniform diameter throughout, and have no valves. These two characteristics make it seem probable that the blood in them can flow in both directions, depending on the animal's needs. After all, the veins supply the anterior vena cava in the thorax, as well as the posterior vena cava in the abdominal cavity, and may thus be said to form an auxiliary connection between the two veins, enabling the blood from the brain to return to the heart through either of them. Spinal veins have also been described in other aquatic animals, i.e. Sirenians (sea-cows, etc.) and Pinniped Carnivores (seals, etc.) and, for the sake of completeness we might add that they have also been found in some terrestrial mammals such as sloths, bats and cats.

We have just discussed four special characteristics of the Cetacean vascular system: the arterial retia in the thorax and neck; the venous retia in the abdominal cavity; the distensions of the hepatic veins and of the inferior vena cava; and the presence of large veins in the vertebral canal. All these characteristics are apparently found in all other aquatic mammals also, though those which do not constantly live in the water – e.g. seals and sea-lions – lack some of them. Clearly, therefore, the retia are an adaptation to an aquatic mode of existence and especially to diving, though it is not easy to say precisely in what way. We need not, therefore, be surprised to learn that many experts have delved into this problem, and that the literature on it is extensive. Still, even the most recent investigations by Harrison and Tomlinson (1956) have failed to provide a complete answer.

We shall not go into the details of all the hypotheses put forward in the course of the last hundred years, but concentrate on the known facts, i.e. that the retia are capable of absorbing and releasing vast quantities of blood. This is particularly true of the arterial retia, and though the structure of the venous retia has not yet been studied sufficiently, we can nevertheless state that they, too, can store blood for some time, as can the special hepatic veins and the inferior vena cava. The spinal veins, moreover, may, as we have seen, enable the blood from the brain to return both to the thorax and to the abdomen so that, if the flow to the thorax is impeded for some reason, congestion in the delicate central nervous system is avoided. Furthermore, blood from the abdomen can, under certain conditions, be diverted to the thorax through the spinal canal instead of the inferior vena cava which normally carries the blood.

All these modifications are obviously associated with possible pressure differences between the thorax and the abdomen, and possibly between both and the brain. Unfortunately we know practically nothing about the nature of such pressure differences, nor have we evolved adequate experimental techniques for determining them. All our arguments must therefore be based on anatomical inferences and on what little we know about pressure differences in terrestrial mammals. Hence, the reader is advised to treat what follows with caution.

Let us imagine that, at a given moment, the pressure in the thorax is greater than that in the rest of the body. In that case, the blood from the abdominal cavity will not be able to return to the heart, since normal flow can only take place if the thorax is at a lower pressure. The blood stowed in the abdomen would have injurious effects, were it not that it can be stored in the venous retia and in the distended hepatic veins. The annular muscle of the inferior vena cava will be closed, preventing more blood being syphoned from the heart into the abdomen, while the blood from the brain and the rest of the head, unable to return to the thorax, will return to the abdomen via the spinal veins. No doubt the walls of the inferior vena cava will be greatly strained by this tremendous influx of blood, but their special structure is adequate to this task. This was shown clearly by A. von Kügelgen, a German histologist, who found that the wall of the vena cava of a Fin Whale is much more liberally endowed with both elastic tissue and muscle tissue than it is in terrestrial mammals, and is thus far more capable of withstanding great pressures than, say, the inferior venae cavae of horses or men.

With increased pressure in the thorax, little blood will be able to pass through the lungs, and hence to the heart. The retia in the thorax are 'shut', and all the available blood will thus go to the brain by the most direct route.

Now, let us imagine the reverse case, i.e. the pressure in the thorax being lower than in the rest of the body. Clearly blood will then be sucked into the thorax from all directions, and the heart would become over-loaded as it tries vainly to distribute blood to the rest of the body against a high pressure gradient. This, too, is prevented by the retia, whose ramified arterioles in the thorax and neck take up most of the blood, thus reducing the pressure of the flow to normal. As we have seen, the structure of the arterial system proper of Cetaceans shows no signs of constant or intermittent high blood pressure, and it is obviously the function of the retia to prevent high pressure from building up. When the pressure in the thorax is low, the blood from the brain can easily return to the heart. Moreover it is quite possible that blood stored in the abdominal cavity returns not only by the inferior vena cava but also along the spinal veins, whenever more blood is needed quickly by the heart.

If we accept this explanation for the presence of the retia and other special vascular characteristics, we naturally want to know under what conditions pressure differences in the Cetacean body arise. We might be tempted to think that they are associated with deep diving, in which the heart slows down and the supply of blood to the muscles and intestines is reduced or stopped. However, since the retia are more highly developed in porpoises and dolphins than they are in Rorquals, Sperm Whales, Bottlenose Whales and other champion divers, this hypothesis must be rejected.

This unexpected state of affairs points to the conclusion that great internal pressure differences occur not so much when the animal swims at great depths as when it makes sudden vertical movements. After all, when a 100-foot whale dives down perpendicularly, the difference in water pressure between its snout and tail is 3 atmospheres – quite sufficient to affect the circulation. Moreover, it is quite possible that, as a result of changes in the rhythm of the heartbeat which occur on surfacing and sounding, further pressure differences arise in the vascular system, and that such differences may also be due to the whale's characteristically violent respiration, which causes the entire lung to contract or expand and to expel or suck in large quantities of air within a very short space of time.

Experiments with terrestrial animals and man have long ago shown that sudden pressure differences in the lung can produce very appreciable pressure fluctuations in the vascular system. This influence of respiratory movement on man's system is demonstrated very clearly by Valsalva's experiment. In this, the mouth and nose are closed and the subject tries to exhale. The pulse rate is accelerated and the arterial pressure raised owing to the great rise in thoracic pressure. Blood pressure changes are more marked still, when air from the lungs is allowed to escape suddenly through an open mouth. Now, if we bear in mind that porpoises and dolphins not only breathe and dive much faster and more frequently than any of the big whales, but that their relative lung capacity is far greater, we may appreciate not only why their retia are so very well developed but also that retia must be adaptations to quick and frequent rather than to deep or long dives. However, our knowledge of the entire subject is still so incomplete that it would be wisest to await experimental proof before we jump to hasty conclusions.

Apart from the retia and their related structures, the vascular system of Cetaceans shows other peculiarities that are only partly associated with pressure differences. Thus, some animals were found to have marked distensions of the aortic arch and of the pulmonary artery. However, the literature is so full of contradictory explanations of this phenomenon, and my own observations are so inconclusive, that a more detailed discussion would be pointless.

Though it is generally held that the internal carotid artery of Cetaceans closes up before birth, just as that of Even-Toed Ungulates, de Kock has shown recently that, at least in porpoises and Pilot Whales, the vessel is still open in adult animals, although its lumen is very narrow. The thick layer of circular muscle in its wall, and the fact that it is innervated, suggest that the vessel plays a part in controlling the flow of the blood.

Some authors hold that the duct (*ductus arteriosus*; see Fig. 90) connecting the aorta and the pulmonary artery in foetuses, which closes up after birth, remains open in adult Cetaceans. They claim that this has some connexion with changes in blood pressure when the animal dives, but I have failed to find any evidence for this hypothesis. I have, in fact, examined the hearts of many adult porpoises and dolphins of different species, and have even managed to dissect the *ductus arteriosus* of twenty Blue and Fin Whales aboard the *Willem Barendsz*, but all the ducts were found to be entirely closed or so constricted that practically no blood could have passed through them. The ducts of adult animals could therefore not have played any part in regulating the pressure of the vascular system. However, while after birth the *ductus arteriosus* of terrestrial mammals very quickly closes up into a band of hard connective tissue, this closure is significantly retarded in Cetaceans as well as in the Common Seal. A very narrow passage may be left open until the age of 8–12 weeks in the Common Seal, 4–14 months in porpoises and dolphins and 5–13 years in Blue and Fin Whales. The explanation of this phenomenon may be found in the fact that the closure of the duct is highly influenced by the oxygen saturation of the blood. Shortage of oxygen in the blood, and perhaps also a rise of the blood pressure in the pulmonary artery, may cause a temporary reopening of the duct. Consequently, respiratory difficulties in the first weeks after birth may prevent or retard its closure. Such difficulties may be expected to occur in all Cetaceans, because they are born in the water and swim and dive immediately after birth. The same difficulties may occur in the Common Seal because the pups of this species are obliged to enter the water a few hours after birth (they are born on sand banks which are flooded at high tide). In most other Pinnipeds the pups generally do not enter the water before they are 3–4 weeks old or even older. All data available at the moment point to the fact that in these animals the duct closes as quickly as in terrestrial mammals.

Since we are discussing embryonic blood vessels, the reader may be interested to know that the *ductus venosus*, i.e. the duct joining the portal and umbilical veins to the inferior vena cava, though present in the early stages of the Cetacean embryo, disappears half-way through the period of gestation. In Blue and Fin Whales, it is found in foetuses less than about $7\frac{1}{2}$ feet in length, but not in others. This peculiarity of the Cetaceans also needs to be investigated further.

Not all the Cetacean retia have an exclusively or predominantly blood-pressure-regulating function. If, for instance, we examine the retia of the brachial artery, i.e. the artery running to the flippers, we are struck by characteristic differences from the other retia. Where the latter consist

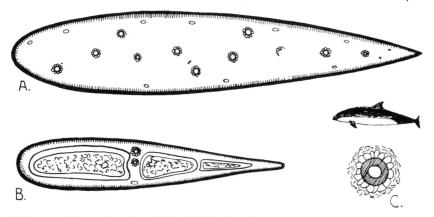

Figure 97. Cross-sections through (A) the flukes (B) the pectoral fin of a Bottlenose Dolphin, showing position of arteries surrounded by a sheet of veins. One such 'sheet' is magnified in C. Small veins not accompanied by arteries are found close under the skin. (Modified after Scholander and Schevill, 1955.)

predominantly of imperceptibly intertwined arterioles with many anastomoses, i.e. of a real network, the brachial artery splits up into a great number of parallel vessels of uniform width with few interconnections (Fig. 95). Along and between these vessels there is a system of similarly constructed brachial veins. As far as is known such special retia occur in all Odontocetes. Mysticetes have not yet been examined in sufficient detail, but Ommanney stated in 1932 that Fin Whales have a single brachial artery surrounded with a net of veins.

Similar retia are also found in Odontocete chevron canals in which the artery carrying blood to the flukes is surrounded with a mixed arterial-cum-venous vascular network. In the flukes themselves, the artery splits up into a very large number of arterioles, all of which are surrounded with a network of mainly longitudinal venules which link up with the retia in the chevron canal (Fig. 97). The flukes also have another multiple system of venules just under the skin. These join up with the superficial caudal veins, which return the blood to the abdominal retia. The chevron canals of Rorquals have only one artery and one vein, but the arteries in the flukes are surrounded with the same kind of venous network as are found in Odontocetes. Arterioles surrounded with venules are also found in the dorsal fin, the flippers and, indeed, throughout the entire integument of Rorquals as well as in the baleen (see Chapter 11).

Their precise significance only became clear during the Second World War, when the Norwegian physiologist P. F. Scholander who, as we have seen, was working in the United States at the time, investigated the effect of exposure on airmen who were forced to bale out over the sea. In this connexion, he studied the regulation of heat losses, particularly in aquatic mammals. He was struck by the fact that the pectoral fins and the flukes are only provided with a thin layer of insulating blubber, and that, therefore, considerable heat losses must occur in these regions. In fact, measurements revealed that the pelvic flippers of seals and the flukes of porpoises were at water temperature, while the temperature of the rest of the body was at least 15 degrees higher. The fins and flukes would thus act like pumps drawing heat from the rest of the body, were it not that the retia prevented them from doing so. In the retia, the warm blood going to, and the cold blood returning from, the flippers and flukes are brought into close contact, and an exchange of heat is effected between them. Thus the arterial blood warms the venous blood returning from the extremities, while all the arterial blood that reaches them has first been cooled by the veins.

It is also possible that under certain conditions, such as great muscular exertion, the body may become overheated. While men can get rid of surplus heat by sweating, Cetaceans have no sweat glands and moreover are surrounded with thick layers of insulating blubber. Hence the excess heat must be lost in a different way, i.e. through the flippers and flukes. Tomilin, investigating an East Siberian Dolphin, found that the temperature of the fins varied by as much as $13 \cdot 5°$ C or $24 \cdot 3°$ F ($20°$ C–$33 \cdot 5°$ C), while the temperature of the rest of the body fluctuated over a maximum range of $0 \cdot 5°$ C. Schevill, working in a warmer climate (Florida), found that the temperature of the fins of a Bottlenose Dolphin was $10°$ C above that of the rest of the integument. Scholander assumes that, during overheating, the circulation in the tail is so regulated that the blood returning from the flukes does not pass through the retia but mainly through the lateral veins of the tail. The arterial blood therefore retains its heat until it reaches the flukes, there to lose it to the sea. Whether similar processes also occur in the flippers still needs to be investigated by careful anatomical examination. It must, however, be mentioned that heat losses are also controlled by similar mechanisms in the entire integument of all Cetaceans (see Chapter 11), and that this type of *retia mirabilia* is also found in sea-cows. Sea-lions and seals, however, do not have them. The only exception is the walrus which has extensive retia in the lower fore and hind limbs. Retia also occur in some terrestrial mammals such as sloths, ant-eaters, and some lemurs, in all of which they have a clear heat-regulating function.

It goes without saying that many scientists who study the blood of Cetaceans do so in the hope of probing some of the mysteries of mammalian life under water. Now, while there is never any shortage of such blood, it must be remembered that most of our experimental material is derived from dead specimens, and has consequently undergone certain changes. Most investigators have been primarily concerned with the oxygen affinity of the haemoglobin in, and the size and number of, the red blood corpuscles. Their diameter in Cetaceans can vary between 7·5 and 10·5 μ (i.e. thousandth parts of a millimetre), depending on the species. The biggest corpuscles are found in Sperm Whales (10·5 μ), which hold the mammalian record. Other Cetaceans have red corpuscles with an average diameter 8·5 μ, which is rather higher than the general average for all mammals taken together. Our own red blood cells have an average diameter of about 7·5 μ, but most other mammals have smaller averages (horse 5·5 μ, goat 3·6 μ). The number of red cells per c.c. of blood varies in Cetaceans between 7 and 11 million, the average being about 9·5, again somewhat higher than the average for mammals of comparable size. Thus in man, the average is 5, and in many other mammals 6 to 7 million cells per c.c. of blood. Hence it is not surprising that in 1939 Knoll came to the conclusion that the ratio of red corpuscles to blood plasma is much greater in Cetaceans than it is in man.

Now the oxygen-carrying capacity of the blood depends not so much on the total volume as on the total surface of all the red blood cells taken together, for the greater the surface area the faster will the red cells be able to take up oxygen in the lungs and to supply it to the tissues. Knoll calculated that in Rorquals this total surface area is one-and-a-half times and, in Sperm Whales, twice that in man – per c.c. of blood, of course. Since, however, we have seen that the total quantity of blood expressed as a ratio of the total size of a given animal does not differ greatly in Cetaceans from that in other mammals, we can apply these figures to the total volume of blood.

Some scientists believe that the haemoglobin content of Cetacean red blood cells is greater than it is in mammals in general, but others have questioned this and ascribed the high figures recorded to experimental errors. I myself investigated a great many Rorqual blood specimens aboard the *Willem Barendsz*, and I never obtained values which differed significantly from those for terrestrial mammals. However, the Japanese biologist Tawara suggested in 1951 that blood pigments other than haemoglobin may also play a part in transporting oxygen.

Attempts have also been made to discover significant differences between the oxygen-binding properties of the red blood cells of Cetaceans and terrestrial mammals. In 1953 Burke submitted all the known data to a critical examination, and suggested that all we could say with certainty was that the haemoglobin of the porpoise and Bottlenose Dolphin contains up to 19 per cent and that of the Fin Whale up to about

14 per cent of oxygen. These figures are of the same order of magnitude
as those found in terrestrial mammals, in the case of which they fluctuate
between 11 per cent and 24 per cent. The only striking differences were
found in seals, for which the figure was 29 per cent. All these remarks
bear out our argument in Chapter 4, viz. that no special reserves of
oxygen are stored in the blood during diving.

The Cetacean muscles, on the other hand, are known to contain 2–8
times as much myoglobin (muscle haemoglobin) as those of terrestrial
mammals, and to have an affinity for oxygen that far surpasses that of
normal haemoglobin. Now we understand why the red blood corpuscles
of Cetaceans cannot have an excessive affinity for oxygen, since, otherwise, they would be unable to surrender enough of this gas to the muscles
which need large reserves of it in dives when their oxygen is cut off. This
is probably also the reason why the haemoglobin of the deepest divers
absorbs the lowest percentage of oxygen, and so shows the greatest
difference from myoglobin. Low oxygen capacity of the blood cells
and high oxygen capacity of the muscles obviously meet the needs of
Cetaceans and other diving mammals admirably. Hence, the main
characteristic of Cetacean blood cells is their exceptionally large surface
area which enables them to effect gaseous exchanges very speedily – a
reasonable arrangement if we consider how little time Cetaceans generally
spend at the surface, and in how short a time the oxygen reserve in their
muscles has to be replenished. Their blood must therefore be considered
not so much an oxygen reservoir for diving, as a quick means of transporting oxygen when surfacing.

To complete the picture, we must say something about the other blood
cells of Cetaceans. Scientists have found nothing unusual here, except an
increased proportion of eosinophil leucocytes in the blood. This phenomenon is not yet understood, but in any case it must be remembered that
practically all the blood examined was taken from animals which were
killed after a desperate struggle and which, moreover, must have lost vast
quantities of blood, with consequent changes in the total blood picture.
This may also explain why some specimens were found to contain an
unusually high percentage of normoblasts. If we remember that the blood
picture in pigs can change significantly after the animals have spent only
one hour in a cattle truck, it seems almost certain that the blood of
Cetaceans captured after a long chase must undergo significant changes also.

No discussion of the vascular system and the blood would be complete
without some mention of the spleen, an organ which plays an important
part in the circulation of all mammals. However, what precisely this part is,
is no clearer today than it was in the day of Claude Bernard, the great
French physiologist who, while examining a candidate, asked him to

explain the function of the spleen. The wretched student was extremely discomfited by this unexpected question and finally stammered out that, though he had once known the answer, somehow he had forgotten it. 'What a terrible pity,' Claude Bernard rejoined, 'because no one before you has ever known it at all.'

For a long time, it was generally believed that the spleen, which is part of the circulatory system, contracted or relaxed to decrease or increase the capacity of the circulatory system. Modern opinion, however, is that the spleen plays a negligible part in regulating the blood flow compared with other organs. Biologists now think that the spleen retains some of the blood passing through it for some time, during which the chemical composition of the blood is changed to form substances which regulate the blood pressure, the breakdown of red blood cells and probably respiration as well. Moreover, the spleen also plays a definite role in the body's defences against bacteria and other harmful organisms, with some of its cells destroying them or counteracting their effect.

Since we know so little about our own spleen it seems strange that we should be discussing that of Cetaceans. In fact, we would have passed over this subject in dignified silence, but for the fact that the Cetacean spleen has a very striking characteristic – it is remarkably small.

True, the spleen of big Rorquals weighs some 6–22 lb., the average being 13 lb., but that is only about 0·02 per cent of the animal's total weight, as against 0·3 per cent in most other mammals. In other words the spleen of the Rorqual is proportionally $\frac{1}{15}$ that of most terrestrial mammals, and so is the spleen of many porpoises and dolphins. Moreover, the spleen of Cetaceans does not have a very distinctive shape. In Rorquals, it is generally elongated, some 60 cm. long, and rather narrow and flat, though many other shapes occur as well. Just as in all other mammals, the spleen has a bright reddish-brown colour and is attached to the stomach by a peritoneal fold. Sometimes one or even more small accessory spleens are also present.

In order to gain a better understanding of the reason why the Cetacean spleen is so small, Miss H. H. L. Zwillenberg, a biology student at Amsterdam University, made a painstaking investigation of their fine structure (1956–7). She came to the conclusion that there is a characteristic difference between the spleen of Odontocetes and that of Mysticetes, as the former have a far greater number of lymph corpuscles, i.e. of white spleen pulp. (In porpoises, for instance, this pulp accounts for 30 per cent of the total spleen content.) This difference is probably due to the two Cetacean sub-orders being descended from terrestrial animals with different types of spleen, though the spleens of both have so many characteristics in common with the spleens of Carnivores and Ungulates that we can safely deduce a particularly close relationship to these mammalian orders. This is further evidence in support of the assumptions we have made on this subject in Chapter 2. The extremely small size of the spleen may be an indication that Cetaceans can largely dispense with those substances in that organ which regulate blood pressure and respiration. It may be assumed that, because of their special method of respiration and their diving habits, this regulation is effected in a different way, with the proviso that our remarks about the spleen apply only to Cetaceans and not to aquatic animals in general. The spleens of seals and sea-lions, for instance, represent an average of 0·45 per cent of the animals' total weight, a much higher figure than that for terrestrial mammals. Hence the small size of the Cetacean spleen may well be associated with the presence of *retia mirabilia*, which are absent or poorly developed in seals and sea-lions. Since the retia play an extremely important part in regulating the blood pressure, it is quite possible that they have relieved the spleen of much of its normal work.

The reader might wonder whether the diminutive size of the Cetacean spleen also vitiates its ability to break down worn red blood corpuscles and to defend the body against bacterial infection. Unfortunately, we cannot give a definite answer to this question. All that is known is that Cetaceans have an exceptional number of very large lymph glands, which are another mammalian line of defence against microbes, and another means of breaking down worn-out red blood cells. When examining the lymph glands of some dolphins under the microscope I saw clear signs of such a breakdown, and it is quite possible that, in Cetaceans, the lymph glands have to some extent taken over this function from the spleen.

So much for the Cetacean spleen, and if what we have said seems somewhat inconclusive, the zoologist's only excuse is that his knowledge of the human spleen is not much greater.

In conclusion we might add that Cetaceans have tonsils, like all other mammals, and in the same place. Little else can be said about them, since this mass of lymphatic tissue has scarcely been examined in Cetaceans. The same may be said of the thymus gland, a dark red lobular organ found in the anterior thorax of foetuses and young animals. In Cetaceans, as in all other mammals, the thymus begins to atrophy with the onset of puberty, after which it gradually disappears. We mention the thymus merely because it, too, consists of lymphatic tissue. Little else is known about its function, though English physiologists have recently discovered that, in man, the thymus may be associated with the pathological condition known as *myasthenia gravis*, the main symptoms of which are extreme fatigue and serious muscular impairment. If the respiratory muscles are affected, this condition may have fatal consequences. Apparently, *myasthenia gravis* occurs in man when the thymus persists in adulthood or when it swells up. Thymus extract appeared to have a similar effect on experimental animals, and, in order to obtain larger quantities of the extract for pathological research, biologists enlisted the help of the Hector Whaling Company. During the 1955 season, P. T. Nowell managed to collect large quantities of thymus extract on board the *Balaena*, and it is hoped that in this way the causes of *myasthenia gravis* may be better understood in the near future.

Figure 98. Bottlenose Dolphin jumping for fish. Photograph: Miami Seaquarium.

FLORIDA IS NOT ONLY a tourist's paradise; it has attractions for naturalists and particularly those interested in marine biology as well. The Marine Studios of Marineland, Florida, has the biggest sea-water aquarium in the world, one of the few containing dolphins and small whales. The aquarium has two tanks – a round one, 80 feet in diameter and 13 feet deep, holding about 400,000 gallons of sea-water, the other quadrangular, 100 feet × 100 feet × 20 feet deep. Visitors can walk all around its edges, and can also go down into special passages along the side of the tank to watch the animals through portholes.

The tanks teem with sharks, rays and other fish, crabs, cuttlefish, turtles and innumerable other creatures. Still, the Bottlenose Dolphins (or Common Porpoises, as the Americans call them) have always been the greatest attraction (Fig. 98). These animals are about ten feet long, black on top and white underneath, and have snouts protruding from their typically bulbous heads. They are quite common off the coast of Florida, where they can be caught easily in nets, so that there is no difficulty in keeping their numbers up – not that this presents a problem, in any case, for they feel so much at home in Marineland that they breed there quite happily. In addition to Bottlenose Dolphins, Marineland also has some specimens of *Stenella plagiodon*, a Spotted Dolphin, and an occasional Pilot Whale. Pilot Whales, which are some twenty-two feet long, nearly black, and with bulging, rounded, foreheads (Fig. 19) occasionally strand on the Florida coast in schools of forty to fifty. While they normally perish fairly quickly in the heat, the fortuitous presence of an expert may often save their lives. We have seen earlier that dolphins can only be transported alive if they are kept moist and cool, so that overheating and skin-blisters which quickly lead to infections are avoided. By taking prompt action, experts in 1948 managed to save a number of stranded Pilot Whales and again in 1958 and then to take them to Marineland. Three of the four animals captured in 1948 survived for only a few days, but the fourth, which lived for another nine months, became Marineland's star turn. Then it was suddenly set upon by the dolphins and fatally injured. Two of the Pilot Whales captured in 1958 were flown to a branch of Marineland in California, where they became acclimatized very soon. In addition, Marineland also kept a single Pigmy Sperm Whale for some time.

Marineland attracted so much public attention that, not surprisingly, similar aquaria have sprung up in other parts of the New World during the last fifteen years: The Living Sea Gulfarium at Fort Walton Beach (Florida); The Lerner Marine Laboratory in Bimini (Bahamas); The Marineland of the Pacific (a Californian branch of Marineland, Florida); and The Ocean Aquarium at Hermosa Beach near Los Angeles, also in California. For some time the Silver Springs Aquarium (Florida) contained two Boutus, caught in the Amazon and transported by air; the other aquaria contain Bottlenose Dolphins, and The Marineland of the Pacific keeps Common Dolphins, some specimens of the Pacific White-beaked Dolphin (*Lagenorhynchus obliquidens*) and a Pacific Pilot Whale (*Globicephala scammoni*). Australian Bottlenose Dolphins are kept in The Coolangatta Aquarium in Sydney and in The Service Paradise Aquarium near Brisbane. In Japan their North Pacific relatives live in an aquarium at Enoshima. However, for our purposes, Florida's Marineland has remained the most important, since it is here that most of the scientific research work on the behaviour of dolphins has been carried out under such ·eminent men as Kellogg and Wood, though during the past few years biologists at The Marineland of the Pacific (amongst them Norris and Brown) have also begun to publish important papers.

In particular, these aquaria have provided a wealth of data on the sense organs, the production of sound, the diet, birth and general behaviour of Cetaceans, to which we shall have to return time and again in the following chapters. We, in Europe, have good reason to feel envious, for few of our zoos or aquaria have large enough tanks to keep dolphins for any length of time. Moreover, capture and transport still seem to present insuperable difficulties over here. Monaco and Plymouth have made some efforts during the last few years to overcome them, but so far with little success, although Monaco kept three Common Dolphins in captivity in 1958. True, there have been sporadic cases of dolphins being kept in captivity in Europe, but such cases are few and far between. Thus the Bottlenose Dolphin which spent a few months at the Biological Station at Arcachon in 1873, and on which Jolyet performed the first experiments on Cetacean respiration, was an exception. The Copenhagen Zoo once managed to keep a porpoise for a short time, and the Westminster Aquarium in London boasted two Belugas at different times – one in 1877 and another in 1878. The first came from Labrador, the second from Newfoundland, but neither survived the five-week journey by ship for very long. Living Belugas were also exhibited during 1909 in a big tank in the docks of Atlantic City, and in 1914 James watched the birth of a young porpoise in Brighton Aquarium. In 1907 New York Aquarium kept a school of Bottlenose Dolphins in a pool 40 feet in diameter and seven feet deep, and some scientific institutes, e.g. Woods Hole Laboratory, also managed to keep an odd Bottlenose Dolphin. In a pool near Namazu (Japan), space was provided not only for different species of dolphin but also for a Little Piked Whale which lived there for a whole month.

Still, Marineland is much more fortunate than European aquaria, in that it is closer to the sea, and in that the transport of dolphins presents comparatively few difficulties. For this reason, special mention must be made of the efforts of W. H. Dudok van Heel (Zoological Station at den Helder) to capture porpoises off Denmark and to transport them alive to Holland (December 1957–January 1958). With the assistance of the director of the Texels Museum, G. J. de Haan, he organized an expedition to Teglgaard near Middelfart where, as we have seen on page 51, porpoises have been caught since the sixteenth century. Though the industry folded up after the Second World War, there were still enough skilled fishermen left to net some twenty porpoises within a few weeks. The animals became used to human contact fairly quickly, and even allowed themselves to be stroked and to be fed by hand. They were taken to Holland in a truck equipped with latex foam mattresses on which the animals were kept wet throughout the journey. Despite the enormous efforts made by the leaders of the expedition – they kept a constant vigil for twenty-four bitterly cold hours – only one of the captured animals reached a basin on Texel alive, to survive for a few months. These porpoises differed from Bottlenose and other dolphins in that they showed clear symptoms of shock when they were lifted out of the water – their heart beat became very irregular, they passed a great deal of urine, and they showed clear signs of having muscle cramp. Most of them died within thirty seconds, and all but one of those that survived the initial shock, died in the truck or very shortly after transport. Although the causes of this shock are not quite clear, it seems that the symptoms occur when the animals are lifted out of deep water (13–20 feet) but not when they are lifted out of shallow water (3–6 feet). Since similar experiences have been reported in the case of Phocaenoid porpoises off California, we may conclude that most porpoises have this special sensitivity.

Using his one survivor, W. H. Dudok van Heel carried out a number of important experiments on the hearing of porpoises (see Chapter 7). The expedition also provided much useful information on the capture and transport of porpoises, and showed that the difficulties involved are such

Figure 99. A female dolphin (Lagenorhynchus obliquidens) *performing tricks in The Marineland of the Pacific, California. Photograph: D. H. Brown, Marineland, California.*

that we in Europe will have to wait quite some time before we can hope to rival American achievements.

Dolphins are general favourites with the spectators because of their entertaining antics. They are extremely lively, keep swimming round the aquarium, jump right out of the water, play with one another and with fishes or floating objects – in short, they are as playful as could be and form a strange contrast to the phlegmatic sea-cows in some European zoos. Like elephants, bears and monkeys, they can be taught all sorts of tricks, though, naturally, we cannot expect them to eat at a table, to ride a bicycle or to brush their teeth – their bodies are just not built that way. But when we read that Flippy, the star turn of Marineland, not only ate out of her keeper's hand and caught fish in mid-air, but that she could also tug at a bell, blow a trumpet, fetch a ball, jump through a paper hoop and, with special harness, pull a boat holding a girl and a dog, we can see why most aquaria are so keen to have them. Skinny, the prima donna at Hermosa Beach, and the dolphins in The Marineland of the Pacific and other aquaria (the Pilot Whale included), are no less agile (Figs. 99 and 100) and learn new tricks all the time. One of them is in fact a dab hand with the hula-hoop. More surprising still is the fact that dolphins in their natural state can also make friends with man. Thus, the dolphin which

Figure 100. Young Bottlenose Dolphins playing basketball. The young male 'scoring a goal' bears scars inflicted by the dominant bull of his school. Photograph: D. H. Brown, Marineland, California.

died on Opononi Beach near Auckland (New Zealand) had been the playmate of children and adults for many years. Opo or Opononi George, as they called him, allowed the children to ride on his back and played ball with them. Similarly, Lamb (1954) described the antics of an Amazonian Boutu which assisted fishermen by driving fish from deep into shallow water. It responded to the men's whistles and would spend hours in the vicinity of the boat. A third example of man's close contact with wild dolphins was cited by Capt. Mörzer Bruins, who reported that in the Bay of Dakar, Bottlenose Dolphins habitually mingle with the bathers, and often try to snatch fish from skin divers.

We might wonder why animals whose mode of life is so different from our own can be tamed so easily. The answer is quite simple. Cetaceans have no natural enemies other than the Killer Whale and therefore need fear little from other aquatic animals below, and nothing from animals above the surface. Hence they are never suspicious and are naturally inclined to be friendly and playful.

They are, moreover, extremely inquisitive and like to investigate everything that goes on around them. This has long been known by seafarers, who will tell you the story of 'Pelorus Jack', a Pilot Whale (or possibly a Risso's Dolphin) which accompanied ships plying between Wellington and Nelson in New Zealand almost every day for thirty-two years. The animal became so much of a national institution that during 1904–14 it was protected by special legislation, infringements carrying a fine of up to £100.

Similar stories are also told about bigger whales, and particularly about Humpbacks, which like to come right up to ships and to swim around and under them in order to investigate them at close quarters. Blue and Fin Whales behave similarly, and especially their young. Whalers have noted that Blue Whales become a little more suspicious before the onset of puberty. It is said that the present size limit for Blue Whales (which are sexually mature at 74–77 feet) was fixed at 70 feet since this limit is easily determined from the animal's behaviour. But adult whales, too, are by no means shy, though old animals may have learned from experience to be wary of man. This may be the reason why the largest proportion of the catch consists of animals which are about to reach or have just reached sexual maturity (see Chapter 14). Sperm Whales, too, are not afraid of man, and have therefore been successfully hunted with even the most primitive equipment. Thus Lt F. A. J. de Boer, third officer aboard the *Piet Hein*, relates that, on 7th June, 1955, he spotted a Sperm Whale swimming very slowly. When a number of blank depth charges were detonated, the animal did not swim any faster but simply changed course, a clear sign that it had noticed the explosions.

Another reason why dolphins are so particularly tractable may well be connected with their being carnivorous. All carnivores have a far wider range of behaviour patterns than herbivorous animals, for they must stalk and capture their prey, while herbivores have merely to go up to their food. In other words, carnivorous animals have to solve many more problems and tackle all sorts of situations in all sorts of special ways, while herbivorous animals find the table already laid for them, or else go hungry. Hence, by and large, carnivores prove the most versatile circus performers, with a far bigger repertoire of tricks than even horses or elephants. More-over, carnivores become very attached to their keepers and can be trained and bribed with food. This is particularly true of fish eaters, which gener-ally devour vast quantities of food and which can be fed at frequent intervals. The dolphins and Pilot Whales at Marineland, for instance, not only know exactly when it is feeding time, but they also learn to come up to eat out of their keeper's hand during the intervals (Figs. 98 and 101). An old female Bottlenose Whale learned to do so within a week, and also to respond to a dinner bell. W. H. Dudok van Heel's porpoises also learnt to eat from his hand very quickly.

Figure 101. Dolphins feeding out of the hand of a diver. Photograph: D. H. Brown, Marineland, California.

Another reason why dolphins can be trained so quickly is their natural playfulness. Not only do they chase one another and other animals in the aquarium, but they also like to throw dead fish and balls into the air, and to catch them as they come down. They can keep this game up for a long time, and they also like to play with all sorts of objects floating on the water (Fig. 102). Thus, some dolphins and Pilot Whales were seen to amuse themselves for more than an hour with a feather of one of the pelicans which shared their tank (Fig. 103). They will fetch stones and other objects for you, and even bring up stones from the bottom of the tank to spit them with great accuracy at the bystanders. One of them is reported to have taken an instant dislike to Roman Catholic priests, spitting stones at them the moment they approached. Other dolphins made up for this lack of manners by great courtesy and consideration, one of them returning a camera a girl had dropped. A photograph of this act appeared in *Life* magazine of March 1959, together with pictures of dolphins playing basketball, stealing handkerchiefs out of visitors' pockets, and many other tricks. Young animals are naturally much more

Figure 102. Bottlenose Dolphin playing with an inflated tyre.
Photograph: F. S. Essapian, Miami Seaquarium.

Figure 103. An adult female Bottlenose Dolphin playing with a pelican feather. Photograph:
D. H. Brown, Marineland, California.

playful than older ones, but they often nag their elders and betters into playing with them. The older generation do not seem to mind, and adult cows have often been seen 'borrowing' calves from other cows to share in the fun.

Nor is this playfulness restricted to captive specimens. We have already spoken of whales turning somersaults (see Chapter 3) while diving[1], but quite apart from such displays of high spirits, they like to play other games as well. Thus T. J. Terpstra reports that on 10th August, 1955, the S.S. *Akkrumdijk* (Holland-America Line) passed a school of fourteen Sperm Whales at 35°N 52°W. While most of the animals swam away when the ship drew near, one Sperm Whale stayed on to play with a drifting plank, diving close beneath it and then turning round to give a number of repeat performances. Capt. Mörzer Bruins reports that cormorants and dolphins regularly play in the Bay of Bahrein, the cormorants swooping down on and pecking at the dolphins as the latter

[1] Dolphins, as is well-known, leap into the air (Fig. 57), and Pilot Whales have often been observed to come halfway out of the water in a vertical position. These actions are performed both during and outside the mating season (see Fig. 196).

surface. The dolphins react by jumping right out of the water. Whether this game, which, by the way, the cormorants also like to play with ducks, is entirely to the dolphins' liking is open to discussion, though dolphins are known to deal summarily with other nuisances. Caldwell (1956) reports that one of the Bottlenose Dolphins in The Living Sea Gulfarium repeatedly picked up a turtle which tried to steal fish from it and dropped it at the other side of the tank.

Another helpful factor in the training of Bottlenose Dolphins is the fact that, just like seals and sea-lions, they are diurnal animals, i.e. they eat and play during the day and rest by night. Hence, like monkeys, horses and dogs, they are closer to man's daily rhythm than, say, hedgehogs or cats which are most active in the dusk or at night. Not that these dolphins are fully awake throughout the day, for after each feed they usually snatch about an hour's 'sleep', the cows floating with their blowhole above water, and the bulls just a little below the surface, to come up for air every so often, and usually opening their eyes as they do so. At night, when they do not feed, they usually sleep for much longer periods. Naturally, wild dolphins may have quite a different diurnal rhythm, possibly influenced by the tides, since, during high water, they enter creeks and bays in search of fish. Layne has stated that Boutus are active day and night, but the porpoise which was kept in Texel for some months used to spend a great deal of its time dozing at the surface. Vincent (1960) reports that the Common Dolphins in Monaco had a daily respiratory rhythm of six and a nightly rhythm of three to four blows per minute.

In any case, the Marineland aquarium has clearly shown that some Cetaceans are in fact nocturnal animals, since when Pilot Whales were first taken there, they spent practically the whole day floating near the surface, their eyes closed and their blowhole, front part of the back and dorsal fin just protruding above the water. For this reason, these animals had to be fed at night-time, though the Pilot Whale which stayed in the aquarium for nine months gradually began to become more active during the day, thus adapting itself to the general pattern. However, when the dolphins started to attack it, it quickly returned to its old nocturnal ways. At Marineland, California, too, a Pilot Whale used to sleep both during the day and during the night, dozing either horizontally or vertically near the surface. Whether this difference between dolphins and Pilot Whales is connected with their diet – the former feeding predominantly on fish and the latter predominantly on cuttlefish – will have to be investigated further. In any case, it appears that the Gangetic Dolphin, which is practically blind, and which feeds off the slimy bottom of the Ganges and its tributaries, is another nocturnal animal, and so, apparently, is the Little Piked Whale, though Kimura and Nemoto (1956), who observed one of these animals for a whole month in a Japanese tank, state that it did not sleep at all but merely increased its respirational and other activities from nightfall until about midnight, thereafter to become more restful again.

The fact that aquatic animals sleep at all may seem strange, since we usually associate the idea of sleep with a supine position, but if we recall that horses and elephants have no difficulty in sleeping on their feet, there is really nothing that need occasion us any surprise. Some fish sleep during the night, while others which are most active during that period (e.g. some sharks) spend their days dozing at the bottom of the sea, or near the surface (e.g. the Basking Shark and the Moonfish). Although seals and sea-lions generally sleep ashore, they, too, can occasionally doze in the water, sometimes with their noses just above the water, but generally floating below the surface and coming up for air at regular intervals. They often sleep with their eyes shut, and give the impression of being very fast asleep indeed, though it is still debatable whether their 'sleeping' is comparable with ours. When we sleep, our blood pressure and respiratory frequency drops, our muscles become relaxed, and there is a decrease in activity of certain nerve centres. It is, of course, extremely difficult to establish the existence of similar phenomena in animals, and particularly in fish and dolphins, though we do know that most terrestrial mammals (some monkeys excluded) sleep much less deeply than we do. Cows, horses and donkeys never seem to sleep properly at all, but to doze gently instead.

The Sperm Whale seems to be the deepest sleeper of all Cetaceans. A number of observers have stated repeatedly that this animal can stay near the surface for hours on end, apparently very fast asleep. This is also borne out by the many stories of ships colliding with sleeping Sperm Whales. Thus, one dark night during the Second World War, the crew of an American destroyer felt a heavy jolt as their ship rapidly lost speed. Thinking that they had been torpedoed, they took to the boats only to discover that there was no apparent damage. Next morning the body of a large Sperm Whale was found right across the bows. A similar experience was had by Capt. A. P. Disselkoen on 22nd March, 1955, aboard the S.S. *Amerskerk*. The ship was making 17 knots west of Cape Guardafui when she suddenly had a mysterious collision. It was found that, just below the water-line, she had struck the head and body of a thirty-two-foot Sperm Whale. The engines had to be reversed to shake off the animal which had been killed by the impact. It seems likely that Sperm Whales were also responsible for the reported collisions of the Russian whaler *Aleut* near the Panama Canal, the 24,000-ton American liner *Constitution* off Genoa, and the *Willem Ruys* (Royal Rotterdam Lloyd) between Cape Town and Colombo (all three in 1956).

Greenland Whales, too, are extensively reported to be rather heavy sleepers, and Capt. Mörzer Bruins tells us that one day in the South Atlantic, as his ship passed a Biscayan Right Whale sleeping at the surface, the animal woke up only when the ship's bow waves lapped over its head. Clearly, such observations may be expected far more frequently in the case of Sperm Whales, Right Whales and Humpback Whales than, for instance, of Fin Whales, since the former are lighter and therefore float more readily at the surface (see Chapter 3). Even so, there are some reports of sleeping Fin Whales, particularly from warmer waters. Unfortunately we still lack information about how non-captive dolphins and porpoises sleep, though Degerbøl and Freuchen report that Narwhals often doze at the surface.

Another reason why dolphins are so easily trained and handled is that they, and indeed all other Cetaceans, are herd animals, and herd animals are known to be naturally far more tractable than others. In his contact with such animals man is always helped by the fact that the animals quickly learn to look upon him as one of their own herd.

Unfortunately, little is known about the exact composition of Cetacean herds, though, from what sparse data we have, it would seem that like herds of terrestrial mammals, Cetaceans congregate in schools of varying sizes. There are first of all the very big schools (100–1,000 animals), some of which are known to be mixed schools consisting of cows and bulls of all ages. Apart from two exceptions, which will be discussed below, nothing resembling a leader has been found in these schools, which is also the case with large herds of terrestrial animals, e.g. some South African zebras.

The largest of these leaderless schools are, or rather used to be, made up of Biscayan Right Whales. Nowadays, these animals are generally seen alone, or in small schools, probably as a result of intense hunting, but formerly they were reported to congregate in very large schools indeed.

Another of the big whales found in large schools is the Fin Whale. Schools of up to 300 (and occasionally of up to 1,000) animals of this species are still not uncommon, though schools of ten to fifteen seem to be the more general rule. Within the school itself, different observers have reported the existence of especially close-knit groups of two to three animals, though they could not determine with any certainty whether these were family units made up of bull, cow and calf, or of cow and two calves of different ages. Zenkovich states in his book on whaling in the U.S.S.R. (German translation 1956) that, during migration, old and young animals usually travel in separate schools, to recombine into larger schools when they have reached their Arctic or Antarctic destination.

Herds of zebras are known to join other herd animals (e.g. antelope and buffalo), and the same may be true of Fin Whales also. On 24th June, 1955, A. Vermeulen, first mate on M.S. *Oberon* (K.N.S.M.) reported that, at 39°N 73°W, he observed a school of about fifty Fin Whales swimming in a north-easterly direction. The animals, apparently on their migration to the north, were accompanied by hundreds of dolphins.

Common Dolphins, Bottlenose Dolphins, False Killers, or dolphins of the genera Prodelphinus, Lagenorhynchus, Orcaella and Steno occur in very large, mixed and apparently leaderless schools. The existence of mixed schools of dolphins, i.e. schools containing bulls, cows and calves of all ages, has been established on many occasions either during mass strandings or during mass catches (see Chapter 1). Though dolphins have often been seen in fairly or even very small schools, schools of about 1,000 strong are by no means rare. In 1955 Tomilin reported that he had seen a school of Black Sea Dolphins from the air, which he estimated at roughly 100,000 animals. Such schools must be considered exceptional, however, and are probably restricted to the breeding grounds of the fish on which the dolphins feed. If food becomes scarce, these large schools break up into smaller ones again. Schools of Little Piked Whale, Humpback Whale, Cuvier's Whale, Risso's Dolphin and of some River Dolphins are usually smaller than 100, and generally consist of ten to twenty animals, the schools being mixed, as far as is known. Boutus live in schools of from three to six, and are sometimes found alone, while Rough Toothed Dolphins of the genus *Sotalia* have been seen in schools of from three to twenty.

Greenland and Blue Whales usually live alone or in small family groups of bull, cow and calf, though Greenland Whales are thought to combine into schools where food is plentiful. Blue Whales, too, live solitary or restricted lives in the Arctic and Antarctic, but in their winter quarters they are said to combine into larger groups. Capt. Mörzer Bruins reported that, on 23rd September, 1953, at 11°15′N 60°20′E, i.e. in the Indian Ocean, he met a school of thirty to fifty Blue Whales, spread over an area of ten miles. Within the school itself, smaller groups of three to four animals could be distinguished.

The Sei Whale appears to lead a more solitary existence and is rarely met in larger groups, while the Pigmy Sperm Whale seems to avoid his fellows almost completely. The Gangetic Dolphin, too, does not apparently like its congeners, though more than one individual may share the same creek.

Amongst terrestrial animals (e.g. mountain zebras, donkeys, sheep and goats), we often find separate herds of males and females. The female herd, which includes immature young males, is sometimes led by a strong male (e.g. in some monkeys and llamas), when it may legitimately be called a 'harem'. Generally, however, the leader, too, is a female.

'Harems' are common in Sperm Whales, where schools of cows and calves are usually led by an old 'steer', as whalers call him. These schools hardly ever leave tropical and sub-tropical waters, while bachelors of all ages migrate in separate schools to the Arctic and Antarctic during the summer. For this reason, the Antarctic catch consists exclusively of male Sperm Whales, and that is why not a single cow has been discovered among the forty-five Sperm Whales stranded on the Dutch coast since 1531. In the mating season, bulls often have violent fights to secure a harem.

Sperm Whales, like elephants, have the occasional rogue male, i.e. a solitary individual which obviously cannot fit into any school, and which is therefore particularly aggressive. Such rogues were Moby Dick, New Zealand Jack, and many other famous whales from the great days of Sperm Whale hunting, all of which tore up men and boats alike, as time and again they eluded their would-be captors.

Belugas, Narwhals and Killers are said to occur in separate schools of males and females, though they generally live in mixed schools. Tomilin reports that in the Barents Sea, Belugas can be found in mixed schools of up to 10,000 animals, while Tarasevich (1958) states that Common Dolphins live in mixed schools during the mating season and in separate schools at other times. Møhl Hansen (1954) states that porpoises occur both in mixed and in separate schools, so that some catches may consist of bulls only. Grey Whales, too, seem to live in separate schools, at least for part of the year, and female schools are often led by an older cow. Hill (1957) thinks that there are clear signs of the existence of a 'harem' type of school among the Bottlenose Dolphins of Marineland, but this theory needs to be investigated further.

Leaders are, however, definitely found in another two species, e.g. in Pilot Whales and in Bottlenose Whales. Pilot Whales usually live in mixed schools of hundreds and even thousands, and male leaders have frequently been reported. No doubt, this is how these animals obtained their name.

A similar situation is said to prevail in the Bottlenose Whales as well, which, because bulls and cows differ in size and shape, and because of their diet and deep diving, have much in common with Sperm Whales. They combine into schools ranging from very small groups to associations of thousands of animals, and they are said to be led by one or more old steers. Here, too, there have been cases of rogue males attacking whalers, particularly in olden times. Mixed herds led by an old male are also found among such terrestrial mammals as wild sheep and wild goats.

Mutual ties between individuals in Cetacean herds seem to be very strong, and the animals definitely rely on them. Thus, in Marineland, when Pilot Whales were first introduced in force, they stayed close together and even slept and awoke together, and Bottlenose Dolphins, once they had become used to their new environment, swam about separately, to join forces the moment anything frightened them. The Pilot Whale of Marineland (California) became aggressive when he was alone in the basin for a fairly long time. When dolphins were introduced, he became friendly again. All this bears out a statement by Uda and Nasu (1956) that, in the Pacific, schools of whales show a perceptible increase in number after hurricanes. The schools probably keep together by making sounds to one another, a method of communication which has been positively established in the case of Black Sea Common Dolphins. Once a school of big whales has become dispersed by hunters, it apparently finds its way back by sounds as well. Whales, like apes, probably produce continuous noises, a subject which we shall investigate more fully in the next two chapters.

Hunting packs, of the kind found in wolves, are known among Killer Whales, and there have been seen attacking dolphins, seals, sea-lions, and even walruses. The Killer Whales first surround their victims, herding them together and cutting off all means of escape. The older dolphins generally form a protective circle round their young, and the Killer Whales, singling out one of the weaker parents, pounce on him. As happens in so many herds, weaker members are often pushed into the most vulnerable spots by their fellows. Occasionally, one or more Killer Whales split their victims' ranks to carry off one of the young. They are, however, careful to avoid old walruses, for which they have a healthy respect. Caldwell states that schools of dolphins of the species *Stenella plagiodon* make organized attacks both on shoals of fish and on big cuttle-fish, though he does not report their method of attack.

The strong ties between members of a particular school often take the form of mutual aid and, particularly, of assistance to wounded animals, to an extent rarely found among terrestrial mammals, which generally leave the weak and sick to their own devices, or actually set upon them. Of terrestrial animals, only elephants have been reported to come to the aid of their wounded. When this happens, two friends hold up their comrade on either side with their bodies and tusks.

The best description of mutual aid between Cetaceans comes from two members of the staff of The Living Sea Gulfarium at Fort Walton Beach in Florida. They noticed that a submarine dynamite explosion had injured a Bottlenose Dolphin in the bay. The animal sank, but immediately two others came to its assistance and, pushing their heads under its flippers, carried it up to the surface for air (Fig. 104). Being unable to blow themselves while thus occupied, they would let go of their wounded comrade from time to time, to return to their work of mercy the moment they had filled their own lungs. The same behaviour was also observed when one of a group of Bottlenose Dolphins which was being put into a tank bumped its head against a wall and sank to the bottom in a dazed state. Similar actions are reported from Marineland, Florida, where two dolphins supported an injured friend for twenty minutes until he had regained sufficient strength to swim alone.

Mutual aid, however, is not the general rule among all Cetaceans, and Schevill, who was present when one of a school of twelve Whitesided

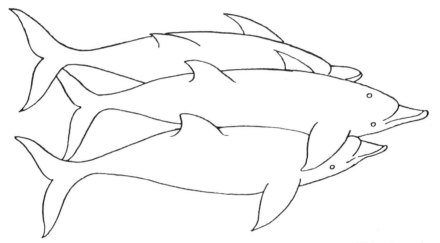

Figure 104. Two Bottlenose Dolphins supporting a wounded congener. (Siebenaler and Caldwell, 1956.)

Dolphins was harpooned off Cape Cod, reports that the others not only ignored the animal, which floated for some ten minutes, but even swam away from it. Jonsgård, too, reports that during the capture of fifty-two of these animals somewhere in Norway, none of them paid any attention to his comrades' fate. The behaviour of their Pacific relatives (*Lagenorhynchus obliquidens*), however, seems to be somewhat more comradely. Hubbs (1953) tells us that an injured individual was surrounded by his friends and carried away from the ship. Brown and Norris (1956) reported a similar experience with this species. On the other hand, Common Dolphins in the North Pacific are said to desert their wounded. During porpoise hunts in Denmark, it appeared that these animals are, in fact, frightened off by their wounded comrade's cry and actually avoid the danger spot for some time.

Some Cetaceans respond to the cry of wounded comrades, and that they come to their assistance from considerable distances, has repeatedly been observed in Killer Whales, Sperm Whales, dolphins and others. In April 1956, when Porto Garibaldi fishermen caught a female dolphin in a net, they were set upon by ten other dolphins and nearly lost their lives. Luckily, they released the female just before the all-male rescue party managed to capsize their small craft. The story was reported in *De Telegraaf* of 26th April, 1956, but the article did not say how the fishermen, in spite of their distress, found time to make sexual distinctions between their attackers. Still, the story of the rescue itself need not be doubted, as those of us who have seen the beautiful French film taken aboard the research ship *Calypso* will understand. In a memorable scene of this film, twenty-seven female Sperm Whales come from miles away to rescue an over-inquisitive calf which has been injured by the ship's screw. In all such cases, the rescuers are unquestionably attracted by distress signals, and the crew of the *Calypso* did in fact hear the calf emitting such sounds.

Mutual aid seems to occur in bigger whales also. Zenkovich (1956) reports at least three cases of Humpback, Greenland and Grey Whales supporting injured animals under the surface, until the helpmates themselves fell victims to the whalers. In the case of the Humpback Whale, this assistance was rendered for forty minutes. In the case of the Grey Whale, Zenkovich observed clearly that the injured animal was a cow, and her rescuers two bulls. He says that he has noticed the same thing on a number of occasions, and that he never saw a Grey cow coming to the assistance of a bull. Whalers have always known that when two Blue Whales are sighted, the female must be shot first, for the male will not desert her and can therefore be caught fairly easily, while the cow does desert her injured mate. Luckily for the whales, gunners cannot usually distinguish the sexes while the animals are swimming, though their inability to do so has the unfortunate consequence that no special measures can be taken to protect the cows. Tomilin (1935) reports that female Grey and Sperm Whales also desert their injured mates, while both sexes of Humpback Whales come to each other's assistance.

Naturally, whales also render assistance to the young, and not only their own. In Marineland, when a new-born calf is slow in swimming to the surface, it is pushed up either by its mother or by another cow. The same behaviour was also displayed towards a still-born calf (Fig. 105), and is said to be quite common among Bottlenose Dolphins in their natural state. Moore (1955) reported a number of instances of Bottlenoses continuing to push a dead calf or at least its head to the surface for days after it was dead. They do this even with other dead animals and, in fact, with all sorts of objects. In Marineland, at least, Bottlenose Dolphins have been observed pushing a turtle or even a small tin to the surface in this

Figure 105. Two female Bottlenose Dolphins, mother and 'aunt', pushing a still-born calf to the surface. Photograph: R. J. Eastman, Marineland of Florida, Miami.

way. On the other hand, Tomilin states that a Common Dolphin will support her calf until it dies, but ignores it from then on. By and large, however, wounded or dead animals and even floating objects seem to arouse some sort of 'lifting' behaviour in Cetaceans, and the game of our Sperm Whale with a plank (see p. 187) may well be explained in this way, and so may the reported instances of dolphins saving human lives. The famous story of Arion and similar tales told through the ages may, there-fore, have been based on at least a modicum of truth. In any case, there is the absolutely authentic story of a dolphin saving the life of a woman off the coast of Florida in 1949. This woman, while bathing, was carried out to sea by a strong current, and was on the point of drowning, when a Bottlenose Dolphin dived under her and pushed her violently towards the surface and then towards the beach, until she could stand on firm ground.

However, not all Cetaceans look after their young in the same way. Sperm Whales are reported to rescue injured calves by taking them into their mouths. Such behaviour was observed by both Olaus Magnus and by Scoresby (1811), and the Old Dartmouth Historical Society at New Bedford (Massachusetts) has an old print depicting it (Fig. 106). We shall return to the nursing of calves in Chapter 13, where we shall discuss the whole question more fully.

Those familiar with the herd life of animals may wonder whether there are social distinctions among Cetaceans, of the kind met in many other herd animals. The problem of social distinctions between animals was first investigated scientifically when the Norwegian scientist Schjelderupp Ebbe studied the social behaviour of chickens. Chickens are known to keep pecking at one another, and it appeared during the investigation that pecking is a way of maintaining a given, or reaching a higher position in the social hierarchy. The chicken that pecks at all the others but is not pecked at itself is at the top of the scale, the one that is pecked at by only the top chicken while pecking at all the others is Chicken No. 2, and so on until we reach the poor animal that is lowest in the social scale which is attacked by everyone while pecking at no one itself. Though the method of asserting social superiority may differ from species to species, all herd animals display similar behaviour patterns: dogs bite, cows butt, etc. True, these patterns are not always equally strictly observed, and even chickens may behave differently, but this is not the place to discuss the entire problem in detail, particularly since the available evidence is far from conclusive. Suffice it to say that the degree of social assertiveness

Figure 106. A Sperm Whale surfacing with a wounded calf in her mouth. Watercolour in the possession of the Old Dartmouth Historical Society, New Bedford, Mass. (Parrington, 1955.)

depends very much on a number of factors, of which space and food resources are the main considerations. If the food supply is profuse over a wide area, biting and butting abate, but when there is keener competition for food, the number of attacks increases greatly. Horses feeding from a trough, for instance, are much more aggressive to other horses than when they are grazing. In general, animals in captivity are more aggressive than animals in their natural state, though some domestic pets seem to have lost all traces of assertiveness.

The most important data on the social behaviour of Cetaceans are once again based on observations of the Bottlenose Dolphins in Marineland. Apparently, these animals assert their social position by lashing out with their tails, by pushing with their snouts, and even simply by adopting a threatening attitude. The White-beaked Dolphins of Marineland in California often show weals inflicted by a congener placed higher in the hierarchy (see Fig. 100). While their social disputes are generally fairly mild, dolphins will occasionally inflict terrible gashes on their fellows, particularly when new animals are added to the tank. The newcomers are apparently expected to fight their way into the herd – just like students who have often to undergo somewhat unpleasant initiation rites.

From observations made in Marineland, it appeared that male Bottlenose Dolphins observe a very strict hierarchical order, mainly based on size. Cows never fight amongst themselves if one or more bulls are present. In the absence of a bull, however, they will assert their place in the hierarchy, the biggest cow usually taking first place, etc.

Naturally, it is almost impossible to investigate whether non-captive Cetaceans behave in the same way, since to do so would involve picking out individuals from a mass of animals swimming about under the surface. All we can say with certainty is that whales and dolphins very often show scars or weals inflicted by their fellows. In Sperm Whales, for instance, the skin is often marked by a number of parallel stripes at intervals corresponding precisely with the gaps between their teeth. I myself was shown such stripes on Ziphiids of the genus *Berardius* at the Japanese whaling station Ayukawa, and my colleague Omura told me that he had seen them repeatedly. Similar scars have often been found on porpoises, and particularly on Common Dolphins, Bottlenose Dolphins, Risso's Dolphins and Rough-toothed Dolphins, where they occur also in the females of the species.

Many healed fractures of ribs and other bones, e.g. vertebral processes, which are commonly found on Cetacean skeletons, must also have been caused in the same way. My book on the Cetaceans (1936) contains a list of seventy-two such fractures found both in recent and also in fossil Cetaceans, but meanwhile the number of known cases of fracture has grown to well over one hundred, in one of which six ribs and five vertebral processes had broken and then healed. That the original injuries were not man-inflicted appears clearly from the fact that they are as frequent in fossil whales and Cetaceans not pursued by man as in those which are hunted by him. As mere bites could not have inflicted such serious fractures, they must be the result of violent strokes of the tail, and since Cetaceans have no enemies apart from Killer Whales, which attack their victims with their teeth and generally kill them in the process, the healed fractures can only have been caused by congeners.

If such scars and fractures were restricted to male animals, one might have thought of fights arising out of sexual rivalry, but social rivalry seems the better explanation, the more so since violent fights over cows have only been reported of Sperm Whales. The evidence also points to the fact that violent fights over food do not occur, so that the social hypothesis seems to fit all the known facts best. Still, it remains an hypothesis, and every observation which increases our knowledge in this field will earn the gratitude of all marine biologists.

All herds are sometimes seized by sudden panic. Thus, cattle will race blindly over the plains, drowning in rivers or falling down gorges on the way. The mass strandings of scores and even of hundreds of Cetaceans are said to be caused in the same way. Such strandings have been observed mainly in the case of Killer Whales, False Killers and Pilot Whales, and seem to occur quite frequently. In 1927, 150 False Killers were found stranded in the Dornoch Firth (Scotland), and in 1929, 167 False Killers ran aground at Velenai (Ceylon). Further recorded mass strandings of False Killers occurred at Zanzibar (1933 – 54 animals); in the Darling District of South Africa (1935 – 200 animals); on St Helena (1936 – 58 animals); and on the coast of Britain (1936 – 75 animals). On 14th March, 1955, 67 Pilot Whales stranded at Westray (Orkneys), and de Kok (1959) reports that the strandings were preceded by a panic during which the animals wounded one another by their uncontrolled movements.

Though Killers may possibly be stranded while pursuing seals or sea-lions into shallow waters, the two other species, which feed mainly on slow-swimming cuttlefish, cannot possibly run aground for the same reasons, nor can Sperm Whales of which mass strandings are also reported. On 14th March, 1784, thirty-two of these giants were stranded at Audierne (South Brittany), and on 27th February, 1954, the Associated Press reported that thirty-four Sperm Whales had been found stranded at La Paz (Gulf of California), whose inhabitants were assailed by the unwhole-some stench of decomposing carcasses for a long period, since twenty-four Sperm Whales had run aground here two weeks earlier.

One of the reasons why these animals become panic-stricken may well be the fact that they suddenly find themselves in shallow waters. How it is possible that this situation occurs fairly frequently, will be explained in Chapter 8. On page 181 we have seen how sensitive porpoises are to depth and Townsend, investigating Bottlenose Dolphins in the New York Aquarium, found that the animals became extremely restless whenever the water dropped below a certain level. Other contributory factors may well be sudden temperature differences, or sudden thunderstorms. The herd instinct is always very marked during such mass strandings. On 22nd May, 1955, when seventeen young Killer Whales stranded on Paraparaumu Beach (New Zealand), unsuccessful attempts were made to save some of them by chasing them back into the sea. The animals would always return and had finally to be abandoned to their fate. The same behaviour has been repeatedly observed in Pilot Whales.

Panic also seizes Californian Grey Whales whenever they are attacked by Killer Whales. Sometimes they have the sense to retire into the Californian bays, where the gigantic breakers form an insurmountable obstacle for their enemies, but often they become so completely paralysed with fear, that they simply float upside down, their white bellies and extended flippers invitingly presented to the attackers. Degerbøl and Nielsen have described similar behaviour on the part of Belugas, which also await the approaching killer as if petrified, though they do not turn upside down. This attitude seems to be much more sensible, for it has been noticed that, in this way, they often manage to escape the killer's attention, possibly because the enemy cannot hear them.

Panic is, however, not common to all Cetaceans, and certainly it is not produced by every type of fear. The animals have, for instance, never been known to become panic-stricken during big whale hunts, even when entire schools are dispersed. During mass captures of dolphins, observers have often been struck by the fact that large groups of these animals allowed themselves to be slaughtered in turn without showing any signs of unrest, let alone of real panic.

No discussion of animal behaviour would be complete without some mention of their sense organs, which, after all, are the animals' main means of contact with the outside world. Animal behaviour is strongly influenced by the nature of the sensory impressions the nervous system receives. Groups of animals may, therefore, be said to inhabit different worlds, human beings, apes and birds living predominantly in a visual world, while dogs, horses, cattle and pigs live primarily in a world of smells. Many of their surprising feats can thus be explained very simply.

Little need be said about the Cetacean sense of smell, for the simple reason that the olfactory organ is either absent or else so rudimentary as to be negligible. The visual sense, though not as poor as was generally believed, is nevertheless not keen enough to be considered very important either. Practically nothing is known about their sense of touch, and their taste, like that of all other animals, is restricted to distinguishing between different kinds of food. The only other sense is hearing, and in fact it appears that Cetaceans, like bats, have a very highly developed ear, which must be considered their most important sense organ. The next chapter is, therefore, devoted to its discussion in detail.

7

Hearing

IN THE AFTERNOON of 29th May, 1956, the stately Senate Chamber of Utrecht University was filled to capacity by a large crowd of friends and relatives who had come to see the degree of Doctor of Medicine being conferred on F. W. Reysenbach de Haan. From the walls, the portraits of famous physicians and surgeons of the past looked down on the candidate, and behind the table sat the present members dressed in sombre black. Everyone must have been puzzled that a thesis entitled *De ceti auditu* – 'On the hearing of Whales' – should have been presented to the faculty of medicine rather than that of science. However, the candidate's sponsor, Prof. Dr A. A. J. van Egmond, explained the reason when he told the audience how the research project had originated and what its real purpose was. It had all started years before when the Otological Clinic in Utrecht received the head of a Rorqual foetus for detailed investigation. The staff of the clinic were reluctant to tackle a subject so little connected with man and what is more, smelling so offensively. Thus the head of the foetus was left undisturbed in its jar of formalin, until, years later, the new assistant, Reysenbach de Haan, decided to do something about it. At just about that time, a school of Pilot Whales had stranded on a beach near Esbjerg in Denmark, and by prompt action it was possible to get hold of two fairly fresh heads. Even so, they had begun to smell by the time they arrived, and de Haan's collaborators were none too pleased when he began dissecting them. Not long afterwards, everyone agreed that his investigations, though of little purely medical interest, were nevertheless of tremendous scientific importance.

The sponsor pointed out that, although famous naturalists, starting with Pliny almost 2,000 years ago, had all speculated about the hearing of Cetaceans, it was not until 1954 that the first reasonable account appeared. This was a reference to Dr F. C. Fraser of the British Museum (Natural History), who together with his colleague, P. E. Purves, had studied the problem for many years and whose preliminary report was published in the Bulletin of the British Museum in 1954. The final report appeared in 1960 (also in the Bulletin).

The reader might wonder what is so peculiar about the hearing of Cetaceans that scholars took 2,000 years even to get to the crux of the problem. After all, the absence of external ears is not so strange in itself, since they serve to capture sound waves through the air, and would not only be quite useless in the water, but also spoil the streamlining of the rest of the body by causing undesirable currents. There is nothing surprising, then, in the fact that Cetaceans have no obvious pinna and have only the smallest of external ear slits (though rudimentary pinnae were discovered in a Beluga and a porpoise). The 'ears' which whalers have the habit of taking home to put on the chimney-piece (Fig. 111) are quite unrelated to pinnae and are in fact the whale's bullae tympani to which we shall return later.

Despite this deficiency, whales have always been known to be very keen of hearing. Thus Pindar, who lived from 522 to 422 B.C., claimed that dolphins could be attracted by a flute or lyre, and Aristotle (384 to 322 B.C.) expressed surprise that these animals fled from all kinds of noises, despite the fact that, according to him, they lacked an auditory passage. (This passage was first discovered and described by Rondelet in the middle of the sixteenth century.) The first Japanese whalers used to drive whales and dolphins into bays by beating against the sides of their boats with wooden hammers, a method akin in principle to that used even now during *Prøyser jag* (see Chapter 3). Formerly, the big whales were 'stalked' by ships with softly purring steam engines, noisy motors being avoided. Nowadays, however, they are hunted with ships with strongly vibrating engines which cause them to take to flight. Fast corvettes then catch up with them. During his whale-marking voyage aboard the catcher *Enern*, Prof. Ruud of Oslo noticed that whales hit by marks showed hardly any reaction, while marks that missed and fell into the water with a loud splash sent them scuttling away with fear. They would dive abruptly and not surface again till they were a long way from the danger spot. Obviously their sense of hearing is far keener than their sense of touch. Similar experiences have been reported with porpoises off Denmark (see Chapter 6), which seemed much more nervous of modern motor-boats than they had been of earlier rowing and sailing boats – the noise of the engines apparently frightens them so much that they dive to great depths. Even a few slaps on the water with a stick are enough to make them change course by as much as 90 degrees. Capt. Mörzer Bruins reported similar behaviour of *Sotalia plumbea*, a marine dolphin from the Persian Gulf.

How keen the Cetacean auditory sense really is, can also be gathered from reports of dolphin hunts off the American coast. Once a school of

Bottlenose Dolphins has been hunted by a particular boat, they subsequently avoid it like the plague, though other boats do not bother them. This delicate differentiation between sounds is often found in cattle, which show clear signs of nervousness when they hear the approach of the vet's car. Cetaceans, however, have a still more sensitive ear, which is best seen from the fact that porpoises, Sperm Whales and at least some of the other Cetaceans apparently react to asdic gear, a kind of underwater radar used for depth sounding and also for locating solid obstacles in the ship's path. Radar and asdic are both used for detecting reflected waves, but while radar emits and receives short radio wave-lengths, asdic emits and receives ultrasonic vibrations. There is nothing mysterious about such vibrations, except that they are too high in pitch to be audible to the human ear. The pitch of a note depends on the number of vibrations its source emits in unit time, and is usually measured in kilocycles (1,000 vibrations) per second. Now the limit of human hearing is between 15 and 20 kilocycles, while monkeys respond to notes up to 33, cats up to 50, mice and rats up to 90, and bats even up to 175 kilocycles per second. These animals can therefore hear a great many sounds that escape us altogether, and would be able to react to asdic vibrations which have a frequency of between 20 and 40 kilocycles.

The hearing of Cetaceans is second only to that of bats. Naturally, their upper auditory limit is very difficult to determine, and all we know of the bigger whales is that some species respond to asdic. However, much more is known about the Bottlenose Dolphins in Marineland Aquarium. In 1953 Schevill and Lawrence taught one of these animals to come up for food in response to a sound signal. The experiment cost 1,200 fish, but, at the end, the two investigators knew that the dolphins could respond to notes up to 153 kilocycles, though their response fell off at 120 kilocycles. Kellogg and Kohler had noticed even earlier that the Bottlenose Dolphins in the big tank were frightened by sounds between 100 and 400 cycles (roughly the range between our lower *c* and upper *a*), but that they merely swam a little more quickly when they heard sounds between 400 cycles and 50 kilocycles.

This acute sense of hearing in Cetaceans is not surprising when we consider how badly developed their other senses are. All the evidence seems to point to the fact that they not only locate their prey by sound, but that sound is also their chief means of communication. We shall return to this subject in greater detail in the next chapter; here we shall merely consider what they can hear and how their auditory organs work, i.e. how sound vibrations reach their inner ear, and how auditory stimuli are transmitted from it to the brain.

Since whales are aquatic animals, we shall begin by comparing their hearing with that of fish. It has long been known that fish, too, respond to sounds, and that, for instance, sharks can be frightened off by shouting. However, the real facts only come to light in the course of the past fifty years through ingenious investigations in which Prof. S. Dijkgraaf of Utrecht played an important part. Now, hearing does not apparently play a major role in the life of fish since, though they can aurally detect under-water vibrations, their ears alone cannot tell them the direction from which the sound comes. As far as we know, fish lack both a middle and an external ear, and sounds must therefore reach their inner ear by bone conduction, i.e. by vibrations of the skull. When this happens, it is impos-sible to tell the direction of the sound, which can only be detected if the right and left ears are acoustically isolated from each other. In other words, only if one ear receives the sound a fraction later than the other, i.e. if there is a slight phase lag and a consequent difference in intensity, can the source of the sound be located with any certainty. The greater the distance between its two ears, the more accurate is a given animal's 'directional hearing'.

The fact that bone conduction makes it impossible to locate a sub-marine source of sound, was proved by Dr Reysenbach de Haan by experiments on himself and a few collaborators. No special apparatus was needed, since man's eardrums and auditory ossicles, which are designed for receiving vibrations of the air, do not function under water, where bone conduction takes over. The experiments showed clearly that men cannot tell the source of a sound under water. The fact that fish seem to be able to do so despite this handicap must probably be attributed to their having a special organ, the so-called lateral organ which, until recently, was erroneously believed to have a purely tactile function. J. W. Kuiper of Groningen has shown that the lateral organ can also respond to sounds, thus providing a measure of acoustic isolation, the details of which are not yet fully understood. From Dr Reysenbach de Haan's experiments, it further appeared that human sound reception deteriorates under water in other respects also, and that the intensity of normal sounds has to be increased by sixty decibels before we can hear them. This corresponds precisely to the loss of hearing we should expect in a man with impaired external and middle ears.

Since bone conduction is, as we have seen, a method of hearing with serious limitations, the famous Dutch anatomist, Petrus Camper, the first scientist (1765) to write a treatise specifically on the hearing of whales (and of Sperm Whales in particular) thought that these mammals might not hear as well below water as at the surface, on the assumption that their ears were similar to those of fish. Since then Schevill and Lawrence's experi-ments in the Marineland Aquarium have shown clearly that Bottlenose

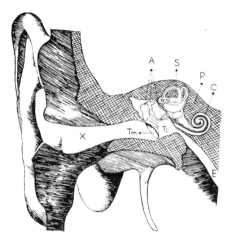

Figure 107. Man's ear. X = external auditory meatus; Tm = tympanic membrane; Tc = tympanic cavity; A = auditory ossicles (malleus, incus, and stapes); S = semi-circular canals (organ of equilibrium); P = petrosal; C = cochlea; E = Eustachian tube (connecting middle ear with the posterior part of the nose). (IJsseling and Scheygrond, 1951.)

Dolphins not only pick up sounds below the surface at distances of eighty feet, but that they can locate the source of the sound, and Dudok van Heel's porpoise experiments at Texel have shown just how accurately they can do so. His observations were made in an echo-free basin after the animal had lost its natural curiosity about the tank and reacted only to sounds representing food signals. By gradually bringing two sources of sound nearer to each other, it was found that the animals could distinguish food signals of 6,000 cycles down to an angle of 16° between the sources. Now, man can distinguish sounds of 1,500 cycles coming from two sources which make an angle of only 8°, but when we consider that sound travels four times as fast in water as it does in air, and that the distance between a porpoise's eardrums is half the distance it is in man, the porpoise's degree of directional hearing can be said to be comparable to man's.

The fact that it took so many centuries before the auditory apparatus of Cetaceans was properly understood may possibly be explained by the persistent fallacy on the part of biologists that there was some connexion between the hearing of fish and Cetaceans and that the latter, too, relied on bone conduction. From Claudius in 1858 to Guggenheim in 1948 and Yamada in 1953, scientists have time and again fallen into the error of thinking that the role of the middle ear and of acoustic insulation, which play such important roles in the hearing of terrestrial mammals, was negligible in Cetaceans. All the greater is Fraser and Purves's achievement in being the first to show that whales hear exactly like other mammals, even though acoustic isolation is produced in a very special way.

In terrestrial mammals the bony skull does not respond to airborne vibrations and the two eardrums are set into independent vibration by atmospheric waves. But, of course, eardrums designed for receiving this type of wave would be useless to Cetaceans, whose ears must be specially modified to their aquatic environment. An auditory apparatus designed for atmospheric vibrations cannot be used in the water and our first problem is therefore to investigate how acoustic isolation of the ears is achieved in Cetaceans. Our second problem is that of the reception of high pitched tones, which makes very special demands on the construction of the auditory apparatus. Before we discuss the special modifications which enable whales to receive, and to receive very acutely, sounds in water, we must first take a closer look at our own ears.

Our external ear – the pinna – picks up atmospheric vibrations and propagates them along the air in the external auditory canal, a fairly wide passage, surrounded partly by the cartilaginous concha and partly by the bone of the skull. The external auditory canal is sealed off by the eardrum about an inch from its beginning, and the eardrum is set into vibration by the air, in the same way as, for instance, the diaphragm of a microphone vibrates when we speak into it. The pinna, the auditory canal and the eardrum jointly make up the external ear (Fig. 107). Behind the eardrum lies the middle ear, surrounded on all sides by cranial bone. It consists of an air-filled space, the tympanic cavity, which communicates with mouth and throat by the Eustachian tube. In this way the pressure inside and outside the eardrum is always equal, thus allowing it perfect freedom of vibration. In a number of mammals the tympanic cavity is evaginated, i.e. it shows a conspicuous globular swelling surrounded by a shell-like protuberance of the tympanic bone, the so-called *bulla tympani*, which may serve to increase the intensity of incoming sounds, though its exact function has not yet been fully understood.

The vibrations of the eardrum are transmitted by a chain of auditory ossicles to the membrane covering the opening of the inner ear, the so-called oval window. The auditory ossicles – malleus (hammer), incus (anvil) and stapes (stirrup) – articulate by means of joints. The handle of the malleus is attached to the eardrum, its head being linked by a small joint with the body of the incus. A process of the incus is joined to the stapes, whose footplate is fitted into the oval window, thus communicating its vibrations to the membrane. Behind the oval window, there is a vestibule which communicates with the auditory sense organs and the semi-circular canals of the inner ear, both embedded in the hardest part of the temporal bone, i.e. the petrosal. The inner ear or labyrinth contains a fluid to which the vibrations of the oval window are transmitted. The vibrations are then picked up by a complicated system of auditory receptors and conducted by the auditory nerve to the brain, where we become conscious of them as sounds.

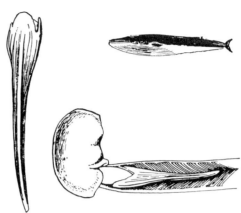

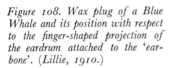

Figure 108. Wax plug of a Blue Whale and its position with respect to the finger-shaped projection of the eardrum attached to the 'ear-bone'. (Lillie, 1910.)

We have already seen that Cetaceans have no obvious pinna, though the fact that very young embryos have a rudimentary external ear points to their distant terrestrial ancestors having had such an organ. All that has remained of it in present-day Cetaceans, however, is the small slit in the skin some distance behind the eye. However, an external auditory meatus running through the blubber from the slit to the middle ear at the base of the skull is found in all Cetaceans. The meatus is S-shaped and not straight as it is in most mammals (Fig. 113), probably to prevent excessive strain during the annual increase of the amount of blubber, which is particularly marked in Rorquals. From the top of the S-bend, a muscle runs to the upper skull, no doubt in order to keep the canal taut when the blubber is too thin. Near the skull, the canal is surrounded by cartilage from which a number of small muscles run to the skull – apparently another remnant from the days when whales still had a movable pinna.

Although the external auditory meatus has so small a diameter (1–5 mm.) that it looks like a piece of string, it is – at least in Odontocetes – an open tube, filled with seawater and discarded epithelium cells over its entire length. The wall of the canal consists of dark epithelium, connective tissue, and some striated muscle. In Mysticetes, the tube is open externally, closed over a generally short central section consisting entirely of connective tissue, and open again over the internal section which can be up to three feet long and perceptibly increases in diameter towards the skull, so that it looks like a funnel. However, the actual channel in this part of the tube is very narrow, since the tube is almost completely filled by the conical 'wax plug' (Fig. 108). Actually, 'wax plug' is a very misleading term since the wax (cerumen) formed by special glands in human ears is an entirely different substance. The wax plug consists of concentric strips of horny

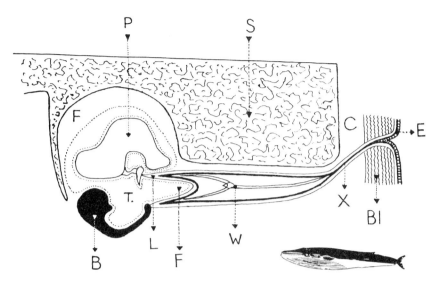

Figure 109. Diagrammatic cross-section through the base of the skull and the ear of a Mysticete. E = epidermis; Bl = blubber; C = connective tissue and muscles; X = external auditory meatus (closed part); W = wax plug; F = finger-shaped projection of eardrum; L = band-shaped ligament of eardrum which receives the sound vibrations and conducts them to the auditory ossicles; T = tympanic cavity; F = foam-filled cavities surrounding the ear-bone; P = petrosal; B = bulla; S = bones of skull. (Reysenbach de Haan, 1956.)

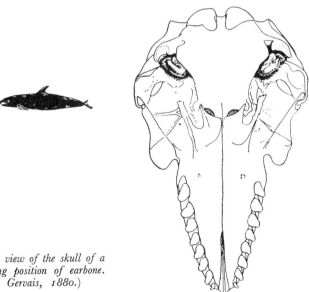

Figure 110. Bottom view of the skull of a False Killer showing position of earbone. (Van Beneden and Gervais, 1880.)

epithelium, rather like the horns of a cow or our own nails, although their structures are not quite analogous. Wax glands proper are present only in the pronounced evagination of the tympanic membrane of Mysticetes, where a thin layer of ear-wax can in fact be found on the inner side of the horn.

The external auditory canal terminates in the thick eardrum which is attached to an ossified ring of the 'ear-bone'. In Odontocetes, this membrane is fairly small and convex, so that it projects like a cone into the tympanic cavity, and is therefore known as the tympanic cone. In Mysticetes the corresponding part of the tympanic membrane is a taut ligament, and the remaining part of the drum projects along the external auditory passage as an elongated, hollow structure, resembling the finger of a glove. Vibrations are, however, transmitted direct to the fairly small ligament. Not to make things too complicated, we shall simply refer to all these structures as the eardrum.

Experts still differ on the way in which vibrations reach the eardrum. Fraser and Purves, who carried out experiments on fresh material, concluded that sound travels far better through the external auditory passage and the 'wax plug' of Mysticetes than through the blubber itself. They attribute this difference to the fact that the connective tissue fibres of the blubber run in all directions, while, in the main, those of the auditory canal run longitudinally along it. They also found that the wax plug is an excellent conductor especially of very high tones, its conductive properties being roughly equivalent to those of wood, and that sound travels through it much better in a longitudinal than in a transverse direction. Reysenbach de Haan, on the other hand, holds that the external auditory passage plays no special part in the transmission of sound, since he found that Cetacean blubber and muscle have the same sound-propagating properties as the water outside. Even so, the auditory passage is by no means a rudimentary organ and consists of apparently well-functioning tissue. Moreover, Yamada has shown that its connective tissue is provided with a great many sense receptors, which probably serve to communicate the state of tension in the passage to the central nervous system. Further experiments in this field are clearly desirable, for all the evidence seems to point to the conclusion that the external auditory passage plays an essential part in transmitting sound from the water to the eardrum.

The eardrum, i.e. the taut membrane dividing the external from the middle ear, is surrounded by an annular part of what, for convenience, we shall call the 'ear-bone', though its proper name is the petro-tympanic bone or the tympano-petro-mastoid. The ear-bone is found on the base of the skull (Fig. 110) and consists, as the Latin name indicates, of two, or if you like of three, bones: the tympanic, the petrosal and the mastoid,

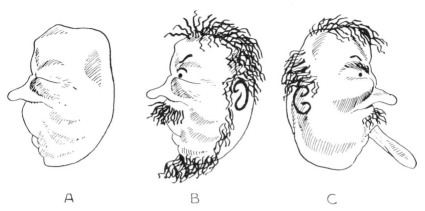

Figure 111. A = the bulla of a Rorqual as whalers remove it from carcasses. B and C = *how they shape it without and with the eardrum.*

which latter is also considered as part of the petrosal (the mastoid process). In Mysticetes, the tympanic is attached by two, and in Odontocetes by only one, very thin, tongue-shaped bone process to the other two bones, and therefore breaks off very easily. It is a shell-shaped bone surrounding a greatly enlarged swelling of the tympanic cavity, which gives it a bladder-like appearance – hence the name bulla tympani, or bulla for short.

It is this bulla which whalers have the habit of taking home with them as souvenirs, not for their biological interest, but because their strange shape so oddly resembles a human face. A small process forms the nose; eyes, ears and a few locks of hair are painted and, straight away, you have a model of a friend's or relative's face or, if your tastes run that way, a caricature of some political figure. If the long projection of the eardrum (see above) is not cut off, the figure looks as if it were smoking a cigar, like Churchill or Sibelius (Fig. 111).

The petrosal is an extremely hard bone close to the opening of the bulla, and may be compared with the petrous portion of the temporal bone of man and other mammals. It surrounds the cochlea and the semi-circular canals of the inner ear, which will be discussed below, and has two processes (the proötic process and the mastoid process, also called the mastoid bone) by which it is joined to the other bones of the skull. Of these two processes, the mastoid is the more important. In Odontocetes it is short, rather flat and broad and attached by two ligaments to the squamosal and occipital bones of the skull. In Sperm Whales, the process is somewhat more highly developed and is mainly lamellar in structure, and in Mysticetes it is a long, knotted bone which fits tightly between the

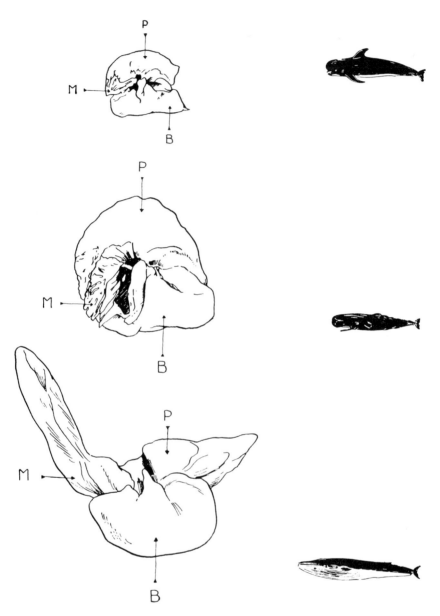

Figure 112. Right ear-bone of a Pilot Whale, a Sperm Whale and a Sei Whale, P = petrosal; B = bulla; M = mastoid process, connecting ear-bone to skull. (Yamada, 1953.)

squamosal and the occipital, thus providing far closer contact with the skull than it does in Odontocetes (Fig. 112).

One of the most striking characteristics of the Cetacean ear-bone is probably the loose way in which it fits into the skull. In all other mammals, the bones surrounding the different auditory organs fit very closely into the other bones of the skull and form an important part of the wall of the brain case. In Odontocetes, on the other hand, the ear-bone is connected so loosely by ligaments to the rest of the skull that in a fresh specimen of, for instance, a porpoise, it can be freely moved with the index finger. In Mysticetes, though the mastoid process fits between the bones of the skull, it is joined to them merely by connective and not by bone tissue. This is the reason why the ear-bone is so easily wrenched out of the other skull bones, and why such bones are sometimes found washed up on the beach. It also explains why most fossil skulls lack the bone, and why fossil ear-bones are so often found by themselves. The great Dutch expert on Cetaceans, Dr A. B. van Deinse of Rotterdam, has described and classified a number of such ear-bones discovered during excavations in Achterhoek and Twente.

This extremely loose connexion between Cetacean ear and other skull bones is one of the main factors in producing the acoustical isolation which is essential for directional hearing under water. What little connective tissue there is will transmit few if any sound vibrations. Acoustical isolation is, moreover, achieved in other ways as well. In the first place, the ear-bone is very hard and massive and hence much heavier than the other bones of the skull, as is immediately apparent if one picks it up in one's hand. Precisely because it is so heavy it will not resonate with the lighter bones – at least not for frequencies above 150 cycles – so that the vibrations transmitted to the rest of the skull via the blubber cannot reach the ear-bone itself.

Secondly, the middle ear is completely surrounded by cavities filled with albuminous foam (Figs. 109 and 113). The cavities are in fact evaginations of the tympanic cavity, with which they communicate by an opening, so that the pressure in both is equal. In Mysticetes, these cavities are generally restricted to the immediate neighbourhood of the ear-bone, but in Odontocetes they may also run on beneath the skull, in two (apical and lateral) directions. Moreover, in Odontocetes the cavities themselves lie embedded in a great deal of fatty tissue, and in Mysticetes in a large mass of hard connective tissue, both of which may act as acoustic isolators, though some investigators doubt if they can keep out sound under water. In any case, it may be said that acoustical isolation is mainly produced by the peculiar albuminous foam with which the cavities themselves are filled. The cavities (air sinuses) are surrounded

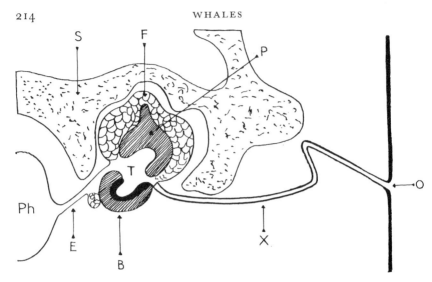

Figure 113. Highly simplified cross-section through a part of a Cetacean head (right side), showing position of ear. O = external auditory orifice; X = external auditory meatus; B = bulla; P = petrosal; S = bones of skull; E = Eustachian tube; T = tympanic cavity; Ph = pharynx; F = foam-filled cavities. (Greatly changed after Reysenbach de Haan, 1956.)

by a well-developed venous plexus. Variations in the amount of blood in this plexus maintain an equilibrium between the hydrostatic pressure, the volume of the gas in the cavities and the blood pressure, when the animals dive.

Because of all the above factors, sound vibrations can reach the middle ear in only one way, i.e. through the eardrum. In other words, the situation is precisely the same as in all terrestrial mammals, though it is achieved by different means. Clearly there is no resemblance here to the auditory system of fish, and hence whales, just like other mammals, can locate the direction of sounds very accurately. In Archaeocetes, however, the ear-bone was probably connected to the rest of the skull by real bone, though we know little about its exact nature. It seems possible, therefore, that these most ancient of Cetaceans may have had difficulties with directional hearing, although there are indications that they had air sinuses (evaginations of the tympanic cavity).

Just as in other mammals, the vibrations of the Cetacean eardrum are transmitted through three auditory ossicles to the oval window of the internal ear. The auditory ossicles themselves are thick, short and very heavy, their weight in porpoises being five times as great as it is in man. Their thickness is best appreciated by examining the stapes, which lacks the characteristic stirrup form which it has in man (and from which it derives its name), but looks rather like a rectangular bone, sometimes with a central hole. The bone is, however, not fused to the petrosal as was formerly thought. The malleus is joined by a thin osseous strip to the ear-bone, and thus much more rigidly held to that bone than it is in most other mammals, where the connexion usually takes the form of a very thin and supple ligament. Mice and bats, however, have a similar osseous strip, which seems to indicate that it is an adaptation for the reception of very high tones. (We all know that the tighter a violin string, the higher is the note it produces.) In order to prevent what small vibrations there are along the walls of the ear-bone from reaching the auditory ossicles by way of this thin strip, the joint between malleus and incus is constructed in an ingenious way so that vibrations of the ear-bone cannot be transmitted to the incus, while those from the eardrum can. Fraser and Purves have investigated this question very carefully, and have constructed an excellent working model in which the special action of the joint can be clearly seen.

Despite their robust structure, the Cetacean auditory ossicles are relatively small, particularly the stapes whose surface area is only one-thirtieth that of the eardrum. On the other hand, the lever of the malleus is very large, and hence the stapes is made to vibrate with thirty times the intensity (amplitude) of the eardrum. The explanation for this is that the pressure of sound waves is much greater, and the amplitude much smaller, in water than it is in air.

The study of the internal ear of any mammal, surrounded as it is by hard bone, is difficult enough, but in Cetaceans the difficulties are almost insurmountable, since here the petrosal is probably the hardest found in the entire animal kingdom, and the most difficult to cut. Chisel and bone-saw merely cause it to splinter, and Petrus Camper, who was not put off by minor difficulties, said of the bone that 'it is just possible to file it down, but it is a most laborious job'. Even so, different biologists have on more than one occasion tackled this 'laborious job', in order to fathom one of the whale's greatest secrets. All of them were struck by the fact that the semi-circular canals are so remarkably small; in porpoises, for instance, they are no larger than they are in hamsters – possibly one of the reasons why so many famous anatomists – the great Camper included – failed to locate them altogether. It must not be thought, however, that mere size determines the efficiency or importance of this organ of equilibrium since even the smallest canals can function very effectively. This became quite clear during the transport of porpoises from Denmark to Holland, for, whenever the truck swerved, the animals immediately tried to regain their equilibrium by moving their flippers.

In contradistinction to the semi-circular canals, the cochlea is well developed and, in fact, rather large compared with that of terrestrial mammals. It normally has two turns.

All sorts of experiments on men and animals have shown that the receptors sensitive to high tones are concentrated in the part of the cochlea nearest the oval window, while the receptors sensitive to low tones are found in the part furthest from the window. If, as we have good reason to believe, Cetaceans can, indeed, hear very high tones, the high-tone receptors ought to have a special structure. Because of the great technical difficulties involved they have so far not been investigated adequately, but even so, as early as 1908 a Viennese scholar, W. Kolmer, who, while on a visit to the Zoological Station at St Andrew's (Scotland), happened to come across a recently killed porpoise, managed to show that a certain number of cells (the so-called supporting cells of Hensen and Claudius) are strikingly big and strongly developed near the oval window. Reysenbach de Haan not only confirmed these findings, but showed that the same cells are very strongly developed in other mammals that are similarly sensitive to high tones, i.e. in bats. He even classified the animals (Cetaceans, bats, mice, cats and men) he had investigated according to the size of these cells and found that it was proportional to the animal's sensitivity to high tones. While we know little about the exact function of these cells, it seems clear, therefore, that they are connected in some way with sensitivity to very high tones.

From what has been said above, it is obvious that Cetaceans have a very highly developed organ of hearing that is particularly sensitive to very high tones. In Chapter 9 we shall discuss how the modifications which produce this sensitivity have affected the structure of the auditory nerve and of the auditory centres in the brain.

I am devoting so much space to hearing in whales because this is, in fact, their most important sense. We shall see later that vision plays only a small, and smell hardly any, part in the whale's life, and that feeding, direction-finding, judging the depth of water and mutual contact are all largely restricted to the ear. Moreover, greater knowledge of the whale's auditory sense is of practical value as well. We have already seen that these animals are set to flight by asdic and that this knowledge is being used in modern whaling. Similarly, it is possible that they might be attracted by special calls, just as birds and stags are. We have seen in Chapter 6 that some Cetaceans are attracted over long distances by the cry of one of their comrades in distress – sounds which we may learn to imitate. Tomilin reported in 1955 that the Turks and the people of the Black Sea coast near Batum attract Bottlenose Dolphins with special whistles – a time-hallowed method already known to Pliny. It is also possible that, since whales may find their krill through the (as yet unknown) sounds these crustaceans are said to make, we may attract them by imitating krill-noises. Best of all, we might discover a special call attractive to the males alone, thus automatically sparing the lives of all females during the whaling season. Before progress is made in this field, we must, however, have thorough knowledge of the sounds which Cetaceans themselves produce, and of the meaning these sounds have for their congeners. We shall examine this problem in the next chapter.

8

The Production of Sounds

URING THE Second World War, the United States was naturally very concerned about the possibility of submarine attacks on her long and vulnerable coastline, and so set up a protective *sofar* barrier to give warning of an enemy approach. Submarines might be invisible, but *sofar* made them audible, as guards with hydrophones glued to their ears listened for suspicious sounds.

In 1942, almost a year after Pearl Harbour, a young *sofar* operator suddenly heard his hydrophone emit a mysterious creaking noise, and saw the hands on the dials of his instruments swinging ominously. The alarm was sounded and naval aircraft and a patrol boat set out to investigate. However, before they could go into action, the instruments had ceased to register the disturbance and it was assumed that the submarine had escaped. A routine report was sent to the Navy Department in Washington and the incident promptly forgotten.

But not by Washington, for there similar reports poured in in alarming numbers. It looked as if enemy submarines could infest U.S. coastal waters without anyone being able to do anything about it. Moreover, coastal patrol vessels off the Aleutians continually reported sounds like those of a ship's screws, or continuous clicking noises of unidentifiable origin. Similar reports came from the Solomon Islands, and there was the strange episode of a mine going off without a ship having been anywhere near it. The Navy Department was greatly perturbed until somebody suggested that the noises might not be caused by enemy naval detachments at all but by fish, perhaps by dolphins.

This explanation seemed fantastic because fishes had for centuries been thought to be mute. Thus in his ode to Melponeme, Horace wrote: 'O mutis quoque piscibus.' To solve the problem, zoologists were called in and asked what they knew about the subject. Unfortunately their knowledge was very scanty. They could quote Aristotle's (350 B.C.) saying that a captured dolphin squeaks and moans above the water, there were some

Figure 114. Odysseus tied to the mast of his ship to resist the enticing song of the sirens (here represented as birds). Note the dolphins in the background. From a Greek painting in the Athens Archaeological Museum. (Grünthal, 1952.)

casual reports of sounds apparently emitted by fishes, and fishermen from the Yellow Sea had reported that they had been woken up by them. All this, however, was not very reliable evidence. The question had never been investigated properly, partly because of lack of apparatus, and partly because of lack of money. But now that the hydrophone had made its appearance, and that the U.S. Navy provided all the resources, zoologists were quite willing to go into the matter. They soon found that the sea was a veritable babel of sounds resembling falling stones, ships' hooters, rattling chains, saws, moans and squeaks. One of the biggest sources of noise was soon identified as the *croaker*, a strange fish capable of a sound as loud as 107 decibels. (Cf. the pneumatic drill's 80 decibels, an aircraft engine's 110 decibels and a thunderbolt's 120 decibels.) Different fish produce their own characteristic noises, as visitors listening to the special loudspeakers installed in some aquaria have been able to hear for themselves. Crustaceans, too, are not silent, and the 'snapping shrimp' found in the Pacific is the loudest of all.

The pitch of the sounds made by all fish so far investigated is rather low – 100–1,500 cycles per second, the noise being most intense at about 350 cycles, i.e. in the region of our upper *a*. (The 'snapping shrimp' emits much higher notes of between 1,000 and 2,500 cycles per second.) Fishes usually produce sounds with their mouths or swim bladders, though their fins may contribute to the general effect. Detailed investigations are still continuing, not only for defence purposes, but also to help the fishing industry to identify large shoals of fish by analysing the noises they emit. To do so, all the different submarine noises had to be classified, including, of course, those produced by Cetaceans.

Aristotle was aware that dolphins could produce sounds at the surface, and it has often been suggested that the enticing melody of the sirens, which forced Odysseus to have himself tied to the mast of his ship lest he respond to their call, was really the song of leaping dolphins. In any case, the ancient Greeks included dolphins when they depicted this scene (Fig. 114). Rapp (1837) says that he heard stranded dolphins bellow like oxen, while the noise of a White-beaked Dolphin stranded on the Dutch coast in 1918 was said to resemble the lowing of a cow. The bigger Cetaceans, however, were always believed to be silent and the great Hunter (1786) asserted unequivocally that they were dumb. Only a few years later, however, Schneider (1795) and Lacepède (1804) mentioned the screams of wounded whales, probably those of Biscayan and Greenland Right Whales, since Rorquals were not generally hunted at that time. In any case, all whales exhale with a whistling noise, which, as we saw in Chapter 4, can be heard from quite a long distance away. At the beginning of this century, a whale (probably a Humpback) put in a regular appearance in a Bermudan bay, and the local population could easily distinguish it by its particularly piercing whistle, probably caused by the presence of a large acorn-shell in its blowhole. From about that period we also have an account by Ravits of a noise resembling a siren being made by a school of forty Humpback Whales. It rose and fell continuously, and Ravits thought that it may have had some connexion with courtship. More generally, all these 'blowing' noises are believed to establish mutual contact, and particularly to re-establish contact with a school when an individual whale has become separated from it.

So far we have only discussed the noises Cetaceans make at the surface, and we shall now investigate whether they can produce underwater sounds as well. Such sounds have been reported long ago, especially in the case of the Beluga, whose scream is, in fact, proverbial in Russia, a noisy man being said to 'squeal like a Beluga'. The Beluga's submarine scream is so loud that it can easily be heard above the surface of the water where it is said to resemble the call of a song bird. Because of this sound and also because of its colour, the Beluga is known among British whalers as the 'Sea Canary'. But apart from 'singing', the Beluga is also reported to growl, roar, and squeal. Submarine sounds of Common Dolphins and Risso's Dolphins have also been heard quite often by listeners outside the water and have even been recorded without special amplifiers. Kullenberg (1947) says that the noise of dolphins swimming seven feet below the surface resembles the piping sounds of fighting or playing mice, and

Figure 115. Two Bottlenose Dolphins approaching the hydrophone in the Marineland Aquarium, Florida. (Photograph: F. S. Essapian, Miami.)

investigators aboard the French research ship *Calypso* have corroborated this statement. How high-pitched these notes really are was fully appreciated by F. C. Fraser who failed to hear them altogether, while his colleagues just could. The real intensity of the sound became apparent when the shrill and piercing cries of newly caught and frightened Bottlenose Dolphins penetrated through the thick glass plates of the Marineland Aquarium in Florida and could be heard in the passages. A loud squeak was also heard by the well-known underwater photographer Hans Hass, when, off the Azores, he filmed the mouth of a harpooned and dying Sperm Whale. The noise was very clear and strong and appeared to come from the throat, and – according to Hass – was certainly not accompanied by movements of the lower jaw. Worthington and Schevill recorded hammering and other noises made by whales off the coast of North Carolina, and the young Sperm Whale which lost its life while investigating the *Calypso*'s screw was heard to emit a shrill whistle.

All these superficial observations tell us little about the real nature and significance of the noises, which have only been studied since 1948, when a number of American biologists began to investigate the sounds made by Pilot Whales, Spotted Dolphins and Bottlenose Dolphins in the Marineland Aquarium and in the Lerner Marine Laboratory, by means of a hydrophone (Fig. 115), while other investigators managed to make a recording of the voice of a Beluga in the Saguenay River near Quebec.

The most frequent noise made by all the species investigated so far is a peculiar shrill whistle (which can be heard without an amplifier) of 7,000–15,000 cycles per second in the Bottlenose Dolphin and of 500–10,000 cycles per second in the Beluga, which have a deeper voice. The sounds are always accompanied by an escape of air bubbles from the blowhole, and undoubtedly serve the animals as a means of communication. It has been observed that young Bottlenose Dolphins keep in constant contact with their mothers by 'whistling', and that contact between individual members of a school is maintained in the same way. Tomilin confirmed these observations in the case of Black Sea Dolphins. Thus dolphins are not only herd animals, but herd animals which communicate with one another. Similarly, large groups of monkeys keep up an incessant chatter, unlike solitary apes (orang-utan, gorilla), which are usually silent.

In Chapter 6 we saw that social distinctions are very important in all herd animals, and in Bottlenose Dolphins, just as in dogs, social superiority is frequently asserted by making threatening noises. Dolphins produce these noises by shutting their jaws vigorously.

During feeding, the Bottlenose often makes a barking noise accompanied by a release of air bubbles. However, such air bubbles are never emitted when the animal occasionally makes a noise which sounds like a miaow. In the mating season, Bottlenoses also produce a weird whine, and, when they investigate some unfamiliar phenomenon, they sound like a rusty creaking hinge. These creaking sounds, which have a frequency of 20–170 kilocycles, appear to be completely supersonic, and we shall return to them later. Meanwhile, it must be noted that it is not only the Bottlenose but other dolphins as well which produce such sounds. The Beluga, in addition, can chirp and make chiming sounds, and the Pilot Whale has been heard whining, belching, and smacking its lips. Its belch was known to Bartholinus who noted as early as 1654 that the Pilot Whale 'horrendum emittit ructum'.

Mysticetes, on the other hand, appear to be much more silent, and it is questionable whether they can emit any underwater sounds at all, though McCarthy, during a trip to the Antarctic in 1946, thought that his asdic picked up definite sounds made by Rorquals. Each sound, he states, resembles a high-pitched whistle whose frequency increases rapidly during the second it persists. The whistling was kept up intermittently for a whole minute. A few *sofar* stations and also some American patrol boats have, moreover, picked up sounds which they claim were emitted by Humpback and other big whales, while a recording of whale noises made at the Biological Station at Woods Hole reproduces an intermittent hum resembling the sound of a ship's screw. This hum, however, may have merely resulted from the animal flailing its tail.

Other investigators, such as Hosokawa (1950), Schevill and Lawrence (1952) and the British biologist Symons, who did research work aboard the *Balaena*, were unable to pick up any Rorqual noises, much as they tried to do so. (The only sound Schevill managed to pick up in 1958 was a 'generator hum' emitted by a Biscayan Right Whale.) Even so, it seems unlikely that Rorquals, whose auditory organs are so well adapted to picking up underwater sounds, should be less capable of emitting noises than dolphins, Sperm Whales and Biscayan Right Whales. No doubt, improved equipment and methods of observation will lead to better results in the future.

In any case, we have seen that dolphins, at least, can produce noises up to 170 kilocycles per second and that they respond to sounds of between 150 and 153,000 cycles per second (see Chapter 7). This would enable them to distinguish clearly between noises emitted by their own species and the low-pitched sounds of fish.

Such high pitch sounds make us think of bats whose ability to find their way about in complete darkness is known to be associated with the high notes they produce, so much so that, as the well-known eighteenth-century naturalist Spallanzani proved, blinded bats lose none of their sureness of flight. The exact mechanism of their flight had long puzzled biologists, particularly when it appeared that the animals' feelers played no part in it. The problem was finally resolved with the discovery of the principle of radar which, as we know, is based on transmitting very short radio waves and receiving them again after they have been reflected by solid objects. Radar is used *inter alia* by ships sailing in thick fog and in the vicinity of icebergs, and the risk of collision is consequently minimized.

Now a great many investigators, including Prof. Dijkgraaf of Utrecht, have shown that the remarkable flying feats of bats are based on a similar principle. Bats emit high-frequency sound waves through their mouths and noses, and pick up any reflected signals by ear. In this way, they manage to avoid obstacles in their path without having to use their eyes. Ultrasonic vibrations are particularly suited to this purpose since they can be beamed in a given direction far better than low-frequency vibrations. What we know about bats leads us to assume that whales and dolphins, whose hearing is so extraordinarily acute and whose other sense organs are so poorly developed, and which, after all, spend much of their time groping in the dark of the lower ocean or under the ice, hear and avoid obstacles in much the same way. Let us see what evidence there is to support this hypothesis.

First of all, there is the pitch of the notes which they emit and to which they are known to respond. Secondly, Kellogg, Kohler and Morris, all American zoologists, discovered in 1953 that, as far as Bottlenose Dolphins are concerned, sounds somewhere between 7 and 15 kilocycles are emitted with continuously changing pitch, while sounds between 20 and 170 kilocycles (i.e. the noises resembling a squeaking door) consist of a series of very short blasts of variable duration. Both effects, i.e. frequency and pulse modulation, are also used in radar; and pulse modulation, in particular, is used in echo-sounding and in asdic.

Further evidence is the fact that whales can be trapped in nets – a time-honoured method used in Japan and elsewhere. The animals never try to break through this fragile barrier and healthy Boutus, porpoises, and River Dolphins of the genus *Sotalia* are known to be capable of avoiding every kind of net. Thus McBride reports that Bottlenose Dolphins give a wide berth to all nets of fine mesh, even when the sea is turbulent or the water muddy. They simply jump out of the water to clear the obstacle, and only when the mesh is ten inches square or more do they ignore its presence and allow themselves to be caught. All this fits in with our asdic hypothesis, just as do Schevill and Lawrence's experiments on the way in which Bottlenose Dolphins find their prey in the dark. At first Schevill and Lawrence failed to discover any form of ultrasonic sound emission used in echo-locating, but during their latest experiments (1956) in a very quiet pool near Woods Hole they did in fact note that, under special conditions, the animals emitted very weak sounds, not normally detectable. Thus, whenever they came near to a fish that was being offered them, they emitted clicking noises with a frequency of between 100 and 200 kilocycles. Even more convincing are experiments carried out by Kellogg in 1958 and 1959 in a specially constructed echo-free pool on the Florida coast. The pool contained turbid water to exclude the visual factor, and the experiments were therefore carried out 'in the dark'. Even so, the Bottlenose Dolphins steered clear of a host of obstacles and produced characteristic clicks or squeaks with frequencies above 100 kilocycles the moment a new obstacle was put into the tank. Worthington and Schevill noted similar sounds being made by a Sperm Whale off Cape Cod. Very convincing experiments have been made by Norris (Marineland of the Pacific) and Wood (Marineland, Florida). They blindfolded Bottlenose Dolphins with rubber suction cups and observed that the animals swam about the tank without any indication of uncertainty. When a fish was thrown into the water the animals emitted their *sofar* sounds and swam unerringly to the food. We may therefore safely conclude that all the evidence points to the fact that whales and dolphins locate objects by a method akin to asdic, at any rate unless and until experiments in which hearing and sound production are excluded – and it has not yet been possible to do this – prove the contrary.

The fact that Cetacean orientation principally relies on echo-location may explain why mass-strandings occur in some species (see page 199). Dudok van Heel has demonstrated that these strandings nearly always occur on very slightly sloping or on muddy coasts. In both cases the echo either comes from everywhere or there is no echo at all, which causes complete lack of orientation.

We must now ask how and where all these supersonic vibrations are produced, particularly since, as we have seen in Chapter 4, Cetaceans lack vocal chords. Actually, animals can produce sounds not only by means of vocal chords but also by vibrating the air in other folds in the lining of their larynx and throat. Various research workers, including F. C. Fraser, have shown that noises are produced whenever air is pumped through the larynx of a dolphin. Moreover, we have already seen that when air escapes or is sucked in through the blowhole and the diverticula beneath it, definite sounds are produced, and that air bubbles are released from the blowhole even when the animal is submerged. While it is questionable whether these bubbles are directly connected with the production of sounds since, as we have seen, Mysticetes have no diverticula, the diverticula of Odontocetes with their numerous folds could certainly act as excellent vibrating membranes. Possibly the laryngeal diverticulum of Mysticetes (see p. 147) may play a similar part, but this question awaits further examination. In any case, we have seen that Cetaceans have a wide enough range of organs to produce all the sounds we have discussed, and that echo-locating is very likely to be an important reason why they produce them.

9

Senses and the Central Nervous System

At the end of Chapter 6 we saw that a thorough understanding of Cetacean behaviour must be based on the study of the sensory organs. We have already discussed their most important sense – hearing – at length so that we can now devote our attention to the other senses and particularly to seeing. To explain what changes the Cetacean eye has undergone in order to adapt to life in the water we shall first take a brief look at the eye of man as a representative terrestrial mammal.

Our own eye lies in a bony case, the orbital cavity. Eyelids, eyelashes and eyebrows protect the delicate tissue of the eyeball against the harmful influences of dust and sweat, while the lachrymal glands continually wash and lubricate the eyeball with a thin film of tears. The tears, after bathing the surface of the eye, are drained from its inner corner into the nose by the lachrymal duct.

The wall of the eye is composed of three coats (Fig. 116), of which the outer sclera is fibrous and preserves the form of the eyeball. From it the seven eye muscles which help to rotate and move the eyeball in its socket run to the orbital wall. The outer coat is transparent in front where it forms the cornea, i.e. the part of the eye which we can see. Below the sclera is found the middle layer or choroid which is dark and richly vascular and contains the main arteries, veins and lymphatic vessels of the eyeball. It completely surrounds the globe except for a small circular opening in front – the pupil. The circular band immediately surrounding the pupil is the mottled iris. The pupil can be dilated or contracted to admit the precise amount of light needed.

The inner layer or retina contains the receptors of sight, and is essentially nervous in structure and function. Light stimuli are transmitted to the brain by way of the optic nerve, whose terminal nerve fibres are distributed over the entire retina. Immediately behind the iris is found the lens, which is suspended in this position by the delicate suspensory ligament which blends with the transparent lens capsule and is attached circumferentially to the interior of the globe through the ciliary body. The latter, which consists of concentric involuntary muscle fibres, also connects the iris with the choroid. The iris divides the eyeball in front of the lens into an anterior and a posterior chamber, both filled with a clear fluid called the aqueous humour. The part of the eyeball behind the lens is filled with a transparent gelatinous substance called the vitreous humour.

The eye functions very much like a camera, though its lens (together with the cornea, the aqueous and vitreous humours, all of which help to refract the incoming light) is far more complex. The iris can be compared with the camera's diaphragm, and the retina with the photographic film or plate. When at rest, our eye is focused at infinity, i.e. the light rays reflected by distant objects form a clear picture on the retina. Now, we all know that when close-up pictures are to be snapped, the lens of the camera must be pulled out, since otherwise the image would form behind the photographic plate and thus become blurred. Some fish and snakes can 'screw out' their lenses in a similar way, but man, for one, cannot, and to look at a nearby object he must accommodate his eye, i.e. change the shape of his lens. The more spherical the lens, the nearer to the front of the eye the image is formed, and the more compressed antero-posteriorly the lens the further from the front of the eye is the image. Accommodation for near vision is effected by contraction of the concentric ciliary muscle and consequent slackening of the suspensory ligament. As the muscle contracts, the choroid is drawn forward and the ciliary processes are brought closer to the lens, thus relaxing its tension.

Visibility under water is much poorer than it is on land, since a great deal of light is absorbed by the upper layers of water. Thus, off our coasts, 90 per cent of white light is absorbed by the time we go down to five fathoms, and only 1 per cent of white light penetrates below twenty fathoms. Below 215 fathoms, the sea is pitch black, no matter how clear the water or how bright the sunshine. Horizontal visibility is further decreased by the scarcity of light-reflecting objects. The well-known ophthalmologist, G. L. Walls, of the University of Michigan, who wrote a book of nearly 800 pages on the vision of vertebrates, therefore assumed that the maximum visibility even in shallow seas is about fifty-six feet. In other words, big whales would be unable to see their own flukes. Since, moreover, many Cetaceans spend part of their time below the ice where only a very small amount of light penetrates, and since many of them are predominantly nocturnal animals, it is not surprising that vision does not play as important a part for them as for other mammals.

Of all Cetaceans, porpoises and dolphins, which feed on fish relatively near the surface, have by far the keenest vision. The Bottlenose Dolphins

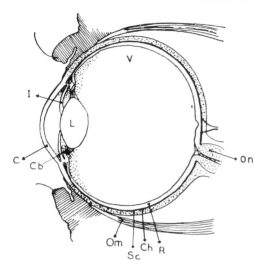

Figure 116. Cross-section through the eye of man. Sc = sclerotic coat; C = cornea; I = iris; L = lens; Cb = ciliary body; V = vitreous humour; Ch = choroid; R = retina; On = ocular nerve; Om = ocular muscle. (IJsseling and Scheygrond, 1951.)

in the Marineland Aquarium certainly rely on their eyesight to capture prey, and at the Woods Hole Biological Station a one-eyed Bottlenose was repeatedly seen turning its head so that its good eye was towards the fish it was pursuing. Now all these dolphins are diurnal animals, but the Pilot Whales in the Marineland Aquarium, which feed on slow-moving cuttle-fish and which are primarily nocturnal, definitely appear to rely on vision to a much smaller extent. Further evidence for the assumption that cuttle-fish-eating and deep-diving whales do not rely on eyesight is that Sperm Whales have very small eyes indeed. Quiring, comparing the weight of the eye of a Humpback Whale with that of a Sperm Whale (both animals weighed approximately forty tons), found that the former weighed 980 grams whereas the latter only weighed 290 grams. Right Whales, too, have relatively small eyes compared with Rorquals, whose eyes are one and a half times as big. According to Gilmore (1958), Grey Whales use their eyes to some extent for finding their bearings in clear water. The smallest Cetacean eye is that of the Gangetic Dolphin, a lead-black animal, some eight feet long, with a forceps-like beak (Fig. 117). It is found in the Ganges and its tributaries, and in the only full description of this animal, Anderson (1878) states that its eye is as big as a pea and has no lens at all. The eye muscles are diminutive, while the optic nerve is exceptionally thin. The Gangetic Dolphin feeds on fish and crabs off the muddy bottom of these rivers, where eyesight would be no advantage to it; besides, it is a nocturnal animal. In captivity, these dolphins generally refuse all food during the day. Other fresh-water dolphins from the same region (species of *Orcaella*) and those relatives of the Gangetic Dolphin

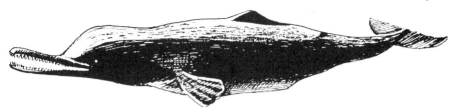

Figure 117. The Gangetic Dolphin is practically blind and finds its food at the bottom of muddy rivers.

from other rivers (e.g. the La Plata Dolphin and the Boutu) which find their prey in less turbid waters have correspondingly better eyes.

But to function at all, however poorly, Cetacean eyes had to undergo certain adaptations to their aquatic environment. Firstly, they need no device to keep their eyeballs moist, and all Cetaceans therefore lack lachrymal glands and ducts. In other words, whales cannot weep. Nor need whales worry about dust and sweat, and so they have no eyebrows or eyelashes, or, for that matter, any hands or paws with which to brush foreign bodies out of their eyes. Other adaptations are also dictated by their aquatic environment, and we shall see that most of these adaptations are more highly developed in Odontocetes than in Mysticetes, possibly due to the greater mobility of the former's prey.

Now a ray of light entering the eye lens on land is refracted differently from one entering the eye under water. An image of an object which would normally form on our retina would form behind it if we looked at the object through water. We can correct this fault by accommodating our lens, but Cetaceans have permanently compensated for their 'longsightedness' by an exceptionally rounded lens, strongly resembling that in fish. In many species the lens is very nearly perfectly spherical (Fig. 118), and even in Rorquals, where the curvature is less pronounced, it is very much more rounded than in terrestrial mammals. A more spherical lens has the same effect as a pair of convex glasses worn under water by a man with normal sight – the rays are bent forward and the image is made to fall on the retina as it would do if he were out of the water without glasses (Fig. 119). The Cetacean's lens also has a greater refractive index than that of terrestrial mammals, and in most species the eyeball itself is oval rather than spherical, thus enlarging the visual field (see below), but at the same time decreasing the distance between lens and retina (thus making them more longsighted). In Rorquals this is partly cancelled out by their having a very much smaller lens than other Cetaceans.

The first scientist to make a thorough study of the Cetacean eye with relatively modern instruments was Dr Matthiessen, Professor of Ophthalmology at the University of Rostock, who spent his long vacation

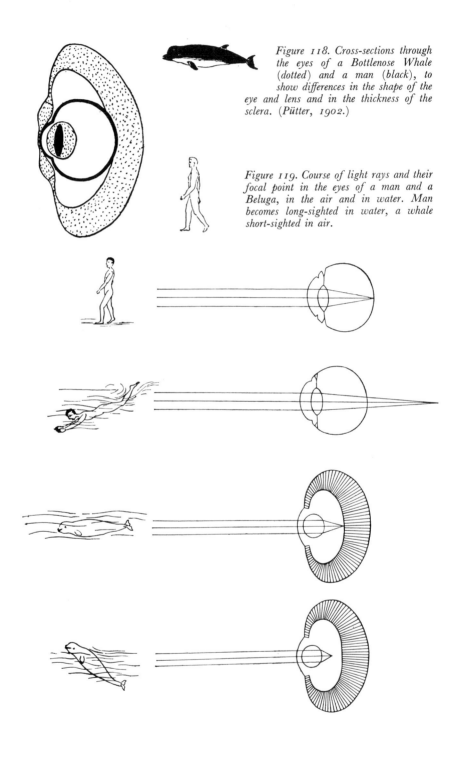

Figure 118. Cross-sections through the eyes of a Bottlenose Whale (dotted) and a man (black), to show differences in the shape of the eye and lens and in the thickness of the sclera. (Pütter, 1902.)

Figure 119. Course of light rays and their focal point in the eyes of a man and a Beluga, in the air and in water. Man becomes long-sighted in water, a whale short-sighted in air.

in 1890 visiting a number of Norwegian whaling stations and collecting specimens. In Tromsö, he met Svend Foyn, the inventor of the harpoon gun and the owner of some of the stations, and discovered that Foyn 'dislikes scientists and cannot bear to have strangers visiting his whaling stations'. Fortunately, other whaling masters proved less intractable, particularly Capt. Bull on Sörväd station (near Hammerfest), who received him most hospitably and entertained him for some weeks. Matthiessen acknowledged his debt to his host and to other helpers in his subsequently published paper, in which he showed, *inter alia*, that the cornea, the aqueous humour and probably also the vitreous humour of the Cetacean eye have the same refractive index as sea water. In other words, they do not bend rays of light entering from the water, and the shape of the cornea can have no influence on the path of the rays. The optical properties of the eye are therefore primarily controlled by the lens.

Because of adaptations to its aquatic environment, the Cetacean eye necessarily functions less efficiently on the surface, where images will form in front of the retina and consequently be blurred – the animals become shortsighted and in need of concave glasses. Some authorities believe that whales and dolphins cannot see anything at all out of the water, but experiments in the Marineland aquaria (Florida and California) have shown that this belief is erroneous, for, as we have seen, Bottlenose Dolphins can catch fish in mid-air (Fig. 120), jump through hoops, pull at a bell-rope, follow the movements of a hand some fifty feet away, and recognize their keepers. In short, they behave in such a way that we must conclude that their eyesight out of the water is fairly good, in fact remarkably good when we consider how well the same eyes enable them to see below the surface. Dudok van Heel made similar observations with porpoises, and Tomilin with Common Dolphins. Moreover, Killer Whales are believed to scan the surface of the sea carefully, and even to pounce upon seals lying on ice-floes, while Rorquals (and particularly Little Piked Whales) have been observed to look up between cracks in the ice (Figs. 222 and 223). The same behaviour has been reported of Grey Whales also.

In Odontocetes, visual acuity is undoubtedly due to lens accommodation, and their ciliary muscles are, in fact, well developed. Mysticetes, on the other hand, seem to lack ciliary muscles, and their eyes can therefore not be accommodated. Matthiessen has, however, inferred that while Mysticetes cannot see clearly above water their retina can, nevertheless, register impressions of moving objects and of outlines. Moreover, Fischer (1946) believes that the shape of their eyes, and also those of Sperm Whales, is such that the distance between lens and retina is greater in the upper and smaller in the lower eye. Aerial images would then be focused

Figure 120. A Bottlenose Dolphin in Marineland, Florida, jumping for fish.

sharply on the lower retina, and aquatic images on the upper retina. However, the whole subject requires further investigation.

Another factor affecting the eye of aquatic animals is water pressure. While the eye, like all other Cetacean tissues, is constructed of extremely incompressible material (see Chapter 4), water pressure may only alter its shape. Now we have seen that the shape of the eye affects the sharpness of the image and the width of the visual field, and since the Odontocete eye, particularly, lacks much of the bony orbit protecting our own eyes, it must have special safeguards against pressure distortion.

Most whalers could tell you and possibly even show you how the shape of the Cetacean eye is maintained, since the eyes, like the 'ears', are often taken home as trophies. The contents of the eye are pulled out through the back, where an opening admits the optic nerve, an electric bulb is fitted in, and light is made to shine through the cornea. While the cornea generally becomes dry and somewhat crinkly, the eyeball itself retains its shape thanks to the enormous thickness of its tough sclera. And it is this coat which guards the eye of living Cetaceans from undue distortion. Its exceptionally hard connective tissue is many scores of times thicker in Rorquals than it is in terrestrial mammals, and even porpoises and dolphins have a particularly thick sclera (Fig. 118).

While sea-water keeps the Cetacean eye permanently moist and clean, the great masses of water which continuously stream past the cornea at great speed naturally expose it to very much more wear and tear than a terrestrial mammal's. True, this disadvantage is less serious than might be thought because the eyes are small and built into a streamlined body, but frictional forces are still great enough to necessitate a special corneal structure. Thus the outer cornea of Cetaceans is cornified, the cornified substance uniting by means of papillae with the living tissue beneath. Because of this cornification, the eye is protected not only against friction but also against the stinging effect of brine. The conjunctiva is also protected by a cornified layer. Nor are these the only means of protecting the Cetacean eye against irritation by salt water, for, though Cetaceans have no tear glands, other glands, e.g. Harderian glands in the outer corners of the eyes and also glands in the conjunctiva of the eyelids, excrete an oily substance which regularly bathes the cornea, thus protecting it and the eyelids against the harmful effects of sea-water. Any surplus oil is washed away by the sea, so that there is no need for special drains such as our own lachrymal ducts. Such ducts have, however, been found in the skulls of Archaeocetes.

Naturally, the eyelids themselves, which can shut off the vulnerable eye from the outside world, are its best protection against superficial injury. That the eyelids of Cetaceans can shut and open is best seen in a newly killed whale, where they·can be moved up and down with ease. Though they look somewhat rigid in Odontocetes, the Bottlenoses of Marineland and other dolphins are known to be capable of shutting their eyes, and the eyelids of Odontocetes and Mysticetes alike are, moreover, provided with well-developed muscles; a set of muscles connected to each of the four *recti* muscles of the eye keeps them open, and an annular muscle shuts them. In theory, therefore, whales and dolphins would not only be able to sleep with their eyes shut, but also to wink, if they chose.

Though the Cetacean pupil can be greatly dilated, the relative smallness of the cornea is a disadvantage in the poor light in which Cetaceans normally move. In animals which live in perpetual twilight, one might have expected to find the exceptionally large eyes of nocturnal animals, e.g. of lemurs. But we have seen why a large eye would be a drawback to Cetaceans. Now, nature has in fact made some amends for these deficiencies by providing Cetaceans with an exceptionally well-developed *tapetum lucidum*, a special layer at the surface of a part of the choroid layer adjacent to the retina. The *tapetum lucidum* contains large quantities of guanine crystals which give it a metallic appearance and enable it to reflect light like a mirror. The eyes of a cat or a horse glow in the dark because they possess a tapetum whose function it is to send light which has passed to the retina back to the retina a second time. In this way vision in the dark is greatly increased, and it is therefore not surprising that in terrestrial mammals a tapetum is found, particularly in carnivores and ungulates which use their eyes day and night, and in lemurs which only spring to life after sunset. Man shares his lack of a tapetum with diurnal apes, pigs and a number of other mammals. In all Cetaceans, however, the tapetum, which forms a blue or green iridescent layer, is extremely well developed, covering almost the entire surface of the choroid, particularly in Mysticetes where, as in seals, it runs as far as the ciliary body. In Odontocetes, though not so large, it is still considerably bigger than in terrestrial mammals.

Another adjustment to the paucity of light under the sea is found in the microscopic structure of the retina, whose receptors of sight consist mainly of modified nerve cells called rods and cones, the ability to see in dim light depending largely upon the rods. Now, many investigators have been able to show that Cetaceans not only have a greater number of rods, but that their rods are bigger than those of terrestrial mammals. Mysticetes appear to have the longest rods of all, possibly because of their deep dives. We might then expect Sperm Whales and Bottlenose Whales to have very long rods also, but unfortunately not enough data are available to test this hypothesis.

It was long believed that Cetaceans lacked the cones found in the retina of terrestrial mammals, but in 1946 Fischer managed to isolate such cones in the retina of a Sperm Whale and a Fin Whale. This discovery was highly significant because many authorities believe that the presence of cones is associated with visual acuity and with colour perception.

A question of great importance for the correct evaluation of Cetacean behaviour is the size of the Cetacean visual field. When we look straight ahead we can take in a field of 160° without having to move our head. A dog covers a field of roughly 250°, and some rodents (e.g. hares and rabbits) can cover 360°, i.e. they can observe everything that goes on around them. Their large visual field, so important in animals threatened from all sides, is, however, offset by loss of stereoscopic vision, which is indispensable for estimating distances correctly and is therefore particularly sharp in hunting animals, or in arboreal animals which jump from branch to branch. Stereoscopic vision occurs when the visual field of the left eye partially overlaps that of the right eye. In man, the stereoscopic field is 120° in a total visual field of 160°, in the dog about 90°, in the horse 60°, and in the rabbit 30° in a forward direction and another 9° in a caudo-dorsal direction.

In other words, hunted animals usually have their eyes placed laterally, whereas hunters, which have to judge their distance from their prey very accurately, benefit from eyes placed more frontally. Thus we might expect Cetaceans, and Odontocetes particularly, to have close-set eyes, were it not that this would vitiate their streamlining. Moreover, frontally placed eyes which stick out of the head would be exposed to exceptional frictional and saline effects, and so Cetaceans must content themselves with small, laterally placed eyes, recessed in the head with consequent loss of field vision. Animals with small snouts, e.g. dolphins, are still best off in this respect, and in Bottlenose Dolphins the visual fields of left and right eyes overlap to some extent so that part of their vision is stereo-scopic. This, together with the flexibility of their heads, undoubtedly accounts for the agility with which they catch fish in and out of the water. An animal like the Pilot Whale with its blunt and bulbous head, has its frontal view greatly obstructed; this applies even more to the Sperm Whale and to Mysticetes. However, all these animals feed on slow-moving cuttlefish or on small shrimps, and good vision is less important to them. A Pilot Whale was seen to refuse food placed directly in front of it, but to respond when the food was moved towards the side.

While the axis of the porpoise's eye at rest appears to be directed towards the side, that of most other Cetaceans is, according to Pütter, directed obliquely downwards and towards the front. Since the Cetacean eye is elliptically flattened, the horizontal visual field is undoubtedly greater than the vertical field. Detailed investigations of the size of the visual field have not yet been made, though Fischer found in 1946 that the Sperm Whale had a horizontal visual field of about 125° on either side of the head (Fig. 121). While the animals are in the water, they are unlikely to see much above the surface, because of refraction and reflec-tion by the water, though some of the tricks of captive Bottlenose Dolphins suggest that they must have some idea of what goes on above the surface while their eyes are still submerged.

Naturally, the total visual field of all mammals can be increased by moving head and eyeball. We have discussed the Cetacean neck and possible head movements in Chapter 3, and need say no more about them. As for the eyeball, we know that the Cetacean eye muscles are fairly well developed. Hunter described all seven as early as 1787, and Hosokawa

Figure 121. Top view of head of Sperm Whale, showing limits of its visual fields. (After Mann Fischer, 1946.)

(1951), who investigated the eye muscles of a number of different species, had little to add except that the four recti muscles were rather small, while the two obliques were of normal size. The eyeballs of living dolphins were, in fact, found to be very mobile.

We have now reviewed the most important characteristics of the Cetacean eye, and can pass on to a discussion of the other senses.

We need not waste much time on the sense of smell which is completely lacking in Odontocetes and rudimentary in Mysticetes. Russian zoologists have admittedly found that the Beluga reacts to smoke and other strong odours, but the lack of an olfactory organ would seem to indicate that the stimuli are received by taste receptors or by some other sense. The fact that Cetaceans cannot smell is not so much due to their aquatic life, as to their descent. Smelling, i.e. the perception of chemical stimuli by means of an organ situated in the nose, is perfectly possible in water, so much so that smell forms an extremely important sense in fish which all have highly developed olfactory organs and nerves. Fish can smell the presence of dissolved particles, and their olfactory organ would thus act very much like our own sense of taste. During the evolution of terrestrial animals, however, there occurred a clear separation between these two senses, the organs of taste remaining organs for the perception of particles dissolved in water, while the organs of smell became specialized as perceptors of particles diffused in the air. Since dry and cold air can have an adverse effect on the tender mucous membrane of the organ of smell, it had to be tucked away safely in the back in the nasal cavity where the air can only get to it after being warmed and moistened in the nostrils. Aquatic mammals, however, would choke if water penetrated to the rear of the nasal cavity, and their olfactory receptors would have had to migrate elsewhere. Why they have not is a debatable question, though the answer may well lie in Dollo's 'law of irreversible evolution' (see page 69). By that law, once terrestrial mammals took to water, their olfactory receptors could not travel back to their original position, and, being useless at the back of the nasal cavity, they simply atrophied. In Mysticetes, a vestigial olfactory organ is still present, probably for smelling above the surface, and sea-cows have a fairly well developed organ of smell, no doubt for the same purpose.

The fact that Mysticetes have retained some sense of smell is inferred primarily from their having small evaginations of the nasal cavity, the ethmoturbinals of other mammals, which are covered with olfactory epithelium. Moreover, their ethmoid, like that of most mammals, has a cribriform plate perforated with small holes, allowing the terminal branches of the olfactory nerve to pass through. The latter, although poorly developed, is present in all Mysticetes and even has a swelling at

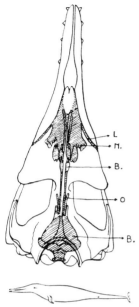

Figure 122. Skull of Archaeocete (Dorudon stromeri) *with brain and nasal cavities drawn in. L = lachrymal duct; N = nasal cavity with distensions and projections; B = olfactory bulb; O = optic nerve; B = brain. (Kellogg, 1929.)*

its extremity, the so-called olfactory bulb which is found in most vertebrates. It is not yet known whether adult Mysticetes have a functioning olfactory nasal epithelium, but the presence of an olfactory nerve makes it likely. Embryos, moreover, have been shown to have olfactory receptors in their nasal epithelium.

Archaeocetes, which lived forty million years ago and which we have discussed at length in Chapter 2, undoubtedly had a very much keener sense of smell than their modern relatives. This is inferred from the structure of their nasal cavity, and particularly from the presence of characteristic lamellae of bone which, in other mammals, are covered by olfactory epithelium (Fig. 122). In modern Odontocetes, on the other hand, all traces of an olfactory organ or nerve are generally absent, though the ethmoid of some of their Miocene ancestors was found to be perforated to admit the olfactory nerve, so that fifteen million years ago these animals may well have been able to smell.

No discussion of the organ of smell would be complete without some remark about Stenson's duct. Vestiges of this duct are found in all Cetaceans, where they take the form of one or two small grooves inside the tip of the upper jaw. These grooves are clearly visible even in adult whales, though they seem to fulfil no function at all. Moreover, there are no traces of the duct itself, let alone of a vomeronasal (Jacobson's) organ.

The sense of taste will be discussed at greater length in Chapter 10, so that we can conclude our survey of the Cetacean senses with a few remarks on the sense of touch. We must pass over the perception of pain and heat stimuli in silence, since very little is known on this subject. Papers on the Cetacean spinal cord usually state that the Cetacean sense of touch and particularly the sensitivity of the skin are poorly developed, but they are surely wrong since, for instance, stranded dolphins have often been observed to react to even the most gentle touch by movements of the body or of the eyelids. Moreover, the Bottlenoses and also the Pilot Whales in the Marineland aquarium love to be stroked by their keepers, and Bottlenoses have been seen stroking each other with their pectoral fins during

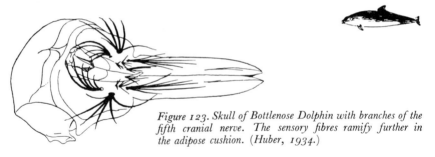

Figure 123. Skull of Bottlenose Dolphin with branches of the fifth cranial nerve. The sensory fibres ramify further in the adipose cushion. (Huber, 1934.)

love play. Like most other mammals, the dolphins in the aquarium like to rub themselves against all sorts of rough surfaces including stones, planks, and even tortoises. They like to have hoses playing on them and delight in having their skins scrubbed with a brush, just as tame elephants and rhinoceroses do. Although the skin of Cetaceans has not yet been fully examined for tactile cells, the presence of a papillary layer in the corium of the skin is evidence that the Cetacean sense of touch is well developed, since, in many other mammals, tactile cells are particularly abundant in these layers.

The adipose cushion – or 'melon' – above the snout of Odontocetes (see Chapter 4) is assumed to be especially sensitive, since it is provided with a number of well-developed branches of the fifth cranial nerve (the trigeminal nerve; see Fig. 123). These branches probably terminate in tactile cells, but unfortunately their role awaits further investigation, which may well show that, in them, Odontocetes have a special means of registering water pressure and flow. Mysticetes, which lack a 'melon', are provided with bristles on their upper jaw which, as we have seen in Chapter 2, may very well serve as 'feelers'.

The Japanese biologists Ogawa and Shida have, moreover, shown that both upper and lower lips of Rorquals are provided with a great number of small 'bumps', particularly at the tip of the snout. These bumps, which have a diameter of about 1 mm., are said to contain a number of tactile cells, which is borne out by the fact that the lips of whales have always been known to be particularly sensitive. The tail and particularly the flukes must be extremely sensitive as well, since dissections of the Cetacean nervous system show the presence of very prominent nerves in these regions. These nerves must have a sensory and probably a tactile function, since there are practically no muscles in this region. Whether they do, in fact, terminate in tactile cells is not known at present.

All in all, we must agree with Jansen's contention (1950) that, together with certain characteristics of the cerebellum, all the facts point to Cetaceans having a well-developed tactile sense.

From the structure of the central nervous system, i.e. the brain and the spinal cord, we can, in fact, draw a great many interesting inferences not only about the senses, but also about propulsion, metabolism and all sorts of other vital processes. The central nervous system is like a switchboard controlling all the functions of an animal, and its structure clearly reflects the animal's behaviour. For this reason, we shall devote the rest of this chapter to a discussion of the Cetacean brain and spinal cord.

The Cetacean central nervous system, like that of all vertebrates, lies inside the braincase and the vertebral column. The spinal cord is, as we have seen in Chapter 5, surrounded by a thick vascular network, and so is part of the brain of Mysticetes. Odontocetes have less highly developed retia in the braincase, though vascular networks are certainly found in the base of their skull and round the large nerves emanating from this region, e.g. the optic nerve. In addition to being cushioned by this mass of blood vessels, the delicate tissue of the central nervous system is protected by meninges, connective-tissue membranes identical with those found in terrestrial mammals. According to Gersh (1938), the epiphysis, a small organ protruding from the roof of the brain, is also very similar to that of terrestrial mammals. This organ is thought to regulate the pressure of the cerebro-spinal fluid.

If we look at the spinal cord of a terrestrial mammal in cross-section, it appears to consist of white matter surrounding an H-shaped mass of grey matter. While the grey matter is made up of nerve cell bodies, the white matter consists of nerve fibres most of which are medullated, i.e. surrounded by a sheath. Thus the grey matter may be said to be the switchboard proper, while the white matter constitutes the plugs and wires carrying messages to and from the rest of the body. Whereas the dorsal horns of the grey matter (in man, the posterior horns of the H-shaped mass) are composed almost entirely of cells which receive sensory stimuli, the ventral roots consist almost entirely of motor cells whose fibres run to the muscles, causing them to contract when necessary.

If we look at a Cetacean spinal cord in cross-section and compare it with that of a typical terrestrial mammal, we are immediately struck by the fact that, particularly in the thoracic and lumbar regions, the ventral (in man, anterior) horns are extraordinarily large while the dorsal (in man, posterior) horns are comparatively small (Fig. 124). The same is true also of the white matter, which is much thicker at the bottom than it is on top, and of the nerve roots emanating from the cord. In other words the motor nerves, i.e. the nerves causing muscles to contract, are much more highly developed in Cetaceans than they are in terrestrial mammals, while the sensory nerves are much less developed, at least in comparison with the motor nerves and possibly, though to a lesser

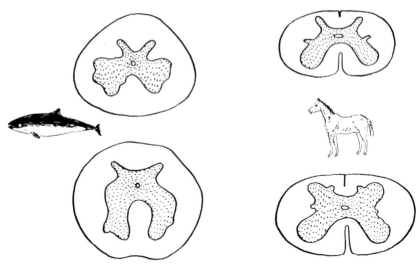

Figure 124. Cross-sections through the spinal cord of a porpoise and a horse. Top: cervical region; Bottom: lumbar region. (After: Hepburn and Waterston, 1904, and Pressy and Cobb, 1929.)

extent, compared with the sensory nerves of other mammals. There is nothing very surprising in this discovery, for we saw in Chapter 3 that a very large proportion of the Cetacean body consists of muscle. From the fact that the sensory apparatus of Cetaceans is relatively small, various biologists have inferred that they have reduced sensitivity, but we have just seen that this inference does not tally with the known facts. True, because of the animal's general shape and the almost complete absence of limbs, the total skin surface is much smaller than it is in terrestrial mammals. Moreover, aquatic mammals need fewer temperature receptors in the skin, since water is not subject to such sudden fluctuations of temperature as the air. This, and also the fact that the ventral horns are exceptionally large, probably explains why the dorsal horns have been taken to be much smaller than they really are.

It may be objected that a strongly developed muscular apparatus must go hand in hand with a well-developed system of proprioceptors and a consequent increase in the size of the dorsal horns. In fact, this is not so, since most proprioceptive reflexes by-pass the cells of the dorsal horns, the nerve fibres from the spinal ganglion which transmit these stimuli going directly to the ventral horns. The size of the dorsal horn is thus not very much affected by the presence of a well-developed system of proprioceptors for registering tensions in muscles and tendons. The Cetacean spinal cord has a very distinct cervical intumescence; the lumbar swelling is much less prominent.

While the first descriptions of the Cetacean brain were written by Ray in 1671 and Tyson in 1680, both of whom dissected a porpoise, the earliest comparative account to have remained of any real value is Tiedemann's (1826). True his description contained some errors, but these were put right twenty years later by Stannius, who also made a study of the brains of porpoises. Mysticete brains are, of course, more difficult to come by, and though Hunter gave a first, superficial, description in 1787, it took many years before a specimen made its first appearance in a laboratory. In 1879, Prof. Aurivilius of the University of Uppsala was sent the brain of a Rorqual by a Norwegian whaling station, but as he considered it too valuable for dissection, he kept it in the museum, where it probably still is to this day. Fortunately, the Norwegian station continued to supply whale brains, and in 1885 Guldberg was able to give a full account, in the course of which he mentioned the great difficulties involved in dissecting so delicate and fragile an organ surrounded by such hard bone. It took him five hours of intensive work to remove the brain from the skull, and even though modern instruments have reduced the time, the removal of a whale's brain is still one of the toughest tasks a zoologist has to tackle. Even so, we now have fairly full descriptions of the brains of a number of Cetaceans.

Everyone looking at the brain of a whale or dolphin for the first time is struck by the fact that the brain is so compressed from front to back (Figs. 125, 126). In Mysticetes, it is as wide as it is long, but in Odonto-cetes its width actually exceeds its length and, in addition, it is very peculiarly curved. All these characteristics do not, however, affect the internal structure and function of the brain, but simply arise from the peculiar telescoping of the Cetacean skull bones which we have discussed in Chapter 2. What does affect the function of the brain is the equally striking fact that the cerebrum is so large and extends so far back that, for instance, in Common Dolphins it completely covers the cerebellum, and in other Odontocetes it covers most of it. (In Mysticetes, on the other hand, the top of the cerebellum is clearly visible.) A third striking characteristic of the Cetacean brain is its exceptionally convoluted appearance. This was first noticed in 1671 by Ray, who thought it pointed to a high state of mental development. The Dutch neurologist, Prof. Jelgersma, was so struck by the resemblance between porpoise and human brains, that he devoted his old age to the comparative study of the brains of porpoises, sea-cows and common otters. In 1934, at the age of seventy-four, he published the results in a book entitled *Das Gehirn der Wassersäugetiere* (The brain of aquatic mammals).

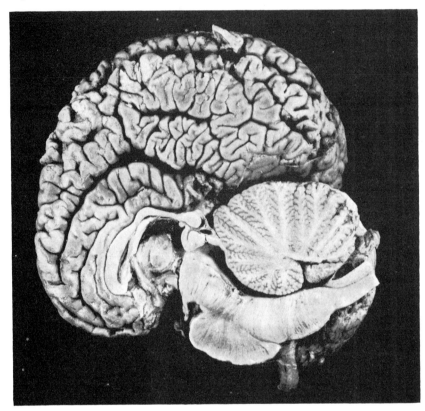

Figure 125. Longitudinal section through the brain of a Bottlenose Dolphin. Photograph: G. E. Pilleri, Bern.

Before discussing the convolutions of the Cetacean brain in greater detail, we must first look at the general function of their brain. We have already seen that Odontocetes lack an olfactory nerve, though vestiges of it can be found in Odontocete embryos and in adult Sperm and Bottlenose Whales, the latter having a small perforation in the ethmoid plate. But in all these animals the olfactory sense is practically non-existent, and we may therefore take it that the olfactory centres of the brain itself would hence be absent or atrophied. In fact, we find that the mammillary body, the anterior nuclei of the thalamus, and the hippocampus are absent. On the other hand, it appears that some parts of the brain which have always been considered as olfactory centres – e.g. the amygdaloid nucleus and the olfactory tubercle – are fairly well developed. We may therefore agree with Breathnach, who published comprehensive papers on this subject in 1954 and 1960, that these organs may have some other unsuspected function. In Mysticetes, the central olfactory system is, of course, more fully developed since they have an olfactory nerve, even though, as we have seen, it does not play a very important part in their lives.

Little can be said about the visual brain centres, as these have not been sufficiently investigated, and as what evidence has been published is largely contradictory. According to Breathnach (1960) they are not as poorly developed as has been previously thought.

The auditory centres, on the other hand, have been investigated more thoroughly, and seem to be particularly well developed – not surprisingly, if we recall how important hearing is in the lives of Cetaceans. All the nuclei and sensory paths associated with the auditory centres, e.g. the nucleus ventralis, the trapezoid body, the superior nucleus of the oliva, the lateral lemniscus, the corpora geniculata and the temporal lobes of the cerebrum, are very large, especially in Odontocetes. Those parts of the brain assumed to assimilate high notes, e.g. the nucleus ventralis, appear particularly well developed, the more so since the nucleus dorsalis which is associated with the assimilation of low notes is so small that even experienced neurologists usually miss it. This, too, is only to be expected from our discussion of the Cetacean ear, and so is the fact that the auditory nerve (the eighth cranial nerve) of Odontocetes is the biggest of all cranial nerves. In Mysticetes, however, it takes second place to the fifth cranial nerve (the trigeminal), of which more will be said later. The central auditory apparatus of Mysticetes, though very much more highly developed than that of terrestrial mammals, is not as effective as that of dolphins, in which certain centres that may well be associated with directional hearing and the reception of high-pitched tones are particularly prominent. Since Mysticetes feed on slow-swimming prey, a minor development of these centres is only to be expected.

The eighth or acoustic nerve also contains vestibular fibres which convey impulses from the semi-circular canals, i.e. from the equilibrating organ. The ratio of vestibular to cochlear fibres is very small, but absolutely the vestibular fibres are no smaller than they are in terrestrial mammals. Some central nervous regions, such as Deiter's nucleus, and probably certain parts of the cerebellum, are well developed in accordance with the important part that balance plays in the lives of Cetaceans.

The trigeminal nerve is, as we have seen, the largest of all cranial nerves in Mysticetes, and the second largest in Odontocetes. This is certainly not due to the presence of a large number of motor fibres, for in neither does chewing of food play an important part. However, the trigeminal not only supplies the muscles of the jaws but also all the tactile bodies in the entire head which, as we know, is supposed to be particularly sensitive in Cetaceans. Moreover, when we consider that the heads of Cetaceans are generally large, constituting as they do one-quarter to one-third of the total length of the body of Mysticetes,then it is understandable that their trigeminal nerve is so inordinately large.

The facial nerve, too, is very thick in comparison with the seventh cranial nerve of terrestrial mammals – no doubt because of the presence of very well-developed blowhole muscles (see Chapter 4). The glosso-pharyngeal (ninth cranial) nerve, which mainly supplies the taste buds of the tongue, is very small, especially in Mysticetes, and the same applies to the twelfth cranial nerve, the hypoglossal, which supplies the muscles of

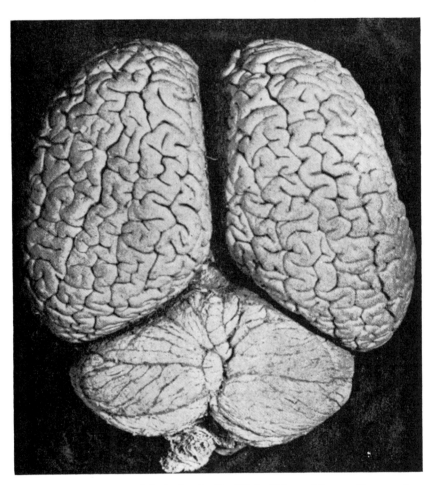

Figure 126. Top view of the brain of a Fin Whale. (Ries and Langworthy, 1937.)

the tongue. In the next chapter we shall see how minor is the part these muscles play – hence their smallness. The remaining cranial nerves show no special modifications and we shall therefore pass over them in silence.

The cerebellum, on the other hand, is so unusual that we shall discuss it at some length. The weight of the cerebellum of adult Rorquals is about 1,300 grams (29 oz.), i.e. about the total weight of the human brain. Now these figures, in themselves, tell us little. The picture becomes clearer when we learn that the weight of the cerebellum accounts for 20 per cent of the total weight of a Rorqual's and other Mysticete's brains, and for 15 per cent in Odontocetes, while it accounts for only about 10 per cent of the brain of terrestrial mammals. This is not at all strange, however, since the function of the cerebellum is primarily the control of voluntary movements. Hence it is always large in agile animals. The lower percentage of the Odontocete cerebellum is not due to a minor development of this part of the brain but to the very extensive development of the cerebrum.

An examination of the Cetacean cerebellum immediately shows that it is as highly convoluted as the cerebrum, the white matter being more highly ramified than it is in any other mammal, man included. In 1950, when J. Jansen, a scientist attached to the Anatomical Institute of the University of Oslo, compared the sizes of various Cetacean lobes with that of other mammals and of man in particular, he came across very striking differences. The enormous development of the lobulus simplex is undoubtedly connected with the high stage of development of the tactile nerves and is further evidence that the tactile receptors may be sensitive to water pressure and flow to which the body must respond. The poor development of the lobus ansiformis is associated with the fact that Cetacean limbs have undergone considerable reduction and the remarkable size of the paraflocculus is due to the role it plays in muscle coordination, a phenomenon to which the great Dutch anatomist Bolk drew attention as early as 1906.

Before discussing the Cetacean cerebrum, we must first look at the total weight of the brain which it largely determines. Now, Cetacean brains have been weighed on many occasions, the highest recorded figure being the brain of a Sperm Whale which weighed 19·6 lb., i.e. the weight of an eight- to nine-month old baby. The record for the brain of a Fin Whale is 18·3 lb., for that of a Humpback Whale (average weight 11 lb.) is 15 lb., and the brain of a 100-ton Blue Whale was found to weigh about 15¼ lb. The brains of the other big whales have still to be weighed, but these four may be said to have larger brains than all other mammals. An elephant's brain has a maximum weight of 11 lb., and the terrestrial mammal with the second biggest brain is man (total brain-weight about 3 lb.). The

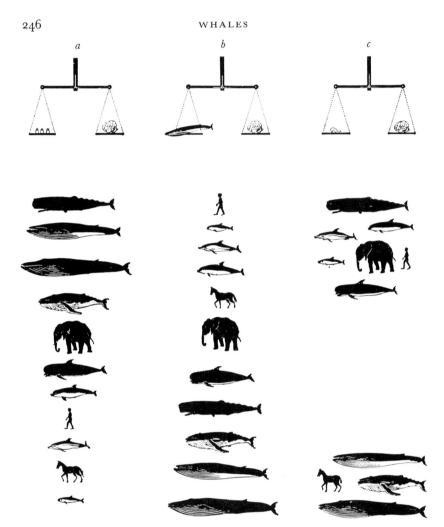

Figure 127. Classification of a number of Cetacea and other mammals according to (a) total weight of brain; (b) ratio of brain to body weight; (c) ratio of brain to brain-stem weight (Wirz's system).

brain of Bottlenose Whales (6·6 lb.), Pilot Whales (4·5 lb.), Belugas (4·2 lb.), Bottlenose Dolphins (4 lb.), Narwhals (3·1 lb.) are bigger than that of man, while that of the Common Dolphin (about 2·2 lb.) and the porpoise (about 1·2 lb.) is smaller.

Clearly mere weight of brain can tell us little about an animal's mental capacities, for otherwise an elephant would be more than three times as intelligent as man, and a Rorqual would have an unheard-of I.Q. If we look instead at the ratio of brain to body weight, we find that the brain of the Blue Whale represents 0·007 per cent, that of the Fin Whale 0·016 per cent, that of the Humpback Whale 0·02 per cent, that of the Sperm Whale 0·03 per cent, that of the Pilot Whale 0·083 per cent, that of the Bottlenose Dolphin 0·225 per cent, that of the Common Dolphin 0·666 per cent, that of the porpoise 0·854 per cent, compared with the elephant's 0·12 per cent, the horse's 0·154 per cent and man's 1·93 per cent. In other words, Rorquals with the biggest brains have the smallest brain to body-weight ratio and porpoises with the smallest brain the highest ratio of all Cetaceans (Fig. 127). From this, we can draw a general inference: the bigger the animal the smaller the ratio of brain to body weight.

This rule applies, by and large, to all animals – the brain of a cat representing 0·94 per cent of its body weight, and that of a lion a mere 0·18 per cent, etc., and can be explained by the fact that the relative size of the brain is determined by the size of the animal's surface rather than by its bulk, since the brain is intimately associated with the functions of a great many sensory organs, the receptors of which lie in a plane. Moreover, the surface of the skin is closely related to a given animal's metabolic rate, which thus affects the size of the brain. Now as a given animal grows larger, its surface area (and hence its brain) becomes smaller with regard to its bulk (or weight) because the surface increases as the square and the bulk as the cube of the increment. Hence the bigger the animal, the larger its brain, but the smaller its brain to body-weight ratio.

However, things are not quite as straightforward as that, as a brief glance at Fig. 127 will show. The Sperm Whale which tops column *a* does not take last place in column *b* as we might have expected it to do, and man does not come last in column *a*, etc. Moreover, Crile and Quiring, comparing the brains of a horse and a Beluga (two animals which happened to have identical weights of 1,150 lb.) found that the former weighed 1·78 lb., while the latter weighed 5·19 lb., though the surface area, and probably also the sensory surface area of the Beluga which, *inter alia*, has no olfactory epithelium, is undoubtedly smaller than that of the horse.

The Dutch expert, Prof. Dubois, who achieved world-wide distinction through his discovery of *Pithecanthropus*, therefore established a formula for relating brain-weight to body-surface. Using his formula, we find that the brains of mammals fall into seven categories. Man, whose brain to surface ratio is the highest, falls into the top category, i.e. the seventh stage of cephalization; *Pithecanthropus* occupies the sixth stage; anthropoid apes the fifth stage; other apes, most carnivores, and ungulates the fourth stage; many rodents, including the rabbit, the third stage; mice and hedgehogs the second stage; and shrews and bats the first stage. Mysticetes would fall into the fourth and Odontocetes into the fifth stage of cephalization, which is only to be expected from the fact that a thirty-five-ton Sperm Whale has a bigger brain than a 55-ton Blue Whale.

More recently, Dubois's classification has been challenged by many biologists who have found that, as more material was being investigated, the dividing line between the different stages became increasingly blurred, and that Dubois's formula itself was open to serious criticism. It appeared that not only the ratio of brain-to-body-weight and brain-to-body-surface, but also the ratio of brain-to-brain-stem, and of cerebellum and cerebrum separately to brain-stem, had to be considered. It is particularly Prof. A. Portmann (Basel) and his students who have shown how much more complicated the whole subject is than used to be thought. This became very clear from the thesis that one of his students, Katharina Wirz, submitted in 1950, which exploded Dubois's theory of the seven stages of cephalization. According to Wirz, mammals must, for the time being, be grouped into three classes of cephalic development, the middle class having two sub-divisions. Insectivores, bats and rodents make up the lowest class, terrestrial carnivores make up the lower sub-division of the intermediate class, Pinniped carnivores (e.g. sea-lions), ungulates, all apes and monkeys and Mysticetes make up the upper sub-division, while Odontocetes, elephants and man constitute the highest class (see Fig. 127). Mlle Wirz thought that of all Odontocetes the porpoise has the most highly developed brain, followed by the Beluga, the Narwhal and finally the dolphin.

Despite the many unresolved problems – e.g. the strange position of elephants on this scale – as far, at least, as Cetaceans are concerned, Mlle Wirz's classification agrees by and large with that of Dubois, and with the results of other biologists, such as Quiring (1943). Even though Cetaceans, because of their streamlined contours, have a relatively small body surface, their brains are more highly developed than those of most mammals, Odontocete brains being superior to those of Mysticetes and almost equalling those of man.

This fact was actually noted by the very first natural scientists to study the brains of porpoises. In 1671 Ray concluded from his studies that these animals must have 'wit and capacity' enough to make Herodotus's story of Arion's miraculous rescue by dolphins (see p. 12) seem credible. The older scholars were reminded of human brains not so much by the size of the porpoise's cerebrum, but rather by the convolutions of its cerebral cortex. (Figs. 126 and 128). These convolutions are not only very striking in appearance, but are an essential criterion for judging the stage of development a given brain has reached. From a number of investigations on mammals it appears that the number of individual convolutions and fissures increases with the size of the brain. This is due to the fact that the grey matter in the brain, i.e. the matter containing the bodies of the nerve

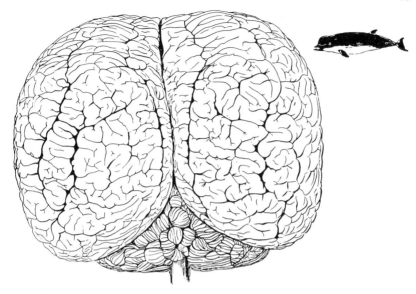

Figure 128. Top view of the brain of a Bottlenose Whale. (Kükenthal, 1889.)

cells and thus the site of cerebration, constitutes a rather thin cover of the cerebral hemispheres. It is, in fact, a surface, with the result that its area decreases (relatively in size) the greater the total mass of the brain becomes. To compensate for this deficiency, the cortex of big animals is thrown up into a correspondingly larger number of folds, thus increasing the total surface area. The fact that the cortex of porpoises shows almost as many folds as the human cortex may possibly be due to its exceptional thinness (Jelgersma, 1934), but we must remember that the number of convolutions is related to the absolute size of the brain, so that it depends not only on the size of the animal, but also on its stage of cephalization.

Must we assume that porpoises, Sperm Whales and dolphins, by virtue of their highly convoluted brains, have mental capacities akin to those of man, and that Adriatic fishermen who claim that dolphins are good Christians are not so far off the mark? While we cannot go all the way with them, we can nevertheless assert that the high development of their brain clearly indicates that these animals have a strongly centralized nervous system, and that many Cetacean reactions are more dependent on the brain than those of other mammals. Some scholars have pointed to the very important role that the acoustic sense plays in their lives, and see in its high degree of development a large contributory factor to the growth of the brain and of the cortex, in particular. On the other hand, sight is

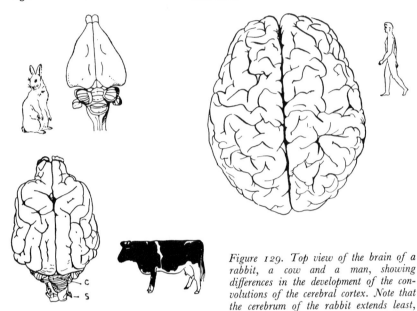

Figure 129. Top view of the brain of a rabbit, a cow and a man, showing differences in the development of the convolutions of the cerebral cortex. Note that the cerebrum of the rabbit extends least, and that of man most, towards the rear. In man the cerebrum completely covers the cerebellum. C = cerebellum; S = spinal cord.

much less developed than it is in most other mammals, and the olfactory sense may be completely absent. The influence of sight on the size of the brain may be shown by the fact that, according to Anderson, the cerebrum of the Gangetic Dolphin is not only much smaller, but has also a significantly smaller number of convolutions than the cerebrum of other Odontocetes (Fig. 130). On page 228 we saw that the eye and the optic nerve of this animal are rudimentary.

Some scientists prefer to ascribe the large Cetacean brain primarily to strong muscle development and to the associated highly differentiated nervous structure. Without further explanation, however, it seems improbable that an animal which propels itself mainly with its tail should need a more highly developed brain than, for instance, a monkey which uses all its limbs so skilfully.

Another important contribution to the solution of the problem of the mammalian brain – which is still far from solved – was offered by Crile and Quiring in 1940. From a careful investigation of the brains of hundreds of different vertebrates, they gained the clear impression that an animal's metabolism has important effects on the development of its brain in general, and of the cerebrum in particular. The higher the metabolic rate, the faster not only the heartbeat and the respiratory rate, but

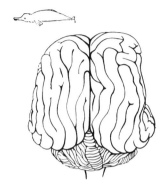

Figure 130. Top view of the brain of a Gangetic dolphin, showing small number of convolutions of the cerebral cortex. Note the marked grooving of the cerebellum which is not affected by the lack of visual power. (Anderson, 1878.)

the greater the rate of excretion, glandular secretion and the need for food. As a result of an increased need for food, the animal has to move about faster and in much more differentiated ways, and will therefore need a more highly developed sensory apparatus. All these factors may contribute to the development of a larger brain. This is borne out by the fact that warm-blooded animals which have to produce their own heat have a higher metabolic rate and a much larger brain than fish and reptiles of comparable size, which obtain their body heat from their environment. Portmann and his colleagues have, moreover, shown recently that the more active a particular species of fish the larger its brain. Here, too, metabolism plays an important part in cerebral development.

In Chapter 11, we shall see that Cetaceans have a very high metabolic rate indeed, with a consequent high food intake and a need for great activity. Hence the metabolic hypothesis would clearly explain their highly developed brain, particularly since Odontocetes, which pursue fast-moving fish, have a very much larger brain than Mysticetes whose prey is so much more slow-moving. Still, as we have seen, the problem is by no means solved, and a great deal of research will still have to be done, before we can explain why, for instance, a porpoise has a brain comparable in mass to that of man.

We shall conclude this chapter by saying a few words about our knowledge of the brains of Archaeocetes, or rather about the lack of such knowledge. The reader might wonder how we can hope to know anything about so perishable an object as the brain of animals which have been extinct for 30 million years. In fact, the brain is surrounded by bone, and in most mammals fills the brain-case so completely that we can take plaster-casts of the brain itself from the case. In that way, we can obtain a fairly accurate idea of the shape and location of the brain, the size of its different parts and of the cranial nerves, and even of its convolutions.

While this method is applicable to Odontocetes, Breathnach showed in 1955 that in Mysticetes, and probably also in Archaeocetes, the brain was surrounded by so many large vascular networks that the plaster casts can no longer be held to provide anything like exact replicas of their brains. Hence, very little can be said about them, at least until further facts come to light.

10

Feeding

THOSE WHO REGARD the elephant as a giant among beasts would be surprised to learn that it is a mere dwarf compared with some extinct reptiles. Thus, we know from fossils that the 70-foot *Brontosaurus* weighed at least 30 tons, and *Branchiosaurus* probably as much as 50 tons, i.e. the weight of a Centurion tank, while elephants weigh a maximum of 10 tons and an average of only 4 tons. But of all animals the biggest is alive to this day – the Blue Whale, great numbers of which are still caught every year. Blue Whales can grow to 100 feet and weigh up to 135 tons, i.e. the weight of four *Brontosauri*, more than thirty elephants, or 1,600 men (Fig. 131). Now, 1,600 men make up the population of a village, and one whale could supply that village with all the fat it needs, i.e. the equivalent of the annual fat yield of the milk of 275 cows.

The record is held by a Blue Whale which tipped the scales at 2,684 cwt. (136·4 tons). When it was caught on 27th January, 1948, by the Japanese whaler *Hashidate Maru*, it proved to be a cow of 'only' 90 feet, so that it seems likely that others are heavier still, even though this particular cow was exceptionally fat.

The average adult Blue Whale weighs 106 tons and is 85 feet long. The average size of the catch is, however, less, since a great many captured whales have not yet attained physical maturity. The average adult Fin Whale, 72 feet long, weighs 58 tons (maximum weight 70 tons). The figures for the Sei Whale are 13 tons average weight, 48 tons maximum (length 47 feet); for the male Sperm Whale 33 and 53 tons respectively (length 47 feet); and for the female Sperm Whale 13 and 14 tons respectively (length 37 feet). All these whales, while much smaller than Blue Whales, are considerably larger than elephants.

An elephant would never be able to support such weights unless it took to the water. In the last chapter we have seen that the heavier an animal, the smaller its relative surface area. Now the power of the legs and of the muscles which help to support the animal is principally a function of the

253

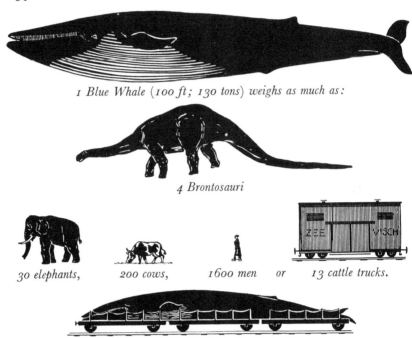

1 Blue Whale (100 ft; 130 tons) weighs as much as:

4 Brontosauri

30 elephants,   *200 cows,*   *1600 men*   *or*   *13 cattle trucks.*

The trucks shown would collapse, since a 30 ft truck can carry a maximum load of 15 tons. Nine such trucks would be needed.

Figure 131. The weight of a whale. (Slijper, 1948.)

surface of their cross-sections, and with increase in total weight a point is reached where the legs would simply collapse under their burden. Hence, once a certain maximum weight is reached, life on land becomes impossible.

The situation is, of course, quite different in the water, where buoyancy counteracts the gravitational pull on the body. No wonder, then, that there is a great deal of evidence that such giant reptiles as the *Brontosaurus*, the *Diplodocus* and the *Branchiosaurus*, whose weight greatly exceeded the terrestrial maximum, spent practically all their life submerged in rivers or swamps.

The reader might wonder whether an aquatic environment imposes no limitations whatsoever on an animal's size, and whether, in millions of years to come, animals could evolve compared with which our Blue Whale would be a mere pigmy. While we cannot be certain, we do know that even aquatic animals cannot exceed certain dimensions, because the surface of the lungs, the intestines, the red blood corpuscles and the kidneys become relatively smaller with increase in total weight. Thus, above a certain point (which is difficult to establish precisely), the organs can no longer deal with essential metabolic processes. In any case, the food supply will probably have a set limit to further growth long before this crucial point is reached.

True, large animals need proportionally less food than their smaller relatives (see Chapter 11), but even so, a large animal must eat more than a small one, and, in fact, food supply faces whales with problems already.

Everyone knows that whales feed on plankton, though few can tell you what plankton really is. *Plankton* is a Greek word meaning 'what drifts', and has come to be applied to all living matter floating in the water which cannot move across large distances by its own exertion, i.e. countless millions of vegetable and animal organisms of all shapes and sizes. Thus, while a large part of plankton is microscopically small, plankton also contains worms, snails, shrimps and the still larger jellyfish. In what follows, we shall deal only with planktonic organisms of up to three inches.

One of the most striking characteristics of this kind of plankton is that, in certain circumstances, it can multiply incredibly quickly, and cover vast areas. In summer, some of our own ditches and pools may become so choked up with it that they look like a mass of thick broth, and aquarists the world over know how difficult it is to keep their aquaria free from this scourge. Because of its abundance, quick growth, and multiplication, plankton forms the ideal food for very large animals, and may even be said to be the *only* food for them, since every other source would soon become exhausted. This is borne out by the fact that the largest fish, i.e. the Basking Shark and the Whale Shark, which may grow to a size of forty and fifty feet respectively, also feed on plankton and particularly on small crustaceans, and so does the biggest ray – the Manta. Even the larger species of two groups of extinct reptiles were found to have had a significant reduction in the size and number of their teeth, and therefore probably fed on plankton as well.

The whale's chief diet in the Antarctic and to a somewhat lesser extent in the Arctic is made up of a particular kind of plankton, called *krill*, which consists of small crustaceans. In the Antarctic krill consists largely of the species *Euphausia superba* Dana, crustaceans with a maximum length of three inches (Fig. 132). In cold waters, where food is particularly abundant, krill multiplies with fantastic rapidity, and a single female is capable of laying 11,000 eggs. No wonder that krill occurs in such profusion that over vast areas the sea looks like red-brown soup. By using special plankton nets, scientists discovered that, while krill occurs down to more than 500 fathoms, the biggest concentrations are found up to five fathoms down. Hence whales do not have to look for their prey as

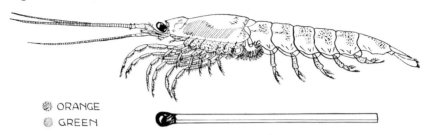

ORANGE
GREEN

Figure 132. Krill, a small crustacean of the species Euphausia superba *Dana is the main food of large Rorquals in the Antarctic. (Modified after Mackintosh and Wheeler, 1929.)*

deep down as was once believed. The reason why they sound as far down as they do is, therefore, something of a mystery (see Chapter 4).

Fresh krill presents a very colourful spectacle since the green of much of its thorax provides a striking contrast with the orange head, appendages and abdomen. The green colour is due to the stomach usually being filled with unicellular diatoms, particularly with *Fragilariopsis antarctica* (Fig. 133). Diatoms, as we might have guessed from their colour, are unicellular plants which like all plants contain chlorophyll, whereby carbonic acid dissolved in the sea can be photosynthesized into organic matter. Diatoms store this food in the form of small droplets of fat, and it is by and large the fat of these microscopic Antarctic diatoms which, after they have successively passed through krill, whales and finally the factories, we buy as margarine or soap.

Because photosynthesis can only take place under the influence of sunlight which, as we have seen in Chapter 9, cannot penetrate to lower reaches of the ocean, diatoms, and hence krill, are mainly found near the surface of the sea.

The orange colour of so many crustaceans arises from the presence of carotene, another substance found predominantly in plants, and largely responsible for the orange colour of carrots. Krill must therefore have derived its carotene, too, from diatoms. Carotene is also present in other planktonic organisms such as worms, snails and small jellyfish, and in the Antarctic a plankton net usually comes up with a rich orange harvest glittering through vitreous bodies. Carotene is a particularly important pigment since it is the precursor of vitamin A which is so abundant in the liver of whales and to a lesser extent in their blubber. Apart from carotene, krill contains so much fully synthesized vitamin A, particularly in the eyes, that whales have no need to convert krill carotene into vitamin A, their needs being fully met as it is. We shall return to this subject in greater detail in Chapter 11 which deals with the liver; here, we shall merely point out that it is because of the presence of carotene that the contents of whale intestines and also whale faeces have a characteristic brick-red colour. Whalers are not very keen on this colour as it darkens the oil, even though it does not affect its quality. However, since oil is generally judged by its colour, the crew of factory ships always see that all intestinal matter is scrubbed off the decks so as not to pollute the boilers.

Euphausia superba, the Antarctic krill, takes two years to reach full maturity after it is hatched out. The stomachs of whales therefore contain krill of different sizes and ages, one-year-old krill being from $1\frac{1}{4}$–$1\frac{3}{4}$ inches long and two-year-old krill from 2–$2\frac{1}{4}$ inches. Whalers, who were formerly misled into believing that because of these differences in size Antarctic krill consisted of two distinct species, called the smaller 'Blue Whale krill' and the larger 'Fin Whale krill', since Blue Whales were thought to feed mainly on the former, and Fin Whales on the latter. Closer investigations have, however, shown that they were wrong and that both 'species' can be found in either whale. Particularly in the Antarctic, there is so much krill that even the greediest whales need never go short. From Mackintoshs's summary of the investigations of the Discovery Committee (1942), it appeared, for instance, that about 75 per cent of captured Blue Whales, 55 per cent of captured Fin Whales, and more than 90 per cent of captured Humpback Whales had their stomachs filled to capacity. In the tropics and sub-tropics, where food is scarce in the areas of the principal land stations, the stomachs of whales are, however, generally quite empty, a subject to which we shall return in a later chapter.

Meanwhile, a word or two about the point raised by animal lovers to the effect that the lives of whales might be spared and the whole procedure

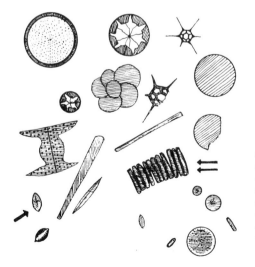

Figure 133. Unicellular plants and animals found in the stomachs of krill. They are predominantly diatoms of which the majority belong to the species Fragilariopsis antarctica *(double arrow). The single arrow points to* Cocconeis ceticola *which is often found on the skin of whales (Barkley, 1946.)*

simplified if the oil for the sake of which they are killed could be obtained direct from krill. In fact, whaling circles have given some thought to this question and have even calculated how much it would cost to extract oil in this way. It appeared that the project was wasteful both of resources and of man-power, and the idea has been shelved, at least for the time being. In future, atomic power may alter the situation, but the subject is still too speculative to deal with at length. It must, however, be added that krill oil as such is not fit for human consumption and would have to be converted first, though it can, of course, be used for industrial purposes, just like sperm oil.

Another difficulty is that krill concentrations are very difficult to locate. Attempts have repeatedly been made to use a 'fish lens', a kind of echo-sounding apparatus, for tracing large swarms of krill, but so far with little success. Whales seem to have the advantage over even our most up-to-date scientific techniques, though there is hope that we may one day be able to wrest their secret from them.

In the Antarctic, krill is so profuse and so strongly concentrated that the stomachs of whales are completely filled with krill and with very little else. Even the odd fish, cuttlefish or penguin which they occasionally swallow must have been a krill-feeder itself and have been sucked in quite accidentally. Only off New Zealand, the Falkland Islands and Patagonia do whales also feed on 'lobster krill', the larvae of crustaceans known as *Munida*, while in the South Pacific, Rorquals augment their diet of krill with two related crustaceans: *Thysanoessa macrura* and *Thysanoessa vicina*.

In Arctic waters, the diet is more varied. While Right Whales and Blue Whales feed mainly on krill like their southern relatives (though Arctic krill is called *Thysanoessa inermis* and *Meganyctiphanes norvegica*), they also feed on Pheropods (*Clio, Limacina*). The Sei Whale with its finer baleen normally restricts itself to a diet of somewhat smaller crustaceans (*Calanus finmarchicus*), though in the Northern Pacific it also feeds on cuttlefish. The Californian Grey Whale, again, seems to be another exclusive krill eater, feeding particularly on amphipods, though since it used to be caught exclusively in Californian, Japanese and Korean waters where its stomach is generally empty, we know little about its diet. The animal is supposed to feed very close to the bottom of the sea.

Northern Fin Whales, Humpback Whales and Little Piked Whales have a far more varied diet. In the above regions, their stomachs were found to contain not only krill and cuttlefish but also herring, mackerel, whiting and other fish. In fact, Fin Whales eat so much herring in the North Atlantic that the Norwegians call them 'Herring Whales' (*Sillhval*). Because of this diet, other fish-eaters may fall accidental victims to them.

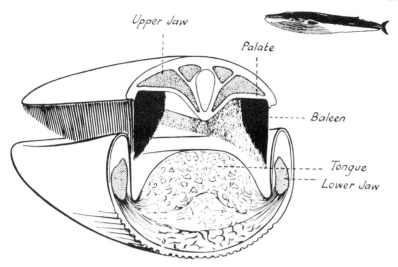

Figure 134. Diagrammatic sketch of the head of a Rorqual showing position of baleen and tongue. (Hentschel, 1937.)

Thus a Humpback whale caught in the North Atlantic was found to have six cormorants in its stomach, with a seventh stuck in its throat. Japanese whalers, too, have more than once discovered cormorants in the stomachs of Fin Whales. Bryde's Whale keeps to an almost exclusive diet of fish (especially pilchard and anchovy) – and not surprisingly, since it lives largely in tropical and sub-tropical waters where there is much less plankton. Moreover, the hairs of its baleen plates are so coarse that it could not function as an effective plankton strainer. Even sharks of up to two feet in length have been found in the stomachs of Bryde's Whales, and there is at least one known case of one of them swallowing fifteen penguins which were themselves hunting for fish. Krill has been found, however, in the stomachs of Bryde's Whales caught off the Bonin Islands.

Obviously, enormous animals like whales cannot get hold of such small fry as krill with ordinary teeth and jaws, and nature has therefore provided them with a structure akin to a plankton net – a strainer through which water can flow freely while krill itself is kept back. In all Mysticetes, this strainer takes the form of horny whalebone or baleen plates, each less than one-fifth of an inch thick. The plates are fringed along their inner edges and descend like side-curtains in two rows from the upper jaw (Fig. 134). The distance between any two plates is under half an inch, and the plates curve slightly backwards, which gives more rigidity and probably has the effect of letting the water flow out more smoothly, and thus obviates unnecessary turbulence.

Figure 135. Humpback on Vancouver Island Station. Note the fringe of the baleen and the Acorn Barnacles on the skin. (Photograph: G. C. Pike, Nanaimo, B.C.)

Figure 136. Biscayan Right Whale on Vancouver Island Station. Note the long baleen and the tongue. (Photograph: G. C. Pike, Nanaimo, B.C.)

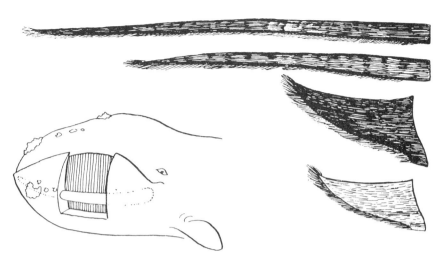

Figure 137. Diagrammatic sketch of the head of a Biscayan Right Whale illustrating position of baleen. A section of the lower lip has been cut away. (Matthews, 1952.)

Figure 138. The baleen of a Greenland Right Whale (top), a Biscayan Right Whale, a Blue Whale, and a Fin Whale (bottom). (Peters, 1938.)

Figure 139. Biscayan Right Whale on Vancouver Island Station. Note the prominent upper lip, the tongue, and the bonnet over the snout. (Photograph: G. C. Pike, Nanaimo, B.C.)

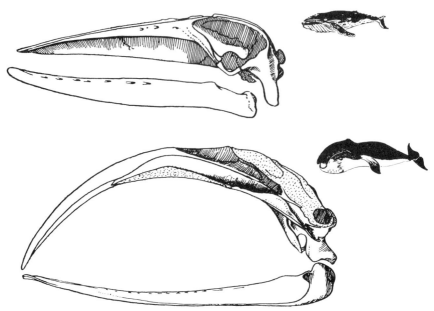

Figure 140. Sections through the skulls of a Greenland Right Whale (below) and of a Humpback (top) showing that Right Whales with their long baleen have strongly arched upper jaws. (After Eschricht and Reinhardt, 1864, and Van Beneden and Gervais, 1880.)

The plates have a fairly straight outer edge, slightly bent to the side, and a rounded inner edge, and are rather broader on top than at the bottom where the plates come to a point. The inner edge is less smooth than the outer, and has a fringe, the hairs of which are thicker and less elastic in some species than in others (Fig. 135). If we examine the mouth of a Whalebone Whale, we find that the inner hairy fringes are intertwined so that it resembles a coarse fibre mat, and it is this mat which acts as the real strainer. In fact Whalebone Whales derive their name of Mysticetes from the Greek *mystax* meaning moustache.

The baleen of Right Whales is long and narrow (Fig. 136), and in the Greenland Right Whale it has an average length of 10 feet and a maximum length of $14\frac{1}{2}$ feet (Fig. 138). In Biscayan Right Whales its maximum length is 8 feet, and in Pigmy Right Whales about $2\frac{1}{4}$ feet. To make room for these long plates, the rostrum of Right Whales has become markedly arched (Figs. 137 and 140), and the slim lower jaw is provided with a 5-feet-high lower lip for sealing the sides of the mouth (Fig. 139). Even when the jaws are wide open, the baleen still stretches to the bottom of the mouth, so that, when the whale shuts its jaws, the tips of the plates are bent inwards. While the large Right Whale's baleen is black, that of the

Pigmy Right Whale is black at the outer and cream on the inner side. The average number of plates on either side of the mouth of Biscayan and Pigmy Right Whales is 230, and that of Greenland Whales about 300.

Californian Grey Whales and all Rorquals have very much shorter plates (Fig. 138), i.e. Blue Whale, $3\frac{1}{4}$ feet; Humpback, $2\frac{1}{2}$ feet; Fin Whale, $2\frac{1}{4}$ feet; Sei Whale, 2 feet; Californian Grey Whale and Bryde's Whale, $1\frac{1}{4}$ feet; and Little Piked Whale, 8 inches. Because of the shorter plates, the rostra of these animals are not arched, nor do they have the specially large lower lip of Right Whales, though the Grey Whale's rostrum is somewhat curved at the top. The Blue Whale has 250–400, the Sei Whale an average of 330, Bryde's Whale 270, the Humpback Whale 300–350, and the Little Piked Whale 300 baleen plates on either side of the mouth. Blue Whales, Sei Whales and Humpback Whales have black plates, Fin Whales have black, blue and cream plates, Bryde's Whales have white and black plates, and the baleen of Little Piked Whales is cream-coloured throughout. The hairy fringe is usually of the same colour as the horny plates, but in Sei Whales it is white, and, moreover, so soft and fine that it looks like wool. This explains their diet of very small food, just as the stiffer structure of the Bryde's Whale baleen explains their diet of fish. The plates at the centre of the row are thickest and longest, those at the ends are shorter and narrower, and the extremities of the row consist of separate hairs.

Baleen is made of the same substance as our own hair and nails or as the horns of cattle. In cross-section, baleen is seen to consist of a homogeneous cortical layer enclosing three to four layers of horny tubes (Fig. 141) which become progressively thinner towards the centre. Knowledgeable readers will appreciate that, from a structural point of view, baleen therefore resembles normal bone or the 'unbreakable' front forks of some bicycles which also consist of a homogeneous outer layer and a number of internal tubes, this construction combining minimum weight with maximum

Figure 141. Cross-section through the baleen of a Fin Whale showing its construction from horny tubes enclosed by cortical layers. (Ruud, 1940.)

strength. A hollow cylinder has practically the same degree of rigidity as a solid one, just as a T-beam has the same strength as a solid beam. Moreover, in the baleen, the tubes allow for inner movement, just like the leaf spring of a motor-car, and are therefore more elastic than a solid tube would be. The tubes run uniformly along the entire length of the baleen and emerge as hair on the inner edge (see Fig. 143). On closer investigation the hair does, in fact, prove to be hollow, and open at the tip where it is constantly worn down by friction. For, needless to say, the plates are exposed over their entire surface, to continuous friction by contact with the water, and on the inside also by movements of the tongue. Similarly, our own epidermis is constantly worn off by rubbing. Like it, and like our hair, the baleen must continuously be replenished at its root, in this case the gum. As the top wears off, new material is continuously being pushed out of the gum, so that the baleen retains an even length, or grows to its proper length in young animals. In order to obtain a better idea of this process, we shall look at the development of the plate in the foetus. At birth a whale has very small and soft baleen plates, and while it is being suckled, it has, in fact, no need of them. Very young foetuses still have completely

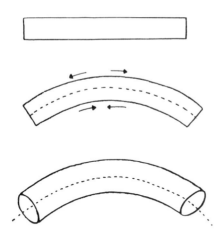

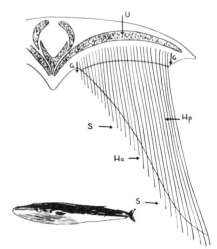

Figure 142. Whenever a solid beam (e.g. a rubber rod) is bent, its convex side becomes longer and its concave side shorter. Thus the rod must withstand tension and compression. In the centre, the length remains constant and no external forces act upon it. A hollow pipe is therefore as strong as a solid one.

Figure 143. Highly diagrammatic sketch of a section through the head of a Rorqual, showing position and structure of baleen. U = upper jaw; G = part of baleen embedded in the gum, where new baleen is formed and pushed out; Hp = horny tubes which emerge on the inner side as hair (Ha). Friction takes place over the entire surface of the baleen protruding from the gum (S).

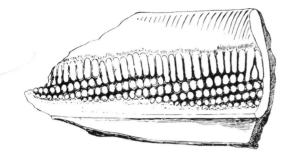

Figure 144. Transverse ridges and papillae on the baleen wall of a 10-foot Fin Whale foetus. They are the first rudiments of the baleen.

smooth and flat gums, which, however, very soon give rise to two longitudinal, fairly wide ridges on either side of the palate, the so-called baleen ridges. In ten-foot embryos of Blue and Fin Whales, the centre of each ledge then throws up an ever larger number of little walls at right angles to the ledge. While the walls spread forward and backward from the centre, small rows of papillae are formed at their extreme edges and soon develop a hairy appearance. The wall – or lamella as it is called – with its papillae is the original baleen (see Fig. 144).

In cross-section, every papilla is seen to consist of an epidermal fold outside a dermal fold made up of connective tissue, blood vessels and nerves. The epidermis then becomes cornified towards the outside, thus turning the round papilla into a cornified tubule (Fig. 145). While the epidermis is made up entirely of a number of layers of living cells at its base, it becomes progressively more cornified in the upper regions of the papilla, until the entire wall of the top of the papilla consists of horn. The reason why the 'hair' is a tubule rather than a solid pipe is explained by the fact that the uppermost cells do not become cornified but die off. In the layers of living cells, cell division takes place mainly longitudinally, so that the papilla keeps growing in length rather than breadth. In adult Mysticetes, the papilla itself is somewhat shorter than the part of the baleen surrounded by gum (see below). In other words, in this region, the baleen itself is still partly made up of living tissue, in the same way that, say, the hoof of a horse (whose structure is analogous to baleen) consists of part-living tissue as well. However, the visible part of the baleen consists exclusively of hollow tubules with cornified walls. The tubules are packed together without any connective tissue, so that they can shift with respect to one another, which, as we have seen, makes the baleen particularly elastic and pliable.

A longitudinal section through the palate will reveal the way in which the cortical layer is constructed (Fig. 145). It appears that the space between any two walls or lamellae, each of which bears four rows of

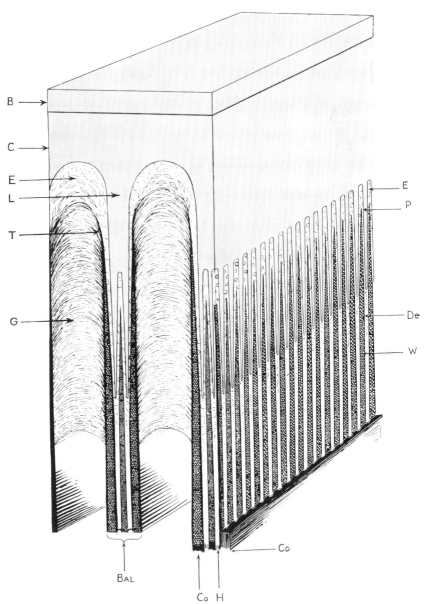

Figure 145. *Diagrammatic sketch of the structure of two baleen plates of a Rorqual separated by gum. B = upper jaw-bone (palate); C = connective tissue of palate; E = epithelium; L = lamella with P = papillae covered with epithelium; De = dead epithelial cells in the hollow part of horn tube; W = wall of two adjoining horn tubes; H = hollow part of horn tube; Co = cortical layer, Bal = baleen consisting of tubes and cortical layer; G = gum; T = region where thickness of cortical layer is determined. (W. L. van Utrecht.)*

cornified papillae, is filled with a peculiar, generally grey, substance – some 4 feet 6 inches thick measured from the palate or along the baleen. This substance, the gum, which consists of non-cornified epidermal cells, is somewhat more delicate than the baleen itself, and, particularly when it is squeezed, looks very much like rubber. In the dermal papillae, which penetrate the gum, van Utrecht discovered arterioles surrounded by networks of venules similar to those found in the dermal papillae of the integument (see Chapter 11). In Chapter 5 we saw that this type of structure may serve for maintaining the body's temperature, and hence its presence in the gum, which comes into constant contact with cold water, is not surprising.

The gum, like all other epidermal tissue exposed to continuous friction, undergoes constant cell division by which worn-off material is continually replenished from the base layers. Because of this cell division and the consequent outward migration of cells, tensions are set up in a specific spot close to the wall of the baleen. These tensions cause cornification of the gum cells. The resulting cornified layer is pushed out with the tubules and the gum, and emerges as the cortical layer of the tubules. The gum itself contributes no further material to the baleen, new material being added exclusively by the cells covering the walls of the baleen where they face the gum, i.e. the cells between the baleen and the special cornified layer which we have just mentioned. The cells of this intercalated layer shift outward with the horn tubules and the cells of the gum, and gradually become cornified. Hence the thickness of the cortical layer is determined by the thickness of this special intercalated layer, which, in turn, is determined by processes that take place in the specific regions shown on Fig. 145. Differences in thickness which may be produced in these regions at any moment are always reflected in the layer, no matter how far it has been pushed out in the course of the years. We emphasize this fact, because the fine structure of the baleen, and particularly of its cortical layers, is an important means of determining a whale's age. We shall return to this question in greater detail in Chapter 14.

We have seen that the baleen acts like a strainer, and we shall now investigate what happens when a whale feeds. While no one has ever seen what exactly happens when a Mysticete swallows its food, we know that there is a marked difference between the feeding of Right Whales with their very long baleen and of Rorquals with their very short baleen and mouths that can be greatly distended from the bottom. Right Whales seem to swim through thick masses of krill with almost constantly open mouths. The water streams into the mouth and through the openings between the baleen plates while the krill is kept back by the hairy fringe. A

Figure 146. Two krill legs (Euphausia superba *Dana*) *greatly magnified to show their straining properties.* (*Barkley, 1940.*)

little later, the mouth is closed for a brief interval, the tongue is brought up and the krill pushed towards the throat in a way that is not yet fully understood. Rorquals, whose mouths can be greatly widened by virtue of their system of external folds and grooves, take in large quantities of krill with one gulp, close the mouth, and contract the muscles of the tongue and the base of the mouth, thus squeezing the water between the baleen and expelling it over the edge of the lower jaw. Once the mouth has been closed, the krill is pushed towards the throat.

We have seen that very large sharks also feed on plankton and particularly on little shrimps. The reader might like to know, therefore, that these animals strain their food in practically the same way as whales; their branchial arches have a complete system of small ossified plates on the inside. It is not known how giant reptiles obtained and strained their aquatic prey, though some species may have used their teeth. On the other hand, they may have had a softer structure analogous to baleen which, being made of more delicate tissue than bone, failed to fossilize. The small capacity of the mouth of these giant reptiles, however, does not support the hypothesis that they were plankton feeders (F. C. Fraser). Krill itself also has a kind of plankton strainer, although its 'mesh' is of course infinitely finer than that formed by the baleen. Krill feeds mainly on smooth diatoms less than 0·04 mm. in size, and their favourite food is

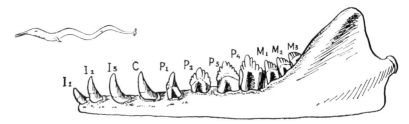

Figure 147. Lower jaw of Basilosaurus cetoides *Owen, a serpent-shaped Archaeocete, showing dentition. I = incisors; C = canines; P = premolars; M = molars.* (*Kellogg, 1936.*)

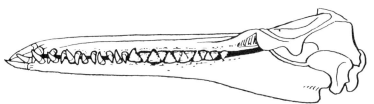

Figure 148. Skull of Squalodon bariense *from the middle Miocene (France; about 15 million years old). (Kellogg, 1928.)*

Fragilariopsis antarctica. Coarse and large diatoms are apparently rejected by means of a complicated system of hair on the legs which acts as a primary filter (Fig. 146). The remaining material, i.e. the small diatoms, passes through a much finer filter and is then swept into the mouth by movements of the legs.

Mysticetes are the only whales which feed on plankton, other Cetaceans having teeth instead of a strainer. Their teeth are, however, quite different from those of terrestrial mammals. The supposed ancestors of our modern whales (see Chapter 2) probably had three incisors, one canine, four premolars and three molars in either jaw, and so had the oldest representatives of the Archaeocetes, e.g. *Protocetus.* Younger forms such as *Basilosaurus* and *Dorudon* had molars with a serrated edge (Fig. 147). F. C. Fraser has shown that these molars have a very close resemblance to those of the recent Crabeater Seal (*Lobodon carcinophagus*). This animal mainly feeds on fairly small crustaceans and these may also have been the main food of the younger Archaeocetes. Serrated teeth are also found in the oldest known Odontocetes, the Squalodonts which, moreover, had a marked lengthening of the jaws (Fig. 148). The ideal set of teeth for fish eaters is, in fact, a long row of even and conical teeth.

In all modern Odontocetes the individual teeth are, in fact, so similar that it is difficult to distinguish them. The posterior part of the row of

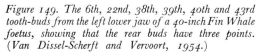

Figure 149. The 6th, 22nd, 38th, 39th, 40th and 43rd tooth-buds from the left lower jaw of a 40-inch Fin Whale foetus, showing that the rear buds have three points. (Van Dissel-Scherft and Vervoort, 1954.)

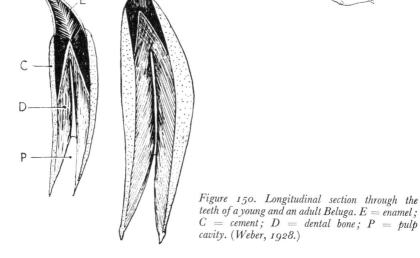

Figure 150. Longitudinal section through the teeth of a young and an adult Beluga. E = enamel; C = cement; D = dental bone; P = pulp cavity. (Weber, 1928.)

tooth-buds found in the connective tissue of the jaws of Mysticete foetuses at a certain stage of their development (see Chapter 2) still resembles the triple crown of the teeth of Archaeocetes, but tooth-buds with more than one cusp do not persist for long (Fig. 149).

The teeth of Odontocetes have only one single root (Fig. 150). The central pulp cavity is generally fairly small and usually disappears after a time, when no further dental growth can take place. Like the teeth of most other mammals, man included, Odontocete teeth consist of dentine surrounded with cement and covered with an enamel cap. In older animals, the crown is often worn down, so much so that the enamel has completely disappeared to reveal dentine stumps. Enamel is altogether lacking in adult Narwhals, Sperm Whales, Pigmy Sperm Whales and all Ziphiidae with the exception of the Bottlenose Whale, though the ancestors of Sperm Whales must have had enamel crowns, since embryos still have enamel organs in their tooth-buds. Cetaceans do not grow a second set of teeth, i.e. they do not shed their 'baby teeth'.

'*Montrez-moi vos dents et je vous dirai qui vous êtes,*' the great Cuvier said at the beginning of the last century, and his epigram applies *a fortiori* to Odontocetes, whose feeding habits are far from uniform. In the first place there are the fish-eaters, e.g. porpoises and most dolphins, the length of whose jaws differs from species to species, though even those with relatively short jaws must be considered long-jawed mammals (Fig. 151). In freshwater dolphins, the two lower jaws have become fused along almost their entire length, thus providing exceptional rigidity. The number of teeth on each side of upper and lower jaws varies from about fourteen (Irawadi

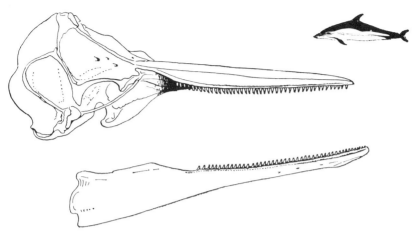

Figure 151. Skull of Common Dolphin with the sharp conical teeth of the real fish-eater. (Van Beneden and Gervais, 1880.)

Dolphin) to sixty-eight (Boutu). The Boutu is, in fact, a most voracious animal which even attacks the notorious pirayas. The teeth of fish-eating dolphins are almost exclusively conical, and generally thin. Porpoises alone have characteristically spatulate crowns (Fig. 152).

Odontocete teeth are used for capturing prey and not for chewing it, since the prey is generally swallowed whole. For this reason, most dolphins

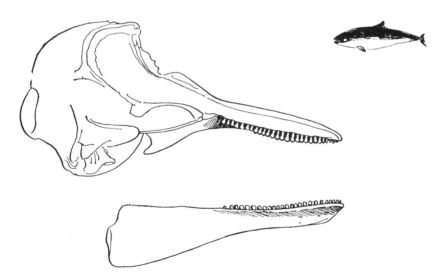

Figure 152. Skull of Porpoise with spatular teeth. (Van Beneden and Gervais, 1880.)

feed on fairly small fish, and Common Porpoises, for instance, restrict their diet mainly to herring, whiting and sole. (There is the reported case of a Bottlenose Dolphin which choked to death because it swallowed a shark nearly four feet long). Stomachs of porpoises and Bottlenoses were found to contain remnants of shrimps and cuttlefish as well. In some areas, cuttlefish even make up the major proportion of a Bottlenose's diet. When eating sepias, they spit out the calcium 'shell' and retain the edible portion. Sea-weed, too, has been found in the stomachs of Bottlenose Dolphins, while the stomach of a river dolphin *Sotalia teuszii* (Cameroons) was found to be completely filled with leaves, fruit and grass.

One of the most notorious marine predators is the Killer Whale or Orca, an animal which may grow to a length of thirty feet. Its back is black with characteristic white or yellow areas behind the eye and the dorsal fin, which, in bulls, is particularly large and pointed. The fin cuts through the water like a knife, but the claim that the Killer slits its victims' bellies open must be dismissed as fable. Killers have, at one time or another, infested every single sea on earth, and most sailors abhor them just as much as they detest sharks. For Killers, too, feed on mammals, and though I myself know of no single instance of a man having been devoured by them, they are known to be notorious slayers of porpoises, dolphins, seals, sea-lions, sea-otters, Narwhals and Belugas. They also eat penguins, and attack young walruses, but keep well out of the way of older specimens – indeed, they prefer the young of all their prey.

The best illustration of the greed of a Killer Whale was provided by the stomach of a specimen caught off one of the Pribylov Islands (Bering Sea), which was found to contain thirty-two full-grown seals. The twenty-foot Killer, weighing eight tons, which was washed ashore at Terschelling (Holland) on 20th July, 1931, was obviously a little less well-fed, for its stomach contained a mere three pregnant porpoises, each with a full-term foétus. Killers also cause a veritable carnage among the relatively slow Arctic Belugas, though, according to Freuchen, a man who studied these animals for twenty years, Killers never devour female Belugas, which they kill and then abandon. The cause of this odd behaviour has never been explained.

Killers do not restrict their attacks to smaller Cetaceans, but attack even the biggest of Blue Whales. While they usually concentrate on young victims, from three to forty of them will band together to fall upon adults also. They dig their teeth deep into the lips, the pectoral fins and particularly into the bottom of the mouth and the tongue of these colossal though lumbering animals tearing out large hunks of flesh and leaving the victim to die of loss of blood before devouring him. The slow Californian Grey Whale is another of their favourite targets, and Andrews

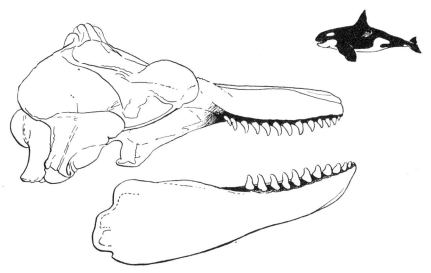

Figure 153. Skull of Killer Whale with few, though big and strong, teeth. The animal eats fish, but generally prefers mammals. (Van Beneden and Gervais, 1880.)

reports that the Grey Whale catch always contained many specimens whose tongues, pectoral fins, and, to a lesser extent, other parts of the body had been damaged by Killers. In the Antarctic, Killers will occasionally follow factory ships and fall upon carcasses waiting to be flensed. They frequently ignore the guns fired by the crew to frighten them off. Killers never seem to follow their prey across the surf, of which they are said to be greatly afraid, probably because, from experience, they have learned that it covers shallow waters.

Nor do Killers restrict their diet to penguins and mammals. They eat a great amount of squid, and Iceland fishermen will tell you that from 1952 onwards the south coast of their country was infested by thousands of Killers for years, and that these animals not only competed with the local fishing industry, but even plundered the nets or ruined them when they themselves became enmeshed. The damage they caused during the summer of 1956 was estimated to amount to about £100,000 and the Government, in despair, had to enlist the help of the U.S. Navy. Depth charges were dropped from an aircraft for three days running and, though only a few of the robbers were killed, the schools disappeared from the fishing grounds.

Even though Killers do not disdain fish, their teeth are not particularly adapted to this diet. True, they have 10–14 conical teeth on each side of the upper and lower jaw (Fig. 153), but the teeth are frequently worn down to small stumps in older animals. Like all other Odontocetes, Killers never chew their prey but swallow it whole or in big pieces. Thus Eschricht, while examining a 21-foot Killer, discovered no less than thirteen complete porpoises and fourteen seals in the first chamber of its stomach (6½ feet × 4¾ feet). A fifteenth seal was found in the animal's throat (Fig. 154). Other carnivores are known to eat comparatively huge meals. Thus the stomach of a wolf weighing 112 lb. was found to contain 20 lb. of meat.

Other Odontocetes have specialized on a diet of cuttlefish, and this is particularly true of Beaked Whales (*Ziphiidae*). Admittedly, some members of this family, e.g. Bottlenose Whales, also feed on herring and krill, but other species feed exclusively on cuttlefish. In contradistinction to fish, cuttlefish are fairly slow and hence easily caught. Moreover they are fairly soft, and their captors can dispense with the long row of sharp teeth characteristic of most fish-eaters. In the Ziphiids, the number of teeth has, in fact, become so greatly reduced that, to all intents and purposes, they can be called toothless, though they are clearly descended from fish-eating ancestors. *Diochoticus*, for instance, a Beaked Whale which lived 18 million years ago and whose fossils were discovered in Patagonia, had long jaws with twenty-three well-developed teeth in the upper and nineteen in the lower jaw. *Mioziphius*, discovered in the Belgian Upper Miocene deposits, and which must have lived about 9 million years ago, still had forty teeth in the upper jaw, while the number of teeth in its lower jaw had by then been reduced to two. On the other hand, *Choneziphius*, another Belgian Upper Miocene fossil, had only a somewhat rudimentary set of sockets in its upper jaw, and only two teeth in its lower jaw.

Present-day Beaked Whales have the long jaws of their ancestors but none of their teeth. They obviously seize the cuttlefish with the edges of their jaws and then squeeze them back to the throat. (In older bulls, and less frequently in adult cows, one or two teeth can occasionally be seen to push through the lower gum.) (Fig. 155.) The only known exception is *Tasmacetus shepherdi*, the first known specimen of which was stranded in New Zealand twenty years ago. It had nineteen fairly well-developed teeth in its upper, and twenty-seven in its lower jaw. This otherwise little known animal therefore had at least some of the striking characteristics of its Miocene relatives. Moreover, it would be wrong to say that other Beaked Whales are completely devoid of all signs of teeth. If we prepare the jaws as carefully as Boschma did, or look at Fraser's excellent X-ray pictures, we notice that the gum of each half of lower and upper jaws may contain thirty-two very small loosely-fitted teeth on both sides (Fig. 156). However, these teeth never break through the gum and are therefore generally missed by casual observers.

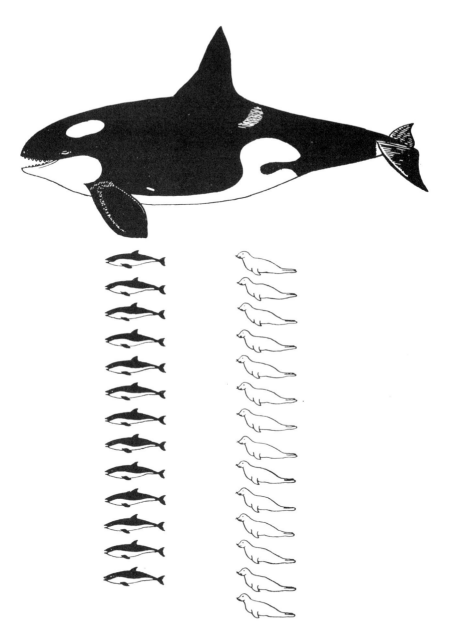

Figure 154. The $6\frac{1}{2}$ feet by $4\frac{3}{4}$ feet fore-stomach of a 24-foot Killer Whale was found to contain 13 porpoises and 14 seals.

False Killers and Pilot Whales live on a mixed diet of fish and cuttle-fish, but the remnants of cuttlefish seem to preponderate in their stomachs. They have fairly short jaws with 8–11 well-developed teeth. Risso's Dolphin would seem to have restricted its diet to cuttlefish to an even greater extent, since it has no more than six pairs of weakly developed teeth in the lower jaw, and no teeth at all in the upper jaw. *Phocaenoides*, a North Pacific relative of our porpoise, which feeds on cuttlefish, has a complete set of teeth, though the teeth have barely broken through.

The Sperm Whale is a mighty cuttlefish feeder. Not that it scorns other food – for even 10-foot long sharks and also odd seals have been found in its stomach – but cuttlefish is unquestionably its favourite diet. Cuttle-fishes are molluscs with characteristic ink-bags and tentacles. The eight-armed Octopods live mainly at the bottom of the sea, while the ten-armed Decapods generally swim from one depth to another. Although Octopods have been found in the stomachs of Sperm Whales, Decapods form their main diet. It is believed that Sperm Whales do not so much go after this prey as swim about with open mouths, enticing the cuttlefish which seem unable to resist the colourful contrast between the Sperm Whale's purple tongue and white gum of the jaws. While the prey is generally some thirty to forty inches long, the skin of Sperm Whales often bears sucker marks of from one to four inches in diameter, showing that the captors must have fought with giant squids (*Architeuthis*). At a whaling station in the Azores, Robert Clarke of the National Institute of Oceanography (England), one the greatest living experts on Sperm Whales, once opened

Figure 155. Skull of the Beaked Whale Mesoplodon gervaisi (*Deslongchamps*) *with only a single tooth in its lower jaw. A typical cuttle-fish eater.* (*Van Beneden and Gervais, 1880.*)

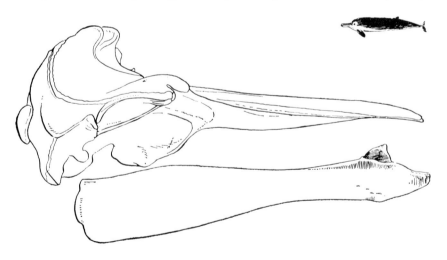

Figure 156. Central part of the left lower and upper jaws of the Beaked Whale Mesoplodon grayi *van Haast (Leyden Museum of Natural History). Note the tooth which has cut through the lower jaw, and the row of teeth hidden in the gum of the upper jaw. (Boschma, 1956.)*

a Sperm Whale's stomach to find a giant squid some thirty-five feet long (tentacles included) and weighing more than 400 lb., i.e. the weight of two adult men and one child.

Sperm Whales do not chew their food either but swallow it whole. To seize their prey, they have 18–30 pairs of teeth in the lower jaw (Figs. 157 and 158), the two halves of which are fused over more than half of their length (Fig. 159). The teeth of the lower jaw lie embedded in a groove, in which a row of sockets can only just be distinguished, but though the teeth are therefore poorly anchored to the bone, every whaler who has tried to take a Sperm Whale tooth home as a souvenir will tell you how difficult it is to wrest it from the exceptionally tough connective tissue of the gum. In this way, the teeth are held firmly in position, and whenever the Sperm Whale closes its mouth the conical ivory-coloured tips fit exactly into a row of corresponding indentations in the palate of the upper jaw. While young teeth are sharp and gently curved, older teeth may become so worn down by friction that they are quite blunt. (We have seen that they lack enamel.) In the pulp cavity, and also in the otherwise smooth dentine of the tooth, there often arise irregular rounded patches of osteodentine. These were described in detail by Neuville (1935) and by Boschma (1938).

Oddly enough, the Sperm Whale's exceptionally good set of teeth does not seem to play as important a part in its life as we might have thought. When a young Sperm Whale is weaned and has to look for its own food, the teeth have not yet broken through, and they do, in fact, only appear when the animal has grown to about twenty-five feet, i.e. when it has reached sexual maturity. Moreover, Sperm Whale teeth often show signs

Figure 157. Lower jaw of a Sperm Whale on board the Willem Barendsz. *(Photograph: Dr W. Vervoort, Leyden.)*

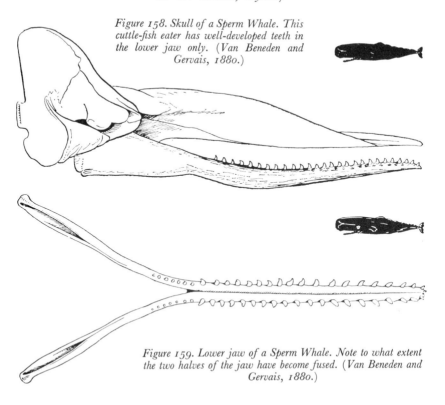

Figure 158. Skull of a Sperm Whale. This cuttle-fish eater has well-developed teeth in the lower jaw only. (Van Beneden and Gervais, 1880.)

Figure 159. Lower jaw of a Sperm Whale. Note to what extent the two halves of the jaw have become fused. (Van Beneden and Gervais, 1880.)

of disease or decay and are frequently covered with barnacles, which shows that they are not fully employed.

The anonymous author of the short article on the Cachalot in the French Encyclopaedia (1771) was the first to point out that Sperm Whales also had teeth in their upper jaws. Petrus Camper described them again fifteen years later, and it is, therefore, all the more astonishing that knowledgeable biologists like Abel (1907), Doflein (1910) and other authors as late as 1928 should still have stressed the absence of these teeth. True, the upper teeth are rather insignificant and generally hidden in the gum, but their presence has been demonstrated quite clearly. In 1938 Prof. Boschma, the Director of the Leyden Natural History Museum, in which the study of Cetaceans has always been pursued very keenly, gave an excellent description of the upper teeth of two Sperm Whales which had stranded near Breskens in 1937. In the bigger of the two animals, he found fifteen small teeth embedded in the gum on either side of the jaw. Their length varied from $2\frac{1}{2}$ to $5\frac{1}{3}$ inches. The first, sixth, twelfth and fifteenth teeth protruded from the gum, but all the others were completely hidden (Fig. 160).

A proper set of upper teeth in sockets was, however, present in some

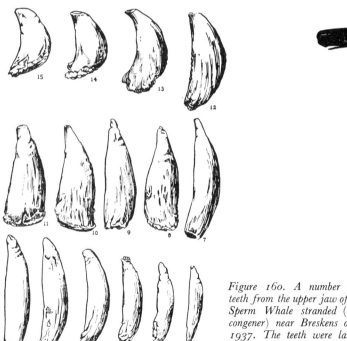

Figure 160. A number of rudimentary teeth from the upper jaw of a 57-foot male Sperm Whale stranded (with a 51-foot congener) near Breskens on 24 February 1937. The teeth were largely hidden in the gum. (Boschma, 1938.)

ancestors of the modern Sperm Whale, e.g. in *Diaphorocetus* and *Idiophorus*, fossils of which were found in Lower Miocene deposits in the Argentine. These animals had fourteen and twenty-two upper teeth respectively. Extinct members of the Sperm Whale family from the Miocene deposits found near Antwerp, e.g. *Scaldicetus caretti* and *Physeterula* of which the Brussels Museum of Natural History has such remarkable fossils, also had a long row of well-developed teeth in the lower and upper jaws. However, at about that period, the animals had already begun to concentrate on a diet of cuttlefish. Thus different fossils dating from within the last ten million years or so had first a continuous groove and subsequently nothing but a few rudimentary teeth in the upper jaw. The teeth of *Placoziphius* from the Miocene deposits of Belgium and Holland had probably begun to be very much like those of modern Sperm Whales. Recent Pigmy Sperm Whales have 9–15 small conical teeth on either side of the lower jaw, and occasionally one or two rudimentary teeth in the upper jaw. Pigmy Sperm Whales, too, feed predominantly on cuttlefish, but supplement their diet with crabs.

The Beluga and the Narwhal, both inhabitants of the Arctic, have a very mixed diet of cuttlefish, shrimps, crabs and fish. Moreover, both types look for their food at the bottom of the sea. The Beluga, whose fish diet consists largely of flounders and plaice, also feeds on halibut, capelin and salmon. It has a fairly good set of from 8–10 teeth on either side of the jaw. The Narwhal (Fig. 40), on the other hand, is completely devoid of teeth, and seizes its prey with the hard edges of its jaw, swallowing it without chewing – like all other Odontocetes. Narwhal embryos, however, have two tooth-buds on either side of the upper jaw, behind which are found four dental papillae, which may occasionally develop into small teeth completely covered by gum. In bulls, one of two left tooth-buds generally develops into the eight-foot spiral tusk, though, occasionally, the tusk can develop from one of the buds on the right side. Moreover, there are also known cases of Narwhals with two tusks, examples of which can be seen in the Zoological Museums of Stockholm, London and Amsterdam. There are some known cases of a cow having a tusk – their tooth-buds, however, rarely break through the gum. In any case their lack of tusks seems to be no disadvantage, since Freuchen, who made a thorough study of Greenland Narwhals, showed that the males use their tusks neither for attack nor for defence. They never break the ice with them either, and during fights in the mating season they are very careful not to get this 'weapon' damaged. It is very fragile, indeed, and once it snaps, infection can set in very quickly. The fragility of the Narwhal tusk is due to the fact that its pulp cavity, which contains living tissue, runs right to the tip of the tusk, whereas in the tusk of, say, the elephant, it stops at the jaw. Possibly, the Narwhal uses its tusk for stirring up fish and other prey at the bottom of the sea, but more probably it is a secondary sexual characteristic comparable in biological significance with a deer's antlers or a man's beard.

The Gangetic Dolphin, too, which, as we saw in Chapter 9, feeds mainly at the bottom of turbid rivers, probably used its long jaws with their strong teeth for stirring up the mud, and it seems likely that the *Eurhino-delphids*, well-preserved fossils of which were discovered in Miocene deposits in America, Japan and Belgium, made a similar use of their long beaks. These $14\frac{1}{2}$ to 16 foot long, completely extinct dolphins had a particularly long, almost needle-shaped, upper jaw and a very much shorter lower jaw (Fig. 161). Both jaws carried a long row of pointed teeth from which we may infer that they were mainly fish-eaters. On the other hand, the section of the upper jaw protruding in front of the lower jaw is toothless, and its function is probably to stir up the slimy or sandy bottom. The fact that these animals, like the Narwhal and the River Dolphins, have a fairly long neck with free cervical vertebrae may also be associated with the same phenomenon.

When we chew our own food, we begin a rather long and complicated chain of processes which together make up the process of digestion. This whole chain of processes takes place inside the alimentary canal, a twisting and turning tube which runs all the way from the mouth to the anus. By the actions of saliva and of gastric and intestinal secretions our food is broken down until it can pass through the wall of the intestine, where it is absorbed by the blood and then assimilated by the body. The secret of this process lies in the effects of certain substances called enzymes (which are contained in the various secretions) on the proteins, fats and carbohydrates which constitute our food.

In Cetaceans, too, the process begins in the mouth. We have already discussed their teeth, baleen and jaws at length, and in connexion with digestion we need only mention one more fact, viz. that, since Cetaceans

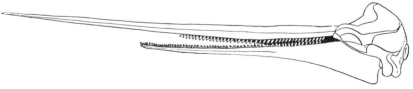

Figure 161. Skull of Eurhinodelphis cocheteuxi *du Bus, from the Upper Miocene (Antwerp). Reconstruction by Abel (1909) from material in the Brussels Natural History Museum. The animal lived some 10 million years ago, probably fed on fish, obtained by churning up the bottom with its long, toothless, beak.*

Figure 162. Lower jaw of Fin Whale used as gateway to the vicarage at Starup near Haderslev (Denmark).

do not chew their food, they naturally have comparatively weak jaw muscles and a simple jaw joint which allows the jaws to move in a vertical direction only, while their lower jaw has a simpler structure than that of terrestrial mammals. Certain processes, e.g. the coronoid process and the angular process, which play such an important part in attaching the muscles which move the lower jaw, were still well developed in Archaeocetes, but are greatly reduced or entirely absent in all other Cetaceans, and particularly in those Odontocetes which feed on cuttlefish, and in all Mysticetes, since Mysticetes do not have to seize their prey but need merely open and shut their mouths. In the course of 35 million years, the lower jaw of these animals has become an extremely simple, arched clasp. In Rorquals the processes can still be distinguished, but in Right Whales they have been reduced to insignificant stubs, and the jaw joint has an extremely simple globular head. The lower jaws of Mysticetes are bent strongly outwards to make room for the baleen. This phenomenon is most striking in Right Whales, whose jaw-bones were often used for gate-posts by whalers of earlier times (Fig. 162). In Holland this custom has recently been revived, and in Schiermonnikoog there is a twenty-one-foot gate made from the jaws of a Blue Whale.

Between the two halves of the lower jaw lies the bottom of the mouth, which, as we have seen, has longitudinal grooves in Rorquals, whose mouths can be considerably distended. We have also seen that these animals need large mouths for ingesting considerable quantities of krill with each gulp. They can do this all the better by virtue of a number of

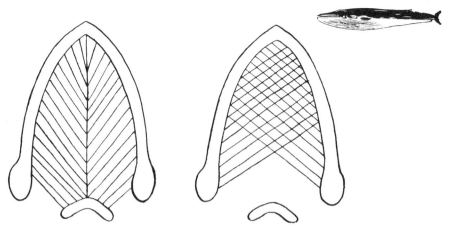

Figure 163. Diagrammatic sketch of the course of the layer of cutaneous muscles between the two lower jaws (right) and of the muscles between the lower jaws and the hyoid bone (left) in a Rorqual.

cutaneous muscles which run diagonally from the centre of the lower jaw to either side of its edges. These muscles consist of different layers running in alternating directions (Fig. 163). The contraction of the bottom of the mouth is greatly aided by the presence of large quantities of elastic fibre in its connective tissue (Sokolov, 1958).

In addition, longitudinal geniohyoid and mylohyoid muscles run from the jaws to the hyoid bone of the tongue. All these muscles are, of course, used for reducing the size of the mouth once the prey has been seized, and for squeezing out the water between the whalebones (Fig. 164). The tongue, too, is important in this process, since it may be said to be part and parcel of the bottom of the mouth.

Whales do, in fact, lack our own freely movable tongue. Odontocete tongues still have a short free tip, and so have those of Mysticete foetuses (Fig. 165), in which, soon after birth, the base grows wider as it grows longer, till finally the tongue is nothing but a massive swelling covering practically the entire bottom of the mouth. The reader will best appreciate how massive it really is if he is told that the tongue of a Blue Whale has the same weight as an adult elephant, i.e. roughly four tons, or 2·5 per cent of the whale's total body-weight – a percentage which is vastly greater than, for instance, in the case of man. Unfortunately for us, Rorqual tongues are not very muscular and are therefore not edible. This is only to be expected of so immovable an organ, which is in fact almost entirely made up of spongy connective tissue. The tongue of Right Whales contains much more muscular tissue than that of Rorquals. This tissue quickly

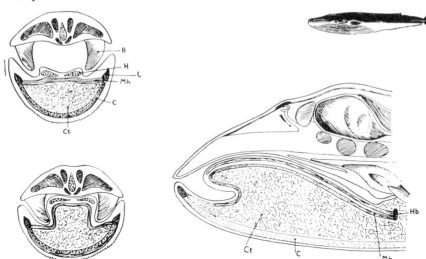

Figures 164–5. (*Left*) *Cross-section through the head of a Blue Whale foetus with open and closed mouth. B = baleen; H = hyoglossus; L = lower jaw; Mh = mylohyoid muscle; C = layer of cutaneous muscle between the two lower jaws; Ct = loose connective and fatty tissue of tongue. (Kükenthal, 1893.) (Right) Longitudinal section through the head of a Blue Whale foetus, in which the tongue still has a free tip. Ct = loose connective and fatty tissue of tongue; C = layer of cutaneous muscle between the two lower jaws; Hb = hyoid bone; Mh = mylohyoid muscle. (Kükenthal, 1893.)*

decomposes after death, when the gases liberated during putrefaction may make the tongue swell out like a balloon. No doubt, this is the reason why some people still believe the fable that whales can inflate their tongues at will to help them swallow their food. The real part played by this rigid organ during swallowing is, in fact, not fully known.

A gustatory sense is said to be entirely absent in most Cetaceans, though rudimentary taste organs have been described in some Odontocetes, whose papillae at the base of the tongue may be considered as taste-buds. In consequence, the ninth cranial nerve (the glossopharyngeal) is rather insignificant in Cetaceans. In fact, all Carnivores which swallow their food whole have a poor gustatory sense. Herbivorous animals, on the other hand, which are in greater danger of swallowing poisons and must therefore select their food more carefully, have a much more highly developed gustatory sense. Small wonder then that very strange objects are often found in Cetacean stomachs. Kleinenberg, for instance, while examining the stomachs of Common Dolphins from the Black Sea, not only found pieces of wood, feathers, paper and cherry stones, but even a bouquet of flowers. On the other hand, it seems that Cetaceans have some means of reacting to the salinity of the water, and some Russian biologists believe that Belugas can detect smoke. Whether these reactions are due to taste or to some other sense is, however, not yet known.

Not only the gustatory sense, but the salivary glands also are usually more highly developed in herbivorous than in carnivorous animals. Not surprisingly, therefore, even the earliest anatomists to study the Cetaceans, e.g. Cuvier, Meckel and Rapp, were struck by the rudimentary form or complete absence of this gland in them.

While no one really believes that Jonah could have lived inside a whale, the one Cetacean stomach he could even have entered is that of the Sperm Whale, for both the pharynx and the oesophagus (normal width 4–5 inches) of all other whales are far too narrow to admit a man. Big Rorquals can probably distend their oesophagus to 10 inches, but even that is not big enough to allow them to swallow a man. Killers, which can swallow seals and porpoises whole, have a much wider oesophagus, and the Sperm Whale which gulps down thirty-four feet long giant squids could certainly have swallowed Jonah. Budker, in his book *Baleines et Baleiniers*, mentions the story of a sailor being swallowed by a Sperm Whale, but there is, of course, no authentic account of anyone ever having emerged alive from such an ordeal.

Through the oesophagus, the food enters the stomach, where the digestive process really starts (in so far as it has not been begun by the action of the saliva in the mouth, as happens in man). In most mammals, and particularly in carnivorous and omnivorous animals, e.g. dogs, pigs and man, the stomach is a single pouch. If we look at its inner lining through a microscope, we see that in a small region near the oesophagus it has the same structure as the epithelium of the oesophagus itself. It consists of stratified squamous epithelium, more or less cornified, but lacks a homogeneous horn layer, such as, for instance, is found in the epidermis. The rest of the stomach is lined with non-cornified epithelium containing a great many fundus glands which mainly secrete hydrochloric acid and the enzyme pepsin which breaks down complex proteins into simpler compounds. In the pyloric region of the stomach (i.e. the region adjoining the duodenum), the fundus glands are replaced by pyloric glands which mainly secrete alkaline mucus.

While the stomachs of herbivorous sea-cows and of Pinnipeds are generally similar in form and structure to those of the Carnivores and Omnivores we have just described, the Cetacean stomach is much more complex, consisting in all species (with the exception of Beaked Whales which we shall discuss separately) of three main compartments which, in Odontocetes, communicate by means of very narrow openings, and in Mysticetes by means of slightly wider openings (Fig. 166). The first and second compartments (forestomach and main stomach) are wide sacs

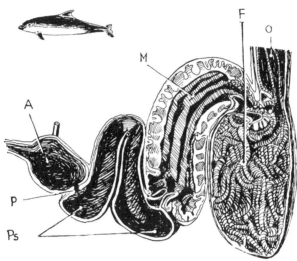

Figure 166. Section of stomach of a Bottlenose Dolphin.
O = oesophagus
F = forestomach
M = main stomach
Ps = pyloric stomach
P = pylorus
A = ampulla of duo-
denum
(Pernkopf, 1937.)

which in big whales can hold well over 200 gallons and a ton of krill (Fig. 167). Peacock (1936), who investigated the stomachs of False Killers, found that their capacity varied from 2–3 gallons, and Vladykov estimated the capacity of the first compartment of a Beluga's stomach at 4·8 gallons. Comparing these figures with those for man ($4\frac{1}{2}$ pints), dogs ($5\frac{1}{4}$ pints), pigs (14 pints), horses (4 gallons), cows (55 gallons), we find that, relatively speaking, the capacity of the whale's stomach cannot be called very large – nor would we expect this of a carnivorous or fish-eating animal. The passage between the first and second compartments (the forestomach and main stomachs) lies close to the entrance of the oesophagus, while the passage to the third (the pyloric) compartment generally lies on the opposite side of the main stomach. The pyloric compartment, which usually resembles a bent tube, is indented to form 2–4 sub-divisions, the last of which communicates with the duodenum through the very narrow pylorus. Near the stomach, the duodenum of most Cetaceans expands into an ampulla which has often been mistaken for yet another compartment of the stomach.

If we investigate the different compartments more closely, we find that the first compartment is lined with hard and generally white or yellow squamous but non-cornified epithelium which contains no glands and hence secretes no juices. The lining of the second compartment has a very much softer and somewhat velvety appearance, and is generally purple in colour. Sometimes a characteristic system of reticular folds can be observed in it, but at other times the folds run parallel. The appearance of the folds is, in fact, determined by the extent to which the stomach is filled and hence stretched. The lining contains fundus glands, and both pepsin and hydrochloric acid have been found in this compartment. Japanese scientists, in particular, have studied the quantity and the effects of these pepsins with a view to applying them to therapeutic purposes. In Europe, pepsin forms the basis of various pharmaceutical preparations, and is generally derived from the stomachs of cattle, but Japan, lacking a pastoral economy, is forced to rely partly on whales for her pepsin supplies.

Apart from pepsin, the second compartment also contains lipase, a fat-digesting enzyme which, though generally secreted by the pancreas, may also be formed in the stomachs of terrestrial animals and of Carnivores, in particular. H. J. Ketellapper, who examined Blue and Fin Whale stomachs *inter alia* for the presence of enzymes, shows that only small traces of lipase were present in them.

The lining of the third compartment, the pyloric stomach, is generally reddish-brown in colour, and looks as velvety as the second. While it may have a few fine folds, it is often very smooth, and contains a large number of normal pyloric glands.

If we compare the Cetacean stomach with that of other mammals,

Figure 167. Whenever the stomach of a whale is accidentally cut open, the krill spills out over the deck. (Photograph: H. W. Symons, London.)

even the most superficial glance will reveal a striking resemblance between Cetaceans on the one hand and Ruminants (camels, cattle, deer, sheep, etc.) and some leaf-eating apes (e.g. the guereza) on the other (Fig. 168). The reader may have learnt at school that a cow has a complex forestomach consisting of paunch (rumen), honeycomb bag (reticulum), and manyplies (psalterium). All these compartments are covered with cornified epithelium and have no glands. They can therefore be compared with the Cetacean forestomach, and are, in fact, anatomically identical with it, but they differ in their physiological function. Thus, the intestinal glands of cattle do not produce enzymes for breaking down the cellulose on which these animals chiefly feed, nor, for that matter, are such enzymes secreted by the glands of any vertebrates. The break-down is therefore effected by the enzymes of millions of unicellular animals and plants which live in the paunch of cattle. No traces of them have ever been found in those of Cetaceans, which must therefore break down their food in a different way.

The secret of the digestion of whales and dolphins must be sought in the highly muscular wall of the forestomach (which in Fin Whales can be up to three inches thick), in the tough lining and the presence of marked pleats in this wall, and finally in the presence of sand and small stones which, at least in some species, are too common to be accidental and must therefore play some part in digestion. Van Beneden, for instance, while investigating the stomach of a Pilot Whale in 1860, discovered a number of pebbles in the first compartment, the biggest weighing 1 ounce, and Malm (1938), while investigating another Pilot Whale, found stones weighing altogether twenty-one pounds. It would therefore appear that, like the muscular stomach of birds, the first Cetacean stomach compartment by contracting forcefully can, with the help of stones and sand, break down the food to suitable dimensions. Cetaceans, like birds, swallow their food whole, so that it must be broken down in the first compartment before passing through the very narrow passage to the second. Moreover, the passage often protrudes like a small snout into the first compartment, thus impeding the passage of large particles even farther. The reason why sand and stones are not found in all Cetacean stomachs may well be that the vertebrae of fish and the chitin armour of crustaceans provide adequate grinding material. In either case, whales 'chew' their food with their stomachs, just as birds do. This is borne out also by the fact that the first stomach division is relatively small in suckling Cetacean calves which have no need to chew their food at all. In adult Odontocetes, the first compartment is by far the largest, but in Mysticetes, which feed on small plankton, the second compartment is bigger than the first.

Clearly, animals which feed exclusively on food as soft as cuttlefish

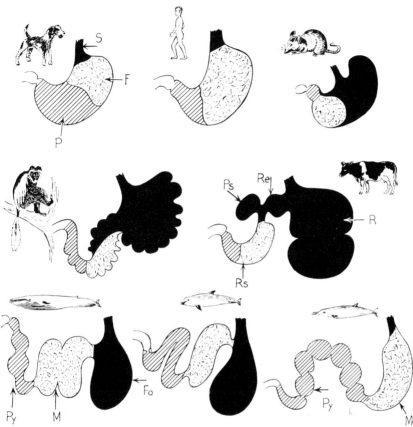

Figure 168. Diagrammatic sketch of the division of the stomach on the basis of the structure of its lining (and particularly of the presence of certain glands) in a dog, a man, a mouse, a guereza, a cow, a Fin Whale, a Bottlenose Dolphin, and a Beaked Whale. S = region of stratified squamous epithelium; F = region of fundus glands; P = region of pyloric glands; R = rumen (paunch); Re = reticulum (honeycomb bag); Ps = psalterium (manyplies); Rs = rennet-stomach; Fo = forestomach; M = main stomach; Py = Pyloric stomach. (Slijper, 1946.)

could easily dispense with the first compartment altogether, since soft food, however large, can be broken down fairly easily by the acid in the stomach – hence the absence of this compartment in all Beaked Whales (Fig. 168), whose pyloric stomach is indented to form up to twelve small chambers instead. Sperm Whales and Pigmy Sperm Whales, whose teeth are very much less reduced than those of Beaked Whales and which are therefore less specialized animals, have the typical first compartment of Odontocetes.

The Cetacean intestine has few points of special interest. Gangetic

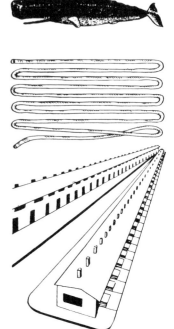

Figure 169. A 55-foot Sperm Whale has an intestine with a true length of 500 feet, i.e., the length of a normal street with 25 houses on either side.

Dolphins and Mysticetes have a very short cœcum which is absent in all other Cetaceans, in which, therefore, there is no clear transition between large and small intestine, both of which look identical as, in fact, they do in most Carnivores.

While watching the flensing of a Cetacean carcass, spectators are invariably struck by the enormous quantities of intestinal matter which appear. Measurements will show that a large Sperm Whale of, say, fifty-five feet long has an intestine some 1,200 feet long (Fig. 169). This is almost two furlongs, i.e. roughly the length of a street with sixty-five houses on either side. However, the intestines of all animals stretch on removal, and we must not be deceived by their apparent length after dissection. Thus man's intestine, which measures 154 inches inside the living body, stretches to about 340 inches at autopsy. At death, the intestinal muscles of all animals relax – they lose their tonus, as biologists say – and automatically stretch to 2–3 times their normal size, particularly when they are pulled out none too gently. If we divide the external measurements by 2·5, our Sperm Whale must have had an intestine about 500 feet long – still the length of a street with twenty-five houses on either side.

Expressed as a percentage of body length, the Sperm Whale's intestine represents 2,400 per cent – a formidable figure indeed. The dead intestines of Fin Whales represent 400 per cent, of Little Piked Whales, Humpback Whales and Bottlenose Whales 550 per cent, of Beaked Whales 600 per cent, of Gangetic Dolphins 730 per cent, of Killers and Bottlenose Dolphins 820 per cent, of Belugas 1,000 per cent, of Narwhals 1,100 per cent, of Risso's Dolphins and Common Dolphins 1,200 per cent, of Whitesided Dolphins 1,400 per cent, and of porpoises 2,200 per cent. By and large, therefore, the smaller the animal, the greater the percentage length of its intestine, which is only to be expected from the fact that as an animal becomes smaller its surface area decreases proportionally to the square of the decrease in length. Hence in a very large animal, the surface area of the intestine becomes too small to carry out its essential task of secreting digestive juices and of absorbing digested foods, and the intestine must therefore grow longer. It is not at all clear why the Sperm Whale is so abnormal in this respect, since its diet of cuttlefish is no different from that of many other Cetaceans whose intestines are about the length we would expect.

If we compare the above figures for Cetaceans with those for mammals of comparable external dimensions, we find that the respective figures are: man – 650 per cent; lion – 390 per cent; sheep – 3,000 per cent; seal – 1,600 per cent as against the smaller dolphin's average of 1,700 per cent. Clearly carnivorous animals have a short, herbivorous animals a long, and omnivorous animals an intermediate intestine. Experiments on various mammals have shown that fish-eaters have much longer intestines than meat-eaters, which may be due to the fact that, while the latter spurn part of the skin and bones of at least their bigger victims, the former, and also the Killer Whale, leave nothing behind. It is quite possible, therefore, that the digestion and absorption of certain substances found in the skin and the skeleton of the prey demand a much larger intestinal surface in the captor. However, too little is known about the digestion of Cetaceans for any final pronouncements to be made on this subject.

The Cetacean pancreas seems to be similar to that of most mammals, both in situation, structure, function and relative weight (i.e. 0·1–0·2 per cent in small, and 0·03–0·15 per cent in large Cetaceans). The organ has, however, not yet been investigated sufficiently, an omission which is the more regrettable since the enzymes it secretes are of great practical interest. In Germany, for instance, the enzyme has been used successfully for leather tanning, and in Japan for other industrial purposes. Investigators are hampered by the fact that the pancreas must be removed immediately after death and that it must then be refrigerated at once.

The Cetacean pancreas generally has one, but occasionally more than one, duct which combines with the bile duct of the liver into one passage entering the duodenum. In many mammals, man included, a branch of the bile duct runs to the gall bladder where part of the bile is temporarily stored, to be poured into the intestine in large quantities whenever it is needed. The fact that all Cetaceans are completely devoid of a gall bladder was already known to Aristotle and Pliny, so that man has known about it for over 2,000 years, though the reason why remains obscure to this day. This is a strange gap in our knowledge, the more so since a great many other mammals belonging to different orders are also devoid of this organ.

No discussion of the Cetacean digestive system would be complete without some mention of *ambergris* (see Chapter 1). The very word has a magic sound and used to conjure up visions of great riches washed up on lonely beaches and bringing unexpected fortune to those who stumbled upon it. In earlier times, ambergris was worth its weight in gold, and as the Dutch East India Company once possessed a piece weighing 975 lb., we need not be surprised that sailors the world over dreamt of making similar finds. By 1953, however, when a piece of ambergris weighing 918 lb. was removed from the gut of a Sperm Whale aboard the *Southern Harvester* in the Antarctic, prices had dropped considerably. Even so, the world market price is still £40 to £70 per lb. since, in spite of the existence of many synthetic substitutes, the high quality scent industry still uses ambergris to a considerable extent.

The West came to know of ambergris through an Arabian merchant who ventured forth to the islands of the Indian Ocean. On the Andaman Islands he traded iron against ambergris, a product that Orientals had long prized as an aphrodisiac. By the Middle Ages, Europeans, too, had begun to use it in love philtres and also as a cure for dropsy and other diseases. As the demand rose while the supply (whose source remained a mystery) lagged behind, prices rose to giddy heights. Avicenna, the famous medieval philosopher and physician, attributed ambergris to eruptions of submarine volcanoes, and Koblio (1667) thought he recognized it as the droppings of a certain seabird. Marco Polo (ca. 1300) who knew that Oriental sailors hunted Sperm Whales for their ambergris, thought that these animals simply swallowed this substance with the rest of their food. It was not until 1724 that Dudley showed that ambergris is formed inside the Sperm Whale, and as late as 1791 the House of Commons was so puzzled by this mysterious substance that they summoned Capt. Coffin, the master of a whaler, to explain exactly what ambergris was.

We do not know what precisely he told his distinguished audience, but then the whole nature of ambergris is shrouded in mystery to this day. It is a waxlike, dark brown or greyish-yellow substance which is as pliable as pitch, though not as sticky. It smells of musk, is highly soluble in organic solvents, and consists of a very complex aliphatic alcohol, ambraïne, mixed with an oily substance. It often contains chitin or other hard parts of cuttlefish which is not surprising as it is found in the intestine of Sperm Whales. It was formerly believed that ambergris was the result of disease or malnutrition, but Robert Clarke, who was present during the discovery of the enormous piece of ambergris in a Sperm Whale caught by the *Southern Harvester* (see above), reported that the animal was extremely healthy and well fed. Actually, ambergris may well be comparable to the intestinal stones of otherwise healthy terrestrial mammals. Cows, for instance, often have stones or big hair balls in their intestines, and the well-known Dutch expert on stranded whales, Dr A. B. van Deinse, examining a stranded porpoise in 1935, discovered no less than twenty glittering white stones in its intestine, the largest of which measured 1 inch $\times$ $\frac{4}{5}$ inch $\times$ $\frac{3}{5}$ inch. The stones consisted of calcium phosphate and many organic compounds. Ambergris may, therefore, be the pathological product of an otherwise normal intestine, its basis being intestinal matter. In fact, a product resembling ambergris has been made experimentally from the faeces of a Sperm Whale.

Metabolism

ALL CETACEANS are gluttons, and the Killer Whale can swallow meals of thirty seals at a time (see Fig. 154). In the Aquaria in Florida and California, Pilot Whales are fed 45–60 lb. of fish and cuttlefish, while Bottlenose Dolphins (and Pacific White-beaked in Marineland, California) consume 'only' 22 lb. of fish a day. They could easily eat more still, since the dolphins which were kept in the New York Aquarium ate 65 lb. of fish a day. Porpoises, too, need a large supply of food. Dudok van Heel found that, in order to keep his animals in good condition, he had to feed them 22–25 lb. of mackerel daily. Nishimoto and his colleagues removed 450 lb. of krill from the stomach of a forty-foot Sei Whale, which the animal must have swallowed shortly before, as the small shrimps were still quite fresh. The stomach of an Antarctic Blue Whale was found to contain nearly one ton of krill (Fig. 167), and we have every reason to assume that this quantity did not represent its full daily ration.

Looking at Fig. 131, you might say that this is not surprising, since animals 1,600 times our own weight must obviously eat correspondingly large quantities of food. Actually, things are not quite as simple as that. The inhabitants of Lilliput, when they found that Gulliver was twelve times their height and therefore weighed 12^3 times their weight, were wrong to think that he would consume 1,728 times as much food as they did – he had a much more economical metabolism than his small hosts. True, a horse eats more than a mouse, but if we work out how much food it needs per pound of body-weight, it appears that the mouse eats about twenty-five times as much as the horse.

To understand this strange phenomenon, we must first ask ourselves why animals have to eat at all. An adult human being who has stopped growing needs food to replenish worn-out tissues. For instance, our skin and the lining of our intestines are continuously exposed to frictional effects, and thousands of red blood cells wear out every day. However, all these losses could probably be made good with only half an ounce of meat a day, and we all know that we would quickly starve to death if we ate no more than that. We eat food, not only to replace cells, but also to obtain energy for the work our body does. The greater the work done, the greater our need for food. Our body may be likened to an internal combustion engine, with a large part of our daily diet acting as the fuel. However, a car needs no petrol when it stands in the garage, while even the idlest of stay-a-beds must eat to keep alive. Even while he is supine on his back, his heart continues to beat, his respiratory system continues to function, and his body temperature is maintained. After all, man lives in an environment some 36° F. colder than his body, and if his temperature dropped below a certain critical level he would quickly die. No matter how warmly we dress, we constantly lose a certain amount of heat which, just like the heat given out by a stove, must be replenished by burning combustible materials – coal or food. To supply the necessary energy for keeping our organs working when our body is at rest, and to supply the necessary heat, we need about 1,800 great calories of food a day, i.e. about two-thirds of our requirements for sedentary or other light work. In other words, most of our food is needed to maintain temperature at its normal level.

Heat is lost primarily through the skin and the greater our external surface, the more heat is lost. For this reason we hunch up when we are cold, and stretch out as far as possible when we feel hot. Now, we have seen that the heavier an animal, the smaller its surface area and its heat losses per unit of body weight. Big animals will therefore lose relatively much less heat than small ones and will therefore need relatively less food. Cetaceans have the additional advantage that their streamlined form, i.e. the absence of protruding limbs, pinnae, etc., reduces their relative surface area still further, as a result of which their metabolism is particularly efficient. On the other hand, they have to overcome far greater environmental difficulties than terrestrial animals, particularly since water conducts heat about twenty-seven times as well as air. Our own body cools down much more quickly in water than in still air of the same temperature. Moreover, when a whale swims, the water flows past its body at speed, with the result that further great heat losses are incurred, just as we are cooled off by a breeze. Nor can whales find any form of shelter or even curl up to decrease their surface area, as, for instance, dogs do when they are cold. If we bear in mind that a normal human being loses consciousness after three hours in water at about 60° F., and after only fifteen minutes in water at about 32° F., we will appreciate what difficulties aquatic mammals have to contend with.

The best solution is, of course, a thick layer of insulating material. Thus

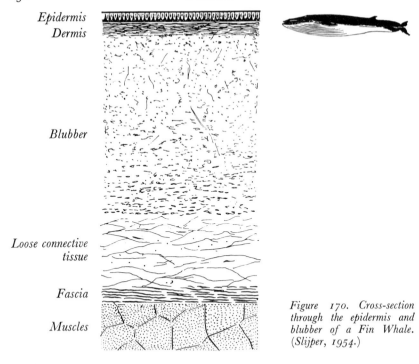

Epidermis
Dermis

Blubber

Loose connective
tissue

Fascia

Muscles

Figure 170. Cross-section through the epidermis and blubber of a Fin Whale. (Slijper, 1954.)

Channel swimmers invariably cover their skins with a thick coat of grease, and whales have a natural thick layer of blubber. We shall now look at this insulating layer in greater detail.

The skin of all mammals, Cetaceans included, consists of an outer epidermis, an inner dermis or corium, and of subcutaneous connective tissue (Fig. 170). The Cetacean epidermis is very thin; in big whales it is made up of a 5–7 mm. thick inner black or white layer of living cells, and an outer cornified layer which is less than 1 mm. thick. (In Chapter 2 we saw that the Cetacean skin is completely devoid of sweat glands and sebaceous glands). The dermis is a thin layer of tough connective tissue immediately under the epidermis, and contains no fat. In porpoises it is only 0·34 mm. thick, and this is the reason why their skins (and the skins of most whales and dolphins as well) cannot be used for leather. The Narwhal, the Beluga, and some River Dolphins form the exceptions, and their skins are, in fact, tanned in some countries.

In the big whales, the only skin suitable for processing is that covering the penis, and though it is of no industrial value, whalers sometimes turn it into useful domestic articles. The epidermis is naturally in close contact with the dermis, since water friction would otherwise tend to pull them

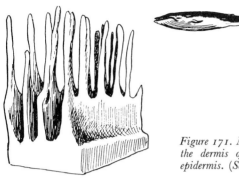

Figure 171. Model of ridges and papillae whereby the dermis of a Rorqual is held fast to the epidermis. (Schumacher, 1931.)

apart. In fact they are joined much like dovetails, with the dermis projecting into the epidermis by means of a great number of longitudinal ridges (Fig. 171). Moreover, every ridge is provided with a host of tall papillae which reach far up into the epidermis where their tips are slightly swollen (Fig. 172). In this way there is a very solid and yet elastic connexion between the two layers, while, thanks to the papillae, the capillaries in them can be brought nearer the surface of the skin. It is also quite possible that the ridges and the papillae may act as touch receptors (see Chapter 9).

Below the whale's dermis lies the blubber, which may be compared with another subcutaneous fatty layer – bacon. The relatively tough blubber is separated from the fascia covering the muscles beneath by a layer of loose connective tissue. In this way the blubber can be moved independently, just as, for instance, our own skin can be moved across the muscles. Hence the blubber can generally be pulled off fairly easily with a winch, and the flensing knife is only an auxiliary tool in removing it. The blubber itself is constructed of hard and fibrous connective tissue which fuses imperceptibly into the connective tissues of the dermis. Individual bundles of fibrous connective tissue are segregated by large concentrations of fat cells.

The number and arrangement of the cutaneous blood vessels play a most important part in maintaining the body's temperature. Parry (1949) who has examined this problem thoroughly in a Fin Whale and a porpoise found that the capillary network in their skins was constructed much more simply than that of man and many other mammals, in whose dermis we find two nets of arteries and four nets of veins. In Cetaceans, the blubber is crossed by simple arterioles which pass straight to the dermis, and there is no network at all. In the dermis, these arterioles run along the bottom of the ridges from which a tiny blood vessel enters each papilla, there to branch out into a capillary network that is most prominent in the distended tips (Fig. 172).

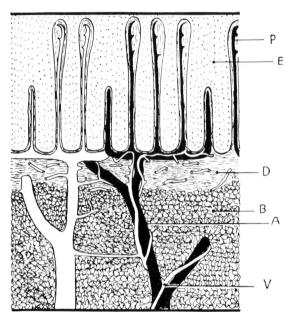

Figure 172. Sketch of the skin of a Porpoise. E = epidermis; D = dermis with venous retia; B = blubber; A = artery surrounded with venules (V); left (white): a large efferent vein; P = dermal papilla reaching almost to the top of the epidermis where it is broadened. The papilla contains arterioles surrounded with a number of venules (see Fig. 173), and capillaries at its tip. (Parry, 1949.)

According to Van Utrecht, the blood is returned by a number of veins which completely surround the tiny arterioles of the papillae (Fig. 173) in much the same way as some larger arteries of Cetaceans are surrounded with veins (see Chapter 5). As a result of this arrangement, which, by the way, is also found in the papillae of the gum (see Chapter 10), as much

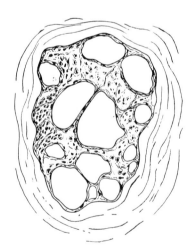

Figure 173. Cross-section through a dermal papilla in the epidermis of a porpoise. The large vessel in the centre is an arteriole surrounded with venules (see Figure 97). (Prepared by W. L. van Utrecht.)

heat as possible is retained by the body. The venules first return the
blood to a rather sparse network in the dermis, and then carry it back
through the blubber. Another set of venules surrounds the arterioles very
much as ivy encircles a tree (Fig. 172). From the fact that Cetaceans have
only half as many papillae per square millimetre of skin as, for instance,
man, we may take it that, despite this elaborate vascular arrangement,
their skin contains relatively less blood than that of other mammals.

In an eighty-nine-foot Blue Whale which tipped the scale aboard the
Hashidate Maru at 136·4 tons, the blubber was found to weigh twenty tons,
i.e. about 15 per cent of the animal's total weight. Actually, its blubber
must have been rather thin, for the normal percentages are: Blue Whale –
27 per cent, Fin Whale – 23 per cent, Sei Whale – 21 per cent, and Sperm
Whale – 32 per cent. In Right Whales, the corresponding figures are
36–45 per cent, and in dolphins 30–45 per cent. Porpoises, too, have a very
thick blubber; that of a number of Danish specimens was found to represent 45 per cent of the total weight. Specimens from the North Sea are
usually leaner, though 60 per cent was measured in one case. The actual
thickness of the blubber varies from species to species, but is greatest in
Right Whales, and especially in Greenland Whales, whose blubber has an
average thickness of twenty inches and, according to Zenkovich (1956),
of twenty-eight inches in some parts. Sperm Whales and Humpback
Whales also have sizeable blubber coats with an average thickness of
five to seven inches. Fin Whales and Blue Whales have coats three inches
and six inches thick respectively, and Sei Whales very much thinner coats
still. Now, all these figures are only rough approximations because blubber
is by no means of even thickness throughout. In large Rorquals, for
instance, it is thickest on the dorsal side of the lumbar and caudal regions,
and thinnest on the flanks. Moreover, blubber increases in thickness from
the front to the back, so that the top and bottom of the tail are particularly
fat. Thickenings of blubber also occur on the upper side of the lower jaw,
in front of the blowhole, at the base of the pectoral fins, and just in front
of the dorsal fin. The blubber is particularly thin round the eyes and a
little to the side of the blowhole, which is probably connected with movements of the eyelids and the walls of the blowhole. While the thickness of
the blubber varies from species to species, and from season to season, the
relative proportions of the blubber remain unchanged. In other words,
differences in blubber thickness from part to part do not depend on food
supplies but on streamlining, which is not so much the result of mere fat
as of the particular distribution of the fatty tissue, just as the details of our
own shape and physiognomy depend largely on the distribution of our
own subcutaneous fat.

According to Heyerdahl (1932), the only scientist to have made a

detailed study of this question, even the *composition* of the blubber changes
from part to part. Thus while its average fat content is 60 per cent in
Rorquals and 45 per cent in Sperm Whales[1], the remainder being connective tissue, a separate analysis of individual parts of the body shows that
the fat content of the blubber is much greater on the dorsal than on the
ventral side, where, in turn, it is greater than on the flanks. The fat
content increases perceptibly from snout to tail – on the dorsal side from
55 per cent to 80 per cent, and on the ventral side from 34 per cent to
72 per cent. In general, we may say that the thicker the blubber the fatter
it is and the less it consists of connective tissue.

In Rorqual embryos the relative thickness of the blubber increases
throughout the period of gestation, right up to birth. In Blue and Fin
Whales, its thickness is 0·75 per cent and 0·6 per cent of the total length
of the embryo respectively, the corresponding figures in adult specimens
being 0·53 per cent and 0·46 per cent. On the other hand, the fat content
of embryonic blubber is only 5–6 per cent. Apparently, the blubber begins
as a 'skeleton' of connective tissue which becomes fattier after birth. This
is not so strange if we bear in mind that the embryo or foetus has no need
of fat as reserve food or as insulation against cold.

In adult Rorquals the relative thickness of the blubber increases with
body length – hence the difference of roughly 14 per cent in the relative
thickness of the blubbers of Blue and Fin Whales, Blue Whales being
roughly 14 per cent longer than Fin Whales. It seems likely that smaller
animals which have a relatively larger skin surface, and thus greater heat
losses, must use a larger percentage of their food intake for preserving
thermal equilibrium by combustion. Moreover, measurements have shown
that pregnant cows have the thickest blubber, while lactating cows have
the thinnest. Clearly, during gestation a reserve is put by against the time
when the suckling calf will make heavy demands on its mother (see
Chapter 13). During the winter season the thickness and the fat percentage
of the blubber of Rorquals decrease considerably. The thinnest animal
ever described was a sixty-five-foot female Fin Whale which ran aground
near Wilhelmshaven on 8th February, 1944. The thickness of much of its
dorsal blubber was no more than 1¼ inches and its fat content varied
between 1·7 per cent and 3·5 per cent.

To get an idea of the insulating properties of blubber, we would have
to know the normal body temperature of Cetaceans. Now, it is extremely
difficult to take the temperature even of porpoises, let alone of big whales,
and we generally have to make do with measurements on freshly killed
carcasses. True, Zenkovich managed to take the temperature of a living

---

[1] In fact the layer of blubber of most Toothed Whales contains not fat but a wax-like
substance (see page 72).

Sperm Whale that was paralysed by a harpoon after an intense chase. The figure he obtained, i.e. 100·7° F., must, however, have been abnormally high, as was the temperature Portier took of a recently killed Killer (98° F.), even though Tomilin took similar temperatures in Black Sea Dolphins (97·7° F.). White measured 95° F. in a porpoise, and Richard 96·1° F. in a dolphin. These figures agree with Laurie's (1933) average of 95° F. in thirty freshly killed Blue and Fin Whales. Parry, Kanwisher (1957), and Slijper took temperatures of 95·9° F. which agreed with those taken by Guldberg in 1900, so that Sudzuki's 97·9° F.–98·6° F. is probably a little on the high side. However, Sudzuki worked with N. Pacific Sei Whales, while the other biologists worked with Blue and Fin Whales. For the time being, at least, we may take it that the average body temperature of Cetaceans in general is about 95·9° F. – a very low figure indeed for a mammal.

This figure is 2·5° F. below that of man, whose temperature is low in turn when compared with that of horses (100·4° F.), of cows and guinea-pigs (101·3° F.), of rabbits, sheep and cats (102·2° F.), and of goats (103·1° F.). Only hedgehogs are known to have an average summer temperature equal to that of Cetaceans, while sloths, opossums and duck-bills (89·6° F.–93·2° F.) are even more cold-blooded. But then the last-named species occupy such a special position among mammals in so many respects, that we may safely say that compared with terrestrial mammals, whales have a very low temperature. Seals and related species certainly have higher temperatures, for Clarke measured 98° F. in an elephant seal. The hippopotamus, on the other hand, has a temperature similar to Cetaceans (96° F.), and sea-cows probably have a lower temperature still. It may be regarded as most advantageous to Cetaceans that their body functions optimally at so low a temperature, since the smaller the difference from the aquatic environment, the less heat (and consquently food) is needed for maintaining thermal equilibrium.

Since heat is lost through the skin, it is important to determine the actual size of the integument. Little is known about this subject apart from the fact that surface areas of 12·4 and 14·5 square feet have been measured in porpoises, of 15·2 square feet in a Common Dolphin, of 143 and 146 square yards in Fin Whales and of 223 square yards in Blue Whales. While the skin of the Blue Whale would therefore cover a tennis court, it is, nevertheless, relatively small compared with the animal's bulk. Thus an elephant whose skin has an area of about 41·8 square yards would, if its mass were as great as a Fin Whale's and its skin surface rose in proportion, cover an area of 480 square yards. Similarly, an average porpoise has a smaller surface area than a man of approximately equal weight, whose skin covers 19·3 square feet. This comparatively much smaller area of the

Cetacean skin surface, due largely to streamlining, has, as we have seen, a considerable effect in minimizing heat losses.

The heat conducting properties of the blubber of a porpoise and a Fin Whale were determined experimentally by Parry (1949). From the result (0·0005 g. cal. per sq. cm. per second per centimetre thickness, at temperature difference 1° C.), together with the known area of the skin and the temperature difference between it and the sea, Parry calculated how much heat the animals would have to produce in order to maintain their temperature. Mammals are believed to be capable of producing forty-five (great) calories per square metre (4·2 calories per square foot) of skin surface per hour. While some biologists think that these figures do not apply to mammals in general, we shall use them here, in the absence of more accurate data. If we do so, we shall find that the amount of heat a porpoise or a Fin Whale at rest loses through its skin considerably exceeds the amount their body is capable of producing in the same time. Hence, the animals cannot possibly stay at rest and must move about rapidly during most of the day if they are not to lose too much heat. As we know from personal experience, the faster we move about, the warmer we get – a fact we use to advantage on a cold winter's day.

Conversely, we get cold when we are scantily dressed, and Cetaceans cool off so much because their blubber coat is not really thick enough to lag them completely under all conditions. Parry has calculated that the Fin Whale would have to have a 5½-inch thick blubber covering if it were to maintain its temperature at rest. Now, that thickness is only found in particularly fat specimens at the end of the Antarctic season.

Why then is the blubber so thin, you may ask, particularly if you remember that these animals store a great deal of fat in other parts of the body, i.e. in the skeleton, between the internal organs, and even in the muscles. We may gain a clearer understanding of this question if we investigate how fat is stored by big Rorquals in the course of the Antarctic season. In the beginning of the season, most fat is stored as blubber, so that the thickness of this layer increases rapidly and thermal insulation is consequently increased. After the middle of January, however, the thickness of the blubber over most parts of the body increases only very slightly. The exception is the back and especially the region immediately in front of the dorsal fin, where the thickness of the blubber still increases significantly. Most of the fat, however, is now laid down elsewhere – at first in the skeleton, then chiefly in the muscles and finally between the organs. This strange way of laying down fat is obviously necessary since if, at the end of the season, the blubber grew any thicker than it does, the animals would become too hot when swimming about; so much so that they might die of heat-stroke in the midst of the ice-cold polar sea.

Cetaceans have, after all, no means of taking shelter or of standing in a breeze when they get too hot, and above all, they cannot lose surplus heat by perspiring, by lolling their tongues, or by increasing their rate of respiration. Moreover, their skin is not as vascular as that of most mammals which, in some parts of the body (e.g. the ears), can give off a great deal of heat direct through the blood. In Cetaceans, the vascular system, as we have seen, has a heat-preserving structure, and the animals must mainly rely on the blood in the fins for liberating heat. According to Tomilin, however, the blood flow to the fins of a dolphin can be so increased that their temperature may be up to 16° F. higher than that of the flanks. Whalers maintain that whales bleed from the tail fin much more profusely after a long hunt than when they are killed quickly. Moreover, the circulation to the skin is probably diverted to the small veins encircling the arteries whenever heat is to be preserved, while this path is short-circuited when heat is to be lost (see p. 298 and Fig. 172). The fact that Cetaceans can, nevertheless, become too hot with serious consequences, appeared clearly during the transport of Bottlenoses and other dolphins from the coast to inland aquaria. Whenever their captors omitted to keep their entire bodies moist with cold water, the animals' temperature rose to as much as 108·5° F., and they died.

However, Cetaceans have one advantage over most terrestrial mammals: their environment, though cold, is usually of even temperature. Diurnal temperature differences, which are particularly marked in deserts and on mountains, do not affect deep water to any great extent, and even the temperature differences between the various layers are nothing like those terrestrial mammals have to contend with. Even the temperature differences between tropical and polar seas are no greater than 45° F. – very much less than the seasonal fluctuation of up to 130° F to which a polar fox or hare is exposed. Moreover, the food of migrating Cetaceans is so distributed in the world's areas as to assist their thermal economy. In the cold polar seas the animals can increase their blubber by feeding off a rich and plentiful diet, while in the tropics, where food is mostly scarce, their girth decreases and a far greater amount of heat is lost. This explains why the Sei Whale, which lives largely in warmer waters and which is the fastest swimmer of all Rorquals, has the thinnest blubber, while the slow Greenland Whale which never leaves the Arctic has the thickest blubber coat of all.

From what has just been said, we may safely infer that Cetaceans have a very high metabolic rate, which enables them to keep in constant motion and thus to maintain their temperature. Even in their sleep they do not keep perfectly still (see Chapter 6) nor do they seem to sleep for long periods, particularly in cold waters. In warmer waters they can, of course, relax a little more, and it is therefore not surprising that most reports of sleeping whales come from lower latitudes. While no one has ever been able to measure the actual metabolic rate of Cetaceans – to do so involves using complicated instruments, and under water the difficulties are even greater – we may get some idea of its extent if we are told that Bottlenose Dolphins in New York Aquarium consumed about 18¾ lb. of herring a day, e.g. 237·5 calories per pound of body weight, while an average working man needs only 116·5 calories. Luckily, most Cetaceans eat food with a high calorific value so that the actual weight of food they have to consume is not so striking.

We might have guessed that Cetaceans would have a high metabolic rate from the size of their brain alone (see Chapter 9). Other organs, too, and particularly their thyroid, suggest very much the same. The extremely complicated processes which keep an animal alive and allow its body to function are controlled, not only by the central nervous system, but also by a number of endocrine glands which pour their secretions directly into the blood stream, in contradistinction to other glands (e.g. the sweat glands) whose products are excreted. The thyroid is one of these endocrine glands, and plays a particularly important role in regulating the metabolic rate. We shall therefore examine it in some detail.

In Cetacean foetuses the thyroid has roughly the same shield-shape as in man, but in adult specimens the gland forms two big lobes, on either side of the trachea close behind the larynx, which are joined by a slender bridge. The gland itself, about fourteen inches long in big whales and dark red, is externally divided into small lobes. Its weight varies between 2¼ and 9 lb., and in adult porpoises between half an ounce and an ounce. These figures, and also the information that the thyroid of Rorquals, dolphins and porpoises represents 0·01 per cent, 0·02 per cent and 0·05 per cent of their body weight respectively, tell us very little in themselves, since surface area and consequently loss of heat per pound of body weight clearly decrease with increase in body size, thus causing a decrease in metabolism and thyroid weight. However, Crile and Quiring (1940) compared the weights of the thyroids of a Beluga and a race-horse, two animals with an identical weight of 1,048 lb., and found that while the former weighed 3½ ozs. the latter weighed only 1⅙ oz. This agrees with the fact that terrestrial mammals the size of porpoises have a thyroid-to-body ratio of about 0·015 per cent as against the porpoise's 0·05 per cent. Comparing the thyroids of a large number of mammals, Crile and Quiring discovered that particularly large thyroids were found only in aquatic mammals and in terrestrial mammals which live in the Arctic, i.e. in animals which lose an inordinate amount of heat and whose metabolism is accordingly high. Human beings, too, have large thyroids, but for quite different reasons which need not concern us here.

Microscopic examinations of Cetacean thyroid glands have shown that the organs may vary in output. This variation may, however, only reflect the intensity of the hunt before the animals were killed. Thyroid extract, which is used extensively for therapeutic purposes, can conveniently be prepared from Cetacean glands. In 1941 Jacobsen established that the effect of the hormone extracted from a given weight of glands was about 67 per cent of the effect of the hormone extracted from the same weight of sheep glands. However, all our existing plant is designed for producing sheep's thyroid extract, and in Western Europe, at least, the switch-over would be too costly to warrant new methods of extraction.

The parathyroid gland, which measures only about $2\frac{3}{4}$ inches $\times$ $1\frac{1}{2}$ inches in large Rorquals, might be overlooked in animals some eighty feet long, were it not for the fact that its grey or pinkish colour sets it off against the dark red of the thyroid. It is found laterally behind either side of the thyroid, and its weight varies from specimen to specimen (from $\frac{1}{3}$ oz. to $4\frac{1}{2}$ ozs. in Fin Whales). Undoubtedly this small gland has the same function in Cetaceans as it has in all mammals, viz. control of the calcium metabolism.

Still more difficult to find are the adrenal (or suprarenal) glands, not because they are particularly small (in large Rorquals each gland measures 8–12 inches $\times$ 6–8 inches $\times$ 2–4 inches, while both glands together weigh from 28 ozs. to 88 ozs.) but because they are so tucked away between the diaphragm and the front of the kidneys that they are extremely inaccessible. Generally, the adrenals are completely hidden by the stomach or the diaphragm, organs which, in such enormous animals, cannot be easily pulled aside.

Bartholinus was the first to describe the adrenals of a porpoise as early as 1654, but it was not until 1787 that Hunter described them in whales, where they are flattish, oval organs, perceptibly lobular on the outside (just like the thyroids) – a clear indication that the lobulation is connected with the absolute size of the organs. (There are no lobes in porpoises and dolphins.) On dissection, the adrenals, like those of all other mammals, prove to consist of a yellowish cortex and a central brownish medulla, from which biologists have managed to isolate cortine and adrenaline respectively. However, the industrial processes involved have proved so complicated and so beset with technical difficulties that there can be no question of a serious exploitation of these Cetacean hormones at the moment. Moreover, the adrenals are too poor in vitamin C ($0 \cdot 125$ ozs. per lb. of gland) to make their extraction an economic proposition.

The porpoise's adrenal glands represent $0 \cdot 04$ to $0 \cdot 08$ per cent of the body weight, those of some dolphins 0·01 to 0·04 per cent and those of Rorquals 0·001 to 0·003 per cent. In other mammals, too, the adrenals decrease in relative weight with increase of body weight. This happens because they are intimately related to the functions of the body surface. In the case of the Beluga and the race-horse mentioned earlier, the adrenal glands weighed 1¼ ozs. and 1¾ ozs. respectively, the race-horse having a bigger gland, no doubt because it is capable of sudden spurts of energy. Similarly, such *Felidae* as cats and tigers which lie in wait for hours, suddenly to pounce upon their prey with all their might, also have fairly large adrenal glands. Such animals may be called 'sprinters' whereas those who have to develop a constant but moderate quantity of energy during a comparatively long time and those who live in a cold climate may be called 'stayers'. Cetaceans in general may therefore be regarded as stayers, and so it is not surprising at all that, compared with most terrestrial animals, they have relatively large thyroids and comparatively small adrenals.

On the floor of the brain, all vertebrates have a small gland – the pituitary. It may be likened to a glandular switchboard since some of its hormones control the function of the other endocrine glands, while others have a direct effect on growth, lactation, sexuality, and other important functions of the body. Some pituitary extracts play an important part in medical therapy, and since the pituitary of cattle weighs no more than 0·07 ozs. (2 gm.), it is not surprising that repeated attempts have been made to exploit the pituitary of Blue Whales (1¼ oz.) and of Fin Whales (just under 1 oz.). True, this small organ lodged in a cavity, the *sella turcica*, in the sphenoid bone at the base of the skull, is very hard to find, but a recent method of cranial dissection has enabled biologists to obtain the pituitary of every captured whale.

In all mammals, the pituitary gland consists of an anterior and a posterior lobe. Fig. 174 shows that the pale yellow stalk by which the organ is suspended from the brain continues as the posterior lobe, the anterior lobe being suspended from a stalk of its own, the so-called *pars tuberalis*, which forms a ring round the posterior stalk and then runs on into the tissue of the anterior lobe. It is dark brown in colour and consists mainly of blood vessels supplying the anterior lobe, which is not as dark as the *pars tuberalis* itself. The anterior lobe accounts for much the largest proportion of the mass of the pituitary, the ratio of anterior lobe, posterior lobe and *pars tuberalis* being 16 : 1 : 0·8.

The fine structure of, and the circulation in, the Cetacean pituitary are similar to those in other mammals, except that the former is distinguished by having a septum between the anterior and posterior lobes. This septum is made up of a fold of tough connective tissue thrown up from the dura

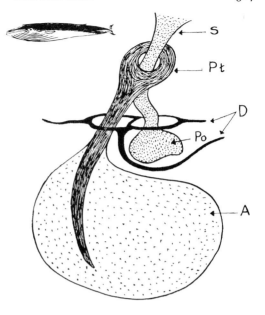

Figure 174. Very diagrammatic sketch of the pituitary gland of a Fin Whale, seen from the left. The anterior lobe is drawn in longitudinal section to show that the pars tuberalis runs into it. S = stalk; Pt = pars tuberalis; Po = posterior lobe; A = anterior lobe; D = dura mater with septum between anterior and posterior lobes.

mater of the brain. In this way, the two lobes are completely separated from each other, and there is no special pars intermedia connecting them, as there is in most other mammals. Prof. Gaillard of Leyden University has shown experimentally that, in all vertebrates, the special tissue of the intermediate lobe can only be formed when the two lobes are in direct contact with each other and not otherwise. The fact that a pars intermedia is also lacking in so ill-assorted a collection of animals as sea-cows, elephants, armadillos and birds, is an indication of how difficult it is to interpret this phenomenon. We shall therefore not attempt any further discussion of it, but merely mention that intermedine, the hormone secreted by the intermediate lobe of those vertebrates which have one, is secreted by the anterior lobe in Cetaceans.

The two lobes of the Cetacean pituitary were found to yield the same hormones as those of other mammals. The first scientist to isolate and prepare these hormones was A. P. Jacobsen, ship's surgeon on the Norwegian factory ship *Kosmos*, on which he sailed to the Antarctic and collected specimens of Cetacean endocrine glands in 1935. On his return, he did research work at Oslo University under the auspices of the Whaling Fund and a private chocolate company which was interested in whale hormones industrially. Jacobsen and many scientists after him succeeded in proving that certain hormones which affect uterine contractions, blood pressure and the excretion of urine can be obtained in adequate quantities from the posterior pituitary lobe of Cetaceans, and that other hormones regulating growth, thyroid secretion, lactation and the function of the sexual organs can be isolated from the anterior lobe. Biologists have found that the anterior lobe, and thus the pituitary gland, is twice its normal mass in pregnant females, and Nishiwaki and Oye (1951) showed that the anterior lobe of Blue Whales and Fin Whales was heavier the smaller a given male or the larger a given female. With the onset of puberty, the gland swells perceptibly in both sexes.

However, Jacobsen failed to find the anterior lobe hormone (A.C.T.H. – adrenocorticotrophic hormone) which stimulates the adrenal cortex. This is not surprising when we consider that the preparation and the effects of this hormone were first tackled successfully in other mammals and man since the Second World War, and that the work was so original that Hench, Kendall and Reichstein were awarded the Nobel Prize for their part in it (1950). A.C.T.H. has important applications in the treatment of arthritis, rheumatism and serious burns, and the results so far achieved with it have been most striking. In the 1949–1950 season, the pituitary of whales was collected for the first time aboard the *Thorshøvdi*, with the object of preparing A.C.T.H. from it, and Holterman, an employee of Nyegaard & Co., Oslo, did in fact succeed in isolating it. In the ensuing seasons a concerted effort by the entire Norwegian whaling fleet yielded approximately 9,000 pituitary glands with a total weight of about 400 lb. Twenty-five thousand ampules of A.C.T.H. were given free of charge to a number of hospitals, and the work continues.

It is only natural that Norwegian scientists should have played a leading part in the study of the endocrine glands of Cetaceans, since Norway not only owns the biggest whaling fleet but is, as we have seen, very poor in cattle, the chief source of hormones in other countries. For similar reasons, Norway and Japan have also made a thorough study of the Cetacean pancreas, an organ that not only secretes enzymes into the intestine (see Chapter 10), but that contains small islands of special tissue (the islands of Langerhans) which secrete the hormone *insulin* into the bloodstream. Insulin regulates the sugar metabolism in the liver and, when the islands do not function properly, too much sugar is found in the blood, and diabetes sets in. By taking regular injections of insulin, diabetics can nowadays live an otherwise normal life. This type of hormone therapy was started in 1922, when Banting and Best managed to isolate chemically pure insulin from the pancreas of cattle, and ever since the demand for insulin has increased by leaps and bounds. Diabetes is, to some extent, a hereditary condition, and the more diabetics are saved and allowed to propagate, the more widespread the condition becomes. Thus it is known that in Canada and Sweden the annual increase in the number of registered diabetics is 14 per cent.

In these circumstances, it is becoming increasingly difficult to meet the ever-growing demand for insulin from normal sources of supply. Of the forty-four member states of the World Health Organization twenty-four reported a shortage of insulin in 1948, amongst them not only Norway and Japan, which lack a pastoral economy, but also France and Switzerland. The great cattle countries of South America, Australia and South Africa can, no doubt, step up their insulin production much further, but the time will probably come when whales will have to be used as well. A Fin Whale has a pancreas weighing an average of seventy-seven pounds, i.e. as much as the glands of about 100 cattle, while the pancreas of a Blue Whale is equivalent in weight to those of 200 cattle. On the other hand, the insulin yield per pound of Cetacean pancreas is only about 50 per cent that of cattle, and the organ must be removed immediately after death and kept refrigerated. For all these reasons, it is still not an economic proposition to embark on the large-scale production of whale insulin. However, the situation may well change, and, if it does, Jorpes (1950) has calculated that the annual Antarctic catch will yield 1,500 tons of pancreas, a quantity sufficient to cover the present insulin needs of a country with a population of about twenty-five million (e.g. Poland, Turkey, or the combined Benelux countries).

No discussion of an animal's metabolism is complete without some mention of the liver, which plays so important a part in it. The liver of Cetaceans is divided into two lobes by a shallow indentation in its lower edge, and it occasionally has an intermediate lobe as well. It is dark red in colour, and in Rorquals it may weigh as much as a ton. It is devoid of a gall bladder (see Chapter 10).

Since the liver plays such an important part in an animal's metabolism, we fully expect its weight to decrease with increase of body mass since, as we have seen, the bigger a given animal the smaller its metabolic rate. However, when we compare the ratio of liver to total body weight of porpoises (average = 3·2 per cent) and dolphins (average = 2·2 per cent) with the corresponding figures for rabbits (4·3 per cent), small dogs (3·3 per cent), large dogs (2·4 per cent), man (2·7 per cent) and horses (1·1 per cent), we may safely say that Odontocetes have an inordinately large liver for their mass. The same is also true of Rorquals and Sperm Whales, which, according to Quiring, have percentages of 0·9 and 1·5 respectively, while the figure for the very much smaller elephant, which might have been expected to have a higher percentage, is only 0·8. Seals (3·9 per cent) have a liver-to-body weight ratio which, size for size, is comparable with those of Cetaceans. The evidence therefore points to the conclusion that aquatic mammals in general and Cetaceans in particular have a very high metabolic rate.

The liver is one of the few Cetacean organs that is regularly processed on factory ships for its yield of vitamin A, which we normally get in butter and other fatty foods and which is an essential part of our diet. Although the quantities of vitamin A found in whales vary from individual to individual (in Blue Whales from 1,000 to 9,000 International Units), the average figures are 4,000 I.U. per gram of liver in Blue Whales, 1,100 I.U. in Fin Whales, and 5,000 I.U. in Sperm Whales. Apart from vitamin A, the liver also contains smaller quantities of the provitamin A, kitol, which is changed into vitamin A by heating. The oil obtained from the blubber, the bones, the flesh and the other organs contains somewhat smaller quantities of vitamin A which, though not lost in the boilers, is destroyed when the fat is hardened, so that it must be put back into margarine.

The liver of whales contains only negligible quantities of vitamin D. We have seen that no equivalent of cod-liver oil (which contains vitamins A and D) can be obtained from whales. On the other hand, the Cetacean liver contains some constituents of vitamin B complex, roughly to the same extent as the liver of cattle, though the constituent used for counteracting anaemia has not yet been discovered. Most mammals, man included, can synthesize their own vitamin D when ultra-violet light falls on the ergosterol in their skin. Now, since ultra-violet rays are absorbed by water fairly close to the surface, Cetaceans must obtain all their requirements of vitamin D from their food and are therefore unable to store large quantities of it in their livers or in other tissues.

Little is known about the presence or needs of vitamin C in Cetaceans, apart from the fact that traces of it have been found in the adrenal glands, and that the epidermis of the Narwhal contains as much as 31·8 mg. per g. of tissue (cf. p. 55). But we do know that the thorax and the abdomen of Rorquals, porpoises and dolphins occasionally contain a peculiar brown fatty tissue which, though Padoa discussed its presence as early as 1929, has not yet been investigated in detail. Now, a similar brown fatty tissue is commonly found in hedgehogs, hamsters, bats and other hibernating animals, where it is known to be capable of storing large quantities of vitamin C. It is therefore quite possible that this tissue plays a similar role in Cetaceans, particularly in Rorquals which eat little or nothing in winter and which would therefore need large reserves of the vitamin.

We have seen how Cetaceans maintain their body temperature, and we must now discuss how they cope with the special problems imposed by their aquatic medium. The first and foremost of these arises from the fact that Cetaceans live in salt water, where thirst can become as oppressive as in the most arid of deserts.

An animal's body consists largely (about 70 per cent) of water with a salt concentration of from about 0·9–3 per cent. If the animal is to stay alive, this concentration must be maintained under all conditions. Aquatic animals without backbones, e.g. crustaceans, squids and water-snails are more fortunate in that, unlike vertebrates, their body fluids have roughly the same salinity as the sea in which they live. Aquatic vertebrates, on the other hand, are quite definitely not so well adapted to their environment. While sharks and rays took to sea water fairly quickly owing to a special adaptation of their blood to the saline environment (urea), bony fishes (*Teleostei*) took 200,000,000 years to do so completely. For a number of reasons not yet perfectly understood, the salinity of the body fluid of vertebrates is very much lower than that of non-vertebrates, and hence well below that of the sea-water. This is true even of marine fishes, which have only a somewhat higher salt concentration than their fresh-water relatives. In a number of places (e.g. the oral epithelium, the intestines, and the gills) the body fluid is separated from the sea-water by only a thin wall which acts as a semi-permeable membrane, i.e. a membrane which will allow water, but not salts, to pass. Since there is a tendency to keep the salt concentration equal on either side of the membrane, water will constantly be withdrawn from a body with a lower salt concentration, thus tending to expose the animal to dehydration in the midst of a sea of water.

Of course, this does not happen in fact, or else bony fish would not have been able to live in the sea for 200,000,000 years. In the first place bony fishes take in water in the form of food and sea-water, thus counteracting the osmotic effects. The sea-water, however, contains more salt than fish blood, and this surplus must be removed. Fish can rid their blood of the extra salt because their gills are provided with special cells for this purpose.

Now, aquatic mammals lack any such special cells and must solve the problem of their low salinity in a different way. The salinity of their blood and other body fluids, though somewhat higher than that of terrestrial mammals, is still considerably lower than that of sea-water, so that whales and dolphins do in fact lose water through the intestines, and other parts of the body. This was shown experimentally by Fetcher in 1940 and in 1942. He pumped just under half a gallon of sea-water into the stomachs of each of two Bottlenose Dolphins and found that after some time, the faeces had a salt concentration equal to that of the blood, so that water must have been withdrawn from the body by the intestines.

From Fetcher's experiments it also emerged that the kidney of these animals can, for very short periods, release urine with a fairly high salt concentration, but from other experiments on whales and dolphins it appears that the salinity of the urine generally corresponds with that of the blood and other body fluids. The kidney cannot therefore be likened to the special salt-excreting cells of bony fishes or to the kidneys of some desert mammals (e.g. the kangaroo rat) whose urine is particularly saline. The only way, therefore, in which Cetaceans can get rid of their surplus salt is to pass large quantities of urine with a consequent waste of water – something these animals which, as we have seen, lose water through their mouths and intestines as it is, and which have to be very parsimonious in their water economy, can ill afford.

Fortunately, not all Cetaceans are equally handicapped in this respect. Those which feed on mammals or birds, like the Killer Whale, and those which feed on fish like most porpoises and dolphins, do not take in highly concentrated salt solutions with their food, and their main problem is their inability to make good any water losses by drinking fresh water as we do. While they cannot help swallowing some sea-water with their food, they do seem to keep it down to an absolute minimum. Seals are said to swallow no sea-water at all, but all we can meanwhile say about Cetaceans is that Mysticetes which feed on krill and those Odontocetes which feed on cuttlefish are in a particularly unfortunate position in that, by eating non-vertebrates, they swallow a diet with the same salinity as sea-water. They will therefore have to pass particularly large quantities of urine and limit all other water losses as much as possible. In this they are greatly helped by the fact that they do not lose water through their skin, which, as we have seen, is devoid of sweat glands. Moreover, the air they inhale is so saturated with water vapour that there is little water loss in the lungs. Irving has calculated that four-fifths of the herring which dolphins eat consists of water, of which a maximum of 20 per cent is lost by the production of faeces and by exhalation, so that 80 per cent can go into the production of urine. In addition, Cetaceans, because of their high metabolic rate, oxydize vast quantities of food with the consequent liberation of large quantities of water, particularly since they oxydize mainly fats whose combustion releases more water than that of carbo-hydrates or proteins. Combustion of fat and minimum evaporation through the skin are probably also the reasons why some desert animals can go without water for such long periods. Clearly, desert and salt water environments are similar in more than one respect.

While various scientists including the physiologist Krogh (1939) agree that Cetaceans must get rid of their surplus salt by the excretion of vast quantities of urine, there is no experimental evidence that they do so in

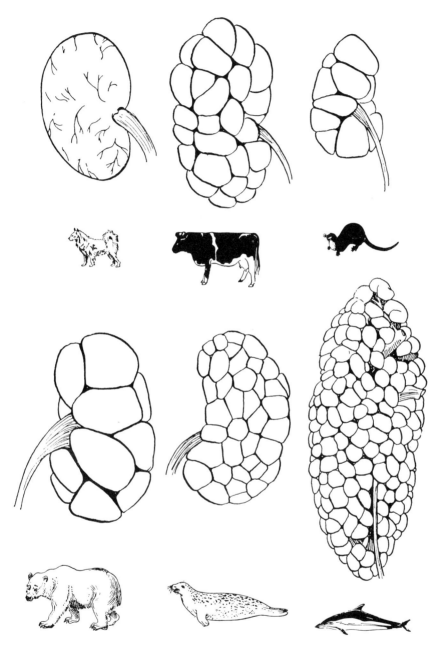

Figure 175. Sketch of the kidneys of a dog, a cow, an otter, a Brown Bear, a seal and a dolphin. (Ellenberger-Baum, 1943, and Anthony, 1922.)

fact. Fetcher's and other scientists' experiments tell us little on this subject, and all we really have to go by is the size and structure of the kidneys.

The ratio of kidney to body weight was found to be 0·44 per cent in two Fin Whales, 0·5 in a Humpback Whale, 1·1 per cent in a Bottlenose Dolphin and a White-sided Dolphin, and 0·84 per cent in several porpoises. While a number of biologists have shown that, with increasing body weight, there is a decrease in the kidney-to-body-weight ratio, comparisons between porpoises and dolphins on the one hand and human beings (0·37 per cent), zebras (0·4 per cent) and a number of deer (0·35 per cent) on the other, or between Rorquals and elephants (0·29 per cent) show clearly that the relative weight of the Cetacean kidney is exceptionally large.

The Cetacean kidneys are found in the same place as they occupy in terrestrial mammals: on the dorsal wall of the abdominal cavity. They are two long, fairly flat and rather broad organs and are surrounded by an outer cortex consisting of connective tissue. From the shape of the cortex alone, we can tell that Cetacean kidneys are divided into a large number of small lobes, called renculi, and thus resemble the calves' kidneys which we buy at the butcher's (Fig. 175). However, the number of such renculi is very much larger in Cetaceans than it is in cattle. Thus the Finless Black Porpoise (*Neomeris phocaenoides*; length 4½ feet) has 150 per kidney, the Common Porpoise 250–300, dolphins about 450, Belugas about 400, and Rorquals about 3,000. Every renculus is really a complete kidney with a cortex, a medulla, a papilla and a calyx of its own. Occasionally, two or more of the lobules become fused, and generally 4–6 of them have a common duct to the ureter which collects all the ducts of all the renculi and finally leaves the kidney on its caudal side. The fine structure and the circulation of the Cetacean kidney do not differ significantly from those of other mammals, some of which also have lobular kidneys instead of the smooth kidneys of man and horses. Lobulated kidneys are found not only in cattle (which have twenty-five to thirty renculi) but also in the rhinoceros, in otters, bears, elephants (eight renculi), seals, sea-lions and sea-cows (see Fig. 175). The dugong, on the other hand, has a smooth kidney.

In seals, the number of lobules is almost as large as in Cetaceans. Now, the greater the number of lobules, the larger the cortex and, since it is in the cortex that saline is removed from the bloodstream, the greater the excretion of urine (it is not quite clear what precisely happens in the medulla, but it seems likely that at least part of the water is returned to the bloodstream here). In animals which excrete a great deal of urine with a salt concentration equal to that of the blood we must therefore expect a strong increase in the cortex, which in turn is evidence that a great deal of urine is being excreted.

This is borne out by the fact that – despite their large mass – Rorquals have a very high kidney-to-body-weight ratio. Unfortunately, other Cetacean kidneys have not yet been studied sufficiently to enable us to come to any definite conclusions on this subject, but it seems reasonable to assume that whales feeding on krill with a salinity equal to that of water will have a larger kidney-to-body-weight ratio than dolphins which feed on fish. In fact, seals with the most highly lobulated kidneys feed mainly on crustaceans. Anderson (1878) found that the eight-foot Gangetic Dolphin which feeds on fresh-water fish and other fresh-water animals with a correspondingly low salt content, had kidneys measuring four inches by three inches, with only about eighty lobules each, while the smaller (five feet) porpoise had kidneys measuring six inches by two inches with 250 lobules each. Unfortunately, nothing is known of the kidneys of the porpoise's own fresh-water relatives.

We conclude this chapter with the brief comment that the Cetacean bladder is comparatively small, even though Yazawa established that that of a Fin Whale can hold $5\frac{1}{2}$ gallons of urine. The urine itself is clear and pale, has an acid reaction and contains the normal mammalian proportion of urea.

12

Distribution and Migration

W E HAVE SEEN that all whales are gluttons which swallow their fatty diet by the ton with never a thought for their figures. But then who can blame them – their table is so often bare. With the onset of winter, when violent gales blow up and the ice floes begin to shift to lower latitudes, a wall is gradually but remorselessly driven between whales and their food and they must migrate to warmer waters. Now while, to us, the tropics conjure up a picture of lush vegetation, most of the blue tropical waters, as a biologist put it, are in fact a 'desert in the sea'.

The colourful wealth of tropical specimens so beloved of all aquarists is a wealth of species and not of individuals. Vast concentrations of plankton, and with them vast concentrations of plankton-feeders, are extremely rare in the tropics. The exceptions are the sea off the Galapagos Islands, the Caribbean Sea, the Arabian Sea (particularly the Gulf of Aden) and a few other places. These waters teem with plankton, fishes and even with squids and, not surprisingly, schools of up to 1,000 dolphins can be found here, together with such predominantly tropical whales as Sei Whales, Bryde's Whales, and female Sperm Whales. Possibly even such true migrating whales as Blue Whales, Fin Whales and Humpback Whales spend at least part of the winter in these regions to supplement their sparse diet.

In any case, to reach these seas, whales have to travel through waters which are extremely barren, and hence the stomachs of whales caught at tropical and sub-tropical whaling stations are nearly always empty. For instance, at Tangalooma, an Australian land station, only one out of 2,000 Humpbacks was found to have food in its stomach, and similar observations are reported from African stations as well. Thus, while migrating whales may get some food on their long journey, they certainly do not get very much, and for at least four months of the year they have to go with almost no food at all. A human being would perish under such

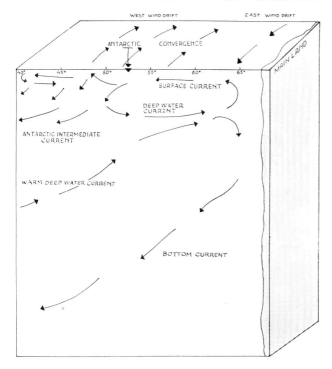

Figure 176. The main ocean currents between 40°S and the Antarctic Continent. (From John after Schubert, 1955)

conditions, but then human beings are built quite differently. Whales are not only the greatest known gluttons; they are also the greatest known fasters. For while such cold-blooded animals as lizards and snakes, and hibernating animals in general, can laze about without food for even longer periods, whales, with their high metabolic rate, have to travel more than 4,000 miles on an empty stomach, some of them pregnant or suckling.

The reader may wonder why whales which can withstand cold so well have to travel for such long distances, when they could simply withdraw to the nearest ice-free sea. The answer is probably that, in order to maintain their temperature, they simply have to move about, and that the heat loss is less in the tropics than in the polar seas. Moreover, newly-born whales have a very thin blubber coat and a relatively large skin surface with a consequently much larger loss of heat, and it is desirable that they should be born in warmer waters. Admittedly, some animals stay in the Arctic or Antarctic throughout the year but it is believed that all of them are either bulls or non-pregnant cows.

Now, since the distribution and migration of animals is largely governed by their food supply, we might look more closely at the distribution of krill, the whales' main source of food, and, in particular, we might find out why krill is so plentiful near the poles and so scarce in the tropics.

All life on earth depends on the presence of plants, since plants alone can synthesize organic matter from carbonic acid and water, with the help of sunlight. Now, while sunlight and water are found throughout the world, carbonic acid is more soluble in cold than in warm water. Thus a bottle of soda water may pop, i.e. release its carbon dioxide, if it is not kept cool enough. Similarly oxygen, which all organisms need for respiration, is more plentiful in cold than in warm water, while, conversely, destructive bacteria prefer warmer temperatures. Consequently, organic matter is more abundant in cold than in warm waters – hence the abundance of vegetable plankton, and animal plankton feeding on it, near the poles. Tropical seas often contain less than 5,000 micro-organisms per gallon of water, while the Antarctic has been known to contain up to 500,000. On the average, the Antarctic is from ten to twenty times as rich in plankton as the tropics.

This difference is not entirely due to the greater abundance of carbonic acid and oxygen, since plants also require nitrates, phosphates and sulphates and can only flourish and propagate their kind if these salts are present in solution. Thus, only where oxygen and carbonic acid occur together with these compounds can we expect the prolific growth of plankton which is known to occur in the polar seas. Now, the distribution of marine salts is mainly governed by sea-currents, and we would therefore do well to examine the nature of these currents in the Antarctic.

The upper 100 fathoms of the Antarctic, which are at 32° F., form an ocean current flowing from the continent to the north (Fig. 176). Along the mainland, a fairly strong and constant easterly wind (Fig. 177) deflects the current to the west, so that it flows in a north-western direction. The direction of the wind farther north – between 40° and 50° S. – becomes westerly and its force much more violent, for these are the 'Roaring Forties' which churn up waves high as houses and which are dreaded by sailors all over the world.

Oceanographers speak of it as the West Wind Drift, and where the cold surface current from the Antarctic meets the West Wind Drift at about 50° to 55° S. (the so-called Antarctic Convergence), the current turns downwards and splits into two (Fig. 176). One branch, the Antarctic intermediate water, flows north at about 400 fathoms below the surface where it can usually be followed right up to the equator, while another branch returns to the Antarctic below 100 fathoms, rises to the surface near the continent, surrenders its heat, and again becomes the original surface current flowing N.W. The current returning to the continent (the so-called deep current) has gained heat because, near the Antarctic

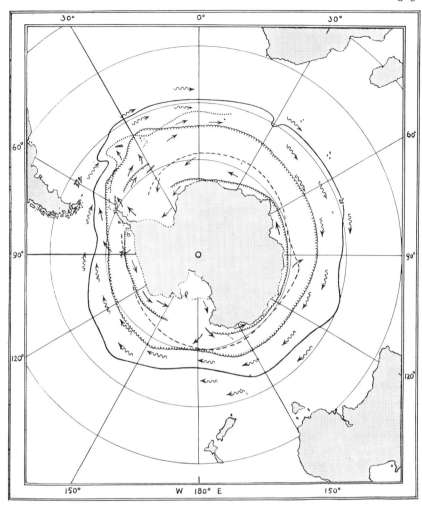

Figure 177. Ocean currents and limits of Antarctic pack ice (see Fig. 178). (Marr, 1956.)

Convergence, a warm current rises up from about 1,500 to about 200 fathoms. This warm deep current from the Atlantic, Indian and Pacific Oceans in the north comes into contact with the cold current returning south, and surrenders some of its heat and a great many salts to it. In this way, the current which returns to the Antarctic at a depth of 100 and 500 fathoms reaches a temperature of up to 34·7° F. and also gains the mineral salts needed for supporting plant life.

Since vegetable plankton which, as we have seen in Chapter 10, consists mainly of diatoms, needs sunlight, it is found chiefly in the upper fifty fathoms, and particularly in the top 5–10 fathoms, where there is, *inter alia*, the greatest concentration of *Fragilariopsis antarctica* (see Fig. 133), krill's chief source of food. For this reason, krill, though present down to 500 fathoms, is most prolific in the top 5–10 fathoms, and it is here that whales chiefly forage for it.

Though plankton is fairly evenly distributed over the entire Southern Ocean, it is particularly abundant south of the Antarctic Convergence. Krill, however, forms an exception because it is rarely found as far to the north as the Antarctic Convergence, where the temperature of the water is apparently too high for it. In the thirties, biologists associated with the Discovery Committee made many long voyages to the Antarctic and collected tens of thousands of plankton, and particularly krill, samples from most areas. The first results were published by F. C. Fraser (1936) in his detailed paper on the distribution and development of the young stages of krill, while Miss Bargmann (1945) dealt with the life history of adolescent and adult krill. In 1956, when, after years of painstaking research, J. W. S. Marr of the National Institute of Oceanography published the first results and a preliminary chart (Fig. 178) of further work on the distribution of krill, experts learnt to their surprise that krill is concentrated in two areas: in the region of the East Wind Drift, i.e. mainly south of 63° S., and in the Weddell Current (Fig. 177). The Weddell Current arises where the East Wind Drift, after having passed the Weddell Sea, is deflected by Graham Land. Augmented by currents from the Pacific, the current then carries vast masses of cold water to the north-east, passes South Georgia, and continues as far as about 55° S. Its influence can be felt as far as 30° E., i.e. about as far as Cape Town. In other words, only between 60° W. and 30° E. and up to 55° S. is krill found in large concentrations, while elsewhere such concentrations are not found beyond 63° S. Moreover, the chart shows clearly that individual concentrations are not uniformly dense, probably as a result of local differences in the direction of the currents and the temperature of the water. One such irregular current, for instance, is found just outside the Ross Sea, where a shelf impedes the return flow of the water.

Whales may reasonably be expected to keep to regions where there are large quantities of krill, and, by and large, this is borne out by the whaling statistics which, *inter alia*, give the number of whales caught per square of ten degrees (Fig. 179). However, the statistics must be regarded with some reserve, for though the annual catch certainly depends on the number of whales in a given area, such factors as weather conditions, distance from the nearest harbour, or intense hunts in past years, may affect the results of whaling expeditions in particular regions. Fortunately, in addition to

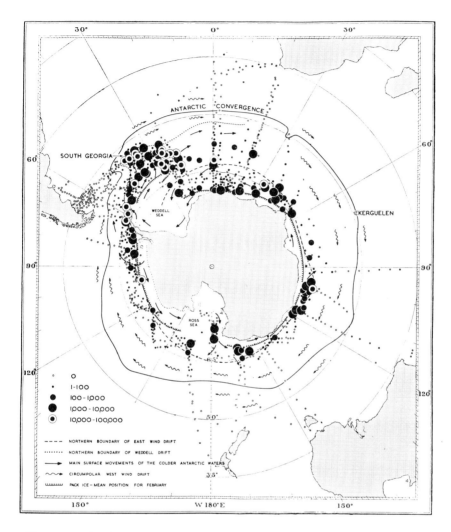

Figure 178. Distribution and concentration of krill in the Antarctic during the present whaling season (January–March). The size of the dots reflects the number of krill caught with one attempt in a plankton net of diameter 1 metre at the surface. (Marr, 1956.)

these statistics, we also have data on the number of whales observed from research ships cruising in various parts of the Antarctic Ocean. The *Norvegia*, for example, patrolled the Antarctic during the entire 1930–1 season, and the *Discovery II* made regular observations from 1933 to 1939, which are compiled in the chart reproduced in Fig. 180.

From all the facts and figures, it appears that by far the largest number of whales occurs between 20° and 70° W. (south of the Atlantic), between 20° and 40° E. (south of Africa), between 80° and 110° E. (south-west of Australia), between 150° and 170° E. (south-east of Australia), between 160° and 140° W. (south-east of New Zealand) and between 110° and 70° W. (south-west of South America). The number of animals caught or observed in the remaining regions and especially between 50° and 70° E. (south of the Indian Ocean) and between 140° and 110° W. (south of the Pacific) is very small, in comparison. From Figs. 178, 179, and 180 we can easily tell that the distribution of krill coincides largely with the distribution of whales, so that we are safe in saying that the latter is governed by the former. Where krill is scarce, whales' stomachs are often empty, and we may assume that most whales merely cross these regions in search of better hunting grounds. According to Beklemishev (1960) the distribution of krill depends on the occurrence of cyclones, causing upwelling water in which the younger stages of krill are brought to the surface. Centres of cyclonic activity appear to coincide with the occurrence of the largest numbers of whales, especially Blue Whales, which feed mainly on young krill.

The above remarks apply primarily to Blue and Fin Whales, whereas the distribution of Humpbacks is known to be confined to even more limited regions south of South America, the Atlantic Ocean, South Africa, West Australia, East Australia and New Zealand (Fig. 181). The explanation for this phenomenon is, as we shall see below, that the Humpback spends the southern winter mainly off the warmer coasts and also migrates up and down these coasts, while Fin and especially Blue Whales seem mainly to winter in, or at least to migrate over, the high sea. Thus the distribution of Humpback Whales is governed not only by the presence of krill but also by the position of the mainland, while that of Blue and Fin Whales probably depends far more on the density of their food. Sperm Whales are caught chiefly to the south of the Atlantic Ocean and south of Africa, but little more is known about their distribution in the Antarctic Ocean.

For statistical purposes, the Antarctic whaling grounds have been divided into six areas (see Fig. 181), viz. Area I: 120° W.–60° W. (the East Pacific Area); Area II: 60° W.–0° (Greenwich) (the Atlantic Area); Area III: 0°–70° E. (the African Area); Area IV: 70° E.–130° E. (the W.

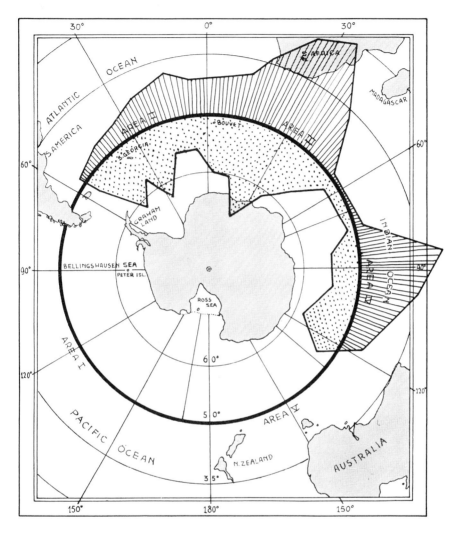

Figure 179. Total number of Blue (hatched) and Fin Whales (dotted) caught in the Antarctic during 1934–1938. Latitude 50° S is taken as the axis, and each degree N or S represents 1,000 animals. (From data by Mackintosh, 1942.)

Australian Area); Area V: 130° E.–170° W. (the E. Australian Area); and Area VI: 170° W.–120° W. (the W. Pacific Area, a recent sub-division of the former Area I, i.e. 170° W.–60° W.). In the accompanying figures, the old division is still observed. The distribution of whales in these areas is far from uniform. We have seen that Humpbacks keep to certain regions, and Sperm Whales, while found in all areas, are caught chiefly at 25° W., 30°–50° W., and 120°–130° E. Starting from Area II, the percentage of captured Blue Whales increases as we move farther east, while that of Fin Whales decreases. Thus, from 1947 to 1954, the percentage of captured Blue Whales was 25 in Area II, 33 in Area III, 36 in Area IV, and 41 in Area V. These figures are corroborated by observations made aboard the *Discovery II*, and it would appear that the differences between the various areas are due more to natural factors than to man's intervention. Possibly the explanation must be sought in ice-conditions, since it is a known fact that most Blue Whales keep to drifting ice while the majority of Fin Whales is found just outside it. Prof. Ruud has estimated that, in the ice, Blue Whales represent 50 per cent, and outside the ice only 10 per cent of the total Blue and Fin Whale population. The causes of this phenomenon are not known.

The statistics also show clearly that the oil yield decreases as we move east from Area II. Now, the oil yield of whales is expressed in barrels per Blue Whale Unit, a barrel being one-sixth of a ton, and a B.W.U. being one Blue Whale, or two Fin Whales, or 2·5 Humpback Whales, or six Sei Whales, all irrespective of length. If we look at the figures for the years after the Second World War, we find an average yield of 135 barrels per B.W.U. in Area II and also in the eastern part of Area I, of 121 barrels in Area III, of 117 barrels in Area IV and of 116 barrels in Area V. As Area I has only been reopened to whalers since the 1955–6 season, the figures for the Pacific part of Area I will not be dealt with here.

The statistical results, in themselves, do not entitle us to assert that whales get fatter towards the Western areas, since they represent weekly totals of oil gained from all whales except Sperm Whales. Now, it is not absolutely certain that Blue Whales are always twice as fat as Fin Whales, as the definition of the B.W.U. might have misled one into thinking.[1] Thus if two Fin Whales were to yield more oil than one Blue Whale, the decrease in the number of barrels per B.W.U. from west to east may well be due to the known fact that the percentage of Blue Whales increases in

[1] In the absence of adequate data, various experts believe that, at least in the second half of the season, Blue Whales do in fact yield roughly twice as much oil as Fin Whales. When the results of Jonsgård's recent investigation into the oil yields of individual Rorquals are completed, we may know more about this subject, even though he worked with specimens caught by Norwegian land stations, which may not be representative of Antarctic Rorquals.

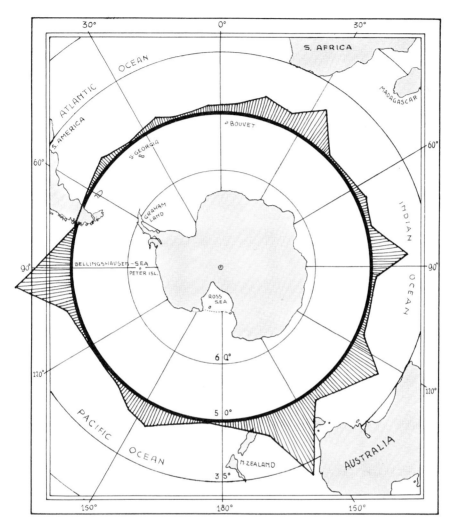

Figure 180. Average number of Blue, Fin and Humpback Whales spotted per day by the Discovery II during 1933–1939. Latitude 50° S is taken as the axis. (From data by Mackintosh, 1942.)

that direction. Since, however, the number of Blue Whales caught annually has decreased so greatly over the past fifteen years that nowadays Blue Whales represent a mere 4–5 per cent of the total catch, this factor cannot influence the yield to any large extent. It might also be argued that the statistics are affected by characteristic differences in length between specimens in different zones, since the bigger a whale the larger, of course, its yield of oil, a factor which the definition of the B.W.U. does not take into consideration. However, no such marked differences have ever been recorded.

To overcome all these statistical difficulties, C. E. Ash, the *Balaena* chemist, has tackled the entire subject in a completely fresh manner. He expressed the yield in barrels per total weight of whale instead of per B.W.U., the weight having first been calculated from the length by using a formula which was established as a result of a great number of measurements and weighings, largely carried out by Japanese biologists. In this way, Ash calculated that, for the years 1947 to 1951, the oil yield per total weight was: Area II – 24·6 per cent, Area III – 22·5 per cent, Area IV – 22·8 per cent, and Area V – 21·2 per cent – a significant decrease from west to east. (Though different factory ships manage to extract different quantities of oil from the B.W.U., due to differences in technique, these differences do not affect Ash's figures to any significant extent.)

There is other evidence as well that whales in the western zones are fatter than those in the east, viz. the chemical composition of their oil. Whale-oil, like most fats, is a compound of glycerol and fatty acids. Now, fatty acids are either saturated (e.g. palmitic acid) or else unsaturated (e.g. oleic acid) when they can add on other hydrogen atoms until saturation is reached. The extent to which unsaturated acids are present in oils or fats is given by their iodine number or value, which expresses the number of grams of iodine absorbed by 100 grams of oil or fat under certain conditions. Thus the higher the iodine number, the greater the percentage of unsaturated fatty acids.

Now, the Norwegian chemist, J. Lund, who has made a very long and detailed study of the iodine number of the oil obtained from various whaling areas, discovered, *inter alia*, that marked differences in this number are found in various parts of the North Atlantic (Norway, Spain, Newfoundland). Such differences are also found in the Antarctic, where the iodine number decreases perceptibly from west to east. Moreover, Lund established that the iodine number in a given area increases in the course of the season as the whales grow fatter. A low iodine number, therefore, seems to go hand in hand with a low oil yield and from it we can thus adduce additional evidence that whales have less fat in the east than in the west. Another factor influencing these differences may well be

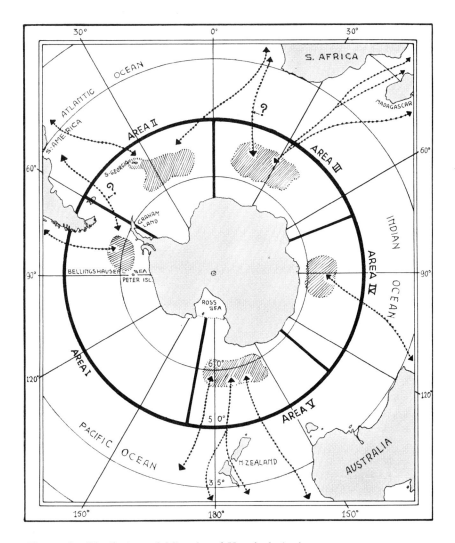

Figure 181. Distribution and Migration of Humpbacks in the Antarctic. (From data by the National Institute of Oceanography, England.)

fluctuations in the composition of krill fat, since experiments on pigs have shown that the iodine number of bacon is largely influenced by their diet. Bacon which is produced on a diet of carbohydrates is more highly saturated, and hence has a lower iodine number, than bacon produced on a fatty diet. Moreover, the iodine number is further influenced by the chemical composition of the particular fat an animal eats. Unfortunately, we do not know sufficient about regional variations of krill fat to come to any definite conclusion on its effects on the iodine number of whale-oil.

A good way to judge the relative fatness of a whale would clearly be to measure the actual thickness of its blubber. We have seen that by expressing the yield in barrels per B.W.U., such factors as length and variations in processing from factory ship to factory ship are completely ignored. Now, from the statistics published annually in the Norwegian *Hvalfangst Tidende* it emerges clearly that the oil output of different factory ships varies greatly. Thus, during the 1955–6 season, factory ships operating in the Antarctic produced an average of 121·6 barrels per B.W.U., the maximum being 152·1, and the minimum 100·9 barrels per B.W.U., and if we look at the individual figures for the past ten years, we see that, while the yield of a given ship varies from year to year, the position of most ships in the list remains fairly constant. Moreover, as the differences in the number of units caught by individual ships have decreased, the differences in the oil output have become more pronounced.

One of the main reasons for these individual differences between ships is the international catch limit imposed on all ships operating in Antarctic waters. Once the total permissible number of whales has been caught the season is closed, and every expedition tries to get as large a share of the quota as possible for itself. The number and the engine capacity of catchers per factory ship has increased steadily since the Second World War (see Fig. 217). Some of the fluctuations shown in Fig. 217 are due to the fact that, during some seasons, whaling companies agreed to limit the size of their catcher fleet. The greater the number of catchers the keener the competition, even amongst the boats belonging to one and the same company, with a consequent lack of discrimination in selecting the catch. As a result a greater proportion of the catch consists of small animals and the yield per B.W.U. drops. Furthermore, if a maximum number of whales must be caught and processed in minimum time, whalers may set to work with less attention to detail and a further drop in yield ensues, particularly since dead whales may not be left in the water for more than thirty-three hours.

Clearly, therefore, the annual statistics published in Sandjeford do not accurately reflect the actual fatness of whales in the different zones or during different seasons, and it is therefore encouraging that the Dutch

Whale Research Group T.N.O. of Amsterdam has been studying this problem for a number of years. With the assistance of Norwegian, English and South African whalers, scientists and institutions, the Dutch team has been able to collect a wealth of data which has been analysed by a number of biologists and mathematicians from the Amsterdam Mathematical Institute. The findings so far have not been particularly striking and the results have been mainly negative. However, from them scientists have discovered what mistakes to avoid in the future choice of specimens, representative body regions and measuring techniques, and though it will take many years before we can hope to have more positive information, it has already emerged that the thickness of the blubber may vary from year to year, probably depending on the abundance of food. Similar observations were made by E. Vangstein, the Director of International Whaling Statistics in Sandjeford, when he investigated the causes of the high yield in the 1951–2 and 1953–4 seasons. (Measurements of blubber thickness may help to remedy shortcomings in processing techniques on certain factory ships, and C. E. Ash has done a great deal of research on this subject.)

Having discussed the distribution of whales in the Antarctic, we shall now look more closely at their migratory habits. We have seen that krill occurs mainly in a certain area surrounding the Antarctic continent and in the Weddell Current. In the summer, these regions are only partly covered with drifting ice, since, towards autumn, the impenetrable limit of polar pack ice is near the mainland (see Fig. 177), except in the Weddell Sea where it extends to about 63° S. In summer, therefore, the pack ice does not keep the whales from their krill, but as the year goes on the ice spreads farther north, and by November (the end of the winter), for instance, it will have reached about 60° S. off Cape Horn or 55° S. south of Cape Town. It therefore stretches almost as far as the Antarctic Convergence, and cuts off all the normal krill concentrations from the whales, the overwhelming majority of which then migrate to the north.

While we know that much, we know little about their final destination or routes, though the answer to this question is important both scientifically and also for practical reasons since, once we know the geographical origin of whales caught by the various tropical and sub-tropical land stations, we should be able to tell to what extent the population of a given Antarctic zone is being reduced in and out of the Antarctic, and, if need be, we could take protective steps. Moreover, if we knew that whales from a particular zone return to it year after year, we could apply regional, rather than total, sanctions.

That whales migrate to the tropics and return to the Antarctic, though not necessarily to the same zone, appears clearly from the fact that they are caught in the Antarctic in the summer alone, and in the tropics only in the winter. Moreover, their migrations have been observed off the South American and Australian coasts, and investigations of their stomach contents and the thickness of their blubber have shown that their diet is largely of Antarctic origin, and that their blubber is thinner in the tropics. Also, the presence of such parasites as barnacles and *Penella* and the peculiar scars (probably inflicted by lampreys which attack whales exclusively in warmer waters) (see Chapter 2) are clear evidence of a sojourn in the tropics, while the film of diatoms (especially *Cocconeis ceticola* Nelson; see also Chapter 2) found particularly on Blue and Fin Whales and occasionally on other species, is clear evidence of a long stay in the Antarctic. Diatom films, which disappear quickly in the tropics, take at least one month to form, and from their thickness together with the presence or absence of spores we can often determine the duration of a whale's stay in the Antarctic more precisely.

All the above is, however, no more than circumstantial evidence, and for direct proof we must use a technique that has long been applied to the study of the migration of fish, birds and bats, i.e. marking. But before we discuss this technique, we must first mention a recent, promising, departure in the study of the migration of whales and, particularly, of the question where they spend the winter: the decision, in 1951, by the National Institute of Oceanography to enlist the Royal Navy and the Merchant Navy as whale spotters. Three years later, the Dutch Whale Research Group T.N.O. began a similar project by calling on all Dutch seamen to report any whales they may have spotted on their journeys, and to use special forms for the purpose. Thanks to the co-operation not only of the Royal Dutch Navy and of all Dutch shipping companies, but of all the crews as well, 4,500 completed forms, reporting about 3,500 separate observations, were received in the first three years, and experts are at present at work interpreting them. Since some regions are crossed by ships more frequently than others, the number of whales reported is converted by a factor based on the number of daylight hours a particular ship has spent in a given region.

The National Institute of Oceanography and also the Dutch Whale Research Group have so far published no more than preliminary reports, from which it appears, *inter alia*, that at least during certain parts of the year whales congregate in particular regions. Thus, large concentrations of Rorquals were found in the Arabian Sea, the Gulf of Aden, off Dakar, in the Caribbean, and near Newfoundland, no doubt because, as we have seen, these areas are particularly rich in food. Capt. Mörzer Bruins reported the presence of large schools of dolphins in the Gulf of Aden as well, and Dutch sailors have described similar concentrations of dolphins off the coast of Venezuela, where larger whales also have apparently occurred in such profusion that a promontory of Margarita Island was christened Punta Ballena.

Sperm Whales, on the other hand, seem to be scarce both in the Caribbean and off Newfoundland, and to congregate in the eastern part of the N. Atlantic, probably because large schools of cows usually keep to the Azores, which thus form a base to which the bulls return every year.

Once the data are interpreted in more detail, we shall undoubtedly know more about the migratory habits of whales, even though a great deal of further research must be done, particularly in areas not usually visited by ships. Important data from New Zealand and Polynesia are likely to be provided by the special team of observers working under W. H. Dawbin (Sydney). In the U.S.A., J. J. Woodburn (Philadelphia) has initiated research similar to that carried out by British and Dutch scientists.

The oldest report on the migration of Rorquals, based on the recognition of marks, dates back to the latter half of the nineteenth century, when Blue Whales caught at Norwegian whaling stations were found to carry fragments of American bomb-lances. In other words, Rorquals migrating north along the American coast may cross over to Norway. Similar incidental observations have been made ever since, of which the most fascinating is probably the discovery in the stomach of a whale killed off New Zealand, on 23rd June, 1954, of a tin of tooth-powder containing a piece of paper with the name and address of one of the crew of the *Willem Barendsz*. The tin had been thrown overboard during the 1953–4 Antarctic season at about 40° E., and the whale must, therefore, have done a great deal of cruising before it was caught.

The systematic marking of whales was begun in about 1920 by the Norwegian biologist, Hjort, who fired copper lances into their blubber, both off the Faroes and off South Georgia. His first attempts were, however, unsuccessful, for it appeared that either because infections set in or else because the blubber shifted across the muscles (see Chapter 11), the marks disappeared from the skin and were lost. The Discovery Committee then developed a new type of mark which cannot be ejected by the body and which was found not to have deteriorated even after being lodged in a whale for twenty-five years. It is a tube, about $10\frac{1}{2}$ inches long, made of stainless steel. The tube has a blunt head (Fig. 182), and is fired from a special gun or from a modified harpoon gun, at a range of, preferably, no more than sixty-five feet. Instructions are stamped on it, and the finder is promised a reward of £1 if the mark and details of its discovery are sent

to the National Institute of Oceanography, which notes all the details and, if requested to do so, returns the mark to the finder.

Whales do not show any signs of reacting to the marks, probably because, to them, they are mere pinpricks. The marks do not damage vital parts and the danger of infection with stainless steel marks is practically nil, particularly since they are nowadays coated with penicillin ointment.

Generally, marks lodge in the large mass of dorsal muscles, where they are so well hidden that most of them are overlooked during the quick processing operations aboard modern whalers. Subsequently, they may be recovered from the boilers, but of the 5,063 marks fired by the *William Scoresby* from 1934 to 1939, only about 370 have been recovered so far, and it seems unlikely that a great many more will be found in the future. The use of mine and magnetic detectors, Geiger counters, etc., for discovering whether a dead whale has a mark lodged in it, have all proved abortive, and not one of Prof. Ruud's special streamer marks, which were provided with conspicuous strands of brightly-coloured nylon threads, has ever been recovered.

The marking of whales is an expensive business, in which the price of every mark ($£2$) is insignificant compared with the enormous cost of a special marking expedition. For this reason, the National Institute of Oceanography was unable to continue the valuable work it began in the thirties. However, it appeared that a good deal of marking could be done from ordinary catchers which often reach the Antarctic before the opening of the season, either for reconnaissance or for Sperm Whale hunting which has no closed season. In this way, Norwegian, Dutch, Australian, Japanese and Russian catchers have been marking whales ever since the last war.

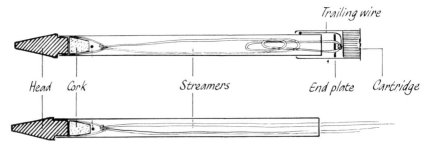

Figure 182. (*Top of page*) Whale mark issued by the National Institute of Oceanography, England. (*Below*) Streamer-mark used by the Enern *during her 1953 expedition.*

During the same time, W. H. Dawbin, calling in the help of small, locally chartered vessels, managed to mark a great number of Humpback Whales together with a few Fin Whales off New Zealand and some South Sea islands. R. Clarke marked whales, and particularly Sperm Whales, off Peru. Russia and Japan use marks of their own, and the Japanese have so far marked well over 1,000 whales in the North Pacific alone. With financial assistance from all Norwegian, British and Dutch whaling companies, it was possible to send the catcher *Enern* on an Antarctic marking expedition towards the end of 1953. On board were Prof. J. T. Ruud and his assistant, P. Øynes, R. Clarke of the National Institute of Oceanography, and the director of the Dutch T.N.O. group, W. L. van Utrecht. The *Enern* sailed from Cape Town via the Antarctic to South Georgia, marking 110 whales on its way. In 1954, on a second journey just before the opening of the season, 243 whales were marked in twenty-eight days, as weather conditions were better that time.

It is a very great pity indeed that funds for large-scale marking expeditions are no longer set aside by the various countries. Marking is not only of paramount scientific importance, but, since it tells us more about the distribution, migration, life span, and perhaps also about the size of the whale population, it is of great commercial value, as well. In Chapter 14, we shall see how life span and size of population affect the determination of the annual catch limit. Meanwhile, we shall discuss the effects of marking on the study of the distribution and migration of whales in the southern hemisphere.

The results of the first survey were published in three reports by Rayner in 1940 and 1948, and by Brown in 1954, from which it emerged that a number of Humpback Whales and three Fin Whales marked in the Antarctic had been caught at tropical and sub-tropical land stations. Two Fin Whales marked in the sub-tropics were caught in Antarctic waters. While this is slender evidence, it nevertheless is positive proof for our assumption that Antarctic whales spend the winter in the tropics. The survey has further shown that Humpbacks occur in five distinct Antarctic populations (see Fig. 181), and that individuals usually return to their respective zones, though, very occasionally, an animal from Area II, having wintered off the West African coast, may return to Area III, and that there is a similar, occasional, interchange between the Australian and New Zealand stocks, as well as between Areas V and I (Bellinghausen Sea). There are two separate Australian Humpback stocks, one off the East Coast and one off the West Coast of the continent. In the 1958-9 season, a mark fired off the East Coast was for the first time returned from a whale caught in Area IV. Fig. 183 shows clearly that Humpbacks migrate along the coasts of the continents, possibly because

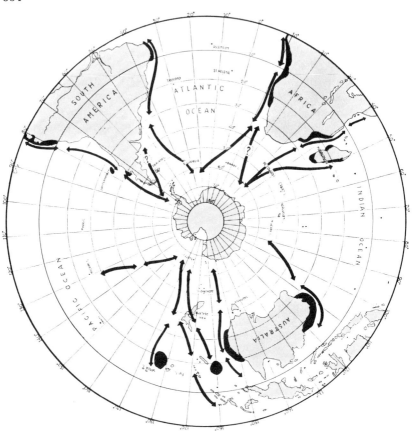

Figure 183. Migratory routes of Humpbacks and main hunting grounds in warm Southern waters. (From data by the National Institute of Oceanography.)

it is desirable for the young to be born in shallow water. The figure, which is based on the whaling statistics, is also corroborated by observations from ships (see p. 330). The whale, which was widely reported not only to have splashed curious spectators who had rowed out to watch in small boats, and to have rammed a pier, but also to have given birth to a calf in Durban Harbour (September 1956), is therefore likely to have been a Humpback – particularly since it was said to have been covered with what appear to have been barnacles. In addition to being found off the continental coasts, Antarctic Humpbacks can also be found in large numbers off the Pacific islands right up to Hawaii, where in winter they have often been observed with their calves. W. H. Dawbin, who has collected a great deal of information on the migration of Humpbacks, concluded that schools from the New Zealand sector migrate north mainly along the east coast, and back mainly along the west coasts of the islands. This phenomenon has not yet been fully explained.

Blue and Fin Whales, whose distribution is probably much more dependent on the abundance of their food supply, do not occur in such closed communities, and there is, therefore, a much greater interchange of individual whales from the various zones. Nevertheless, it seems clear from Brown's chart that the vast majority of these animals remain faithful to their Antarctic home grounds, and return there year after year. Thus, in 1952, seven marks dated between 1935 and 1938, were recovered from Antarctic Rorquals in almost the same spots in which they had originally been fired. Naturally, the longer the interval between the firing and the recovery of a given mark, the greater the chance of the whale having shifted its habitat, but the greatest shift so far observed in Fin Whales is 50° E. or W. In other words, while some animals may occasionally move to an adjacent area, there are no recorded reports of movements across an entire area into one that is not contiguous. Blue Whales seem to be a little more cosmopolitan, for shifts of up to 87° (i.e. passing two area limits) have been observed. Interchanges of Blue and Fin Whales have been reported between Areas I and II, III and IV, and to a lesser extent IV and V, but hardly ever between Areas II and III, where the Greenwich meridian seems to act as an insurmountable barrier! However, there is one recorded incident of a Blue Whale covering 1,900 miles between Areas II and IV in forty-seven days.

However, the shift from one area to another rarely occurs in the Antarctic itself, for marks recovered in the same year in which they were fired always show that what shifts there are take place over small distances. Thus, whenever a given whale moves to another zone, it does so only after having spent one or more winters in the tropics, where it probably joins a congener or a school from a neighbouring sector. The precise winter quarters and migratory routes of Blue and Fin Whales are, as we have seen, not adequately known, but it is hoped that when all the observations mentioned on p. 330 are fully analysed, we shall understand the subject much better. It seems likely that, by and large, they migrate at least partly to areas rich in food, e.g. the N.W. coast of Africa, the Bay of Bengal and the Gulf of Aden, and that their routes take them not so close to the mainland as those of the Humpback. This applies particularly to Blue Whales; some sub-tropical whaling stations in South Africa and South America still manage to capture Fin Whales. However, their catch consists mainly of young animals. Mature individuals seem to avoid coastal waters altogether, and tropical whaling stations (e.g. Gaboon) rarely catch any Fin Whales at all. Blue Whales, on the other hand, are often observed off

Tristan da Cunha in the southern winter, and it is there that the Southern Right Whale cow seems to give birth to her young.

Figures of the annual catch, as well as blubber measurements, indicate that the migrations of Blue, Fin and Humpback Whales do not coincide, and that the Fin Whale returns to the Antarctic a little later in the spring than the Blue Whale. Thus the percentage of Fin Whales caught increases perceptibly as the Antarctic season advances. Air temperature, too, seems to be a factor influencing the time of migration. For instance, if the average September air temperature over South Georgia is lower than $32 \cdot 4°$ F., Blue Whales will pass the island earlier than Fin Whales, but if it is above $32 \cdot 9°$ F., Fin Whales will pass by first. During the first half of January, i.e. just before they begin to migrate north, the number of Humpbacks in the Antarctic seems to be at its maximum. There are indications that cows accompanied by calves, and thus unable to keep up with their congeners, arrive in the Antarctic somewhat later and that they possibly stay there somewhat longer. In any case, Chittleborough states that pregnant Humpback cows, at least, are late in passing the Australian coast in the course of their migration to the north.

The percentage of the catch represented by pregnant Blue and Fin Whale cows decreases as the season advances, a phenomenon that is the more striking since at the start of the season, when the embryos are small, cases of pregnancy might be more easily overlooked by the inspectors. While the explanation might be that pregnant cows arrive or leave earlier, it seems more likely that the drop in the percentage is due to the fact that, as the season advances, cows wean their calves to an increasing extent, at which stage they may be caught. In this way, the percentage catch of 'resting' cows is increased, and that of pregnant cows drops automatically. There are indications that pregnant Fin Whale cows stay longer in the Antarctic than pregnant Blue Whale cows, possibly because the former give birth to their calves about one month later than the other.

The increase in the percentage of immature animals caught as the Antarctic season advances is probably due to their late arrival or late departure, but may also be caused by the fact that they have just grown big enough to exceed the size limit.

It has already been pointed out that not the entire Antarctic population migrates into warm waters during the winter season. A small part, at least, appears to stay behind at about 50° S. On the other hand, recent observations seem to suggest that during the summer season not all Rorquals migrate into the cold waters of the Antarctic. A certain number of them obviously stay behind in the temperate waters of about 40° S., or even closer to the equator.

So far we have restricted our remarks to the migration of Humpback,

Blue and Fin Whales in the southern hemisphere, and we shall now examine their migratory habits in the northern hemisphere. Now, all three species are found over all the oceans of the world, though not to the same extent. Thus we have seen that, in tropical and sub-tropical waters, Humpbacks keep much closer to the coasts of the continents than Blue and Fin Whales – no doubt one of the reasons why Humpbacks have been caught in large number in Gaboon (Equatorial Africa) – and why a number of them have been observed in Indonesian waters.

The fact that Antarctic Blue and Fin Whales cross the equator is borne out by strandings in Ceylon and on the Indian coast, by observations in the Arabian Sea, and by some of the records made by Dutch officers who, reported, *inter alia*, that on 23rd September, 1953, 30–50 Blue Whales in groups of 3–4 were seen over an area of about ten square miles in the Indian Ocean (at 11°15′ N. and 60°20′ E.) and that the love-play of a school of ten Fin Whales was observed on 9th June, 1955, at 18°13′ N. and 20°12′ W. (in the Atlantic). We are entitled to assume that all these whales were of Antarctic origin, for Arctic Rorquals are much farther north at that time. It is even highly probable that South Atlantic Rorquals spend the (southern) winter in the Caribbean and off the N. African coast.

It is generally held that southern Humpback, Blue and Fin Whales form a population distinct from their Northern counterparts. While both groups can be found in warm waters every year, their chances of inter-mingling are small, since at least the majority visit these waters at appointed times of the year. During the winter, most of the northern whales are in warm waters and most of the southern whales in the Antarctic, while in summer (winter in the Southern hemisphere) a great number of the northern whales are in the Arctic and the majority of the southern whales move up towards the equator. However, occasional interchanges seem, nevertheless, to occur and Zenkovich (1956), who believes that such inter-changes are more common in the Pacific than in the Atlantic, bases this opinion, *inter alia*, on the fact that a Rorqual caught off New Zealand was found to be covered with northern whale lice (amphipods) while southern parasites (*Penella* included) have been found on Blue and Fin Whales caught off Japan, the Kuril Islands and Kamchatka.

Despite the fact that the two groups are segregated, they show no external or internal differences, so that there is no reason to refer to separate strains. However, they do show certain behavioural differences. We have seen that Antarctic Blue Whales keep mainly inside, and Antarctic Fin Whales mainly outside, the zone of drifting ice, and while their counter-parts in the N. Atlantic seem to behave similarly, those in the N. Pacific do not. Japanese scientists have gone very thoroughly into this subject, and in 1955 Omura reported that, though Blue Whales are never found

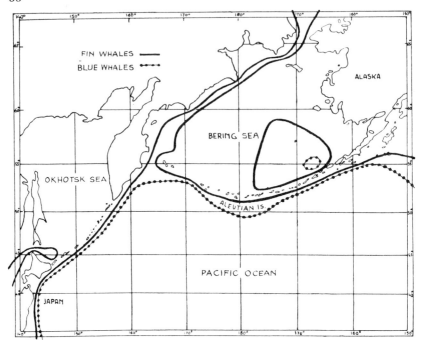

Figure 184. Northern limits of Blue and Fin Whales in the N. Pacific. (Omura, 1955.)

north of the Aleutian and the Komandorskie Islands, Fin Whales penetrate deep into the Bering Sea (Fig. 184). The reasons for this difference in behaviour are not yet plain, but must probably be sought in the distribution of their food.

It is moreover believed that the Antarctic, in addition to being larger, is also more plentiful in plankton supplies than the Arctic, and that Antarctic plankton is richer in fats. In the absence of more detailed investigations, scientists base this opinion on the fact that northern whales are generally smaller and thinner than their southern counterparts.

A. Jonsgård, Prof. Ruud's chief collaborator, who made a special study of this subject, found that the average length of Fin Whales caught in the Antarctic was 68 feet for males and 72 feet for females, the corresponding figures in the N. Atlantic being 60 feet and 66 feet, and in the North Pacific 59 feet and 64 feet. Antarctic Fin Whales were found to attain sexual maturity at 63 feet and 66·5 feet respectively and, assuming that their northern counterparts attain it at the same age, the corresponding figures for the N. Atlantic and the N. Pacific are only 58 feet and 61 feet

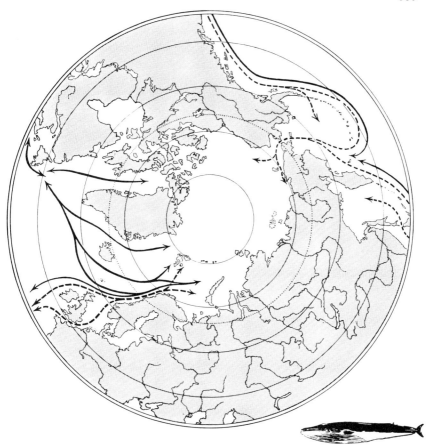

Figure 185. Coastal migration of Blue Whales (black lines) and Fin Whales (dotted lines) in the northern hemisphere. Little is known about their migrations across the open seas. In these waters, the migrations of Humpback and Biscayan Right Whales largely correspond with that of Blue Whales, but in the Pacific they correspond with that of Fin Whales.

respectively. These findings were confirmed by Japanese biologists. Jonsgård also found that during the summer of 1952, the oil yield expressed in barrels per B.W.U. was: Norway, 61–66; British Columbia, 71; and Kamchatka, 64; as against the Antarctic average of about 120. The hypothesis that all these differences are due to the food situation is borne out by observations that Blue, Sei and Sperm Whales in the N. Pacific are all correspondingly smaller at sexual maturity than their southern counterparts.

Northern and southern Rorquals differ not only in physical development but probably in migratory habits as well, since the northern groups appear to keep much closer to the coast. Thus northern Blue Whales migrate north along the American East coast, past Newfoundland and Labrador, and then proceed through the Davis Strait to Baffin Bay, or else cross over to Spitsbergen, with some whales taking the Denmark Strait and others travelling between Iceland and the Faeroe Islands and between the Faeroes and Scotland (Fig. 185). The last group, in particular, passes the Norwegian coast where, formerly, Rorquals were caught in fairly large numbers. These whales probably migrate south along more or less the same routes, and these routes are also taken by Humpbacks in the western N. Atlantic. Thus some Rorquals, on their way to and from America, have to pass the northern coasts of Europe. As for those on the eastern side of the N. Atlantic, it is known that Humpbacks avoid the North Sea and the Channel and swim round Britain on their journeys north and southwards. Thus, while no Humpback has ever stranded in Holland or Belgium, some Humpbacks have in fact been washed ashore in Britain. This is also true of Blue Whales, though they have very occasionally been spotted in the North Sea. On the other hand, more than forty-five Fin Whales have been reported stranded on the Dutch coast alone, and strandings are more common still in Britain. Fin Whales probably take to the North Sea more readily because their diet includes herring which is plentiful in that sea. Apart from that, we really know very little about their N. Atlantic migratory route, and it seems likely that at least some of them keep clear of the coasts.

There are quite a number of indications that some Rorquals do not engage in long distance migration even in the North Atlantic. During the summer season a significant number of Rorquals have been observed still in waters between 30° and 40° N., whereas during the winter the northern limit of the population lies at about 50° N., although animals have occasionally been observed farther north. During the winter, the southern limit lies at about 10° N.

Distinct migratory routes have also been discovered in the N. Pacific (Fig. 185). Japanese observers state that Fin Whales migrate along the Japanese East coast and also through the Sea of Japan, while other Rorquals stick almost exclusively to the East coast route. From quite a number of data, clear indications appear that at least part of the Western stocks of North Pacific Rorquals migrate into the Indian Ocean by the Malacca Strait or Sunda Strait route. Others obviously winter in Indonesian waters, where Antarctic whales can be observed as well. While all Pacific Fin Whales look the same, Japanese scientists, and particularly Dr. Fujino, have shown that N.W. Fin Whales can be distinguished from their N.E. congeners by their blood groups. Fin Whales seem to have about twelve different blood groups, one of which was found to be par-

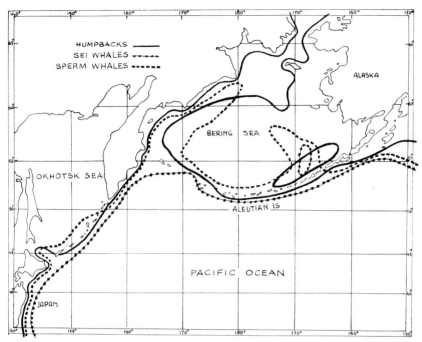

Figure 186. Northern limits of Humpbacks, Sei Whales, and Sperm Whales in the N. Pacific.
(Omura, 1955.)

ticularly marked in, for instance, animals caught off Kamchatka, but absent in those caught N.E. of the Aleutian Islands. This may indicate that, although some interchanges between the N.E. and N.W. groups in the Bering Sea have been established by marks, such interchanges are rare, and that, in the autumn, each group generally returns south along a specific route. The same is probably true of Blue Whales and Humpbacks as well, although Japanese observers found that Humpbacks occasionally cross over from the American to the Asian side, and vice versa.

Like the three Rorquals we have discussed, the Sei Whale is a true cosmopolitan and frequents all seas, except the very cold ones. While it moves towards the poles in the spring, and towards the equator in the autumn, the Sei Whale keeps well clear of the ice, and is rarely found north of the Aleutian Islands (Fig. 186) or south of South Georgia. As a rule, it reaches the Antarctic fairly late, and leaves it fairly early, so that no Sei Whale has ever been found completely covered with a film of diatoms (which takes at least six weeks to form). In some seasons (e.g. 1957–8 and 1958–9) an exceptional number of Sei Whales were caught in the Antarctic, probably because they migrated farther south than they usually do. Apparently not all Sei Whales participate in this migration, because Dawbin observed that schools of Sei Whales can be observed throughout the year between 35°–37° S. and 174°–176° E. Off the Norwegian coast (where Sei Whales generally occur together with coalfish, which the Norwegians call *seje* – hence the whale's name) they manage to reach higher latitudes because the Gulf Stream increases the temperature of the water, but even here they keep outside the Arctic proper. Very little is known of the Sei Whale's actual migratory route, except that it seems to avoid the North Sea, so much so that only one individual was ever found stranded on the Dutch coast (the former Zuider Zee – 1811).

Bryde's Whale which, until quite recently, was invariably confused with the Sei Whale, probably has a larger distribution in waters between 30° N. and 30° S. than investigations so far have definitely established. It has been caught and observed off the East African and the West African coast, south of 30° N., in the Bay of Bengal, in the Strait of Malacca, off the West coast of Borneo, off the Bonin Islands, off South California, once off Grenada and once (12th July, 1959) off Curaçao (both West Indies), and also off Australia, where three specimens were caught in Shark Bay (October 1958). Migrations north or south have never been established.

Little Piked Whales and Biscayan Right Whales have a very similar geographical distribution to Blue and Fin Whales. Both occur in all seas, and both migrate to warmer waters in the autumn and back to colder waters in the spring, but the Little Piked Whale penetrates much farther into the ice than the Biscayan Right Whale. In fact, these miniature Rorquals are believed to venture farther into the polar drifting ice than any other Balaenopterids (see Figs. 223 and 224). However, the behaviour of Little Piked Whales and Biscayan Right Whales differs from that of Blue and Fin Whales, in that the former apparently avoid very warm waters, say, between 25° N. and 25° S., where their presence is extremely rare, though a few Little Piked Whales have been reported stranded in Ceylon, Manila and other areas within these latitudes. In spring, Little Piked Whales travel along the Norwegian coast as far as the Barents Sea, but newly weaned calves are left behind in Norwegian waters.

We owe most of our knowledge about the distribution and migration of Sperm Whales to C. H. Townsend, who collated data on 36,908 Sperm Whales, caught by American whalers between 1761 and 1920, from log books kept in New Bedford Library. As a result of his investigations, modern whaling statistics, and a number of other observations, we can say that the Sperm Whale, too, is a cosmopolitan, though harem-type schools of females and young bulls led by an old steer (see Chapter 6) rarely leave warm waters, and are generally restricted to latitudes between 40° S. and 40° N. Mature bulls, on the other hand, unless they are the leaders of a harem, migrate north or south in the spring and return to warmer waters in the autumn. Older males go closer to the poles than younger ones, and are often caught near the ice. How far north or south they migrate depends largely on the abundance of cuttlefish, and Tomilin (1936) reported that, for instance, in the Bering Sea they rarely pass beyond 62° N. (Cape Navarin), where the sea becomes fairly shallow and cuttlefish correspondingly scarce (Fig. 186). Off Kamchatka, and particularly off the Komandorskie Islands, cuttlefish are particularly abundant, which probably explains why some cows have been known to venture at least as far as S.W. Kamchatka (about 52° N.). In the N. Atlantic, on the other hand, females generally do not travel so far north, and no Sperm Whale cow has been reported stranded farther north than about 54° N., where a school of nine males and eight females stranded on Neuwerk Island, near Hamburg, in December, 1723. A predominantly female school of thirty-two ran aground on 14th March, 1784, near Audierne (Southern Brittany; 48° N.). All Sperm Whales stranded on the British and Belgian coasts, however, were bulls, and so were the individuals making up all the forty-seven strandings on the Dutch coast recorded since 1255, including the most recent stranding in 1953. Male Sperm Whales have been caught everywhere in the Antarctic but mainly at about 25° W., between 30° and 50° E. and between 120° and 130° E.

While calves do not journey as far afield as their fathers, they nevertheless begin to travel over vast distances fairly early on, since even harem schools migrate, though only within the warmer regions, moving closer to the polar boundaries in the spring and nearer to the equator in the autumn. Nor are the schools evenly distributed, some areas being particularly populous, probably because of the peculiar distribution of cuttlefish. Cuttlefish abound at the confluence of cold currents and tropical waters, e.g. off S.W. Africa, and off the West coast of S. America where the cold Benguella Current and the Humboldt Current respectively carry up cold water from the south. The sea teems with cuttlefish, especially where the Humboldt Current mixes with equatorial waters, i.e. off the coast of Peru and off the Galapagos Islands, and it is here that Sperm Whales appear in very large concentrations. No wonder that whaling stations in Chile and Peru top the list of Sperm Whale hunters by accounting for 27 per cent of the total catch (see Fig. 15). (Twenty per cent of Sperm Whales are caught in the Antarctic, 18 per cent off Japan and Korea, and 15 per cent off South Africa.)

The fact that so many Cetaceans roam over such vast areas is not surprising when we consider that their diet is found in most seas and that

Figure 187. The Indian Porpoise, Neomeris phocaenoides *(Cuv.), is an almost entirely black animal and lacks a dorsal fin. (Kellogg, 1940.)*

there are few obstacles to their free movement. Most cosmopolitan of all are Bottlenose Whales, Killers, Cuvier's Dolphins, Pigmy Sperm Whales, False Killers, and Risso's Dolphins, the last three of which are, however, rarely found in coastal waters. While little is known of the migratory habits of most of them, Bottlenose Whales in the N. Atlantic, for one, are known to migrate north in the spring, sometimes as far as Spitsbergen. In the autumn they have been seen off the Cape Verde Islands, our only indication of how far south they may go. It is quite possible that some of them reach the equator, there to intermingle with the southern species, but we have no reliable information to this effect. What we do know is that, during the autumn migration, they occasionally cross the North Sea. No less than fourteen of the seventeen Bottlenose Whales that have been washed ashore in Holland since 1584 were discovered during August and September; the last incident was reported from Flushing (19th August, 1958) when a living Bottlenose was released from the wreckage of a ship by a diver.

The Pilot Whale and the Bottlenose Dolphin also have a fairly universal distribution, at least if we consider all their different types as belonging to the same species. Actually, *Globicephala melaena,* for instance, i.e. the N. Atlantic and Mediterranean Pilot Whale which occurs in European waters and also off the East coast of America, from Greenland right down to Virginia, is different in external appearance from *Globicephala macrorhyncha,* which has much shorter pectoral fins and which has been observed from Virginia down to the Gulf of Mexico and off the West Indies. The N. Pacific Pilot Whale (*Globicephala scammoni*) also has short pectoral fins. The Southern Pilot Whale, which occurs in all waters south of 30° S. and along the Pacific coast of S. America up to the equator, appears to be identical with the N. Atlantic type (Davies, 1960). This northern strain of the Atlantic Pilot Whale can be found close to the Canadian coast during most summers, but keeps more to the open seas in winter,

Figure 188. The Chinese River Dolphin, Lipotes vexillifer *Miller, from Tung Ting Lake. (Kellogg, 1940.)*

probably due to movements of its food and particularly of the cuttlefish, *Illex illecebrosus*.

Similar migratory movements have also been established in the case of the Common Dolphin and of the Pacific White-sided Dolphin (*Lagenorhynchus obliquidens*). Of the former, Capt. Mörzer Bruins observed that in summer it visits Algerian waters in large schools, while it is extremely rare in the winter. The migration of the Pacific White-sided Dolphin is, according to Brown and Norris (1956), connected with the migration of the anchovies on which they feed. In winter and spring these animals keep close to the coast, and in autumn they move far out to sea.

Various strains and species of Bottlenose Dolphin seem to have different feeding habits as well. According to Capt. Mörzer Bruins, the N. Atlantic species (*Tursiops truncatus*) always keeps to within the top 100 fathoms, whereas *Tursiops aduncus* (a Red Sea and Indian species) generally keeps to deeper waters.

While some Bottlenose Dolphins have been observed as far north as Spitsbergen, the Common Dolphin keeps to more temperate seas, and is rarely found much farther north than Iceland and Finmark.

A scattered distribution is shown by the genera *Berardius* (two species in the Atlantic part of the Antarctic and the N. Pacific respectively), *Lissodelphis* (N. Pacific and southern seas) and *Feresa* (Pacific, S. Atlantic, and probably Australia – stranding of two unknown dolphins near Sydney – reported by Dawbin in 1959.)

Other Cetaceans keep to far more restricted areas. Thus most dolphins of the genera *Stenella* (*Prodelphinus*) and *Sotalia* keep generally to tropical and sub-tropical waters, although at least three representatives of *Stenella* have stranded on the British coast. *Sotalia*, which looks like a small

Figure 189. Commerson's Dolphin from the Straits of Magellan, one of many species of the genus Cephalorhynchus. (*Kellogg, 1940.*)

Bottlenose Dolphin, is particularly fond of estuaries and is rarely found far from the coast, while species of *Steno* (Rough-toothed Dolphins) which occur in most warm seas, generally prefer deep water. The Finless Black Porpoise, sometimes called the Indian Porpoise (see Fig. 187) is also found over a wide area, from the Cape of Good Hope to Japan. It prefers coastal waters, and especially likes lagoons and estuaries, so much so that, in China, it travels up the Yangtze Kiang beyond the Tung Ting Lake, more than a thousand miles from the sea.

Dolphins of the genus *Orcaella* are coastal species with an even more restricted distribution. They are mainly found in the Bay of Bengal, and off Malacca and Thailand. Fresh water dolphins of the family *Platanistidae*, all of which have unusually long and slender jaws, are all confined to tropical and sub-tropical rivers, e.g. the Susu or Gangetic Dolphin (*Platanista gangetica*) which lives in the rivers Ganges and Indus; the Amazonian Dolphin or Boutu (*Inia geoffrensis*) which is found in the Upper Amazon; the La Plata Dolphin (*Stenodelphis blainvillei*) which occurs in the River Plate; and the Chinese River Dolphin (*Lipotes vexillifer*) from the Tung Ting Lake (see Fig. 188).

Other Cetaceans are confined entirely to Arctic or Antarctic regions. Thus Greenland Whales, Belugas and Narwhals occur in Arctic waters alone, the Beluga being confined to regions north of the Polar Circle, at least in Europe. In N. America and E. Asia, its southern boundaries are 60° N. and 50° N. respectively. Belugas are rarely found south of these boundaries, and the same is largely true of Greenland Whales and

Figure 190. Wilson's Hourglass Dolphin, Lagenorhynchus wilsoni *Lillie, as seen on 14th April 1947 at 48°59′ S, 6°36′ E. Drawing by H. van der Lee. (From Bierman and Slijper, 1948.)*

Narwhals, though the former have been observed off Cape Cod, and one specimen of the latter was washed ashore in what was then the Zuider Zee. The Pigmy Right Whale (*Caperea (Neobalaena) marginata*), dolphins of the genus *Cephalorhynchus*, which have a striking black and white coloration (Fig. 189), and some species of the genus *Lagenorhynchus* (Fig. 190) which are also white and black, are all restricted to the cold south, where they have been seen over wide areas between the northern limit of drifting ice and the latitude of Cape Town.

Exclusively North Pacific species are *Lagenorhynchus obliquidens*, and representatives of the genus *Phocaena*, related to our Common Porpoise. Another North Pacific Cetacean is the Californian Grey Whale which

Figure 191. Beaked Whale, Mesoplodon mirus True, *a species that has only rarely been observed in the Atlantic. (Kellogg, 1940.)*

travels from the Bering Sea down to Southern California (about 20° N.) on the American side, and from the Sea of Okhotsk to Korea (35° N.) in the Western Pacific. Gilmore (1960) has shown that the American stock travels southward far from the coast, but that they are close to the coast when they go northward. In so doing they swim most of the time with the current. It seems likely that, not so long ago, the Grey Whale was far more widespread and that it occurred in the N. Atlantic as well. From recent finds of bones of the Californian Grey Whale in the Wieringermeer polder and other parts of the former Zuider Zee first described by A. B. van Deinse and G. C. A. Junge in 1937, together with other fossil material, we know that the Grey Whale must have frequented the N. Atlantic between 4000 and 500 B.C., and probably till fairly recently, since the 'Scrag Whale' described by Dudley off New England in 1825 may well have been a Californian Grey Whale.

Exclusively North Atlantic species are the White-sided Dolphin *Lagenorhynchus acutus*, the White-beaked Dolphin *Lagenorhynchus albirostris*, two Beaked Whales: *Mesoplodon bidens* and *Mesoplodon europaeus* (see Fig. 191), together with the Common Porpoise, with which we must conclude our discussion of the distribution and migration of Cetaceans.[1] Despite the fact that porpoises are so common, we know little about their migration except that they travel as far north as the Davis Strait, Greenland, Spitsbergen and the White Sea. Off the American coast, porpoises have been observed as far south as 38° N., and specimens have also been washed ashore near Dakar. Porpoises are true coast-lovers, and are found in the Baltic, the Mediterranean and the Black Sea and quite a long way up the larger rivers. Thus porpoises have been caught in the Rhine (near Cologne), the Nethe (near Lierre), the Seine, and the Meuse (near Venlo). It is also known that the North Sea population increases in the spring to reach a maximum in July and August when the young are born, and that, from November to February, porpoises desert the Baltic Sea. Unfortunately, we have no idea what connexion there is between these movements themselves, or between them and a possible migration to the south.

---

[1] It is not yet clear whether the rare N. Pacific porpoise *Phocaena vomerina* belongs to the same species as the Common Porpoise.

13

Reproduction

ALL THOSE INTERESTED in whaling are quite naturally concerned to know how many whales can be caught annually without causing serious depopulation. In the next chapter we shall see that it will probably take many years before there is complete certainty on this subject. One thing, however, is clear: any further knowledge must be based on the study of Cetacean reproduction, and on the rate at which these animals multiply. Hence it is not surprising that when applied biologists turned their attention to Cetaceans at the beginning of the twentieth century, reproduction took pride of place in their investigations. Since 1925–30, when Risting, Mackintosh and Wheeler laid the foundations of this branch of zoology, a spate of publications has constantly added to our knowledge of it.

Despite all the work that has been done on the subject, a considerable area remains shrouded in mystery. This is only to be expected in view of the difficulties encountered in studying the reproductive processes of terrestrial mammals, which, in contrast to whales, generally display much more than just a part of their head or back to the observer, and which do not migrate from the poles to the equator, while hiding the secrets of their intimate life under a screen of sea. In the case of whales, therefore, biologists are largely restricted to gathering what information they can from whale carcasses.

Even on superficial examination, we are struck by the fact that the testes, i.e. the male sex glands, are not found in an external pouch, as they are in most mammals. In fact, they cannot be seen from the outside at all, and only when the abdominal cavity has been opened and the intestines removed or pushed aside, do we find them behind, and lateral to, the kidneys, in the form of two fairly elongated cylindrical organs with a white, smooth and shiny surface (Fig. 192). But even when we have found them, the testes at least of the big whales are difficult to handle for closer examination, since in Blue Whales they may be more than two

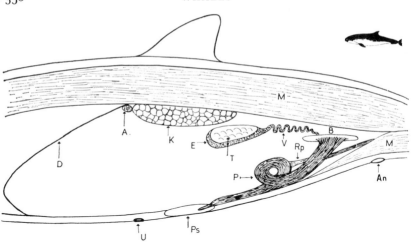

Figure 192. Diagrammatic left view of the sexual organs of a male porpoise. M = muscles of the back; D = diaphragm; A = adrenal gland; K = kidney; T = testicle; E = epididymis; V = vas deferens; B = pelvic bone; Rp = retractor penis muscle; P = penis; Ps = genital slit; U = umbilicus; An = anus.

feet six inches long and weigh up to 100 pounds. (The testes of Fin Whales, Sei Whales and Sperm Whales weigh sixty, fifteen and twenty-five pounds respectively.) We have seen that their position inside the body is an advantage in streamlining, but whether streamlining demands that they be placed precisely where they are is a debatable point, the more so since the testes of male sea-cows, of some insectivores, of elephants, sloths and armadillos are in the same position.

The fine structure of the testes is, by and large, no different from that of the testes of all mammals, and so is that of the spermatozoa which, in even the largest whales, are no larger than man's. From detailed microscopic investigations it appears that while small quantities of semen may well be produced by whales throughout the year, a marked increase occurs during the mating season.

The spermatozoa are conveyed from the testes by a highly convoluted duct, first to the epididymis which, in whales as in many other animals, is an elongated organ close to the testes. From the epididymis they are conveyed farther by the vas deferens, a tube which is convoluted either over its initial section or else over its entire length, but is devoid of all evaginations in which such accessory genital glands as the vesicular and bulbo-urethral glands are normally found. (The only accessory genital gland in Cetaceans is the prostate gland.) The vas deferens combines with the ureter, and then, just as in other mammals, enters the penis from below, and terminates at its tip.

In form, structure and position, the Cetacean penis is very similar to that of bulls and other male ruminants (rams, goats, stags, etc.) in all of which this organ is completely hidden beneath the abdominal skin, and in all of which it resembles a thin, hard rope. (The pizzle which was formerly used for flogging was, in fact, a bull's penis.) In whales and dolphins, the penis, at its base, consists of two arms (the crura) which are attached to the pelvic bones. The arms fuse into the very long rope-like body which is cylindrical or oval in cross-section. In large Rorquals, it can be as long as ten feet with a diameter of up to 1 foot (Fig. 192). A slit, just posterior to the umbilicus, allows the anterior part of the penis, which is surrounded by a fold of the abdominal skin, to be pushed out. In whales, as in ruminants, the retraction of the penis into the penis slit is brought about by a pair of strap-like muscles (the *retractores penis*). When the penis is retracted and flaccid, the organ assumes an S-shaped position inside the skin, but when the muscles (which are attached to the top of the S) slacken, the penis may become erect, due partly to the elasticity of the particularly hard and tough connective tissue of its shaft, and partly to turgidity caused by the sudden influx of blood into a mesh-work of blood spaces (cavernous spaces).

If we look at the penis of any mammal in cross-section, we see that, inside its thick wall, it contains special spongy tissue (the *corpus cavernosum penis*), in which small arterioles carry blood to the venous sinuses. By distension of the arterioles and simultaneous contraction of the efferent venules, large quantities of blood can be stored in the organ, with the result that it lengthens and becomes tumescent, a prerequisite for copula-tion. A similar spongy structure (the *corpus spongiosum*) surrounds the urethra, which lies in a separate groove, and is also found under the skin of the anterior shaft which, though it has a simple pointed tip in most Cetaceans, can yet be compared with the rounded *glans* of other mammals. While the spongy tissue of the outer skin and that surrounding the urethra consists entirely of blood vessels, the central corpus cavernosum penis of Cetaceans is riddled with strands of tough and elastic connective tissue, with a consequent reduction of cavernous (spongy) tissue proper. The penis of whales and dolphins (like that of ruminants) becomes erect not so much through an influx of blood, as through the elasticity of its tough tissue. On the other hand, the penis of odd-toed ungulates (i.e. horses), Carnivores, and apes, becomes tumescent primarily through the influx of blood, and consequently their *corpora cavernosa penis* consist mainly of cavernous tissue (Fig. 193). Cetaceans have no os penis.

The correspondence between the genital organs of male Cetaceans and even-toed ungulates makes us suspect, straight away, that there is a similarity in the way they copulate. We all know that bulls, rams, or stags

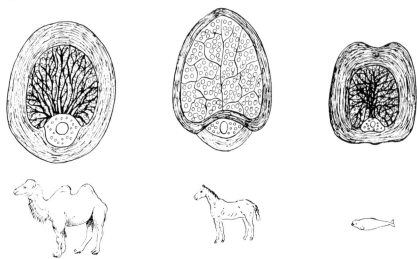

Figure 193. Cross-section through the penis of a camel, a horse, and a Beluga to show the similarity in structure between the camel and the Beluga. The horse has a much thinner sheath of connective tissue and its large corpus cavernosum penis consists mainly of blood vessels, while that of the other two animals consists mainly of connective tissue.

copulate with astonishing rapidity, and that the whole process lasts no more than a few seconds, while horses take minutes, and Carnivores anything from fifteen minutes upwards. Bears often copulate for forty-five minutes and martens for more than an hour.

However, while it seems likely that whales copulate like even-toed ungulates, it is extremely difficult to test this hypothesis. First, it is difficult to observe the mating habits of aquatic animals (particularly if the action is as short as we believe it to be), and secondly, Rorquals, at least, mate mainly in tropical waters, where whalers are few and far between. Even so, we have countless reports on this subject – the first dating back to more than 100 years ago. After some introductory love play, whales are said to dive, to swim towards each other at great speed, then to surface vertically and to copulate belly to belly. In so doing, their entire thorax, and often part of their abdomen, as well, are said to protrude out of the water. They then drop back into the sea, with a resounding slap, that can often be heard far away. The authenticity of all the many reports is vouched for by the drawings of one such observation which Nishiwaki and Hayashi published in 1951 (Fig. 194). They saw one and the same pair of Humpbacks repeating the action a number of times within the space of three hours. Similar observations were also made in 1947 by the crew of one of the catchers of the *Willem Barendsz*, by Capt.

P. G. V. Altveer, Master of the *Eemland* (Royal Dutch Lloyd – 25th
September, 1955, off the South American coast between Salvador and
Rio de Janeiro), and by Capt. H. J. Stiekel, Master of the *Merak N*, who
observed courtship in a school of about ten Rorquals at 18° N. and 20° W.,
on 9th June, 1956. G. Huisken, who served as stoker on S.S. *Molenkerk*,
reports that, in March 1948, on a journey between Karachi and Aden, he
observed some members of a school of about 200 Sperm Whales behaving
similarly.

Scammon (1847), however, described another method of mating, viz.
copulation at the surface, bellies lying horizontally. This type of copulation, too, has been reported on many occasions, for instance by the crew
of the factory ship *Balaena*, by Hubbs of Californian Grey Whales and
Humpbacks, by Burns (1953) of Grey Whales, and by Ruspoli of Sperm
Whales (1955). Huey, who saw it twice from about 200 feet away in Grey
Whales, reported that the pectoral fins protruded out of the water, that
the flukes were submerged, and that each act of copulation lasted for

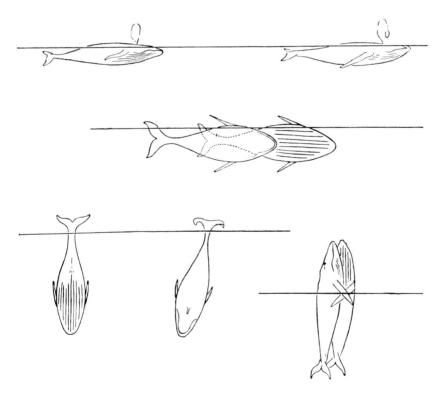

Figure 194. Humpbacks mating. (Nishiwaki and Hayashi, 1951.)

thirty seconds. Clearly, only in this position could mating continue for
half a minute, or even for only ten seconds as observed in Sperm Whales
by Ruspoli. It must be much shorter in the vertical position, in which the
couple have to jump out of the water. Actually, despite the many reports
to the effect that the couple separate after they have jumped out of the
water it is not yet certain that they really copulate while they jump, since
jumping may well be no more than a part of their love play.

In any case, in Cetaceans – as in most mammals – prolonged love play
precedes the final act. Unlike many mammals, e.g. polecats and even
donkeys in which courtship is exceedingly rough, Cetacean couples display
great tenderness. Humpbacks, Bottlenose Whales and Pilot Whales are
said to stroke their partners with their entire bodies and their flippers, as
they gently glide past each other. Humpbacks have also been seen to give
their partners playful slaps with their long pectoral fins. According to
Scammon these slaps can be heard miles away on quiet days. Brown and
Norris noticed that the male Bottlenoses in the Marineland Aquarium
(California) had erections whenever the cow brushed past under their
pectoral fins. Occasionally, bulls will bite the cows' flukes playfully, and,
in Florida, six-week-old Bottlenoses were observed playing their first
sexual games and attempting to copulate with older congeners of both
sexes and also with other animals in the tank, e.g. sharks and turtles.
Such precocious behaviour is found in most terrestrial mammals as well,
and so is masturbation, for which Bottlenoses in the Marineland
Aquarium were observed using ropes or jets of water.

Copulation proper has been observed both in the aquarium at Florida
and also in that at California, where male Bottlenoses were seen to
approach their mates by coming up from beneath them and bending their
tails upwards as they did so. In the final position (which was maintained
for two to ten seconds), the anterior part of the bull's body was more or
less at right angles to that of the cow (see Fig. 195). Immediately after
copulation, the cows were heard to emit a series of piping sounds which

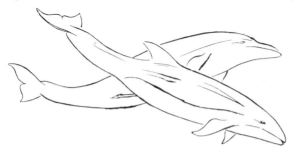

*Figure 195. Mating of a
male Bottlenose Dolphin
with a female White-
beaked Dolphin* (Lagen-
orhynchus obliquidens) *in Marineland of the Pacific* (Calif.). (*Diagram by D. H. Brown,
based on one of a number of observations.*)

were accompanied by an escape of air bubbles from the blowhole. While some animals were seen to copulate only once and then to go their separate ways, others repeated the act a number of times in the space of half an hour. In the Californian aquarium, Brown and Norris observed that Bottlenose bulls made sexual advances not only to cows of their own species but also to *Lagenorhynchus obliquidens*, a N. Pacific White-beaked Dolphin, which they approached fifty times within thirty minutes, though only a few of these approaches resulted in copulation. Apparently the White-beaked cows were in season while the Bottlenose cows in the tank were not. Nothing is known about any offspring of such mixed unions (if, indeed, they are ever born), except that Fraser (1940) described three skeletons discovered in Ireland which looked very much like crosses between Bottlenose and Risso's Dolphins.

There are few other descriptions of the mating of dolphins. Hamilton (1945), Nishiwaki (1958) and Caldwell (1955) have reported fairly quick acts of copulation in a lateral surface position on the part of Rough-toothed Dolphins (*Steno rostratus*), Killer Whales, and Spotted Dolphins (*Stenella plagiodon*), and Wilcke and his colleagues (1953) believe that they have observed the mating of *Lagenorhynchus obliquidens* off the coast of Japan, but have given no details. A Dutch fisherman reported that he saw two porpoises copulating in the vertical position off Texel (January 1958), and Spencer described the same behaviour in two Belugas (Hudson Bay) as early as 1889. According to Vladykov, four Belugas often pursue one and the same cow.

One of the best descriptions we have comes from Th. Carels, first mate

Figure 196. Pilot Whale surfacing after vertical copulation (Photograph: Th. Carels.)

Figure 197. Section of vagina of a porpoise, showing annular folds, resembling funnels with their mouths directed towards the cervix (C). (Pycraft, 1932.)

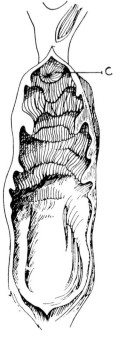

C

on the meteorological ship *Cumulus*, who, on 18th April, 1959, observed a school of about twenty Pilot Whales at love play close to the ship, which was then at 52° N., 20° W. Every so often, five or six animals would surface vertically right up to their pectoral fins, while other pairs would swim side by side, occasionally biting each other's mouths playfully. They would then dive under and assume an almost horizontal position, belly to belly. After about twenty seconds, one or both partners would emerge vertically out of the water (see Fig. 196 and p. 187).

While all the available evidence, therefore, indicates that Cetaceans copulate very quickly, reliable data are still scarce. Biologists would much welcome any further information on this subject gathered at first hand.

In all Cetaceans, the external female genitalia are contained in an elongated genital slit, just anterior to the vent (Fig. 42 and 213). While the outer part of the vagina is smooth and contains some longitudinal folds, lined with vaginal epithelium, the interior part is provided with a number of prominent annular folds (Figs. 197 and 198), which give the vagina the appearance of a chain of successive funnels with their mouths directed towards the cervix. While their exact function is by no means clear, these peculiar folds, which are not found in any other mammals, may serve for keeping water out of the womb, and also for providing extra space to allow the foetus to be born. They may also play some part during copulation.

Like that of terrestrial mammals, the uterus of most Cetaceans protrudes into the vagina by means of a snout-like cervix (Figs. 197 and 198) provided with a very thick and rigid wall, thus causing the passage to the uterus to become very narrow and very twisted, and the uterus to be practically sealed off. (Narwhals and possibly Beaked Dolphins, as well, are said to lack a definite cervix.) The uterus itself consists of a short corpus dividing into the two uterine horns, which run parallel for a short part of their length, and then bend respectively to the right and the left, curving first upwards and then downwards, to continue as the oviducts (Fig. 198). The oviducts, which receive the ova formed in the ovaries

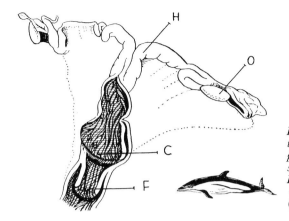

Figure 198. Female reproductive organs of the Common Dolphin with uterus and vagina in section. F = annular fold (see Figure 197); C = cervix; H = uterine horn; O = ovary. (Pycraft, 1932.)

and carry them to the uterus, are straight tubes in some species, and twisted to a varying extent in others.

The Cetacean ovaries are roughly in the same place as the testes of the opposite sex, but even though they are much smaller organs, the ovaries of Rorquals can be up to one foot long and can often weigh as much as twenty-two pounds. On one occasion, the British whaler *Balaena* caught an eighty-three-foot pregnant Blue Whale each of whose ovaries weighed sixty-five pounds. The ovaries of Odontocetes resemble those of other mammals, but Mysticetes have ovaries whose appearance is far more akin to those of birds. In adolescent Mysticetes, they are fairly flat organs provided with a varying number of grooves, but in adults they resemble an enormous bunch of grapes (Fig. 199). If one of the 'grapes', i.e. a follicle with a diameter of from $1\frac{1}{4}$ to 2 inches, is cut, a fairly transparent fluid spills out, and keen eyes can often make out the ovum, a tiny spot, 0·1–0·2 mm. in diameter, near its inner wall – the beginnings of a future colossus weighing 100 tons.

By and large, the ovaries of most mammals are constructed on the same pattern: a large number of ova, each in a follicle of its own. When a given female is not in season, her follicles are 'immature' and so devoid of internal moisture that the walls come into close contact with the ova inside. As the follicle matures, it becomes distended by the accumulation of fluid, and moves outwards to the surface of the ovary, from which it begins to protrude. At the height of oestrus, the pressure in the follicle becomes so great that, for instance in Fin Whales, it increases to about three inches in diameter. Then its wall bursts in a definite spot, and the ovum is discharged. It is subsequently caught in the funnel-shaped opening of the oviduct where it may be fertilized by a spermatozoon, and then travel on to the uterus. In multiparous (i.e. litter-producing) mammals, a number of follicles mature and protrude from the ovary simultaneously, but in uniparous animals such as man, horses and cattle, only one follicle generally matures at a time.

Oddly enough, whales, though uniparous, have a number of protruding follicles even when they are not in season; hence the resemblance of their ovaries to bunches of grapes (Fig. 200). Nevertheless, only one of these follicles normally matures during one season. In Blue and Fin Whales this mature follicle is almost invariably found in the anterior part of the ovary, where the wall of that organ is thinnest. It is this follicle which subsequently bursts (or ovulates) and which alone liberates an ovum that can be fertilized and reach the uterus, there to develop into a foetus. However, just like women, mares and cows, female whales, too, can give birth to twins and triplets. This means that more than one follicle can mature simultaneously, or that one and the same follicle can discharge a number of ova.

Once ovulation has taken place, fertilization usually ensues in most animals living in their natural habitat. During gestation and lactation, other follicles do not reach full maturity and are consequently somewhat smaller. Some, at an earlier stage of their development, return to the inside of the ovary, while others, though retaining their alveolar shape,

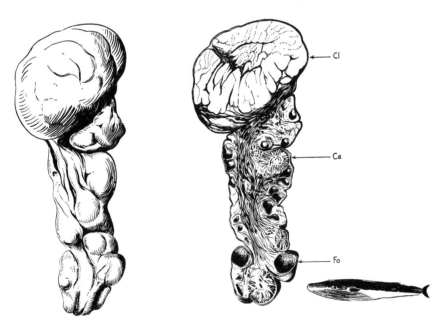

Figure 199. Ovary of pregnant Fin Whale. Left: external view; right: longitudinal section. Cl = corpus luteum which is pink rather than yellow; Ca = corpus albicans; Fo = follicle.

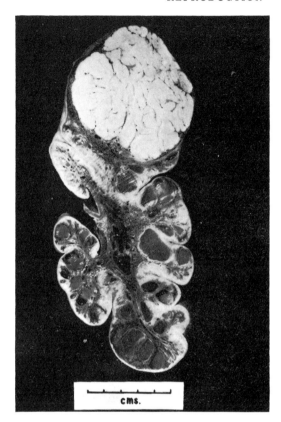

Figure 200. Longitudinal
section of Humpback ovary
with corpus luteum (top).
The fluid in the follicles has
coagulated. Left: a corpus
albicans. (Photograph: Dr
R. G. Chittleborough, Ned-
lands, Australia.)

lose a little of their moisture and become less taut. Others may suffer
degeneration (atresia) so that the ova in them never arrive at the possibility
of fertilization. Occasionally the ovaries, especially of old cows, display
particularly large follicles, but these must be considered pathological
phenomena.

Our description of the Cetacean ovary applies exclusively to animals
that are not pregnant. In pregnant Rorquals, for instance, one of the
ovaries bears a spherical mass with the dimensions of a small football
(Figs. 199 and 200), the so-called corpus luteum (yellow body). (Actually,
the corpus luteum of Rorquals is pink, unlike that of Odontocetes and
most other mammals which is yellow). In Blue Whales the corpus luteum
has a diameter of 8 inches, and an average weight of $5\frac{3}{4}$ lb. (minimum
$1\frac{3}{4}$ lb.; maximum $16\frac{1}{2}$ lb.). In Fin Whales, its average diameter is
$4\frac{1}{2}$ inches, and its average weight is 2 lb. ($14\frac{1}{2}$ oz.–6 lb.). The corresponding
weights in Humpback Whales are $1\frac{3}{4}$ lb. (19 oz.–$4\frac{1}{2}$ lb.); in Sperm Whales
$1\frac{3}{4}$ lb. ($17\frac{1}{2}$ oz.–2 lb. 10 oz.). In smaller Odontocetes and in many other

mammals the corpus luteum is frequently larger than the rest of the ovary. The most superficial observation will show that the surface of the corpus luteum displays an annular structure of diameter up to $2\frac{1}{4}$ inches, surrounding a hollow of diameter about $\frac{1}{5}$ inch. The hollow is the spot where the follicle has ruptured to release the ovum. In other words, the corpus luteum is simply a ruptured follicle whose wall has greatly increased in size and formed new tissue. It is this tissue which produces progestin, a hormone which stimulates and strengthens adhesion of the fertilized ovum to the uterine wall. The corpus luteum of big whales yields from thirty to forty milligrams of progestin per kilogramme of organ, and whale progestin, together with whale oestrin (a hormone produced by the cells lining the maturing follicle), is in fact put to good use by the pharmaceutical industry in a number of countries.

After ovulation, the follicles of all mammals produce corpora lutea which, as we have seen, swell to an immense size if the ovum is subsequently fertilized. In dogs, cats, pigs and other mammals, the corpus remains large and active right up to the end of gestation, but in horses, cattle and sheep its function is taken over by the placental tissue about halfway through pregnancy, when the corpus degenerates. Degeneration also occurs whenever ovulation is not followed by fertilization and pregnancy, but in that case the corpus begins to undergo recessive changes some ten days after ovulation. In either case, the glandular yellow (or pink) tissue quickly disappears until no more than a fairly degenerate type of white connective tissue (hyaline-sclerotic tissue) remains, the so-called corpus albicans (white body) (Figs. 199 and 200). In big whales the corpora albicantia are generally made up almost exclusively of the thickened elastic walls of the arteries which originally supplied the corpus with blood, and which have subsequently been squashed together.

In all Cetaceans, the corpus luteum continues to function throughout pregnancy, but degenerates soon after the young is born so that during the second half of the period of lactation only the corpus albicans remains. After a few years, the latter disappears completely in terrestrial mammals, and also in seals and sea-lions, so that, for instance in cattle, it is unlikely that more than three corpora albicantia could be found at one time in one and the same cow. However, in the few Odontocetes examined so far (Dolphins, Pilot Whales) and in all Rorquals, it appears that the corpora albicantia, while diminishing in size, never disappear completely. Thus in Rorquals, where they start out with a brown colour and a diameter of three to five and a half inches, the corpora fade and shrivel until finally they have a diameter of a quarter to half an inch. By virtue of their persistence, the corpora albicantia enable biologists to diagnose how often ovulation has occurred in a given whale. Such diagnoses are impossible in other animals, and whale biologists are therefore in a specially favourable position. Unfortunately, the corpora albicantia give no indication whether pregnancy followed a given ovulation. True, some biologists (e.g. Zemski, 1957) claim that from the size, shape and structure of the corpora, one ought to be able to tell whether a given white body was associated with pregnancy or not, but so far the evidence has remained inconclusive. However, research into this problem is being continued and it may well be possible one day to tell how many calves a given whale has given birth to.

Whenever ovulation goes hand in hand with mating, the ovum liberated from the follicle is likely to meet spermatozoa in the upper oviduct. Some of these will penetrate the membrane of the egg cell, and when one fuses with the cell itself, the ovum is fertilized and is forced into the uterus by contractions of the muscular walls of the oviduct. During its journey, which may take a few days, the ovum develops into a tiny vesicle. At the same time, the lining of the uterus is being prepared to receive it, so that, on arrival, it can become attached to the uterine wall.

In all Odontocetes so far investigated, the fertilized ovum was almost invariably attached to the distended left horn of the uterus, while the smaller right horn was found to contain a part of the allantois (Figs. 201 and 209). Sleptsov (1940) states that in only 17 per cent of the 635 pregnant dolphins and Belugas which he investigated was the embryo found in the right horn. In Mysticetes, on the other hand, the foetus may develop in either horn, though it appears from investigations of Blue and Fin Whales that there is a slight balance (60 to 65 per cent) in favour of both the right ovary and the right horn.

Like that of man, apes, horses and cows, the Cetacean ovary usually produces no more than one ovum at one time. Occasionally, however, more than one ovum may be discharged, when twins or multiplets may develop. In whales, we know a great deal about this subject, since the uterus of every captured female is investigated carefully for the presence of embryos. If the embryos are very small, they may well escape the watchful eyes of the inspectors, but larger foetuses rarely do. From whaling statistics it appears that the percentage of twins conceived by Blue, Fin, Sei and Humpback Whales are 0·68, 0·93, 1·09, and 0·39 of total pregnancies respectively. These figures correspond by and large with those found in man (1·3 per cent), horses (1·1 per cent) and cows (0·5 to 1·9 per cent). According to Kimura (1957) about $33\frac{1}{3}$ per cent of Fin Whale twins are uniovular. Multiplets seem to be more common in whales than in man and in larger domestic animals, for triplets, and to a lesser extent even quadruplets and sextuplets, have all been described in the literature. It is, of course, impossible to say whether the entire

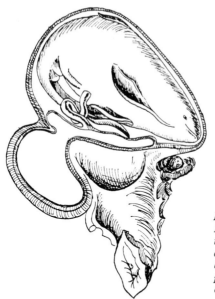

Figure 201. Pregnant uterus of a Common Porpoise seen from beneath. The embryo is in the left uterine horn, while the right horn contains the allantois (one of the two embryonic membranes) which forms part of the porpoise's placenta. Note the short umbilical cord. (Wislocki, 1933.)

litter would have been viable, but in any case, while sextuplets have also been described in cattle, horses have never been known to produce more than four foals simultaneously. (Man holds the record with octuplets.)

The Cetacean placenta, i.e. the tissue by which the embryo is attached to the wall of the uterus, is called *diffuse* and epithelio-chorial, by which biologists mean that it is uniformly distributed across the inner walls of both uterine horns and that maternal and foetal tissues do not become fused, their respective vascular systems being separated by two capillary walls and two epithelial layers. Because of this separation, whales lose less blood when they give birth than, for instance, human beings in whom there is a much more intimate association between the two tissues and a consequent laceration when they are separated at birth. Nevertheless, slight bleeding at birth has been observed in a Bottlenose Dolphin at Marineland, due to the fact that foetal and maternal tissue adhere in such a way that when they are separated some damage is unavoidable. Slight bleeding also occurs in horses, pigs and camels which have the same type of placenta.

Unlike man, whose embryo is surrounded with an amnion alone, Cetaceans (like Ungulates and Carnivores) have two embryonic membranes both filled with fluids: the amnion which surrounds the embryo and the allantois which lies outside. While a small part of the allantois is generally found in the uterine horn containing the embryo and the amnion, by far its largest part fills the 'sterile' horn where it forms part of the placenta (Fig. 201).

Since whales and dolphins cannot rear their young in caves or nests or other sheltered spots, young whales must be able to surface for air, to follow their mothers, and to keep warm (unlike dogs they cannot snuggle up to their dam for comfort), the moment they are born. The only thing their mother can do for them, is to feed them and, like the young of most mammals, the Cetacean calf will begin to hunt for its mother's teat within half an hour of its birth. Suckling apart, the young Cetacean is more or less left to his own devices, and is born with fully open eyes, alert ears and other senses, and enough muscle power to swim about quickly. All this implies that, just like a calf or a foal, it must have fairly large dimensions at birth.

Thus a newly-born Blue Whale is about twenty-five feet long, and may weigh more than two tons (Fig. 202), and a newly-born Fin Whale may measure twenty feet and has an average weight of over 4,000 lb. Grey Whales measure fifteen feet at birth and weigh about 1,500 lb. Newly-born Sei, Humpback and Sperm Whales .measure up to fifteen feet,

Figure 202. Whales have gigantic calves. An 18-foot female foetus removed from a Blue Whale carcass during the 1947–1948 season, on board the Willem Barendsz.
(Photograph: Dr W. Vervoort, Leyden.)

sixteen feet and fourteen feet respectively. The newly-born Mysticete is approximately 30 per cent its mother's length, and in Odontocetes the corresponding figure may be up to 45 per cent. Similar percentages are found also in other mammals whose young are born more or less complete.

Accordingly, the weight at birth represents a fairly high percentage of the mother's weight. For Rorquals, the figures are 5–6 per cent, and for dolphins 10–15 per cent, i.e. they are of the same order as those for Ungulates (8–10 per cent) and seals.

In most orders of mammals, there is a definite relation between the duration of the gestation period and the size of the young at birth, since the rate of foetal growth is the same in all of them. Thus, horses carry their young for eleven months, camels for twelve months, giraffes for fourteen–fifteen months, rhinoceroses for eighteen–nineteen months, and elephants for as much as twenty to twenty-two months. However, Huggett and his collaborators (1951, 1959) have shown that every Cetacean species has its own rate of foetal growth, so that, for instance, a 4,000-lb. Blue Whale baby develops in exactly the same time (ten-eleven months) as a twelve-pound baby of a porpoise. The reason for this characteristic must mainly be sought in the food-situation. Investigations of terrestrial mammals have shown that the mating season makes great physical demands on the bull, while lactation makes similar demands on the cow. Similarly heavy demands are made on the young when it is weaned and has to fend for itself. Hence there is evidence that mating, lactation and weaning often coincide with periods of plenty.

In big Rorquals, mating takes place shortly after they have returned well-fed to the tropics, and lactation begins ten–twelve months later when the cow can once again draw on the reserves stored up during the southern summer. The calves are weaned in the Antarctic where they can feed to their heart's content. The period of gestation of these big animals is therefore extremely short and they have an exceptionally high rate of foetal growth. Similar factors are said to determine the periods of gestation and the mating season of porpoises and dolphins as well, and further investigations of the food supply of Sperm Whales will probably explain why their period of pregnancy is so long. According to many sources from various areas, Sperm Whales carry their young for sixteen months, and a gestation period of sixteen months was also determined by Nishiwaki and his colleagues for N. Pacific Killer Whales.

The development of the Cetacean embryo can often be followed during one whaling expedition, when countless pregnant females are caught with foetuses at different stages of growth. This was particularly true in earlier times, when the season lasted from November to April, but even nowadays, when the season lasts from the beginning of January to the

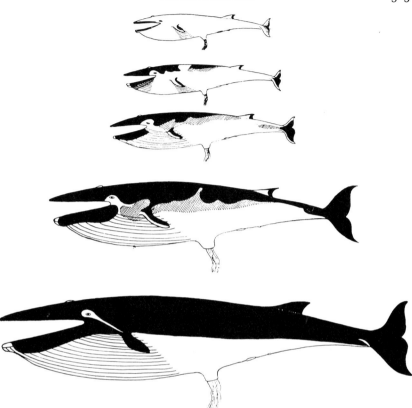

Figure 203. Development of colour pattern and grooves in Fin Whales. The lengths of the foetuses shown are respectively 95.11, 110, 125, 220, and 400 cm.; they are therefore not drawn to scale.

middle of March, much knowledge can be gained on one trip. Naturally, we miss the first stages (see Fig. 23) which develop in warmer waters, and which must therefore be studied at tropical or sub-tropical whaling stations. It is here that we must investigate the development of the general shape and of the different organs which – just as in man and large domestic animals – takes place during the first two and a half to three months after fertilization. If we assume that fertilization takes place on, say, 1st July, then, by the 1st October, the young whale will be about one foot long, and most of its organs formed. Although the head is still bulbous, and arched downwards, and though the abdomen protrudes, the general form is that of the adult Rorqual, and all the fins are present.

On the other hand, the characteristic grooves on throat and thorax, the whalebone and the pigment of the skin are still unformed. The absence

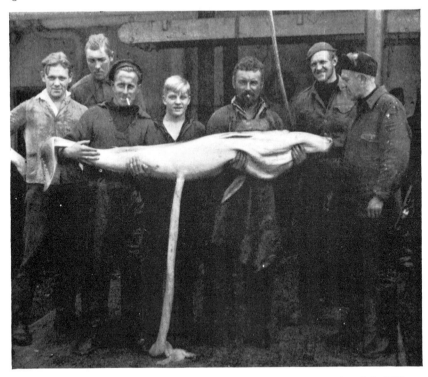

Figure 204. The 192 cm. female foetus of a Fin Whale, photographed aboard the Willem Barendsz *on 11 January, 1947. The umbilical cord is 120 cm. long. (Photograph: J. P. Strijbos, Heemstede.)*

of this pigment causes the blood vessels beneath to lend their colour to the epidermis so that the foetus looks pink. At the beginning of January, the foetuses of Blue and Fin Whales are from 27 to 31 inches long, 5 to 6 months old, and weigh from 13 to 15 lbs. It is at this stage that the first grooves appear between the pectoral fin and the umbilicus (Fig. 203). These grooves are soon joined by the appearance of others at the bottom of the mouth, and both sets eventually become fused to run for about 45 inches from the tip of the snout to the umbilicus. Pigment first appears at about the same stage (i.e. when the foetus is about 30 inches long), in the form of a dark strip along the under and upper jaw, and particularly at the tip of the snout, together with other dark strips at the edge of the dorsal fin and the flukes. Thereafter, irregular dark areas arise on the back and on the pectoral fin, but only when the foetus is about 13 to 14½ feet long does it have the pattern with which it will be born. Meanwhile the number of grooves increases, and the grooves grow more pronounced.

By the time the foetus has grown to about 9 to 10 feet, the first lamellae appear on the whalebone ridge (see Chapter 10).

During the first four months in the uterus, the Cetacean embryo develops at about the same rate as that of other mammals (see p. 364), but in the subsequent three months, the embryo of a Blue Whale may grow from 2 feet to over 6½ feet, and its weight may increase from 8 lb. to 5 cwt. (Fig. 204; see also Naaktgeboren, Slijper and van Utrecht, 1960). Huggett and Widdas (1951), who did extensive research on the intra-uterine development of various mammals, have calculated that the rate of growth during these three months is two and a half times that of most terrestrial mammals and ten times that of men and apes. This is probably due to the fact that the mother (but not the Sperm Whale mother – see p. 364) has adequate supplies of food for only four to five months (Laws, 1959).

Now let us turn our attention to the termination of pregnancy, i.e. birth. The fact that the Cetacean calf (like that of the sea-cow and most hippopotami, but unlike that of seals, sea-lions and sea-otters) is born under water and that the whole process is thus normally invisible to us, makes biologists all the more indebted to such institutions as the Marine-land Aquarium, where they can view, photograph and film the event to their heart's content. (There was only one precedent, viz. in 1914 when a still-born porpoise saw the light of day in Brighton Aquarium. In Marineland, too, six pregnancies of Bottlenose Whales ended in mis-carriages or still-births, but on seven occasions viable Bottlenose calves were born, while the birth of a viable Spotted Dolphin was also observed.) These studies in the Marineland Aquarium and some of Sleptsov's observations on the birth of dolphins caught in nets off the Black Sea coast together with investigations of cows which obviously died in labour, are, in fact, the only available data on the birth of Cetaceans. No one has ever witnessed the birth of a Rorqual, and all our knowledge is based on examination of three cows which died in labour.

The abdomens of pregnant Bottlenose Dolphins in the Marineland Aqua-rium are said to protrude in characteristic places a few months before birth. These animals are so tame that they allow divers to place their hands against them and feel clear movements of the foetus. Sometimes these movements can be observed visually as well. During the last months of pregnancy, the cows have a tendency to keep to themselves, and they become far less playful. With the onset of labour, the cow starts to swim very much more slowly than she usually does, while other cows keep constantly by her side, surround her from time to time, and give the impression of being intensely interested in her. Similar behaviour has also been observed in cows and other herd animals, and must be attributed

Figure 205. The birth of a Bottlenose Dolphin in the Marineland Aquarium, Florida.
(Photograph: R. J. Eastman, Miami.)

to a protective instinct which ensures that the cow in labour is not left behind or attacked by enemies when she is most helpless. In the Marineland Bottlenoses, the first labour pains lasted for thirty to sixty minutes; they were followed by violent contractions of the abdominal wall, and then the flukes of the calf suddenly appeared from the genital slit (Fig. 205).

We might not have expected the tail to emerge first, since, normally, human babies, calves, foals, indeed the young of most uniparous mammals, are born head first (Fig. 206), breech presentations being signs of a difficult birth. Now, it might have been possible to argue that captive Bottlenoses are atypical and are born tail first only because of unnatural environmental factors, were it not a fact that of twenty-five Cetacean births and still-births which have been observed, only one was a head presentation. The exception was reported by Essapian in an otherwise normal young Bottlenose, born in Marineland (Florida). Vladykov also reported a head presentation in a Beluga, though on evidence that requires further investigation. Fig. 205 gives a good idea of the normal birth of a Bottlenose, and the same position has been observed not only in various dolphins, but also in some Mysticetes including a Humpback Whale (Dunstan, 1957). The question, therefore, arises why Cetaceans differ so radically from terrestrial mammals in this respect. The answer can be found by following up the various suggestions of Prof. de Snoo, formerly Professor of Obstetrics at the University of Utrecht, who was struck by the fact that uniparous animals, whose offspring are always relatively large, usually produce their young head first, while multiparous animals whose offspring is much smaller usually produce 50 per cent of their young tail first, and 50 per cent head first. Now, if the offspring is small, it can usually slip through the mother's pelvis fairly easily, and it is born fairly quickly. In uniparous animals, on the other hand, whose young are born large, the process of birth lasts much longer, and here it may be a question of life or death whether the young emerge head or tail first. While we do not know precisely what produces the first respiratory stimulus, it seems probable that, in addition to cessation of the umbilical blood stream, the dryness and low temperature of the air outside the mother's body play an important part. Moreover, the danger of rupture of, or strangulation by, the umbilical cord is much greater in caudal than in head presentation. Thus the first breath might be taken when, during a caudal presentation, part of the body has emerged and the head has not, with a consequent intake of blood, mucous, and amniotic fluid. The danger of choking or of becoming infected by what are partly non-sterile fluids is obviated by head presentations in which the nostrils always emerge first, so that every veterinary surgeon who can turn a caudal presentation round before or during birth will invariably do so.

To find out how the final position of the foetus is assured, we shall look at mammals with a two-horned uterus, and ignore those with a uterus simplex (i.e. the primates) since the discussion would otherwise take us too far afield. Now, in mammals with a uterus bicornis (e.g. horses, cattle, and deer), the embryo has a fairly small head, a long and very mobile neck, and relatively heavy hind-quarters. Fig. 206 shows clearly that most of the uterus with the major part of the foetus occupies the lower front of the abdomen, while the passage through which the foetus is eventually expelled is higher up. Because the space inside the abdomen is restricted, because only its lower front can be distended, and probably also because of the distribution of the embryo's mass and the gravitational effects on it, the heavy rump of the foetus drops to the lower part of the uterus and the abdomen, while the head naturally points to the cervix and the pelvis.

This position is also ensured by the fact that the wall of the uterus keeps contracting at regular intervals throughout pregnancy and particularly during birth, when the contractions become intense and are felt as labour pains. The original contractions are much gentler and probably go

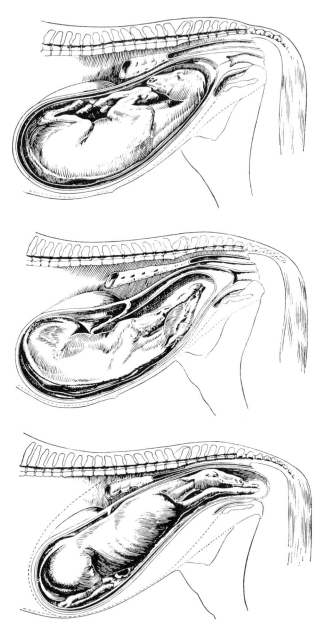

Figure 206. Position of foal before (top) and during birth (centre and bottom). (Stoss, 1944.)

unnoticed by the mother. These and the later contractions are called peristaltic contractions, i.e. wave-like contractions throughout the entire uterus, starting at the apex of the horn and continuing right up to the cervix. It would appear that these peristaltic contractions have a tendency to pull the lightest and least rigid parts of the foetus with them and thus to bring them nearer the cervix and the genital slit. With the onset of labour pains shortly before birth, the neck and the fore-legs are stretched out, so that the head is born resting on these limbs.

There is, however, one serious danger associated with peristaltic contractions, viz. the danger of compressing the umbilical cord which joins the foetus to the placenta and consists of blood vessels. Since the cord is very light and mobile (Figs. 204, 208, and 212), there is a tendency for it to be driven towards the cervix, just like the head, with the consequent risk of a fatal compression when the head, in passing through the narrow cervix, presses against it. Alternatively, the umbilical cord may wind round the throat of the foetus, and cut off the blood supply to its head. To minimize these risks, the umbilical cords of all the animals in question are exceptionally short, i.e. they represent from 20–60 per cent the total length of the foetus, unlike the umbilical cord of man and other primates (which have no peristaltic contractions of the uterus) where the corresponding figures range from 100–200 per cent.

As far as Cetaceans are concerned, we do not know whether the contractions of the uterus are, in fact, peristaltic, but we do know that the structure of their uterine walls and particularly the arrangement of longitudinal and annular muscles in them are identical with the structure of the uterus of those mammals in which peristaltic movements are known to occur, and unlike the uterine structure of primates in which the uterus simplex contracts as a whole. It seems likely, therefore, that peristaltic movements occur in the Cetacean uterus as well, the more so since the umbilical cord represents about 40 per cent of the foetus's average length at birth. Moreover, conditions in the abdominal cavity are almost identical with those found in Ungulates. True, the genital slit is not as far above the uterus as it is in Ungulates, but Fig. 207 shows clearly that the passage from the uterus to the vagina (the cervix) is dorsally placed and that the uterus itself occupies a lower position.

For all these reasons, we might have expected Cetacean calves to be born head first, were it not for the fact that the shape of the Cetacean foetus differs so characteristically from that of terrestrial mammals. In Cetacean foetuses, the head and thorax are the most bulky and also the most rigid parts, as they have hardly any neck to speak of and as their hindquarters and long tail are light and very mobile (Fig. 210). For this reason, the head and neck are forced to the lower front of the uterus, while the tail

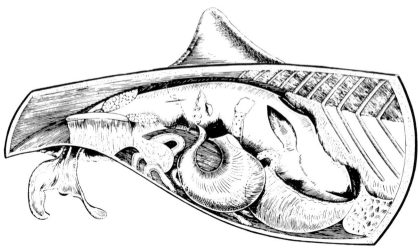

Figure 207. Right view of abdominal cavity of a 4-foot porpoise which drowned while giving birth in a shrimpers' net (Texel, 7 July 1955). Note the position of the foetus in the vagina and the left uterine horn, the top of which has become emptied.

In the foregound: the right uterine horn and ovary. Above the foetus's tail the pelvic bone and cervix can be seen clearly. The hatched line right of the cervix indicates the spot where the embryonic membranes are torn. (Slijper, 1936.)

is forced towards the cervix, i.e. the calf is born tail first, as, indeed, observations show it is.

From investigations of pregnant Cetaceans it has, however, appeared that in some the final position is taken up very shortly before birth, and that some foetuses face the cervix during most of the period of pregnancy. Possibly, the situation changes quite a few times during pregnancy, and, in any case, even if dissections reveal that the foetus faces the genital slit, the tail may nevertheless emerge first, since, as Fig. 207 and 208 show, the top of the uterine horn is attached to the abdominal wall close to the pelvis. As the foetus becomes larger, the uterus therefore slumps forward and causes the foetus to curve and sometimes even to double up. Towards the end of pregnancy, however, the snout is almost always at the top of the uterine horn, while the tail lies close to the cervix (Fig. 209). Sleptsov (1940) found this position in most of the 635 pregnant dolphins and Belugas mentioned earlier. The observations of W. van Ubrecht have shown that in Fin Whales tail positions become more frequent as the period of gestation advances. In the course of two months he found tail positions only. My colleague, R. G. Chittleborough, who investigated many Humpbacks in an advanced stage of pregnancy, also discovered a clear preponderance of tail positions.

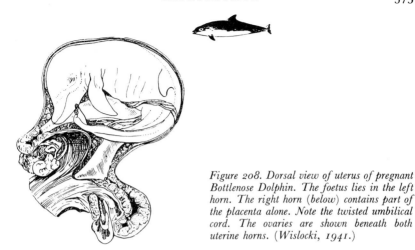

Figure 208. Dorsal view of uterus of pregnant Bottlenose Dolphin. The foetus lies in the left horn. The right horn (below) contains part of the placenta alone. Note the twisted umbilical cord. The ovaries are shown beneath both uterine horns. (Wislocki, 1941.)

The enormous intestines and other organs which are laid bare in flensing big whales, often make it difficult to determine the correct position of the foetus, and things are not made any easier by the flood of amniotic fluid which, as in other mammals, gushes forth when the uterus is dissected. (In Cetaceans, the foetal membranes are shed near the cervix (Fig. 207) during birth, so that Cetaceans, unlike, for instance dogs and cats, are born without them).

The fact that 50 per cent of seals and sea-lions are born in the same position goes to confirm that our explanation of the reason for Cetaceans being born tail first is correct. Now, the former have a similar uterine structure to Cetaceans, the only difference being that their foetuses (Fig. 210) have a very heavy and very rigid body, while their neck, head, pelvis and hind limbs are extremely motile. In their case, it is therefore a matter of pure chance which of these motile parts is forced towards the cervix.

The reader may wonder whether there is no danger of the Cetacean dorsal or pectoral fins catching against, for instance, the pelvic bones during birth, thus causing the foetus to be stillborn or the mother to die. Now, the pectoral fins lie flat against the body and their tip, at least in Odontocetes, lies just in front of (and is therefore born after) the animals' point of maximum girth (Fig. 210), so that the cervix and the very mobile pelvis (see p. 59) are sufficiently distended to allow them to pass (Fig. 211). In Mysticetes, the situation is less favourable. Dunstan (1957) noticed in a Humpback cow, killed while giving birth, that the pectoral fins of the foetus had folded forward about the shoulder joint, but other Rorqual foetuses cannot do this. Their pectoral fins, sunken in a depression of the skin, are more rigid than those of Humpbacks. The dorsal fin, too,

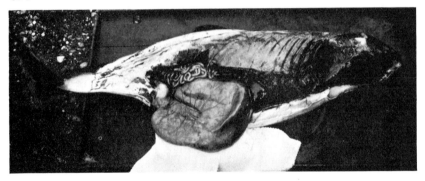

is pressed close to either side of the body, so that it does not protrude, and the flaccid flukes are neatly tucked in. It has sometimes been stated that, because their fins and flukes have not yet acquired their final rigidity, newly-born Cetaceans are poor swimmers during the first few days after their birth, and dolphin hunters from Yalta and the coast of Novorossiysk even claim that their umbilical cord remains attached to the mother for that period. However, all these claims must be discounted, since observations in the Marineland Aquarium have shown clearly that the umbilical cord snaps off during, or immediately after, birth, and that the young can swim very efficiently from the start, even though it takes some weeks before the dorsal fin and flukes become erect and rigid.

The birth of Cetaceans is shrouded in more legend than just this. Thus both Lütken (1887) and Pedersen (1931) were told by the inhabitants of

Figure 209. Section of a 5-foot. female porpoise, caught off Den Helder on 19 March 1937. Top: The 2-foot. foetus in the left uterine horn. Below: Uterus cut open. The foetus lies in the tail position, but the uterine horn is so bent that its snout, as well, is directed towards the mother's tail. (Photograph: D. van der Zweep, Utrecht.)

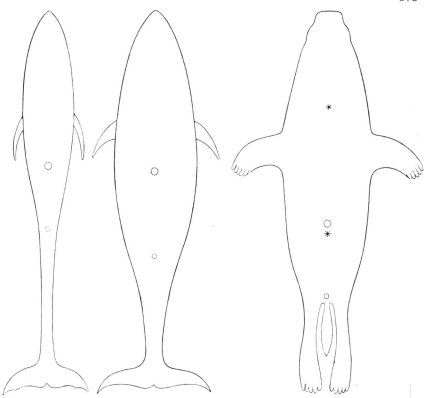

Figure 210. Outlines of fully-developed foetuses of a Blue Whale (left), a Porpoise (centre) and a seal (right). The umbilicus and anus are ringed. The rigid part of the seal's body lies between the two stars. (Slijper, 1956.)

the coast of Greenland that in Narwhals and Belugas the tail of the foetus emerges from four to six weeks before birth, so that the foetus can practise swimming against the day of its birth. Strangely enough, the same story has been told in a number of scientific books and papers, not only by such palaeontologists as Abel (1935), van der Vlerk and Kuenen (1956), and by Ley, who calls himself a 'romantic naturalist', but also by Krumbiegel (1955) in his textbook on the biology of mammals.

But fable apart, there still remains the problem why Cetaceans do not choke if, as we have said, breathing may be stimulated the moment the umbilical cord ruptures or any part of the body (in their case the tail) comes into contact with an environment that is colder than, or, in any event, different from, the womb, while the head is still in the mother's body. Actually since Cetaceans only breathe when their blowhole breaks surface, water cannot act as a stimulus in their case, while air does, so that there is no special danger to Cetaceans in being born tail first.

Compared with other mammals, Cetaceans have a fairly thick umbilical cord (Fig. 212), in which the blood vessels are twisted tightly, thus increasing its rigidity (cf. Figs. 208 and 209). On the other side, the cord is studded with strange brown knobs, the so-called amnion pearls, and though such knobs are found in various terrestrial mammals as well, their function is still unknown. Naaktgeboren and Zwillenberg have shown that they appear under the influence of some substances regulating growth and differentiation of the embryonic skin. In most other mammals (e.g. the cow) they disappear before birth, and the fact that this is not so in whales may be correlated with a different way of cornification due to the absence of hair. The part of the umbilical cord nearest the foetus's abdomen is clearly thickened (Fig. 203), and covered with normal cutaneous tissue. It is where this tissue gives way to the rest of the cord that the epithelium and connective tissue rupture at birth in some species, probably because the epithelium develops a number of invaginations shortly before (Common Porpoise). This weakens the area in question. The umbilical arteries and veins rupture just inside the umbilicus, where they have a weak spot. In this way, the cord snaps when a certain strain is imposed upon it, just like the cord of foals or calves, and unlike the cord

Figure 211. Final phase in the birth of a Bottlenose Dolphin in the Marineland Aquarium, Florida. (Photograph: R. J. Eastman, Miami.)

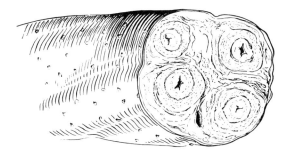

Figure 212. Section of umbilical cord of a Fin Whale foetus. Note the two veins, the two arteries, and the urachus which lie embedded in jelly-like connective tissue. The amnion pearls can be seen on the outer coat.

of puppies and kittens which has to be bitten off by the mother. In Cetaceans, the cord becomes strained the moment the snout has left the mother's body, i.e. when the new whale is fully born.

All biologists who have watched this process are agreed that it takes a fairly long time for the after-birth – i.e. the placenta, the rest of the umbilical cord and the foetal membranes – to be expelled. Sleptsov mentions one and a half to two hours, James speaks of four hours, and McBride and Kritzler (Marineland Aquarium) had, on one occasion, to wait for ten hours after birth before the after-birth emerged. Occasionally the umbilical cord fails to rupture, in which case it probably pulls the placenta behind it, with fatal consequences for the calf, since the cow generally fails to bite the cord off and the heavy placenta dragging behind the calf prevents it from coming up for air. During July and August, dead newly-born porpoises are quite often washed up on the North Sea coast, their placenta attached to an unruptured cord. Though it is by no means certain whether these animals choked to death or died of other causes, it seems reasonable to assume – until the matter is investigated further – that choking was responsible for some of the deaths at least.

In most terrestrial mammals, herbivores included, the mother generally swallows the after-birth, probably so as not to allow the nest to become fouled, or not to betray the presence of her offspring. Moreover, the after-birth provides the mother with food, thus enabling her to stay with her young instead of having to forage for prey the moment it is born. It is also thought that the placenta, in particular, contains certain substances which stimulate lactation. In Cetaceans which cannot foul their nest, the after-birth is abandoned, and the cow shows no interest in it at all, devoting all her attention to the calf which must be persuaded to the surface at the earliest possible moment. We have seen that young Bottlenoses in the Marineland Aquarium were able to keep up with their mothers straight after birth, that they surfaced within ten seconds of being born, or else were pushed up by their mothers, probably because, without air in their lungs, calves tend to sink to the bottom. (In Chapter 6, we saw that Cetacean mothers also push up their still-born calves.) Moreover, the mother would often be supported in this and subsequent tasks by another cow, and the two adults would often keep away from the rest of the herd, shepherding the young calf between them. Such 'aunts' occur in other mammals also, particularly in elephants, and also in hippopotami, in which the mother entrusts her young to another female while she herself goes in search of food. In the Marineland Aquarium, a mother Bottlenose was even observed being assisted by two 'aunts', while on another occasion all the cows in the tank took turns pushing a dead calf to the surface for four hours.

Maternal ties are particularly close in Cetaceans, whose young always keep extremely close to the mother and often swim just behind her dorsal fins or beneath one of her pectoral fins. This method of swimming was observed both in Bottlenoses, and also in Humpbacks whose behaviour the Australian biologist R. G. Chittleborough and his colleagues managed to photograph from a helicopter. In the feeding grounds, however, young Cetaceans may swim far away from their mothers. Young Humpbacks also seem to have an 'aunt', and in Bottlenoses the 'aunt' is often the only cow which the mother allows near her calf, interposing her own body between the calf and any other curious interloper, just as many other animals can be seen doing in the Zoo. The Cetacean mother may keep in almost constant touch with her calf by sounds, and, whenever she dozes off, the calf may sleep under her tail.

When attacked, the Cetacean mother will immediately come to her calf's assistance, and formerly a great many whalers lost their boats and even their lives after they had killed or wounded a calf. There are many reports of the mother and calf not abandoning each other even after one of them has been killed. Long ago, whalers often took advantage of this fact but, nowadays, even if there were no express prohibition, gunners would consider it beneath their dignity to shoot at a calf or at the mother accompanying it.

Two weeks after they are born, young Bottlenoses in Marineland usually make their first attempt to leave their mother's or their aunt's side and to swim round the tank on their own, and even to chase after fish. Of course, the fish get away, since the calves have hardly cut their teeth and are, in any case, not yet weaned. Only when they are five or seven months old do many of the calves begin to accept pieces of squid and later to swallow fish, but they continue to be suckled, all the same, until they are from twelve to twenty months old, while others keep to an exclusive diet of milk throughout that time. Weaning is often accompanied

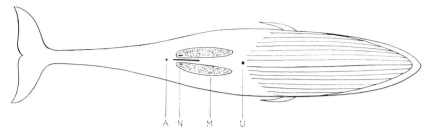

Figure 213. Ventral sketch of Rorqual showing position of mammary glands. U = umbilicus;
M = mammary gland; N = nipple; A = anus. The female genital opening lies between
the two nipple-slits.

by difficulties, with the calf bringing up the first fish it eats, and the mother
massaging its belly with her snout. In the other Odontocetes which have
been studied, the period of lactation lasts for about one year, with the
exception of the porpoise and the Beluga (eight months). Right Whales
and Grey Whales also suckle their young for about a year, and Rorquals
for a shorter period, viz. Humpbacks about ten months, and Blue and Fin
Whales five to seven months (see the Table on pages 384–5). These
differences, as we have seen, may well be associated with the availability
of food resources.

By difficulties, with the calf bringing up the first fish it eats, and the mother

Whales have a shorter period of lactation than many other large
mammals. Thus the bison and other undomesticated
bovines have a period of lactation of about two years, the
dromedary of from eight to eighteen months, the rhinoceros
of fourteen months, and the elephant of as much as three
years. Suckling Cetacean calves rarely leave their mothers'
company, and, whenever the mother comes up for air, the
calf's blow can be seen as a small jet by the side of the
mother's larger one.

By international agreement, a cow accompanied by a
calf may not be killed, and it is the task of the inspectors
aboard all factory ships to see that this clause of the
agreement is scrupulously observed, and that breaches are
promptly reported; when this happens, captain and crew
of the catcher are deprived of their premium. Since the
catchers are usually miles away from the factory ships,

Figure 214. Mammary gland of Humpback,
showing large ducts. (Lillie, 1915.)

breaches can only be detected by careful examination of the mammary glands of all female carcasses.

We have seen that, on either side of the genital slit, all cows have two further openings in which the nipples are recessed (Figs. 42 and 213). When air is pumped into the carcass of a Rorqual, the nipples are occasionally forced out, and they probably do so to a lesser or greater extent whenever a calf is being suckled. Like other male mammals, Cetacean bulls, too, have a pair of small nipples, which, in their case, are set in two small slits near the anus. According to Yablokov (1957), male Belugas excrete a substance from their mammae which other Belugas can clearly perceive. In very young (one inch long) porpoise embryos, Kükenthal discovered no less than eight rudimentary nipples, in separate groups of four on either side. Six of these nipples subsequently disappear and a single pair is left. The presence of the rudimentary mammae would seem to indicate that the terrestrial ancestors of Cetaceans had four pairs of nipples and that they were probably multiparous.

Cetaceans have no protruding udders like cows, and their mammary glands are two long, fairly small, and fairly flat organs, which are inclined to each other at a slight angle (Fig. 213). Their tips are generally not far from the umbilicus, and their average dimensions in 'resting' Rorqual cows are about 7 feet by 2 feet 6 inches by $2\frac{1}{4}$ inches. During lactation, their thickness increases from $2\frac{1}{4}$ inches to a maximum of one foot, and their colour changes from pink to golden brown. If the glands are strongly distended, the nipples can be seen from the outside.

Each mammary gland is divided into countless lobes and lobules, all of which lead by narrow ducts into a central lactiferous duct, which becomes strongly distended close to the nipple (Fig. 214). In Cetaceans, this duct may be compared with the cistern in a cow's udder, by which the cow accumulates sufficient milk to be able to pour it into the suckling calf's mouth. In whales, similar jets of milk often shoot from the nipples of carcasses, when whalers call them 'milk-filled' – generally a reliable criterion that the animal was lactating. Now, lactation means that the secretory cells of the gland are producing milk, which generally indicates that the cow was accompanied by a calf and that a breach of international agreements has been committed.

An inspector will therefore have to report the crew, even though the cow may have been shot in good faith, i.e. even though the calf was some distance away and the gunner failed to spot it, or even though the calf had been weaned shortly before. This may lead to unnecessary recriminations, and, to avoid these, the Dutch Whale Research Group T.N.O. began a detailed histological study of the mammary glands of Blue and Fin Whales in 1947, using material collected on board Dutch, British and

Norwegian whalers. The research was chiefly carried out by E. W. van Lennep and W. L. van Utrecht (who published a preliminary paper on this subject in 1953) and later by W. A. Smit. Starting from the known fact that, in other mammals, certain histological characteristics of the glandular cells are criteria of lactation and of recent cessation of lactation, the Dutch biologists found that, in the vast majority of cases where milk had gushed from the nipples or had been found in the nipples during dissection, the histological picture, too, showed that the cow had been lactating. In one case, however, lactation was diagnosed histologically, when the carcass had not been 'milk-filled', while, conversely, a few milk-filled carcasses proved, on histological examination, to have stopped their secretory activity. In the first case, the calf had probably just sucked the cow dry, or else the milk had been lost while the carcass was being dragged through the water, and, in the others, some milk must have remained in the ducts even after weaning. Further investigations are proceeding, particularly with a view to establishing some relationship between the histological picture and such macroscopic characteristics as thickness, colour, flexibility of the tissue, etc. The final results may well help the inspectors to make their diagnoses with greater accuracy, and, meanwhile, we must take it that using present-day criteria (presence of milk during dissection of the gland, or gushing nipples), their errors cancel out, since they diagnose approximately the same number of false cases of lactation as of false cases of weaning, so that there is unlikely to be any change in the *total* number of reported breaches. In any case, the number of transgressions during recent years has been a mere 0·3 per cent of the total number of animals killed – not a bad figure when we consider the difficulties under which the whaling industry has to work.

All biologists without exception are agreed that Cetacean calves are always suckled under water, though sometimes so close to the surface that they can be seen (Fig. 215). Sea-cows, sea-otters and hippopotami also suckle their young under the surface, though hippopotami can feed their young on land as well. Seals, sea-lions, and the Pigmy Hippopotamus on the other hand, invariably suckle their young on land. In the latter, as in all terrestrial mammals, the young pump the milk from the nipple by means of a sucking reflex (cf. a milking machine), or else the milk is gently squeezed out of the nipple by a massaging action of the lips (c.f. milking a cow or goat by hand). However, neither method is applicable under water, and Cetaceans and hippopotami therefore have to squirt their milk into the calf's mouth.

While suckling their young, Cetaceans move very slowly; the calf follows behind and approaches the nipple from the back (Fig. 216). The cow then turns a little to the side, so that the calf has easier access to the

Figure 215. Humpback suckling two calves. From a drawing by Scammon. (Norman and Fraser, 1928.)

nipple, which has meanwhile emerged from its slit. Since the calf lacks proper lips, it has to seize the nipple between the tongue and the tip of its palate. We have seen that the tongues particularly of young Mysticetes are very much more muscular than those of older specimens, and that their tips are free. With this free tip, which in some Odontocetes has a scalloped edge, the calf presses the nipple from beneath and from the sides against the palate. In this way, and also because of the arrangement of the muscles in the tongue, the tongue becomes doubled up so that the milk can spout straight into the throat. Once the calf lets go, the milk often continues to spout from the teat for a further six seconds or so, so that we gain the clear impression that the milk flows under fairly great pressure, probably due to contraction of the cutaneous muscles with which the mammary gland is surrounded, or else because the lobes themselves are filled with a surfeit of milk, which contractions of the myo-epithelial cells surrounding the individual lobuli force through the nipple. (The presence of myo-epithelial cells in the mammary glands of Cetaceans was established by W. A. Smit.) While most Cetacean calves squeeze the nipple between tongue and palate, Sperm Whales may well form the exception, since, because of the peculiar shape of their heads and lower jaws, it seems unlikely that they can do so. They probably seize the nipple with the corners of their mouths, but no one has ever reported seeing them do so.

The Bottlenoses in the Marineland Aquarium usually start looking for their mothers' nipples some seventy-five minutes after birth, though some took as long as four hours about it. The first feed was taken fifteen to thirty minutes after the first attempt, and for the first two weeks the calf was suckled roughly once every twenty-six minutes, day and night. Sheep feed their young at about the same rate (twenty-two times in sixteen hours of daylight), while piglets are suckled once every hour or so. During each feed, the young Bottlenose took one to nine sucks, each lasting for only a few seconds, since the calf cannot stay under water for more than half a minute at a time. Other mammals suck for far longer periods, e.g. newly-born lambs, which take from 50 to 250 seconds (older lambs – 30 seconds), but in Cetaceans, in which the cow spouts her milk into the calf's mouth, thus obviating the need for sucking, the calf obtains a

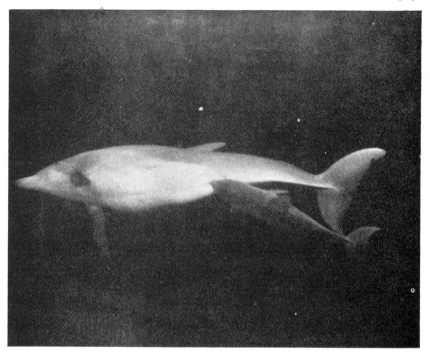

Figure 216. A young Bottlenose Dolphin being suckled. Marineland Aquarium, Florida. (Photograph: R. J. Eastman, Miami, Florida.)

maximum quantity of milk in a minimum time. By the time the young Bottlenoses were six months old, the number of feeds was reduced to about seven times a day. Sea-cows which generally stay submerged for longer periods were observed suckling their calves for ten minutes at a time.

It is impossible to say how much milk a Cetacean calf ingests with each feed, and the literature is full of contradictory statements which vary from three and a half pints to fifty gallons. Considering that primitive cattle like zebu and water-buffalo cows produce about fourteen pints of milk a day, and considering also the composition of Cetacean milk (see below) and the high metabolic rate of young whales, we may, however, take it that some 130 gallons is by no means an overestimate of the daily milk production of large whales. Each of the forty daily feeds would then produce about three and a quarter gallons of milk, a figure which is, of course, subject to revision on closer investigation.

Cetacean milk has a creamy white colour, and is occasionally tinted pink. It often has a slightly fishy smell and its taste is reminiscent of a mixture of fish, liver, Milk of Magnesia and oil. For these reasons, whale's

Species[1]		Mating Season	Date of Birth	Gestation Period (in months)	Lactation Period (in months)	Sexual Maturity Attained at...years ♂	Sexual Maturity Attained at...years ♀
Greenland Whale	NA	Feb.-Mar.		9–10	12		
Grey Whale	NP	Dec.	Dec.	11–12	5	4½	4½
Blue Whale	S	May-June	Apr.-May	10¾	7	4½	4½
	NP						
Fin Whale	S	Apr.-Aug.[2]	June-July[2]	11¼	6	5	6[3]
	NA						
	NP	Nov.-Jan.[4]				5¼	5¼
Sei Whale	S	May-Aug.	May-Aug.	12	5	1½	1½
	NP	Nov.					
Bryde's Whale	S	All year	All year				
Little Piked Whale	NP	Feb.-Mar. and Aug.-Sept.					
	NA	Jan.-May	Nov.-March	10	4½	2	2
Humpback	S	Aug.-Sept.	July-Aug.	11–12	10½	4½	4½
	NP					5	5
Sperm Whale	S	Aug.-Dec.	Dec.-Apr.	16		1¾?	1¼?
	NA	Mar.-May	July-Sept.	16	13		
	NP	Jan.-May	May-Aug.	16	12	4½	4½
Pigmy Sperm Whale				9	12		
Bottlenose Whale	NA		Mar.-May				
Beaked Whale[9]		Mar.-Apr.	Mar.-Apr.	12	12		
Berardius	NP	Feb.	Dec.	10		3	3
Beluga	NA	April-June	April-June	12	8	3	1½-2
Narwhal	NA	All year	All year				
Killer	NA	Nov.-Jan.			12		
	NP	May-July[5]		11–12			
Pilot Whale	NA	Autumn		13–16		13	6
Bottlenose Dolphin	NA	Feb.-Apr.	Feb.-Mar.	12	16		6
Common Dolphin	B			11			3
Gangetic Dolphin	I	July-Sept.	Apr.-July	9			
Common Porpoise	NA	July-Oct.	Mar.-July	8–10	8	1¼	1¼

[1] N.A. = North Atlantic; N.P. = North Pacific; S = Southern hemisphere; B = Black Sea; I = India.
[2] Maximum in June-July. Laws reports that the average birth-day of first-born calves is 21st July, and of subsequent calves 8th June. A small number of calves are conceived and born in Nov.-Dec.
[3] Varying from 3–8 years.

Interval between successive births (in years)	Estimated Life (in years)	Estimated number of offspring per cow	Length of Animal in feet and in (metres) at					
			Birth	Weaning	Sexual Maturity ♂	Sexual Maturity ♀	Physical Maturity ♂	Physical Maturity ♀
	40		13 (4)				51 (15·5)	51 (15·5)
	20	8	14 (4·5)				48 (14·5)	50 (15·5)
3	30	10	24 (7½)	52·5 (16)	74 (22·5)	77 (23·5)	81 (24·7)	87 (26·5)
					70 (21·3)	74 (22·5)		
6	30	12	22 (6·5)	39 (12)	63 (19·2)	66 (19·9)	68 (20·8)	74 (22·5)
					58 (17·6)	61 (18·6)	63 (19·2)	70 (21·3)
	25		21 (6)		62 (19)	66 (19·9)		
	30	12	15 (4·5)	27 (8·5)	44 (13·5)	47 (14·5)	49 (15)	54 (16·5)
					43 (12·8)	45 (13·5)		
					39½ (12·3)	39 (12)		
ne-2)	30		9 (2·7)	16 (5)	22 (6·7)	24 (7·3)		29 (8·8)
	25	15	14 (4·2)	26 (8)	36 (11)	39 (12)	44 (13·7)	45 (14)
					38 (11·5)	39½ (12·3)		
			13 (4)	20 (6)	38 (11·5)	30 (9·5)	51 (15)	38 (11)
	25	6	13 (4)	22 (6·7)				
				21 (6·5)	31 (9)	29 (8·5)		
					11 (3·3)	11 (3·2)	15 (4·5)	13 (4)
						21 (6·5)	26 (8)	23 (7)
			10 (3)					
			6 (1·8)	10 (3)				
			15 (4·5)		32 (9·6)	33 (10)	39 (11·7)	40 (12)
	20	15	5 (1·6)		10 (3)	10 (3)	13 (4)	13 (4)
	20	6					18 (5·5)	18 (5·5)
	20	15	8 (2·5)				30 (9)	15 (4·5)
			9 (2·8)					
	25[6]	5–6	6 (1·8)		16 (4·8)	12 (3·6)	20 (6)	15 (4·5)
	20	8						
	25	15						
	15	10	2¼ (0·7)		3½ (1·1)	3½ (1·1)	5¾ (1·8)	5¾ (1·8)

[4] According to Japanese investigators, mating takes place all year, but is most intense in December.

[5] Probably all year, with maximum intensity during May-July.

[6] Probably senile after 18th year.

[7] Resting period of one year after every three pregnancies.

[8] Resting period of one year after every 4–5 pregnancies.

[9] Mesoplodon bidens (Sowerby).

milk is not at present fit for human consumption, despite the enormous yield, and despite the milk's high fat content.

Analyses of the milk of Blue, Fin, Humpback, Grey and Sperm Whales and of porpoises, Belugas and Pilot Whales show that the composition of Cetacean milk is: water, 40–50 per cent; fat, 40–50 per cent; protein, 11–12 per cent; lactose, 1–2 per cent; salts and vitamins, 1 per cent. The Beluga's milk was shown to have an exceptionally large proportion of water (66 per cent) and small proportion of fat (22 per cent), possibly owing to experimental errors, and the Sperm Whale's milk fat, just as the oil from its liver, was found to be a real fat and not a wax-like product like sperm oil and spermaceti.

If we compare these figures with those for other mammals, it becomes clear why whale milk has the thick appearance of condensed milk. For, while whale milk has a water content of only 40–50 per cent, the milk of most domestic animals has a water content of 80–90 per cent. Whale milk is therefore three to four times as concentrated as the milk of cows, goats and also of human beings. For this reason, young whales can be suckled for shorter periods, and the mother loses less water, with which, as we saw in Chapter 10, she has to be most economical. The fat content of the milk of terrestrial mammals which varies from 2 per cent (human being) to 17 per cent (reindeer), is about 4 per cent in cattle and about 9 per cent in bitches, while the milk of seals has much the same fat content as that of Cetaceans, which is not surprising when we consider that the combustion of fat releases not only a maximum of energy but also a maximum of water, both of which are required to an exceptional degree by marine mammals. In Chapter 10 we saw that the blubber of newly-born Cetaceans contains relatively little fat, and thus offers relatively poor protection against the cold, while their relatively large body surface exposes them to far greater heat losses than mature animals. Thus a high metabolic rate together with the ingestion of concentrated foodstuffs is a *sine qua non* of their survival.

On the other hand, the sugar content of milk which varies in most mammals from 3 to 5 per cent, and which in man and elephants may be as high as 6 to 8 per cent, is very low in Cetaceans and also in seals, whose milk is often practically devoid of sugar. We have seen why aquatic mammals must oxidize fats rather than sugar, but whether this is the only reason for the small percentage of sugar in their milk requires further investigation. Cetacean milk contains roughly twice as much protein as that of the average terrestrial mammal. In Rorquals, the need for extra proteins may well be due to the quick rate of growth of their calves (see below), but the same explanation can certainly not be offered in the case of dolphins, which grow no more quickly than other mammals. Moreover the milk of rabbits and rats also has a protein percentage of about 13.

In fact, the rate of growth is not so much related to the protein percentage of the milk as to the total amount of protein ingested daily – a subject on which we still know very little. On the other hand, Gregory and his colleagues were able to determine that the vitamin A and B content of Blue and Fin Whale milk, and also the proportion of potassium, magnesium and chlorine in it, did not differ significantly from that of the milk of terrestrial mammals.

Calcium and phosphorus, however, do in fact occur in greater concentrations in the milk of Blue and Fin Whales than in that of terrestrial mammals, possibly because an inordinate amount of bone must be grown within six to seven months, during which time Blue Whales, for instance, grow from twenty-five feet to fifty feet, i.e. more than one and three-quarter inches a day. In the same period their weight increases from two to twenty-three tons, i.e. about two hundredweight a day. In fact, Blue Whales grow so fast that they double their birth weight within seven days, the corresponding figures for dogs, pigs, rhinoceroses, cows and horses being nine, fourteen, thirty-four, forty-seven and sixty days respectively.

We started this chapter by pointing out that those concerned with whales are particularly interested in their reproductive processes, since, once it is known how many calves a given cow can produce in a given time, a check can be kept on the population level.

To do so, we must first know at what age whales reach sexual maturity. Now, while examinations of the sexual organs clearly show whether a given whale is mature and thus ready to copulate, the determination of its actual age is extremely difficult (see Chapter 14). The table on p. 384 must therefore be treated with some reserve, particularly since more recent investigations have shown time and again that Rorquals attain sexual maturity later than was formerly thought. At present, it is believed that, as the table shows, average propoises become sexually mature at about fifteen months, that Blue and Fin Whales reach puberty at between four and a half and six years, and Bottlenose Dolphins only after five to six years, with cows and bulls becoming sexually mature at about the same age. The Pilot Whale seems to occupy a very special position in the table and we would do well to suspend judgement on it until more thorough investigations have been made. Humpback cows generally start ovulating when they are four and a half years old, but do not always conceive during the season in which they reach maturity. Now, the age of sexual maturity depends largely on size, and large animals generally mature later than small ones. Seeing that water-buffaloes become mature at about two years, American and European bisons and chamois and tapirs at about three, camels and zebus at four and elephants at only eight or ten, we are forced to conclude that large Cetaceans are singularly precocious for their size.

Female seals – which are, of course, much smaller – only reach maturity at four, and male seals possibly later still. Like these Pinnipeds, Cetaceans continue to grow after that, but only to a small extent; the length at sexual maturity being about 85 per cent of their final length.

Another question which interests whalers is how often Cetaceans are in season, and how many ova are liberated during their oestrous phase. It is said that Narwhal, False Killer and N. Pacific Killer bulls and cows may be in season throughout the year. The same appears to be true for Bryde's Whales, because they live exclusively in warm waters and do not have a definite migration (Best, 1960). In other species, the bulls show signs of slight sexual activity throughout the year, but their activity becomes far greater when the cows are in season, as well. Even when the oestrous phase of cows is prolonged, this phase is divided into periods of minimum and maximum activity, of which the latter usually lasts for two or three months. In most Cetaceans, mating takes place in winter or early spring – our summer or autumn in the case of southern species – i.e. at a time when migrating species are always in warmer waters. Belugas and porpoises alone mate in May and in the middle of the summer respectively, probably because they never travel over large distances.

Most observers think that Humpbacks, Common Dolphins, Pilot Whales and False Killers conceive after the first ovulation, or else ovulate again a few weeks later, and so on, so that all cows of these species are likely to be pregnant by the end of the season. On the other hand, Laws' most recent investigations of Fin Whales (confirmed by Naaktgeboren, Slijper and van Utrecht; 1960) show that cows ovulate a single time during May to July, and that, if fertilization has not taken place, another ovulation takes place five months later. However, the chances of the ovum being fertilized are so good that we may take it that practically all cows which were on heat during the southern winter season have conceived before they migrate back to Antarctic waters.

Another important question is whether cows can conceive immediately or shortly after they have given birth to a calf, or whether no ovulation occurs during lactation. In some terrestrial mammals, e.g. hamsters, the female cannot conceive while she is suckling her young, wild cattle cannot conceive during the first three months of lactation, and in man this 'sterile' period often lasts no longer than six weeks. Other mammals, however, ovulate immediately or shortly after giving birth – in fact, the situation differs from species to species. In the case of Pinniped Carnivores, walruses, for instance, ovulate one year after they have weaned their calves, while sea-lions, which suckle their young for ten months, can be fertilized one month after they have given birth. Young seals are weaned a few weeks after birth, and their mothers can conceive shortly later, or even during, lactation.

In Cetaceans, just as in Pinniped Carnivores, the situation also differs from species to species.

Thus, Common Dolphins, Porpoises, Killers and Belugas were found to be capable of conceiving immediately or very shortly after they had given birth, so that the cows of these species generally produce offspring every year. The same is true of Little Piked Whales, although in their case, cows occasionally miss a year. Black Sea Dolphins are said by Kleinenberg frequently to produce offspring for three successive years, and then to miss the fourth; Belugas have a resting period after every 4–5 pregnancies (Kleinenberg, 1960).

Unfortunately for whalers, the big whales, unlike their smaller relatives, do not produce offspring annually, probably because they lack sufficient food during part of the year. Milk which is rich in fats and proteins makes heavy demands on the mother's reserves, so much so that the blubber layer of lactating cows is always very thin (see Chapter 11). In these circumstances, it would be fatal if a new embryo were to make further demands on her strength while she was still suckling the calf, and we have, in fact, clear indications that Rorqual and Sperm Whale cows do not generally ovulate during lactation. Humpbacks are more generous to whalers, for Chittleborough found that Australian Humpback cows could conceive immediately after birth, or during the early stages of lactation. The cows could therefore produce one calf a year and according to Zemski N. Pacific Humpbacks do, in fact, have four calves every five years. Grey Whales, too, can, according to Hubbs, conceive shortly after they have given birth. All these findings are corroborated by the fact that, in both species, greatly reduced populations can be brought to normal strength in a relatively short space of time.

Laws has calculated that 12 per cent of Fin Whales ovulate about two months after they have given birth, while the remainder only ovulate again at the end of lactation, i.e. four months later, when they are either back in the Antarctic or on the way there. At that time, most of the bulls are, however, sexually inactive (at least in cold waters), so that mating is rare, and the ova usually remain unfertilized. Mating generally takes place once the animals have migrated to warmer waters, i.e. in about May. Laws found that 77 per cent of all conceptions take place from April to August; 17 per cent in September and March, and only 6 per cent from October to March. As a result of 'void' ovulations, the number of corpora albicantia (see p. 360) increases by 2·8 every two years. (In Humpbacks, one by every year; Chittleborough 1960). Since some cows conceive in the early stages of lactation, we might expect the average

interval between two successive births to be less than two years, and the
fact that the calculated interval is as much as 2·16 years must mean that
some cows do not conceive even during the winter following weaning.
It seems reasonable to assume that most of these are cows which, in the
year before, conceived soon after giving birth, and thus overtaxed their
strength.

Sperm Whales have their next oestrous phase only seven months after
weaning their calves, so that they produce offspring once every three
years. Narwhals, too, seem to have a similarly long interval between
successive births, while Blue Whales and Humpbacks' (just like Fin
Whales) are known to miss a season occasionally, and thus to have an
interval of more than two years between successive births. Other Cetaceans also miss a season from time to time, with Common Dolphins
'resting' after every three births.

With the help of all these data we should be able, by and large, to
calculate how many calves a given whale or dolphin cow can produce
during her lifetime, if we also knew her average life expectancy, and her
average fertile life. We shall return to these questions in the next chapter
in greater detail, but we may say, straight away, that while we have well-
founded arguments showing that senility plays hardly any role in the
life of Cetaceans, we know very little indeed about their average life-
span. The relevant figures in the table (p. 384) are therefore based on
inferences from other mammals. Crude approximations though these
figures are, they nevertheless show that Cetaceans cannot produce a
great many offspring, the figures varying from six to fifteen, and we would
do well to assume that Rorqual cows bear a maximum of twelve calves.
(These figures agree, by and large, with what we know of undomesticated
bovines, i.e. bisons.)

14

Whales and Whaling

by Richard J. Harrison FRS
Professor of Anatomy, University of Cambridge

THE HISTORY of modern whaling (since the introduction of harpoon guns after 1864) has been divided into separate phases, each one overlapping the next, brought about partly by changes in the area of operation and partly by technical advances. The last thirty years of the nineteenth century were marked by activity in the North Atlantic conducted at first from land stations in North Norway. Catches reached a peak in 1885. A second phase dates from 1904 when a land station was established at South Georgia and increasing exploitation of the southern population of whales commenced. Factory ships moored in harbours were introduced at this time. The next phase began during the late 1920s with the great development of pelagic whaling; factory ships operated on the high seas without need for land stations or moorings. Pelagic whaling did not supersede other methods entirely, as shore-based whaling continued but with changes in place and degree of activity. It has, however, been the principal factor causing the virtual exhaustion in a commercial sense of the southern stocks of baleen whales. It has also been responsible for the emergence of a more determined conservationist attitude 'to save the whale'. This has resulted in stringent attempts to regulate all aspects of whaling at national and international levels.

Early this century efforts to regulate whaling from land stations were at national level only and it was not until 1931 that the League of Nations drew up a Convention for the Regulation of Whaling. Two years previously a Bureau of International Whaling Statistics had been instituted in Norway to obtain details of catches. The Convention did not come into force until 1935 and not all countries adhered to it. More effective limitation of pelagic whaling was brought about by economic factors leading to agreements among whaling companies.

International conferences held in 1937 and 1938 had some effect in that minimum lengths were set, thus protecting young animals; total protection was given to two species (Right and Grey whales) and temporary protection to one (Humpback). A limit was placed on the operation of factory ships in certain waters, a shortened catching season introduced in the Antarctic, and a sanctuary established in the Pacific sector of the Antarctic. Arrangements to appoint inspectors were also instituted. Details are given in International Agreement for the Regulation of Whaling, 1937, Cmd 5487, London: H.M.S.O. and Protocol amending, 1938, Cmd 5887.

An overall limit to the total Antarctic catch was agreed upon in 1944 and 1945 (Cmds 6510 and 6725). This type of restriction had become more practicable, and a ceiling could be put on the catch well below any earlier level, because of loss of factory ships during the Second World War. A year later an even more important step was taken with the founding of the International Whaling Commission (I.W.C.) at a meeting in Washington. The establishment of the Commission has been described as being in itself a creditable act of international statesmanship. From its inauguration, however, the Commission's recommendations and their amendments have had numerous critics. Many have considered that the interests of the whaling industry were given priority over the advice of scientists and the warnings of conservationists.

The International Whaling Commission meets every year, when delegates of sixteen (1976) nations together with their expert advisers sit round a conference table in London or in the capital of any of the other member states. The needs of the different countries rarely change, and the same is largely true of the delegates. Most of the delegates know one another and one another's problems well. The conference proceeds in private and at the end of the session a *communiqué* is handed to the press.

The main discussions always revolve round the steps which must be taken to prevent the whale population from being reduced too drastically in any part of the world, so that whaling remains a profitable occupation. It is not the Commission's object to preserve whales for the sake of nature conservancy but it is in a good position to conserve the stock of whales since, by its very purpose, it goes much further than mere conservation. Not only does it attempt to preserve whales from extinction, but over and above this it tries to keep their number up to a level which should enable future generations to derive benefit from this source of fats, proteins and other valuable substances. It must try to balance the individual needs of member states, and at the same time protect whales without killing the industry.

The regulations controlling whaling are set out in the Schedule of the International Whaling Convention. They can be amended as the deliberations of the I.W.C. determine each year. Quotas are set for the total number of each species that may be caught, and more recently the numbers allowed from particular stocks in certain prescribed areas of the southern hemisphere and elsewhere are decided. Other matters controlled are the length of the season, the smallest and largest size that may be caught, the taking of females with calves and the use of carcasses. What has aggravated opinion against the I.W.C. is that member countries can lodge objections within a few months of any amendment being agreed, and so obtain a let-out. The presence of inspectors to record all details of the catch, sex, length, dimensions of foetuses and other useful statistics, as well as observers to report on infringements, have helped in theory at least to keep control of affairs. The various difficulties facing the I.W.C., which can operate only by persuasion, have been stated by Mackintosh (1965) and in Schevill (1974). In an authoritative book on the Blue Whale, Small (1971) is critical indeed of the I.W.C. and presents much evidence to support his adverse comments. The tragedy of the virtual disappearance of 'the largest animal known to have lived on land or sea since the beginning of time' is set out with every grim detail authenticated. These books also give histories of the activities of the Commission and, of course, there is considerable information in its Reports. The Permanent Commission for the Regulation of Marine Resources of the South Pacific, of which Chile, Ecuador and Peru are members, regulates whaling within their 200-mile zone. There are also other local treaties regulating affairs in several other countries' home waters.

Many conferences, discussion groups, workshops and meetings of learned societies have been held in recent years besides those of the I.W.C. to consider various aspects of cetology. Several of their reports are listed in the Bibliography: an especially important meeting took place in Bergen, Norway, in 1976 arranged by the Food and Agriculture Organization (F.A.O.) of the United Nations. There is no lack of literature, and reports abound, but are we getting more accurate information? There are many difficulties to overcome and Slijper referred to many of them in his original chapter. Most of his topics and comments are retained here because they are still relevant. Some scientists feel that matters will not really advance until new techniques are adopted to survey whales and study their life at sea. Use of satellites, establishment of fixed ocean stations, fitting of telemetry devices, injection of radioactive markers, controlled breeding in sanctuaries, intensive research on the whale's brain and its behaviour are some: all would be expensive but not impossible. Until these and other approaches are developed, the I.W.C. will have to continue as best it can on scientific advice that has to weigh the evidence derived from several but not necessarily reliable sources.

A whale is killed by firing a harpoon, about 2 m in length and over 50 kg in weight, from a gun mounted on the raised foredeck of the catcher boat into the animal at a range of between 20 and 30 m. The harpoon is fitted with barbs which spread open after it has entered the whale: an explosive charge is detonated by a time fuse. A line attached to the harpoon unravels as it strikes home and is later used to pull the dead whale close to the catcher boat by use of a winch. The carcass is then inflated with air to prevent it sinking and is marked for identification, and often devices are fixed to it, such as radar reflectors or signalling systems, to aid swift recovery after the catcher boat has spent most of the day pursuing other whales. Other methods of killing whales have been investigated but have been found too hazardous, too expensive, not always effective or just impracticable. Once again the I.W.C. have been castigated for not devising a solution to yet another problem in whaling. Whether brought ashore or to a floating factory, processing of the carcass must be performed expeditiously before deleterious *post-mortem* changes develop. Modern techniques of processing concentrate on rapid treatment to extract the now commercially valuable materials.

Quite apart from depredation by man, Slijper was concerned about the actual risk of whales becoming extinct. He thought that whales and dolphins will have to disappear from the earth some time, just like so many thousands of other animals which lived in prehistoric times, and which, after they had lived on earth for some millions or some tens of millions of years, disappeared with only fossils as their trace. He argued that all species and genera, man included, will eventually disappear, and in the case of cetaceans he tried to predict whether, geologically speaking, their time is running out or not.

Slijper compared the natural history of cetaceans, past and present, with that of other orders of animals, and got the clear impression that Mysticetes had passed the peak of their evolution many millions of years ago, and that they are much on the decline. The strongest evidence for this contention is their enormous size. In Chapter 2 it was shown that, twenty-five million years ago, Mysticetes were much smaller, and the history of the entire animal kingdom indicates that the emergence of giant forms is a certain sign of an approaching end. Another factor which, in geological time, endangers their existence is their highly specialized structure and *modus vivendi*. To take but two examples of this specialization: their almost exclusive diet of small 'shrimps' (krill), and a highly specialized whalebone apparatus which has become associated with this type of diet. If changes in the climate, or in the ocean currents, or depredation by man, should ever cause krill to disappear, Mysticetes would have to die out, since there is no other suitable food in adequate quantities and, even if there were, Mysticetes would be unable to obtain it.

Another factor militating against their long-term survival is somewhat paradoxical: most cetaceans live under optimum biological conditions. They have few enemies, are not too adversely affected by parasites, and up to now have had as much food as they need. In this way, weak and deformed animals have an excellent chance of survival, which is borne out by the many healed fractures and pathological bone processes which are found in cetacean carcasses (whose owners continued to live despite their impairment). Under less favourable conditions, Slijper argued that such weakened specimens would be quickly destroyed, but, as it is, their weak or pathological constitution may be transmitted (now considered unlikely) to future generations, until the whole species degenerates, and finally becomes extinct. From that point of view as well cetaceans would become extinct in the near (geologically speaking) future, even if man left them severely alone. In fact, a number of more recent species have already become extinct, e.g. the Atlantic Grey Whale, and this before man had begun to hunt it.

It might be argued, however, that, geologically speaking, whales have at least as good a chance of surviving as man, unless, of course, man eradicates them first, as, indeed, he has done with other species. Now while this danger is by no means imaginary, it is far smaller than is generally believed. Greenland Right Whales and Biscayan Right Whales have been greatly reduced in number by intensive hunts in past centuries, but they have not disappeared, and protective measures over fifty years *should* have enabled the population to increase once again.

In the Antarctic, the danger of eradicating whales is definitely smaller than it is in the Arctic, not only because the available space is larger (the sea accounts for 90 per cent of the area between 50°S. and 65°S., and only for 39 per cent of the area between 50°N. and 65°N.), but also because expeditions to the Antarctic are much more costly. Obviously, expeditions to the Antarctic can pay only if the catch is very large. A big reduction of the whale population would thus automatically curb the industry. Seeing that some 1,500 Blue Whales, 25,000 Fin Whales and 1,250 Humpback Whales were still caught during each year in the 1950s, this danger of extinction seemed remote, and in 1958 Slijper thought it might have been possible to keep the Antarctic industry going on, say, Fin Whales and others, while eradicating Blue Whales or Humpbacks. A critical reduction of the Humpback stock would have had serious economic repercussions, Slijper argued, since tropical and sub-tropical whaling stations (i.e. in Gaboon and Australia) caught few other whales. However, the pelagic catch of southern Humpbacks has indeed been prohibited since 1963 and it seems that there has been an increase in their population. The absolute protection of Grey Whales in the Northern Pacific has had a similar effect, and Gilmore (1960) estimates that while the Grey Whale population off the American coast was reduced from 25,000 to 200 during 1840–1938, their number had grown to 6,000 by 1960. Humpbacks and Grey Whales have an exceptionally small interval between successive births, and can therefore increase more rapidly than, say, Blue or Fin Whales. Sperm Whales, too, are in no great danger of extinction, since the official minimum size limit spares enough of the cows to keep the population at its present level.

Slijper realized that in the case of Blue Whales, there was greater cause for anxiety. The time had seemed ripe for their total protection in the North Atlantic. In the North Pacific, however, the situation then looked somewhat better, since the nations directly concerned, Japan and Russia, did not seem to be too worried. In the Antarctic, however, the outlook was rather bleak. At the beginning of the thirties 75 per cent of the total catch still consisted of Blue Whales, but by 1950–1951 this figure had dropped to 25 per cent, and by 1960 to only 6 per cent. The last figure, however, was partly the result of protective measures. Thus while the Fin Whale season then opened on 7 January, the Blue Whale season only opened on 1 February. Moreover, as we saw in Chapter 12, Blue Whales keep more to the polar ice belt than Fin Whales and, since the last war, expeditions have not ventured as far south as they used to, not only in order to safeguard their increasingly costly ships, but also because modern super-catchers operate much more efficiently on the open sea than in the ice. Of course, it might be argued that they stayed outside the ice belt simply because it is no longer economical to go in search of a diminishing Blue Whale population.

The yield of a Blue Whale is more or less equivalent to that of two Fin Whales, and whalers have naturally preferred to kill one whale instead of two for the same yield. The investigations of the Discovery Committee showed that while Fin Whales outnumbered Blue Whales as early as the thirties, the gap in numbers has grown so large since the war that Fin Whales and other species have had to bear the full brunt of whaling. It was right to ask whether their numbers justified an annual catch of about 25,000 animals. A principal task of the International Whaling Commission and the biologists attached to its scientific sub-committee was to decide this question (see Small, 1971, for criticisms).

Unfortunately, this task is far from simple, for, though all the member states are agreed that protective measures are *desirable*, an industry which has invested large capital in a whaling fleet and which gives employment to many is not so much concerned with whether prohibitive steps are desirable, as with whether they are absolutely *unavoidable*. And that question is, of course, far more difficult to decide. The dangers of giving rash opinions are best shown from the addresses which Sir Sidney Harmer, one of the greatest experts on whales, presented to the Linnaean Society in 1928 and 1930. Though Sir Sidney stated then that the final disaster could be expected very soon, and despite the enormous catches of the thirties, whales have continued to survive and are still caught. All the evidence and the data used must be most rigorously assessed.

All final decisions were based primarily on the International Whaling Statistics which, since 1930, have published detailed information on all whales caught in the Antarctic. The seasons have become steadily shorter ever since 1932, and particularly since the Second World War. While 16,000 Blue Whale Units (B.W.U.) were caught annually by fifteen expeditions in 121 days immediately after the war, the quota of 15,000 units was caught in only 58 days during 1955–1956, which was, however, an exceptionally short season. (Since then the season has been extended to 70 days, as it was in the preceding year. In 1959–1960 the season was very long and the catch figures were bad.) This short duration of the season might lead one to suspect that the whale population had strongly increased, particularly when we consider that although the number of permitted B.W.U. fell by 1,000, the actual number of captured Baleen Whales has increased by 4,250 since 1946–1947. (This is due to the fact that Fin Whales account for an increasing proportion of the catch, and that, in the definition of the B.W.U., two Fin Whales are equivalent to one Blue Whale.)

However, Slijper pointed out that these suspicions are not necessarily correct, since whaling techniques, too, changed radically during 1950–1960. Factory ships, whose average tonnage in 1946 was 13,212, had an average capacity of 16,093 tons in 1955, and thus a far greater potential output. Moreover, we can see at a glance from Fig. 217 that the number of catchers per factory ship increased from 9 to 15 and their average horse-power from 1,302 to 1,945. (The slight drop during 1953–1955 was due to the agreed limitation of the number of catchers per factory ship, since then repealed, and again introduced in 1957–1958.) Nor can we go very much by the average number of whales caught per catcher per day, since the number of B.W.U. per Catcher's Day's Work (C.D.W.) tends to increase with the increasing capacity of the catcher, and to decrease with the increasing number of catchers per factory ship, as the number of carcasses a given factory ship can process is, of course, limited. Needless to say, the statistics do not tell us how many hours a given catcher is kept idle because the mother ship has its hands full (all carcasses must be processed within thirty-three hours, and stores cannot be accumulated) nor how many catchers are used as buoy-boats for towing dead whales to

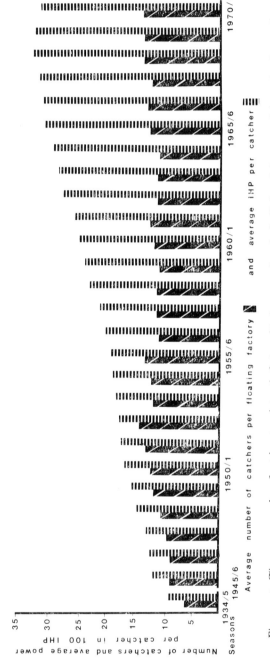

Figure 217. *The average number of catchers per Antarctic factory ship has approximately doubled, and the power of the catchers has nearly quadrupled since 1934. In this time the average gross tonnage of each catcher has increased from 256 in 1934 to 824 in 1970.* (*From data supplied by* International Whaling Statistics.)

Average number of catchers per floating factory ▨ and average IHP per catcher ▦

Number of catchers and average power per catcher in 100 IHP

Seasons 1934/5   1945/6   1950/1   1955/6   1960/1   1965/6   1970/1

35 30 25 20 15 10 5

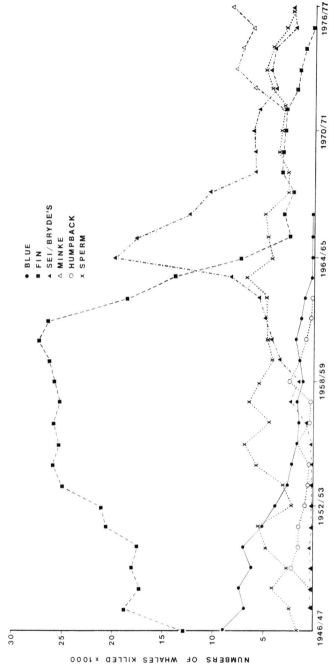

Figure 218. Numbers of whales killed by the combined pelagic whaling fleets in the Antarctic seasons 1946–1947 to 1976–1977. (From data supplied by International Whaling Statistics.)

the factory ships. Moreover, it will generally take longer to capture two Fin Whales than to capture one Blue Whale, and so a comparison of annual catch results did not necessarily lead to reliable conclusions about whale populations.

While, therefore, an increase in B.W.U. per C.D.W. cannot be interpreted as meaning that the number of whales has increased in recent years, it does not *a fortiori* entitle us to say that the number has dropped. In the seasons 1959–1960 and 1960–1961 the figures for B.W.U. per C.D.W. were extremely low (0.72 and 0.68). On the other hand, catching conditions were quite abnormal because there was no overall limit and because many expeditions reported extremely bad weather. A small body of experts on fishery statistics started to study the problem on a new basis, but seem to have treated whales too much like fish.

One argument that has been cited in favour of a drop in population is the decrease in average length of the annual catch and the increase from 13.8 per cent to 30 per cent of the proportion of sexually immature animals in it. In fact, the average length of captured Fin Whales has decreased since 1947–1948 (with the exception of the 'fat years', 1951 and 1952, when it was back to normal). Now an increase in the proportion of young animals in the catch may be interpreted with equal justification as a sign of reduction of the adult population, as of an increase in propagation. Moreover, by virtue of the international overall catch limit of a fixed number of units, competition was naturally increased, with the result that every expedition tried to bag as much of the total quota as quickly as it could. This caused an increase of the number of catchers per factory ship and consequently an increase of Olympic-type competition between the catchers. There was no time for selecting large animals only. Younger animals are less experienced and more inquisitive than adults, and are therefore more easily caught (which applies also to different types of game). Thus Arseniev (1958) reported Russian gunners as stating that adult Rorquals are not only more difficult to approach than immature animals, but that they become more and more suspicious as the season advances.

It is clear that the *International Whaling Statistics* alone cannot tell us how many whales may be caught annually without endangering either the species or the future of the industry. To arrive at the correct answer, we should have to know how many animals there are, how many of them are killed annually, or die of natural causes, and how many calves are born each year. It is only on the question of how many are killed that the statistics tell us anything at all.

The whale population was initially estimated by two methods: whale marks and regional counts. If, say, a few thousand whales are marked before the beginning of the season, and if, for instance, 5 per cent of the catch marks are subsequently recovered, it might be reasonably assumed that the few thousand marked animals represent 5 per cent of the total population. It is doubtful if this method does, in fact, lead to reliable estimates, since the Antarctic population is not static (see Chapter 12) and since many marks are overlooked during processing (see page 332). Thus Ruud estimated that the proportion of marks overlooked in this way is 50 per cent, while Japanese sources have put the figure at 25 per cent.

The other method, direct counts, was thought to be more promising. Naturally, it is impossible to count every single whale, but regional counts can be made from ships and helicopters, and, by combining the results from different representative areas, we may form a fair idea of the total population. The leader of the British whaling research team, Dr N. A. Mackintosh, and his collaborator, S. G. Brown, tried to use this method in order to estimate the Fin Whale population before the Second World War. They based their findings on regular observations made aboard the *Discovery II*, which cruised through a number of Antarctic regions from 1933–1939. Making allowances for special conditions, both biologists calculated that the maximum number of Fin Whales inhabiting the southern hemisphere at the time was 255,000. However, Symons (1956) and Ruud (1956) have both advised great caution in accepting this figure, since it is not known how systematically the *Discovery II* covered the given area, how expert her observers were (and whaling observations demand years of experience), and how many whales took to flight at the ship's approach. During these six years the crew of the *Discovery II* actually *saw* only 1,900 Fin Whales (or 315 per annum), i.e. the average number *captured* by a single catcher during that time. Hence Mackintosh and Brown's count was based on the observed presence of only 0.13 per cent of the estimated total population – a clear indication that their count can, at best, only give us an idea of the order of magnitude of the Fin Whale population.

More recent efforts to convert sighting records into estimates of population have taken account of the deficiences of visual scanning, the diving time of animals, duration of blows, sea and weather conditions, number of observers, reaction to ships and the precise region scanned in respect of the expected whale density.

From 1959 to 1962 the I.W.C. underwent some vicissitudes, with certain member states withdrawing and then rejoining. For these seasons there were no effective limits to catches in the Antarctic, and nations set their own quotas. 1962 was an important year as it marked the serious consideration of scientific advice for management purposes. A special scientific committee (of Three, later Four) had been formed in 1960 by the I.W.C; its report caused the I.W.C. to reduce the quota for 1963–1964 to 10,000 B.W.U. It also protected the Blue Whale throughout most of the Antarctic and the Humpback Whale throughout the southern hemisphere. In fact only 8,429 B.W.U. were taken and it was clear that the recommendations of the Committee of Three had not been taken seriously enough. Much lower quotas (4,000 down to 2,000 B.W.U.) were put forward for 1964–1965 and for later years, but these were unacceptable to those nations still whaling in the Antarctic: a voluntary quota of 8,000 B.W.U. was instituted yet not reached. For 1965–1966 the I.W.C. adopted a policy based on sustainable yields, totally protected the Blue Whale and set a quota of 4,500 B.W.U. for Fin and Sei whales in the Antarctic. This had been reduced progressively, in line with revision of scientific estimates of stock, from 3,200 B.W.U. in 1967–1968 to 2,300 B.W.U. in 1971–1972. Scientific advice had also had effect from 1966 in controlling commercial whaling in the North Pacific, at first by agreement between countries involved, and eventually limited to Japan and the U.S.S.R. Later on, by 1971, the policy of not going above the sustainable yield became adopted and within the framework of I.W.C. proposals.

The policy of the I.W.C. during recent years has been to regulate whaling to ensure conservation of stocks by assessing available scientific advice and then setting a quota for the stocks of each species. It is easy to understand the earlier lack of attention to scientific advice: whales were more plentiful, there was pressure by the whaling industry and others with a commercial interest, the advice had not been tested and even the experts differed, so an *ad hoc* approach seemed adequate. To many it seemed that the I.W.C. dragged its feet, did not take advice and vacillated in face of what were the obvious policies. In fairness to the I.W.C., it has tried to regulate the availability to nations of a biological product and its powers of enforcement are virtually nil. Public opinion has, however, exerted an increasing pressure on commercial whaling. In 1972 came the serious proposal for a ten-year moratorium on all commercial whaling. It had been discussed more and more as the years passed and whale stocks became depleted, and then came the call from the U.N. Conference on the Human Environment. A moratorium for ten years should allow stocks to recover, should reverse the drift to extinction of endangered species and would enable time for a comprehensive review of whaling policies. Whales inhabit international waters and are the heritage of mankind. Why should they be killed for the manufacture of animal feeding stuffs, fertilizer, cosmetics, margarine and oil for lubrication and tanning when adequate substitutes exist (such as wax from Jojoba shrubs) or could be found? If Japan needs more protein could it not import

Australian sheep and beef rather than subsidize a declining and unpopular industry? Moreover whales are gentle, intelligent creatures, harmless to man and not deserving to be slaughtered so inhumanely.

The arguments presented to support a moratorium at most seem cogent enough to persuade nations to initiate such an experiment, and at least should cause interested parties to reflect on, and review, their attitudes. One basic argument concerns whether man enjoys a right to kill any form of animal for food, clothing and other products. If it is accepted that man may farm terrestrial mammals, provided he manages his stock and provides for its welfare, then he should be free to farm the sea with similar provisos. The statement that cetaceans are intelligent needs careful asssessment, and the I.W.C. itself became interested in the matter in 1978. The allegation is based on certain facts and a good deal of sweeping speculation. The facts about the anatomy of the dolphin brain have been stated by Morgane and Jacobs (1968), who conclude that the quality of the cerebral cortex has yet to be shown to be that of an animal displaying intelligence. Wilson (1975) in his book *Sociobiology, The New Synthesis*, reviews other aspects of dolphin behaviour and concludes that 'there is no evidence whatever that delphinids are more advanced in intelligence and social behavior than other animals. In intelligence the Bottle-nosed Dolphin probably lies somewhere between the dog and the rhesus monkey.' He remarks on the large size of the brain of the Sperm Whale: 'Perhaps the Sperm Whale is really a genius in disguise; the possibility cannot be totally discounted.' Wilson is, however, more inclined to associate the large cetacean brain with mimicry, recognition by individuals of their own group at a distance, use of echo-location for orientation and detection of prey which has preadapted cetaceans for a well developed system of auditory communication. We contend that the excellent anatomical and physiological adaptations to diving and to successful existence in the oceans must have evolved along with an associated ability to receive, analyse and store sensory information (mainly auditory) vital to survival of both individuals and groups of cetaceans.

The United States took an important, even if criticized, decision in cetacean conservation when in 1972 it passed a Marine Mammal Protection Act (P.L. 92–522, 21 October 1972). In the Act, Congress declared a national policy to maintain marine mammal populations at optimum sustainable levels, while also ensuring a healthy and stable marine ecosystem. A Marine Mammal Commission was established with a committee of scientists to advise it by reviewing information, making recommendations on permits, supporting research, holding conferences and identifying depleted, endangered and threatened stocks. The essential provision in the Act calls for a moratorium on taking and importing of marine mammals and their products except by certain Indians, Aleuts and Eskimos for subsistence or native handicrafts and clothing. The Act does, however, provide for permits to allow taking of certain species for scientific research and public display.

Quite apart from the effect on commercial whaling, the Act's provisions identified several other issues, some of which have been the cause of much discussion and conflict of opinion. One of these concerned the status of the Bowhead Whale which has been over-exploited throughout its range and which has been hunted for centuries by Alaskan Eskimos for subsistence purposes. It had become clear that the Bering Sea stock had been hunted to such an extent that in 1977 it was between 6 and 10 per cent of its original size. The Marine Mammal Commission accordingly recommended that the Bowhead Whale stock be designated as depleted. Meanwhile the I.W.C. had estimated that the stock size had fallen to between 600 and 2,000 animals, and had noted that hunting had increased. What was of particular concern was the observation that all stocks of the Bowhead Whale had been protected totally from commercial whaling, yet no increase in numbers had occurred. It appeared that the species could be destined to become extinct and therefore the I.W.C. declared that exploitation must cease altogether. This caused more than a little trouble in view of legal action by the Eskimo representatives and the desire of those concerned to do right for their particular cause. It was accordingly proposed that a strict conservation programme be introduced with a limited quota of whales (so many retrieved and so many struck, whichever should come first). Eventually the I.W.C. agreed in 1977 that aboriginal hunters be allowed to land 12 or strike altogether 18 whales, whichever came first, but no calves and whales with calves should be taken or struck. Several other points were emphasized: the need for review of the stock, for control of hunting techniques, that Canada and the U.S.S.R. would not hunt Bowheads and that measures should be taken to preserve the Beluga as that might well be hunted more if the taking of Bowhead Whales were restricted.

Another problem that arose from the introduction of the Marine Mammal Protection Act concerns the governing of the incidental taking of marine mammals in the course of commercial fishing operations. This applies in particular to the incidental taking of Eastern Spinner Dolphins and other dolphins associated with commercial Yellowfin Tuna fishing. The nature of the tuna-fishing technique and the way in which Spinner and Spotted Dolphins accompany the tuna mean that large numbers of dolphins are entrapped and die during netting operations. The estimated dolphin mortality in 1972 was 348,000 (U.S. and foreign); it fell to 143,900 in 1976 but the Commission considered that the Eastern **Spinner**

Dolphin was depleted under the Act. No fishing on pure schools of Eastern Spinners would be allowed by the Commission because estimates indicated that numbers had reached the lower limit of optimum sustainable population. A general permit was to be issued containing limitations on the total number of animals that could be killed and the numbers 'taken' by pursuit and encirclement. Various interested parties naturally objected to or challenged the proposed regulations and went to Court. There were also non-U.S. interests, increasing year by year, to be considered and requests were made for effective agreements. Behavioural studies, experiments with gear and modified catching systems had shown that the kill rate could be much reduced. Dolphins had been observed lying passively on the net, under water and seemingly dead; these 'sleeping' animals would certainly be trapped and die if the net were brought in too soon. It was found to be possible to remove these temporarily stunned animals from the net if the backdown arrangement were maintained until they came to the surface. Eventually, late in 1977, final regulations were passed for 1978–1980 which recognized the depleted status of the Eastern Spinner Dolphin, advocated use of effective gear (super-apron system) and set total quotas declining ('Ratcheting') from 51,945 animals in 1978 to 31,150 in 1980.

Yet another problem besetting the U.S. Commission is that of the deliberate taking of small cetaceans alive for display purposes. A wide variety of species have been exhibited in zoos and marinelands in many countries, but the species easiest to catch alive, to transport, to maintain and to train to perform simple manoevures on command is the Bottlenose Dolphin. Other species can certainly provide attractive displays but there are all kinds of difficulties to be overcome and a high mortality of captive specimens means continual return to the ocean for replacements. Indeed, some species are so difficult to catch safely and maintain successfully that experienced catchers feel these types should never be taken alive. The syndrome known as 'capture shock' is more apparent in species such as *Phocoena*, *Delphinus* and especially *Lagenodelphis*. Live-capture techniques have improved steadily but all require skill in seamanship and handling of gear and specimens. It is also easier to take specimens in certain waters and for many years the majority of Bottlenose Dolphins (*T. truncatus*) required for display and research have come from off Florida. There is, therefore, the danger, even if global numbers were not threatened, for a small local population to be over-exploited. This also applies to the Killer Whale, immature specimens having become increasingly in demand as tank size has expanded, and the population in Puget Sound and thereabouts has become of concern. It will be obvious that live capture of cetaceans should be done by experienced persons, and particular care taken of animals during transport. Standards must be set for size of tank or pool, number of animals in each, water turnover and quality, provision of properly thawed fish for food and adequate veterinary care. The total number of Bottlenose Dolphins taken alive over the past twenty years is virtually impossible to assess because of unrecorded accidents on capture and during transport. It has been estimated that at least 600 were taken off Florida between 1970 and 1973, and in 1975 there were about 1,000 throughout the world in holding tanks or on display. This last estimate includes a relatively small number of animals recognized as *T. gilli* and *T. aduncus* from the Pacific. Longevity in captivity has varied greatly, from days to over twelve years. Not surprisingly efforts have been made to breed from captive dolphins but the high incidence of still-births, the peri-natal and neo-natal mortality, and the failure of about 60 per cent of captive-bred animals to reach even their first birthday has been depressing. For some unknown reasons captive breeding has been more successful in a few marinelands than in most others.

The number of Bottlenose Dolphins captured alive from certain areas has fallen considerably since the Marine Mammal Protection Act was passed. Better husbandry and increasing veterinary skill has reduced mortality. Regular monitoring of weight and length, food intake, blood and other characteristics has enabled animals to be maintained on selected growth patterns.

The basic information needed to make responsible decisions on all the above stocks is that of their number and their potential for sustaining losses by capture. Far fewer Killer Whales are taken for display than Bottlenose Dolphins, so why worry? Indeed Killer Whales are predators of other marine mammals such as seals and porpoises, are said to attack whalebone whales, and have been often shot for their disturbance of fishing and damage to nets. If left to multiply would they become even more of a nuisance? Other matters on which we have no information are to what extent Killer Whales migrate, whether individuals join other populations, and whether particular schools keep to limited regions all the time. Of course these and other questions can be asked about other species and the U.S. Marine Mammal Commission has instigated numerous reviews and assessments to improve knowledge on those cetacean types found in its waters.

Another important event which could have a positive effect on conservation of cetaceans took place in Washington in 1973. It was the Convention on International Trade in Endangered Species of Wild Fauna and Flora (C.I.T.E.S.) and is sometimes known as the Washington Treaty or

Convention. It came into force first during 1975 and in 1976 in the U.K. (H.M.S.O. Cmnd 5459). Eighteen countries entered into agreement almost at once, others joined soon afterwards, and by mid 1978 forty-six countries had become party to the Convention, although a few expressed reservations. The major provisions refer to international trade (defined as export, re-export, import and introduction from the sea). They cover animals and plants (alive or dead) and also any readily recognizable parts or derivatives in which there is or could be trade. The principal objective is, of course, to stop or control trade in those species which are at risk of extermination by man taking them from the wild. Obviously there are degrees of risk for each species and so three Appendices were established which list species under various levels of regulation.

Appendix I contains those species threatened with extinction which are or may be affected by trade, and trade in those species must be authorized only in exceptional circumstances.

Appendix II contains those species not necessarily now threatened with extinction but may become so unless trade is regulated. It also includes other species which must be subject to regulation in order that trade in specimens already in Appendix II may be controlled effectively.

Appendix III contains species within the jurisdiction of a particular country which need the cooperation of other countries to control trade.

Each country has to form a Scientific Authority to advise on the species and to review from time to time the basis on which decisions have been made. A Management Authority authorizes the issue of permits for export and import from or into that country. There are certain exceptions, one of which as far as cetaceans are concerned relates to specimens bred in captivity, and another allows scientific exchange. Certain other international agreements take precedence, especially where they cover marine species included on Appendix II, but Appendix I has priority.

Those cetacean species that were on Appendix I in early 1978 were as follows:

> *Platanista gangetica*
> *Eschrichtius robustus*
> *Balaenoptera borealis* (also Appendix II)
> *Balaenoptera musculus*
> *Balaenoptera physalus* (also Appendix II)
> *Megaptera novaeangliae*
> *Balaena mysticetus*
> *Eubalaena spp.*

Some stocks of *B. borealis* and *B. physalus* are also on Appendix II: *Pontoporia blainvillei* and *Monodon monoceros* are on Appendix III. Proposals are being put forward that all cetaceans not on Appendix I should be on Appendix II.

The cetacean materials in which trade is restricted in the United Kingdom under the Endangered Species (Import and Export) Act 1976 (Modification) Order 1977 are as given in Schedule 3:

Whale meat, whale offals (fresh, chilled, frozen, salted, in brine, dried or smoked, whether or not fit for human consumption). Whale bone, unworked or simply prepared but not cut to shape, and hair and waste thereof. Whale fat and whale oil (other than sperm oil) whether or not refined; and such oil boiled, oxidised, dehydrated, sulphurised, blown or polymerised by heat in vacuum or inert gas, or otherwise modified; and such fat and oil wholly or partly hydrogenated, or solidified or hardened by any other process but not further prepared. Whalemeat extracts and whalemeat juices.

Narwhal tusks and the teeth of all animals, unworked or simply prepared, but not cut to shape, and powder and waste thereof.

It is not easy to reach agreement on the biological status of any species and particularly so as regards cetacean species. A rare plant, for example, may be found only in a locality of small area and the number of specimens in existence on a certain day might be assessable with accuracy. With cetaceans it is much more difficult to assess population size, geographic range, reproductive rates, mortality and the effects of catching. When the reader's eyes reach this sentence, and whatever the date, nobody will have more than a rough estimate for each species of how many whales or dolphins there are alive.

To calculate the annual recruitment, we must know at what age animals reach puberty, how much later a given cow has her first calf, the normal life expectancy of the cow, how many calves she can have throughout her life, and the ratio of bulls to cows. To start with the last point, whaling statistics which indicate, *inter alia*, the sex of foetuses, suggest that the same number of Rorqual and Sperm Whale bulls and cows are born annually, and that this ratio is subsequently maintained.

In Chapter 13 we saw that, by examining their reproductive organs, we can tell whether whales have reached sexual maturity or not, and that whaling statistics and other data enable us to estimate the interval between successive births. In basing our calculations on these data, however, we must bear in mind that, for instance, the figures on page 384 are only reliable if our estimates of the age of the animals are correct. Now, while we cannot tell the precise age of a given whale, we have methods of estimating it, and since all our conclusions depend on the accuracy of these methods, we must examine them closely.

Overall length can tell us something about the age of young animals, but it is no indication of the age of mature ones. We shall say little about Mackintosh and Wheeler's method (1929), since their age determinations by means of examining the degree of healing of external scars applies to maximum periods of three years, and can, moreover, give rise to grave misinterpretations. Another method suggested by Mackintosh and Wheeler which was subsequently used by many other biologists (Wheeler, 1930; Laurie, 1937; Peters, 1939; Zemski, 1940) is far more promising. This method is based on counts of corpora albicantia in the ovaries (see Fig. 199, page 358 and Fig. 200, page 359). In Chapter 13 we saw that these corpora are indications of ovulations and that in whales they never disappear. Counts of the corpora albicantia of Fin Whale cows have shown a distinct periodicity from which it appears that 2.8 corpora albicantia are formed every two years (Laws; page 389), and that the age of a cow can therefore be estimated fairly accurately from the number of corpora albicantia in a given ovary, provided that the age at sexual maturity is known and provided that the ovary is behaving normally.

In 1948, Nishiwaki and Hayashi discovered that in whales, as in many other animals, man included, the colour of the lens of the eye changes with increasing age. The lens is colourless in young animals and gradually turns a golden colour. (The absorption of light can be measured with a photometer.) However, since no particular tint could be associated with a given age, and since, moreover, there was no measurable periodicity, this method is of no practical significance.

One characteristic which shows gradual, periodic, changes is the thickness of the baleen plates, in which ridges and grooves across the surface can be made out with the naked eye (Fig. 219). In some baleen plates the ridges are so regularly spaced that William Scoresby in 1820 suspected that the ridges might be akin to the annual rings found in the horns of cattle, and in the scales and otoliths (ear stones) of fish, in all of which they are used for age determination. By simply opening a whale's mouth we should therefore be able to tell its age. However, things are not quite as simple as that, and it took Ruud, and Tomilin who worked independently, until 1940 to perfect an instrument for measuring the thickness of baleen plates accurately, and Hirata until 1959 to perfect a photographic method.

Whalebone is formed inside the gum, from which it is continually replenished to compensate for frictional effects. In other words, the oldest whalebone is always at the extremity, and the whole baleen plate consists of material formed over a limited number of years. In a seven-year-old whale, for instance, probably nothing of the whalebone formed during the first year of its life has remained, and the extremity of the baleen plate consists of material formed during its second or third year. On page 265,

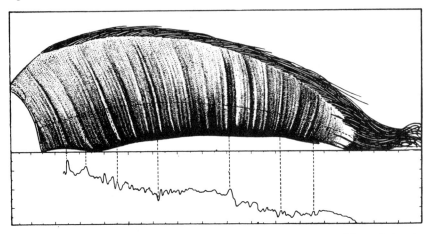

Figure 219. The baleen of a Blue Whale, showing ridges and grooves. The variations in thickness measured with special apparatus are reproduced on the graph.

we saw that the cornified tubules which constitute the innermost part of the baleen plate are of uniform diameter throughout, so that the thickening of the baleen plate towards the gum rests exclusively on increases of thickness of the cortical layer. Baleen plates are naturally thicker at the base, since the extremity has been exposed to friction longer than the rest.

The plates are not thickened uniformly. Thus the lines shown in Figs. 219 and 220 are made up of so many crests and troughs which can be seen with the naked eye. If we assume that frictional effects are equal over the entire surface of the baleen plate, the ridges must be due to the different quantities of horn deposited in the cortical layer from time to time. On page 267 and in Fig. 145, we have seen that the thickness of the cortical layer is determined in a narrow area of the gum. Every difference in thickness corresponds with differences in horn production during a limited time. Why new horn should not be laid down continuously is not quite clear, but is most probably due to periodic metabolic changes. Unfortunately we know little about similar processes in other animals, except that, in human beings, malnutrition and other factors cause the growth of hair and nails to be impaired or even to be discontinued.

In Mysticetes, and particularly in migrating Rorquals, annual metabolic and frictional changes are only to be expected. In cold water, where food is plentiful, large fat reserves are stored up and the whalebone is exposed to maximum friction, while in the tropics where food is scarcer, the whalebone is used to a lesser extent, and the animal becomes thin. The annual return to the Antarctic taxes the strength of the underfed

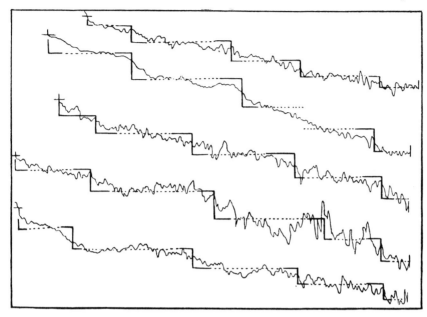

Figure 220. Variations in thickness in the baleen plates of a Fin Whale, showing Prof. Ruud's annual levels. (Ruud, 1945.)

animals, with further metabolic changes. Other contributory periodic disturbances are birth, lactation, weaning and mating.

Ruud has been investigating baleen plates for many years, and believes that, in the thickness of the plates, there occur different levels which are associated with annual alternations of a 'storing metabolism' in cold waters and a 'consumptive metabolism' in warm waters. Every level (or period) would then represent a year in a whale's life, but, because of friction, only six to seven years will be represented on whalebone at one time. Ruud also thinks that we can tell from the angle between individual horny tubes (they converge to the whalebone 'top' which is formed in the foetus) whether the original whalebone is still present, or else how many years have been 'rubbed off'. More recent investigations of Fin Whales by Mrs C. van Utrecht-Cock cast doubt on the correctness of Ruud's interpretation of the so-called annual levels. She believes that the characteristic recurrence of certain crests and troughs across the whalebone ridges is a far better indication for dividing the baleen curves into periods, each typical group of tops representing a certain event in every season. In order to deduce even the most recent events in the history of the whalebone (which can be checked by the ovaries, by the age of a calf, etc.) investi-

Figure 221. Longitudinal section of a 'wax plug' from the auditory passage of a Blue Whale, showing 'annual rings'. (Purves, 1955.)

gations have included that part of the baleen which is found inside the gum. This has enabled Mrs van Utrecht-Cock to distinguish special tops which, probably, are correlated with ovulations. The more or less regular occurrence of these ovulation tops in the curves of the baleen plates agreed with the initial conclusion of Laws that the Fin Whale shows an average ovulation rate of 2.8 per two years. Recent work, however, has shown that Fin Whales display an ovulation rate of 0.68 per annum (Gambell, 1973). Further researches on the baleen plates showed that Ruud's age estimates are on the low side, and moreover that the age determinations are only reliable up to an age of four years (i.e. only in immature animals). For older animals it is better to rely on the corpora albicantia or on another method, first suggested by Purves, and subsequently applied by him and Mountford to mature and immature whales.

This method is based on investigations of the structure of the wax plug, which, as we saw in Chapter 7, is found in the inner part of the external auditory passage of Mysticetes. The plug, which must be freed carefully from the surrounding tissue, looks like an elongated cone (see Fig. 108, page 208, and Fig. 221) and consists of layers of cornified epithelium. The plug, particularly in Blue Whales, is often marked by alternate dark and light laminae, which are suggestive of regular formation. One light and one dark lamina together constitute a growth layer. Apparently the plug grows thicker all the time because the cranial sutures of Mysticetes (just like those of elephants) do not close until late in life, thus the skull and the inner part of the auditory passage keep expanding. To compensate for this expansion, one or two new layers of cornified epithelium are formed across the plug, and Purves believed that the alternate bands around the plug arose from annual periods of maximum growth and maximum rest. Ichihara (1959) pointed to an alternation of fatty and keratinized degeneration of the epithelium. Since the bands are by and large made up of the same type of tissue as is found in horns, nails and whalebone, it seems likely Purves is right in assuming that they, too, arise from annual or periodic metabolic changes. Thus, during migrations to and from the Antarctic, growth could be arrested, and two annual laminae could be formed, while a single lamina only could be formed when, for instance, the southward migration alone influences the metabolism significantly. Other factors, too, might influence the formation of the laminae and Chittleborough and Best (1960) were able to show the presence of laminae in the wax plugs of Bryde's Whales, though that species does not have the marked migratory rhythm of Blue, Fin and Humpback Whales, and though it seems to have no restricted breeding season.

Fifty-two laminae have been found in a Blue Whale, and if we take it that the laminae are bi-annual, Blue Whales have a life expectancy of at least twenty-six years. Nishiwaki (1952) reported that he counted eighty-six laminae in the wax plugs of a Fin Whale, which may mean that Fin Whales live up to forty-three years. From Purves's and Nishiwaki's reports, it appears that the average age of the animals is higher than the average age found by Ruud with the baleen method. The wax plug method has the advantage that the plugs are not worn down by friction, so that all the laminae laid down from birth should be countable, while the whalebone method is, according to Ruud himself, unreliable for periods longer than five years, and quite useless for estimating the age of old whales. However, it is very difficult to make reliable counts of early laminae; immature whales display laminae which are not formed annually.

By means of the ear-plug and other methods it is possible to estimate when whales reach sexual and physical maturity. Human beings stop growing between the ages of twenty-two and twenty-six, after which the last epiphyses – the thin bony plates on the superior and inferior faces of each vertebra – fuse solidly with the middle mass of the centrum. Now, since growth can only take place while some cartilage divides the epiphyses from the centrum, their fusion is equivalent to physical maturity. In all animals, fusion begins in the cervical and caudal regions, the anterior thoracic vertebrae being the last to grow together. Thus, by examining its vertebral column, we can tell what degree of physical maturity a given whale has reached, and biologists now believe that Fin Whales are physically mature at between twenty-five and thirty years, but this is always subject to revision under different conditions.

Biologists can use three methods of estimating the age of baleen whales (corpora albicantia, baleen periods, and ear-plug bands), and while there is some measure of agreement between the results obtained by the several methods, it must be stressed that none of them is conclusive. To be conclusive, any method would have to be tested on an animal whose real age was known beforehand, and this would mean marking of calves which is not always to their advantage.

Dawbin, however, who marked a large number of Humpback calves off New Zealand, does not agree with this opinion, and points out that two of the animals marked by him were caught twelve and nineteen months later in unimpaired condition. In one of these, the actual age at capture, i.e. about three years, could be established with a fair amount of accuracy, and investigations of the baleen plates and the ear plugs indicated that one ring was laid down annually in the baleen, and two growth layers in the ear plugs. This was thought to have been confirmed by a Humpback marked one year old (but it could have been older) in 1954 and captured in 1959 (Chittleborough, 1960). Five ear plugs taken at Japanese floating factories from marked Fin Whales of an age of at least twenty-seven years indicated, however, that the annual rate of deposition is less than 1.5 growth layers a year. Examination of monthly samples of Fin Whale ear plugs by Roe (1967) has provided even more definite evidence that only one lamina of each type is formed in a year, and suggests that the lamination in ear plugs of young whales may vary or be misleading. Lockyer (1972, 1974) has demonstrated a transition between irregular lamination and more even spacing at sexual maturity.

Until recently, the age determination of Odontocetes by examination of layers in the dentine was not verified by examination of an animal of known age. But in 1959, Sergeant, inspecting the teeth of four Bottlenose Dolphins of known age in the Marineland Aquarium (Florida), concluded that, for reasons not yet fully understood, the number of years concurred with the number of layers in each tooth. Sperm Whales, on the other hand, were at first said to form two layers of dentine a year; later this estimate had to be altered to one per year. There is, however, no definite conclusive evidence to decide in sperm teeth the exact rate of layer formation and which lamina is related to growth. Failure to reach conclusions has been due partly to the different ways in which tooth sections have been described.

The exact age of a whale still remains difficult to assess, but we have some information on their life expectancy. The common belief is expressed in the opinion of the great Cuvier, who, in his *Histoire naturelle des Cétacés* (1936), wrote: '*La durée de leur vie doit être considérable si l'on en juge par analogue avec celle des autres animaux à mammelles*' (The duration of their lives, judged by that of other mammals, must be considerable). In saying so Cuvier was probably thinking exclusively of their dimensions. It is generally correct to say that large animals grow older than small animals, but not quite to the extent that popular belief would have it. Thus elephants certainly never grow older than seventy years. Moreover, there are exceptions to this general rule, e.g. bats which live until they are twenty years old, and this despite their small size, from which we might have inferred that their life expectancy was three years at most (the maximum age of mice). The explanation for all this is probably that maximum age is determined largely by metabolic rate, which decreased with increasing size (see Chapters 9 and 11).

Whales, on the other hand, are moving about most of the time even when they are 'asleep' (see page 189). Their metabolic rate could be exceptionally high for their size. It is now known that Rorquals reach puberty at six to ten years of age depending on the species and the year of catch. Mammals in general become sexually mature at about one-eighth to one-sixth their maximum age. We can therefore estimate that the life span of a Rorqual ought to be at least thirty-six to forty-eight and could reach eighty years. The oldest mark found in the carcasses of Fin Whales had lodged there for thirty-seven years, and the animals must, therefore, have been at least several years older, and a number of other Fin Whales have had marks recovered from them after intervals of up to thirty years. A Fin Whale whose age was determined by corpora albicantia, was at least forty-five years old; it was thought that the ovulation rate declined in older females, which is probably true for some Sperm Whale populations but not now for Fin Whales. Variations in ovarian activity will obviously reduce the reliability of corpora counts for ageing purposes.

Counts of growth layers in ear plugs, or of dentinal layers in Sperm Whale teeth, could give more accurate indications of life span. In Fin Whales some ear plugs have over ninety layers, and in Sei Whales over fifty and occasional ones possibly up to seventy. Symons and Weston (1957) mention a Humpback that was twenty-nine years old, and although this species appears to be relatively old at physical maturity (with thirty corpora), it probably has a similar longevity. From the days of Greenland whaling, when harpoons used to be marked with the year in which they were used, we know that Greenland Whales and Biscayan Right Whales can live until forty years at least. Sperm Whales are known from a mark to live until they are at least thirty-two, but animals with over sixty dentinal rings have been reported, but for obvious reasons no marked Blue Whale has been found much older than twenty. These figures do not, of course, indicate the maximum age these animals could reach, since none of the whales in question died of natural causes.

Some other Odontocetes can apparently reach the same age. Thus 'Pilot Jack' or 'Pelorus Jack' (some claim it was a Risso's Dolphin, others a Bottlenose Dolphin) is said to have accompanied ships plying between Wellington and Nelson (New Zealand) for twenty-five years. Sleptsov estimated that the much smaller Common Dolphin lives for fifteen years;

Bottlenose Dolphins can live to well over twenty years according to their teeth.

Because our knowledge of the life span of whales is incomplete, we cannot be sure whether they remain fertile throughout life, or whether cessation of ovarian activity sets in at a particular age, as it does in human females. It has been asserted that Pilot Whales exhibit lack of reproductive activity in old age; Bottlenose Dolphins estimated to be about twenty-five years old show no ovarian activity and it has also been lacking in old captive females but factors other than senescence are probably operating. True, our knowledge of this aspect of wild life is somewhat scanty, but most wild animals can propagate their kind throughout their lives, or else have only the briefest periods of senility. It does seem possible that the fertility of whales, like that of other mammals, decreases with old age, but when do whales reach old age?

With the help of data on the time of sexual maturity, on the maximum life expectancy, and on the frequancy of successive births (see page 389), Slijper therefore arrived at the tentative figures of a cow's normal number of offspring shown in his table, which was based on the assumption that the cow is allowed to live out her span. Recent work (some of which is quoted in the Bibliography) has amended many of these figures in the light of better information and the use of new techniques.

We have still to investigate the annual decrease in a whale population through natural causes. The problems are considerable, for if we can occasionally witness the birth of a cetacean, its death always occurs in the depths of the ocean, so that we have virtually no observations on this point. Hence all our knowledge is based on inferences from other mammals, and since this knowledge is often scanty and moreover not at all referable to cetaceans, what we know with any degree of certainty is very little indeed.

Slijper assumed that cetaceans have a higher mortality rate during the first year of life than during subsequent years: he considered this to be similar to the rate in all terrestrial mammals, including the large European Bison, investigated so far. Cetaceans, like other mammals, can suffer damage at birth and from the after-effects of weaning. Birth under water is hazardous in that the neonate must surface to take its first breath within minutes of parturition. It must have the strength to swim, the ability to keep near its mother and to suck successfully at her nipple, again under water. During the first year the young are at their most helpless, they can succumb to disease, parasites and enemies.

Gilmore (1958) reports the finding of a number of still-born young baby whale carcasses on the beaches of Californian lagoons, but of only a very occasional adult carcass. The infantile mortality rate during the first year of the life of terrestrial mammals is estimated by various sources at from 15 to 50 per cent of the total number of births in a given year, and as high as 40–50 per cent in llamas, red deer and foxes. The figures for seals are also said to be of that order; here the high infantile death rate is largely due to parasites and Killer Whales. It seems reasonable to conclude that young cetaceans fare no better than young seals. Young dolphins and even young whales have to add sharks to the list of their natural enemies, while all cetaceans are known to be susceptible to serious infestation, particularly during the first month after weaning.

Births in captive delphinids have increased in recent years both from pregnant females taken from the ocean and from those which have conceived in captivity. There have been several deliberate efforts by enterprising institutions to breed dolphins from captive animals in order to obviate taking from the wild. Still-births, premature birth of weak young as well as the onset of disease in apparently full-term healthy neonates have indicated a lack of understanding of required birth conditions in captivity, and for that matter in the wild.

Their first birthday over, most cetaceans have left the worst behind them. Naturally, they can still meet with fatal accidents, and porpoises, for instance, have died in large numbers in the Baltic when the sea froze over before they had migrated, while Little Piked (Minke) Whales are believed to perish from similar causes in the Antarctic. Figs. 222 and 223 show photographs taken in 1955 by members of a British Antarctic expedition based on Graham Land. On crossing the frozen Crown Prince Gustav Channel between James Ross Island and Graham Land, they noticed holes in the ice, which 120 Little Piked Whales had opened, so that they could come up for air. They also observed sixty Killers and one *Beradius*. The whales had obviously been cut off from the open sea when the Channel had frozen, and in the course of a few weeks holes several kilometres long were seen to shrivel down to a few metres. All the Killers and many Rorquals had disappeared after four months. They may have died but the possibility that they had travelled sixty-five kilometres under ice to the open sea was considered more likely.

Natural mortality is not caused by whalers but by predators, starvation, accidents, disease and the effects of parasites. The only predator attacking large whales is said to be the Killer Whale but there are few authentic accounts of packs of Killers at work on *live* whales. There is more evidence of Killers, and sharks, preying on calves in the warm waters in which they are born. Perhaps the presence of a ship distracts Killers: yet there are many reports by whalers of a pack tearing away at towed or moored carcasses of whales. The examination of stomach contents confirms that

Figure 222. Little Piked Whales cut off by ice. Probably the last phase in their attempts to keep the ice open for breathing.

Figure 223. The Little Piked Whales in the ice came so close to the edge that they could be petted.

Killers prey on fish, pinnipeds, small cetaceans such as porpoises and Belugas. Polar bears and walruses have also attacked Belugas and Narwhals.

Nobody has yet suggested that starvation has been a direct cause of death of cetaceans in the wild. On the contrary it is maintained that even when the population is at a maximum there is enough food in the seas to maintain adequate nutrition (Mackintosh, 1965). It is more likely that some other factor is causing undernourishment such as wounds, disease or parasites, and the resulting debility ensures that the whale becomes victim to yet further disasters. It is just not known how many cetaceans succumb from such causes, but strandings give some information about cetaceans which have got into difficulties for one reason or another. The possible explanations for this phenomenon have been discussed on pages 199–200 but, whatever the chief one may be, the number of cetaceans lost each year by stranding is insignificant. Mass strandings, particularly of dolphins, do indeed occur with spectacular and distressing results but insufficient in total to have any effect on the survival of all but the rarest species. Evidence of disease, such as parasitic infestation often with secondary infection by pathogenic organisms, has been reported in many stranded individuals. It would be unlikely that all members of a school would be equally incapacitated and not one able to take avoiding action. Far from being altruistic, or a death urge to feel support of land, mass stranding behaviour seems most disadvantageous and frankly pointless. There are over a quarter of a million miles of coastline to the world's seas and unless there are a great many unobserved mass strandings, they are uncommon occurrences. One explanation which could be investigated profitably is that a school is a closely related composite that habitually traverses a more or less defined course over its territory guided by certain perceptible features or factors. Deviation from this 'learnt' course, in chasing prey or because of a change in feature or factor (such as weather or water characteristic), results in random sallies, usually successful, to get back on a safe course.

Cetaceans are afflicted with many varieties of endoparasite and ectoparasite (see Chapter 2). There are several important works listing these numerous parasites, and some are quoted in the Bibliography. Many types of endoparasite are encountered. Trematodes are found in the liver, stomach and intestine, bile duct and in the air sinuses (*Nasitrema*). *Braunina cordiformis*, a stomach fluke, is one of the commonest parasites of the Bottlenosed Dolphin. Cestodes frequent the stomach and intestines (*Diphyllobothrium*) and the blubber (*Phyllobothrium*). Nematodes are common in the lungs (*Halocercus*), heart (*Pseudalius*) and also in the air sinuses

(*Pharurus* and *Stenurus*). Examples from the nematode Family Heterochei-lidae are encountered in the stomach and intestine (*Anisakis* and *Contra-caecum*). *Crassicauda crassicauda* (Family Crassicaudidae) is more common in Rorquals where it is found in muscle, kidneys, ureters and other parts of the uro-genital system. Spiny-headed worms of the Phylum Acantho-cephala also occur in marine mammals: the genus *Bolbosoma* is found in cetaceans in the intestine. Internal parasites are certainly present in many stranded cetaceans; indeed they may be an important cause of stranding. Cetaceans may, however, succumb to parasitic infestation more readily when weakened by some other cause such as trauma or undernourishment. Healthier animals may establish an equilibrium between themselves and their parasites. It probably depends just where the parasites are located and how much their presence interferes with important bodily functions such as digestion and echolocation. It is essential that cetaceans brought into captivity be examined and treated for parasitic infestation. It is not unlikely that animals caught easily had been weakened by such infestation; if so, and they be treated success-fully, it could be argued that being taken into captivity had prolonged their lives. Several types of ectoparasite are described in Chapter 2, but although they can give rise to a 'dirty' as opposed to a 'clean' skin they do not themselves cause death of their hosts.

Cetaceans in the wild were thought by Slijper to be relatively free of serious disease. Ross Cockrill, Rewell and Willis, and Stolk have described some inflammatory conditions, a number of tumours and two instances of cirrhosis of the liver in Rorquals, and in 1959 pneumonia was diagnosed in a Fin Whale (South Georgia). Round or oval masses are occasionally found on the organs or between muscles of Rorquals (Fig. 224). They are known as 'husks' and weigh from a few grams to a kilogram. These masses have a fibrous or calcified capsule containing what often appears like a yellowish cheese-like substance. Ross Cockrill (1960) thinks that they are degenerated encapsulated stadia of internal parasites but they do not seem to cause much damage. Serious pathological conditions are rarely found in whales, as was discovered by a team of six veterinary surgeons and eight assistants led by W. Ross Cockrill. During 1947–1952, this team investigated 12,000 carcasses aboard various factory ships, and had to reject only two because of pathological lesions. 'Whales are prob-ably among the healthiest of living creatures,' he wrote, and he found very few instances where pathological lesions might have shortened life appreciably, but suggested that there might be diseases confined to immature whales, or to particular ocean areas, and that catchers could have ignored emaciated or obviously sick whales. Mackintosh also com-ments on the occurrence of only an occasional emaciated whale in the

Figure 224. Hard, spherical and oval masses in the muscles of a rorqual. (Photograph: W. Ross Cockrill, Rome.)

many carcasses seen by him. Some of the whales that are stranded on beaches also show varying degrees of emaciation but the total for any year is small and the cause of death difficult to ascertain.

Their healthy state is also borne out by the fact that they can survive many fractures. Many museums contain cetacean bones once fractured and subsequently healed (Fig. 225), and Slijper was able in 1936 to cite seventy-two instances of such fractures. Since that time the number of known healed fractures has increased considerably. Some are healed multiple fractures of ribs and vertebral processes, together with vertebral conditions such as ankylosing spondylitis and spondylitis deformans in which successive vertebrae may become fused (Fig. 226). Dental disease and infections of the jaws are also known in Odontocetes and particularly in Sperm Whales and Killers (Figs. 227 and 228), and so are individuals with cogenital defects, e.g. the 160 cm White-sided Dolphin whose spine had a hump which was probably congenital. In most cases, human intervention cannot be blamed, since many of the fractures are found in species that are not commonly hunted and in fossils dating back to a time when man did not exist. Probably most fractures are caused by contact between

Figure 225. Right ribs of a Bottlenose Dolphin in the Brussels Museum. The 3rd, 4th, 5th and 6th ribs are broken but the fractures have healed in the form of pseudarthroses.

animals of the same species (perhaps at mating time), just like the many superficial scars found on the skin of captive dolphins (Fig. 100, page 183) and in many species in the wild. Some fractures could have been caused by Killers or Swordfish. In 1952, Ruud reported how a 34 cm bone originating from the rostrum of a Swordfish had produced an abscess in the skin of a 22 m Blue Whale. A similar bone was discovered in a Blue Whale in 1959 and there are other reports of abscesses in various species probably of similar origin. There is nothing remarkable about whales and dolphins fighting among themselves, what is unexpected is that the resulting serious injuries and fractures heal up again. Clearly even the weak and injured among them can survive, because of the favourable circumstances in which they live, and perhaps because cetaceans can tolerate in water injuries that would cripple and kill a land mammal.

From analogies with other mammals, Slijper decided that the death rate in the years immediately following the first was of the order of 2–5 per cent of the total age group in question. Naturally, this percentage increases with old age since whales, after all, are not immortal, and, like

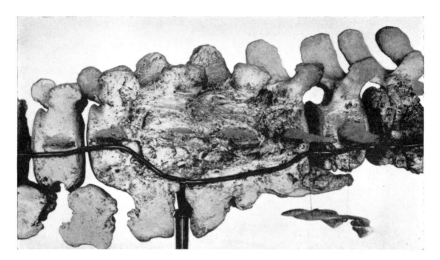

Figure 226. Lumbar and caudal vertebrae of a Greenland Right Whale in the Brussels Museum, showing serious symptoms of spondylitis deformans. Bottom right: Pelvic bone with rudimentary femur. Bottom left: chevrons.

Figure 227. Festering sore and compound fracture of the lower jaw of a Sperm Whale aboard the Willem Barendsz, *1951–1952 season. (Photograph: N. J. Teljer.)*

Figure 228. Lower jaw of a Sperm Whale with an old fracture pseudarthrosed at an angle of 90°. Aboard the Willem Barendsz, *1951–1952 season. (Photograph: N. J. Teljer.)*

most animals, few of them live to the maximum age. Unfortunately, we do not yet know precisely at what age the death rate rises perceptibly.

However, there is one method by which the natural death rate of individual age groups can be assessed, viz. by investigating the age distribution of a given population. By investigating, say, 1,000 animals of the annual catch, and by establishing how many of them are below the ages of 1, 2, 3, 4, etc., we can calculate the average death rate (from natural *and* man-made causes) for every age level, provided only that, first, the ages are very accurately determined (and as we have seen this is not possible in cetaceans), and that, secondly, we know whether the population is static, increasing, or decreasing. Now, on the second point we have even less certainty than on the first, since to establish it is after all the whole purpose of the investigation. Moreover, we must be sure that our 1,000 specimens were, in fact, a random sample (i.e. a sample that is truly representative and not selected in any special way) of the annual catch, and that the annual catch, in turn, is truly representative of the total population. In other words, the percentages of the various age-groups, from the youngest to the oldest, must accurately reflect the corresponding percentages in the annual catch, which, in turn, must reflect the percentages of the total population. This must be done by considering the size limit. From the degree of correspondence of the length distribution of the catch on the one hand, and the sample on the other, we can decide if the sample is in fact a random sample of the catch. It is, however, unlikely that the catch, in turn, is a random sample of the total population. While some biologists believe that, undersized animals apart, the catch is in fact representative, especially since, in view of past keen competition, gunners had no time to select particularly large and fat specimens and shot at whatever came in sight, others believe that what does come in sight first is the younger specimens which are less suspicious of ships (see p. 184), so that the catch consists of a preponderance of younger animals. No wonder, therefore, that some calculations on the death rate of individual age groups are not generally accepted.

Recently, some biologists have tried to establish whether the Rorqual population is static or not by theoretical calculations. To do so, they estimate the population at the beginning of a particular year, and then add the expected annual increase and deduct the expected deaths from natural causes and the annual catch.

Ottestad (Norway) based his estimates on the assumption that, in 1910, when Antarctic whaling first began, the Antarctic Rorqual population was constant and at its maximum. This being the case, we can establish what the annual death rate must be to keep the population static. The moment whaling began, death by capture must naturally be added to death from natural causes, and the total population will therefore have decreased. Hunting may cause the number of births to increase and the number of deaths from natural causes to decrease, since by increasing the space available for the surviving animals, hunters provide them with more food, and enable them to grow stronger and to produce stronger offspring, more capable of resisting enemies and other adverse circumstances. Other factors, too, play a role in this process, but to a far lesser extent. In the case of Rorquals, intervention by man may have had the additional effect of increasing the Fin Whale population, since from 1910 onwards the hunt was primarily directed at Blue Whales, thus increasing the space (and the food) available to other species. Hence it is not impossible that the Fin Whale population may have gone up appreciably between 1910 and 1930.

Methods of population assessment changed when scientists applied the techniques used in fish population studies. There are still problems to overcome in that any formula or ideal model representing a population is only as good as the accuracy of the information used and when all the factors causing corrections are understood and can be estimated with some degree of certainty. The methods use the size of the catch and the catch-per-unit-of-effort with allowances for recruitment and mortality in a season and in successive seasons. Data about age composition, reproduction and behaviour can also be incorporated. Comparisons are made between actual catches and theoretically expected catches. The type of basic mathematical model that can be constructed and which has been used in baleen whale studies is:

$$\mathcal{N}_{t+1} = (\mathcal{N}_t - C_t)e^{-M} + R_{t+1}$$

where $\mathcal{N}$ = catchable stock size; C = catch; R = recruits; t = season; M = coefficient of natural mortality. Estimates of recruitment have to be obtained from age composition data. The population is estimated from the above equation by computing the value for the population which minimizes the sum of the squares of the differences between actual catches and those expected from the population. The principal techniques of assessing whale populations are outlined by Gambell (1976) who provides many useful references. The Reports of the International Whaling Commission show how these mathematical models have been used, and recent issues include computer programs (see also Allen, 1973). While their introduction has been of value there are certain almost insurmountable difficulties in refining the methods. Catch records can be used with some confidence but it is another matter when trying to characterize the catch-effort. Boats vary in their power, equipment and methods of operation, gunners are human and thus not equally skilful. Modern aids to navigation, for tracking whales (and for avoiding bad conditions) affect effort statistics as do day length and for how many days a catcher is at work. It would be simpler if each stock under consideration were an isolated unit, quite independent of other stocks of the same species, and they did not overlap or intermingle at certain times of the year. Similarly if each catcher hunted only whales of one species then it would be easier to assess the effort and not have to apportion it. There is the possibility that one or more of the correction factors introduced carries a deliberate or unintentional weighting so that there is a danger that the investigator demonstrates what he wishes to demonstrate for purposes external to the capabilities of his model. While everyone agrees that there are never enough data, nor sufficient time to process what is available before change occurs, another cogent problem is to determine what the critical minimum population is for each stock below which level disaster is inevitable.

Several expressions using the basic concept of sustainable yield have been much in vogue in recent years, and have also been criticized because of difficulties of being sure about which animals bring about recruitment, and whether or not one can consider a particular stock of one species alone or if the total population of all species in a region must be used for calculations. Furthermore, if one starts arguing that a natural population, considered as a single unit, was sustained by the carrying capacity of the environment one hundred years ago, is one justified in assuming that matters could be just the same today? Theoretically, in a state of equilibrium, the rate of reproduction produces recruits which replace those dying of natural causes and the total population remains steady. Now reduce the total by catching some animals; there will follow an increase in the rate of reproduction with or without a decrease in death from natural causes until the additional new recruits rebuild the depleted population. If these extra animals are removed by catching, the population will remain at the depleted level but will continue to reproduce at the increased rate and continue to provide a sustainable catch indefinitely. Thus the overall or gross recruitment minus the natural deaths gives a net recruitment which is the sustainable yield. As Mackintosh (1965) has explained: 'in properly controlled exploitation we are diverting to human uses organic material which would otherwise go into building the stock up to its maximum or natural level'. At this level, as already stated, the recruitment rate equals that of mortality. If the stock is reduced to lower and lower levels, then the surplus falls until in absolute numbers it approaches zero. Somewhere between these extremes there will be a maximum sustainable yield (M.S.Y.) and a corresponding stock size. If, therefore, catchers were to take only a fraction of the M.S.Y., then some recruits would be added to the stock and it would increase. It will be seen that varying results will come about according to the particular level of the stock when a catch greater or less than the sustainable yield is taken. Now, when whales are considered the decisions are much more complicated. It takes time for a newly recruited whale to enter the system and then to play a part in creating new recruits. Whatever the skill of gunners in selecting their targets, the pressure of circumstances can encourage them to strike at targets of opportunity which will satisfy demand. How can a nearly mature female whale be distinguished from an older one of similar size which is contributing to recruitment? It might not matter in an abundant population but in the strict conditions of an exploited stock the damage done by removing a number of young breeding females could have lasting effects.

Several other types of yield can be defined, of which the currently fashionable replacement yield (R.Y.) is one. It applies only to a particular year and refers to that catch which will leave the population at the end as it was at the start of that year. A maintainable yield is defined as the catch which can be taken year after year.

The I.W.C. makes use of the sustainable yield model for management purposes and for full details recent *Reports* should be consulted. It is obviously necessary to classify stocks on the best available evidence so that quotas may be set that will not be above the sustainable yield. Three types of stock are recognized. An Initial Management Stock is one which may be reduced in a controlled manner to reach M.S.Y. level or other appropriate level: it has been proposed that it shall be defined as a stock more than 20 per cent of M.S.Y. stock level above M.S.Y. level, and further that catching for such stocks shall not be more than 90 per cent of M.S.Y. as far as this is known. A Sustained Management Stock is one which is or should be maintained at M.S.Y. level or at a determined optimum level, say that which is not more than 10 per cent of M.S.Y. stock level below M.S.Y. and not more than 20 per cent above that level. A stock has to remain at a stable level for a long period and provide almost constant catches before it can be classified as a Sustained Management Stock. The third type is a Protection Stock which is below a Sustained Management Stock and therefore one which is below, say, 10 per cent of M.S.Y. stock level below M.S.Y. and should be fully protected. Blue, Humpback, Right and Grey Whales are now under complete protection. Recent estimates suggest that the Grey Whale stock in the eastern Pacific has recovered from only a few hundred in the 1930s to about 6,000 in 1959–1960 and to around 11,000 in 1971: since then coastal watchers report that numbers have stabilized with slight increases up to 1976. The population in the mid nineteenth century was about 25,000 so that a further increase ought to be expected as long as poaching and interference by sight-seeing pleasure trips is controlled. These figures are of interest in that they show the powers of recovery of one exploited cetacean species and also because they give some guidance at least in thinking about recovery of other species. A ban on hunting Southern Blue and Humpback Whales for ten years will not allow enough time for the stocks to reach M.S.Y. levels; protection for over thirty and, more likely, forty years appears more realistic. As regards southern Fin Whales, Gambell (1976) has estimated the present stock to be between 83,000 to 97,000 and that the M.S.Y. level ought to be 209,000 to 248,000. Again it will take far longer than ten years to reach the M.S.Y. level even if all catching ceased.

The 29th Annual Meeting of the I.W.C. was held in Canberra, Australia in June 1977 and it was agreed that the new management and conservation policy adopted two years earlier would be maintained. Whale stocks would continue to be classified into three categories: (a) protected management, (b) sustained management and (c) initial management. Latest scientific advice would decide into which category a stock would be placed. Quotas were set for stocks of all species that could be caught in the North Atlantic and North Pacific in 1978 and in the southern hemisphere in the season 1977–1978. The Commission also decided to take control of medium-sized whales including Bottlenose, Beaked, Pilot and

Killer Whales. Bottlenose Whales in the North Atlantic were added to the list of totally protected species.

For the North Atlantic the quotas fixed (with the previous year's figures in brackets) were: Sperm 685 (685); Minke 2,555 (2,483); Fin 459 (455); Sei 84 (132). For the North Pacific: Sperm, male 0 (4,320), female 763 (2,880) – but these catches were amended at a later meeting to over 6,000 (7,200); Bryde's 524 (1,000); Minke 400 (541). For the southern hemisphere: Sperm, male 4,538 (3,894), female 1,370 (897); Minke 5,690 (8,900); Sei 771 (1,863). The total quota set was therefore initially much lower at 17,839 than that for the previous year (28,050) but was raised by the amended quota for North Pacific Sperm whales.

The 30th Annual Meeting in London recommended yet another apparent reduction of about 5 per cent in the initial total quota for the 1978–1979 and 1979 seasons.

Recent years have seen increasing discussion about the economic value of cetaceans to man. While there will undoubtedly continue to be a demand for edible whale products, which will increase if stocks recover, and increase even more if whale meat can be made more palatable, there is another use of cetaceans by man which has started to impinge on the deliberations of the I.W.C. Conservation problems, curiosity about leviathans, expanding demand for leisure pursuits, travel and hobbies and the encouragement of better education have stimulated interest in identifying, counting and watching the behaviour of cetaceans. The number of persons who have watched the migrating Grey Whales off California must be very considerable. Trips are organized to particular regions to get close to whales: it might not be long before sight-seeing parties tour the feeding areas used by baleen whales much as they now drive through game reserves. While not yet an established secondary industry, when added to the films, photographs, recordings, maps, magazines and books, models and toys manufactured for what must be a potentially enormous market, whale-watching could become big business. Encouraging though all this could be for 'saving the whale', it might have the opposite effect in one respect, and that is to expose cetaceans to increasing underwater noise. This is already happening to the surviving Grey Whales with high-speed motor boats tearing across breeding lagoons. A whale sanctuary ought to be free of man-made noise.

It would be a singularly unobservant person who was today unaware of the widespread interest in whales and the concern about their future. The Bibliography at the end of this book indicates the increase in scientific papers on every aspect of cetology. Popular accounts of whales, dolphins and porpoises are to be found in every bookshop. There have been films

about Melville's Sperm Whale 'Moby Dick' and on the alleged intelligence of Bottlenose Dolphins. Numerous documentaries have been shown
on television and the many articles in magazines, such as the accounts in
the *National Geographic* (Dec. 1976, vol. 150 (6), 722–751; 752–767), have
drawn attention to the diminishing stocks of whales. Groups have been
formed to advocate conservation and protection of whales, and brave
persons have endeavoured to stop the harpoon gunner finding his mark
by placing their little boats between the catching vessel and the whale in
his sights. Any meeting of the I.W.C. is now usually an opportunity for a
demonstration outside the building. The 30th Annual Meeting in London
in 1978 saw a demonstration inside the building when it was reported
that blood from an abattoir was hurled at the Japanese delegation. *The
Times* of 26 June 1978 ran an advertisement stating that in 1977 over
30,000 whales were killed for profit. It named Australia, Brazil, Denmark,
Iceland, Japan, Norway and the U.S.S.R. as being actively involved in
whaling within the limited regulations of the I.W.C., and stated that
Chile, Cyprus, North Korea, Peru, Portugal, South Korea, Spain and
Taiwan operated outside these regulations. Whaling had been banned
by France in 1954, by Panama in 1956, by the United Kingdom in 1963,
by Argentina, The Netherlands and New Zealand in 1964, by Canada
and the U.S.A. in 1972, and by South Africa in 1976. There are, of course,
many maritime countries which, like Mexico, have never engaged in
whaling, but not a few have been content to import whale products.

Slijper, in 1958, considered that all the arguments about the stocks of
whales, the recommended catch, the imposing of restrictions and even
complete protection of a population were based on very little evidence. He
pointed out that while, at that time, more than one country was finding it
very costly to indulge in whaling, others were not so pessimistic and that
Japan and Russia were extending their whaling fleets. He also referred
to the concern felt by some scientists that the catch had been increased
after 1956 from 14,500 to 15,000 B.W.U. and that this catch was far too
high. Slijper advised scientists to keep cool over the contentious issues and
to continue with investigations on the structure and ecology of the animals
concerned. There are, however, some aspects of scientific advice on this
kind of problem that are not always clearly understood. A scientist makes
his observations, collects facts and information, draws his samples, tests
his initial hypotheses over a period of time. He then needs more time to
analyse his findings and draw conclusions about what was happening at
the time and place his data were acquired. He then has to present advice
on what could be happening now, or might happen in the future, based
on what he found in the past and on certain assumptions. Besides the basic
quantitative and qualitative deficiencies that could be present from the

start, the skill of the investigator and the validity of his techniques have to be assessed, and also, by no means unimportant, the comprehensibility of his report. All these points are clearly demonstrated in the application of scientific principles in studying cetaceans and advising about their status in the future. There is no doubt that the past twenty years have seen an increase in knowledge about cetaceans and a better use of scientific advice although there must be reservations about it always being understood. The status of whale stocks in 1978 is not altogether as good as it was thought to be in 1958. On the other hand, the stocks of some species have increased; no species is threatened with immediate extinction; protection of particular populations has been introduced; control of the import of whale products is being more widely adopted; a review of whaling policies has been instigated by several countries; more attention is being paid to possible exploitation of small cetaceans for display purposes; the much-criticized I.W.C., even if now facing financial problems, has slightly reduced the recommended quota; and many more people know about the existence of a whale problem. It was Slijper's earnest hope that this book would awaken wider interest in cetological research, we trust it will contrive to do so for many years.

CLASSIFICATION OF THE CETACEA

1 Archaeoceti

Lower Eocene – Upper Oligocene. Dissimilar teeth. Nostrils not situated on top of head (with one exception). Skull symmetrical. Arterial grooves run in front of transverse processes of caudal vertebrae.

A PROTOCETIDAE. Middle Eocene. Primitive types. 2–9 m. *Protocetus, Pappocetus, Eocetus.*

B DORUDONTIDAE. Upper Eocene – Lower Miocene. Non-serpentine shape. Up to 6 m. *Dorudon, Zygorhiza, Phococetus, Kekenodon.*

C BASILOSAURIDAE. Upper Eocene – Lower Oligocene. Serpentine shape. 12–21 m. *Prozeuglodon, Basilosaurus, Platyosphys.*

D PATRIOCETIDAE. Upper Oligocene. Nostrils have migrated backwards. *Patriocetus.*

2 Mystacoceti (baleen whales; whalebone whales)

Middle Oligocene – Recent. Whalebone. Nostrils on top of head. Skull symmetrical. Arterial grooves run in front of transverse processes of caudal vertebrae.

A CETOTHERIIDAE. Middle Oligocene – Lower Pliocene. Primitive types. 2.5–10 m. *Aglaocetus, Cophocetus, Mesocetus, Mixocetus, Cetotherium, Parietobalaena.*

B RIGHT WHALES (*Balaenidae*). Lower Miocene – Recent. Dorsal fin absent, no grooves, long whalebone.

    1 Bowhead *or* **Greenland Right Whale** [*Balaena mysticetus* (L.)]. 17 m. Arctic Ocean.

    2a Northern Right Whale, Black Right Whale, Biscayan Right Whale [*Eubalaena glacialis* (Müller)]. 16 m.

    2b Southern Right Whale [*Eubalaena australis* (Desm.)]. 16 m. Antarctic waters, bays of southern land masses.

433

3 Pygmy Right Whale [*Caperea marginata* (Gray)]. 6 m. Antarctic Ocean: southern hemisphere.

c GREY WHALES (*Eschrichtiidae*). Post-glacial – Recent. Dorsal fin absent, 2–4 grooves, short baleen.

1 Californian Grey Whale [*Eschrichtius robustus* (Lilljeborg) = *E. gibbosus* (Erxleb.)]. 14 m. North Pacific.

d RORQUALS (*Balaenopteridae*). Upper Miocene – Recent. Dorsal fin, 40–100 grooves, short baleen.

1 Blue Whale [*Balaenoptera musculus* (L.)]. 30 m. Universal, including Pygmy Blue [*B. m. brevicauda*].

2 Fin Whale [*Balaenoptera physalus* (L.)]. 23 m. Universal.

3 Sei Whale [*Balaenoptera borealis* (Lesson)]. 15 m. Universal.

4 Bryde's Whale [*Balaenoptera edeni* (Anderson)]. 15 m. Tropics and sub-tropics.

5 Minke Whale (*Little Piked Whale*, or *Lesser Rorqual*) [*Balaenoptera acutorostrata* (Lacép.)]. 10 m. Universal, but rare in tropics.

6 Humpback Whale [*Megaptera novaeangliae* (Borowski) = *M. nodosa* (Bonnat.)]. 15 m. Universal.

3   Odontoceti (toothed whales)

Upper Eocene – Recent. Recent types have uniform teeth. Nostrils on top of skull. Skull of recent types asymmetrical. Arterial grooves run behind transverse processes of caudal vertebrae.

a SQUALODONTIDAE. Upper Eocene – Lower Pliocene. Teeth still differentiated. Molars with jagged edges. Includes the *Agorophiidae* (Upper Eocene). *Squalodontidae* proper only known from Upper Oligocene – Upper Miocene.

b SPERM WHALES (*Physeteridae*). Lower Miocene – Recent. Older types with well-developed teeth on both jaws. After Upper Miocene strong reduction of teeth in upper jaw. Cuttlefish eaters.

1 Sperm Whale [*Physeter catodon* (L.) = *P. macrocephalus* (L.)]. Male 17 m, female 12 m. Universal.

2 Pygmy Sperm Whale [*Kogia breviceps* (de Blainv.)]. 4 m. Universal.

3 Dwarf Sperm Whale [*Kogia simus* (Owen)]. 2.5 m. Tropical and sub-tropical waters.

c BEAKED WHALES (*Ziphiidae*). Lower Miocene – Recent. Older types with well-developed teeth in both jaws. After Upper Miocene strong reduction of teeth. Most recent types have only 1–2 visible teeth in lower jaw. Pointed beak. Two longitudinal grooves on throat. Cuttlefish eaters.

1a Northern Bottlenose Whale [*Hyperoodon ampullatus* (Forster)]. 10 m. Primarily in high latitudes of North Atlantic.

1b Southern Bottlenose Whale [*Hyperoodon planifrons* (Flower)]. 10 m. All southern oceans, circumpolar.

2 Cuvier's Beaked Whale [*Ziphius cavirostris* (Cuv.)]. 9 m. Universal.

3 Mesoplodon. There are 12 species currently recognized (Moore, 1976), but the taxonomy of the genus is based upon very little material and consequently poorly defined. Some species have a wide distribution (e.g. *M. densirostris*, tropical and temperate seas of the world), while others are very restricted in distribution. Thorough studies may reduce the number of species. 4–7 m.

4a Arnoux's Beaked Whale [*Berardius arnuxi* (Duvernoy)]. 10 m. Southern oceans.

4b Baird's Beaked Whale [*Berardius bairdi* (Stejneger)]. Max. size 13 m. Offshore waters of the North Pacific.

The two species of *Berardius* appear to be well separated geographically, but are not markedly different from one another morphologically.

5 Shepherd's Beaked Whale [*Tasmacetus shepherdi* (Oliver)]. 7 m. Circumpolar distribution in southern temperate waters.

D EURHINODELPHIDAE. Miocene. Very long beaks. Anterior upper jaw devoid of teeth. Articulation of ribs and vertebrae as in *Ziphiidae*. 4–5 m. Probably fed on fish off the bottom.

E HEMISYNTRACHELIDAE. Miocene – Pliocene. Short beak. They look like dolphins, but rib articulation as in *Ziphiidae*.

F RIVER DOLPHINS (*Platanistidae*). Lower Miocene – Recent. Very long and slender beaks. Lower jaws fused over large area. River inhabitants.

1 Ganges Susu [*Platanista gangetica* (Roxburgh)]. 3 m. Ganges, Brahmaputra and Indus river systems. Some specialists recognize the Indus River Dolphin as a separate species, *P. indi* or *P. minor*.

2 Boutu [*Inia geoffrensis* (de Blainv.)]. 2 m. Found in all main rivers in the Orinoco and Amazon basins.

3 Franciscana [*Pontoporia blainvillei* (Gerv.)]. 1.7 m. Coastal species, occurs from Shubut, Argentina north to Ubataba, Brazil.

4 White Flag Dolphin [*Lipotes vexillifer* (Miller)]. 3 m. Tung Ting Lake and the Yangtze River, People's Republic of China.

G DOLPHINS IN THE WIDER SENSE (*Delphinidae sensu lato*). Lower

Miocene – Recent. Mainly fish eaters and maritime. Lower jaws fused only at the tip.

a Acrodelphidae. Miocene. Very long beaks.

b Monodontidae. Pleistocene – Recent. No clear dorsal fin. All cervical vertebrae free.

   1 **White Whale** or **Beluga** [*Delphinapterus leucas* (Pallas)]. 5 m. Arctic and subarctic, shallow waters and estuaries.

   2 **Narwhal** [*Monodon monoceros* (L.)]. 5 m. High Arctic, mainly in deep waters. Absent from north Siberian shelf and rare in north Alaskan sector.

c Porpoises (*Phocoenidae*). Miocene – Recent. Generally clear dorsal fin. Some cervical vertebrae fused. Teeth spatular. No beak.

   1 **Common Porpoise** (U.S.A.: Harbor Porpoise) [*Phocoena phocoena* (L.)]. 1.6 m. North Atlantic and Pacific oceans, latitudes to Mexico and Gulf of California.

   2 **Phocoena spinipinnis, P. dioptrica,** South America; **P. sinus,** Gulf of California. All rare.

   3 **Dall's Porpoise** [*Phocoenoides dalli* (True)]. 2 m. North Pacific coast from Baja California to eastern Honshu, Japan, Bering Sea, Sea of Okhotsk, Sea of Japan.

   4 **Finless Porpoise** [*Neophocaena phocaenoides* (Cuv.)]. 1.6 m. East and South-East Asia, along coast and in major rivers.

d Dolphins in the stricter sense (*Delphinidae sensu stricto*). Miocene – Recent. Generally clear dorsal fin. Some cervical vertebrae generally fused. Conical teeth. Beak often present.

   1 *Kentriodon, Delphinodon*. Miocene types clearly distinct from present types. Pliocene types resemble recent types more strongly.

   2 **Killer Whale** [*Orcinus orca* (L.)]. 9 m. Universal. Sexual dimorphism.

   3 **False Killer Whale** [*Pseudorca crassidens* (Owen)]. 5 m. Tropical and warm temperate waters.

   4 **Pygmy Killer Whale** [*Feresa attenuata* (Gray)]. 2.4 m. Tropical and warm temperate waters.

   5 **Melon-headed Whale** or **Electra** [*Peponocephala electra* (Gray)]. 2.8 m. Tropical and warm temperate waters.

   6 **Irrawaddy Dolphin** [*Orcaella brevirostris* (Gray)]. 2.4 m. South-East Asia and northern Australia.

   7 **Pilot whales**

7a Long-finned Pilot Whale [*Globicephala melaena* (Traill)]. Males (6 m) larger than females (5 m). Northern and Southern hemisphere populations are widely separated geographically – Northern ranges from Greenland, Iceland and Barents Sea to the east and west Atlantic; Southern occurs mainly north of the Antarctic Convergence in the cold currents associated with the West Wind Drift.

7b Short-finned Pilot Whale [*Globicephala macrorhynchus* (Gray)]. Males (5.4 m) larger than females (4 m). Tropical and low temperate waters.

8 Risso's Dolphin [*Grampus griseus* (Cuv.)]. 4 m. Universal in tropical to temperate seas.

9 Bottlenose Dolphin [*Tursiops truncatus* (Mont.)]. There appear to be two morphologically distinct forms – large (4 m) and small (3 m). World-wide in temperate to tropical waters, mainly coastal. In general, the large form occupies colder waters than the small form.

10 Common Dolphin [*Delphinus delphis* (L.)]. 2.5 m. World-wide in warm temperate and tropical waters. Morphologically distinct populations exist.

11 White-sided Dolphin [*Lagenorhynchus*]. 1.6 m to 3 m. *L. acutus* (Gray) (White-sided Dolphin) and *L. albirotris* (Gray) (White-beaked Dolphin) in North Atlantic; *L. obliquidens* (Gill) in North Pacific; *L. cruciger* (Quoy and Gaimard) with a number of strains, in southern waters, such as *L. australis* (Peale).

12 Stenella (Prodelphinus). A number of species between 50°N and 40°S. Mostly tropical. 1 m to 3 m.

13 Rough-toothed dolphin [*Steno bredanensis* (Lesson)]. 2.5 m. Mostly tropical and sub-tropical waters.

14 Cephalorhynchus. Southern waters. Species recognized are *C. heavisidei*; *C. eutropia*; *C. hectori* and *C. commersoni*.

15 Right Whale Dolphins

15a Southern Right Whale Dolphin [*Lissodelphis peroni* (Lacép.)]. Circumpolar distribution, mainly north of the Antarctic Convergence.

15b Northern Right Whale Dolphin [*Lissodelphis borealis* (Peale)]. 3 m. North Pacific Ocean, mainly in cooler offshore waters.

16 Tucuxi [*Sotalia fluviatilis* (Gervais and Deville)]. 1.5 m. Coast of South America. Coastal animals enter rivers.

17a Indo-Pacific Humpbacked Dolphin [*Sousa chinensis* (Osbeck)]. 3 m. East Africa, Red Sea, Arabian and Persian

Gulfs, India, Indonesia, northern Australia, New Guinea and Indo-China. Subpopulations have been recognized.

17b Atlantic Humpbacked Dolphin [*Sousa teuszii* (Kükenthal)]. West African coast.

18 Fraser's Dolphin [*Lagenodelphis hosei* (Fraser)]. Apparently a tropical species. Eastern tropical Pacific, central Pacific, Sarawak, Japan, Taiwan, eastern Australia, and South Africa.

Bibliography

A complete bibliography of the Cetacea would comprise over 10,000 references. The following list should be considered as an introduction to the literature on cetaceans in which reference is made to classical works, to many important recent publications and to those which themselves contain useful bibliographies.

The Bibliography is divided by subject, as the chapters of the text:

General reading

ALPERS, A. (1960). *A Book of Dolphins.* John Murray, London.

ASH, C.E. (1962). *Whaler's Eye.* Macmillan, New York.

COUSTEAU, J. Y. and DIOLE, P. (1975). *Dolphins.* Cassel, London.

GASKIN, D. E. (1972). *Whales, Dolphins and Seals.* Heineman, Auckland.

HARRISON, R. J., and KING, J. E. (1965). *Marine Mammals.* Hutchinson, London.

HOWELL, A. B. (1930). *Aquatic Mammals.* C. C. Thomas, Baltimore. Reprinted (1970) Dover, New York.

MATTHEWS, L. H. (ed.) (1968). *The Whale.* Allen and Unwin, London.

MATTHEWS, L. H. (1978). *The Natural History of the Whale.* Weidenfeld and Nicolson, London.

NORMAN, J. R., and FRASER, F. C. (1948). *Giant Fishes, Whales and Dolphins.* 2nd ed. Putnam, London.

NORRIS, K. S. (1974). *The Porpoise Watcher.* W. W. Norton, New York.

SCHEFFER, V. B. (1969). *The Year of the Whale.* Charles Scribner's Sons, New York.

SCHEFFER, V. B. (1976). *A Natural History of Marine Mammals.* Charles Scribner's Sons, New York.

SMALL, G. L. (1971). *The Blue Whale.* Columbia Univ. Press, New York, 248 pp.

WOOD, F. G. (1973). *Marine Mammals and Man. The Navy's Porpoises and Sea Lions.* R. B. Luce, Washington.

Chapter 1. Historical Introduction (pages 11–57)

1. *History of the study of cetaceans*

ALDROVANDUS, U. (1613). *De Piscibus Libri V et de Cetis liber unus.* Bologna.

ALLEN, J. A. (1882). Preliminary list of works and papers relating to the mammalian Order Cete and Sirenia. *Bull. U.S. Geol. and Geogr. Survey,* **6**, 399–562.

ANDERSON, J. (1878). *Anatomical and Zoological Researches Comprising an Account of the Zoological Results of Two Expeditions to Western Yunnan 1868–1878.* B. Quaritch, London.

ARISTOTLE. *Historia Animalium.* Trans. (1910). D'Arcy W. Thomson, Oxford.

BARTHOLINUS, T. (1654). *Historiarum anatomicarum rariorum Centuria. I and II (Anatome tursionis).* Hafniae.

BELON, P. (1551). *L'Histoire naturelle des estranges poissons marins.* Paris.

BELON, P. (1553). *De Aquatilibus.* Paris.

BENEDEN, P. J. VAN (1889). *Histoire naturelle des Cétacés des mers d'Europe.* Bruxelles.

BENEDEN, P. J. VAN, and GERVAIS, P. (1880). *Ostéographie des Cétacés vivants et fossiles.* Paris.

CUVIER, G. (1817). *Le Règne animal.* Paris.

DEWHURST, H. W. (1834). *The Natural History of the Order Cetacea, and the oceanic Inhabitants of the Arctic Regions.* London.

FRASER, F. C. (1977). Royal fishes: the importance of the dolphin. In *Functional Anatomy of Marine Mammals,* ed. R. J. Harrison, vol. III, pp. 1–44. Academic Press, London.

HUNTER, J. (1787). Observations on the structure and oeconomy of whales. *Philos. Trans.,* **77,** 371–450.

KLEIN, J. T. (1740). *Historiae Piscium Naturalis.* Missus primus. Also (1741) Missus secundus. Gedani.

LACÉPÈDE, B. G. E. (1804). *Histoire naturelle des Cétacés.* Paris.

MAJOR, D. J. (1672). De anatome Phocaenae vel Delphini septentrionalium. *Misc. Med.–Phys. Acad. Nat. Curios.,* **3,** 22–32.

MARTENS, F. M. (1675). *Spitzbergische oder Groenlandische Reise-Beschreibung gethan im Jahr 1671.* Hamburg.

RAPP, W. (1837). *Die Cetaceen.* Stuttgart.

RAY, J. (1671). An account of the dissection of a porpess. *Philos. Trans.,* **6,** 2274–2279.

RONDELET, G. (1554). *Libri de Piscibus Marinis.* Lugduni.

SCHÄFER, W. (1956). Wale auf norwegischen Felsbildern im Lichte meerespalaontologischer Beobachtungen. *Natur u. Volk,* **86,** 233–240.

TYSON, E. (1680). *Phocaena, or the Anatomy of a Porpess.* London.

2. *Texts on cetacean species*

ALLEN, J. A. (1908). The north Atlantic right whale and its near allies. *Bull. Amer. Mus. Nat. Hist.,* **24,** 227–329.

ANDREWS, R. C. (1909). Observations on the habits of the finback and humpback whales of the eastern north Pacific. *Bull. Amer. Mus. Nat. Hist.,* **26,** 213–226.

ANDREWS, R. C. (1914). Monographs of the Pacific Cetacea. I. The Californian gray whale (*Rhachianectes glaucus* Cope). *Mem. Amer. Mus. Nat. Hist.,* **1,** 229–287.

ANDREWS, R. C. (1914). Monographs of the Pacific Cetacea. II. The sei whale (*Balaenoptera borealis* Lesson). *Mem. Amer. Mus. Nat. Hist.,* **1,** 291–388.

BEDDARD, F. E. (1900). *A Book of Whales.* John Murray, London.

BENJAMINSEN, T. (1972). On the biology of the bottlenose whale, *Hyperoodon ampullatus* (Forster). *Norw. J. Zool.,* **20,** 233–241.

BEST, P. B. (1960). Further information on Bryde's whale (*Balaenoptera edeni* Anderson) from Saldanha Bay, South Africa. *Norsk Hvalf.-Tidende,* **49,** 201–215.

BEST, P. B. (1967–1970). The sperm whale off the west coast of South Africa. Parts 1–5. *Investl. Rep. Div. Sea Fish.,* (1967) **61,** 1–27; (1968) **66,** 1–32; (1969) **72,** 1–20; (1969) **78,** 1–12; (1970) **79,** 1–27.

BEST, P. B. (1974). Two allopatric forms of Bryde's whale off South Africa. *Rep. Int. Whal. Commn.* (Special issue 1), 1977, pp 10–35.

BRYDEN, M. M., HARRISON, R. J., and LEAR, R. J. (1977). Some aspects of the biology of *Peponocephala electra* (Cetacea: Delphinidae). 1. General and reproductive biology. *Aust. J. Mar. Freshwater Res.*, **28**, 703–715.

BUSNELL, R.-G., PILLERI, G., and FRASER, F. C. (1968). Notes concerning the dolphin *Stenella styx* Gray 1846. *Mammalia*, **32**, 192–203.

CLARKE, R. (1956). Sperm whales of the Azores. *Discovery Rep.*, **28**, 237–298.

COLLETT, R. (1909). A few notes on the whale *Balaena glacialis* and its capture in recent years in the north Atlantic by Norwegian whalers. *Proc. Zool. Soc. Lond.*, 91–98.

DAVIES, J. L., and GUILER, E. R. (1957). A note on the pygmy right whale, *Caperea marginata* Gray. *Proc. Zool. Soc. Lond.*, **129**, 579–589.

DAWBIN, W. H., NOBLE, B. A., and FRASER, F. C. (1970). Observations on the electra dolphin *Peponocephala electra*. *Bull. Brit. Mus. (Nat. Hist.) Zoology*, **20** (6), 175–201.

DEGERBØL, M., and NIELSEN, N. L. (1930). Biologiske Iagttagelser over og maalinger av Hvidhvalen (*Delphinapterus leucas* (Pall.)) og dens Fostre. *Meddelelser om Gronland*, **77**, 119–144.

DEINSE, A. B. VAN, and JUNGE, G. C. A. (1937). Recent and older finds of the California gray whale in the Atlantic. *Temminckia Leiden*, **2**, 161–184.

DOROFEEV, S. V., and FREIMANN, S. J. (1935). The marine mammalia of U.S.S.R. far East. Resources and commercial use. *Trans. Inst. Fish. Ocean. U.S.S.R. (V.N.I.R.O.)*, **3**, 1–276.

ESCHRICHT, D. F. (1862). On the species of the genus Orca inhabiting the Northern Seas. *Oversigt Kong. Danske Vidensk. Selsk. Forhandl.*, 151–188. Trans. by Flower, W. H. (1866), Ray Society, London.

ESCHRICHT, D. F., and REINHARDT, J. (1861). Om nordhvalen (*Balaena mysticetus*). *Kong. Danske Vidensk. Selsk. Skrifter* (**5**) *Naturw. Math. Afd.*, **5**, 433.

ESCHRICHT, D. F., REINHARDT, J., and LILLJEBORG, W. (1866). On the Greenland right whale (*Balaena mysticetus*, Linn.). In Flower, W. H., *Recent Memoirs on the Cetacea*. Ray Society, London.

FISCHER, P. (1881). Cétacés du sud-ouest de la France. *Actes Soc. Linn. Bordeaux*, **35**, 1–217.

FREUND, L. (1912). Walstudien. *Sitz. Ber. Kais. Akad. Wiss. Wien, Math. Naturw. Kl.*, **121**, 1103–1189.

GIHR, M., and PILLERI, G. (1969). On the anatomy and biometry of *Stenella styx* Gray and *Delphinus delphis* L. (Cetacea, Delphinidae) of the western Mediterranean.

In *Investigations on Cetacea*, ed. G. Pilleri, vol. I, pp. 15–65. Berne.

HENTSCHEL, E. (1937). Naturgeschichte der nordatlantischen Wale. *Handb. Seefischerei Nordeuropas* (3), No. 1, 1–54.

ICHIHARA, T. (1966). The pygmy blue whale, *Balaenoptera musculus brevicauda*, a new subspecies from the Antarctic. In *Whales, Dolphins and Porpoises*, ed. K. S. Norris, pp. 79–111. University of California Press.

JONSGÅRD, Å. (1966). Biology of the north Atlantic fin whale *Balaenoptera physalus* (L). Taxonomy, distribution, migration and food. *Hvalråd. Skr.*, **49**, 1–62.

JONSGÅRD, Å., and LYSHOEL, P. B. (1970). A contribution to the knowledge of the biology of the killer whale *Orcinus orca* (L). *Nytt Mag. Zool.*, **18**, 41–48.

KELLOGG, R. (1928). The history of whales, their adaptations to life in the water. *Quart. Rev. Biol.*, **3**, 29–76, 174–208.

KELLOGG, R. (1938). Adaptation of structure to function in whale, cooperation in research. *Carnegie Inst. Washington Publ.*, **501**, 649–682.

LEGENDRE, R. (1943). Notes cétologiques à propos d'une *Balaenoptera acutorostrata* Lacépède observée à Concarneau. *Bull. Inst. Ocean. Monaco*, 856.

LILLIE, D. G. (1914). Cetacea. The British Antarctic (Terra Nova) expedition. *Nat. Hist. Rep. Zool.*, **1**, (3), 85–124.

LÖNNBERG, E. (1923). Cetological notes I and II. *Ark. Zool.*, **15**, 1–18.

MACKINTOSH, N. A., and WHEELER, J. F. G. (1929). Southern blue and fin whales. *Discovery Rep.*, **1**. 257–540.

MATTHEWS, L. H. (1937). The humpback whale, *Megaptera nodosa*. *Discovery Rep.*, **17**, 7–92.

MATTHEWS, L. H. (1938). The sperm whale, *Physeter catodon*. *Discovery Rep.*, **17**, 93–168.

MATTHEWS, L. H. (1938). Notes on the southern right whale, *Eubalaena australis*. *Discovery Rep.*, **17**, 169–181.

MATTHEWS, L. H. (1938). The sei whale, *Balaenoptera borealis*. *Discovery Rep.*, **17**, 183–290.

MÖRZER BRUYNS, W. F. J., and BAKER, A. N. (1973). Notes on Hector's dolphin, *Cephalorhynchus hectori* (van Beneden) from New Zealand. *Records Dom. Mus. Wellington*, **8** (9), 125–137.

NISHIWAKI, M. (1963). Taxonomical consideration on genera of Delphinidae. *Sci. Rep. Whales Res. Inst., Tokyo*, **17**, 93–103. Also a revision (1964) **18**, 171–172.

OLSEN, Ø. (1913). On the external characters and biology of Bryde's whale (*Balaenoptera brydei*), a new rorqual from the coast of South Africa. *Proc. Zool. Soc. Lond.*, 1073–1090.

OMURA, H. (1958). North Pacific right whale. *Sci. Rep. Whales Res. Inst., Tokyo*, **13**, 1–52.

OMURA, H. (1959). Bryde's whale from the coast of Japan. *Sci. Rep. Whales Res. Inst., Tokyo*, **14**, 1–33.

PERRIN, W. F. (1975). Variation of spotted and spinner porpoise (genus *Stenella*) in the eastern tropical Pacific and Hawaii. *Bull. Scripps Inst. Oceanogr. California*, **21**, 1–206.

PERRIN, W. F., BEST, P. B., DAWBIN, W. H., BALCOMB, K. C., GAMBELL, R., and ROSS, G. J. B. (1973). Rediscovery of Fraser's dolphin *Lagenodelphis hosei*. *Nature (Lond.)*, **241**, 345–350.

PIKE, G. C. (1962). Migration and feeding of the gray whale (*Eschrichtius gibbosus*). *J. Fish. Res. Bd. Can.*, **19**, 815–838.

PILLERI, G., and GIHR, M. (1973–74). Contribution to the knowledge of the cetaceans of southwest and monsoon Asia (Persian Gulf, Indus Delta, Malabai, Andaman Sea and Gulf of Siam). In *Investigations on Cetacea*, ed. G. Pilleri, vol. V, pp. 95–149. Berne.

RAWITZ, B. (1900). Ueber *Megaptera boops* Fabr. nebst Bemerkungen zur Biologie der norwegishen Mystacoceten. *Arch. Naturg.*, **5**, 71–114.

REINHARDT, J. (1862). *Pseudorca crassidens*. Om en for den Dansk fauna ny delphinart. *Oversigt over det Kongelige Danske Videns. Selsk.* Forhandl., 189–218.

RICE, D. W., and WOLMAN, A. A. (1971). The life history and ecology of the gray whale (*Eschrichtius robustus*). *Spec. Publ. Am. Soc. Mammal.*, no. 3, 1–142.

RICHARD, J. (1936). Documents sur les Cétacés et les Pinnipèdes: provenant des campagnes du Prince Albert Ier de Monaco. *Rés. Camp. sci. Albert I, Fasc.*, **94**, 1–71.

SERGEANT, D. E. (1963). Minke whales, *Balaenoptera acutorostrata* Lacépède of the western North Atlantic. *J. Fish. Res. Bd. Can.*, **20**, 1489–1504.

SERGEANT, D. E. (1973). Biology of white whales (*Delphinapterus leucas*) in western Hudson Bay. *J. Fish. Res. Bd. Can.*, **30**, 1065–1090.

TOMILIN, A. G. (1957). Cetaceans. Mammals of the U.S.S.R. *Akad. Nauk Moscow*, vol. 9, 1–756.

TRUE, F. W. (1889). A review of the family Delphinidae. *Bull. U.S. Nat. Mus.*, **36**, 1–191.

TRUE, F. W. (1904). The whalebone whales of the western north Atlantic compared with those occurring in European waters. *Smiths. Contr.*, **33**, 1–332.

WYMAN, J. (1863). Description of a whitefish or white whale (*Beluga borealis* Less.). *J. Boston Nat. Hist. Soc.*, **7**, 603–612.

ZEMSKY, V. A., and BORONIN, V. A. (1964). On the question of the pygmy blue whale taxonomic position. *Norsk Hvalf.-Tidende*, **53**, 306–311.

3. *History of whaling*

ADAMS, J. E. (1975). Primitive whaling in the West Indies. *Sea Frontiers*, **21**, 303–313.

BEALE, T. (1839). *The Natural History of the Sperm Whale, to which is Added a Sketch of a South-Sea*

Whaling Voyage. John van Voorst, London.

BENNETT, F. D. (1840). *Narrative of a whaling voyage around the globe from the year 1833 to 1836.* Vols. I and II. Richard Bentley, London.

BRANDT, K. (1940). Whale oil. An economic analysis. Food Res. Inst. Stanford Univ. Calif. *Fats and Oils Studies*, **7**, 241.

BUDKER, P. (1957). *Baleines et Baleiniers.* Paris. Eng. trans. (1958). *Whales and Whaling*, Harrap, London.

CLARKE, R. (1952). Electric whaling. *Nature (Lond.)*, **169**, 859–860.

CLARKE, R. (1954). Open boat whaling in the Azores: the history and present methods of a relic industry. *Discovery Rep.*, **26**, 281–354.

CRISP, D. T. (1962). The tonnages of whales taken by Antarctic pelagic operations during twenty seasons and an examination of the blue whale unit. *Norsk Hvalf.-Tidende*, **51**, 389–393.

DAWBIN, W. H. (1954). Maori whaling. *Norsk Hvalf.-Tidende*, **43**, 433–445.

DOW, G. F. (1925). *Whale Ships and Whaling.* Salem, Mass.

FELTMAN, C. F., and VERVOORT, W. (1949). Walvisvaart. *Noorduijn's Wet. Reeks*, **35**, Gorinchem.

FRASER, F. C. (1964). Whales and whaling. In *Antarctic Research. A Review of British Scientific Achievement in Antarctica*, eds. R. Priestley, R. J. Adie, and G. de Q. Robin. Butterworths, London.

GARDI, R. (1948). *Chasse à la Baleine*, ed. Attinger. Paris.

HARMER, S. F. (1928). The history of whaling. *Proc. Linn. Soc. Lond.* Session, **140**, 51–95.

HARMER, S. F. (1931). Southern whaling. *Proc. Linn. Soc. Lond.* Session, **142**, 85–163.

INTERNATIONAL WHALING COMMISSION (1950–1977). Reports 1–27. Office of the Commission. Cambridge.

IVERSEN, B. (1955). Whaling activity in Iceland. *Norsk Hvalf.-Tidende*, **44**, 598–606.

JENKINS, J. T. (1921). *A History of the Whale Fisheries*, pp. 1–336. Witherby, London.

JENKINS, J. T. (1948). Bibliography of whaling. *J. Soc. Bibliography nat. Hist.*, **2**, 71–166.

JONSGÅRD, Å. (1974) On whale exploitation in the eastern part of the north Atlantic ocean. In *The Whale Problem: a Status Report*, pp. 97–107, ed. W. E. Schevill. Harvard University Press.

MCVAY, S. (1974). Reflections on the management of whaling. In *The Whale Problem: a Status Report*, pp. 369–382, ed. W. E. Schevill. Harvard University Press.

MILLAIS, J. G. (1907). From Placentia Bay to Spitsbergen: a Naturalist aboard a North Atlantic whaler. From 'Newfoundland and its untrodden ways'. London. Extracts printed in *Nature Canada*, **2** (4), 3–8 (1973).

MOL, T. and BREE, P. J. H. VAN (1969). A short contribution to the history of whaling in Japan during the 17th century. *Sci. Rep. Whales Res. Inst., Tokyo*, **21**, 125–129.

OMURA, H., MAEDA, K., and MIYAZAKI, I. (1953). Whaling in the adjacent waters of Japan. *Norsk Hvalf.-Tidende*, **42**, 199–212.

PEDERSEN, T. and RUUD, J. T. (1946). A bibliography of whales and whaling. *Hvalråd. Skr.*, **30**, 1–32.

PIKE, G. C. (1954). Whaling on the coast of British Columbia. *Norsk Hvalf.-Tidende*, **43**, 117–127.

RISTING, S. (1922). *Av Hvalfangstens Historie*. Kristiana.

SCAMMON, C. M. (1874). *The Marine Mammals of the Northwestern Coast of North America together with an account of the American Whale Fishery*. J. H. Carmany, San Francisco. Reprinted (1968) Dover, New York.

SCORESBY, W. (1820). *An Account of the Arctic Regions with a history and description of the northern whale-fishery*. 2 vols. Archibald Constable, Edinburgh. Reprinted (1969) David and Charles, Newton Abbot.

STARBUCK, A. (1878). The American whale fisheries. *Rep. U.S. Comm. Fish for 1875–76*. Part IV, Appendix A.

WILKE, F., TANIWAKI, T., and KURODA, N. (1953). *Phocoenoides* and *Lagenorhynchus* in Japan with notes on hunting. *J. Mammal.*, **34**, 488–497.

ZENKOVICH, B. A. (1954). *Vokrug sveta za kitami*. (Round the world after whales.) Moscow.

Chapter 2. Evolution and External Appearances (pages 58–92)

1. *General anatomy, comparative anatomy, and measurements*

ASH, C. E. (1952). The body weights of whales. *Norsk Hvalf.-Tidende*, **41**, 364–374.

BENHAM, W. B. (1901). On the anatomy of *Cogia breviceps*. *Proc. Zool. Soc. Lond.*, **2**, 107–134.

BESHARSE, J. C. (1971). Maturity and sexual dimorphism in the skull, mandible, and teeth of the beaked whale, *Mesoplodon densirostris*. *J. Mammal.*, **52**, 297–315.

BJARNASON, I., and LINGAAS, P. (1954). Some weight measurements of whales. *Norsk Hvalf.-Tidende*, **43**, 8–11.

BOUVIER, E. L. (1892). Observations anatomiques sur l'*Hyperoodon rostratus*. *Ann. Sci. Nat. (7) Zool.*, **13**, 259–320.

BRODIE, P. F. (1975). Cetacean energetics, an overview of intraspecific size variation. *Ecology*, **56**, 152–161.

BRYDEN, M. M. (1972). Growth and development of marine mammals. In *Functional Anatomy of Marine Mammals*, ed. R. J. Harrison, vol. I, pp. 1–79. Academic Press, London.

BURMEISTER, G. (1869). Descripcion de cuatro espècies de Delfinidés. *Anal. Mus. Publ. Buenos Aires*, **1**, 367–445.

BURNE, R. H. (1952). *Handbook of Cetacean Dissections*. British Museum (Nat. Hist.), London.

CARTE, A. and MACALISTER, A. (1868). On the anatomy of *Balaenoptera rostrata*. *Phil. Trans. R. Soc. Lond.*, **158**, 201–261.

CLARKE, M. R. (1978). Structure and proportions of the spermaceti organ in the sperm whale. *J. mar. biol. Ass. U.K.*, **58**, 1–17.

CLARKE, R., and PALIZA, O. (1972). Sperm whales of the southeast Pacific. Part III: Morphometry. *Hvalråd. Skr.*, **53**, 1–106.

COWAN, D. F. (1966). Observations on the pilot whale *Globicephala melaena*: organ weight and growth. *Anat. Rec.* **155**, 623–628.

DANOIS, E. LE (1910). Recherches sur l'anatomie de la tête de *Kogia breviceps* Blainv. *Arch. Zool. Exp. Gen.* (5) **6**, 149–174.

DANOIS, E. LE (1911). Recherches sur les viscères et le squelette de *Kogia breviceps* avec un résumé de l'histoire de ce cétacé. *Arch. Zool. Exp. Gén.* (5) **6**, 465–489.

DE SMET, W. M. A. (1977). The regions of the cetacean vertebral column. In *Functional Anatomy of Marine Mammals*, ed. R. J. Harrison, vol. III, pp. 59–80. Academic Press, London.

FREUND, L. (1912). Walstudien. *Wien SitzBer. Ak. Wiss. Mat. Nat. Kl.*, **121**, 1103–1182.

FUJINO, K. (1955). On the body weight of the Sei whales located in the adjacent waters of Japan (II). *Sci. Rep. Whales Res. Inst., Tokyo*, **10**, 133–141.

HARRISON, R. J., and THURLEY, K. W. (1974). Structure of the epidermis in *Tursiops*, *Delphinus*, *Orcinus* and *Phocoena*. In *Functional Anatomy of Marine Mammals*, ed. R. J. Harrison, vol. II, pp. 45–71. Academic Press, London.

HOWELL, A. B. (1927). Contribution to the anatomy of the Chinese finless porpoise *Neomeris phocaenoides*. *Proc. U.S. Nat. Mus.*, **70**, art. 13, 1–43.

HUBER, E. (1934). Anatomical notes on Pinnipedia and Cetacea. *Carnegie Inst. Washington Publ.*, **447**, 105–136.

KASUYA, T. (1973). Systematic consideration of recent toothed whales based on the morphology of the tympano-periotic bone. *Sci. Rep. Whales Res. Inst., Tokyo*, **25**, 1–103.

LILLIE, D. G. (1910). Observations on the anatomy and general biology of some members of the larger Cetacea. *Proc. Zool. Soc. Lond.*, 769–792.

LOCKYER, C. (1976). Body weights of some species of large whales. *J. Cons. int. Explor. Mer.*, **36**, 259–273.

LÖNNBERG, E. (1910). The pelvic bones of some Cetacea. *Ark. Zool. Stockholm*, **7**, no. 10, 1–15.

MCCANN, C. (1974). Body scarring on Cetacea–odontocetes. *Sci. Rep. Whales Res. Inst., Tokyo*, **26**, 145–155.

MACHIN, D. (1974). A multivariate study of the external measurements of the sperm whale (*Physeter catodon*). *J. Zool.*, **172**, 267–288.

MACHIN, D. and KITCHENHAM, B. L. (1971). A multivariate study of the external measurements of the humpback whale (*Megaptera novaeangliae*). *J. Zool.*, **165**, 415–421.

MILLER, G. S. (1923). The telescoping of the cetacean skull. *Smiths. Misc. Colls.*, **76**, no. 5, 1–70.

MURIE, J. (1865). On the anatomy of a fin whale (*Physalus antiquorum* Gray) captured near Gravesend. *Proc. Zool. Soc. Lond.*, 206–227.

MURIE, J. (1871). On Risso's Grampus, *Grampus rissoanus* (Desm.). *J. Anat. Physiol.*, **5**, 118–138.

MURIE, J. (1873). On the organization of the caa'ing whale *Globicephalus melas*. *Trans. Zool. Soc. Lond.*, **8**, 235–301.

NEMOTO, T. (1955). White scars on whales. (I). Lamprey marks. *Sci. Rep. Whales Res. Inst., Tokyo*, **10**, 69–77.

NEUVILLE, H. (1928). Recherches sur le genre Steno et remarques sur quelques autres Cétacés. *Arch. Mus. d'Hist. Nat. Paris* (6), **3**, 69–242.

NISHIWAKI, M. (1950). On the body weight of whales. *Sci. Rep. Whales Res. Inst., Tokyo*, **4**, 184–209.

NOBLE, B. A., and FRASER, F. C. (1971). Description of a skeleton and supplementary notes on the skull of a rare porpoise *Phocoena sinus* Norris and McFarland 1958. *J. nat. Hist.*, **5**, 447–464.

OMURA, H. (1950). On the body weight of sperm and sei whales located in the adjacent waters of Japan. *Sci. Rep. Whales Res. Inst., Tokyo*, **4**, 1–13.

OMURA, H. (1957). Report on two right whales caught off Japan for scientific purposes under Article VIII of the International Convention for the Regulation of Whaling. *Norsk Hvalf.-Tidende*, **46**, 373–390.

OMURA, H. (1975). Osteological study of the minke whale from the Antarctic. *Sci. Rep. Whales Inst., Tokyo*, **27**, 1–36.

PIKE, G. C. (1951). Lamprey marks on whales. *J. Fish. Res. Bd. Can.*, **8**, 275–280.

PING, C. (1926). On some parts of the visceral anatomy of the porpoise *Neomeris phocaenoides*. *Anat. Rec.*, **33**, 13–28.

QUIRING, D. P. (1943). Weight data on five whales. *J. Mammal.*, **24**, 39–45.

RAVEN, H. C. (1942). Some morphological adaptations of cetaceans for life in water. *Trans. N.Y. Acad. Sci.*, Ser. II, **5**, 23–29.

RIDEWOOD, W. G. (1901). On the structure of the horny excrescence known as the 'bonnet' of the southern right whale (*Balaena australis*). *Proc. Zool. Soc. Lond.*, 44–47.

SATAKE, Y. and OMURA, H. (1974). A taxonomic study of the minke whale in the Antarctic by means of the hyoid bone. *Sci. Rep. Whales Res. Inst., Tokyo*, **26**, 15–24.

SCHULTE, H. VON W. (1916). Monographs of the Pacific Cetacea. II. The Sei whale (*Balaenoptera borealis* Lesson). 2. Anatomy of a foetus of *Balaenoptera borealis*.

Mem. Am. Mus. Nat. Hist. n.s., **1**, 389–502.

SCHULTE, H. VON W. (1917). The skull of *Kogia breviceps* Blainv. *Bull. Amer. Mus. Nat. Hist.*, **37**, 361–404.

SCHULTE, H. VON W., and SMITH, M. DE F. (1918). The external characters, skeletal muscles and peripheral nerves of *Kogia breviceps* (Blainville). *Bull. Amer. Mus. Nat. Hist.*, **38**, 7–72.

SERGEANT, D. E., and BRODIE, P. F. (1969). Body size in white whales, *Delphinapterus leucas. J. Fish. Res. Bd. Can.*, **26**, 2561–2580.

SIMPSON, J. G., and GARDNER, M. B. (1972). Comparative microscopic anatomy of selected marine mammals. In *Mammals of the Sea, Biology and Medicine*, ed. S. H. Ridgway, pp. 298–418. C. C. Thomas, Illinois.

SLEPTSOV, M. M. (1939). On the problem of the asymmetry of the skull in Odontoceti. *Zool. Zh.*, **18**, 367–384.

SLIJPER, E. J. (1936). Die Cetaceen, vergleichend-anatomisch und systematisch. *Capita Zoologica*, **7**, 1–590.

SLIJPER, E. J. (1938). Die Sammlung rezenter Cetacea des Musée Royal d'Histoire Naturelle de Belgique. *Bull. Mus. R. Hist. Nat. Belg.*, **14**, no. 10, 1–33.

SLIJPER, E. J. (1939). *Pseudorca crassidens* (Owen), ein Beitrag zur vergleichenden Anatomie der Cetaceen. *Zool. Meded. Rijksmus. Leiden*, **21**, 241–366.

SLIJPER, E. J. (1958). Organ weights and symmetry problems in porpoises and seals. *Arch. néerl. zool.*, **13**, suppl. 1, 97–115.

STRUTHERS, J. (1889). *Memoir on the Anatomy of the Humpback whale.* Maclachlan and Stewart, Edinburgh. (Reprinted from *J. Anat. Physiol.*, 1887–1889, **22**, 109–125, 240–282, 441–460; **23**, 308–335, 358–373.)

TURNER, W. (1872). An account of the great finner whale stranded at Longniddry. *Trans. R. Soc. Edinb.*, **26**, 197–251.

TURNER, W. (1892). The lesser rorqual (*Balaenoptera rostrata*) in the Scottish seas, with observations on its anatomy. *Proc. R. Soc. Edinb.*, **19**, 36–75.

UTRECHT, W. L. VAN (1959). Wounds and scars in the skin of the common porpoise, *Phocaena phocaena (L.)*. *Mammalia*, **23**, 100–122.

WATSON, M. and YOUNG, A. H. (1879). The anatomy of the northern beluga (*Beluga catadon*) Gray; *Delphinapterus leucas* (Pallas) compared with that of other whales. *Trans. R. Soc. Edinb.*, **29**, 393–434.

WILLIAMSON, G. R. (1972). The true body shape of rorqual whales. *J. Zool.*, **167**, 277–286.

WILLIAMSON, G. R. (1973). Counting and measuring baleen and ventral grooves of whales. *Sci. Rep. Whales Res. Inst., Tokyo*, **25**, 279–292.

WINN, H. E., BISCHOFF, W. L., and TARUSKI, A. G. (1973). Cytological sexing of Cetacea. *Marine Biol., Berl.*, **23** (4), 343–346.

WINSTON, W. C. (1950). The largest whale ever weighed. *Nat. Hist. N.Y.*, **59**, 393–399.

YAMADA, M. (1956). An analysis in mass osteology of the false killer whale, *Pseudorca crassidens* (Owen). Pt. 1. *Okajimas Folia Anat. Jap.*, **28**, 453–463.

ZENKOVICH, B. A. (1937). Weighing of whales. *C.R. Ac. Sci. U.S.S.R.*, **16**, 177–182.

2. *Embryology*

BROMAN, I. (1938). Über die existenz eines rätselhaften Sinus retromandibularis bei jungen Walembryonen. *Morph. Jb.*, **81**, 1–7.

BURLET, H. M. DE (1913–1917). Zur Entwicklungsgeschichte des Walschädels. *Morph. Jb.*, **45**, 523–556; **47**, 645–676; **49**, 119–178; **49**, 393–406; **50**, 1–50.

DANOIS, E. LE (1911). Description d'un embryon de *Grampus griseus* Gray. *Archs. Zool. Exp. Gén.*, **8**, 399–420.

EALES, N. B. (1950). The skull of the foetal narwhal, *Monodon monoceros* L. *Philos. Trans.*, **235** B, 1–33.

GILL, E. L. (1927). An early embryo of the blue whale. *Trans. R. Soc. S. Africa Cape Town*, **14**, 295–300.

GULDBERG, G. (1899). Neue Untersuchungen über die Rudimente von Hinterflossen und die Milchdrüsenanlage bei jungen Delphinembryonen. *Int. J. Anat.*, **16**, 301–321.

GULDBERG, G., and NANSEN, F. (1894). On the development and structure of the whale. Part I, On the development of the dolphin. *Bergens Mus. Skrifter.*, **5**, 1–70.

KAMIYA, T., and MIYAZAKI, N. (1974). A malformed embryo of *Stenella coeruleoalba*. *Sci. Rep. Whales Res. Inst., Tokyo*, **26**, 259–263.

KARLSEN, K. (1962). Development of tooth germs and adjacent structures in the whalebone whale (*Balaenoptera physalus* L.) with a contribution to the theories of the mammalian dentition. *Hvalråd. Skr.*, **45**, 1–56.

KAWAMURA, A., and KASHITA, K. (1971). A rare double monster of dolphin, *Stenella caeruleoalba*. *Sci. Rep. Whales Res. Inst., Tokyo*, **23**, 139–140.

KOCKAPAN, C., and KEIL, A. (1976). Zur Zahnstruktur bei Feten vom Weisswall (*D. leucas* Pallas 1776). *Sber. Ges. Naturf. Freunde, Berlin*, **16** (1), 44–47.

KÜKENTHAL, W. (1914). Untersuchungen an Walen (Tl.2). *Jena Z. Med. Naturwiss.*, **51**, 1–122.

LEGENDRE, R. (1926). Notes sur un foetus de dauphin. *Bull. Soc. zool. France*, **51**, 84–91.

MUELLER, E. (1971). Comparative embryological investigation based on a *Balaenoptera physalus* of 90 mm in length. *Investigations on Cetacea*, ed. G. Pilleri, vol. III, pt 2, pp. 203–215. Berne.

MÜLLER, H. C. (1920). Zur Entwicklungsgeschichte von *Phocaena communis* Less. *Archiv. Naturgesch.*, A.**7**, 1–113.

NAAKTGEBOREN, C. (1960). Die Entwicklungsgeschichte der Haut des Finnwals, *Balaenoptera physalus* (L.). *Zool. Anz.*, **165**, 159–167.

NISHIWAKI, M. (1957). Very small embryo of Cetacea. *Sci. Rep. Whales Res. Inst., Tokyo*, **12**, 191–192.

OGAWA, T. (1953). On the presence and disappearance of the hind limb in the cetacean embryos. *Sci. Rep. Whales Res. Inst., Tokyo*, **8**, 127–132.

OGAWA, T., and KAMIYA, T. (1957). A case of the cachalot with protruded rudimentary hind limbs. *Sci. Rep. Whales Res. Inst., Tokyo*, **12**, 197–208.

PILLERI, G. and WANDELER, A. (1962). Zur Entwicklung der Korperform der Cetacea (Mammalia). *Rev. Suisse Zool.*, **69**, 737–758.

SINCLAIR, J. G. (1962). An early dolphin embryo (*Stenella caeruleoalbus*) in serial sections. *Sci. Rep. Whales Res. Inst., Tokyo*, **16**, 83–87.

SINCLAIR, J. G. (1969). Embryogenesis of dolphin gonads. *Texas Rep. Biol. Med.*, **27**, 489–496.

SINCLAIR, J. G. (1969). Early development of the cetacean pituitary gland. *Texas Rep. Biol. Med.*, **27**, 1065–1076.

SLEPSTOV, M. M. (1955). Some pecularities in the development of Cetacea in the early embryonic stages. *Trud. Inst. Okeanol.*, **18**, 48–59.

STRUTHERS, J. (1893). On the rudimentary hind limb of a great fin whale, (*Balaenoptera musculus*) in comparison with those of the humpback whale and the Greenland right whale. *J. Anat. Physiol.*, **27**, 291–335.

TOBAYAMA, T., UCHIDA, S., and NISHIWAKI, M. (1970). Twin foetuses from a blue white dolphin. *Sci. Rep. Whales Res. Inst., Tokyo*, **22**, 159–162.

3. Phylogeny and relationships between cetaceans

ABEL, O. (1914). Die Vorfahren der Bartenwale. *Denkschr. Akad. Wiss. Wien*, **90**, 155.

ANTHONY, R. L. F. (1926). Les affinités des cétacés. *Annls. Inst. Océanog. Monaco*, **3**, 93–134.

BORRI, C. (1932). Sul valore della morfologia dei Cetacei come prova dell' evoluzione. *Atti Soc. Toscana Sci. Nat. Mem.*, **42**, 248–265.

BOYDEN, A., and GEMEROY, D. (1950). The relative position of the Cetacea among the orders of mammalia as indicated by precipitin tests. *Zoologica (N.Y.)*, **35**, 145–151.

BREE, P. J. H. VAN (1971). On the taxonomic status of *Delphinus pernettensis* de Blainville, 1817. (Notes on Cetacea, Delphinoidea II.) *Beaufortia*, **19**, 21–25.

BREE, P. J. H. VAN (1971). On *Globicephala sieboldii* (Gray, 1846), and other species of pilot whales. (Notes on Cetacea, Delphinoidea III.) *Beaufortia*, **19**, 79–87.

BREE, P. J. H. VAN (1971). On skulls

of *Stenella longirostris* Gray, 1828, from the eastern Atlantic. (Notes on Cetacea, Delphinoidea IV.) *Beaufortia*, **19**, 99–106.

BREE, P. J. H. VAN (1973). On the description and the taxonomic status of *Delphinus holboellii* Nilsson, 1847. (Notes on Cetacea, Delphinoidea VI.) *Beaufortia*, **20**, 129–134.

BREE, P. J. H. VAN (1973). *Neophocaena phocaenoides asiaeorientalis* (Pilleri & Gihr, 1972), a synonym of the preoccupied name *Delphinus melas* Schlegel, 1841. (Notes on Cetacea, Delphinoidea VII.) *Beaufortia*, **21**, 17–24.

DOHL, T. P., NORRIS, K. S., and KANG, I. (1974). A porpoise hybrid: *Tursiops x Steno. J. Mammal.*, **55**, 217–221.

DUGUY, R., and ROBINEAU, D. (1973). Cétacés et phoques des côtes de France. Guide d'identification. *Annales Soc. Sci. nat. Charente-Marit. Suppl.*, 1–93.

FLOWER, W. H. (1884). On whales, past and present and their probable origin. *Proc. Roy. Inst. Gr. Brit.*, **10**, 360–376.

FUSE, N. (1925). Serologische Untersuchungen über die verwandschaftlichen Beziehungen verschiedener Walarten. *Jap. J. med. Sci. Trans. Biochem.*, **1**, 1–4.

HAYASI, K. (1927). Weitere Untersuchungen über die Verwandschaftsverhaeltnisse zwischen den verschiedenen Walarten. *Jap. J. med. Sci. Trans. Biochem.*, **1**, 127–129.

HERSHKOWITZ, P. (1966). Catalogue of living whales. *Bull. U.S. Nat. Mus.*, no. 246, 1–259. Washington, D.C.

KÜKENTHAL, W. (1922). Zur Stammesgeschichte der Wale. *SitzBer. Akad. Wiss. Berlin.* 72–87.

MOORE, J. C. (1968). Relationships among the living genera of beaked whales with classifications, diagnoses and keys. *Fieldiana: Zool.*, **53** (4), 209–298.

PAQUIER, V. (1895). Remarques à propos de l'évolution des Cétacés. *Arch. Zool. Exp. Gén. Sér. 3*, **3**, 289–296.

PILLERI, G., and GIHR, M. (1972). Contribution to the knowledge of cetaceans of Pakistan with particular reference to the genera *Neomeris*, *Sousa*, *Delphinus* and *Tursiops* and a description of a new Chinese porpoise ·(*Neomeris asiaorientalis*). In *Investigations on Cetacea*, ed. G. Pilleri, vol. IV, 107–162. Berne.

PILLERI, G., and GIHR, M. (1975). On the taxonomy and ecology of the finless black porpoise, *Neophocaena* (Cetacea, Delphinidae). *Mammalia*, **39**, 657–673.

WINGE, H. (1918). Udsigt over Hvalernes indbyrdes Slaegtskab. *Vidensk. Medd. Dansk. Naturh. Foreningen*, **70**, 59–142. Trans. by G. S. Miller in *Smiths. Misc. Coll.* 1921, **72**, 1–67.

4. *Fossil cetaceans*

ABEL, O. (1902). Les Dauphins longirostres du Boldérein (Miocène supérieur) des environs d'Anvers. *Mém. Mus. R. Hist. Nat. Belg.*, **2**, 101–188.

ABEL, O. (1914). Die Herkunft der Bartenwale. *Verh. zool.-bot. Ges. Wien.*, **64**, 4–10.

ABEL, O. (1914). Die Vorfahren der Bartenwale. *Denkschr. Akad. Wiss. Wien. Math.Naturw.*, **90**, 155–224.

ABEL, O. (1931). Das Skelett der Eurhinodelphiden aus dem oberen Miozän von Antwerpen. *Mém. Mus. R. Hist. Nat. Belg.*, **48**, 191–334.

ABEL, O. (1938) .Vorläufige Mitteilungen über die Revision der fossilen Mystacoceten aus dem Tertiär Belgiens. *Bull. Mus. R. Hist. Nat. Belg.*, **14**, 1–34.

BARNES, L. G. (1973). *Praekogia cedrosensis*, a new genus and species of fossil pygmy sperm whale from Isla Cedros, Baja California, Mexico. *Contributions Sci.* no. 247, 1–20.

BENEDEN, P. J. VAN (1872). Les Baleines fossiles d'Anvers. *Bull. Acad. R. Belg.*, **34**, 6–20.

BORESKE, J. R., GOLDBERG, L., and CAMERON, B. (1972). A reworked cetacean with clam borings: Miocene of north Carolina. *J. Paleontol.*, **46**, 130–139.

BRANDT, J. F. (1873). Untersuchungen über die fossilen und subfossilen Cetaceen Europas. *Mém. Acad. St. Petersburg*, **20**, 206–329.

BREATHNACH, A. S. (1955). Observations on endocranial casts of recent and fossil cetaceans. *J. Anat.*, **89**, 532–546.

CAPELLINI, G. (1865). Balenottere Fossili del Bolognese. *Memorie dell' Instituto di Bologna*, Serie 2, **4**, 315–336.

CAPELLINI, G. (1875). Sui Cetoterii Bolognesi. *Mem. dell' Academia delle Scienze dell Ist. di Bologna*, serie 3, **5**, 595–626.

FLEISCHER, G. (1976). Hearing in extinct cetaceans as determined by cochlear structure. *J. Paleontol.*, **50**, 133–152.

FRAAS, E. (1904). Neue Zeuglodonten aus dem unteren Mitteleocän von Mokattam bei Cairo. *Geol. Pal. Abhandl. N.F.* Bd. 6, H. 3, 199–220.

HALSTEAD, L. B., and MIDDLETON, J. (1972). Notes on fossil whales from the Upper Eocene of Barton, Hampshire. *Proc. Geol. Ass.*, **83** (2), 185–190.

KELLOGG, R. (1927). *Kentriodon pernix*, a miocene porpoise from Maryland. *Proc. U.S. Nat. Mus.*, **69**, 1–55.

KELLOGG, R. (1928). The history of whales. *Quart. Rev. Biol.*, **3**, 29–174.

KELLOGG, R. (1934). A new cetothere from the modelo formation at Los Angeles, California (Contribut. to Palaeont. III). *Carnegie Inst. of Wash. Publ.* no. 447, 83–104.

KELLOGG, R. (1936). A review of the Archaeoceti. *Carnegie Inst. Washington*, publ. no. 482, 1–366.

KELLOGG, R. (1965). Fossil marine mammals from the miocene Calvert formation of Maryland and

Virginia. *Bull. U.S. nat. Mus.*, **247**, 1–45 and 47–63.

KEYES, I. W. (1973). Early oligocene squalodont cetacean from Damaru, New Zealand. *New Zealand J. mar. freshw. Res.*, **7** (4), 381–390.

KUHN, O. (1935). Archäoceten aus dem norddeutschen Alttertiär. *Zbl. f. Min. Geol. Paläont. Stuttgart*, **6**, 219–226.

PAPP, C. VON (1905). *Heterodelphis leiodontus* nova forma aus den miocänen Schichten des Comitates Sopron in Ungarn. *Mitt. Jb. Königl. Ungarischen Geol. Anstalt*, **14**, 2. H, 23–60.

PIA, J. (1937). Von den Walen des Wiener Miozäns. *Mitt. Geolog. Ges. Wien*, **29**, 357–428.

STROMER, E. VON (1903). Zeuglodon-Reste aus dem oberen Mittelcoän des Fajum. *Beitr. Pal. Öst.-Ung.*, **15**, 59–100.

STROMER, E. VON (1908). Die Archaeoceti des Aegyptischen Eozäns. *Beitr. Pal. Geol. Öst.-Ung.*, **21**, 106.

THENIUS, E. (1958). The whale in Austria – a witness of the past. *Norsk Hvalf.-Tidende*, **47**, 172–178.

TRUE, F. W. (1912). The genera of fossil whalebone whales allied to *Balaenoptera*. *Smiths. Miscell. Coll.*, **59**, no. 6. 8 pp.

WILSON, L. E. (1973). A delphinid (Mammalia, Cetacea) from the Miocene of Palo Verdes Hills, California. *University Calif. Publs. geol. Sci.*, **103**, 1–34.

ZIGNO, M. E. BARON A. DE (1876).

Sopra i resti di uno Squalodonte. *Memorie R. ist. Venet. Sci*, **20**, 17–35.

Chapter 3. Locomotion and Locomotory Organs (pages 93–116)

1. Locomotion

CHITTLEBOROUGH, R. G. (1958). Southern right whale in Australian waters. *J. Mammal.*, **37**, 456–457.

COLAM, J. B., and HILL, A. V. (1950). The horsepower of a whale. *Discovery Norwich*, **11**, 374.

ESSAPIAN, F. S. (1955). Speed-induced skin folds in the bottlenosed porpoise. *Breviora*, **43**, 1–4.

FEJER, A. A., and BACKUS, R. H. (1960). Porpoises and the bow-riding of ships under way. *Nature (Lond.)*, **188**, 700–703.

GAWN, R. W. L. (1948). Aspects of the locomotion of whales. *Nature (Lond.)*, **161**, 44–46.

GRAY, J. (1936). Studies on animal locomotion. VI. The propulsive powers of the dolphin. *J. Exp. Biol.*, **13**, 192–199.

GRAY, J. (1948). Aspects of the locomotion of whales. *Nature (Lond.)*, **161**, 199–200.

GUNTER, G. (1943). The swimming speed of *Tursiops*. *J. Mammal.*, **24**, 521.

HAYES, W. D. (1953). Wave riding of dolphins. *Nature (Lond.)*, **172**, 1060.

HAYES, W. D. (1959). Wave-riding

dolphins. *Science*, **130**, 1657–1658.

HERALD, E. S., BROWNELL, R. L. JR, FRYE, F. L., MORRIS, E. J., EVANS, W. E., and SCOTT, A. B. (1969). Blind river dolphin: first side-swimming cetacean. *Science*, **166**, 1408–1410.

HERTEL, H. (1969). Hydrodynamics of swimming and wave-riding dolphins. In *The Biology of Marine Mammals*, ed. H. T. Andersen, pp. 31–63. Academic Press, New York and London.

HILL, A. V. (1950). The dimensions of animals and their muscular dynamics. *Sci. Prog.*, **38**, 209–230.

HOWELL, A. B. (1927). Contributions to the anatomy of the Chinese finless porpoise. *Proc. U.S. Natl. Mus.*, **70**, Art. 13, 1–43.

HOWELL, A. B. (1930). Myology of the narwhal (*Monodon monoceros*). *Am. J. Anat.*, **46**, 187–215.

KERMACK, K. A. (1948). The propulsive powers of blue and fin whales. *J. Exp. Biol.*, **25**, 237–240.

LANE, F. W. (1943). Speed of dolphins. *J. Mammal.*, **24**, 292–293.

LANG, T. G. (1966). Hydrodynamic analysis of cetacean performance. In *Whales, Dolphins and Porpoises*, ed. K. S. Norris, pp. 410–432. University of California Press.

LANG, T. G. (1966). Hydrodynamic analysis of dolphin fin profiles. *Nature (Lond.)*, **209**, 1110–1111.

LANG, T. G., and NORRIS, K. S. (1966). Swimming speed of a Pacific bottlenose porpoise. *Science*, **151**, 588–590.

MATTHEWS. L. H. (1948). The swimming of dolphins. *Nature (Lond.)*, **161**, 731.

PARRY, D. A. (1949). The swimming of whales and a discussion of Gray's paradox. *J. Exp. Biol.*, **26**, 24–34.

PARRY, D. A. (1949). The anatomical basis of swimming in whales. *Proc. Zool. Soc.*, **119**, 49–60.

PERSHIN, S. V. (1969). Hydrodynamic characteristics of Cetacea and average swimming speed of dolphins in natural conditions and in captivity. *Bionica*, **3**, 5–12. (In Russian.)

PURVES, P. E. (1963). Locomotion in whales. *Nature (Lond.)*, **197**, 334–337.

SLIJPER, E. J. (1946). Comparative biologic-anatomical investigations on the vertebral column and spinal musculature of mammals. *Verh. Kon. Ned. Akad. Wet. Nat. Sec.* 2, **42**, No. 5, 1–128.

SLIJPER, E. J. (1961). Locomotion and locomotory organs in whales and dolphins (Cetacea). *Symp. Zool. Soc. Lond.*, **5**, 77–94.

STASS, I. I. (1939). Recording of the dolphin's body movement in the sea. *Dokl. Akad. Nauk. S.S.S.R.*, **24**, 536–539.

STASS, I. I. (1939). Once more on the recording of the movements of the dolphin in the sea. *Dokl. Akad. Nauk. S.S.S.R.*, **25**, 668.

WILLIAMSON, G. R. (1972). The true body shape of rorqual whales. *J. Zool., Lond.*, **167**, 277–286.

WOODCOCK, A. H. (1948). The

swimming of dolphins. *Nature (Lond.)*, **161**, 602.

WOODCOCK, A. H., and MCBRIDE, A. F. (1951). Wave-riding of dolphins. *J. Exp. Biol.*, **28**, 215–217.

WYRICK, R. F. (1954). Observations on the movements of the Pacific gray whale *Eschrichtius glaucus* (Cope). *J. Mammal.*, **35**, 596–598.

Chapter 4. Respiration (pages 117–153)

1. Respiration and diving

CADENAT, J. (1959). Notes sur les Delphinides ouest-africains. VI. Le gros dauphin gris (*Tursiops truncatus*) est-il capable de faire des plongées profondes? *Bull. Inst. Français Afrique noire*, **21**A, 1137–1143.

CALDWELL, D. K. (1955). Notes on the spotted dolphin *Stenella plagiodon*, and the first record of the common dolphin, *Delphinus delphis* in the Gulf of Mexico. *J. Mammal.*, **36**, 467–470.

CLARKE, M. R. (1978). Buoyancy control as a function of the spermaceti organ in the sperm whale. *J. mar. biol. Ass. U.K.*, **58**, 27–71.

FRASER, F. C., and PURVES, P. E. (1955). The 'blow' of whales. *Nature (Lond.)*, **176**, 1221–1222.

GILMORE, R. M. (1960). Census and migration of California gray whale. *Norsk Hvalf.-Tidende*, **49**, 409–431.

GUNTHER, E. R. (1949). The habits of fin whales. *Discovery Rep.*, **25**, 113–142.

GUREVICH, V. S., and KOROL'KOV, YU. I. (1973). A roentgenological study of respirative act in *Delphinus delphis*. *Zoologicheskij Zh.*, **52**, 786–789.

HARRISON, R. J., and RIDGWAY, S. H. (1976). *Deep Diving in Mammals*. Meadowfield Press, Durham, England, *Zool. Ser.* **7**, 1–51.

HEEZEN, B. C. (1957). Whales entangled in deep sea cables. *Norsk Hvalf.-Tidende*, **46**, 665–681.

HUI, C. A. (1975). Thoracic collapse as affected by the *retia thoracica* in the dolphin. *Resp. Physiol.*, **25**, 63–70.

IRVING, L., SCHOLANDER, P. F., and GRINNELL, S. W. (1941). The respiration of the porpoise *Tursiops truncatus*. *J. Cell. Comp. Physiol.*, **17**, 145–168.

JOLYET, F. (1893). Recherches sur la respiration des Cétacés. *C. R. Séances Soc. Biol. Fil.*, **5**, 655–656.

KLEINENBERG, S. E. (1956). Particulars of the respiration of Cetacea. *Akad. Nauk. Uzbeck. S.S.S.R. biol.*, **41**, 366–380. (Russ. no summ.).

LAURIE, A. H. (1933). Some aspects of respiration in blue and fin whales. *Discovery Rep.*, **7**, 363–406.

LAURIE, A. H. (1935). Physiology of whales. *Nature (Lond.)*, **135**, 823.

LENFANT, C., KENNEY, D. W., and AUCUTT, C. (1968). Respiratory functions in the killer whale *Orcinus orca* (Linnaeus). *Am. J. Physiol.*, **215**, 1505–1511.

MEDWAY, W., MCCORMICK, J. G.,

RIDGWAY, S. H., and CRUMP, J. F. (1970). Effects of prolonged halothane anaesthesis on some cetaceans. *J. Am. vet. med. Ass.*, **157**, 576–582.

OLSEN, C. R., HALE, F. C., and ELSNER, R. (1969). Mechanics of ventilation in the pilot whale. *Resp. Physiol.*, **7**, 137–149.

PARKER, G. H. (1932). The respiratory rate of the common porpoise. *J. Mammal.*, **13**, 68–69.

RANCUREL, P. (1964). Note sur la plongée profonde de *Tursiops truncatus*. *Océanographie*, **2**, (4), 135–141.

RIDGWAY, S. H., SCRONCE, B. L., and KANWISHER, J. (1969). Respiration and deep diving in the bottlenose porpoise. *Science*, **166**, 1651–1654.

SCHOLANDER, P. F. (1940). Experimental investigations on the diving respiratory function in diving mammals and birds. *Hvalråd. Skr. Oslo*, **22**, 1–131.

SPENCER, M. P., GORNALL, T. A., III, and POULTER, T. C. (1967). Respiratory and cardiac activity of killer whales. *J. Appl. Physiol.*, **22**, 974–981.

TOMILIN, A. G. (1948). On the biology and physiology of Black Sea dolphins. *Zool. Zh.*, **27**, 53–64. (In Russian.)

TRUE, F. W. (1909). Observations on living white whales. *Smith. Miscell. Coll.*, **52**, 325–330.

2. *Lungs*

BARBOSA, J. M. (1914). Sphincters bronchiques chez le dauphin (*Delphinus delphis*). *Compt. Rend. Acad. Sci. Paris*, **159**, 455–458.

BAUDRIMONT, A. (1955). Structure des veines pulmonaires et circulation fonctionelle du poumon du dauphin commun, *Delphinus delphis* L. *Bull. microsc. appl.*, **5**, 57–78.

BAUDRIMONT, A. (1959). Sur la signification du double réseau capillaire respiratoire des mammifères marins. *Arch. Anat (Strasbourg)*, **42**, 89–117.

BÉLANGER, L. F. (1940). A study of the histological structure of the respiratory portion of the lungs of aquatic mammals. *Am. J. Anat.*, **67**, 437–469.

BONIN, W., and BÉLANGER, L. F. (1939). Sur la structure du poumon de *Delphinapterus leucas*. *Trans. R. Soc. Canada*, **33**, sect. 5, 19–22.

ENGEL, S. (1954). Respiratory tissue of the large whales. *Nature (Lond.)*, **173**, 128–129.

FANNING, J. C., and HARRISON, R. J. (1974). The structure of the trachea and lungs of the South Australian bottle-nosed dolphin. In *Functional Anatomy of Marine Mammals*, ed. R. J. Harrison, vol. II, pp. 231–252. Academic Press, London.

FIEBIGER, J. (1916). Über Eigentümlichkeiten im Aufbau der Delphinlunge, und ihre physiologische Bedeutung. *Anat. Anz.*, **48**, 540–565.

GOUDAPPEL, J. R., and SLIJPER, E. J. (1958). Microscopic structure of the lungs of the bottlenose whale. *Nature (Lond.)*, **182**, 479.

HAYNES, F., and LAURIE, A. H. (1937). On the histological structure of cetacean lungs. *Discovery Rep.*, **17**, 1–6.

ITO, T., KOBAYASHI, K., and TAKAHASHI, Y. (1967). Histological studies on the respiratory tissue of the dolphin lung. *Arch. histol. jap.*, **28**, 453–470.

LACOSTE, A., and BAUDRIMONT, A. (1926). Sur quelques particularités histologiques du poumon du dauphin et leur adaptation fonctionelle à la plongée. *Bull. Station Biol. Arcachon, Bordeaux*, **23**, 87–140.

LACOSTE, A., and BAUDRIMONT, A. (1933). Dispositifs d'adaptation fonctionelle à la plongée dans l'appareil respiratoire du marsouin (*Phocaena communis* Less.). *Arch. Anat. Histol. Embryol.*, **17**, 1–48.

MURATA, T. (1951). Histological studies on the respiratory portions of the lungs of Cetacea. *Sci. Rep. Whales Res. Inst., Tokyo*, **6**, 35–47.

NEUVILLE, H. (1921, 1922, 1923). Sur l'appareil respiratoire des cétacés. I–IV. *Bull. Mus. Hist. nat. Paris*, **27**, 209–215, 396–403; **28**, 27–34; **29**, 35–39.

VLADIMIROV, V. L. (1973). The morphology and some particulars on the branching of the large bronchi in sperm whales. *Izvestiya tikhookean. naucho-issled. Inst. ryb. Khoz. Okeanogr.*, **87**, 198–204. (In Russian.)

WISLOCKI, G. B. (1929). On the structure of the lungs of the porpoise (*Tursiops truncatus*). *Am. J. Anat.*, **44**, 47–78.

WISLOCKI, G. B. (1942). The lungs of the Cetacea with special reference to the harbor porpoise (*Phocaena phocoena*, Linnaeus). *Anat. Rec.*, 84, 117–123.

WISLOCKI, G. B., and BÉLANGER, L. F. (1940). The lungs of the larger Cetacea compared to those of smaller species. *Biol. Bull.*, **78**, 289–297.

YAMASAKI, F., TAKAHASHI, K., and KAMIYA, T. (1977). Lungs of franciscana (*Pontoporia blainvillei*), with special references to their external aspects, weights and bronchial ramifications. *Okajimas Fol. anat. jap.*, **53**, 337–358.

3. *Nasal passage, pharynx, larynx*

ANTHONY, R., and COUPIN, F. (1930). Recherches anatomiques sur le vestibule de l'appareil respiratoire du *Mesoplodon*. *Mem. Inst. Español Oceanog.*, **14**, 1–40.

BAER, K. E. VON (1826). Die Nase der Cetaceen erlautert durch Untersuchung der Nase des Braunfisches (*Delphinus phocaena*). *Isis Oken*, **19**, 811–847.

BEAUREGARD, H., and BOULART, R. (1882). Recherches sur le larynx et la trachée des Balénides. *J. Anat. Phys., Paris*, **18**, 611–634.

BENHAM, W. B. (1901). On the larynx of certain whales. (*Cogia,*

Balaenoptera, and *Ziphius*). *Proc. Zool. Soc. Lond.*, 278–300.

BLEVINS, C. E., and PARKINS, B. J. (1973). Functional anatomy of the porpoise larynx. *Amer. J. Anat.*, **138**, 151–164.

BOENNINGHAUS, G. (1902). Der Rachen von *Phocaena communis*. Eine biologische Studie. *Zool. Jahrb. Anat.*, **27**, 1–98.

CLARKE, M. R. (1970). Function of the spermaceti organ of the sperm whale. *Nature (Lond.)*, **228**, 873–874.

GRACHEVA, M. S. (1971). A contribution to the structure of the larynx in *Tursiops truncatus*. *Zool. Zh.*, **50**, 1539–1545.

GRUHL, K. (1911). Beiträge zur Anatomie und Physiologie der Cetaceennase. *Jena Z. Naturw.*, **47**, 367–414.

HEIN, S. A. A. (1914). The larynx and its surroundings in *Monodon*. *Verhand. Kon. Akad. Wetensch., Amsterdam*, sect. 2, **18**, 4–54.

HINTON, M. A. C. (1936). Some interesting points in the anatomy of the freshwater dolphin *Lipotes* and its allies. *Proc. Linn. Soc. Lond.*, 148th session, 183–185.

HOSOKAWA, H. (1950). On the cetacean larynx, with special remarks on the laryngeal sac of the sei whale and the aryteno-epiglottideal tube of the sperm whale. *Sci. Rep. Whales Res. Inst., Tokyo*, **3**, 23–62.

HUBER, E. (1934). Anatomical notes on Pinnipedia and Cetacea. *Carnegie Inst. Wash. Publ.*, No. 447, 105–136.

KERNAN, J. D., and SCHULTE, H. VON W. (1918). Memoranda upon the anatomy of the respiratory tract, foregut and thoracic viscera of a foetal *Kogia breviceps*. *Bull. Am. Mus. Nat. Hist.*, **38**, 231–267.

LAWRENCE, B., and SCHEVILL, W. E. (1956). The functional anatomy of the delphinid nose. *Bull. Mus. Comp. Zool. Harvard*, **114**, 103–151.

LAWRENCE, B., and SCHEVILL, W. E. (1965). Gular musculature in delphinids. *Bull. Mus. Comp. Zool. Harvard*, **133**, 1–65.

PILLERI, G., GIHR, M., PURVES, P. E., ZBINDEN, K., and KRAUS, C. (1976). On the behaviour, bioacoustics and functional morphology of the Indus river dolphin (*Platanista indi* Blyth, 1859). In *Investigations on Cetacea*, ed. G. Pilleri, vol. VI, pp. 13–141. Berne.

PURVES, P. E., and PILLERI, G. (1973). Observations on the ear, nose and throat and eye of *Platanista indi*. In *Investigations on Cetacea*, ed. G. Pilleri, vol. V, pp. 13–57. Berne.

QUAY, W. B., and MITCHELL, E. D. (1971). Structure and sensory apparatus of oral remnants of the nasopalatine canals in the fin whale (*Balaenoptera physalus* L.). *J. Morph.*, **134**, 271–280.

RAVEN, H. C., and GREGORY, W. K. (1933). The spermaceti organ and nasal passages of the sperm whale (*Physeter catodon*) and other odontocetes. *Am. Mus. Novitates*, **677**, 1–18.

RAWITZ, B. (1900). Zur Anatomie des Kehlkopfes und der Nase von *Phocaena communis* Cuv. *Int. Mschr. Anat. Physiol.*, **17**, 245–354.

SCHENKKAN, E. J. (1971). The occurrence and position of the 'connecting sac' in the nasal tract complex of small odontocetes (Mammalia, Cetacea). *Beaufortia*, **19**, 37–43.

SCHENKKAN, E. J., and PURVES, P. E. (1973). The comparative anatomy of the nasal tract and the function of the spermaceti organ in the Physeteridae (Mammalia, Odontoceti). *Bijd. tot de Dierk.*, **43**, 93–112.

Chapter 5. Heart, Circulation, and Blood (pages 154–178)

1. *Heart, circulation, blood, spleen, lymphatic organs*

ANDREWS, J. C., DILL, F. J., MASUI, S., and FISHER, H. D. (1973). The chromosome complement of the narwhal (*Monodon monoceros*). *Canadian J. Genet. Cytol.*, **15** (2), 349–352.

ARNASON, U., and BENIRSCHKE, K. (1973). Karyotypes and idiograms of sperm and pygmy sperm whales. *Hereditas*, **73** (1), 67–74.

BARNETT, C. H., HARRISON, R. J., and TOMLINSON, J. D. W. (1958). Variations in the venous systems of mammals. *Biol. Rev. (Camb.)*, **33**, 442–487.

BRESCHET, G. (1836). Histoire anatomique et physiologique d'un organe de nature vasculaire découvert dans les Cetacea. Bechet Jeune, Paris. 1–82.

CAVE, A. J. E. (1977). Coronary vasculature of the bottlenosed dolphin. In *Functional Anatomy of Marine Mammals*, ed. R. J. Harrison, vol. III, pp. 199–215. Academic Press, London.

ELSNER, R., PIRIE, J., KENNEY, D. D., and SCHEMMER, S. (1974). Functional circulatory anatomy of cetacean appendages. In *Functional Anatomy of Marine Mammals*, ed. R. J. Harrison, vol. II, pp. 143–159. Academic Press, London.

FAWCETT, D. W. (1942). A comparative study of blood vascular bundles in the Florida manatee (*Trichechus latirostris*) and certain cetaceans and edentates. *J. Morphol.*, **71**, 105–124.

FUJINO, K. (1953). On the blood groups of the sei, fin, blue and humpback whales. *Proc. Jap. Acad.*, **29**, 183–190.

GALLIANO, R. E., MORGANE, P. J., MCFARLAND, W. L., NAGEL, E. L., and CATHERMAN, R. L. (1966). The anatomy of the cervicothoracic arterial system in the bottlenose dolphin (*Tursiops truncatus*) with a surgical approach suitable for guided angiography. *Anat. Rec.*, **155** (3), 325–338.

GERACI, J. R., and MEDWAY, W. (1973). Simulated field blood studies in the bottlenosed dolphin

Tursiops truncatus. 2. Effects of stress on some hematologic and plasma chemical parameters. *J. Wildl. Dis.*, **9**, 29–33.

HAMLIN, R. L., JACKSON, R. F., HIMES, J. A., PIPERS, F. S., and TOWNSEND, A. C. (1970). Electrocardiogram of bottle-nosed dolphin (*Tursiops truncatus*). *Amer. J. Vet. Res.*, **31**, 501–505.

HARBOE, A., and SCHRUMPF, A. (1952). The red blood cell diameter in blue whale and humpback whale. *Norsk Hvalf.-Tidende*, **41**, 416–618.

HARRISON, R. J., and TOMLINSON, J. D. W. (1956). Observations on the venous system in certain Pinnipedia and Cetacea. *Proc. Zool. Soc. Lond.*, **126**, 205–233.

IRVING, L. (1939). Respiration in diving mammals. *Physiol. Rev.*, **19**, 112–134.

KANWISHER, J. (1960). Cardiograph of a whale. *Norsk Hvalf.-Tidende*, **49**, 561–565.

KING, R. L., JENKS, J. L., and WHITE, P. D. (1953). The electrocardiogram of a Beluga whale. *Circulation*, **8**, 387–393.

KNOLL, W. (1940). Blut und embryonale Blutbildung bei den Walen. *Z. Fisch. Hilfswiss.*, **39**, 1–12.

KOCK, L. L. DE (1959). The arterial vessels of the neck in the pilot whale (*Globicephala melaena* Traill) and the porpoise (*Phocaena phocaena* L.) in relation to the carotid body. *Acta Anat.*, **36**, 274–292.

KOLCHIN, S. P., and BEL'KOVICH, V. M. (1970). Some characteristics of the heart function in dolphins. *Zh. evol. Biokhim. Fiziol.*, **6**, 411–417. Translated in: *J. evol. Biochem. Physiol.*, **6**, 335–340. (In Russian.)

KÜGELGEN, A. VON (1955). Über den Wandbau der Vena cava caudalis, eines erwachsenen Finnwales. *Zeitschr. Zellf.*, **41**, 435–459.

LACOSTE, A., and GOUELMINA-RISTITCH, M. (1926). Sur quelques particularités de structure des branches intra-hépatiques de la veine porte chez le Dauphin. *C.R. Soc. Biol., Paris*, **94**, 185–190.

LENFANT, C. (1969). Physiological properties of blood of marine mammals. In *The Biology of Marine Mammals*, ed. H. T. Andersen, pp. 95–116. Academic Press, New York.

MACKAY, J. Y. (1886). The arteries of the head and neck and the rete mirabile of the porpoise (*Phocoena communis*). *Proc. R. Philos. Soc. Glasgow*, **17**, 366–377.

MOSKOV, V. M., SCHIWATSCHEWA, T., and BONER, S. (1969). Vergleichshistologische Untersuchung der Lymphknoten der Säuger. Die Lymphknoten des Delphins. *Anat. Anz.*, **124**, 49–67.

NELSON, G. J. (1971). The lipid composition of the blood of marine mammals. 2. Atlantic bottlenose dolphins, *Tursiops truncatus* and two species of seals, *Halichoerus grypus* and *Phoca vitulina*. *Comp. Biochem. Physiol.*, **40** (B), 423–432.

NELSON, G. J. (1973). The lipid

composition of the blood of marine mammals. 3. The fatty acid composition of plasma and erythrocytes of Atlantic bottlenose dolphin, *Tursiops truncatus*. *Comp. Biochem. Physiol.*, (B) **46**, 257–268.

OMMANEY, F. D. (1932). The vascular networks (retia mirabilia) of the fin whale (*Balaenoptera physalus*). *Discovery Rep.*, **5**, 327–362.

QUAY, W. B. (1954). The blood cells of Cetacea with particular reference to the beluga *Delphinapterus leucas* Pallas, 1776. *Säugetierk. Mitt.*, **2**, 49–54.

RICHARD, J., and NEUVILLE, H. (1896). Foie et sinus veineux intrahépatiques du *Grampus griseus*. *Bull. Mus. Hist. Nat., Paris*, **2**, 335–337.

RIDGWAY, S. H., SIMPSON, J. G., PATTON, G. S., and GILMARTIN, W. G. (1970). Hematologic findings in certain small cetaceans. *J. Am. vet. med. Ass.*, **157**, 566–575.

ROWLATT, U., and GASKIN, D. E. (1975). Functional anatomy of the heart of the harbor porpoise, *Phocaena phocaena*. *J. Morph.*, **146**, 479–494.

SCHOLANDER, P. F. (1940). Experimental investigations on the respiratory function in diving mammals and birds. *Hvalråd. Skr.*, **22**, 1–131.

SCHOLANDER, P. F. (1955). Evolution of climatic adaptation in homeotherms. *Evolution*, **9**, 15–26.

SCHOLANDER, P. F., and SCHEVILL, W. E. (1955). Counter-current

vascular heat exchange in the fins of whales. *J. Appl. Physiol.*, **8**, 279–282.

SLIJPER, E. J. (1962). Foramen ovale and ductus arteriosus botalli in aquatic mammals. *Mammalia*, **25**, 528–570.

SOMMER, L. S., MCFARLAND, W. L., GALLIANO, R. E., NAGEL, E. L., and MORGANE, P. J. (1968). Hemodynamic and coronary angiographic studies in the bottlenose dolphin (*Tursiops truncatus*). *Amer. J. Physiol.*, **215**, 1498–1505.

SPOEL, S. VAN DE (1963). The vascular system in the kidney of the common porpoise (*Phocaena phocaena* L.). *Bijd. Dierk.*, **33**, 71–81.

STANNIUS, F. H. (1841). Über den Verlauf der Arterien bei *Delphinus phocaena*. *Arch. Anat. Physiol., Lpz.*, **8**, 379–402.

TAWARA, T. (1951). On the respiratory pigments of whale (Studies on whale blood II). *Sci. Rep. Whales Res. Inst., Tokyo*, **3**, 96–101.

TOMILIN, A. G. (1951). Thermoregulation in Cetacea. *Priroda*, **6**, 55–58.

TRUEX, R. C., NOLAN, F. G., TRUEX, R. C., JR, SCHNEIDER, H. P., and PERLMUTTER, H. I. (1961). Anatomy and pathology of the whale heart with special reference to the coronary circulation. *Anat. Rec.*, **141**, 325–353.

UTRECHT, W. L. VAN (1958). Temperaturregulierende Gefässsysteme in der Haut und anderen epidermalen Strukturen bei Cetaceen. *Zool. Anz.*, **161**, 77–82.

VEDVICK, T. S., and ITANO, H. A. (1976). Partial characterization of the haemoglobin from Hubbs' beaked whale (*Mesoplodon carlhubbsi*). *Comp. Biochem. Physiol.*, **55**B (1), 65–68.

WALMSLEY, R. (1938). Some observations on the vascular system of a female fetal finback. *Publ. Carnegie Inst. Washington*, **496**, 107–178.

WHITE, P. D., and KERR, W. J. (1915–1917). The heart of the sperm whale with special reference to the AV conducting system. *Heart*, **6**, 207–216.

WILSON, H. S. (1879). The rete mirabile of the narwahl. *J. Anat. Physiol.*, **14**, 377–398.

ZWILLENBERG, H. H. L. (1958). Die mikroskopische Anatomie der Milz der Furchenwale. *Acta Anat.*, **32**, 24–39.

ZWILLENBERG, H. H. L. (1959). Über die Milz des Braunfisches (*Phocaena phocaena* L.). *Z. Anat. Entwicklungsgesch.*, **121**, 9–18.

Chapter 6. Behaviour (pages 179–201)

1. *Behaviour*

ANDERSEN, S. (1969). Epimeletic behavior in captive harbor porpoise, *Phocaena phocaena* (L.). In *Investigations on Cetacea*, ed. G. Pilleri, vol. I, pp. 203–205. Berne.

BEL'KOVICH, V. M., KRUSHINSKAYA, N. L., and GUREVICH, V. S. (1969).

The behavior of dolphins in captivity. *Priroda*, **11**, 18–28.

BEST, P. B. (1970). Records of the pygmy killer whale, *Feresa attenuata*, from southern Africa, with notes on behaviour in captivity. *Ann. S. Afr. Mus.*, **57**, 1–14.

BROWN, D. H. (1960). Behavior of a captive Pacific pilot whale. *J. Mammal.*, **41**, 342–349.

BROWN, D. H., and NORRIS, K. S. (1956). Observations of captive and wild cetaceans. *J. Mammal.*, **37**, 311–326.

BROWNELL, R. L., JR (1964). Observations of odontocetes in central Californian waters. *Norsk Hvalf.-Tidende*, **53**, 60–66.

BUSNEL, R.-G. (1973). Symbionic relationship between man and dolphins. *N.Y. Acad. Sci.*, **35**, 112–131.

CALDWELL, D. K. (1955). Notes on the spotted dolphin *Stenella plagiodon*, and the first record of the common dolphin, *Delphinus delphis*, in the Gulf of Mexico. *J. Mammal.*, **36**, 467–470.

CALDWELL, D. K. (1956). Intentional removal of a disturbing object by an Atlantic bottlenose dolphin. *J. Mammal.*, **37**, 454–455.

CALDWELL, M. C., and CALDWELL, D. K. (1966). Behavior of marine mammals. In *Mammals of the Sea*, ed. S. H. Ridgway, pp. 419–465. C. C. Thomas, Springfield.

CALDWELL, M. C., and CALDWELL, D. K. (1966). Epimeletic (caregiving) behaviour in Cetacea. In *Whales, Dolphins and Porpoises*, ed. K. S. Norris, pp. 755–789.

University of California Press.

CONDY, P. R., VAN AARDE, R. J., and BESTER, M. N. (1978). The seasonal occurrence and behaviour of killer whales *Orcinus orca*, at Marion Island. *J. Zool. Lond.*, **184**, 449–464.

CUMMINGS, W. C., and THOMPSON, P. O., (1971). Gray whales, *Eschrichtius robustus*, avoid the underwater sounds of killer whales, *Orcinus orca*. *Fishery Bull. U.S. natn. ocean. atmos. Admn.*, **69**, 525–530.

EVANS, W. E. (1971). Orientation behavior of delphinids: radio telemetric studies. *Ann. N.Y. Acad. Sci.*, **188**, 142–160.

GUNTER, G. (1942). Contributions to the natural history of the bottle-nosed dolphin, *Tursiops truncatus* (Montagu), on the Texas Coast, with particular reference to food habits. *J. Mammal.*, **23**, 267–276.

GUNTHER, E. R. (1949). The habits of fin whales. *Discovery Rep.*, **25**, 113–142.

HUBBS, C. L. (1953). Dolphin protecting dead young. *J. Mammal.*, **34**, 498.

JONSGÅRD, Å., and NORDLI, O. (1952). Concerning a catch of white-sided dolphins (*Lagenorhynchus acutus*) on the west coast of Norway, winter 1952. *Norsk Hvalf.-Tidende*, **41**, 229–232.

KIMURA, S., and NEMOTO, T. (1956). Note on a minke whale kept alive in aquarium. *Sci. Rep. Whales Res. Inst., Tokyo*, **11**, 181–189.

KRITZLER, H. (1952). Observations on the pilot whale in captivity. *J. Mammal.*, **33**, 321–334.

LAWRENCE, B., and SCHEVILL, W. E. (1954). *Tursiops* as an experimental subject. *J. Mammal.*, **35**, 225–232.

LAYNE, J. N., and CALDWELL, D. K. (1964). Behavior of the Amazon dolphin *Inia geoffrensis* (Blainville), in captivity. *Zoologica*, **49**, 81–108.

LILLY, J. C. (1961). *Man and Dolphin.* Doubleday, New York.

MCBRIDE, A. F., and HEBB, D. O. (1948). Behavior of the captive bottlenose dolphin, *Tursiops truncatus. J. Comp. Physiol. Psychol.*, **41**, 111–123.

MCBRIDE, A. F., and KRITZLER, H. (1951). Observations on pregnancy, parturition and postnatal behavior in the bottlenose dolphin. *J. Mammal.*, **32**, 251–266.

MOORE, J. C. (1955). Bottlenosed dolphins support remains of young. *J. Mammal.*, **36**, 466–467.

NORRIS, K. S. (1965). Trained porpoise released in the open sea. *Science*, **147**, 1048–1050.

PERRIN, W. F., and HUNTER, J. R. (1972). Escape behavior of the Hawaiian spinner porpoise (*Stenella* cf. *S. longirostris*). *Fish. Bull.*, **70**, 49–60.

PILLERI, G. (1969). On the behavior of the Amazon dolphin, *Inia geoffrensis*, in Beni (Bolivia). *Rev. Suisse Zool.*, **76**, 57–91.

PILLERI, G. (1970) Observations on the behaviour of *Platanista gange-*

tica in the Indus and Brahmaputra Rivers. In *Investigations on Cetacea*, ed. G. Pilleri, vol. II, pp. 27–60. Berne.

PURRINGTON, P. (1955). A whale and her calf. *Nat. Hist.*, **65**, 363.

SAAYMAN, G. S., and TAYLER, C. K. (1973). Some behaviour patterns of the southern right whale *Eubalaena australis. Z̧. Säuget.*, **38**, 172–183.

SAAYMAN, G. S., TAYLER, C. K., and BOWER, D. (1973). Diurnal activity cycles in captive and free-ranging Indian Ocean bottlenose dolphins (*Tursiops aduncus* Ehrenburg). *Behaviour*, **44**, 212–233.

SCHEVILL, W. E. (1956). *Lagenorhynchus acutus* off Cape Cod. *J. Mammal.*, **37**, 128–129.

SIENBENALER, J. B. and CALDWELL, D. K. (1956). Cooperation among adult dolphins. *J. Mammal.*, **37**, 126–128.

SLIJPER, E. J. (1958). Das Verhalten der Wale (Cetacea). *Handb. Zool. Band.*, 8, **10**, 1–32.

STARRETT, A., and STARRETT, P. (1955). Observations on young blackfish, *Globicephala. J. Mammal.*, **36**, 424–429.

TAYLER, C. K., and SAAYMAN, G. S. (1973). Imitative behaviour by Indian ocean bottlenose dolphins (*Tursiops aduncus*) in captivity. *Behaviour*, **44**, 286–298.

TOMILIN, A. G. (1935). Maternal instinct and sexual attachment in whales. *Bull. Soc. Nat. Moscou (Biol.) N.S.*, **44**, 351–361.

TOWNSEND, C. H. (1914). The porpoise in captivity. *Zoologica (N.Y.)*, **1**, 289–299.

TRUE, F. W. (1909). Observations on living white whales *Delphinapterus leucas*, with a note of the dentition of *Delphinapterus* and *Stenodelphis. Smith. Misc. Coll.*, **52**, 325–330.

Chapter 7. Hearing (pages 202–217)

1. *Hearing*

BEL'KOVICH, V. M., and SOLNTSEVA, G. N. (1970). Morpho-functional peculiarities of the acoustic organ in dolphins. *Zool. Zh.*, **49**, 275–282. (In Russian, English summary.)

BOENNINGHAUS, G. (1904). Das Ohr des Zahnwales. *Zool. Jahrb. Abt. Anat. Ontog. Thiere*, **19**, 189–360.

DENKER, A. (1902). Zur Anatomie des Gehörorgans der Cetacea. *Anat. Hefte*, **19**, 424–448.

DUDOK VAN HEEL, W. H. (1959). Auto-direction finding in the porpoise (*Phocaena phocaena*). *Nature (Lond.)*, **183**, 1063.

DUDOK VAN HEEL, W. H. (1963). Sound and Cetacea. *Netherl. J. Sea Res.*, **1**, 407–507.

FRASER, F. C., and PURVES, P. E. (1954). Hearing in cetaceans. *Bull. Br. Mus. (Nat. Hist.) Zool.*, **2**, 103–114.

FRASER, F. C., and PURVES, P. E. (1960). Hearing in cetaceans. Evolution of the accessory air sacs and the structure and function of the outer and middle ear in recent cetaceans. *Bull. Br. Mus. (Nat. Hist.) Zool.*, **7**, 1–140.

JOHNSON, C. S. (1966). Auditory thresholds of the bottlenosed porpoise (*Tursiops truncatus* Montagu). *U.S. Naval Ordnance Test Station Report* T.P. 4178. 37 pp.

KELLOGG, W. N., and KOHLER, R. (1952). Reactions of the porpoise to ultrasonic frequencies. *Science*, **116**, 250–252.

KOLMER, W. (1908). Über das häutige Labyrinth des Delphins. *Anat. Anz.*, **32**, 295–300.

MCCORMICK, J. G., WEVER, E. G., PALIN, J., and RIDGWAY, S. H. (1970). Sound conduction in the dolphin ear. *J. Acoust. Soc. Am.*, **48**, 1418–1428.

PURVES, P. E., and PILLERI, G. (1973–1974). Observations on the ear, nose, throat and eye of *Platanista indi*. In *Investigations on Cetacea*, ed. G. Pilleri, vol. V, pp. 13–57. Berne.

PURVES, P. E., and VAN UTRECHT, W. L. (1963). The anatomy and function of the ear of the bottle-nosed dolphin, *Tursiops truncatus*. *Beaufortia*, **9**, 241–256.

REYSENBACH DE HAAN, F. W. (1958). Hearing in whales. *Acta Otolaryngol. Suppl.*, **134**, 1–114.

REYSENBACH DE HAAN, F. W. (1966). Listening under water: thoughts on sound and cetacean hearing. In *Whales, Dolphins and Porpoises*, ed. K. S. Norris, pp. 583–596. University of California Press.

RIDGWAY, S. H., MCCORMICK, J. G., and WEVER, E. G. (1974). Surgical approach to the dolphin's ear. *J. Exp. Zool.*, **188**, 265–276.

SCHEVILL, W. E., and LAWRENCE, B. (1953). Auditory response of a bottlenosed porpoise, *Tursiops truncatus*, to frequencies above 100 Kc. *J. Exp. Zool.*, **124**, 147–165.

SCHEVILL, W. E., and LAWRENCE, B. (1953). High frequency auditory response of a bottlenosed dolphin, *Tursiops truncatus* (Montagu). *J. Acoust. Soc. Am.*, **25**, 1016–1017.

SYMONS, H. W. (1956). Some observations on the ear of blue and fin whales. *Norsk Hvalf.-Tidende*, **45**, 37–45.

WEVER, E. G. MCCORMICK, J. G., PALIN, J., and RIDGWAY, S. H. (1972). Cochlear structure in the dolphin, *Lagenorhynchus obliquidens*. *Proc. Nat. Acad. Sci.*, **69**, 657–661.

YAMADA, M. (1953). Contribution to the anatomy of the organ of hearing in whales. *Sci. Rep. Whales Res. Inst., Tokyo*, **8**, 1–79.

Chapter 8. The production of sounds (pages 218–225)

1. Sound production and echolocation

ANDERSEN, S., and PILLERI, G. (1970). Audible sound production in captive *Platanista gangetica*. In *Investigations on Cetacea*, ed. G. Pilleri, vol. II, pp. 83–86. Berne.

AU, W. W. L., FLOYD, R. W., PENNER, R. H., and MURCHISON, A. E. (1974). Measurements of echolocation signals of the Atlantic bottlenose dolphin, *Tursiops truncatus* Montagu, in open waters. *J. Acoust. Soc. Amer.*, **56**, 1280–1290.

BARHAM, E. G. (1973). Whale's respiratory volume as a possible resonant receiver for 20 Hz signals. *Nature (Lond.)*, **245**, 220–221.

BATESON, G. (1966). Problems in cetacean and other mammalian communication. In *Whales, Dolphins, and Porpoises*, ed. K. S. Norris, pp. 569–579. University of California Press.

BEAMISH, P., and MITCHELL, E. (1971). Ultrasonic sounds recorded in the presence of a blue whale *Balaenoptera musculus*. *Deep-Sea Res.*, **18**, 803–809.

BEAMISH, P., and MITCHELL, E. (1973). Short pulse length audio frequency sounds recorded in the presence of a Minke whale (*Balaenoptera acutorostrata*). *Deep-Sea Res.*, **20**, 375–386.

BEL'KOVICH, V. M., BORISOV, V. I., GUREVICH, V. S., and KRUSHINSKAYA, N. L. (1969). The ability of echolocation in *Delphinus delphis*. *Zool. Zh.*, **48**, 876–884.

BUSNEL, R.-G., and DZIEDZIC, A. (1968). Étude des signaux acoustiques associés à des situations de détresse chez certain cétacés odontocètes. *Annls. Inst. océanogr., Monaco*, **46**, 109–144.

BUSNEL, R-G., ESCUDIE, B., DZIEDZIC, A., and HELLION, A. (1971). Structure des clics doubles d'écholocation du globicéphale

(Cétacé odontocète). *C. r. hebd. Séanc. Acad. Sci., Paris*, **272**, 2459–2461.

CALDWELL, D. K., and CALDWELL, M. C. (1970). Echolocation-type signals by two dolphins, genus *Sotalia*. *Q. J. Fla Acad. Sci.*, **33**, 124–131.

CALDWELL, M. C., and CALDWELL, D. K. (1971). Statistical evidence for individual signature whistles in Pacific whitesided dolphins *Lagenorhynchus obliquidens*. *Cetology*, **3**, 1–9.

CUMMINGS, W. C., FISH, J. F., and THOMPSON, P. O. (1972). Sound production and other behavior of southern right whales, *Eubalena glacialis*. *Trans. San Diego Soc. Nat. Hist.*, **17**, 1–14.

CUMMINGS, W. C., and THOMPSON, P. O. (1971). Underwater sounds from the blue whale, *Balaenoptera musculus*. *J. Acoust. Soc. Amer.*, **50**, 1193–1198.

EVANS, W. E. (1973). Echolocation by marine delphinids and one species of fresh-water dolphin. *J. Acoust. Soc. Amer.*, **54**, 191–199.

EVANS, W. E., and MADERSON, P. F. A. (1973). Mechanisms of sound production in delphinid cetaceans: a review and some anatomical considerations. *Am. Zool.*, **13**, 1205–1213.

FISH, J. F., SUMICH, J. L., and LINGLE, G. L. (1974). Sounds produced by the gray whale, *Eschrichtius robustus*. *Marine Fish Rev.*, **36**, 38–45.

FRASER, F. C. (1947). Sound emitted by dolphins. *Nature (Lond.)*, **160**, 759.

KELLOGG, W. N. (1958). Echo ranging in the porpoise. *Science*, **128**, 982–988.

KELLOGG, W. N. (1959). Auditory perception of submerged objects by porpoises. *J. Acoust. Soc. Am.*, **31**, 1–6.

KELLOGG, W. N. (1961). *Porpoises and Sonar*. University of Chicago Press.

LILLY, J. C. (1968). Sound production in *Tursiops truncatus* (Bottlenose dolphin). *Annls. N.Y. Acad. Sci.*, **155**, 321–341.

LOVE, R. H. (1973). Target strengths of humpback whales *Megaptera novaeangliae*. *J. Acoust. Soc. Am.*, **54**, 1312–1315.

NORRIS, K. S. (1964). Some problems of echolocation in cetaceans. In *Marine Bioacoustics*, ed. W. M. Tavolga, pp. 317–336. Pergamon Press, London.

NORRIS, K. S. (1969). The echolocation of marine mammals. In *The Biology of Marine Mammals*, ed. H. T. Andersen, pp. 391–423. Academic Press, New York.

NORRIS, K. S., PRESCOTT, J. H., ASADORIAN, P. V., and PERKINS, P. J. (1961). An experimental demonstration of echolocation behavior in the porpoise, *Tursiops truncatus* (Montagu). *Biol. Bull.*, **120**, 163–176.

PAYNE, R., and PAYNE, K. (1971). Underwater sounds of southern right whales. *Zoologica (N.Y.)*, **56**, (4) 159–165.

PAYNE, R., and WEBB, D. (1971). Orientation by means of long range acoustic signaling in baleen whales. *Ann. N.Y. Acad. Sci.*, **188**, 110–141.

PILLERI, G., ZBINDEN, K., GIHR, M., and KRAUS, C. (1976). Sonar clicks, directionality of the emission field and echolocating behaviour of the Indus dolphin (*Platanista indi*, Blyth, 1859). In *Investigations on Cetacea*, ed. G. Pilleri, vol. III, pp. 13–43. Berne.

POULTER, T. C. (1968). Vocalization of the gray whales in Laguna Ojo de Liebre (Scammon's Lagoon), Baja California, Mexico. *Norsk Hvalf.-Tidende*, **57**, 53–62.

SCHEVILL, W. E., and LAWRENCE, B. (1949). Underwater listening to the white porpoise (*Delphinapterus leucas*). *Science*, **109**, 143–144.

SCHEVILL, W. E., and LAWRENCE, B. (1956). Food-finding by a captive porpoise (*Tursiops truncatus*). *Brevoria*, **53**, 1–15.

SCHEVILL, W. E., and MCBRIDE, A. F. (1956). Evidence for echolocation by cetaceans. *Deep-Sea Res. Oceanog. Abstr.*, **3**, 153–154.

SCHEVILL, W. E., and WATKINS, W. A. (1962). Whale and porpoise voices, a phonograph record. Woods Hole Oceanogr. Inst., Mass.

SCHEVILL, W. E., WATKINS, W. A., and RAY, C. (1969). Click structure in the porpoise, *Phocaena phocaena*. *J. Mammal.*, **50**, 721–728.

TAVOLGA, W. N. (1964). *Marine Bio-acoustics*. Pergamon Press, New York.

TOMILIN, A. G. (1955). On the behaviour and sound communications of cetaceans. *Trudy Akad. Nauk SSSR, Inst. Okeanol.*, **18**, 28–47. (*Fish. Res. Bd. Canada*, Transl. Ser. **377**, 1–41.)

VINCENT, F. (1960). Études préliminaires de certaines émissions acoustiques de *Delphinus delphis* L. en captivité. *Bull. Inst. Océanogr., Monaco*, **57**, 1–23.

WATKINS, W. A., and SCHEVILL, W. E. (1974). Listening to Hawaiian spinner porpoises, *Stenella* cf. *longirostris*, with a three-dimensional hydrophone array. *J. Mammal.*, **55**, 319–328.

WATKINS, W. A., and SCHEVILL, W. E. (1975). Sperm whales (*Physeter catodon*) react to pingers. *Deep-Sea Res.*, **22**, 123–129.

WOOD, F. G. (1953). Underwater sound production and concurrent behaviour of captive porpoises, *Tursiops truncatus* and *Stenella plagiodon*. *Bull. Mar. Sci. Gulf Caribb.*, **3**, 120–133.

WORTHINGTON, L. V., and SCHEVILL, W. E. (1957). Underwater sounds heard from sperm whales. *Nature (Lond.)*, **180**, 291. (See also: *Norsk Hvalf.-Tidende*, **46**, 573, 1957.)

Chapter 9. Senses and the Central Nervous System

(pages 226–282)

1. *Vision*

DAWSON, W. W., and PEREZ, J. M. (1973). Unusual retinal cells in the dolphin eye. *Science*, **181**, 747–749.

DRAL, A. D. G. (1977). On the retinal anatomy of Cetacea (mainly *Tursiops truncatus*). In *Functional Anatomy of Marine Mammals*, ed. R. J. Harrison, vol. III, pp. 81–134. Academic Press, London.

DRAL, A. D. G., and BEUMER, L. (1974). The anatomy of the eye of the Ganges river dolphin *Platanista gangetica* (Roxburgh, 1801). *Z. f. Säugetierk.*, **39**, 143–167.

HERMAN, L. M., PEACOCK, M. F., YUNKER, M. P., and MADSEN, C. J. (1975). Bottlenosed dolphin: double-slit pupil yields equivalent aerial and underwater diurnal acuity. *Science*, **189**, 650–652.

HOSOKAWA, H. (1951). On the extrinsic eye muscles of the whale, with special remarks upon the innervation and function of the musculus retractor bulbi. *Sci. Rep. Whales Res. Inst., Tokyo*, **6**, 1–33.

HULKE, J. W. (1867). Notes on the anatomy of the retina of the common porpoise: (*Phocoena communis*). *J. Anat. Phys.*, **2**, 19–25.

JAMIESON, G. S. (1971). The functional significance of corneal distortion in marine mammals. *Can. J. Zool.*, **49**, 421–423.

MCFARLAND, W. N. (1970). Cetacean visual pigments. *Vision Res.*, **11**, 1065–1076.

MANN, F. G. (1946). Ojo y visión de

las Ballenas. *Biologica Santiago Fasc.*, **4**, 23–81.

MATTHIESSEN, L. (1893). Über den physikalisch-optischen Bau der Augen vom Knölwal (*Megaptera boops*, Fabr.) und Finnwal (*Balaenoptera musculus*, Comp.). *Zeitschr. vergl. Augenheilk.*, **7**, 77–101.

PILLERI, G. (1964). Zur Morphologie des Auges vom Weisswal, *Delphinapterus leucas* (Pallas). *Hvalråd. Skr.*, **47**, 3–16.

PILLERI, G., and WANDELER, A. (1970). Ontogeny and functional morphology of the eye of the fin whale, *Balaenoptera physalus*. In *Investigations on Cetacea*, ed. G. Pilleri, vol. II, pp. 179–229. Berne.

PÜTTER, A. (1903). Die Augen der Wassersäugetiere. *Zool. Jahrb. Abt. Anat. Ontog. Tiere.*, **17**, 99–402.

ROCHON-DUVIGNEAUD, A. J. F. (1940). L'œil des Cétacés. *Arch. Mus. Hist. Nat., Paris*, Sér. 6, **16**, 57–90.

SIMONS, D. (1977). Analysis of an experiment on colour vision in dolphins. *Aquatic Mamm.*, **5**, 27–33.

WALLS, G. L. (1963). *The Vertebrate Eye and its Adaptive Radiation.* 2nd edition. Hafner, New York and London.

2. *Smell*

ADDISON, W. H. F. (1915). On the rhinencephalon of *Delphinus delphis* L. *J. comp. Neurol.* **25**, 497–522.

BREATHNACH, A. S., and GOLDBY, F. (1954). The amygdaloid nuclei, hippocampus and other parts of the rhinencephalon in the porpoise (*Phocaena phocaena*). *J. Anat.*, **88**, 267–291.

EDINGER, T. (1955). Hearing and smelling in cetacean history. *Monatsschr. Psychiat. Neurol.*, **129**, 37–58.

FILIMONOFF, I. N. (1963). On the so-called rhinencephalon in the dolphin. *J. Hirnforsch.*, **8**, 1–23.

JACOBS, M. S., MORGANE, P. J., and MCFARLAND, W. L. (1971). The anatomy of the brain of the bottlenose dolphin (*Tursiops truncatus*). Rhinic lobe (Rhinencephalon). I. Paleocortex. *J. comp. Neurol.*, **141**, 205–272.

YABLOKOV, A. W. (1957). On the Organs of Chemical Perception in Odontoceti. *Sborn. Nauch. Rabot. M. G. U., Moscow.* (In Russian.)

3. *Sense of touch*

JAPHA, A. (1912). Die Haare der Waltiere. *Zool. Jahrb. Abt. Anat. Ontog. Tiere*, **32**, 1–42. (Also Techn. Transl. no. 1537, National Research Council of Canada, Ottawa, 1972.)

LING, J. K. (1977). Vibrissae of marine mammals. In *Functional Anatomy of Marine Mammals*, ed. R. J. Harrison, vol. III, pp. 387–415. Academic Press, London.

OGAWA, T., and SHIDA, T. (1950). On the sensory tubercles of lips and of oral cavity in the sei and the fin whale. *Sci. Rep. Whales Res. Inst., Tokyo*, **3**, 1–16.

PILLERI, G. (1974). Side-swimming, vision and a sense of touch in *Platanista indi. Experentia*, **30**, 100–104.

4. *Nervous system*

BREATHNACH, A. S. (1953). The olfactory tubercle, prepyriform cortex and precommissural region of the porpoise (*Phocaena phocaena*). *J. Anat.*, **87**, 96–113.

BREATHNACH, A. S. (1955). The surface features of the brain of the humpback whale (*Megaptera novaeangliae*). *J. Anat.*, **89**, 343–354.

BREATHNACH, A. S. (1960). The cetacean central nervous system. *Biol. Rev.* **35**, 187–230.

DART, R. A. (1923). The brain of Zeuglodontidae (Cetacea): with a note on the skulls from which the endocranial casts were taken by C. W. Andrews. *Proc. Zool. Soc. Lond.*, 615–654.

ENTIN, T. I. (1973). Histological investigation of the occipital cortex of the dolphin. *Arkhiv. Anat. Histol. Embriol.*, **65**, 92–100. (In Russian with English summary.)

FLANIGAN, N. J. (1966). The anatomy of the spinal cord of the Pacific striped dolphin, *L. obliquidens*. In *Whales, Dolphins, and Porpoises*, ed. K. S. Norris. University of California Press.

GERSH, I. (1938). Note on the pineal gland of the humpback whale. *J. Mammal.*, **19**, 477–480.

GRÜNTHAL, E. (1942). Über den Primatencharakter des Gehirns von *Delphinus delphis. Monatsschr. Psychiat. Neurol.*, **105**, 249–274.

GULDBERG, G. A. (1886). Über das Centralnervensystem der Bartenwale. *Forhandl. Videnskaps-Selskabet Christiania*, **4**, 1–154.

HEPBURN, D., and WATERSTON, D. (1904). A comparative study of the grey and white matter, of the motor-cell groups, and of the spinal accessory nerve, in the spinal cord of the porpoise (*Phocaena communis*). *J. Anat. Physiol.*, **38**, Pt I, 105–118, Pt II, 295–311.

JANSEN, J., and JANSEN, J. K. S. (1953). A note on the amygdaloid complex in the fin whale (*Balaenoptera physalus* L.). *Hvalråd. Skr.*, **39**, 3–14.

JANSEN, J., and JANSEN, J. K. S. (1969). The nervous system of Cetacea. In *The Biology of Marine Mammals*, ed. H. T. Andersen, pp. 175–252. Academic Press, New York.

JELGERSMA, G. (1934). *Das Gehirn der Wassersäugetiere.* J. A. Barth, Leipzig.

KAMIYA, T., and PIRLOT, P. (1974). Brain morphogenesis in *Stenella coeruleoalba. Sci. Rep. Whales Res. Inst., Tokyo*, **26**, 245–253.

KOJIMA, T. (1951). On the brain of the sperm whale (*Physeter catodon* L.). *Sci. Rep. Whales Res. Inst., Tokyo*, **6**, 49–72.

LANGWORTHY, O. R. (1931). Factors

determining the differentiation of the cerebral cortex in sea-living mammals (the Cetacea). A study of the brain of the porpoise, *Tursiops truncatus. Brain,* **54,** 225–236.

LANGWORTHY, O. R. (1932). A description of the central nervous system of the porpoise (*Tursiops truncatus*). *J. comp. Neurol.,* **54,** 437–500.

LANGWORTHY, O. R. (1935). The brain of the whalebone whale, *Balaenoptera physalus. Bull. Johns Hopkins Hospital,* **57,** 143–147.

MCFARLAND, W. L., MORGANE, P. J., and JACOBS, M. S. (1969). Ventricular system of the brain of the dolphin, *Tursiops truncatus,* with comparative anatomical observations and relations to brain specializations. *J. comp. Neurol.,* **135,** 275–367.

MORGANE, P. J., and JACOBS, M. S. (1972). Comparative anatomy of the cetacean nervous system. In *Functional Anatomy of Marine Mammals,* ed. R. J. Harrison, vol. I, pp. 117–244. Academic Press, London.

OGAWA, T., and ARIFUKU, S. (1948). On the acoustic system in the cetacean brains. *Sci. Rep. Whales Res. Inst., Tokyo,* **2,** 1–20.

OSEN, K. K., and JANSEN, J. (1965). The cochlear nuclei in the common porpoise, *Phocaena phocaena. J. comp. Neurol.,* **125,** 223–257.

PILLERI, G., and GIHR, M. (1970). The central nervous system of the mysticete and odontocete whales. In *Investigations on Cetacea,* ed. G. Pilleri, vol. 2, pp. 89–127. Berne.

PRESSEY, H. E., and COBB, S. (1928). Observations on the spinal cord of *Phocaena. J. comp. Neurol.,* **47,** 75–83.

RAWITZ, B. (1903). Das Zentralnervensystem der Cetaceen. I. Das Ruckenmark von *Phocaena communis* Cuv. und das Cervicalmark von *Balaenoptera rostrata* Fabr. *Arch. mikr. Anat.,* **62,** 1–40.

RAWITZ, B. (1909). Das Zentralnervensystem der Cetaceen. II. Die Medulla oblongata von *Phocaena communis* (Cuv.) Less. und *Balaenoptera rostrata* Fabr. Zugleich ein Beitrag zur vergleichenden Morphologie der Oblongata der Säuger. *Arch. mikr. Anat.,* **73,** 182–260.

RAWITZ, B. (1910). Das Zentralnervensystem der Cetaceen. III. Die Furchen und Windungen des Grosshirns von *Balaenoptera rostrata* Fabr. *Arch. mikr. Anat.,* **75,** 225–239.

RIES, F. A., and LANGWORTHY, O. R. (1937). A study of the surface structure of the brain of the whale (*Balaenoptera physalus* and *Physeter catodon*). *J. comp. Neurol.,* **68,** 1–48.

RIESE, W. (1925). Über die Stammganglien der Wale. *J. Psychol. Neurol.,* **32,** 21–28.

STANNIUS, H. (1846). Über den Bau des Delphingehirnes. *Abh. Geb. Naturwiss.,* **1,** 1–16.

TIEDEMANN, F. (1827). Das Hirn des Delphins mit dem des Menchen verglichen. *Z. Physiol.*, **2**, 251–263.

WILSON, R. B. (1935). The anatomy of the brain of the whale (*Balaenoptera sulfurea*). *J. comp. Neurol.*, **58**, 419–480.

WIRZ, K. (1950). Studien über die Cerebralisation zur Quantitativen Bestimmung der Rangordnung bei Säugetieren. *Acta Anat.*, **9**, 134–200.

Chapter 10. Feeding (pages 253–293)

1. *Food, feeding habits and digestion*

AKIYA, S., and TEJIMA, S. (1948). Studies on digestive enzyme in whale. *Sci. Rep. Whales Res. Inst., Tokyo*, **1**, 3–7.

BAALSRUD, K. (1955). Utilization of plankton. *Norsk Hvalf.-Tidende*, **44**, 125–133.

BOSCHMA, H. (1938). On the teeth and some other particulars of the sperm whale (*Physeter macrocephalus* L.). *Temminckia, Leiden*, **3**, 151–278.

BOSCHMA, H. (1951). Rows of small teeth in ziphioid whales. *Zool. Meded.*, **31**, 139–148.

BROWN, S. G. (1968). Feeding of sei whales at South Georgia. *Norsk Hvalf.-Tidende*, **57**, 118–125.

CLARKE, R. (1954). A great haul of ambergris. *Norsk Hvalf.-Tidende*, **43**, 450–453.

CLARKE, R. (1955). A giant squid swallowed by a sperm whale. *Norsk Hvalf.-Tidende*, **44**, 589–593.

DISSEL-SCHERFT, M. C. VAN, and VERVOORT, W. (1954). Development of the teeth in fetal *Balaenoptera physalus* (L.) (Cetacea, Mystacoceti). I–II. *Proc. Kon. Akad. Wet., Amsterdam Ser. C*, **57**, 196–210.

DONALDSON, B. J. (1977). The tongue of the bottlenosed dolphin (*Tursiops truncatus*). In *Functional Anatomy of Marine Mammals*, ed. R. J. Harrison, vol. III, pp. 175–197. Academic Press, London.

FITCH, J. E., and BROWNELL, R. L., JR (1968). Fish otoliths in cetacean stomachs and their importance in interpreting feeding habits. *J. Fish. Res. Bd. Can.*, **25**, 2561–2574.

FITCH, J. E., and BROWNELL, R. L., JR (1971). Food habits of the franciscana *Pontoporia blainvillei* from South America. *Bull. mar. Sci.*, **21**, 626–636.

FRASER, F. C. (1936). Vestigial teeth in specimens of Cuvier's whale (*Ziphius cavirostris*) stranded on the Scottish coast. *Scottish Naturalist*, 153–157.

FRASER, F. C. (1936). On the development and distribution of the young stages of krill. *Discovery Rep.*, **14**, 1–192.

HARRISON, R. J., JOHNSON, F. R., and YOUNG, B. A. (1970). The oesophagus and stomach of dolphins (*Tursiops, Delphinus, Stenella*). *J. Zool. Lond.*, **160**, 377–390.

HOSOKAWA, H., and KAMIYA, T. (1971). Some observations on the cetacean stomachs, with special considerations on the feeding habits of whales. *Sci. Rep. Whales Res. Inst., Tokyo,* **23**, 91–101.

ISHIKAWA, Y. (1950). Protein digestive power of sperm whale pancreatic enzyme. II. *Sci. Rep. Whales Res. Inst., Tokyo,* **3**, 71–78.

ISHIKAWA, Y., and TEJIMA, S. (1948). Protein digestive power of sperm whale pancreatic enzyme. *Sci. Rep. Whales Res. Inst., Tokyo,* **2**, 55–60.

KAWAMURA, A. (1974). Food and feeding ecology in the southern sei whale. *Sci. Rep. Whales Res. Inst., Tokyo,* **26**, 25–144.

KLEINENBERG, S. E. (1938). Some data on the feeding of *Tursiops tursio* Fabr. in the Black Sea. *Bull. Soc. Nat. Moscow Sect. Biol.,* **47**, 406–413.

MACKINTOSH, N. A. (1973). Distribution of post-larval krill in the Antarctic. *Discovery Rep.,* **36**, 95–156.

MARR, J. W. S. (1962). The natural history and geography of the Antarctic krill (*Euphausia superba* Dana). *Discovery Rep.,* **32**, 33–464.

MILLER, G. S. (1929). The gums of the porpoise *Phocoenoides dalli* True. *Proc. U.S. Nat. Mus.,* **74**, (26), 1–4.

MORII, H. (1973). Yeasts predominating in the stomach of the marine little toothed whales. *Bull. Jap. Soc. scient. Fish.,* **39** (3), 333.

MÖRZER BRUYNS, W. F. J. (1973). On abnormal teeth in the strap-toothed whale, *Mesoplodon layardi*

(Gray, 1865). *Säugetier. Mitt.,* **21** (1), 75–77.

NEMOTO, T. (1970). Feeding pattern of baleen whales in the ocean. In *Marine Food Chains,* ed. J. H. Steele, pp. 241–252. Oliver and Boyde, Edinburgh.

NEMOTO, T., and NASU, K. (1958). *Thysanoessa macrura* as a food of baleen whales in the Antarctic. *Sci. Rep. Whales Res. Inst., Tokyo,* **13**, 193–199.

NEUVILLE, H. (1935). Remarques à propos du développement des dents du cachalot (*Physeter macrocephalus* L.). *Ann. Sci. Nat. (Zool.),* (10) **18**, 171–195.

NEUVILLE, H. (1936). Le pancréas des Cétacés et les théories 'insulaires'. *Livre Jubilaire Eugene-Louis Bouvier, Paris,* 19–23.

PERRIN, W. F., WARNER, R. R., FISCUS, C. H., and HOLTS, D. B. (1973). Stomach contents of porpoise, *Stenella* spp., and yellowfin tuna, *Thunnus albacares,* in mixed species aggregations. *Fishery Bull. U.S. natn. ocean. atmos. Admn.,* **71** (4), 1077–1092.

QUAY, W. B. (1957). Pancreatic weight and histology in the white whale. *J. Mammal.,* **38**, 185–192.

RAE, B. B. (1965). The food of the common porpoise (*Phocaena phocaena*). *J. Zool.,* **146**, 114–122.

RICE, D. W. (1968). Stomach contents and feeding behavior of killer whales in the eastern north Pacific. *Norsk Hvalf.-Tidende,* **57**, 35–38.

RUUD, J. T. (1932). On the biology

of southern Euphausiidae. *Hval-råd. Skr.*, **2**, 1–105.

SLIJPER, E. J. (1946). Die physiologische Anatomie der Verdauungsorganc bei den Vertebraten. *Tabulae Biologicae*, I, p. 1, **21**, Digestion, 1–81.

SMITH, G. J. D. (1972). The stomach of the harbor porpoise *Phocoena phocoena* (L.). *Can. J. Zool.*, **50**, 1611–1616.

SOKOLOV, V. E., and VOLKOVA, O. V. (1973). Structure of the dolphin's tongue. Israel Progm scient. Transl., Jersualem No. 22056, 119–127. Translated from: *Morphology and ecology of marine mammals*, eds. K. K. Chapskii and V. E. Sokolov. Izdatel'stvo 'Nauka', Moskva 1971.

TAKAHASHI, K., YAMASAKI, F., and KAMIYA, T. (1975). Some notes on the pancreas of Franciscana (La Plata dolphin), *Pontoporia blainvillei. Okajimas Fol. anat. jap.*, **52**, 27–38.

WATKINS, W. A., and SCHEVILL, W. E. (1976). Right whale feeding and baleen rattle. *J. Mammal.*, **57** (1), 58–66.

WHITE, J. R. (1970) Thiamine deficiency in an Atlantic bottlenosed dolphin (*Tursiops truncatus*) on a diet of raw fish. *J. Amer. Vet. Med. Ass.*, **157** (5), 559–562.

WILKE, F., and NICHOLSON, A. J. (1958). Food of porpoises in waters off Japan. *J. Mammal.*, **39**, 441–443.

YABLOKOV, A. V. (1958). The cetacean dental structure and type of teeth. *Bull. Soc. Nat.*

Moscou, **63**, 37–48.

YABLOKOV, A. V. (1958). On the morphology of the digestive tract in toothed Cetacea. *Zool. Zh.*, **37**, 601–611. (In Russian.)

Chapter 11. Metabolism (pages 294–315)

1. *Layer of blubber, body temperature, metabolism*

ASH, C. E. (1955). Comparing the fatness of whales. *Norsk Hvalf.-Tidende*, **44**, 20–24.

ASH, C. E. (1955). The fin whales of 1954–5: blubber thickness and factory efficiency. *Norsk Hvalf.-Tidende*, **44**, 264–275.

CLARKE, M. R. (1978). Physical properties of spermaceti oil in the sperm whale. *J. mar. biol. Ass. U.K.*, **58**, 19–26.

GULDBERG, G. A. (1900). Über die Körpertemperatur der Cetaceen. *Nyt. Mag. Naturvid.*, **38**, 65–70.

HAMPTON, I. F. G., and WITTON, G. C. (1976). Body temperature and heat exchange in the Hawaiian spinning dolphin, *S. longirostris. Comp. Biochem. Physiol.*, **55**A, 195–197.

IRVING, L. (1969). Temperature regulation in marine mammals. In *The Biology of Marine Mammals*, ed. H. T. Andersen, pp. 147–174. Academic Press, New York.

ITO, S., and TSUYUKI, H. (1974). Fatty acid component of different blubber oil of finless porpoise. *Sci. Rep. Whales Res. Inst., Tokyo*, **26**, 303–306.

KANWISHER, J., and LEIVESTAD, H. (1957). Thermal regulation in whales. *Norsk Hvalf.-Tidende*, **46**, 1–5.

KANWISHER, J., and SUNDNES, G. (1965). Physiology of a small cetacean. *Hvalråd. Skr.*, **48**, 45–53.

KANWISHER, J., and SUNDNES, G. (1966). Thermal regulation in cetaceans. In *Whales, Dolphins and Porpoises*, ed. K. S. Norris, pp. 397–409. University of California Press.

KERMACK, K. A. (1948). The propulsive powers of blue and fin whales. *J. Exp. Biol.*, **25**, 237–240.

KROGH, A. (1934). Physiology of the blue whale. *Nature (Lond.)*, **133**, 635–637.

MCGINNIS, S. M., WHITTOW, G. C., OHATA, C. A., and HUBER, H. (1972). Body heat dissipation and conservation in two species of dolphins. *Comp. Biochem. Physiol.*, **43**, 417–423.

MACKAY, R. S. (1964). Deep body temperature of untethered dolphin recorded by ingested radio transmitter. *Science*, **144**, 864–866.

PARRY, D. A. (1949). The structure of whale blubber and a discussion of its thermal properties. *Q. J. Microsc., Sci.*, **90**, 13–25.

PORTIER, P. (1938). *Physiologie des Animaux Marins*. Flammarion, Paris.

SLIJPER, E. J. (1948). On the thickness of the layer of blubber in antarctic blue and fin whales. I, II and III. *Proc. Kon. Ned. Akad.*

Wet., Amsterdam, **51**, 1033–1045, 1114–1124, 1310–1316.

TOMILIN, A. G. (1951). On the thermal regulation in cetaceans. *Priroda*, **6**, 55–58.

TSUYUKI, H., and ITOH, S. (1970). Fatty acid components of black right whale oil by gas chromatography. *Sci. Rep. Whales Res. Inst., Tokyo*, **22**, 165–170.

VARANASI, U., and MALINS, D. C. (1971). Unique lipids of the porpoise (*Tursiops gilli*): differences in triacyl glycerols and wax esters of acoustic (mandibular canal and melon) and blubber tissues. *Biochim. biophys. Acta*, **231**, 415–418.

2. Endocrine organs

ANON. (1951). A.C.T.H. from whale pituitaries. *Norsk Hvalf.-Tidende*, **40**, 439–448.

ARVY, L. (1971). Endocrine glands and hormonal secretion in cetaceans. In *Investigations on Cetacea*, ed. G. Pilleri, vol. III (2), pp. 229–300.

BENZ, F., SCHULER, W., and WETTSTEIN, A. (1951). Adrenocortico-tropic hormone in the pituitary gland of the whale. *Nature (Lond.)*, **167**, 691.

CRILE, G. C., and QUIRING, D. P. (1940). A comparison of the energy-releasing organs of the white whale and the thoroughbred horse. *Growth*, **4**, 291–298.

GEILING, E. M. K. (1935). The hypophysis cerebri of the finback (*Balaenoptera physalus*) and sperm

(*Physeter megalocephalus*) whale. *Bull. Johns Hopk. Hosp.*, **57**, 123–142.

HANSTRØM, B. (1944). Zur Histologie und vergleichenden Anatomie der Hypophyse der Cetaceen. *Acta Zool.*, **25**, 1–25.

HARRIS, G. W. (1947). The hypophysial portal vessels of the porpoise (*Phocoena phocoena*). *Nature (Lond.)*, **159**, 874–875.

HARRISON, R. J. (1969). Endocrine organs: hypophysis, thyroid and adrenal. In *The Biology of Marine Mammals*, ed. H. Andersen, Chapter 9, pp. 349–390. Academic Press, New York.

HARRISON, R. J., and YOUNG, B. A. (1970). The thyroid of the common (Pacific) dolphin, *Delphinus delphis bairdi*. *J. Anat.*, **106**, 243–254.

HENNINGS, H. (1950). The whale hypophysis with special reference to its ACTH-content. *Acta Endocr.*, **5**, 376–386.

HOLZMANN, K. (1960). Die neurosekretorische Verknüpfung von Hypothalamus und Hypophyse bei *Balaenoptera borealis*. *Zeit. Zell.*, **51**, 185–208.

JACOBSEN, A. P. (1941). Endocrinological studies in the blue whale *Balaenoptera musculus* L. *Hvalråd. Skr.*, **24**, 1–84.

JORPES, J. E. (1950). The insulin content of whale pancreas. *Hvalråd. Skr.*, **35**, 1–15.

KOIDE, A., and MATSUOKA, Y. (1970). Studies on Fin whale pancreatic proteases. 3. Properties of purified Fin whale amionic chymotrypsin. *J. Biochem.*, Tokyo, **68**, 1–7.

NEUVILLE, H. (1928). Remarques sur les annexes branchiales des Delphinidés. *Bull. Mus. Nat. Hist.*, **6**, 422–428.

PAPKOFF, H., and LI, C. H. (1958). The isolation and characterization of growth hormone from anterior lobes of whale pituitaries. *J. biol. Chem.*, **231**, 367–377.

SINCLAIR, J. G. (1970). Early development of the cetacean pituitary gland. *Texas Rep. Biol. Med.*, **27**, 1065–1076.

SVERDRUP, A., and ARNESEN, K. (1952). Investigations on the anterior lobe of the hypophysis of the finback whale (*B. physalus* L.). *Hvalråd. Skr.*, **36**, 1–15.

TAMURA, H., and UI, N. (1970). Origin of the multiple components of whale thyroid-stimulating hormone. *Biochim. Biophys. Actc*, **214**, 566–568.

TERAO, T., YAMASHITA, S., and UKITA, T. (1970). Studies on the inactivation of whale pancreatic ribonuclease W_1 with idodoacetate. *Biochim. Biophys. Acta*, **198**, 45–55.

VALSØ, J. (1938). The hypophysis of the blue whale (*Balaenoptera musculus* L.). *Hvalråd. Skr.*, **16**, 6–30.

WISLOCKI, G. B., and GEILING, E. M. K. (1936). The anatomy of the hypophysis of whales. *Anat. Rec.*, **66**, 17–41.

YOUNG, B. A., and HARRISON, R. J. (1970). Ultrastructure of the dolphin adenohypophysis. *Z. Zellforsch.*, **103**, 474–482.

3. *Liver and vitamins*

ARVY, L. (1971). The enzymes of Cetacea. In *Investigations on Cetacea*, ed. G. Pilleri, vol. III, pp. 301–314. Berne.

BRAEKKAN, O. R. (1948). Vitamins in whale liver. *Hvalråd. Skr.*, **32**, 1–25.

GRILLO, M. A., and SISINI, A. (1976). Urea cycle enzymes in the liver of the river dolphin, *Platanista indi*. In *Investigations on Cetacea*, ed. G. Pilleri, vol. VII, pp. 139–145. Berne.

KRINGSTAD, H., and LIE, J. (1940). En undersokelse over Vitam B-innholdet; lever av nise. *Tids. Hermetikinindustri, Stavanger*, **8**, 164.

PATHAK, S. P., SUWAL, P. N., and AGARWAL, C. V. (1956). Component acids of Suinsh blubber and liver fats. *Biochem. J.*, **62**, 634–637.

RODHAL, K. (1949). Vitamin sources in arctic regions. *Norsk Polarinst., Skr.*, **91**, 1–64.

URMANOV, M. I., and KUZ'MIN, A. A. (1973). On the morphology of the liver of large whales. *Izvestiya tikhookean. nauchno-issled. Inst. ryb. Khoz. Okeanogr.*, **87**, 205–215.

WAGNER, K. H. (1939). *Vitamin A und B carotin des Finn, Blau and Spermwals*. J. A. Barth, Leipzig.

YAMASAKI, F., TAKAHASHI, K., and KAMIYA, T. (1972). Liver and bile-passage of Ganges dolphin, *Platanista gangetica*. *Okajimas Fol. anat. jap.*, **49**, 365–390.

4. *Kidneys and water balance*

ARVY, L. (1973–1974). The kidney, renal parasites and renal secretion in cetaceans. In *Investigations on Cetacea*, ed. G. Pilleri, vol. V, pp. 231–310. Berne.

CAVE, A. J. E. (1977). The reniculus in *Hyperoödon* and *Orcinus*. In *Investigations on Cetacea*, ed. G. Pilleri, vol. VIII, pp. 103–120. Berne.

CAVE, A. J. E., and AUMONIER, F. J. (1967). The reniculus of *Tursiops truncatus, Stenella longirostris* and other cetaceans. *J. roy. microscop. Soc.*, **86**, 323–342.

DAUDT, W. (1898). Beiträge zur Kenntnis des Urogenitalapparates der Cetaceen. *Jena. Z. Naturwiss.*, **32**, 231–312.

EICHELBERGER, L., LEITER, L., and GEILING, E. M. K. (1940). Water and electrolyte content of dolphin kidney and extraction of pressor substance (Renin). *Proc. Soc. Exp. Biol. Med.*, **44**, 356–359.

FETCHER, E. S. (1939). Water balance in marine mammals. *Q. Rev. Biol.*, **14**, 451–459.

FETCHER, E. S. (1940). Experiments on the water balance of the dolphin. *Am. J. Physiol.*, **133**, 274–275.

FETCHER, E. S., and FETCHER, G. W. (1942). Experiments on the osmotic regulation of dolphins. *J. Cell. Comp. Physiol.*, **19**, 123–130.

GIHR, M., and KRAUS, C. (1970).

Quantitative investigations on the cetacean kidney. In *Investigations on Cetacea*, ed. G. Pilleri, vol. II, pp. 168–176. Berne.

KAMIYA, T. (1958). How to count the renculi of the cetacean kidneys with special regard to the kidney of the right whale. *Sci. Rep. Whales Res. Inst., Tokyo*, **13**, 253–267.

KROGH, A. (1939). *Osmotic Regulation in Aquatic Animals*. Cambridge University Press.

MALVIN, R. L., and RAYNER, M. (1968). Renal function and blood chemistry in Cetacea. *Amer. J. Physiol.*, **214**, 187–191.

OMMANNEY, F. D. (1932). The urogenital system of the fin whale (*Balaenoptera physalus*) with appendix: the dimensions and growth of the kidneys of blue and fin whales. *Discovery Rep.*, **5**, 363–465.

TEFLER, N., CORNELL, L. H., and PRESCOTT, J. H. (1970). Do dolphins drink water? *J. Amer. Vet. Med. Assoc.*, **157**, 555–558.

Chapter 12. Distribution and Migration (pages 316–348)

1. *Geographic distribution, migration*

BIERMAN, W. H., and SLIJPER, E. J. (1947). Remarks upon the species of the genus *Lagenorhynchus*. I. *K. Ned. Akad. Wetensch. Verh. Afd. Nat.*, **50**, 1353–1364.

BIERMAN, W. H., and SLIJPER, E. J. (1948). Remarks upon the species of the genus *Lagenorhynchus*. II. *K. Ned. Akad. Wetensch. Verh. Afd. Nat.*, **51**, 127–133.

BOWEN, S. L. (1974). Probable extinction of the Korean stock of the Gray whale (*Eschrichtius robustus*). *J. Mamm.*, **55**, 208–209.

BROWN, S. G. (1954). Dispersal in blue and fin whales. *Discovery Rep.*, **26**, 355–384.

BROWN, S. G. (1957). Whales observed in the Indian Ocean. *Mar. Observer*, **27**, 157–165.

BROWN, S. G. (1959). Whales observed in the Atlantic Ocean. Notes on their distribution. *Norsk Hvalf.-Tidende*, **48**, 289–309.

CADENAT, J. (1959). Rapport sur les petits cétacés ouest-Africains. Résultats des recherches enterprises sur ces animaux jusq'au mois de mars 1959. *Bull. I.F.A.N.* Sér. A, **21**, 1367–1409.

CHITTLEBOROUGH, R. G. (1959). Australian marking of humpback whales. *Norsk Hvalf.-Tidende*, **48**, 47–55.

CLARKE, R., AGUAYO, A. L., and PALIZA, O. (1968). Sperm whales of the south-east Pacific. Pts. 1 and 2. *Hvalråd. Skr.*, **51**, 1–80.

CLARKE, R., and RUUD, J. T. (1954). International co-operation in whale marking, the voyage of the Enern to the Antarctic, 1953. *Norsk Hvalf.-Tidende*, **43**, 128–146.

COWAN, I. MCT. (1939). The sharp-headed finner whale of the eastern Pacific. *J. Mammal.*, **20**, 215–225.

DAUGHERTY, A. (1966). Marine

mammals of California. Calif. Dep. Fish Game, Sacramento.

DAVIES, J. L. (1960). The southern form of the pilot whale. *J. Mammal.*, **41**, 29–34.

DAWBIN, W. H. (1956). Whale marking in south Pacific waters. *Norsk Hvalf.-Tidende*, **45**, 485–508.

DEINSE, A. B. VAN (1946). De recente Cetacea van Nederland van 1931 tot en met 1944. *Zool. Meded. Rijksmus. Nat. Hist.*, **26**, 139–210.

DEINSE, A. B. VAN, and JUNGE, G. C. A. (1937). Recent and older finds of the California gray whale in the Atlantic. *Temminckia, Leiden*, **2**, 161–188.

FOOT, D. C. (1975). Investigation of small whale hunting in northern Norway, 1964. *J. Fish. Res. Bd. Canada*, **32**, 1163–1189.

FRASER, F. C. (1934–1974). Report on Cetacea, stranded on the British Coasts. **11**, 1934; **12**, 1946; **13**, 1953; **14**, 1974. *British Museum (Nat. History)*.

GASKIN, D. E. (1968). Distribution of Delphinidae (Cetacea) in relation to sea surface temperatures off eastern and southern New Zealand. *N.Z. J. Mar. Freshwater Res.*, **2**, 527–534.

GILMORE, R. M. (1958). *The Story of the Gray Whale*. San Diego.

HARMER, S. F. (1927). Report on Cetacea stranded on the British coasts from 1913 to 1926. *Brit. Mus. (Nat. Hist.)*, 1–91.

HARRISSON, T., and JAMUH, H. G. (1958). Pigmy sperm whale (*Kogia breviceps*) in Borneo. *Nature (Lond.)*, **182**, 543.

HIRASAKA, K. (1937). On the pigmy sperm whale, *Kogia breviceps* (Blainville). *Mem. Fac. Sci. Agric. Taihoku Imp. Univ.*, **14**, 117–142.

HOLM, J. L., and JONSGÅRD, Å. (1959). Occurrence of the sperm whale in the Antarctic and the possible influence of the moon. *Norsk Hvalf.-Tidende*, **48**, 161–182.

JONSGÅRD, Å. (1951). Studies on the little piked whale or minke whale (*Balaenoptera acutorostrata* Lacépède). Report on Norwegian investigations carried out in the years 1943–1950. *Norsk Hvalf.-Tidende*, **40**, 209–232.

JONSGÅRD, Å. (1952). On the growth of the fin whale (*Balaenoptera physalus*) in different waters. Preliminary report from the state institute for whaling research. *Norsk Hvalf.-Tidende*, **41**, 57–65.

JONSGÅRD, Å. (1962). On the species of dolphins found on the coast of northern Norway and in adjacent waters. *Norsk Hvalf.-Tidende*, **51**, 1–13.

KASUYA, T. (1971). Consideration of distribution and migration of toothed whales off the Pacific coast of Japan based upon aerial sighting record. *Sci. Rep. Whales Res. Inst., Tokyo*, **23**, 37–60.

KAWAMURA, A., and SATAKE, Y. (1976). Preliminary report on the geographical distribution of the Bryde's whale in the north Pacific with special reference to the structure of the filtering apparatus. *Sci. Rep. Whales Res. Inst., Tokyo*, **28**, 1–35.

KELLOGG, R. (1928). What is known of the migrations of some whalebone whales. *Smithson. Inst. Ann. Rep.*, 467–494.

KLEINENBERG, S. E. (1956). Marine mammals of the Black and Azov Seas. *Akad. Nauk. S.S.S.R., Moscow*, 1–288. (In Russian.)

LAYNE, J. N. (1965). Observations on marine mammals in Florida waters. *Bull. Fla State Mus.*, **9**, 131–181.

LUND, J. (1951). Charting of whale stocks in the Antarctic 1950/51 on the basis of iodine values. *Norsk Hvalf.-Tidende*, **40**, 384–386.

MACKINTOSH, N. A. (1942). The southern stocks of whalebone whales. *Discovery Rep.*, **22**, 197–300.

MACKINTOSH, N. A. (1946). The natural history of whalebone whales. *Biol. Rev.*, **21**, 60–74.

MARCUZZI, G., and PILLERI, G. (1971). On the zoogeography of Cetacea. In *Investigations on Cetacea*, ed. G. Pilleri, vol. III, (1), pp. 101–170. Berne

MATSUURA, Y. (1936). On the lesser rorqual found in the adjacent waters of Japan. *Bull. Jap. Soc. Sci. Fish., Tokyo*, **4**, 325–330. (In Japanese.)

MERCER, M. C. (1973). Observations on distribution and intraspecific variation in pigmentation patterns of odontocete Cetacea in the western north Atlantic.

J. Fish. Res. Board Can., **30** (8), 1111–1130.

MITCHELL, E. (1975). Porpoise, dolphin and small whale fisheries of the world. Status and problems. *IUCN Monogr.*, **3**, 1–129. Morges, Switzerland.

MOORE, J. C., and PALMER, R. S. (1955). More piked whales from southern north Atlantic. *J. Mammal.*, **36**, 429–433.

OGAWA, T. (1937). Studien über die Zahnwale in Japan. *Bot. Zool., Tokyo*, **5**, 25–34, 409–416, 591–598. (In Japanese.)

OHSUMI, S., and MASAKI, Y. (1975). Japanese whale marking in the North Pacific, 1963–1972. *Bull. Far Seas Fish. Res.*, **12**, 171–219.

OMURA, H. (1955). Whales in the northern part of the north Pacific. *Norsk Hvalf.-Tidende*, **44**, 323–342; 395–405.

PEARSON, J. (1935). The whales and dolphins of Tasmania. Part 1. External characters and habits. *Pap. Proc. R. Soc. Tasmania*, 163–192.

PERRIN, W. F. (1975). Variation of spotted and spinner porpoise (Genus *Stenella*) in the eastern Pacific and Hawaii. *Bull. Scirpps Inst. Oceanogr. Univ. Calif.*, **21**, 1–206.

PIKE, G. C. (1953). Preliminary report on the growth of finback whales from the coast of British Columbia. *Norsk Hvalf.-Tidende*, **42**, 11–15.

PILLERI, G., and GIHR, M. (1972).

Contribution to the knowledge of the cetaceans of Pakistan with particular reference to the genera *Neomeris*, *Sousa*, *Delphinus* and *Tursiops* and a description of a new Chinese porpoise (*Neomeris asiaeorientalis*). In *Investigations on Cetacea*, ed. G. Pilleri, vol. IV, pp. 107–162. Berne.

RAYNER, G. W. (1948). Whale marking. II. Distribution of blue, fin and humpback whales marked from 1932–1938. *Discovery Rep.*, **25**, 31–38.

ROBINEAU, D. (1973). Sur deux rostres de *Mesoplodon* (Cetacea, Hyperoodontidae). *Mammalia*, **37** (3), 504–513.

ROSS, G. J. B. (1977). The taxonomy of bottlenosed dolphins *Tursiops* species in South African waters, with notes on their biology. *Annls. Cape Prov. Mus. (Nat. Hist.)*, **11**, 135–194.

RUUD, J. F. (1952). Catches of Bryde-whale off French Equatorial Africa. *Norsk Hvalf.- Tidende*, **41**, 662–663.

SCHEFFER, V. B., and SLIPP, J. W. (1948). The whales and dolphins of Washington State, with a key to the cetaceans of the west coast of North America. *Am. Midl. Nat.*, **39**, 257–337.

SCHULTZ, W. (1970). Ueber das Vorkummen von Walen in der Nord- und Ostsee (Ordn. Cetacea). *Zool. Anzeiger.*, **185**, 172–264.

SERGEANT, D. E., and FISHER, H. D. (1957). The smaller Cetacea of eastern Canadian waters. *J. Fish. Res. Bd. Can.*, **14**, 83–115.

SERGEANT, D. E., MANSFIELD, A. W., and BECK, B. (1970). Inshore records of Cetacea for eastern Canada, 1949–1968. *J. Fish. Res. Bd. Can.*, **27**, 1903–1915.

SLIJPER, E. J. (1938). Die Sammlung rezenter Cetacea des Musée Royal d'Histoire Naturelle de Belgique. *Bull. Mus. R. Hist. Nat. Belg.*, **19** (10) 1–33.

SLIJPER, E. J., and UTRECHT, W. L. VAN. (1959). Observing whales from ships. *Norsk Hvalf - Tidende*, **48**, 101–117.

SUTCLIFFE, W. H., JR. and BRODIE, P. F. (1977). Whale distribution in Nova Scotia waters. *Fish. Mar. Serv. Tech. Rep.*, **722**, 1–83.

TOWNSEND, C. H. (1935). The distribution of certain whales as shown by logbook records of American whaleships. *Zoologica, (N.Y.)* **19**, 1–50.

VANGSTEIN, E. (1954). Concerning the oil-output in antarctic pelagic whaling. *Norsk Hvalf.-Tidende*, **43**, 57–67.

ZAVERNIN, I. U. P. (1966). Effect of hydrometeorological conditions on commercial whale concentrations in the Antarctic. *Izvestia Inst. ryb. Khoz. Okeanogr.*, **58**, 209–221.

ZENKOVICH, B. A. (1969). Whaling in Antarctic and north Pacific waters and estimates of the stocks. In *Morskie mlekopitaivshchie (Marine Mammals)*, Moscow, Nauka, pp. 5–23.

Chapter 13. Reproduction (pages 349–390)

1. *Reproductive organs*

ANTHONY, R. (1922). Recherches anatomiques sur l'appareil génito-urinaire mâle du *Mesoplodon* et des Cétacés en général. *Mem. Inst., Español Oceanografia*, **3**, Mem. 2a, 35–116.

BEAUREGARD, H., and BOULART, R. (1882). Recherches sur les appareils génito-urinaires des Balaenides. *J. Anat. (Paris)*, **18**, 158–201.

BRODIE, P. F. (1972). Significance of accessory corpora lutea in odontocetes with reference to *D. leucas. J. Mamm.*, **53**, 614–616.

CHITTLEBOROUGH, R. G. (1954). Studies on the ovaries of the humpback whale, *Megaptera nodosa* (Bonnaterre), on the Western Australian coast. *Aust. J. Mar. Freshw. Res.*, **5**, 35–63.

DEMPSEY, E. W., and WISLOCKI, G. B. (1941). The structure of the ovary of the humpback whale. *Anat. Rec.*, **80**, 243–257.

HARRISON, R. J. (1949). Observations on the female reproductive organs of the caa'ing whale *Globicephala melaena* Traill. *J. Anat.*, **83**, 238–253.

HARRISON, R. J., and MCBREARTY, D. A. (1974–1975). Reproduction and gonads of the black finless porpoise, *Neophocaena phocaenoides*. In *Investigations on Cetacea*, ed. G. Pilleri, vol. V, pp. 225–230. Berne.

HARRISON, R. J., and MCBREARTY, D. A. (1978). Ovarian appearances in captive delphinids (*Tursiops* and *Lagenorhynchus*). *Aquatic Mamm.*, **5**, 100–110.

HARRISON, R. J., and RIDGWAY, S. H. (1971). Gonadal activity in some bottlenose dolphins (*Tursiops truncatus*). *J. Zool.*, **165**, 355–366.

LAWS, R. M. (1954). Giant ovaries of a blue whale. *Nature (Lond.)*, **173**, 1003.

LAWS, R. M. (1957). Polarity of whale ovaries. *Nature (Lond.)*, **179**, 1011–1012.

LENNEP, E. W. VAN (1950). Histology of the corpora lutea in blue and fin whale ovaries. *Proc. K. Ned. Akad. Wet., Amsterdam*, **53**, 593–599.

MATTHEWS, L. H. (1948). Cyclic changes in the uterine mucosa of balaenopterid whales. *J. Anat.*, **82**, 207–232.

MATTHEWS, L. H. (1950). The male urinogenital tract in *Stenella frontalis* (G. Cuvier). *Atlantide Rep.*, **1**, 223–247.

NISHIWAKI, M. (1953). Hermaphroditism in a dolphin (*Prodelphinus caeruleo-albus*). *Sci. Rep. Whales Res. Inst., Tokyo*, **8**, 215–218.

OHSUMI, S. (1964). Comparison of maturity and accumulation rate of corpora albicantia between the left and right ovaries in Cetacea. *Sci. Rep. Whales Res. Inst., Tokyo*, **18**, 123–148.

ROBINS, J. P. (1954). Ovulation and pregnancy corpora lutea in ovaries of the humpback whale. *Nature (Lond.)*, **173**, 201–203.

SLIJPER, E. J. (1938). Vergleichend-mikroskopische-anatomische Untersuchungen über das Corpus cavernosum penis der Cetaceen. *Arch. neerl. Zool.*, **3**, suppl., 205–218.

SLIJPER, E. J. (1966). Functional morphology of the reproductive system in Cetacea. In *Whales, Dolphins and Porpoises*, ed. K. Norris, pp. 277–319. University of California Press.

ZEMSKI, V. A. (1956). Methods of establishing traces of corpora lutea of ovulation and pregnancy in the ovaries of fin whales. *Bull. Soc. Nat. Moscow Biol.*, **61**, 5–13.

2. *Mating*

BROWN, D. H., and NORRIS, K. S. (1956). Observations of captive and wild cetaceans. *J. Mammal.*, **37**, 311–326.

ESSAPIAN, F. S. (1962). Courtship in captive saddle-backed porpoises, *Delphinus delphis*, L. 1758. *Z. Säugetierk.*, **27**, 212–217.

HAMILTON, J. E. (1945). Two short notes on Cetacea. I. Coitus. *Steno rostratus. Proc. Zool. Soc. Lond.*, **114**, 549.

HUFFMAN, W. E. (1970). Notes on the first captive conception and live birth of an Amazon dolphin in North America. *Underwater Nat.*, **6**, 9–11.

PILLERI, G. (1971). Beobachtung ueber das Paarungsverhalten des Ganges-delphins, *Platanista gangetica. Rev. Suisse Zool.*, **78**, 231–234.

SLIJPER, E. J. (1938). Vergleichend-anatomische Untersuchungen über den Penis der Säugetiere. *Acta néerl. Morphol. Norm. Path.*, **1**, 375–418.

TAVOLGA, M. C., and ESSAPIAN, F. S. (1957). The behavior of the bottlenosed dolphin (*Tursiops truncatus*): mating, pregnancy, parturition, and mother-infant behavior. *Zoologica*, **42**, 11–31.

TORMOSOV, D. D. (1972). Breeding places of sperm whales in the southern hemisphere. *Trudy atlant. nauchno-issled. Inst. ryb. Khoz. Okeanogr.*, **81**, 91–94.

3. *Gestation, birth, placenta*

CALDWELL, M. C., and CALDWELL, D. K. (1972). Behavior of marine mammals. In *Mammals of the Sea : Biology and Medicine*, ed. S. H. Ridgway, chapter 6, pp. 419–465. C. C. Thomas, Illinois.

DUNSTAN, D. J. (1957). Caudal presentation at birth of a humpback whale, *Megaptera nodosa* (Bonnaterre). *Norsk Hvalf.-Tidende*, **46**, 553–555.

ESSAPIAN, F. S. (1953). Birth and growth of a porpoise. *Nat. Hist.*, **62**, 392–399.

ESSAPIAN, F. S. (1963). Observations on abnormalities of parturition in captive bottle-nosed dolphins, *Tursiops truncatus*, and concurrent behavior of other porpoises. *J. Mammal.*, **44**, 405–414.

GAMBELL, R., LOCKYER, C., and ROSS, G. J. B. (1973). Observations on the birth of a sperm whale calf. *South Afr. J. Sci.*, **69** (5), 147–148.

GILMORE, R. M., and EWING, G. (1954). Calving of the California grays. *Pac. Discovery*, **7**, 13–15.

GRAY, K. N., and CONKLIN, R. H. (1974). Multiple births and cardiac anomalies in the bottle-nosed dolphin. *J. Wild. Dis.*, **10**, 154–157.

HOEDEMAKER, N. J. T. C. (1935). Mitteilung über eine reife Plazenta von *Phocaena phocaena* (Linnaeus). *Arch. neerl. Zool.*, **1**, 330–338.

JAMES, L. H. (1914). Birth of a porpoise at the Brighton aquarium. *Proc. Zool. Soc. Lond.*, 1061–1062.

MORTON, W. R. M., and MULHOLLAND, H. C. (1961). The placenta of the ca'ing whale *Globicephala melaena* (Traill). *J. Anat.*, **95**, 605, and **96**, 417.

SLEPTSOV, M. M. (1940). On some particularities of birth and nutrition of the young of the Black sea porpoise, *Delphinus delphis. Zool. Zh.*, **19**, 297–305.

SLIJPER, E. J. (1949). On some phenomena concerning pregnancy and parturition of the Cetacea. *Bijdr. Dierkd.*, **28**, 416–448.

SLIJPER, E. J. (1956). Some remarks on gestation and birth in Cetacea and other aquatic mammals. *Hvalråd. Skr.*, **41**, 1–62.

TURNER, W. (1872). On the gravid uterus and on the arrangement of the foetal membranes in the Cetacea. *Trans. r. Soc. Edinb.*, **26**, 467–504.

VAN HEEL, DUDOK W. H., and METTIVER MEYER, M. (1974). Birth in dolphins (*Tursiops truncatus*) in the Dolfinarium, Harderwijk, Netherlands. *Aquatic Mammals*, **2**, 11–22.

WISLOCKI, G. B. (1933). On the placentation of the harbor porpoise (*Phocaena phocaena* (Linnaeus)). *Biol. Bull.*, **65**, 80–98.

WISLOCKI, G. B., and ENDERS, R. K. (1941). The placentation of the bottle-nosed porpoise (*Tursiops truncatus*). *Am. J. Anat.*, **68**, 97–125.

ZEMSKY, V. A., and BUDYLENKO, G. A. (1973). Humpback whale's 'Siamese twins'. *Priroda, Mosk.* (3) 124–125. (In Russian.)

4. Mammary glands, lactation and milk

ARVY, L. (1973–1974). Mammary glands, milk and lactation in cetaceans. In *Investigations on Cetacea*, ed. G. Pilleri, vol. V, pp. 157–202. Berne.

BRODIE, P. F. (1969). Duration of lactation in Cetacea: an indicator of required learning? *Amer. Midland Nat.*, **82**, 312–314.

GREGORY, M. E., KON, S. K., ROWLANDS, S. J., and THOMPSON, S. Y. (1955). The composition of the milk of the blue whale. *J. Dairy Res.*, **22**, 108–112

LAUER, B. H., and BAKER, B. E. (1969). Whale milk I. Finwhale (*Balaenoptera physalus*) and beluga whale (*Delphinapterus leucas*) milk:

gross composition and fatty acid constitution *Can. J. Zool.*, **47**, 95–97.

LENNEP, E. W. VAN, and UTRECHT, W. L. VAN (1953). Preliminary report on the study of the mammary glands of whales. *Norsk Hvalf.-Tidende*, **42**, 249–258.

OHTA, K. *et. al.* (1955). Composition of fin whale milk. *Sci. Rep. Whales Res. Inst., Tokyo*, **10**, 151–167.

PEDERSEN, T. (1952). The milk fat of sperm whale *(Physeter catodon)*. *Norsk Hvalf.-Tidende*, **41**, 300; also milk of *Megaptera* (1952). *Norsk Hvalf.-Tidende*, **41**, 375–378.

WHITE, J. D. C. (1953). Composition of whales' milk. *Nature (Lond.)*, **171**, 612.

5. *Sexual cycle, reproduction, growth*

BRINKMANN, A. (1948). Studies on female fin and blue whales. Report on investigations carried out in the Antarctic during the season 1939–1940. *Hvalråd., Skr.*, **31**, 1–38.

BRODIE, P. F. (1971). A reconsideration of aspects of growth, reproduction and behavior of the white whale *(Delphinapterus leucas)*, with reference to the Cumberland Sound, Baffin Island, population. *J. Fish. Res. Bd. Can.*, **28**, 1309–1318.

CHITTLEBOROUGH, R. G. (1955). Aspects of reproduction in the male humpback whale, *Megaptera nodosa* (Bonnaterre). *Aust. J. Mar. Freshwater Res.*, **6**, 1–29.

CHITTLEBOROUGH, R. G. (1955). Puberty, physical maturity and relative growth of the female humpback whale, *Megaptera nodosa* (Bonnaterre). *Aust. J. Mar. Freshwater Res.*, **6**, 315–327.

CHITTLEBOROUGH, R. G. (1958). The breeding cycle of the female humpback whale, *Megaptera nodosa* (Bonnaterre). *Aust. J. Mar. Freshwater Res.*, **9**, 1–18.

CHITTLEBOROUGH, R. G. (1960). Apparent variations in the mean length of female humpbacks at puberty. *Norsk Hvalf.-Tidende*, **49**, 120–124.

CHUZHAKINA, E. S. (1955). The reproductive cycle of sperm whales. *Trudy Inst. Okeanol.*, **18**, 95–99. (In Russian.)

FISHER, H. D., and HARRISON, R. J. (1970). Reproduction in the common porpoise *(Phocoena phocoena)* of the North Atlantic. *J. Zool.*, **161**, 471–486.

FRAZER, J. F. D., and HUGGETT, A. ST G. (1959). The breeding season and length of pregnancy in four species of large whales. *Proc. Int. Congr. Zool.*, **15**, 311–313.

FRAZER, J. F. D., and HUGGETT, A. ST G. (1973). Specific foetal growth rates of cetaceans. *J. Zool.*, **169**, 111–126.

GAMBELL, R. (1968). Seasonal cycles and reproduction in sei whales of the southern hemisphere. *Discovery Rep.*, **35**, 31–134.

GAMBELL, R. (1973). Some effects of exploitation on reproduction in whales. *J. Reprod. Fert.*, Suppl., **19**, 531–551.

GILMORE, R. M. (1960). A census of the California gray whale. *U.S. Fish Wild. Serv. Spec. Sci. Rep. Fish.*, **342**, 1–30.

HARRISON, R. J. (1969). Reproduction and reproductive organs. In *The Biology of Marine Mammals*, ed. H. T. Andersen, pp. 253–348. Academic Press.

HARRISON, R. J., BOICE, R. C., and BROWNELL, R. L., JR (1969). Reproduction in wild and captive dolphins. *Nature (Lond.)*, **222**, 1143–1147.

HARRISON, R. J., and BROWNELL, R. L., JR (1971). The gonads of the South American dolphins, *Inia geoffrensis, Pontoporia blainvillei* and *Sotalia fluviatilis. J. Mammal.*, **52**, 413–419.

JONSGÅRD, Å. (1958). Taxation of fin whales (*Balaenoptera physalus* (L.)) at land stations on the Norwegian west coast. *Norsk Hvalf.-Tidende*, **47**, 433–439.

KASUYA, T., MIYAZAKI, N., and DAWBIN, W. H. (1974). Growth and reproduction of *Stenella attenuata* in the Pacific coast of Japan. *Sci. Rep. Whales Res. Inst., Tokyo*, **26**, 157–226.

KLEINENBERG, S. E., and YABLOKOV, A. V. (1960). On biology of reproduction of the Beluga in the Northern Seas of U.S.S.R. *Trudy Polar Inst. Sci. Res. Fisheries*, **12**, 165–173.

KRAMER, G. (1954). Über relatives Wachstum bei Bartenwalen. *Zool. Anz.*, **152**, 58–64.

LAWS, R. M. (1956). Growth and sexual maturity in aquatic mammals. *Nature (Lond.)*, **178**, 193–194.

LAWS, R. M. (1958). Recent investigations on fin whale ovaries. *Norsk Hvalf.-Tidende*, **47**, 225–254.

LAWS, R. M. (1959). On the breeding season of southern hemisphere fin whales, *Balaenoptera physalus* (Linn.). *Norsk Hvalf.-Tidende*, **48**, 329–351.

LAWS, R. M. (1959). The foetal growth rates of whales with special reference to the fin whale, *Balaenoptera physalus* (Linn.). *Discovery Rep.*, **29**, 281–308.

MATSUURA, Y. (1941). Statistical studies of whale foetuses. 3. Sperm whale in the adjacent waters of Japan. *Bull. Jap. Soc. Sci. Fish.*, **9**, 142–144.

MØHL HANSEN, M. (1954). Investigations on reproduction and growth of the porpoise (*Phocaena phocaena* (L.)) from the Baltic. *Vidensk. Medd. dansk. naturh. Foren. Kbh.*, **116**, 369–396.

NAAKTGEBOREN, C., SLIJPER, E. J., and UTRECHT, W. L. VAN (1960). Researches on the period of conception, duration of gestation and growth of the foetus in the fin whale, based on data from international whaling statistics. *Norsk Hvalf.-Tidende*, **49**, 113–119.

NISHIWAKI, M. (1955). On the sexual maturity of the antarctic male sperm whale (*Physeter catodon* L.). *Sci. Rep. Whales Res. Inst., Tokyo*, **10**, 143–149.

NISHIWAKI, M. (1959). Humpback

whales in Ryukyuan waters. *Sci. Rep. Whales Res. Inst., Tokyo,* **14**, 49–87.

NISHIWAKI, M., and HANDA, C. (1958). Killer whales caught in the coastal waters off Japan for recent 10 years. *Sci. Rep. Whales Res. Inst., Tokyo,* **13**, 85–86.

OHSUMI, S., NISHIWAKI, M., and HIBIYA, T. (1958) Growth of fin whale in the northern Pacific. *Sci. Rep. Whales Res. Inst., Tokyo,* **13**, 97–133.

OMURA, H., and SAKIURA, H. (1956). Studies on the little piked whale from the coast of Japan. *Sci. Rep. Whales Res. Inst., Tokyo,* **11**, 1–37.

RIDGWAY, S. H., and BENIRSCHKE, K. (1977). Breeding dolphins; present status, suggestions for the future. *U.S. Marine Mammal Commission Rep.* No. MMC–76/07.

SERGEANT, D. E. (1962). The biology of the pilot or pothead whale *Globicephala melaena* (Traill) in Newfoundland waters. *Bull. Fish. Res. Bd. Can.,* **132**, 1–84.

SLEPTSOV, M. M. (1940). Determination de l'âge chez *Delphinus delphis* L. *Bull. Soc. Nat. Moscou Sect. Biol.,* **49**, 43–51. (In Russian.)

SYMONS, H. W. (1955). The fetal growth rate of whales. *Norsk Hvalf.-Tidende,* **44**, 519–525.

SYMONS, H. W., and WESTON, R. D. (1958). Studies on the humpback whale in the Bellingshausen Sea. *Norsk. Hvalf.-Tidende,* **47**, 53–81.

TORMOSOV, D. D. (1973). The onset of sexual maturity in sperm whales in the southern hemisphere. *Trudy atlant. nauchno-issled. Inst. ryb. Khoz. Okeanogr.,* **51**, 83–90. (In Russian.)

Chapter 14. Whales and Whaling (pages 391–431)

1. Age determination

BEST, P. B. (1960). Further information on Bryde's whale (*Balaenoptera edeni* Anderson) from Saldanha Bay, South Africa. *Norsk. Hvalf.-Tidende,* **49**, 201–215.

CHITTLEBOROUGH, R. G. (1959). Determination of age in the humpback whale, *Megaptera nodosa* (Bonnaterre). *Aust. J. Mar. Freshwater Res.,* **10**, 125–143.

CHITTLEBOROUGH, R. G. (1959). *Balaenoptera brydei* Olsen on the west coast of Australia. *Norsk Hvalf.-Tidende,* **48**, 62–66.

CHITTLEBOROUGH, R. G. (1960). Marked humpback whale of known age. *Nature (Lond.),* **187**, 164.

CHRISTENSEN, I. (1973). Age determination, age distribution and growth of bottlenose whales, *Hyperoodon ampullatus* (Foster), in the Labrador Sea. *Norw. J. Zool.,* **21**, 331–340.

DAWBIN, W. H. (1959). Evidence on growth-rates obtained from two marked humpback whales. *Nature (Lond.),* **183**, 1749–1750.

DAWBIN, W. H. (1959). New Zealand and south Pacific whale marking and recoveries to the end of 1958. *Norsk Hvalf.-Tidende,* **48**, 213–238.

GASKIN, D. E., and BLAIR, B. A. (1977). Age determination of harbour porpoise, *Phocoena phocoena* (L), in the western North Atlantic. *Can. J. Zool.*, **55**, 18–30.

ICHIHARA, T. (1959). Formation mechanism of ear plug in baleen whales in relation to glove-finger. *Sci. Rep. Whales Res. Inst., Tokyo*, **14**, 107–135.

ICHIHARA, T. (1966). Criterion for determining age of fin whale with reference to ear plug and baleen plate. *Sci. Rep. Whales Res. Inst., Tokyo*, **20**, 17–82.

JONSGÅRD, Å. (1969). Age determination of marine mammals. In *The Biology of Marine Mammals*, ed. H. T. Andersen, pp. 1–30. Academic Press, London and New York.

KASUYA, T. (1972). Growth and reproduction of *Stenella caeruleoalba* based on the age determination by means of dentinal growth layers. *Sci. Rep. Whales Res. Inst., Tokyo*, **24**, 57–79.

KASUYA, T. (1977). Age determination and growth of the Baird's beaked whale with a comment on the fetal growth rate. *Sci. Rep. Whales Res. Inst., Tokyo*, **29**, 1–20.

LAWS, R. M. and PURVES, P. E. (1956). The ear plug of the Mysticeti as an indication of age with special reference to the north Atlantic fin whale (*Balaenoptera physalus* Linn.). *Norsk Hvalf.-Tidende*, **45**, 413–425.

LOCKYER, C. (1972). The age at sexual maturity of the southern fin whale (*Balaenoptera physalus*) using annual layer counts in the ear plug. *J. Cons. CIEM*, **34** (2), 276–294.

LOCKYER, C. (1974). Investigation of the ear plug of the southern sei whale *Balaenoptera phyaslus*, as a valid means of determining age. *J. Cons. int. Explor. Mer.*, **36**, 71–81 also: (1972). **34**, 276–294 (age at sexual maturity).

MIKHALEV, JU. A. (1977). Method for graphical record of surface relief of decalcinated sections of sperm whale teeth with the aim to determine their age. *Rep. Int. Whal. Comm.*, **27**, 356–362.

NIELSEN, H. G. (1972). Age determination of the harbour porpoise *Phocoena phocoena* (L.) (Cetacea). *Vidensk. Meddr. dansk naturh. Foren.*, **135**, 61–84.

NISHIWAKI, M. (1950). Determination of the age of Antarctic blue and fin whales by the colour changes in crystalline lens. *Sci. Rep. Whales Res. Inst., Tokyo*, **4**, 115–161.

NISHIWAKI, M. (1952). On the age-determination of Mystacoceti, chiefly blue and fin whales. *Sci. Rep. Whales Res. Inst., Tokyo*, **7**, 87–119.

NISHIWAKI, M., ICHIHARA, T., and OHSUMI, S. (1958). Age studies of fin whale based on ear plug. *Sci. Rep. Whales Res. Inst., Tokyo*, **13**, 155–169.

NISHIWAKI, M., and YAGI, T. (1953). On the age and the growth of teeth in a dolphin (*Prodelphinus caeruleo-albus*). *Sci. Rep. Whales Res. Inst., Tokyo*, **8**, 133–146.

NISHIWAKI, M., and YAGI, T. (1954). On the age determination method of the toothed whale by the study of the tooth. *Proc. Japan. Acad.*, **30**, 399–404.

OHSUMI, S. (1977). Age-length key of the male sperm whale in the north Pacific and comparison of growth curves. *Rep. Int. Whal. Comm.*, **27**, 295–304.

PURVES, P. E. (1955). The wax-plug in the external auditory meatus of the Mysticeti. *Discovery Rep.*, **27**, 293–302.

PURVES, P. E., and MOUNTFORD, M. D. (1959). Ear plug laminations in relation to the age composition of a population of fin whales (*Balaenoptera physalus*). *Bull. Br. Mus. (Nat. Hist.) Zool.*, **5**, 125–161.

ROBINS, J. P. (1960). Age studies on the female humpback whale, *Megaptera nodosa* (Bonnaterre), in Australian waters. *Aust. J. Mar. Freshwater Res.*, **2**, 1–13.

RUUD, J. T. (1940). The surface structure of the baleen plates as a possible clue to the age of whales. *Hvalråd. Skr.*, **23**, 1–24.

RUUD, J. T. (1945). Further studies on the structure of the baleen plates and their application to age determination. *Hvalråd. Skr.*, **29**, 1–69.

RUUD, J. T., JONSGÅRD, Å., and OTTESTAD, P. (1950). Age studies on blue whales taken in Antarctic seasons 1945/46, 1946/47 and 1947/48. *Hvalråd. Skr.*, **33**, 1–63.

SERGEANT, D. E. (1959). Age determination in odontocete whales from dentinal growth layers. *Norsk Hvalf.-Tidende*, **48**, 273–288.

TOMILIN, A. G. (1945). The age of whales as determined from their baleen apparatus. *C. R. (Doklady) Ac. Sci. U.S.S.R.*, **49**, No. 6, 460–463.

2. *Predators, parasites and pathology*

ARNOLD, P. W., and GASKIN, D. E. (1975). Lungworms (Metastrongyloidea: Pseudaliidae) of harbor porpoise *Phocoena phocoena* (L. 1758). *Can. J. Zool.*, **53**, 713–735.

CANNON, L. R. G. (1977). Some aspects of the biology of *Peponocephala electra* (Cetacea: Delphinidae). II Parasites. *Aust. J. Mar. Freshwater Res.*, **28**, 717–722.

DAILEY, M. D., and BROWNELL, R. L., JR (1972). A checklist of marine mammal parasites. In *Mammals of the Sea. Biology and Medicine*, ed. S. H. Ridgway, Chapter 9, 528–589. C. C. Thomas, Illinois.

DAILEY, M. D., and PERRIN, W. F. (1973). Helminth parasites of porpoises of the genus *Stenella* in the eastern tropical Pacific, with descriptions of two new species: *Mastigonema stenellae* gen. et sp. n. (Nemotoda: Spiruroidea) and *Zalophotrema pacificum* sp. n. (Trematoda: Digenea). *Fishery Bull. U.S. natn. ocean. atmos. Admn.*, **71**, 455–471.

DELYAMURE, S. L. (1968). Helminthofauna of Marine Mammals

(Ecology and Phylogeny). *Acad. Sci. U.S.S.R*, Moscow 1955. Jerusalem, Israel Program for Scientific Translations. 522p.

DE SMET, W. M. A., and BULTINCK, J. (1972). A case of invasive acanthosis in the skin of the penis of a sperm whale (*Physeter catodon* L.). *Acta zool. path. antverp.* No. 55, 91–102.

GERACI, J. R., and GERSTMANN, K. E. (1966). Relationship of dietary histamine to gastric ulcers in the dolphin. *J. Am. Vet. Med. Assoc.*, **149**, 884–890.

GILMARTIN, W. G., ALLEN, J. F., and RIDGWAY, S. H. (1971). Vaccination of porpoises (*Tursiops truncatus*) against *Erysipelothrix rhusiopathiae* infection. *J. Wildl. Dis.*, **7**, 292–295.

GILMORE, R. M. (1959). On the mass strandings of sperm whales. *Pacific Nat.*, **1**, 9–16.

GREENWOOD, A. G., HARRISON, R. J., and WHITTING, H. W. (1974). Functional and pathological aspects of the skin of marine mammals. In *Functional Anatomy of Marine Mammals*, ed. R. J. Harrison, vol. II, 73–110. Academic Press, London.

JONSGÅRD, Å. (1955). Recent investigations of whale parasites. *Norsk Hvalf.-Tidende*, **44**, 258–260.

JONSGÅRD, Å. (1962). Three finds of swords from swordfish (*Xiphias gladius*) in Antarctic fin whales (*Balaenoptera physalus* (L)). *Norsk Hvalf.-Tidende*, **51**, 287–291.

KLONTZ, G. W. (1970). Medical care

of newly captured killer whales. *SWest. Vet.*, **23**, 267–269.

LOTH, E. (1931). Sur les fractures guéries des os des Cétacés et Siréniens. *Bull. Inst. Océan. Monaco*, **571**, 1–8.

MARKOVSKI, S. (1955). Cestodes of whales and dolphins. *Discovery Rep.*, **27**, 377–395.

MICHEL, C., and BREE, P. J. H. VAN (1976). On two strandings of the beaked whale *Mesoplodon densirostris* (de Blainville, 1817) on Mauritius. *Z. Säugetierk.*, **41** (3), 194–196.

MIGAKI, G., DYKE, D., VAN and HUBBARD, R. C. (1971). Some histopathological lesions caused by helminths in marine mammals. *J. Wildl. Dis.*, **7**, 281–289.

MIGAKI, G., VALERIO, M. G., IRVINE, B., and GARNER, F. M. (1971). Lobo's disease in an Atlantic bottle-nosed dolphin. *J. Am. Vet. Med. Ass.*, **159**, 578–582.

OHSUMI, S. (1972). Catch of marine mammals, mainly small cetaceans, by local fisheries along the coast of Japan. *Bull. Far Seas Fish. Res. Lab.* No. 7, 137–166.

REES, G. (1953). A record of some parasitic worms from whales in the Ross Sea area. *Parasitology*, **43**, 27–34.

RIDGWAY, S. H. (1968). The bottlenose dolphin in biomedical experimentation. In *Methods of Animal Experimentation*, ed. W. I. Gay, vol. III, p. 387. Academic Press, New York.

ROBSON, F. D., and BREE, P. J. H. VAN (1971). Some remarks on a mass stranding of sperm whales *Physeter macrocephalus*, Linnaeus, 1758, near Gisborne, New Zealand on March 18, 1970. *Z. Säugetierk.*, **36**, 55–60.

ROSS COCKRILL, W. (1960). Pathology of the Cetacea. A veterinary study on whales. *Br. vet. J.*, **116**, 133–144, 175–190.

SCHMIDT. G. D., and DAILEY, M. D. (1973). Zoogeography and the generic status of *Polymorphus* (*Polymorphus*) *cetaceum* (Johnston et Best, 1942) comb. n. (Acanthocephala). *Proc. helminth. Soc. Wash.*, **38** (1), 137.

SLIJPER, E. J. (1931). Verletzungen und Erkrankungen der Wirbelsäule und Rippen bei den Cetaceen. *Anat. Anz.*, **71**, 156–185.

STOLK, A. (1952, 1953, 1962). Some tumours in whales. I, II, III. *Proc. Kon. Ned. Akad. v. Wet., Amsterdam*, C **55**, 275–278; C **56**, 369–374; C **65**, 250–268.

STOLK, A. (1953). Hepatic cirrhosis in the blue whale *Balaenoptera musculus*. *Proc. Kon. Ned. Akad. Wet., Amsterdam* C **56**, 375–378.

SWEENEY, J. C., and RIDGWAY, S. H. (1975). Common diseases of small cetaceans. *J. Amer. Vet. Med. Ass.*, **167**, 533–540.

TAYLOR, R. J. F. (1957). An unusual record of three species of whale being restricted to pools in Antarctic sea-ice. *Proc. Zool. Soc. Lond.*, **129**, 325–331.

UYS, C. J., and BEST, P. B. (1966). Pathology and lesions observed in whales flensed at Saldanha Bay, South Africa. *J. Comp. Path.*, **76**, 407–412.

3. *Population studies*

ALLEN, K. R. (1973). The computerized sperm whale population model. *Rep. Int. Commn Whal.*, **23**, 70–74.

ALLEN, K. R. (1974). Recruitment to whale stocks. In *The Whale Problem: a Status Report*, ed. W. E. Schevill, pp. 352–358. Harvard University Press.

ARSENIEV, B. A. (1958). Relation between the number of observed and the number of captured whales in Antarctic whaling. *Trudy Inst. Fish. Ocean. Moscow*, **33**, 96–100.

BANNISTER, J. L. (1969). The biology and status of the sperm whale off Western Australia – an extended summary of results of recent work. *Rep. int. Comm. Whal.*, **19**, 70–76.

BEST, P. B. (1974). Status of whale populations off the west coast of South Africa, and current research. In *The Whale Problem: a Status Report*, ed. W. E. Schevill, pp. 53–81. Harvard University Press.

BROWN, S. G. (1973). Whale marking – progress report 1972. *Rep. int. Commn. Whal.*, **23**, 49–54; and (1972). **22**, 37–40.

CHAPMAN, D. G. (1974). Estimation of population size and sustainable yield of sei whales in the Antarctic. *Rep. int. Commn Whal.*, **24**, 82–90.

DAWBIN, W. H. (1960). The composition of the New Zealand whale catch in 1959. *Norsk Hvalf.-Tidende*, **49**, 401–409.

DOI, T., and OHSUMI, S. (1970). On the maximum sustainable yield of sei whales in the Antarctic. *Rep. int. Commn Whal.*, **20**, 88–96.

GAMBELL, R. (1976). Population biology and the management of whales. In *Applied Biology*, ed. T. H. Coaker, pp. 247–343. Academic Press, London.

GAMBELL, R. (1976). World whale stocks. *Mammal Rev.*, **6**, 41–53.

GILMORE, R. M. (1960). Census and migration of the California gray whale. *Norsk Hvalf.-Tidende*, **49**, 409–431.

HARMER, S. T. (1931). Southern whaling. *Proc. Linn. Soc. Lond.*, **142**, 85–163.

HYLEN, A., JONSGÅRD, Å., PIKE, G. C., and RUUD, J. T. (1955). A preliminary report on the age composition of antarctic fin whale catches 1945/46 to 1952/53 and some reflections on total mortality rates of fin whales. *Norsk Hvalf.-Tidende*, **44**, 577–589.

IVASHIN, M. V. (1973). Marking of whales in the southwestern hemisphere (Soviet materials). *Rep. int. Commn Whal.*, **23**, 174–191.

JONSGÅRD, Å. (1955). The stocks of blue whales (*Balaenoptera musculus*) in the northern Atlantic Ocean and adjacent Arctic waters. *Norsk Hvalf.-Tidende*, **44**, 505–519.

JONSGÅRD, Å. (1974). On whale exploitation in the eastern part of the north Atlantic Ocean. In *The Whale Problem: a Status Report*, ed. W. E. Schevill, pp. 97–107. Harvard University Press.

MACHIDA, S. (1974). The voyage of the Konan Maru No. 16 to the Antarctic whaling grounds. *Sci. Rep. Whales Res. Inst., Tokyo*, **26**, 289–302.

MACKINTOSH, N. A. (1942). The southern stocks of whalebone whales. *Discovery Rep.*, **22**, 197–300.

MACKINTOSH, N. A. (1965). *The Stocks of Whales*, pp. 1–232. Fishing News (Books), London.

MACKINTOSH, N. A. and BROWN, S. G. (1956). Preliminary estimates of the southern populations of the larger baleen whales. *Norsk Hvalf.-Tidende*, **45**, 469–480.

MITCHELL, E. D. (1974). Present status of northwest Atlantic fin and other whale stocks. In *The Whale Problem: a Status Report*, ed. W. E. Schevill, pp. 108–169. Harvard University Press.

NASU, K. and SHIMADZU, Y. (1970). A method of estimating whale population by sighting observation. *Rep. int. Commn Whal.*, **20**, 114–129.

OHNO, M. and FUJINO, K. (1952). Biological investigations on the whales caught by the Japanese antarctic whaling fleets 1950–51. *Sci. Rep. Whales Res. Inst., Tokyo*, **7**, 125–188.

OHSUMI, S., and FUKUDA, Y. (1972). A population model and its application to the sperm whale in the north Pacific. *Rep. int. Comm. Whal.*, **22**, 96–110; also OHSUMI, S. (1972). **22**, 69–90; **23**, 192–199 (recruitment rate of Antartic fin whales); **24**, 91–101.

OMURA, H. (1973). A review of pelagic whaling operations in the Antarctic based on the effort and catch data in 10° squares of latitude and longitude. *Sci. Rep. Whales Res. Inst., Tokyo*, **25**, 105–203.

OTTESTAD, P. (1956). On the size of the stock of antarctic fin whales relative to the size of the catch. *Norsk Hvalf.-Tidende*, **45**, 298–308.

RUUD, J. T. (1954). Observations on the use of size limits in the regulation of whaling. *Norsk Hvalf.-Tidende*, **43**, 192–198.

RUUD, J. T. (1956). International regulation of whaling. A critical survey. *Norsk Hvalf.-Tidende*, **45**, 374–387.

SERGEANT, D. E. (1966). Populations of large whale species in the western north Atlantic with special reference to the fin whale. *Fish. Res. Bd. Canada, Circ.* No. 9, 31pp.

SMALL, G. L. (1971). *The Blue Whale.* Columbia University Press.

VANGSTEIN, E. (1956). Whaling operations in the antarctic season 1955–6. *Norsk Hvalf.-Tidende*, **45**, 349–374.

WHEELER, J. F. G. (1934). The stock of whales at South Georgia. *Discovery Rep.*, **9**, 351–372.

WINN, H. E., EDEL, R. K., and TARUSKI, A. G. (1975). Population estimate of the humpback whale (*Megaptera novaeangliae*) in the West Indies by visual and acoustic techniques. *J. Fish. Res. Bd. Can.*, **32**, 499–506.

English	German	Norwegian	Dutch
Greenland Right Whale	Grönlandwal	Grønlandshval[5]	Groenlandse Walvis
Biscayan (N. Atlantic) Right Whale	Nordkaper	Nordkaper[6]	Noordkaper
Pigmy Right Whale	Zwergglattwal	Dvergretthval	Dwergwalvis
Californian Grey Whale	Grauwal	Gråhval	Grijze Walvis
Blue Whale	Blauwal	Blåhval	Blauwe Vinvi
Fin Whale[1]	Finnwal	Finhval[7]	Gewone Vinv
Sei Whale	Seiwal	Seihval	Noordse Vinv
Bryde's Whale	Brydewal	Brydehval	Bryde's Vinvi
Little Piked (Minke) Whale	Zwergwal	Vågehval[8]	Dwergvinvis
Humpback	Buckelwal	Knølhval	Bultrug
Sperm Whale	Pottwal	Spermhval	Potvis
Pigmy Sperm Whale	Zwergpottwal	Dverg-Spermhval	Dwergpotvis
Bottlenose Whale	Entenwal[4]	Naebhval[4]	Butskop
Beluga	Weisswal	Hvidfisk	Beluga
Common Porpoise[2]	Meerschwein	Nise	Bruinvis
Killer (Orca)	Schwertwal	Spaekhogger	Orca[9]
Pilot Whale	Grindwal	Grindhval	Griend
Bottlenose Dolphin[3]	Grosser Tümmler	Tumler	Tuimelaar
Common Dolphin	Delphin	Delphin	Dolfijn

[1] Razorback. [2] American: Harbor Porpoise. [3] American: Common Porpoise. [4] Dögling (German and Danis

French	Japanese	Russian
aleine franche	Hokkyoku Kujira	Grenlandskii Kit
aleine des Basques	Semi Kujira	Nastoiashchii Kit
aleine franche naine	Kosemi Kujira	
aleine grise	Koku Kujira	Seryi Kit
orqual bleu	Shironagasu Kujira	Sinii Kit
orqual commun	Nagasu Kujira	Seldianoi Kit
orqual de Rudolf	Iwashi Kujira	
aleine de Bryde	Nitaci Kujira	
etit rorqual	Koiwashi Kujira (Minku)	Malyi polosatik kit zalivov
légaptère	Zatô Kujira	Gorbatyi kit
achalot	Makkô Kujira	Kashalot
achalot nain	Komakkô	Karlikovyi Kashalot
ypérodon		Butylkonos
elphinaptère blanc	Shiro Iruka	Belukha
Iarsouin	Nezumi Iruka	Morskaya Svin'ya
paulard	Shachi	Kosatka
lobicéphale noir	Gondô Kujira	Grindy
ouffleur	Handô Iruka	Afaliny
auphin	Ma Iruka	Del'finy-belobochka

letbak.   [6] Retthval.   [7] Swedish: Sillhval.   [8] Minkehval.   [9] Zwaardvis.

IMPERIAL AND METRIC EQUIVALENTS

Linear Measure

1 inch.	2·54 centimetres
1 foot (12 inches)	30·48 centimetres
1 yard (3 feet)	0·9144 metre
1 fathom (6 feet)	1·8288 metres
1 mile (1,760 yards). .	1·6093 kilometres

Capacity Measure

1 pint	0·568 litre
1 quart (2 pints)	1·136 litres
1 gallon (8 pints)	4·546 litres

Avoirdupois Weight

1 ounce	28·35 grams
1 pound (16 ozs.)	0·4536 kilogram
1 stone (14 lb.)	6·35 kilograms
1 quarter (28 lb.)	12·7 kilograms
1 cwt.	50·8 kilograms
1 ton (20 cwt.)	1,016 kilograms

Index

Latin names of animals are not given in this Index but will be found on pages 433–8.